# A METHODOLOGICAL PRIMER
# for
# POLITICAL SCIENTISTS

# A METHODOLOGICAL PRIMER FOR POLITICAL SCIENTISTS

by

Robert T. Golembiewski

William A. Welsh

William J. Crotty

Rand McNally & Company

Chicago

Rand McNally Political Science Series


Printed in U.S.A. by Rand McNally & Company
Library of Congress Catalog Card Number 67:14692

# PREFACE

It seems unusually inappropriate to assign authorship of this volume to three men. For this volume is intimately in-stream in three major senses. Thus it patently rests on the industry and skill of countless scholars, insofar as it reflects what has gone before. Moreover, *A Methodological Primer for Political Scientists* profited from the good works and kindnesses of many diverse contributors, insofar as the authors and their analytical framework were open to contributions and were successful in assimilating them. Finally, the volume will require the commitment of many researchers, insofar as it will successfully influence that which is to come.

Words fail in expressing the various senses in which this book could never have come to be if we were left to our own resources. We trust that in-context acknowledgements will reflect the diverse aids we took, sought, and received. Particular note may be made here of the office of General Research and the Social Science Research Institute, both of the University of Georgia, which generously supported this effort. Sandra Daniel, Gloria Hawkins, Renate Black, Sigrid Sanders, Joanne Hayes, Elizabeth Landrum, and Carol Mathes provided the necessary and massive typing and clerical services. Jackie Hall and Susan Sewell helped in the final stages.

When mentioning resources which contributed to this book, we three would be remiss did we fail to acknowledge the herculean efforts of George S. Parthemos, Vice-President for Instruction here at Georgia, and did we neglect the skill he devoted to achieving in practice his vision of academic excellence. He brought us and our colleagues together, and has labored to free us to be the best that we can be. No administrator can do more.

Robert T. Golembiewski
William A. Welsh
William J. Crotty

# TABLE OF CONTENTS

# A METHODOLOGICAL PRIMER
# for
# POLITICAL SCIENTISTS

## INTRODUCTION

This book will not please everyone, that much is already certain. "You young political scientists and your methodological interests," one of our older and respected colleagues chided us in the early days of work on this manuscript, "y'all remind me of nothing more than children who just discovered their fingers and are only dimly aware of the uses that can be made of their digits. That is, the journals are full of sophisticated methodological disquisitions and trivial results." The pique has real professional roots. Thus our colleague claims that advanced age prevents him from learning "new methodological tricks." But he nonetheless counts himself an eager recipient of any "new findings."

This book acknowledges both the wisdom and overstatement of our mature friend. Essentially, the position here is a simple one. It may be adumbrated briefly in terms of three assertions. First, to be sure, the journals have been over-full of expositions and discussions of *techniques;* but, second, only niggardly attention has been given to what may properly be called *methodological issues*. Third, this volume sees this connection between the two assertions above: the preoccupation with technique and the neglect of methodology help explain the general failure within Political Science to provide "new findings" compelling enough to satisfy our abrasive and admired colleague.

The position sketched above is not orthodox opinion, but it does seem to be gaining supporters. And this increasing support has solid foundations. As Douglas Price explained:

> Over the past decade or so many political scientists have struggled to learn statistics, but few—if any have evidenced much interest in the broader problems of the "philosophy of science." This is regrettable, and as research becomes more elaborate and more professionalized there will be an increasing need for sophisticated critics of measurement techniques, theory-building, and the rest of the logic inquiry.[1]

Price's plea does not recommend a return to what David Easton called the "hyperfactualism" that characterized the social sciences in the period between the two world wars. Then, the preoccupation with "methods"—techniques for gathering and processing "hard" data—had the effect of obscuring methodological guidelines such as, for example, that data are no better than the theoretical system that motivated their gathering. Price calls for disciplining methods or techniques to methodology, and we heed his call. Nothing else will suffice if political scientists are to move further toward what Easton described as "gradually becoming accustomed to an image of ourselves as an integrated part of the total scientific enterprise that pursues an understanding of man in society."[2]

Our present purpose, then, is to fill a major gap in Political Science. Useful results depend upon a viable empirical methodology, attention to which has been rare; hence the lack of theories in Political Science which describe, explain, and permit prediction. Moreover, as Somit and Tanenhaus note, "most American political scientists are largely unfamiliar with the origins and early evolution of their discipline."[3] The lack of methodological concern, as a consequence, has co-existed with a strong tendency toward circular discovery–neglect–rediscovery sequences, as contrasted with a cumulative building upon earlier contributions. Methodological inattention and evolutionary myopia contributed to a common result. As Somit and Tanenhaus conclude: "American political scientists have paid a heavy price in time, effort, and controversy for their failure to attend more closely to their past."[4]

Our approach to helping fill this major gap in Political Science emphasizes empirical methodology simply defined, following Kaufman, as the "analysis of scientific procedure."[5] To put it somewhat differently, Political Science must emphasize methodological issues, for the "unity of all science"—as the physical scientist Pearson put it long ago in his renowned *The Grammar of Science*—"consists alone in its method."[6] "It is one thing to demand autonomy of inquiry," was Meehan's way of making a similar point, "and quite another matter to argue for autonomy of method."[7]

Acute practical reasons urge an emphasis upon methodological issues, as well as the fact that cumulative empirical work demands it. Only moderate methodological advances have been made of late. Moreover, there is some reason to fear the possibility of a kind of empirical Dark Ages embodied in the definition of *political science* as philosophical wisdom alone. Men of goodwill do differ as to the probability of such a backsliding from advances of recent years toward developing an empirical approach to a science of politics. Undeniably, however, existing methodological advances have been made under conditions of disciplinary expansion that have been unusually (and perhaps uniquely) favorable. How long the boom-town atmosphere will continue is a debatable issue, but in any case prudence dictates shoring-up the real advances made under the prevailing heady influence. Finally, Political Science must run faster just to stand still, so great is the increasing need for attention to methodology. Meehan explained that "some knowledge of the nature and form of scientific explanation, of the meaning and use of scientific methods, techniques, and constructions, and of the various other aspects of scientific inquiry, is already an essential part of the intellectual equipment of any adequately trained political scientist and the need for this training seems very likely to increase rapidly in the near future."[8]

Reinforcing disciplinary advances is particularly necessary because they suffer from serious inadequacies, methodologically viewed. To illustrate the broader range of these inadequacies, consider two consequences of the present expansionist days in the discipline: a plethora of newly developed "scope and methods" courses, and sometimes even of positions within departments of Political Science for specialists therein; and an increasing number of young Ph.D's. having skills and an awareness of techniques that are literally astounding even against the background of recent disciplinary history. Such advances have been tethered short, however. Favorable conditions and all, epigrammatically, scope and methods courses have emphasized scope. In a similar vein, various analytical capabilities and computational skills have proved more valuable for "counting" than as supports for a methodology of "sciencing" the empirical content within the discipline of Political Science. The difference between "counting" and "sciencing" is enormous, as later analysis will take pains to demonstrate.

The limited purpose here has a straightforward rationale, then. Further encouragement of political scientists toward a methodology capable of exploiting reality still demands attention. Meehan expressed one aspect of this unfilled need. "The paucity of material on theory in political science is astonishing," he observed; "virtually everything available on the subject comes from philosophy of science or sociology."[9] Much of the borrowing, further, has been unfortunate and indiscriminate. Rather than a methodology appropriate for an empirical science—for example, and for example only—much of the discipline inclines toward the systems approach of an early Talcott Parsons. Similarly, increasing emphasis has been given functionalism, and particularly so in comparative politics. Typically, such methodological postures were imported into Political Science from other disciplines, particularly from Sociology and Economics. There is a further similarity, unfortunately. Even if one acknowledges the historical usefulness of either a Parsonian or a functional approach, developments in their parent disciplines over the last decade have established that these two approaches do not themselves constitute a viable methodology for empirical research. What is more significant, these two approaches are not congenial to a viable empirical methodology. A kind of cultural lag hypothesis explains why similar conclusions have not yet deeply penetrated into Political Science.[10]

The next four paragraphs outline the ways in which this volume argues for the acceptance of a viable empirical methodology in Political Science. First, this book will argue a thesis in terms specific enough to be of use at present stages of development of various areas of the discipline. In a negative sense, the extreme to be avoided is a spiraling-off into issues that are real enough but which only complicate achieving the limited—and in many senses, the primitive—purposes of this book. Positively, this volume attempts to act upon the conviction that what the political scientist "needs most is a direct confrontation of methodological problems immediately relevant to his own discipline."[11]

Second, this book specifically includes many significant areas of inquiry within Political Science. Some significant areas must be omitted, but only because of limited resources of time and skill. The extreme to be avoided is a weak articulation of methodological issues with specific substantive areas within the discipline. Perhaps flippantly, methodology out-of-context is shunned here as much as context-without-methodology is condemned.[12]

This in-context emphasis on methodological issues sharply distinguishes this volume from such useful (and rare) approaches as Meehan's recent *The Theory and Method Of Political Analysis.* His motivation was understandable, since he hoped "by framing the study in broad and abstract terms, to avoid the bottomless pit of *ad hominem* argument and academic provincialism."[13] We, in contrast, shall run the risks of "*ad hominem* argument and academic provincialism," for we hope that framing our study in specific and concrete terms will contribute directly to building our methodological guidelines into on-going research.

Third, this book will attempt to be constructive in the full sense. That is, the argument attempts to "go somewhere" by using the existing sub-literatures as springboards into empirical inquiry. The extremes to be avoided are dual: mere carping on the one hand; and on the other hand, a punitive holding up of a vision of a methodological Promised Land without specifying how one can get from "here" to "there." The standard operating procedure is to be methodologically oriented-in-context, and to be research-oriented over-all. In short, our procedure is to methodologically develop specific substantive areas rather than to talk about methodology in the abstract.

This sketch of the purpose of this book also implies what the volume is not. Generally, the volume does not come from the same mold as many existing treatments of research methods available to the political scientist. There are dual advantages to this difference. Basically, these treatments deal with research in Psychology or Sociology and perhaps even with "social relations" or "the behavioral sciences."[14] Despite a variable commonality of interest, therefore, much of the content of these volumes on research methods does not directly relate to the training and interests and problems of most political scientists. In addition, most of the available treatments only gently treat basic methodological issues. Rather they tend toward a preoccupation with research settings; research design; techniques for gathering data; and techniques for analyzing data. This characterization is generally accurate,[15] although some efforts vary the format by especial emphasis upon a specific class of techniques[16] or upon a "policy integration" which also encompasses the application of research findings.[17] Despite the considerable virtues of such an emphasis upon techniques or generalized research loci,[18] that emphasis better suits the present development stage of (let us say) Psychology than Political Science.

Five outer boundaries more particularly circumscribe the areas neglected by this volume. First, the treatment is not overly concerned with the design of specific experiments, although this emphasis is present now and again. Second, the interest here is not basically in techniques of gathering or interpreting data, although some techniques will get more than passing attention. Third, the individual chapters do not pretend to an exhaustive review of all of the literature within their respective areas. Although the chapters do purport to adequately represent the various sub-literatures, their basic aim is to provide a methodological orientation for exhaustive review and analysis of the sub-literatures. If the methodological orientation proves useful in general, that is, we will be pleased to accept the responsibility for misreading the literature in specifics. We trust this responsibility need not be shouldered very often, of course. Fourth, and perhaps most worthy of note, this methodological primer is not presumed to include all of the diverse interests of political scientists. Rather, this volume's methodological thesis is deemed necessary grounding *only* for empirical research in the discipline. We may neglect certain interests of political scientists, that is, but we do not thereby exclude them from the realm of Political Science. Fifth, our attention will generally be directed no further back historically than to what Somit and Tanenhaus call the "middle years" of the development of Political Science, beginning roughly with the Twenties.

No complicated rationale underlies these "is-nots." The first three tasks can be accomplished more appropriately elsewhere, as in other social science literatures.[19] As for the fourth limiting boundary, no empirical orientation suffices to encompass the research activity that is and rightly should be considered within the domain of Political Science.[20] The fifth boundary condition is purely one of convenience. Many contemporary issues in Political Science were not newly hatched during the discipline's middle years,[21] and we stress the contemporary only because that is where we are and because it simplifies our analysis.

Even if the boundary conditions of this volume are reasonable, this effort nonetheless requires complementing in at least three ways in any comprehensive scope and methods approach. First, the present empirical emphasis requires a companion stress on normative issues and their methodology. In the same way, Aristotle's *Politics* needed his normatively oriented *Ethics.* Although preliminary efforts are made at several points to describe specifically how a healthy Political Science must be methodologically prepared to integrate the "is" and the "ought," the full association of the empirical and the normative is hardly exploited below. The present argument methodologically attempts to avoid the dominance of either "is" or "ought," however, whether in derivations of what purportedly exists from some statement of the desirable or in transmutations of the existing into the desirable.

With tongue in cheek a little, then, one can conceive of a companion volume to this book. Its working title is *A Methodological Primer for* POLITICAL *Scientists.* Short of that, the mutual involvement of teaching staff with philosophic interests in a scope and methods offering can achieve many of the same objectives.

Second, the present volume requires complementing via detailed reading in the several sub-literatures dealt with below, and particularly via extending the methodology to areas of Political Science that are not specifically considered here. This may be an unnecessary admonition to readers who quarrel with our treatments of the sub-literatures! But the volume is intended to serve as a methodological yardstick against which the empirical achievements of the various disciplinary areas can be estimated, and it should be used as such. In this sense, the volume should well complement many scope and methods offerings. Their common emphasis is upon the several substantive areas of inquiry in Political Science, that is, upon "power" or "public interest" or what have you. The present methodological interests will be applied directly to a number of these problem areas, thereby providing immediate methodological counterpoint to the substantive sub-literatures. Moreover, our methodological approach also will be transferable basically to problem areas not directly considered here.

Third, this volume sets the stage for subsequent development of skills of research design and analysis, but it merely sets the stage. Acting on the methodological orientation developed below often will require sophisticated skills and techniques in gathering, analyzing, and interpreting data. This volume basically provides motivation and support for the use and development of various techniques and skills; it does little of the heavy work.

There are many ways in which these needed complements to this volume can be provided. One attractive scope and methods package at the graduate level would be tripartite, for example. *A Methodological Primer for Political* SCIENTISTS would set the standards for empirical inquiry and sketch useful lines of development in various disciplinary areas; a second "hardware" phase would introduce the student to selected techniques and particularly to the machining of data; and a third phase would be a kind of practicum in which the student and staff would be confronted with a relevant and manageable empirical inquiry that would require the working out of specific problems of design, implementation, and analysis. A full course year, at least, would be necessary for such a sequence.

Whatever these complementary studies may involve, the effort seems worth the candle. This volume has a dual vision of the discipline: as one operating on the basis of a viable empirical methodology in appropriate areas, and as one in which the debilitating warfare between proponents of the "facts" and "wisdom" gives way to a direct linking of the two orientations on appropriate problems, to mutually supportive efforts to solve problems more unique to each orientation.

## NOTES

1. From a book review by Douglas Price, in the *Journal of Politics,* 27 (February, 1965), 196.

2. *Varieties of Political Theory* (Englewood Cliffs, N.J.: Prentice-Hall, 1966), p. 8.

3. Albert Somit and Joseph Tanenhaus, *The Development of American Political Science: From Burgess to Behavioralism* (Boston: Allyn and Bacon, 1967), p. 2.

4. *Ibid.,* p. 3.

5. Felix Kaufman, *Methodology of the Social Sciences* (New York: Oxford University Press, 1944), p. vii.

6. Karl Pearson, *The Grammar of Science* (London: J. M. Dent, 1937), p. 16.

7. Eugene J. Meehan, *The Theory and Method of Political Analysis* (Homewood, Ill.: The Dorsey Press, 1965), p. 8.

8. *Ibid.,* p. v.

9. *Ibid.,* p. 167.

10. The required dialectic is clearly underway, however, as in Don Martindale (ed.), *Functionalism in the Social Sciences,* Monograph 5 (Philadelphia: American Academy of Political and Social Science, February, 1965).

11. This advice was given by Leonard Broom to behavioral scientists in his introduction to Abraham Kaplan, *The Conduct of Inquiry: Methodology for Behavioral Science* (San Francisco: Chandler, 1965).

12. Specifically, that is, this volume will not strive for the degree of generality attempted by such contributions as that of Roy G. Francis, *The Rhetoric of Science* (Minneapolis: University of Minnesota Press, 1961), or by Kaufmann, *op. cit.*

13. Meehan, *op. cit.,* p. 17.

14. Specific areas within Political Science, however, have begun the development of research methods appropriate to their own problems. This is most strikingly the case in two volumes edited by Glendon Schubert, *Judicial Decision-Making* (New York: The Free Press of Glencoe, 1963) and *Judicial Behavior: A Reader in Theory and Research* (Chicago: Rand McNally, 1964).

15. See, for example, Maurice Duverger, *An Introduction to the Social Sciences with Special Reference to their Methods* (New York: Praeger, 1964); Leon Festinger and Daniel Katz, *Research Methods in the Behavioral Sciences* (New York: The Dryden Press, 1953); William J. Goode and Paul K. Hatt, *Methods in Social Research* (New York: McGraw-Hill, 1952); Marie Jahoda, Morton Deutsch, and Stuart W. Cook, *Research Methods in Social Relations* (New York: The Dryden Press, 1951), Vols. I and II; and Paul F. Lazarsfeld and Morris Rosenberg (eds.), *The Language of Social Research* (Glencoe, Ill.: The Free Press, 1955).

16. Paul F. Lazarsfeld, *Mathematical Thinking in the Social Sciences* (Glencoe, Ill.: The Free Press, 1953).

17. Daniel Lerner and Harold Lasswell (eds.), *The Policy Sciences* (Stanford, Calif.: Stanford University Press, 1951).

18. Considerable evidence also establishes the dangers to empirical research of such emphasis, as detailed in Robert T. Golembiewski, *The Small Group: An Analysis of Research Concepts and Operations* (Chicago: University of Chicago Press, 1962), especially Chapters 2 and 3.

19. Russell L. Ackoff, *The Design of Social Research* (Chicago: University of Chicago Press, 1953); F. Stuart Chapin, *Experimental Designs in Sociological Research* (New York: Harper, 1955); and J. C. Townsend, *Introduction to Experimental Method for Psychology and Social Science* (New York: McGraw-Hill, 1953).

20. This conclusion agrees with that of commentators such as Sheldon S. Wolin, *Politics and Vision: Continuity and Innovation in Western Political Thought* (Boston: Little, Brown, 1960), especially pp. 1–27.

21. For example only, the present interest with "functionalism" in Political Science has roots which go back at least to A. Lawrence Lowell, "The Physiology of Politics," *American Political Science Review,* 4 (1910), 1–15.

# PART ONE

## Some Methodological Guidelines in Context

# i

# Toward Increasing the Relevance of Three Contemporary Approaches to a Science of Politics

This volume derives its motivation and its goals from a common observation: Contemporary Political Science, we are told, is a growing babel of approaches that will help achieve scientific status for the discipline—if they do not first irrevocably fragment its practitioners. To facilitate the former end and to discourage the latter are the twin goals of this book.

The mechanics of approaching this chapter's goals are straightforward. First, three major approaches in Political Science will be shown to fall short in various ways of a simple set of standards for scientific research. Second, specific modifications will be outlined which can make the three approaches carriers of a greater relevance in the scientific study of politics. Subsequent chapters will extend this general approach in three ways: by sharpening the methodological criteria which empirical research must meet; by measuring a number of areas of Political Science against these criteria; and by developing the specific ways in which some existing fields of Political Science can be re-oriented methodologically.

This chapter suggests the nature and tone of the full volume. It spotlights the broad constructive purposes of the total effort; it suggests the dimensions of the critical argument; and it begins the task of outlining and applying the specific methodological criteria that empirical work in Political Science must meet. From one important perspective, more specifically, the chapter's limited sample of approaches to Political *Science* permits compound emphases. The legitimate value to a science of politics of each of the three approaches, within the limits of a viable methodology for empirical work, will be stressed. The common neglect of these methodological limits also will be emphasized, for the disciplinary consequences are not trifling. The value to a science of politics of each of the three approaches is depreciated thereby, that is, if indeed each does not take on negative values. Moreover, ample evidence suggests that the development of each approach suffers because methodological guidelines are not respected.

The implied analytical tightrope may be made explicit. Ours is the constructive purpose of attempting here to build upon three major scholarly ways in which political scientists have functioned. What follows may induce defensiveness and even hostility, however. For the need to reorient three major approaches to Political Science rests upon a critical argument; and no one enjoys the goring of his own ox. Emphasizing our intentions may help avoid the worst. We argue only that the direction of the three approaches has been awkward. We do not reject the value of the approaches; and we certainly do not intend to hold an academic courtmartial for the purpose of drumming any of the approaches out of the discipline. The point may be put more positively, perhaps. As we will attempt to show, all three approaches can be so modified as to contribute directly to the development of a science of politics.

Emphasizing *three* approaches to a science of politics does imply further costs and cautions, patently. In terms of the costs of selectivity, for example, the present sample suffers from all of the liabilities of its kind, and perhaps more. At the very least, however, the sample includes some significant strains of contemporary work and illustrates the liabilities of a still wider family of effort. Moreover, caution should prevent over-interpretation of the three approaches selected; that is, they do not always refer to some group of scholars, but rather to ways of scholarly functioning. Even at that, the typologies are not watertight categories. For example, many scholars have functioned comfortably within more than one of the three approaches of special interest below.

## I. METHODOLOGICAL GUIDELINES: SOME CRITERIA FOR EMPIRICAL SCIENCE

Judging the scientific usefulness of any approach requires a set of criteria, of course. Three such criteria will serve our purposes here. They constitute base-line minima, as it were, and the failure of any approach to meet any one criterion provides sufficient grounds for assigning a low probability to the likelihood of its supporting a science of politics. The specific criteria are:

i. any approach should be methodologically compatible with existing work in the physical and behavioral sciences, or at least it should not peremptorily reject or exclude that which has proved methodologically useful in other areas of study;

ii. any approach should seek its (dis)confirmation in events external to the theoretical systems developed; in this sense, any approach should be self-correcting rather than self-sealing, whether the external events are experimental or natural; and

iii. research techniques must be oriented toward isolating the dimensions of reality useful for descriptive and predictive purposes; this requires both an emphasis upon nominal definition and upon operational definition of dimensions of reality.

No attempt will be made here to support these criteria. Some part of this enterprise has been brought off specifically elsewhere,[1] and subsequent chapters give attention to relevant issues. Moreover—despite questions about emphasizing these particular criteria rather than others —any useful list of guidelines would have to include the three criteria above.

## II. THE PHILOSOPHIC PERSUASION

Political Science has given only incomplete attention to even such rough methodological guidelines as those above, as may be demonstrated by considering a first major contemporary approach to the study of politics—the "philosophic persuasion." We shall build content into the term on a piecemeal basis. "Philosophic persuasion" is perhaps better illustrated than defined, indeed, as shall be done presently. Moreover, the designation "philosophic persuasion" is not an entirely happy one. For "philosophic know-nothing" seems to apply more fully to some scholars of this general persuasion, so pronounced and exclusive is their persuasion. The term does not imply or intend derogation; rather, it describes. We hasten to make clear that the philosophic know-nothings —the extreme abreactors from the scientific persuasion—know much, and often profoundly. Like that political coalition of long ago intent on reserving the privilege of governance to native Americans, however, the philosophic know-nothings are similarly intent on regaining and reserving disciplinary hegemony for "native *political* scientists," i.e., those schooled in the great tradition of political philosophy *and* preoccupied with it. Hence the designation here to refer to a range of opinion within the philosophic persuasion that is particularly relevant to explaining the disciplinary lack of service to methodological guidelines in Political Science.

Scholars of the philosophic persuasion are no great friends of a science of politics, as they have made increasingly clear of late. Indeed, the tone of a number of recent major volumes[2] suggests that opponents of the orientation feel emboldened to move in for the kill, so vulnerable have the proponents of the scientific approach left themselves by their failure to deliver on their promises. Almost certainly, if this interpretation is too extreme, the pendulum is swinging the other way.[3] Thus the balance of power in at least one of the most influential schools has changed so radically that it proved possible in 1962 to excoriate publicly both founding father and several home-grown proponents of the new science of politics (and to do so with a jesuitical zeal).[4] Significantly, also, the last few years have accorded the science of politics a widening spiral of critical attention.[5] Perhaps most important, the great mass of *political* scientists—those "centrists" about whom Strauss has written—seem less inspired by promises of the glorious coming of a science of politics. That is to say, the centrist seems increasingly predisposed to let the activist opposition have its turn at calling the disciplinary tune.[6]

Not all observers read the signs in the same way, to be sure. Dahl, for example, has argued that the books can be closed on the successful acceptance of the "behavioral orientation" and that now we can get down to the details of developing the new science of politics as we advance from recently won beachheads.[7] And Eulau gives support to Dahl's position,[8] although he is less strident in claiming victory because he does not really acknowledge that there was a war or that fighting it was necessary.

The neo-prominence of the philosophic persuasion was long in the making and has accelerated rapidly of late,[9] whatever power status one is willing to assign them. The last major assault on the science of politics, in fact, was a phenomenon of the immediate post-World War II era. It stressed the role of values in political analysis, and particularly in Public Administration.[10] Proponents of this point of view won their battle, but that is all.

In large part, the philosophic persuasion lodges a valid and major charge against the political *scientist*—his marked historical tendency to fall into "scientism." As Hayek developed the point with great finesse, scientism refers to the uncritical extension into the social sciences of habits of thought appropriate only for the natural sciences or (we might add) of habits of thought equally inappropriate for both social and natural sciences.[11] Scientism also often implies the naive belief that all problems are amenable to scientific solution or, at least, that only problems capable of scientific solution are interesting or relevant problems. At its best, then, the philosophic persuasion is akin to the English Idealists, as their position is described by Collingwood. English Idealism, he explained, was not directed against science. Rather it was a revolt against that philosophy "which claimed that science was the only type of knowledge that existed or ever would exist. It was not a revolt against the intellect, it was a revolt against the theory which limited the intellect to the kind of thinking characteristic of natural science."[12]

The justice of the rejection of scientism by the philosophic persuasion is patent. The "American science of politics" is shot through with value premises, like it or not, as Crick demonstrates in *The American Science of Politics* (see footnote 2 below). The only alternatives are to be more *or* less specific about these values. An important aspect of work in Political Science, then, must involve intensive philosophical analysis to suggest crucial areas for empirical research, to guide the uses to which such research is put, and increasingly to add more detail to the picture of that Good Society which empirical research can help us attain. Political Science, adequately conceived, cannot tolerate the notion that only problems amenable to empirical resolution are interesting or relevant problems.

The rejection of scientism by the philosophic persuasion makes good sense from several other perspectives, in addition. Rightly, that is, scholars stress the multi-dimensional dangers of any blanket denial that the science of politics must have significant aspects that are value-loaded. We note but three dimensions of these dangers. First, neglect of the significant roles of values will leave the student wallowing in indecision and non-evaluation in areas where a value-free attitude is inappropriate and self-defeating.[13] Political Science—dealing as it does in significant part with the definition of the good life and with ways and means of attaining it—must therefore walk a narrow line. It must bring together empirical and normative considerations at crucial points. And the discipline also must avoid the dual and subtle temptations of deriving the purportedly existing from some definition of the desirable, or of defining the desirable in terms of the existing.

Second, as one perceptive critic noted, "political objects" by and large exist only in the normatively charged realm of "human opinion."[14] A radical value-free orientation thus may have the awkward consequence of reducing "political objects" to sub-political determinants, which runs the risk that the "political will disappear altogether."[15] Segregationist attitudes may be associated with specific empirical roots such as toilet-training practices, for example. But such hypothetical empirical co-variants hardly exhaust the levels of discourse applicable to the associated attitudes. Nor can sub-political determinants be neglected, although they must be kept in their limited, empirical places. In other words, political scientists must in part be concerned with applied questions. And knowledge of sub-political determinants may be crucial in prescribing how normatively desirable political attitudes can be fostered, or how normatively undesirable attitudes may be changed. Many factors argue against relying on other disciplines for the isolation of such subpolitical determinants. The unique training and interests of political scientists in such research are likely to be served best by political scientists themselves.[16]

Third, as Berns puts the point, "... the behavioral scientist's interest in ... factual research and in the widespread search for subpolitical causes of behavior ... is part of the behavioral scientist's denial of man's rationality, and of man's nature ...."[17] Overstatement notwithstanding, Berns' barb concerning presumed intent does have a point that strikes deeply in some cases. Clearly, moreover, methodologically inelegant empirical work also deserves censure. The same holds for normatively insensitive applications of factual research designed to prey on man's weaknesses rather than to help remedy them, which applications can truly be said to deny man's nature. But all these reservations concern factual research in practice rather than in principle, as it were. Consequently, Berns diminishes the impact of his point. For he can be read as implying that factual research ought to be foresworn because it somehow inherently denies man's rationality, and this apparently whether or not the research is methodologically adequate or predictively useful. This is know-nothingness with a vengeance. At the very least, oppositely, one could also argue that factual research can support and sustain man's rationality by providing him with a picture of reality that permits man more effective pursuit of his political goals. And what could be more subversive of man's rationality than severely limiting his quest for knowledge of the world around him?

We are led to borrow Schaar's ringing words, which he put to quite the opposite use. Arguments like that of Berns about the primacy of values can have the serious, although unintended, consequence of rendering "intelligence cautious just where it must be bold, dumb where it should be articulate."[18]

Such considerations illustrate the need for a disciplinary mix of normative and empirical emphases, while they also spotlight the delicacy of that integration. These matters will be left in their present state of undress, but only because they will receive detailed attention in subsequent chapters.

If its adherents lead from a position of clear strength, the philosophic persuasion commonly does not let well enough alone. Thus a Berns can begin with relative tolerance by arguing that "the political can better be seen by minds that do not draw this distinction [between the normative and empirical] too sharply," but his argument inexorably grinds to the conclusion that the "interest in factual research ... is part of the behavioral scientist's denial of man's rationality, of man's nature." Such expansionist arguments leave little room for the more delicate treatment of values required in empirical work. This required treatment excludes all values but the values of science from the processes of developing conclusions; and it includes a wide range of normative considerations in such questions as the selection of research problems, the treatment of research subjects, and the choice of uses to which results will be put.

That matters tend toward extremes is not surprising, however, for we refer to a war, not a skirmish. The issues and their formulations are as political as they are analytical, since their resolution influences (if not determines) who gets which scarce resources. Moreover, ideological differences add further spice to the contest. For instance, Strauss maintains that all (or almost all) behavioralists, i.e., political *scientists,* are "liberals." Their vocal analytical opposition is ideologically "conservative," this teacher also notes, albeit not so uniformly as the opposition is "liberal." The generalization of opposed ideologies is a useful one, although it can be misleading.[19] Given that this is a revolution and not a debate, the ideological difference is understandable. No doubt more personal factors also helped compound the controversy. For example, behavioralists often neglect pointedly to give the philosophically oriented a place on the disciplinary research frontiers (as was the case in the 1955 Brookings Lectures, for example) or—when they do acknowledge such work—they do so in a condescending manner.[20] That the behavioralists are young men, in the main, helps matters not a bit. But such is the way of revolutions of the left, of the have-nots.

Analytical detachment, then, would have required phenomenal scrupulosity by both proponent and opponent. The rarity of such scrupulosity is evidenced by the fact that even moderate formulations of limits on the role of values in Political Science tend to be viewed with suspicion and scorn. Hence Berns took Rothman to task even for taking this position: It is "vital for the healthy growth of [our] discipline" that we "separate political science from political philosophy so that factual research [will] not continue to be the stepchild of normative reflections . . . ."[21] The reasons for Berns' concern must remain problematic. But notice that the quotation contains two emphases which are quite independent: a methodological emphasis that empirical work must not be a derivative of normative considerations, and an apparent organizational emphasis that may imply a redefinition of the discipline. The distinction is not made by Berns, however, and his scholarly guns hammer away at Rothman's position as at a monolith. Now monolithic Rothman's position may be, and many other behavioralists may want to define political philosophy out of the profession. However, there are no good reasons for assuming a one-to-one correspondence between the two emphases. Certainly there is no methodological reason for rejecting the first emphasis. One accepts it simply because that is the way sciences have developed. The development is the same for contemporary Political Science and medieval chemistry, which had to curb the alchemist and bring out the scientist in the likes of Theophrastus Bombastus ab Hohenheim. Political philosophers, particularly, should not confuse a necessary methodological insight with an arbitrary (and we argue, mischievous) redefinition of the boundaries of their discipline.

There are sins of both commission and omission in the over-enthusiastic presentation of the case of the philosophic persuasion, to employ terminology congenial to them. On the former head, as we understand it, the philosophic persuasion maintains that scientism evades important issues, or that science cannot answer significant (even *the* significant) questions. There seems little to quarrel with here. We, at least, are happy to concede both points. But adherents of the philosophic persuasion also seem to argue that no issues but their issues are important. What other interpretation, for example, to put on Strauss's astringent comment about the "new science of politics"? Strauss noted: ". . . one may say of it that it fiddles while Rome burns. It is excused by two facts: it does not know that it fiddles, and it does not know that Rome burns."[22] To be sure, the entire body of Strauss's writing does not harp on this theme, and some of the work is valuable theoretical undergirding indeed for a science of politics.[23] But certainly the words quoted here were not lightly chosen. More to the point, the words illustrate a significant and apparently growing opinion.[24]

Following Bentley's warning, our purpose is not to snip definitions or to nip at ambiguous terminology. But if Strauss implies that the philosophic persuasion holds a monopoly on wisdom, or even on wisdom-provoking questions, a firm disclaimer is appropriate. Consider the applicability of Strauss's comment in the area of one of our particular interests, the study of large-scale productive organizations. If anything, its huge literature has been criticized for paying too much attention to issues of value, as in the debate over the "social responsibility" of government and especially business organizations. The point may be put more specifically. There are those who know that Rome burns, e.g., in the sense that individual freedom will be secured (if anywhere) only in large-scale organizations, and that this securing grows ever more difficult. And there are those who—if they despair of an organizational equivalent of the City of God on Earth—nonetheless realize that much fiddling with detailed behavioral investigations implies (for example) approaches to Judaeo-Christian ideals in organizations. The vehicles are specific structural innovations and managerial techniques that do not require sacrificing either employee satisfaction or effectiveness.[25]

The immediate point may be put sharply. In organizational analysis, then, fiddling with empirical data can well serve those concerned with values. Indeed, this understates the general case. No one can doubt the importance of the philosophical analysis of Judaeo-Christian ideals through the centuries, but preachment is most likely to be effective when tied to ways and means that permit practical advantage to coincide with preachment. And philosophic analysis, of whatever degree of acuity, is not up to this full demonstration. Neglect of the interaction of philosophical and empirical orientations, consequently, implies a sin of omission.

Omission has other interesting facets. It is instructive that in a recent volume the degree of detailed attention and loving care lavished on the "history of science" in several disciplines bore a distinct and direct relation to the relative sophistication of the several disciplines considered.[26] In order, Physics, Chemistry, Medicine, Psychology, and Economics reflected decreasingly insightful attention to the history of their science, and this by people increasingly preoccupied with other interests. Political Science was not represented.

If analytical experience is to constitute really nourishing fodder, to state the implied point, a discipline is well advised to develop specialists in its own methodological history who have the perspective of breakthroughs in other problem areas. Political theorists and political philosophers seem particularly adapted to such a role for which Plato and Aristotle early provided *raison d'être* aplenty in their methodological interests. In point of fact, however, political theorists have tended of late to flee from such an opportunity. Harvey Glickman aptly expressed this change in perspective within the classical tradition. He wrote:

> The writers of "the Great Books" in political theory were passionately interested in how politics were actually carried on; otherwise they would have had no basis for political prescription.
>
> Somehow in recent years, the mantle of theory slipped from the writers who tried to understand events to scholars who reported, translated, classified and analysed ideas and argued about the ethics of previous writers. Political theory, so embodied, was really a combination of intellectual history and ethics; it had deserted empiricism for scholasticism.[27]

Glickman's perceptions are significant as well as sharp. From what available data tell us,[27a] for example, scholars in Political Science place a low value on the desertion of empiricism for scholasticism by students of the philosophical persuasion. Specifically, the field of Political Theory is seen as having contributed the least to the development of Political Science in recent years, at least in the eyes of the sample of scholars who recently responded to an extensive questionnaire exploring the state of the discipline.

Political scientists have not devoted telling attention to the methodological experiences of their own and other disciplines, and the trend within the philosophical persuasion isolated by Glickman plays an important role in explaining that neglect. Of course, recent days have seen the beginnings of interesting work on the history of science of the discipline,[28] but neglect has been the general rule. The consequences have been profound, and indeed paradoxical.

Adherents of the philosophic persuasion exercised a massive impact on methodological work in absentia, as it were, but the point can only be sketched here. Thus adherents of the philosophic persuasion rightly stress the common lack of historical perspective of those developing a science of politics, who consequently spend much time going over or neglecting old ground. This myopia is in large part a consequence of methodological inattention and neglect of disciplinary evolution, however, both of which might have been remedied by aggressive efforts on the parts of scholars with the training and interests of the philosophic persuasion. Exceptions to this generalization exist, in both by-gone days and the present.[29] But the generalization holds rather more than less. The consequences of methodological and evolutionary neglect also may be illustrated negatively. Given appropriate attention, that is, there would be far less borrowing of analytical vehicles from other disciplines after they had been rejected or while they are being subjected to serious criticism. The record of such maladoptions is long but not distinguished. Consider Simon's choice of logical positivism, the rather widespread flirtations with Parsons' action systems, and the present emphasis upon functionalism.

To establish further that the common emphasis is decidely elsewhere than upon comparative methodology, consider only that product of the most influential school of the philosophic persuasion—the *Essays on the Scientific Study of Politics*. That volume contains critical essays dealing with the work of several students prominently associated with the development of a science of politics, including Herbert A. Simon, Harold D. Lasswell, and Arthur F. Bentley. Those essays imply that the only major requirements for scientific analysis are careful writing, the lack of contradictions within a piece and between several pieces, and the like. At least, the *Essays* never specify any other criteria, nor are they much concerned with the matter (with only occasional exceptions in the essay on voting studies). However noteworthy such characteristics may be in other kinds of efforts, they are of no special importance in empirical science. To be sure, the *Essays* could have made the case that much of the work reviewed was innocent of the requirements of science. But this the *Essays* did not do. At best they made the point that the work reviewed was bad political philosophy, to which charge all of the excoriated authors no doubt would gladly plead guilty. Hence the pages of the *Essays* are full of the industrious burning of houses to roast pigs, if not verbal cockroaches, of crucifying science on the cross of literary elegance and precision in exposition.

For a variety of reasons, then, adherents of the philosophic persuasion are not likely to facilitate the development of a science of politics, as matters now stand, and some of them may wish to sabotage it. Developing viable places for both value-free and value-loaded effort has been a major accomplishment of all scientific effort, as has been the growth of a body of workers with methodological interests and perspectives. The philosophic persuasion makes small effort in either direction. The value question is commonly raised in an all-or-nothing form by adherents of the philosophic persuasion. They also have had a longstanding and a general aversion to methodological issues, which has the common effect of insulating them against much that is going on in the discipline now. The dual failure permits little optimism that this first approach can meet Criterion i. Consequently, the first approach is unlikely to facilitate the development of a science of politics, unless appropriate reorientations are made.

## III. THE MODEL-BUILDERS

Archeologists of disciplines in some far-off time may identify our age in Political Science as that of the model-builder. Much of the sharply increased contemporary work in international relations and comparative administration reflects this preoccupation, for example. Models of conflict at various conceptual levels, models of kinds of societies, simulation models for international gaming, and attempts to program the budget process—these are but a sparse sampling of the relevant effort.

The proclivity toward model-building has been most marked in allied disciplines, and especially in Economics, but its export to Political Science well suited a long-existing market. Thus the recent disciplinary enthusiasm for efforts such as that by the economist Downs has historical roots in model-building which has preoccupied some students of politics since the breed began. Rousseau, for example, quite clearly set for himself a model-building enterprise in his *du social contrat,* his goal being the intuition of those conditions under which man would be absolutely unfettered by external human controls, with no thought as to whether or not these conditions ever did or could or would or should obtain.[30] And Rousseau has much company, even if few are the subjects of as much controversy as he.

Imported or domestic, however, much contemporary model-building will prove to be love's labor lost in Political Science. This does not slight the central role of model-building in the development of any science. Ample evidence suggests, unfortunately, that much of the model-building in Political Science has but faint chance of contributing to a science of politics. Indeed, this model-building in effect avoids precisely those methodological issues whose resolution must precede large-scale scientific effort, particularly those issues related to Criterion ii. Hence the contemporary fascination with certain kinds of model-building may do a grievous disservice to scientific development in the discipline.

There are many traps associated with model-building. Not the least of them is the simple (but often neglected) datum that there are at least two basic types of models, each having its own uses and liabilities. Rousseau's work may be taken to reflect both types. His *du social contrat* typifies a utopian model; his *On the Government of Poland* is reality-based. The point of departure of the latter effort is the existing world of flesh-and-blood people in a particular society with its own particular culture and experiences. Given these empirical factors, Rousseau argues, the government of Poland was a tolerably unique approach in the real world to that ideal model he developed in his *contrat* of the generalized conditions under which men would probably be absolutely free. That is, man can be free where and only where *I* = *They* and the fetters of control over man by men do not exist, by definition.

Rousseau's work serves double duty. It illustrates the uses and abuses of the two types of models. Utopian work, carefully distinguished, may serve as an analytical standard against which existing conditions may be compared. Rousseau's work also implies that confusing the two types of models is an analytical sin, mortal in gravity. Thus, one must avoid the assumption that, for example, Rousseau in the *contrat* is describing any existing society, or any society that man is likely to see for any length of time in any larger aggregate, or even a society in which Rousseau would like to live. This means that much sport made of Rousseau is so much applesauce. The *contrat* in its largest part—granted that Rousseau, like all men, lets his attention wander at times—is merely that model of that logically developed society in which the *I* and the *They* are in consensual harmony. Therefore, by definition, the *I* is completely free of the restraints imposed upon him by *Them*. Now, Rousseau knows full well that this *I-They* harmony can exist only under very special conditions of size, of technology, and the like, and so he tells the reader what these conditions are and how they reinforce one another. Oppositely, *On the Government of Poland* indicates how the ideal model of the *contrat* was approached, and the degree to which it was approached, under actual conditions then extant in Poland. Both types of models have their uses, therefore, but the usage of each must be strictly limited.

A similar point holds for other models that are formally defined only. Consider *game theory*.[31] Per se, it has little predictive value. For there are very few nontrivial real-life "games" that can now be analyzed in the detail required by the gaming approach. But game theory will generate concepts necessary to explain the trivial cases. In turn, appropriate empirical testing may establish the validity of such concepts in explaining and predicting behavior in more complex situations. Of course, much of the model-building in Political Science can serve such a purpose, but only if the models are built so as to permit (and to facilitate) testing.

Much model-building in Political Science gives every evidence of wanting the best of all possible worlds, and thereby of getting, more or less typically, the worst of them. For example, the common failure to distinguish types of model-building implies the likely abort of relevant work in Political Science. Consider the classic difficulty with Plato. How to understand the patent differences between his *Laws* and the *Republic*? Without the acknowledgment that Plato had the virtuosity to play more than one game, understanding comes hard. But the hard way it has been, with few exceptions. Because the *Republic* and the *Laws* do differ, it has been frequently argued that Plato wrote the *Laws* after he had gone to seed. He *really* meant the *Republic*, in contrast, which he wrote while still full of the juice of life. As Sabine—certainly an influential, he—wrote: "It is plausible to see in the [Republic] the enthusiasm of Plato's first maturity . . . and in the [Laws] the disillusionment which came with age . . . ."[32]

Explanations in terms of geriatries—whether correct or merely convenient—foreclose a crucial methodological issue. Plato's two efforts, simply, are different types of theories. At least Plato is usually quite clear that the *Republic* describes a utopian state built upon, and leading toward, the assumption of incredible capabilities in its ruling elite. Hence his allusions to the *Republic* as an "ideal." Hence also his recognition that philosopher-kings do not exist and that their selection would be chancy in the extreme if they did exist.[33] Why, then, did he trouble to write the *Republic*? As an alternative hypothesis, Plato could have written the *Republic* to demonstrate what an impossible set of conditions constrain monarchial governance interpreted in extremis. Considerable text in one standard English translation, indeed, supports this hypothesis.[34] The *Republic*, then, could have been written first as an extended demonstration that one must face the practical problem of organizing a city-state, which the *Laws* proceed to do without resorting to synthetic philosopher-kings.

Whatever Plato's motivation in writing whichever book first, his curious treatment in the discipline suggests that the failure to distinguish types of models in Political Science may amount to a kind of disciplinary learned incapacity. So much work in Political Science is (implicitly or explicitly) prescriptive that it seems difficult for students to read a piece that attempts to be strictly descriptive or one that attempts to develop logically a few abstract propositions. Hence the enthusiasm for such breathless questions: Was Plato (Rousseau, et al.) a TOTALITARIAN or a DEMOCRAT?[35] The *Republic* and the *Laws*, respectively, give comfort to both positions. But this is not because Plato was necessarily either one or the other, whatever that means when applied to a non-contemporary. Plato simply employed different kinds of models in the two efforts.

Consequently, the point of contention is not nearly so much the classical tradition versus something else, as some have dramatically argued, but, what is to be done with the classical tradition? Typically, the question is neglected. The methodological insights of classical writers are obscured in the rush to relate their efforts to some contemporary substantive great issue or other, often at the expense of attenuating the point of the original effort. The tragedy is that while there are great problems of relating treatments of substantive great issues over time, the pressing methodological issues today must begin with just those problems grappled with by the classical authors.

The difficulties with model-building do not end with this long-standing insensitivity to types of models. Thus—with the economists taking the lead—many political scientists have made a method of insensitivity. The economist Milton Friedman, for example, simply went further than most. He boldly put the point in print. Friedman noted:

> . . . The relation between the significance of a theory and the "realism" of its "assumptions" is almost the opposite of that [expected.] Truly important and significant hypotheses will be found to have "assumptions" that are wildly inaccurate descriptive representations of reality, and, in general, the more significant the theory, the more unrealistic the assumptions . . . .[36]

Only in a footnote does Friedman disavow an argument for the converse proposition that the usefulness of a theory will vary directly as does the bizarreness of its basic propositions. Friedman's is not a solo voice by any means. Anthony Downs made the same point at a meeting of the American Political Science Association, and received warm support from the audience.[37] Moreover, entire subject-matter areas relevant to Political Science—e.g., traditional organization theory in Public Administration—were developed as derivations from implicit propositions that (at least) had no clear grounding in observable phenomena. The orthodox literature of executive-legislative relations has been generated, albeit more argumentatively, by similar underlying propositions. These propositions—even when they are explicitly recognized, which is seldom—usually are accepted as beyond question.[38] In Gouldner's term, indeed, a "metaphysical pathos" of an awkward kind vitiates much research in Political Science and at least forecloses some significant issues, if it does not in fact predetermine the results of the research. The extended demonstration of one facet of this point, we take it, occupied Crick in his *The American Science of Politics.*

Only the hypothesis that much model-building in Political Science is ascientific explains to us the general support for Friedman's position. Briefly, a physicist would find that position fantastic. The point may be made at greater length. The goal of model-building in any science is to predict what we do not know from some comely organization of what we do know. Much model-building in Political Science, oppositely, tells us what we do know based upon what we do not know (e.g., one of Friedman's theoretical constructs). Or, alternately, the model-building enterprise amounts to a kind of scholarly baptismal service. New names, that is, are given wholesale to existing insights.

The conclusion and evidence above may seem precious, so let chapter and verse be cited. Consider these major propositions of one typical approach to model-building in Political Science:

1. define a "system" in terms of "... a set of points, a line, or a zone comprised of a set of subsystems which habitually exchange greater amounts of information and/or energy, or exchange them at higher rates, with each other or with intermediate subsystems linking them interdependently with other systems or sets of subsystems";
2. assume that a "society" is a "system";
3. assume that some politically defined entity is a "society" with a constituent "political system";
4. then one can generate such "hypotheses": "In the less developed societies, the limited resources available to groups other

> than the political system is such that they are unable to exercise effective controls over the political system; the political system thus is more likely to be autocratic, and 'constitutionalism' and limited government are rare."[39]

These propositions exemplify the weaknesses of a formidable volume of literature, although this particular set has the advantage of greater sharpness than much of its kind.[40] Tersely, what we do not know and perhaps what we cannot conceive of in more than metaphorical terms (items 1-3), we are asked to assume. What we can be pretty certain about, as a very general proposition (item 4), we are offered as an hypothesis. This sketches the misuse of model-building.

Such model-building efforts inspire only a superficial confidence. To be sure, they do carry some of the raiment of rigorous work. Moreover, such models can be elegantly done, and this with comforting consistency with what is already known. And all this can be done, given a subtle misuse, while submerging crucial methodological issues and requiring only tools traditionally in the kit of the political scientist, particularly "intuitive" ones. Hence the popularity of macroscopic models in political science—decision-making models, conflict models, general learning-theory models, systems models, the pressure-group models, and so on. Hence also their undistinguished record for generating cumulative empirical research, despite great expenditures of talent, ingenuity, and other resources in short supply.

Given the nature of garden-variety models, little hope can be held out for happier outcomes. That is, such models usually are not tested against external events; they seldom are formulated in terms permitting external testing, or even in terms encouraging it; and these models sometimes are formulated in ways that are self-fulfilling and thus defy testing. Consequently, Criterion ii is not met in much model-building in Political Science.

There are further grounds for the pessimism of our evaluation. The basic propositions of such models often are of unestablished validity, and indeed they may be in heated dispute. Moreover, these propositions are often part of some macroscopic model that is less amenable to analysis than (let us say) what the sociologist Merton called "middle-level theory." The scope of such models being what it commonly is, even the most careful analysis is likely to be shot through with a large number of implicit propositions dealing with reality or desirable states of affairs. Such propositions are beyond testing in many cases, even if their formulators have an active interest in verification and replication. A profusion of alternative models, that is to say, is highly probable.

The work of Fred W. Riggs is typical of model-building in the discipline. To a significant degree, his typologies rise above testing, or pre-empt it. Moreover, when testing efforts are made, they strongly tend to be indirect and very delicate, seeking confirmation in external models whose validity is also unestablished. For example, Riggs notes that: "The foregoing arguments support the idea that [the sociologist David Riesman's concept of] inner-direction may be an important pattern of motivation among the elites of transitional societies. Our position would be strengthened *if we could find any logical reason* why inner-direction should be regarded as characteristic for personality direction in the prismatic world [read 'transitional societies,' or 'underdeveloped areas']."[41] That Riesman's typology rests on shaky supports makes problematic the value of Riggs' enterprise, even if he could find "any logical reason" for it and even if a "logical reason" sufficed to empirically support a complex verbalization.

Our case against model-building applies generally, but we can make it more specific here in two ways. First, we stress the advantages of model-building which surely exist. Second, we note the limited sense in which our comments apply to one variety of model-building, namely simulation.

The value of the typical model-building enterprise should be underscored, even though its value to scientific effort is strictly limited. Rapoport thus concludes that the typical model-building enterprise at best aids in recognizing and categorizing phenomena, which are but components of scientific effort. The theoretician consequently enlarges his conceptual repertoire and may facilitate his search for variables and their lawful relations, even "when he is a long way from a successful theory." To equate the typical model-building effort to science, however, is akin to restricting "medicine . . . to diagnosis, while problems of prognosis, prophylaxis, and treatment remained untouched." Rapoport elaborated his point in terms that enrich our analysis. He noted that:

> . . . All such programs, in fact, are aimed toward the creation of a *taxonomy*. Their successful completion enables the "theoretician" to "diagnose" observe phenomena as members of theoretically established categories. Clearly, such programs succeed only to the extent of delineating entities to be talked about—i.e., the *subjects* of supposedly meaningful assertions. They do not touch upon the problem of determining what is to be said about the entities. They do not deal with the *predicates* of assertions. Recognition, not prediction, is the end product of systematic taxonomy.[42]

Our case against the typical model-building effort is less apt for one variety of the species, the variety called *simulation,* which makes use of the speed and power of computers and often requires complex mathematical manipulations.[43] Simulations of this kind may be designated as "little man, much machine" systems. Let us concentrate on the analytical uses of such narrowly defined simulation, temporarily neglecting "much man, little machine" systems such as early versions of the international game developed at Northwestern. Basically, for present purposes, simulation can be taken to involve the putting of experiential data into the memory banks of a computer, let us say the maintenance records of a SAC base. Various "decision rules" concerning the priorities to be given certain types of maintenance orders then can be tested against the computer's inputs of (for example) the actual experience of maintenance demands over some period of time. The various "decision rules" then may be compared in terms of their usefulness for accomplishing the business at hand, that is, getting a plane into the air as quickly as possible after maintenance is required. Such a simulation thus has the purpose of indicating which decision rule permits the lowest turn-around time.

Simulation has much to recommend it in the wide variety of cases in which it is applicable. First, simulation can provide answers that were once beyond calculation, or required so much manpower and such cumbersome calculations that they were never attempted. Thus one simulation run on a SAC base's maintenance record demonstrated that of the several decision rules for servicing aircraft that were compared, the unsophisticated 'first come, first served' rule was as good as any. A similar demonstration without the computer would have been very difficult.

Second, simulation is useful even in cases where less elaborate operations provide clear enough answers, in the sense that it permits estimates of costs and benefits. Thus one simulation of SAC maintenance operations demonstrated the awkwardness of a basic 9–5 work schedule. This is clear enough to the unaided intellect, given that most flights are made during the daylight hours and that many demands for maintenance consequently would have to wait overnight for service. The simulation, however, also attached relatively firm costs to various alternative work schedules, thereby permitting a judgment of just how comparatively costly a conventional work schedule was in terms of increased turn-around time.

Third, simulation is convenient in that it "collapses" time. Thus, on a relatively simple model, five minutes of computer time may simulate one month of experience. The possibilities for experimentation, then, are patently substantial.

Fourth, methodological developments promise perhaps a two-thirds reduction in programming time in the near future. *Simscript*, for example, may have that much of an advantage over *Fortran*. As programming comes to utilize "near-English," although this is a longer-range proposition, even further reductions in programming time may be expected.

However, simulation has its significant liabilities as a technique for contributing to an empirical science of politics. Some troublesome, but surmountable, features may be sketched briefly. First, experience with simulation has been concentrated in relatively narrow areas, for example, in scheduling the work of a job-order shop. More complex simulations are less well explored. Indeed, so undeveloped is the art that the most ambitious simulation thus far attempted—that of a large and diversified business organization—was programmed successfully, but no one has yet been able to design an experiment that can exploit the program. Third, machine simulation requires tremendous expenditures of time, as the political scientist is likely to view such matters. Perhaps five programming man-years, for example, may be required for even a moderately complex simulation.

One further factor more significantly limits simulation for research purposes appropriate to Political Science. Thus, in one sense, simulation studies are particularistic even when all relevant data have been fed into the computer. For example, a simulation model appropriate for one SAC base's maintenance operations need not be appropriate for others. Differing behavioral factors may lead to different experiential records, and such factors have been neglected in existing simulations. For example, whether a specific airbase has high-cohesiveness or low-cohesiveness work units will make a very significant difference in its record.

In the usual case, of course, not all relevant data are fed into a simulation program (which is hardly surprising). Moreover, the simulation is not likely to point up the fact (which is very significant). In this sense, simulation basically requires the existence of those concepts and operations whose development is the major early burden of scientific work. Simulation is not likely to generate even the need for such work, as, for example, by yielding deviant cases which may be explained by developing appropriate intervening variables. Such a consequence is not impossible, but it is unlikely. For any single simulation model probably will replicate its experimental results with only a few sets of experiential data to check the consistency of the results. Hence there is fairly high probability that deviant cases will go unobserved. Moreover, even if the deviant cases are isolated, the simulation effort often will approximate using a 16-inch cannon to hunt ducks. The weapon dwarfs the target.

Where only formal properties suffice for a simulation exercise, or where only established empirical concepts and their corresponding operations are involved, this bias of simulation is less important or is of no consequence.

A conclusion seems appropriate, therefore. Model-building has a mixed appropriateness, given the nature of the data with which Political Science must deal. This conclusion rests upon two factors. First, there are significant problems with testing the results of simulation runs against actual experience in scientifically useful ways. Many practical purposes, however, can be well served by simulation runs. Second, and more important, Political Science plays to a major weakness of "much machine, little man" simulations, since the discipline has only begun to develop concepts and operations appropriate to its empirical interests.[44] These two factors imply that Criteria ii and iii will be unevenly met by model-building via mathematical simulations.

## IV. THE MATHEMATIZERS

One must speak cautiously about the uses in Political Science of the several mathematics. This caution is appropriate for several reasons. There are an incredible variety of mathematical and statistical approaches to a wide variety of subjects of interest to political scientists. Thus mathematical techniques have been applied to court cases, election results, party strength, and so on; and proto-mathematical attempts have been made to supplement verbal analyses in areas of political philosophy. The present usefulness of mathematics in Political Science also covers an enormous range. Finally, there can be no doubt that every science must resort to increasingly more refined mathematical operations.[45]

Certain general comments, however, can be of value in outlining the very real constraints on today's use of mathematics in Political Science. Although these constraints are often neglected, the position here is not that all mathematics are irrelevant under all conditions at all stages of development of a science of politics, but that other work now has a definite priority. This moderate position applies particularly to the use of mathematics in constructing models. The argument here applies with much diminished force to the testing of models; and it applies even less to the common use of mathematics or statistics to facilitate description. Distinguishing these three uses of mathematics is important both in concept and practice. Much valuable contemporary work in Political Science, for example, involves mathematical or statistical manipulations in what can be called natural-history classification.[46] The comments below refer basically to the mathematical building of deductively formulated theory, to which natural-history classification is a necessary and preliminary step. The following chapter will add detail concerning these types of theory.

Given a restricted focus on deductively formulated theory, three factors particularly limit the application of mathematics in Political Science. First, any mathematics—even the mathematics of simple integers—is itself a model built upon arbitrary assumptions. Many of these assumptions are so fine and subtle that they still elude the most intensive analysis. The point holds even for the simplest of mathematical operations, for example. And, many of the more powerful computational techniques—which are themselves models—raise significant questions about whether they create information or merely much "noise" from the multitudinous successive approximations they require.[47]

A crucial limit on applications of the mathematics to theory-building then, is the degree to which the properties of any specific data universe coincide with the properties of the particular mathematical model (and its associated computational techniques) to be applied to that universe. Prosaically, the use of Euclidean geometry in planning a transoceanic flight has little to recommend it; its use in making a breadbox is another matter. Perhaps more revealingly, linear algebra is a particularly useful model for solving a wide range of problems, particularly given such computational models as the simplex method in linear programming. Even after careful selection of the problem, however, reality usually must be 'smoothed' somewhat to fit the mold of the mathematical and computational models.

The trick, as usual, is knowing how far one can go before such smoothing falsifies reality. This encourages cautious mathematical applications to many problem areas in Political Science. For we have little experience with the smoothing problem. Moreover, many "solutions" cannot be tested independently, or at least cannot be tested easily. There should be far more building of disciplinary breadboxes, that is, than mathematical planning of transoceanic flights. Certainly, at least, there is ample evidence that the use in Political Science of various mathematical models has encouraged some smoothing that gives too much to the mathematical model and too little to reality.[48] Relatedly, many areas of relevance to Political Science clearly invite mathematical and statistical analysis to facilitate description or natural-history classification.

Second, there is a related way of making the same point. When we build a breadbox we know the significant physical dimensions—length, width, and height—that a useful formal model must encompass. Knowing these dimensions, we can then determine that Euclidean geometry can be extended so as to permit the handling of these dimensions, and that solid geometry does the job even better in the immediate space in which we live. Bluntly, however, we are far from the knowledge of those dimensions that are relevant for describing many phenomena of interest to the political scientist. In analyzing a legislative roll-call, for example, direction (yea or nay) and magnitude (percentage yeas) seem patently useful dimensions. But other dimensions seem both obvious and important, although they are analytically elusive. The differential intensities with which legislators vote yea or nay, for example, fall in this category. And still other dimensions may be significant although they elude our present comprehension. Isolating such dimensions, then, is a necessary preliminary to constructing mathematical models.

Third, reality imposes almost irreversible constraints on the movement from scientific law to scientific measurement to mathematical statements of quantitative relations. Kuhn put the point in these terms: "The road from scientific law to scientific measurement can rarely be travelled in the reverse direction."[49] Nature, then, is a jealous mistress of her secrets. In the absence of a notion of lawful relations, quantification and mathematical manipulation will tend to be abortive, if not cruelly self-fulfilling. Without such theoretical orientations toward data, Kuhn explains, the sheer volume of phenomena would overwhelm the researcher. Given such orientations, he continues, "phenomena fall into a pattern, take on form and relative importance, and can be grappled. The major zigs in the zig-zag course of science result from shifts in such orientations." Not that such orientations are some be-all and end-all. They merely furnish the basis for detailed analysis; they cannot take the place of such analysis.

The point may be put otherwise. Typically, goes this argument, scientific progress follows such an order: insight about empirical regularities → measurement → quantification → mathematization.

The preceding progression needs little qualification, but it does require some. That is, the constraints imposed by nature are only almost irreversible. Thus an important parameter may thrust itself forward as a mathematically determined invariant even though its existence was not anticipated. Rapoport illustrated the point:

> For example, the energy and the entropy changes in a system reveal themselves as "state variables" in the thermodynamic sense by being represented as certain line integrals independent of the path of integration. Here a mathematical invariance points to a physical "reality." Once this is recognized, one naturally hunts for other invariants, and a number have proved their conceptual usefulness, e.g., the Helmholtz work function, the enthalpy, etc.[50]

Given the priority commonly dictated by nature, then, the isolation of the theoretically important "somethings" to measure must precede useful measurement and mathematical manipulations of subtlety and power. Various mathematical and statistical techniques may help meet this priority, to be sure, thereby helping meet Criterion III. But the burden of proof is on these models and not on reality.

## V. TOWARD GREATER RELEVANCE: A CASE STUDY

It is disingenuous and uncharitable even to imply that scholars utilizing the three approaches to Political Science—the philosophic persuasion, the model-builders, and the mathematizers—have been wasting their time at their respective labors. Rather, the problem is one of the direction that these several efforts have tended to take. For with some modifications, work of all three types can be made more relevant to the scientific study of politics. Specifically, work of all three types can be made to meet the demands of the three criteria for scientific work suggested above. How this might be done, moreover, is not obscure.

Consider contemporary Anthropology. In many significant particulars, its developmental problems are akin to those faced in Political Science. Recent developments that promise a convenient way out of such difficulties in Anthropology, then, are of some significance for political scientists.

Like Political Science, Anthropology suffers an embarrassing richness of competing models. These may be classified, following Gouldner and Peterson, as Single-Factor Theories and Multiple Causation Theories.[51] Unfortunately, the virtues of the two types of models are not complementary. Rather, their inadequacies tend to compound one another. For Single-Factor Theories—stressing one explanatory element such as climate, geography, natural resources, technology, and the like—suffer from defects of both conception and execution. Conceptually, such theories explain the variation in many dependent variables in terms of one independent variable. This neglects the many ways in which the dependent variables influence one another, for example, as well as the ways in which the dependent factors influence the independent variable. In practice, Single-Factor Theories struggle all too obviously against their conceptual inadequacies. Such theories, as Parsons concluded, "had a notorious tendency to overreach the facts."[52] Multiple causation—including the various versions of functionalism—tends in contrast to degenerate into this awkward operational dictum: Everything influences everything else. Acting on this dictum commonly raised (and neglected) the major question of the relative significance of the many variables and left a heritage of an enormous number of covariants which threatened to overwhelm researchers.

Like Political Science, also, Anthropology is enlivened by pervasive and contrasting orientations to data. Thus one major school stresses the primary role of moral beliefs, values, and norms in interpreting anthropological data. And another major school persistently stresses the primacy of technology, despite the many contrary arguments raised since Marx's time and, indeed, since at least the time of Heraclitus. Thus the acute contemporary observer E. H. Carr was not deterred by the critical literature. "Experience shows," he noted, "that the structure of society at any given time and place, as well as the prevailing theories about it, are largely governed by the way in which the material needs of society are met."[53]

As in Political Science, matters could only get worse without a change of direction. Conventional tools permitted no definitive choice between the many competing models of the two types. Meanwhile, proponents of the several models continued to generate data that had the more or less self-fulfilling tendency to support the particular theory that induced the research. For the scientist suffers as does mortal man: The questions he asks will influence (if not determine) the answers he gets. Gouldner and Peterson at once put the problem pointedly and sketch the required research strategy in these terms:

> Ironically, however, this very accumulation of data creates an embarrassment of riches for the would-be builder of theory. There is scarcely any theory which is not lent seeming support by judicious illustrations selectively drawn from this treasurehouse of data. Conversely, there is no theory which is not seemingly controverted by the selection of equally partial data. The abiding problem is how the growing mass of data may either be mobilized as a whole, or else somehow reduced to manipulable essentials, or how it may be systematically brought to bear on theory.[54]

A sophisticated mathematical technique—factor analysis—promises a way out of the anthropologist's bind. Thus, in general, the technique permits the isolation of some parsimonious set of dimensions necessary to reproduce the matrix of the statistical intercorrelations of a larger number of variables. At the same time, factor analysis permits a judgment of the relative importance of particular dimensions in accounting for the variation in that matrix of intercorrelations. The technique, that is, helps avoid the difficulties associated with both Single-Factor Theories and Multiple Causation.

Gouldner and Peterson applied factor analysis to the intercorrelations of ratings of some 59 traits for a large number of societies for which the Yale Cross-Cultural Files provide data.[55] Four dimensions were considered particularly important in reproducing the derived correlation matrices: "Lineality," "Sex Dominance," "Level of Technology," and "Norm-sending." Factor analysis demonstrated that these four accounted for the bulk of the differences observed in the 59 traits scored for 71 "primitive or pre-industrial societies."

Factor analysis, like all techniques, may settle some issues while raising others. For example, the naming of any factors isolated is diversely arbitrary. That is, factor analysis only provides clues as to which traits characterize some dimension and how much they "load" that dimension.

**TABLE I.1 Factor T: Level of Technology**

| *Item* | *Varimax-Loading* | *Trait* |
|---|---|---|
| 16 | .760 | Pottery |
| 11 | .705 | Use of grain for food |
| 28 | .696 | Prevalence of war |
| 14 | .654 | Mining and smelting metals |
| 20 | .577 | Slavery |
| 13 | .551 | Domesticated animals other than herded |
| 18 | .546 | Weaving |
| 22 | .450 | Money or a standard medium of exchange |
| 10 | .442 | Agriculture |
| 29 | .427 | Codified laws |

Source: Adapted from *Technology and The Moral Order* by Alvin W. Gouldner and Richard A. Peterson, copyright (c) 1962 by The Bobbs-Merrill Company, Inc., reprinted by permission of the publisher.

Table I.1 illustrates the major trait loadings for the factor "Level of Technology." A loading of 1.00, for example, would mean that a particular trait was a perfect measure of that dimension. Naming the factor would be no great problem in such a case. Normally, as in Table I.1, the various traits only imperfectly measure the underlying dimension. The analyst, then, must identify the dimension in terms of those traits that contribute the heaviest loadings to it. In Table I.1, many of the heaviest loadings are contributed by traits with a clear relation to level of technology (e.g., items 11, 14, 13, 18, and 22). Other traits (e.g., 16 and 29) can be shown to have such a relation, although it is not obvious. Finally, the full-fledged definition of other traits (e.g., item 10) makes clear their relation to the level of technology. Demonstrations of these two conclusions are beyond the scope of the present effort.[56] There seems little question, however, about the labeling of the factor in Table I.1.

The interpretation of factor loadings can be more conjectural. Thus Factor A—Apollonianism, or Norm-sending—may seem to have a high loading of traits relevant to religion or magic. But several items (26, 29, and 30) refer to the centralization of authority, which implies a high degree of what may be called "impulse control." Other traits (e.g., items 51, 56, and 57), appropriately enough, suggest institutional ways of here-and-now reinforcement of high levels of impulse control through ceremonies and rituals emphasizing the promise of a future reward, as in appropriate solemnization and careful preparation for the journey into the after-life. Item 44, and the negative loading it contributes to Factor A, also supports the interpretation of this factor as relating to impulse control. The negative sign of the factor loading, roughly, means that

**TABLE I.2 Factor A: Apollonianism, or Norm-Sending**

| *Item* | *Varimax-Loading* | *Trait* |
|---|---|---|
| 51 | .707 | Elaboration of ceremony and ritual |
| 26 | .545 | Power vested in chief |
| 57 | .540 | Attractiveness of future life |
| 50 | .510 | Organized priesthood |
| 44 | —.491 | Marriage by capture |
| 15 | .462 | Metals secured from outside |
| 29 | .437 | Codified laws |
| 56 | .433 | Elaboration of mortuary ceremonies |
| 30 | .403 | Authority vested in judges |

Source: Adapted from *Technology and The Moral Order* by Alvin W. Gouldner and Richard A. Peterson, copyright (c) 1962 by the Bobbs-Merrill Company, Inc., reprinted by permission of the publisher.

the reduced incidence, or absence, of marriage by capture contributes to Factor A. In similar terms, even some other traits that imply a religio-magical complex (e.g., item 50) may be interpreted as part of the institutionalized system necessary to reinforce impulse control.

In sum, factor analysis pointed up the interrelations of the empirical and the normative. Factor A may be interpreted reasonably as tapping the realm of moral beliefs, values, and norms. While Factor T lends credence to the positions of students like Marx, then, Factor A contributes considerable support to those who seek an explanation of the differences between societies in other than materialist terms.

Factor analysis can be put to further service. It permits a judgment as to the relative significance of the several factors in accounting for the differences observed between the several societies. Recall that four factors were considered capable of explaining the bulk of these differences. What is the order of priority of these factors? Various operations, too detailed to report on here, suggest that not only are Factor A and Factor T most important, but also that they are related positively and significantly. As Gouldner and Peterson conclude: "... the higher the level of technology, the higher the degree of demanded impulse control ..."[57]

There are sharp limitations on even the most useful of techniques, of course, and factor analysis is no exception. Notice, however, that factor analysis has convenient limitations as far as the disciplinary development of Political Science is concerned. Thus the technique leaves much work for the model-builders in Anthropology who must explain the relation of Factors A and T in terms that permit empirical verification. Factor analysis also leaves matters in the hands of those who will study both technology and value systems, so as (among other goals) to isolate increasingly more refined traits or variables, to provide new data, and to analyze the implications and the interplay of values.

## VI. CONCLUSION

There is a convenient way, then, of arranging matters so that the three significant approaches in Political Science discussed earlier can contribute with mutual profit to the development of a science of politics. To be sure, some uses of factor analysis have been attempted in areas of interest to political scientists,[58] but none so neatly illustrates the technique's ability to tie together the three major approaches to Political Science analyzed above. Moreover, there are enormously wider fields that invite cultivation. Many problems in comparative government and comparative administration, for example, are amenable to the approach that shows so much promise in Anthropology. Indeed, the classification of types of societies that has both sparked and accompanied the contemporary interest in comparative administration is a problem cut from the same cloth as that confronting Anthropology.[59] Existing classifications in Political Science, however, tend to suffer from the model-building liabilities sketched earlier.[60]

There are difficulties with the approach outlined here, of course, several of which may be emphasized briefly. First, note that the argument has shifted focus from methodological issues to a technique. This shift in focus has its temporary advantages. Primarily, applications of factor analysis have the effect of enforcing appropriate methodological changes on all three approaches. Consider our three minimal criteria for scientific work. The application of factor analysis spotlights the integration of "fact" and "value" emphases required at certain stages of study, and it also implies their segregation at other stages. Moreover, any factor-analytical application must be tested against data external to the derived dimensional model, as in replicative and predictive studies. Indeed, this puts the point too passively. Rather, the basic purpose of factor analysis is to suggest dimensions of reality which can then be operationally and conceptually refined and tested for predictive usefulness. That is, factor analysis is by basic design not a be-all and end-all technique. Its very development is rooted in the processes of empirical inquiry. Hence it is designed to facilitate movement from the natural-history stage of development, and from the intuition of empirical regularities that is the product of this early phase of scientific inquiry. The technique helps isolate those "somethings" that are necessary to order reality, to permit scientific description in terms of a parsimonious set of concepts, laws, and theories. Finally, since factor analysis provides a first-approximation of the dimensions of reality necessary to account for the variance within some batch of data, the technique therefore places attention squarely on what is the basic scientific issue.

In at least three complex senses, then, factor analysis encourages a methodological orientation that is consistent with the three present criteria for scientific work: methodological compatibility with existing scientific effort in other areas of inquiry; external (dis)confirmation; and a basic focus on isolating dimensions of reality. Hence the earlier assertion that the shift to technique in this chapter has methodological advantages.

The illustration of a technique also implies more general methodological lessons. The experience in Sociology and Anthropology with Multiple Causation is particularly relevant to a major contemporary trend in Political Science. Of course, "functionalists" of various stripes have been the major carriers of that approach to reality. Therefore the problems in Sociology and Anthropology with functionalism, and work such as that of Gouldner and Peterson designed to resolve such difficulties, both have a clear relevance for Political Science. For functionalism is getting a major build-up in the discipline,[61] and there is no need to repeat mistakes that other disciplines already have made.

Second, factor analysis can be abused as well as used. For example, the technique requires quantified data, and this implies its several problems. Some relatively painless accommodations are possible in early work, however. Thus Gouldner and Peterson took a direct and uncomplicated approach to quantification. They made use of simple rank-orders to distinguish societies on the several traits, based upon ratings on simple scales made by trained anthropologists drawing on the available descriptive literature. These rank-orders were intercorrelated and provided the matrices for the factor analysis. A similar approach would be applicable (for example) in many areas of comparative administration. There is, of course, no guarantee of the validity or reliability of the approach to quantification chosen by Gouldner and Peterson.

Substantial advantages serve to counterbalance the dangers of misuse, fortunately. Beginning the dialectic of moving toward quantification and mathematization has much to recommend it, to cite an obvious point.

Moreover, as with all techniques, the usefulness of factor analysis will be greatest after problems of theoretical significance have been identified, after appropriate concepts for their examination have been developed, and after relevant data have been collected. In addition, however, factor analysis provides some internal tests of a self-correcting kind which help in such endeavors as well as depend upon them.[62]

Replication is a related problem in factor analysis. That is, the results of a factor analysis are "soft" in at least two senses. The substantive meaning of any dimensions isolated may be elusive, a matter of particular moment when attempts are made to test the predictive usefulness of the dimensions, and their operational definition consequently becomes necessary. Then too, the results of factor analysis may vary significantly, depending upon the particular data included in any two "similar" studies. The associated issues are thorny, but they have been met with some success in limited areas.[63]

Third, factor analysis certainly is not the only technique appropriate for the satisfactory analysis of political data. A Dahl can do well enough with non-mathematical tools, for example.[64] Moreover, certain other techniques—such as hierarchical decomposition—which avoid some of the difficulties associated with factor analysis will be discussed later. Factor analysis does have substantial advantages for certain purposes under rather specific conditions, however, and that is the only point at issue here. Note, for example, that factor analysis directs attention to co-variation in nature. Thus it helps avoid some troublesome issues associated with causal inference, with which variables are dependent and which independent, and so on.[65] Certain aspects of causal inference will be raised later in context; hence bare mention here will suffice.

## NOTES

1. Robert T. Golembiewski, "Toward the Administrative Sciences: Methodological Directions for Public Administration," *International Review of Administrative Sciences,* 30, No. 2 (1965), 113–23.

2. David Butler, *The Study of Political Behavior* (London: Hutchinson, 1958); Bernard Crick, *The American Science of Politics* (Berkeley and Los Angeles: University of California Press, 1959); and Herbert J. Storing (ed.), *Essays on the Scientific Study of Politics* (New York: Holt, Rinehart, & Winston, 1962).

3. The amplitude of the effect may be judged by comparing two significant period pieces, such as *Research Frontiers in Politics and Government,* 1955 Brookings Lectures (Washington, D.C.: Brookings Institution, 1955), and James C. Charlesworth (ed.), *The Limits of Behavioralism in Political Science* (Philadelphia: American Academy of Political and Social Science, 1962). The latter volume, which is less breathless about Political *Science,* was circulated very widely (and without charge).

4. Storing, *op. cit.*

5. The dimensions of the spiral are suggested dramatically by comparing the sharply increasing acidity of this progression of work: Butler's *The Study of Political Behaviour;* Crick's *The American Science of Politics;* and Storing's *Essays on the Scientific Study of Politics.* The most recent major critical effort escalates the spiral in many respects. For example, its editors sharply phrase one of their volume's differences with Storing's work. Storing is said to see behavioralists as "naive"; but Charles A. McCoy and John Playford see the methodology of behavioralism as "a pathological condition." *A Political Politics: A Critique of Behavioralism* (New York: Crowell, 1967), p. 10.

6. This is our judgment. McCoy and Playford, *op. cit.,* p. 9, seem to agree. They note: "many (perhaps most) political scientists are still unreconstructed" on the issue of the behavioral approach. In opposition, however, note that Herbert A. Simon does make the "Political Science Hall of Fame" detailed in Albert Somit and Joseph Tannenhaus, *American Political Science: A Profile of a Disicipline* (New York: Atherton Press, 1964), p. 73.

7. Robert A. Dahl, "The Behavioral Approach," *American Political Science Review,* 55 (December, 1961), 763–72.

8. Heinz Eulau, *The Behavioral Persuasion in Politics* (New York: Random House, 1963).

9. Early rumblings of discontent can be seen in Eric F. Voegelin, *The New Science of Politics* (Chicago: University of Chicago Press, 1952) and in the various exchanges in the professional journals between the Waldos, Simons, Hallowells, et al.

10. Paul Appleby's *Policy and Administration* (University, Ala.: University of Alabama Press, 1949) played a major role in stressing the intimate relations of policy and administration.

11. See Frederich V. Hayek's series beginning with "The Counter-Revolution of Science," *Economica,* 8 (New Series) (February, 1941), 9–36.

12. Quoted in Crick, *op. cit.,* p. 213.

13. Christian Bay, *The Structure of Freedom* (Stanford, Calif.: Stanford University Press, 1958), p. 8, works himself into such an uncomfortable corner when he writes: "The social scientist who strictly limits himself to the role of an observer of human behavior can only report what it appears that men actually do want, or in fact believe they ought to want. Statements about what men ought to want would amount to a projection of the observer's own values. . . ." Bay's position is incisively analyzed by Walter Berns, "The Behavioral Sciences and the Study of Political Things," *American Poltical Science Review,* 55 (September, 1961), pp. 550–59.

14. Harry V. Jaffa, "The Case Against Political Theory," *Journal of Politics,* 22 (May, 1960), 259.

15. Berns, *op. cit.,* p. 550.

16. Witness the neglect of a political machine by psychologists in the modern path-finding study of voting: Paul F. Lazarsfeld, Bernard Berelson, and Hazel Gaudet, *The People's Choice* (2nd ed.;

New York: Columbia University Press, 1948,) p. xxvii.

17. Berns, *op. cit.*, p. 558.

18. John H. Schaar, "Some Ways of Thinking About Equality," *Journal of Politics*, 26 (November, 1964), 868.

19. Strauss, "An Epilogue," in Storing, *op. cit.*, p. 308. Most self-avowed political *scientists* do seem classifiable as "liberal," and in this sense Strauss is correct. Strauss goes farther, however, and argues that the science of politics "rests on a dogmatic atheism" (p. 322). In contrast, true empirical endeavor seems to us necessarily based upon value propositions—like the existence of Truth and of an ordered universe—that are essentially conservative in at least some contemporary meanings of that term. Christian Bay's "Politics and Pseudopolitics: A Critical Evaluation of Some Behavioral Literature," *American Political Science Review*, 59 (March, 1965), 39–51, directs attention to some aspects of this value-nexus of empirical science. The following chapter stresses this necessary grounding of science in values.

20. See, for example, Robert L. Peabody, and Nelson W. Polsby (eds.), *New Perspectives on the House of Representatives* (Chicago: Rand McNally, 1963), pp. 237–39.

21. Berns, *op. cit.*, p. 550. Rothman's words are from his review of *Introduction a la Science Politique*, in the *American Political Science Review*, 53 (December, 1959), 1120.

22. Strauss, "An Epilogue," in Storing, *op. cit.*, p. 327.

23. Leo Strauss, *Natural Right and History* (Chicago: University of Chicago Press, 1953).

24. That the opinion has significant adherents is clear in much of the data summarized by Somit and Tannenhaus, *op. cit.*, especially pp. 14–17. That the opinion is growing is our own judgment.

25. Robert T. Golembiewski, *Men, Management, and Morality* (New York: McGraw-Hill, 1965).

26. Harry Wolfe, *Quantification:* A. *History of the Meaning of Measurement in the Natural and the Social Sciences* (Indianapolis, Ind.: Bobbs-Merrill, 1961).

27. Harvey Glickman, "Political Science," in Robert A. Lystad, *The African World* (New York: Praeger, 1965), p. 139. See also David Easton, *The Political System* (New York: Knopf, 1953).

27a. Somit and Tanenhaus, *op. cit.*, p. 55.

28. See, for example, Roland Young, *Approaches to the Study of Politics* (Evanston, Ill.: Northwestern University Press, 1958); Charles Hyneman, *The Study of Politics* (Urbana: University of Illinois Press, 1959); and Vernon Van Dyke, *Political Science: A Philosophical Analysis*, (Stanford: Stanford University Press, 1960). By way of contrast, see also Edwin G. Boring, *History, Psychology, and Science* (New York: Wiley, 1963).

29. There are early exceptions to this generalization, of course, most notably Plato and Machiavelli. Among contemporaries, Arnold Brecht has given significant attention to methodological issues, particularly in his *Political Theory* (Princeton, N.J.: Princeton University Press, 1959). And the first major published work of Fred M. Frohock, *The Nature of Political Inquiry* (Homewood, Ill.: Dorsey, 1967) reflects just the kinds of contributions to empirical analysis that can be made by adherents of the philosophic persuasion.

30. Rousseau did not unfailingly stick to his last. But note his approach to the proposition he takes as an empirical given: Man was born free and yet is everywhere in bondage. How this change in fact did come about, Rousseau cannot detail. But how this change may be creditably explained in terms of a utopian construct—now that is a problem he believes he can illumine.

31. The narrow definition of game theory is accepted here. Commentators like Martin Shubik, however, lean toward a definition that encompasses the whole of behavioral-mathematical analyses of human choice. See Shubik's *Game Theory and Related Approaches to Social Behavior* (New York: Wiley, 1964).

32. George H. Sabine, *A History of Political Theory* (2nd ed.; New York: Holt, 1950), p. 39.

33. Sabine's classic history of political philosophy sometimes approaches this position in evaluating Plato. Speaking of the *Laws*, for example, Sabine notes that

in that "theory Plato tried to come to grips with political actualities in a way that he never approached" in the *Republic. Ibid.,* p. 67. However, Sabine does not develop the methodological distinction between goal-based, empirical and utopian theories. Plato seems to do better on this score. For example, he noted at one point in his *Laws* that: "Thus we shall have as an accomplished fact and waking reality that result which we treated . . . as a mere dream, when we constructed a kind of picture of the union of reason and the head—*if,* that is to say, we have the members carefully selected and suitably trained . . . and thus finally made into wardens, the like of whom we have never before seen in our lives for excellence in safeguarding." Emphasis added. That "if" is not supported by any great optimism. See *The Laws,* translated by R. G. Bury (London: Heinemann, 1926), II, 569.

34. See particularly the close of the argument, *ibid.,* Vol. II, sec. 969 A-D. See also such points as sec. 945 ff. in the same volume.

35. Thomas L. Thorson (ed.), *Plato: Totalitarian or Democrat?* (Englewood Cliffs, N.J.: Prentice-Hall, 1963).

36. Milton Friedman, *Essays in Positive Economics* (Chicago: University of Chicago Press, 1953), p. 14.

37. Anthony Downs, *An Economic Theory of Democracy* (New York: Harper, 1957).

38. These propositions are isolated and analyzed in James Burnham, *Congress and the American Tradition* (Chicago: Regnery, 1959). The less explicit orthodoxy may be found in the American Political Science Association, *Toward A More Responsible Two-Party System* (New York: Rinehart, 1950).

39. John T. Dorsey, Jr., "The Information-Energy Model," pp. 8, 13. Paper presented at Meeting of the American Political Science Association, St. Louis, Mo., September 6–9, 1961.

40. Easton introduces his attempt to isolate a "political system" from a broader "environment" in a way that illustrates the present point. He notes at one point that he can only imply "that there is some kind of boundary between a political system and its environment." David Easton, *A Framework For Political Analysis* (Englewood Cliffs, N.J.: Prentice-Hall, 1965), p. 47. The same point is illustrated, if more subtly, by James M. Buchanan and Gordon Tullock, *The Calculus of Consent: Logical Foundations of Constitutional Democracy* (Ann Arbor: University of Michigan Press, 1962).

41. Fred W. Riggs, *Administration in Developing Countries: The Theory of Prismatic Society* (Boston: Houghton Mifflin, 1964), p. 91. For a similar but more detailed evaluation of Riggs's work, see Joseph La Palombara, "Public Administration and Political Change: A Theoretical Overview," in Charles Press and Allan Arian (eds.), *Empathy and Ideology: Aspects of Administrative Innovation* (Chicago: Rand McNally, 1967), esp. pp. 92–95.

42. Anatol Rapoport, "The Use of Theory in the Study of Politics," in Edward H. Buehrig (ed.), *Essays in Political Science* (Bloomington: Indiana University Press, 1966), pp. 12, 13, 21.

43. Perhaps the best-known computer simulation using significant inputs from players is analyzed in Kalman J. Cohen, William R. Dill, and Alfred A. Kuehn, *The Carnegie Tech Management Game* (Homewood, Ill.: Irwin, 1964). A "more man" system is discussed in Harold Guetzkow, et al., *Simulation in International Relations* (Englewood Cliffs, N.J.: Prentice-Hall, 1963).

44. Political scientists, however, have participated in very creative uses of computerized simulation techniques. We have in mind particularly Ithiel de Sola Pool, Robert P. Abelson, and Samuel Popkin, *Candidates, Issues and Strategies: A Computer Simulation* (rev. ed.; Cambridge, Mass.: The M.I.T. Press, 1965).

45. See, generally, James C. Charlesworth (ed.), *Mathematics and the Social Sciences* (Philadelphia: American Academy of Political and Social Science, 1963).

46. This awareness is refreshingly present in William H. Riker and Donald Niemi, "The Stability of Coalitions on Roll Calls in the House of Representatives," *American Political Science Review,* 56 (March, 1962), especially 64–65.

47. Oskar Morgenstern, "Limits to the Uses of Mathematics in Economics," in Charlesworth, *op. cit.*, p. 29.

48. Wallace Mendelson, "The Neo-Behavioral Approach to the Judicial Process: A Critique," *American Political Science Review*, 57 (September, 1963), 593–603.

49. Quoted in R. W. Gerard, "Quantification in Biology," pp. 205–6, in Woolf, *op. cit.*

50. Anatol Rapoport, "In Search of Quantifiable Parameters of Group Performance," in *First Conference in System Engineering* (New York: Wiley, 1960).

51. Alvin W. Gouldner and Richard A. Peterson, *Notes on Technology and the Moral Order* (Indianapolis, Ind.: Bobbs-Merrill, 1962), especially pp. 2–8.

52. Talcott Parsons, *Essays in Sociological Theory Pure and Applied* (Glencoe, Ill.: The Free Press, 1949), p. 24.

53. E. H. Carr, *The New Society* (Boston: Beacon Press, 1959), p. 19.

54. Gouldner and Peterson, *op. cit.*, p. 12.

55. The study employed data from the Files reported in Leo W. Simmons, *The Role of the Aged in Primitive Society* (New Haven, Conn.: Yale University Press, 1945).

56. Gouldner and Peterson, *op. cit.*, pp. 24–27.

57. *Ibid.*, p. 36.

58. Duncan MacRae, Jr., *The Dimensions of Congressional Voting* (Berkeley and Los Angeles: University of California Press, 1958); John G. Grumm, "A Factor Analysis of Legislative Behavior," *Midwest Journal of Political Science*, 7 (November, 1963), 336–56; Arthur S. Banks and Robert S. Textor, *A Cross-Polity Survey* (Cambridge, Mass.: Massachusetts Institute of Technology, 1963); Somit and Tannenhaus, *op. cit.*, and others. Pathfinding work is also in process at Northwestern University.

59. Fred Riggs, *The Ecology of Public Administration* (New York: Asia Publishing House, 1961).

60. The recent work of Banks and Textor, *op. cit.*, permits optimism about an improvement of the situation in this area.

61. Theodore Lowi, "Toward Functionalism in Political Science," *American Political Science Review*, 57 (September, 1963), 570–83, for example, adopts the approach. Common use of functionalism also has been made in the study of international relations and comparative government, and political scientists generally are more favorable to functionalism than are other social scientists. On both points, see Don Martindale (ed.), *Functionalism in the Social Sciences* (Philadelphia: American Academy of Political and Social Science, 1965), especially pp. 84–126.

62. For an illustration, see Robert T. Golembiewski's *The Small Group: An Analysis of Research Concepts and Operations* (Chicago: University of Chicago Press, 1962), pp. 74–86.

63. Particular success has been achieved in the study of small groups, as in the isolation of functional roles and the dimensions of leadership behavior. *Ibid.*, pp. 104–10 and 128–44.

64. Robert A. Dahl, *Who Governs?* (New Haven, Conn.: Yale University Press, 1961).

65. The emphasis upon co-variation rather than "causality" traces most directly to Karl Pearson, *The Grammar of Science* (London: J. M. Dent, 1937).

# ii

# Some Building Blocks of Empirical Science: Methodological Directions for Public Administration

The value of the preceding chapter is also its greatest fault. It stresses scope and generality, with some profit, it is hoped. But that chapter pays for value received in the neglect of key methodological elements and lack of specificity, and these are significant costs. These costs cannot, and fortunately need not, be suffered long.

The purpose here is to begin the task of reducing these costs and to do so within one of Political Science's major fields of inquiry—Public Administration. This field serves to spotlight crucial methodological issues that did not receive due attention because of Chapter I's focus on the usefulness of one analytical technique for sketching the possible integration of three approaches to a science of politics. Three specific tasks preoccupy this chapter. First, it develops the notion of developmental stages in scientific inquiry and in the history of disciplines. Second, the chapter provides detail on the crucial (and related) problems of conceptual and operational definition of dimensions of reality. Third, the chapter sharpens some methodologically useful distinctions between types of theories in Political Science by isolating three ways in which empirical and normative considerations must be integrated by a viable methodology for empirical work.

## I. THE NEED FOR METHODOLOGICAL PROGRESS: PUBLIC ADMINISTRATION AS REPRESENTATIVE OF A DISCIPLINE

The accelerating drive toward the development of the administrative sciences threatens to leave Public Administration behind. As the sociologist Whyte explained the successful infiltration of traditional disciplinary

This chapter originally appeared under the title "Toward the Administrative Sciences: Methodological Directions for Public Administration," *International Review of Administrative Sciences*, 30 (No. 2, 1964), 113–23. Modifications have been made to suit the present analysis.

boundaries: "Call it poaching if you will, but such an invasion is vitally needed."[1] Hence this effort, which outlines the methodological orientation required for scientific inquiry. The emphasis will be upon outlining the approach to reality which has proved useful for analytical purposes. Little attention will be devoted to justifying the outline in any sophisticated sense, which is the concern of the philosophy of science. The material to be presented is not novel. It is there for the taking in the literatures of the physical and life sciences, and less clearly in the behavioral sciences that have sprouted so profusely of late. If such methodological information is in the public domain, however, it has been relatively untapped by students of Public Administration or Political Science.[2] And nothing less than widespread knowledge and application will suffice.

These allusions to narrowness of focus and breadth of application may be given more content. The specific problems and needs derived from an interest in Public Administration constitute the warp of the work. These problems and needs are not unique to the discipline, however. Nor is the discipline somehow insular. Consequently, although the focus here is narrow, the methodological comments will apply with equal force to other subject-matter areas within Political Science which are amenable to empirical analysis. Even outlining all these areas would be an impossible burden here. Epigramatically, however, this analysis is crucial to (let us say) Aristotle's *Politics*. His *Ethics* can (for many purposes) get along quite well without it.

There is more point than convenience to the narrow focus here, however. The development of Public Administration, which to an extent is peculiarly its own, has brought students of the subject closer to the problems of empirical analysis than is the case with many other areas of Political Science.[3] Although this development has its patent deficiencies, it provides both a valuable and convenient base upon which to build and it also aids in communicating knowledge to those trained in the discipline. For example, Public Administration experienced an anti-science reaction by its own philosophic know-nothings, and this as early as the immediate post-World War II period. There are ample signs that the discipline has largely refined the contributions of lasting value from this reaction, and that it is once again seeking a more useful concept of science and its underlying methodology. Our phrasing is anthropomorphic, but the real probability is nonetheless that attention to methodology in Public Administration will serve as a powerful catalyst to the ferment undoubtedly going on. Relatedly, Public Administration plateaued as an area of concentration after World War II. Today, however, it radiates all the signs of sharply-intensifying activity.[4] This activity can at once gain further impetus from, as well as be sustained by, methodological concern.

## II. SCIENCE AND PUBLIC ADMINISTRATION: PAST FAILURE AND A HOPEFUL PROPOSAL FOR A SYNTHESIS

The specific *Why?* and the *What?* of this building and communicating within the context of Public Administration may be expressed in three working propositions which outline the present area of concern. They are:

1. Public Administration as a discipline is at a crucial stage in its development;
2. If Public Administration is to develop further, a different and more rigorous methodology must be employed wherever possible; and
3. Methodological development in Public Administration implies research which both provides training in the appropriate methodology and yields results that are not trivial in terms of the long-standing interests of the discipline.

These working propositions have not preoccupied students of Public Administration. Indeed, their handling of such propositions may be characterized fairly in this way:[5] admit Proposition 1; discuss 2, if at all, polemically in terms of the possibility or impossibility of a science of Public Administration; and never get around in a comprehensive fashion to the investigations implied by Proposition 3.

The science versus art conflict in Public Administration reflects this unsatisfactory state of affairs. Such a controversy is a keystone in the preliminary struggle of any discipline toward a more rigorous methodology. Public Administration has not moved beyond this preliminary effort. The four central phases in the discipline's history of science versus art controversy explain this arrested development: a shower of papers in the twenties and thirties which attempted to endow the new discipline with the attributes of science by literary fiat[6]; a more sophisticated rebirth of interest in the question in the late forties and early fifties which centered around a value-free approach[7]; a counterattack by advocates of the public policy approach which reached maximum intensity in the late forties and emphasized the place of value elements in administration[8]; and a contemporary slackening of interest in which the dominant fashion-by-ennui is that Public Administration reflects aspects of both science and art, without clear specification of exactly what is meant[9].

These four phases culminate in a methodological dead-end. The early contributions did not establish a viable approach to a science of

Public Administration, for they were hopeful rather than searching. They reflected the desire for the prestige of fields called sciences rather than a commitment to their methodology.

The failure of the later "scientific approach" to attract significant support or to achieve a definite place in the discipline is more complex. But certain elements in that failure seem clear and important enough to be briefly noted here:

1. The injunction to become "scientific" was quite general, with no clear indication of where or how this was to come about.
2. Many students of Public Administration argued—or suspected—that the value-free study area proposed for scientific Public Administration was quite unlike the one necessary to encompass Public Administration as it really is.[10]
3. The attempt to set up a value-free area of concern for Public Administration which was part of this later scientific approach was interpreted as a redefinition and severe contraction of disciplinary boundaries.
4. The later approach unnecessarily linked science in Public Administration with logical positivism, which has attracted strong opposition.
5. Some public policy-ers interpreted the later approach as neo-traditional and as threatening to re-establish in slightly different terms the politics versus administration dichotomy against which they had raised strong and successful objection.[11]
6. The later scientific approach has failed to produce significant results in the discipline. Moreover, the model of the later value-free approach—Simon's *Administrative Behavior*—is a global treatment of decision-making.[12] This area is one in which value elements are most important in practice, and thus it is a poor strategic point at which to apply such an approach.
7. Some students perceived that—whatever the relative merits of the two concepts—*decision-making* was intended as a substitute for *public policy* in the core definition of Public Administration.[13] This gave a decided "political" cast to the debate over science in the area, for it was generally recognized that public policy was congenial to the traditional interests and approaches of *political scientists.* Decision-making implied something quite different, even if the specific dimensions of the differences were unclear.

The traditional doubts about any science of human behavior also threw some weight on the scales already over-balanced against a vaguely defined plea for science in Public Administration.

Thus the problems of empirical analysis have been approached in Public Administration—if unsatisfactorily. A careful analysis is required to avoid the scholarly potholes that remain as evidence of this early industry, and as road-blocks to methodological change.

## III. SCIENCE: A THREE-WAY APPROACH[14]

Part of the difficulty in science's failure to find a secure place in Public Administration has been the general lack of discussions of science that can bear critical examination. Those students who left a record of their understanding of science generally did so briefly. This section will attempt to remedy this oversight somewhat by sketching a three-element working model of empirical science.

### A. The Problem

Much of the discussion of science in and out of Public Administration mistakenly begins and ends with *the* scientific method. Science, however, begins not with a method but with a problem (i.e., any hitch for which one does not have an explanation). This obvious point is often neglected, as is the obvious implication to which it leads: emphasis on the problematic situation means that instead of a method of science (see below) one must speak of *specific methods* and their relation to the types of problems under consideration. The same is true of any specific technique. Consequently, a field of inquiry is not excluded from scientific status because it does not utilize the methods or techniques of any field of inquiry generally recognized as a science.

Nevertheless, certain general phases in the scientific handling of any specific problem can be isolated. These general phases comprise a four-sequence model. The sequences are:

1. The analysis of the particular problem which induces inquiry;
2. The Baconian inductive observation of those data which problem-analysis suggests are relevant;
3. The development of hypotheses suggested by the relevant data; and
4. The experimental or observational test of hypotheses and their logical consequences, a successful test demonstrating the provisional usefulness of the underlying theoretical system, and rejection implying the need to modify or reject the underlying theory.

Care must be exercised, however, not to extend the interpretation of this paradigm too far. For certain problems (roughly, in the physical sciences) have been more vigorously and successfully attacked in this fashion than other problems (roughly, in the social sciences). Experience with these more-developed areas should be a valuable source of information for the treatment of other areas. The fact that a problem has not been approached in this four-stage fashion, however, does not establish its scientific untouchability. It was Einstein, after all, who explained that politics is more complicated than physics.

**B. The Methods**

The many injunctions in the literature of Public Administration to apply the method(s) of science to administrative problems proved abortive, and the consequence is not at all surprising. For although a significant volume of this literature defines science in terms of its method, the meaning is usually not clear.[15]

Treatments of scientific method in the general literature of science are more informative. But even there the range of treatments is wide. For example, the noted physicist Bridgman tersely noted that: "The scientific method, is nothing more than doing one's damndest with one's mind, no holds barred."[16] This treatment, if concise, lacks content. Of the more developed approaches, three are particularly noteworthy. They are: Bacon's inductive method; Descartes' deductive method; and the hypothesis-testing method of Cohen and Nagel.[17] The apparent lack of agreement of these three developed approaches has been put this way by Northrop:

> "whereas in initiating inquiry Bacon placed the emphasis upon collecting data, and Descartes upon rationalistic logical deduction from what is indubitable, Cohen and Nagel urge us *immediately* to propose hypotheses and check them by determining whether predictions made upon the basis of them are confirmed."[18]

The disagreement about methods is more apparent than real, however. For an issue exists only on the assumption that there is *a* method. This assumption is untenable on several grounds. For example, the problematic situation determines the method. Thus empirical methods are neither necessary nor appropriate for certain problems which raise only questions of logical consistency. Moreover, all three of the methods cited above are required at the several stages of development of a particular problem area (roughly a discipline), as the following sub-section emphasizes.

If the relation of methods to problems seems patent, Public Administration did not avoid making a monolithic choice. Consider one central and consistent assumption of Simon's early position (which most influenced students of the discipline): that the method of science and the method of logic are (at least to a significant degree) one and the same. This is an unfortunate emphasis; to illustrate, traditional logic is preoccupied with class, or property, concepts while many concepts used in science are relational.[19] For similar reasons (among others), the noted student of science Felix Kaufmann concluded that "methodology must be clearly distinguished from deductive logic and recognized as an autonomous rational discipline" with its own criteria of adequacy.[20]

### C. The Stage of Development

The situational appropriateness of various methods has a clear import for "science." Realistically, science must be conceived as an interdependent series of developmental stages rather than as a discontinuous, science–non-science model. Three such developmental stages are adequate for present purposes.[21] These stages focus upon: (1) problem-area analysis, (2) natural-history classification, and (3) deductively formulated theory.

These stages may be described briefly. In problem-area analysis, first, the emphasis is straightforwardly upon determining which questions must be asked, and what data are necessary, to understand the problem area. Here, as Leo Strauss rightly notes, science must rest on "pre-scientific knowledge." The natural-history stage, second, sees the beginning of cumulative research. The basic method is Baconian induction, as contrasted with what might be called "informed intuitive search," and the product is a rough classification. The criteria for classification are qualitative and tend to emphasize surface characteristics, their complete meaning being found (as Northrop put it) "in factors which can be immediately apprehended." The stage of deductively formulated theory, third, builds upon the results of the second stage while developing concepts which cannot be immediately apprehended.[22] The concepts in this stage are said to exist by virtue of being the products of a complex process. To begin, a model of what is proposed to exist, is developed. This model, analyzed deductively, yields propositions whose validity may be tested by experiment or observation. Positive experimental or observational results constitute grounds for according a tentative reality to the concepts and their relations which generated the successful tests. This status is frozen only as long as replications and extensions of the initial results also prove possible. Failure at any point requires that a new model be developed and subjected to the same procedure.

As suggested above, then, the stage of development of a discipline as well as the problematic situation requires attention, for one or more of the methods considered above characterizes each of the stages. That is, the inductive method characterizes the problem-area analysis stage, and so on.

The implied neatness of interaction of stage and method, however, should not be overdone. Perhaps this simple illustration $\begin{matrix} & 2 & \\ \swarrow\!\!\nearrow & & \nwarrow\!\!\searrow \\ 1 & \longleftrightarrow & 3 \end{matrix}$ conveys a more accurate picture of the dynamics of the total sequence than the $1 \rightarrow 2 \rightarrow 3$ picture suggested by the three stages. Attempts to include progressively larger problem areas in deductively formulated theory imply still greater complexity. For the extension of the problem area covered by deductively formulated theory may (and always seems to) require more than the mere accumulation of more experimental data under old concepts. The process is roughly this: New problems must be analyzed; new data may have to be gathered under new concepts of the natural-history stage (concepts by apprehension); and changes in the existing theory and in the basic concepts of the third stage of inquiry (concepts by postulation). Consider the argument between Galilei and the Inquisitor. Their dispute did not concern the occurrence or nonoccurrence of eclipses. Rather, it concerned derivations from two deductively formulated theories purporting to explain the same phenomenon. Galilei's system postulated the revolution of the earth around the sun; the Inquisitor's system postulated that the earth must be the center of the universe. On the level of sense data, there was nothing to choose between the systems: the postulates of neither system could be apprehended directly. Derivable from Galilei's system, however, were certain propositions that explained and predicted a phenomenon—eclipses—explainable by the Inquisitor's system only as acts of God. For the prediction of eclipses, then, Galilei's theory was a useful one and the Inquisitor's was not.

The scientist could not be satisfied by the greater usefulness of Galilei's theory. The scientific dialectic did not cease with the disconfirmation of one theoretical system by its inability to predict external events. That test did not resolve the issue because Galilei's postulates could not be tested directly. Consequently, they were not necessarily the only ones which could account for eclipses. The problem then was to demonstrate that no other theory or derived postulates could explain the same phenomena. This problem was vexing. The only practical test —ascertaining whether the original hypothetical statements could be extended to account for apparently related phenomena—could never positively confirm Galilei's postulates. Consequently, only failure to extend the model successfully had a clear interpretation. Negative results might force modification of the original model, or they might inspire the development of another mother theory. As Albert Einstein expressed this process of asymptotic approximation of reality:

> Science is the attempt to make the chaotic diversity of our sense-experience correspond to a logically uniform system of thought. In this system single experiences must be correlated with the theoretic structure in such a way that the resulting coordination is *unique and convincing.*[23]

Moreover, even preliminary work requires sophistication enough. For example, it is far from accurate to think of the natural-history stage as a "pure fact"-gathering stage which merely supplies the grist for the theoretical mills of the final stage. In contrast, scientifically useful facts are not pure, or immediately apprehended. Rather they are simplifications of such data brought under concepts implying relations in propositional form.[24] Consequently, even in preliminary stages one is already dealing with a low level of theory rather than with pure fact.

Even early in the scientific process, then, a prime feature is the interaction of inductive methods in handling our sense-experience and deductive methods in determining the correspondence of those experiences with logical systems. The product of the natural-history stage is a system of what may be called a middle-level theory, that is, as contrasted with the high-level theory of the third stage. Galilei's system illustrates the importance of this middle-level theory. It was based upon apprehended data reported in terms of such concepts by apprehension as *darkness, brightness, time, position,* and *phases,* and also upon the repeated confirmation of certain low-level theoretical relations involving these concepts and the sun and the moon. The development of such middle-level theory is thus of crucial importance in a science, and section IV of this chapter will deal with it in some detail.

These considerations outline the methodological frame necessary for scientific effort. In sum, science should be used as a verb rather than a noun, as a doing rather than a being: a doing in the sense of isolating and solving problems; developing appropriate concepts and techniques of study, and encompassing problem areas within theoretical networks of increasing comprehensiveness in a self-correcting manner. The role of theory is significant in this doing. Briefly, some of the uses of theory are:

1. *Aggregative,* theory indicates the set relations which are regarded as existing in some empirical data universe;
2. *Suggestive,* theory suggests possible empirical relations other than those for which it specifically provides;

3. *Predictive,* theory permits the prediction of relations in some empirical data universe; and
4. *Corrective,* theory permits continuous internal retesting by the comparison of conclusions derived from the properties of the theory with empirical observations.

This brief discussion, however, does not suffice to reconcile science and Public Administration methodologically. A consideration of the fact versus value question and a more detailed look at the place of concepts by apprehension in science and theory are necessary to complete the task.

## IV. EMPIRICAL SCIENCE: THE PROBLEMS OF FACT AND VALUE

The early development of the several natural sciences depended upon the separation of two classes of questions: What is the case? and, What ought to be the case? These may be called questions of fact and value, respectively. Development of the social sciences as natural sciences also depends upon the consistent distinction of these questions.

The observation is not novel for the political scientist, of course. Aristotle clearly separated the two questions in his *Politics* and *Ethics;* Bacon lauded Machiavelli for his achievement in keeping the distinction in *The Prince;* and injunctions to separate the two questions as a precondition to scientific development of the study of politics or of Public Administration have been common in the literature.[25] Indeed, as many complain, some behavioralists are only too prone to separate fact from value and to neglect the latter.

The weight of this awareness, however, has not been sufficient to impress the distinction on the work of many students of Public Administration. Most students continue to work both sides of the street, often implicitly and at the same time.[26] Among the unsuccessful attempts to establish a fact-value distinction in Public Administration, Simon's work is particularly relevant here. The impact of his work has been great.[27] Partly because of Simon's acknowledged stature and partly because of his essentially one-man advocacy of a fact-value distinction in the discipline following World War II, *the* distinction and *the* place of this distinction in a science of Public Administration generally have been confused in the literature with *his* distinction and its place in *his* science of Public Administration. Thus the fact-value distinction in the discipline was the target of criticisms aimed at Simon's choice of a metaphysical vehicle and his argument in general. As in the case with the broader science versus art question, however, advocate and opponent have set aside the fact versus value question. Apparently the scholarly warfare was considered unrewarding.

This unsatisfactory truce is broken here. The task has been begun. On the fact side, that is, part of the difficulty students have had with Simon's position stems from his preoccupation with low-level decision-making and the apparently firm facts associated with it. However, facts are soft. Indeed, they are considered to exist only so long as concepts are developed and increasingly more inclusive theoretical statements of the empirical relations of such concepts are verified. The process is similar for physical facts and social facts.

The task of separating the analytical baby from the bath water, however, remains to be completed. Thus emphasis here is upon the value side of the fact versus value question and its place in a science of Public Administration. To begin, it is necessary to isolate two general classes of sub-processes within the broader scientific process: (1) the process toward conclusions and the conclusions themselves; and (2) those processes which do not directly affect the development of the conclusions. Included in the latter class are: the selection of the problem for investigation, the limitation of the uses of human and other materials involved, and the determination of what shall be done with the results. In Class 1, a particular set of values—the values of science—should be observed.[28] Values in any sense—the term has been promiscuously applied to referents ranging from the Commandments to economic cost—may be pertinent to Class 2 of the scientific process.

In contrast, the overwhelming weight of early opinion in Public Administration took the untenable position that a technical definition of the field—as administration rather than politics—precluded the consideration of values. As for Simon, his approach via logical positivism made the necessary pertinence of values in Classes 1 and 2 impossible. Indeed, it has been argued that Simon's system logically prevented him from studying anything in any fashion. Value elements are involved in all research from the decision to study onward, that is, and excluding values consequently is as crippling to empirical analysis as it is to philosophic analysis.

Moreover, values play a more important role than that outlined above. Consider their part in the fundamental distinctions between types of research. Thus empirical investigations must be distinguished in terms of the incidence or non-incidence of certain goal-values in Class 2 of the scientific process:

1. An empirical category, which has as its object the description and explanation of selected features of the real world; and
2. A goal-based, empirical category, which presupposes a given goal,

> and attempts to indicate conditions necessary to, or resulting from, the achievement of that goal through a description and explanation of the real world.

In methodological terms, with one significant exception, these first two categories of research must respect the guidelines for empirical work sketched in Chapter I. That qualification: The goals or values in the second category are normative givens whose validity cannot be established by empirical analysis.

A third type of research also is important—although derivative models do not necessarily have empirical counterparts—because certain important methodological cautions are appropriate. This rational or utopian category includes argument by logical analysis or development of propositions from statements of values, definitions, and axioms which may be wholly or partially independent of the empirical world. Consequently, utopian systems do not meet the criterion for external (dis)-confirmation established for empirical work in Chapter I. An example or two will illustrate the genre. On the systematic level of interest, such work is best illustrated by plane geometry. In the social area, Max Weber's work on bureaucracy similarly argues from a set of values to the nature of *an* ideal bureaucracy (in the sense of optimum attainment of those goals). He was not primarily concerned with whether or not this system did or ever would correspond to an empirical system.

To begin making an important distinction, attempts *to apply* a utopian model must be monitored carefully. Utopian work must be handled gingerly, that is, with both empirical elements and value elements playing prominent roles in the process. The properties of the system must be judged against our values to determine their desirability, and the system's propositions must be checked against empirical data to determine the degree to which they mirror reality. This is not just so much hair-splitting. The application of these two tests to the traditional theory of organization, for example, demonstrates that this point has a vital relevance to problem areas of interest to the student of Public Administration.[29] For the present, suffice it to note that, *when applied,* utopian models must follow the same methodological guidelines as goal-based, empirical work.

The *development* of a utopian model, in contrast, is literally fancy-free in comparison with that of an empirical model. In terms of the utopian system per se, neither empirical nor normative testing is relevant. The system *as a system* is judged only by the comprehensiveness and rigor of its development from its base of goals, definitions, and axioms. The nature of the values, definitions, and axioms is irrelevant.

The distinction between utopian models *as used* and *as developed* is significant. Thus failure to distinguish between work of this kind as *used* (e.g., as a model after which certain relations are patterned) and as *system* has been the source of considerable confusion. Some students have been seduced by the methodological convenience of developing utopian models, in sum, while they were uninhibited by the methodological constraints which should hedge applications of such models. Model-building in Political Science, as Chapter I shows, often reflects this uncomfortable combination.

The literature is strewn with evidence of the disregard of these types of theories and, consequently, of values. To illustrate, a purported empirical datum (which may be part of an empirical theory) may be interpreted as a necessary and desirable guide for behavior (which guide should be expressed as a goal-based, empirical theory). More commonly, a utopian approach is considered to be empirical. Traditional organization theory, for example, reflects both oversights. Similarly, the labored explanations of why Plato's *Republic* and his *Laws* are so different reflect such methodological imprecision. More consistently than not, Plato distinguished a utopian model (the *Republic*) from a goal-based, empirical model (the *Laws*). Many of his critics have done less. Popper's *The Open Society and Its Enemies,* for example, leans heavily on a confusion of types of theory.

These considerations imply a clear point for present purposes. A fully developed discipline of Public Administration, then, would have three theoretical emphases. One emphasis would be upon empirical theory, or basic research. The prime goal is the search for what is related to what under which conditions. A second emphasis would be upon a goal-based, empirical theory, or a policy orientation. Such theories focus upon how it is that one gets what one is after, given the relations which exist in the world or which may be induced. Utopian systems of theory constitute a third emphasis. They may aid work in other areas, if care is exercised. This restricted role contrasts sharply with the historic, if often unconscious, preoccupation with utopian theorizing in the social sciences generally, and in Public Administration particularly.

Values must have an important place in a fully developed discipline of Public Administration, in sum. The place of values is limited in empirical theory, to be sure. But their importance in goal-based, empirical theory—that is, in the policy orientation which always must be central in the discipline—can hardly be over-emphasized. Students of the discipline certainly must devote considerable attention to the Good Life, to the preferential order of values as they appear in policies. An empirical theory may help sharpen the contrast between sets of values, but it cannot make the choice. Once a choice of desired states of affairs is made, an empirical theory will point the direction of the actions necessary to implement the decision, if that theory is a "good" one.

Needless to say, then, our approach does not imply the triviality of value questions in Public Administration. Modern counterparts of Aristotle's *Ethics* always must occupy many students. The position here is simply this, in abstract: The scientific study of empirical relations is an important—and in Public Administration a neglected—area of concern; moreover, much important work in this area can be done before any significant agreement about values is achieved; and, finally whatever else, there is no excuse for confusing value problems and empirical ones.

Only limited areas of Public Administration will support the proposed empirical approach at present, which further supports the place of values in the discipline. This boundary condition was neglected by earlier pleaders for a science of Public Administration. Contemporary proponents of a scientific approach need not run the same risk. This is the sense, for example, of spotlighting small-group analysis for the student of Public Administration and of Political Science generally.[30] The small-group literature shows what may be done with the empirical approach, and also spotlights its methodological demands. Moreover, the small group is significant in many areas of interest to political scientists: in the study of organization, of voting and opinion study, of juries and judges, and the like. At the same time, the use of small-group results and techniques forces the student to learn and practice the methods of empirical research. This combination of relevance and training gives substantial impetus to the drive toward an empirical science of politics.

There need be no enmity, in short, between value and empirical emphases. Indeed, the two can be mutually supportive. Thus values may be important empirical data.[31] This is not to say that values can be proved or disproved. But they can be determined (an empirical task); they can be analyzed for implications, inconsistencies, or consequences (a rational task); or they can be compared with actual behavior (a combination of these tasks). Moreover, values may serve as *givens* for empirical judgments. That is, the incidence of beliefs that segregation is divinely ordained is an important empirical datum in any judgment of a realistic policy for the implementation of the Supreme Court decision in a specific city. Finally, the processes associated with developing a sense of values and acting in terms of it certainly are within the scope of empirical analysis. As Scott broadly made the point:

> It has been said that values—the bases of moral judgments—cannot be studied empirically [because] empirical inquiry is limited to existential propositions concerning means-ends relationships; the

> ends themselves cannot be chosen on empirical grounds, and therefore cannot be the object of scientific inquiry . . . . [However,] the human process of evaluation and moral judgment, of arriving at ultimate values against which means are assessed, *is* a matter amenable to empirical inquiry, since the aim of the study is not to choose among ends, but to investigate the psychological processes of choosing—how it develops, and its consequences for human behavior.[32]

## V. SCIENCE: CONCEPTS BY APPREHENSION AND OPERATIONS

Public Administration as a discipline has accomplished much of the necessary work in its problem-analysis stage. Consequently, any significant methodological developments in the discipline must move Public Administration into the natural-history stage. An understanding of the stage is therefore of particular importance to students of the discipline, especially since the literature has seldom gone beyond the preliminary science versus art and fact versus value problems raised by the abortive attempts to establish the discipline as a science.

Two notes introduce the objects of analysis and relate them to earlier discussion. First, the development of the major elements of the natural-history stage—*concepts by apprehension* and *operations*—becomes necessary when the use of everyday language begins to pay diminishing returns because of its lack of precision and scope. The problems are similar for the physical and social sciences. Second, a viable empirical methodology rests upon the processes of nominal and operational definition. Consequently, these processes constitute crucial methodological touchstones for empirical work and for goal-based, empirical work as well. Utopian work *qua* system can be operationally foot-loose, and—although nominal definition is often carefully attended to in utopian systems—the only tether on developing nominal definitions is one's fancy. Reality holds a tighter rein on empirical work. This implies a further compelling convenience of utopian theorizing against whose temptations methodological consciences must remain steadfast.

The development of concepts by apprehension may seem deceptively simple. The concepts of this type and their corresponding operations with which we are most familiar (e.g., weight, grams on a balance; height, meters on a measuring rod; and the like) seem natural. Their consistent, if historically brief, use also creates a strong impression of their always-and-ever existence. Such concepts, however, are merely convenient constructs which have been developed only with enormous effort. Moreover, they may be the proverbial flies of a summer whose autumn is predictive failure.

The magnitude of the difficulty of developing concepts by apprehension may be suggested by the tasks involved: (1) the determination of which aspects of a given slice of empirical experience are significant; and (2) the development of clearly defined, non-overlapping, and unidimensional concepts—or nominal definitions—for these aspects.[33]

The development process, then, may be described as a maximizing solution of these two tasks. A solution comes dearly, and then only tentatively. That is, much work must be devoted to testing proposed concepts to determine whether they help make order of experience. Moreover, any concept must be continually evaluated in terms of its applicability to broader sets of relations. There seems no finite limit to the process, although some concepts permit satisfactory prediction and explanation for many purposes.

Two recurring themes in conceptual definition may be stated broadly. First, the importance of concepts by apprehension in the natural-history stage of a discipline is great. Second, their development is a delicate and demanding business.

That the significance of concepts by apprehension cannot be overemphasized requires little support. Indeed, concepts are the very stuff of empirical work. As Merton notes: "concepts, then, constitute the definitions (or prescriptions) of what is to be observed; they are the variables between which empirical relationships are to be sought."[34] No concepts, in sum, no sciencing.

The delicacy and demands of nominal definition may be sketched in equally brief compass. Every observation is mediated by the sense impressions which intervene in complex ways between the observer and the real object. This is not some gossamer distinction. As Pearson put it long ago, sense impressions are filtered by "inferences and associations" stored within the observer. Scientists do not go about counting the leaves on trees, after all, although the dimension of *number* is one of their sense impressions as they stand in a forest. The basic questions of nominal definition consequently are two. What sense impressions are descriptively and predictively useful? And what inferences and associations of the observer—what working model of reality—should direct selection from among multitudinous sense impressions?[35]

The importance and the problems of the development of concepts by apprehension also may be illustrated simultaneously. Thus the degree of solution of the problems of conceptualization triggers a network of effects. For example, the degree of solution significantly determines the nature of results obtained when concepts are embodied in hypotheses and empirically tested. Consider, to illustrate, a nominal conceptualization that taps two or more orthogonal classes of phenomena. To simplify considerably, a number of replicatory tests might yield inconsistent results. For the weights of the several classes of phenomena included might vary from test to test and—depending on the distributions by weights—the observed relations would vary or might be contradictory from study to study. Moreover, the solution of the two problems of conceptualization also determines how far and how fast the development of middle-level theory—that is, the system expressing the relations existing between concepts by apprehension—may proceed and how soon the development of deductive theory may begin.

These comments suggest the importance of the operational definition of concepts by apprehension. To indicate briefly the function of the operational definition, we note that concepts are not phenomena themselves. They refer to phenomena via construction from various sense impressions. An important element in the usefulness of any concept is thus the set operations by which that concept is to be measured. Two separate elements are involved: The *validity* of the operation (does the operation refer to the same aspect of reality as the concept?); and the *reliability* of the operation (what is the degree of consistency between independent observations of the same material?).

The reliability and validity of all operations pose devilish problems. We must be selective here, but two examples should suggest the nature and significance of the broader family of underlying problems. First, determining operational validity is a complex and delicate matter. Thus the face-validity of the operation is a factor. Ultimately, however, the test is the twofold usefulness of the operation: in consistent prediction of specific empirical relations; and in the more and more comprehensive explanation of the real world. Thus the problem of operational validity is tied to operational reliability and the consistency, clarity, and significance of the nominal definition which the operation is intended to tap.

Second, the reliability of operations poses reinforcing complications. In some cases, operational reliability constitutes little challenge. For example, observers might be trained together and the consistency of their observations might be determined by judging the degree of interobserver agreement in categorizing some standard stimuli.[36] But it is far more difficult to attempt to equilibrate the responses of experimental subjects whose self-ratings on a questionnaire indicate "high satisfaction" with their performance on an experimental task. And—like it or not—much behavioral research must depend on such self-reports by human actors. As an approximation only, the researcher can settle for the meaning provided by consistent co-variations of high satisfaction with other variables. As he raises his standards concerning the variance he wishes to account for, the researcher must account for response set, interviewer effect, and numerous other ways of conceptualizing factors that might influence individual self-reports.[37]

Our position here is definitely not that scientific research in Political Science must be hamstrung by subjectivity of observers or participants who report only their own culture-boundedness. Operations useful in behavioral research can be "harder." Consider the use of "unobtrusive" operations for gathering data about behavior. For example, a researcher interested in the relative numbers of people who visited two exhibits in a museum might utilize observers or self-reports by visitors. Both approaches have their awkward features as reliable operations. A possible unobtrusive measure would be the relative amount of wear on asphalt flooring-tiles around the two exhibits. Such measures cut through many of the problems of reliability implicit in operations using observers or participant reports.[38] Validity is still an important issue, however. For example, the wear on tiles at one site might be affected by the fact that many people approach that exhibit, shuffle their feet in discomfiture, and quickly move on. A more soothing exhibit might attract more visitors who stayed longer but with less agitation. What is being measured is still at issue, patently, although how it is being measured raises relatively few problems.

Even the selective illustration above establishes that the development of nominal-operational pairs is a complex business, then. One must juggle an equation of four variables. These four variables are: the conceptual, or nominal, definition; the reliability of the operations which define it; the validity of these operations; and the level of theory in which the concept may be imbedded. Even this puts the matter too simply, however, for only temporary solutions exist.

This complexity may be illustrated by considering the development of the concept *cohesiveness*, a dimension that will prove increasingly useful in understanding behavior in organizations. The following chapter will survey the problems of nominally and operationally defining the dimension, but brief commentary here will reinforce the substance of the preceding discussion while it lays the groundwork for the following chapter.

Let us develop a methodological micro-history. Early nominal conceptualizations stressed that cohesiveness referred to the *positive attractions* of a group for its members and, consistently, early operations measured liking among members. Some results supporting this early approach were obtained, but conflicting results soon forced both conceptual and operational modifications. For example, conceptually, cohesiveness was refined to refer to the *resultant attraction* of a group. For no doubt some of the conflicting early findings were due to the fact that positive attractions might be counterbalanced or overweighed by features that made the group unattractive. Relatedly, in terms of specific operations, "partial" measures such as those based upon personal liking were displaced by "resultant" measures derived from answers to such questions: How much do you want to remain a member of this group? These changes were reflected in more consistent results.

All this seems resonable enough, although one may wonder why researchers did not see the obvious at the start. Hindsight does make things rather more clear, but significant open questions concerning cohesiveness still remain. Thus high cohesiveness is associated with either high or low productivity. This is reasonable, since high cohesiveness implies significant control over the behavior of group members, and since both high and low productivity imply a high degree of control of member behavior. In an applied sense, however, greater specification of the conditions—leadership style, personality characteristics, organization structure, and so on—under which cohesiveness will be associated with one of the other of these productivity levels is clearly desirable. This suggests the magnitude of the work yet to be done. And one should not be surprised if both conceptual and operational changes in cohesiveness are required to do the job. Nor should one be surprised if these changes seem obvious afterward.

The problems of the scientific handling of empirical data thus do not promise early or effortless solution. However, posing of problems in this form is in itself an enormous step toward a more rigorous methodology and cumulative research. At least the metaphorical elastic yardstick will be an inadequate tool. Although concepts can be labeled subjective, they are so in a special sense only. Hypothesized relations between concepts may be tested in replicatory studies, since their operations are specified. Logical derivations from any positive findings, in turn, may be confirmed or refuted. These are the bases for consistent and cumulative disciplined effort. That is, this serious business of attempting to leap-frog over the shoulders of concepts and their operations from lesser to greater comprehensiveness, of uncovering and accounting for more and more empirical relations, has a twofold function. It demonstrates the scientific usefulness (or reality) of concepts and their operations. Moreover, it spins the web of an increasingly broad theory, or a convincing and unique explanation, of empirical relations.

Nominal and operational definitions, then, constitute an alternative to the pessimistic scholarly tradition which holds that one must adopt a *Weltanschauung*—a world-view—and interpret reality in terms of it. It is this tradition, in the final analysis, which must be outgrown by work toward a scientific area in Public Administration and toward a Political Science.[39]

## VI. CONCLUSION

These considerations are not meant to cheapen the descriptive studies of life in administrative organizations that have enriched our knowledge, or to imply that they are passé. The works of the Macmahons, Milletts, Druckers, Dimocks, and the rest have and will continue to have real significance. Such work also has its limits, however. Thus it is simply a matter of fact that increasing attention must be devoted to moving into the natural-science stage, and beyond, if Public Administration is to hold its own in contributing to the development of the administrative sciences.

## NOTES

1. William F. Whyte, "Small Groups and Large Organizations," in John H. Rohrer and Muzafer Sherif (eds.), *Social Psychology at the Crossroads* (New York: Harper, 1951), p. 311.

2. For two interesting exceptions, see Charles Hyneman, *The Study of Politics* (Urbana: University of Illinois Press, 1959), especially pp. 75–108 and 151–73; and Vernon Van Dyke, *Political Science: A Philosophical Analysis* (Stanford, Calif.: Stanford University Press, 1960), especially pp. 191–205.

3. Chapter VII, in fact, argues that Public Administration as a discipline was on the very threshold of moving into the development of empirical theories of the middle-range and beyond before a strong anti-science reaction set in.

4. Developments in both training and research support this evaluation of the condition of Public Administration. The training developments in the public service have been many and varied, but for our purposes it suffices to note only that the demands for training have grown so explosively as to create an environment that cannot help but stimulate increased activity by students of Public Administration and to make the field hyper-attractive to large numbers of professionals-to-be.

Research also has been bullish. By any standards, the recent production has been noteworthy. As a sampling only, the reference here is to such pieces of work as: W. Lloyd Warner, Paul P. Van Riper, Norman H. Martin, and Orvis F. Collins, *The American Federal Executive* (New Haven, Conn.: Yale University Press, 1963); Franklin P. Kilpatrick, Milton C. Cummings, Jr., and M. Kent Jennings, *The Image of the Federal Service* (Washington, D. C.: Brookings Institution, 1964); Dean E. Mann, *The Assistant Secretaries* (Washington, D.C.: Brookings Institution, 1965); David T. Stanley, *Changing Administrations* (Washington, D. C.: Brookings Institution, 1965); and John J. Corson and R. Shale Paul, *Men Near the Top* (Baltimore, Md.: Johns Hopkins University Press, 1966).

5. For Propositions 1 and 2 it is simpler to list exceptions or quasi-exceptions, there being so few. In this spirit, on Proposition 1 see Frederick C. Mosher, "Research in Public Administration: Some Notes and Suggestions," *Public Administration Review*, 16 (Summer, 1956), 169–78. For a notable exception to the usual loose treatment of Proposition 2, see Dwight Waldo, *The Administrative State: A Study of the Political Theory of American Public Administration* (New York: Ronald Press, 1948, especially pp. 185–86.

Proposition 3 is difficult to support in brief compass. Briefly, however, note that the well-known exchange between Robert A. Dahl, "The Science of Public Administration: Three Problems," *Public Administration Review*, 7 (Winter, 1947), 1–11, and Herbert Simon, "A Comment on 'The Science of Public Administration,'" *Public Administration Review*, 7 (Summer, 1947), 200–203, is developed without supporting findings or research techniques.

6. See William F. Willoughby, "The Science of Public Administration," especially p. 39, in John Mabry Matthews and James Hart (eds.), *Essays in Political Science in Honor of Westel Woodbury Willoughby* (Baltimore: The Johns Hopkins Press, 1937).

7. This was largely a one-man effort. Herbert A. Simon, *Administrative Behavior: A Study of the Decision-Making Processes in Administrative Organization* (preliminary edition; Chicago: Illinois Institute of Technology, 1945) and (New York: Macmillan, 1947 and 1956); and with Donald Smithburg and Victor A. Thompon, *Public Administration* (New York: Knopf, 1950).

8. The most influential work in this approach is Paul H. Appleby's *Policy and Administration* (University, Ala.: University of Alabama Press, 1949), especially p. 10.

9. Dwight Waldo, *The Study of Public Administration*, Doubleday Short Studies in Political Science (Garden City, N. Y.: 1955), p. 2. Whether it be gain or loss, the issue is not even raised

in many more recent sources. This is the case for example with Felix Nigro, *Modern Public Administration* (New York: Harper and Row, 1965).

10. See Appleby, *op. cit.;* and Marver Bernstein, "The Scope of Public Administration," *Western Political Quarterly,* 5 (March, 1952), 124–37.

11. For one interpretation of this effect of Simon's work, see Norton E. Long, "Public Policy and Administration: The Goals of Rationality and Responsibility," *Public Administration Review,* 14 (Winter, 1954), especially 22.

12. Simon, *Administrative Behavior, op. cit.*

13. Martin Landau, "The Concept of Decision-Making in the 'Field' of Public Administration," in Sidney Mailick and Edward H. Van Ness (eds.), *Concepts and Issues in Administrative Behavior* (Englewood Cliffs, N. J.: Prentice-Hall, 1962), pp. 1–28.

14. This section draws heavily on several sources, some of which are mentioned in the footnotes. Other sources include: David Bohm, *Causality and Chance in Modern Physics* (New York: Harper, 1957); Edwin G. Boring, *History, Psychology, and Science,* edited by Robert I. Watson and Donald T. Campbell (New York: Wiley, 1963); Robert Brown, *Exploration in Social Science* (Chicago: Aldine, 1963); Albert Einstein and L. Infeld, *The Evolution of Physics* (New York: Simon and Schuster, 1938); Ernest Nagel, *The Structure of Science* (New York: Harcourt, Brace and World, 1961); F. S. C. Northrop, *Science and First Principles* (New York: Macmillan, 1932), and *The Logic of the Sciences and the Humanities* (New York: Macmillan, 1948); Henri Poincaré, *The Foundation of Science: Science and Hypotheses,* translated by George Bruce Halstead (New York: The Science Press, 1913); and Hans Reichenbach, *Atom and Cosmos,* translated by Edward S. Allen (London: Allen and Unwin, 1932).

15. Marshall E. Dimock, "Scientific Method and the Future of Political Science," in Matthews and Hart, *op. cit.,* p. 198, strikes a familiar discord when he notes that: "in my view science is a method rather than a degree of systematization of results . . . scientific method is simply a tool." But the tool is left unexplored.

16. P. W. Bridgman, "The Prospect for Intelligence," *Yale Review,* 34 (Spring, 1945), 450.

17. Francis Bacon, *Works,* Vol. III (Boston: Brown and Taggart, 1862), "Novum Organum: Aphorisms Concerning the Interpretation of Nature and the Kingdom of Man," Aphorism XIV: "Our only hope . . . lies in a true induction." Descartes wrote: "The long chains of simple and easy reasonings by means of which geometers are accustomed to reach the conclusions of the most difficult demonstrations, had led me to imagine that all things, to the knowledge of which man is competent, are mutually connected in the same way . . . ." René Descartes, *A Discourse on Method and Selected Writings* (New York: Dutton, 1951), p. 16. Finally, Morris Cohen and Ernest Nagel, *An Introduction to Logic and Scientific Method* (New York: Harcourt, Brace, 1934), pp. 199, 200–201, note that: "It is an utterly superficial view . . . that the truth is to be found by studying the facts . . . . We cannot take a single step forward in any inquiry *unless we begin with a suggested explanation or solution* of the difficulty which originated it." (Their emphases.)

18. Northrop, *Science and First Principles,* p. 11.

19. Carl G. Hempel, *Fundamentals of Concept Formation in Empirical Science,* Vol. II, No. 7, International Encyclopedia of Unified Science (Chicago: University of Chicago Press, 1952), especially pp. 4–7.

20. Felix Kaufmann, *Methodology of the Social Sciences* (New York: Oxford University Press, 1944), p. vii.

21. Northrop, *The Logic of the Sciences and the Humanities,* for (1), pp. 28–39; for (2), pp. 35, 60; and for (3), pp. 60–61.

22. Thus at the beginning of the *Principia,* Newton distinguished "perceived space" and "mathematical space," which correspond to a "concept by apprehension" and a "concept by postulation," respectively. See his Propositions I and II.

23. Albert Einstein, "Considerations Concerning the Fundaments of Theoreti-

cal Physics," *Science,* 91 (May 24, 1940), 487. (Emphasis added.)

24. Richard C. Sheldon, "Some Observations on Theory in Social Science," in Talcott Parsons and Edward A. Shils (eds.), *Toward a General Theory of Action* (Cambridge, Mass.: Harvard University Press, 1951), pp. 36–37, makes this point with the qualification that "While it is true that all observation is in terms of a conceptual scheme and that a fact is a sense datum in terms of a conceptual scheme, this does not mean that one must have a fully worked-out theory to do any observation at all."

25. The distinction was made picturesquely in the paper which is widely considered as Public Administration's birth certificate, Woodrow Wilson's "The Study of Administration," *Political Science Quarterly,* 2 (June, 1887), 197–222. He used the example of borrowing a thug's clever knife-sharpening technique without borrowing his motive.

26. The unsettled state of the literature is reflected in Dwight Waldo, "The Administrative State Revisited," *Public Administration Review,* 25 (March, 1965), especially 13–14.

27. Waldo reflects this impact when he devotes more than nine pages of a 70-page pamphlet, *The Study of Public Administration,* to analyze the position that Simon sketched in his *Administrative Behavior.*

28. Robert Merton, *Social Theory and Social Structure* (Glencoe, Ill.: The Free Press, 1949), pp. 309 ff., lists four important characteristics of the "set of cultural values and mores governing the activities termed scientific": universalism; sharing of results; disinterestedness; and organized scepticism.

29. An application of the literature to organization theory may be found in Robert T. Golembiewski, *Behavior and Organization* (Chicago: Rand McNally, 1962).

30. Robert T. Golembiewski, *The Small Group: An Analysis of Research Concepts and Operations* (Chicago: University of Chicago Press, 1962); and Sidney Verba, *Small Groups and Political Behavior* (Princeton, N.J.: Princeton University Press, 1961).

31. For an illustration of the importance of values in administration and of their empirical treatment, see Peter M. Blau, *The Dynamics of Bureaucracy* (Chicago: University of Chicago Press, 1955).

32. William A. Scott, *Values and Organizations* (Chicago: Rand McNally, 1965).

33. For a fuller discussion of some of these problem areas, See William J. Goode and Paul K. Hatt, *Methods in Social Research* (New York: McGraw-Hill, 1952), pp. 41–53; and Merton, *op. cit.,* pp. 87–90.

34. Merton, *op. cit.,* pp. 41–44.

35. Karl Pearson, *The Grammar of Science* (London: J. M. Dent, 1937), pp. 38–39.

36. The method of determining reliability may be a significant problem, however, especially in the early development of a specific operation. See Launor F. Carter, William Haythorn, Beatrice Meirowitz, and John Lanzetta, "The Relation of Categorizations and Ratings in the Observation of Group Behavior," *Human Relations,* 3 (July, 1951), 239–54.

37. Consider the significant question of the role a respondent should assume in responding to a questionnaire. The marked effects of variations in such role-taking have been demonstrated many times. For example, see M. T. Orne and F. J. Evans, "Social Control in the Psychological Experiment: Antisocial Behavior and Hypnosis," *Journal of Personality and Social Psychology,* 1 (1965), 189–200.

38. The use of a wide variety of such "unobtrusive" operations has been brilliantly assayed recently. See Eugene J. Webb, Donald T. Campbell, Richard D. Schwartz, and Lee Sechrest, *Unobtrusive Measures: Nonreactive Research in the Social Sciences* (Chicago: Rand McNally, 1966).

39. Robert T. Golembiewski, "Toward the New Organization Theories: Some Notes on 'Staff,'" *Midwest Journal of Political Science,* 5 (August, 1961), 237–59.

iii

# Empirical Science at the Micro-Level: Cohesiveness as Concept and Operation

This third chapter furthers the pattern of increasing resolution and decreasing scope already established by the first two chapters. The first chapter considered three major approaches to a science of politics in terms of a few rudimentary methodological criteria at the disciplinary level. The second chapter reduced its field-of-view to an area within Political Science in an attempt to sharpen many methodological details within Public Administration which also have a discipline-wide applicability. This third chapter permits microscopic methodological exploration of a single dimension of reality—the cohesiveness of small social groupings—and suggests extensions to a broader range of political phenomena. Again the purpose is to gain greater discrimination at the cost of narrowed scope. In addition, the chapter hopes to breathe into the analysis some sense of the dynamics of insight, tinkering, and experimentation that characterize conceptual and operational definition.

While it specifically illustrates the development of a concept and operation at the microscopic level, the methodological analysis of cohesiveness also has broader uses. First, although the analysis will be nested directly in an organizational context most congenial to Public Administration, the conceptual-operational experience with cohesiveness has a wide relevance to issues within Political Science. Some significant aspects of the operations of legislative committees, for example, can be studied profitably in terms of cohesiveness. Then too, voting studies should profit from the specification of the differential cohesiveness of small informal groupings that have been shown to exercise great in-

This chapter was originally published as "Management Science and Group Behavior: Work-Unit Cohesiveness," *Journal of the Academy of Management,* 4 (August, 1961), 37–99. Major modifications have been made for present purposes. For detailed consideration of many relevant studies, see Albert J. Lott and Bernice E. Lott, "Group Cohesiveness as Interpersonal Attraction: A Review of Relationships with Antecedent and Consequent Variables, *Psychological Bulletin,* 64 (October, 1965), 259–309.

fluence on social behavior in a bewildering diversity of contexts.[1] However, voting studies have not dealt directly with group variables.

The costs of the failure to make explicit provision for group properties in research designs in Political Science seem formidable. For example, the neglect of group properties in voting studies derives in no small measure from the fact that the required research design does not lend itself conveniently to survey research, which has been the vehicle for most behavioral studies of voting. Convenience is not cheaply served in this case. The groups referred to in available studies usually are categoric ones, such as "labor union member,"[2] but we have not yet developed satisfactory dimensions for differentiating large groupings.[3] Studying patterns of voting within families avoids many of these difficulties, but where this tack has been taken, differences between families have not been specified.[4] Since everything we know establishes that much behaviorally significant data is missed when only undifferentiated groups are considered,[5] the analysis of cohesiveness below can contribute directly to remedying what seems a major blind spot of politically relevant research such as that on voting.

In addition to such direct transfer possibilities, the methodological dissection of cohesiveness will illustrate the processes of developing other concepts and operations, which illustration will apply to macroscopic as well as microscopic phenomena. Our micro-analysis also will draw attention to the dangers of attempting to apply to macroscopic phenomena the concept-operation pairs appropriate for more simple levels. Both these lessons seem of direct relevance to the political scientist, whose historic interests have centered around large aggregates, but with little attention to the processes of operational definition. This is a dangerous combination.

## I. THE ROLE OF SMALL-GROUP PROPERTIES IN PUBLIC ADMINISTRATION AND THE MANAGEMENT SCIENCES

Awareness of the multiple bases of human behavior has developed gradually over the past half-century from demonstrations of the influence of groups upon behavior. The burgeoning small-group literature is a recent product of this awareness. In contrast to the descriptive nature of the early group literature, the experimental study of ad hoc collectivities characterizes recent work. Sociologists and psychologists have spearheaded this research, the goal of which is to develop concepts and operations for the detailed description of group behavior.

The rigorous study of the small group is immediately relevant to the management sciences, which fact accounts for the attention given that literature in Public Administration.[6] Two features of this relevance deserve emphasis. First, the relevance of the small group derives from the traditional emphasis in organization theory upon formal organization and the individual.[7] The stress on *informal organization* since the thirties departs radically from this orthodoxy, but definitions of the concept have been generally diverse and uniformly general. Small-group analysis provides substantive content for the concept informal organization, thereby recognizing both the value and the limits of the bulk of organizational analysis of the last two or three decades. The three panels of small-group variables clearly imply the considerable magnitude of the increased specificity possible in treating informal organization:

1. *a structural panel,* which includes variables relevant to the description of the relations which exist between group members, e.g., leadership status;
2. *a style panel,* which includes variables relevant to the description of modes of group behavior, e.g., a group with a permissive style of supervision; and
3. *a population panel,* which includes variables relevant to the description of the properties of group members which are significant for group functioning.

Concurrently, small-group analysis provides a model of research methods necessary in behavioral studies in the management sciences specifically, and more generally within Political Science.

The present purpose is to analyze the development of a single dimension relevant to explaining and predicting small-group behavior, the better to exploit the convenience inherent in the study of small units. The focus is upon *cohesiveness,* a strategic concept indeed in small-group analysis. Its analysis provides a useful illustration-in-depth. But the argument does have a dysfunctional narrowness as well. That narrowness can be but partially remedied here by brief suggestions of the broader webs of relations which cohesiveness will help explore.

## II. COHESIVENESS: CONCEPTUAL DEVELOPMENT

Cohesiveness taps a basic property of the small group: its "stick-togetherness," or the member loyalty which defines the group system. Several overlapping but distinct conceptions of cohesiveness have been employed, however. Three general classes of such meanings may be noted:

1. the attraction of a group for its members;
2. the coordination of the efforts of members; and
3. the level of motivation of group members to perform a task with zeal and efficiency.

The three meanings could not be included in a single concept. Thus the general restriction of the concept to Meaning 1 constituted the first major clarification of cohesiveness. Meanings 2 and 3 do not appear to be unidimensional. They have also been interpreted with an external bias, while Meaning 1 seems truly a group property. The failure to validate hypotheses derived from Meanings 2 and 3 substantiates these observations. Such hypotheses proposed that groups characterized by a high internal "togetherness" (for example) will have high output on an experimental task. Mixed experimental results revealed the too-facile association of a group characteristic with a measure of performance that has an extra-group basis. That is, a small group characterized by high cohesiveness could be a high producer—that is, more able to control member behavior than a group with low cohesiveness. Or, a small group could be a low producer, i.e., more able to resist extra-group demands than low-cohesiveness groups.

Early conceptual clarification was centered upon cohesiveness conceived as *attraction*, therefore, but the emphasis developed in awkward ways. The earliest modern formulation of cohesiveness held that it "is the total field of forces which act on members to remain in the group . . . ."[8] The deficiencies of this conceptualization may be summarized:

1. The concept emphasizes the "total field of forces" rather than the group, with (as will be shown) important consequences for operational definitions of cohesiveness.
2. The concept is not unidimensional, since the "total field of forces" might contain a preponderant weight of elements (such as a prison sentence) which would permit this, as well as the converse, formulation: The greater the forces acting upon individuals to stay in a group, the less attractive the group is to those individuals.
3. It is impossible to measure the "total field of forces" directly, and each indirect operational definition is (at best) a partial measure of, or (at worst) not related to, the "total field of forces."

More recent work has remedied some of these conceptual problems. For example, the major progressive development conceptualized cohesiveness as a group property. The nominal definition provided, in a subtle but significant change, that "cohesiveness is a . . . property of groups, the attraction which it has for its members, or the forces which are exerted on the members to stay in the group . . . ."[9] The emphasis here, unlike that in the earlier version, is upon a potentially measurable phenomenon, member attraction-to-group. But the second difficulty noted above still prevails. As a result, cohesiveness was further clarified, on the basis of experimental findings, to be a function of the individual members'

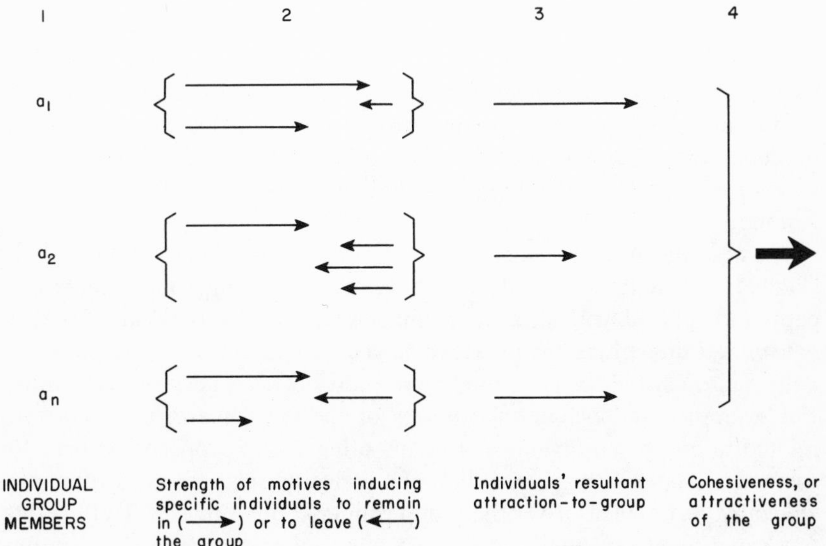


FIGURE III.1 Conceptual Schema for Group Cohesiveness.

*resultant* attraction-to-group.[10] The resultant scores for individuals are a function of two classes of factors: group properties, and the motivational states of the persons involved, which are a function of personal needs and characteristics. As Libo put it, cohesiveness "may be hypothesized as a function of the degree to which there is a correspondence between the need structure of all the individual members and the need-satisfying potency in the group."[11] Variables in all three small-group research panels, then, are relevant to cohesiveness. Figure III.1 schematically outlines this final conceptualization.[12]

## III. COHESIVENESS: OPERATIONAL PROBLEMS

The conceptual clarification of cohesiveness, however, did not solve operational problems. That is, deciding upon *what* was to be measured did not solve the problem of *how* it was to be measured. But the clarification did permit a clear indication of what operational developments were necessary. The linkages between conceptual and operational definition, then, are vital and complex.

To develop the point, early operational definitions of cohesiveness usually were based on indexes of sociometric choice (e.g., indexes developed from answers to questions such as: Who are your friends in Group *x*?). Promising results prompted a series of studies of natural-state groups which utilized a number of similar (but not identical) sociometric operational definitions of cohesiveness. The results of such studies may be briefly noted. Some strongly confirmed predicted relations of cohesiveness and other variables; others supplied positive but unexciting support; and others yielded unexpected and contradictory results.[13]

Gross and Martin concluded that such mixed results indicated the "logical and methodological inadequacies" of existing cohesiveness concepts and operations.[14] These inadequacies were of several kinds. The early *conceptual* difficulties have been reviewed. A number of *operational* difficulties also existed. In part, they were induced by conceptual difficulties. For example, the sociometric choices of individuals are not necessarily related to group cohesiveness, or to any other group property. At best, the sociometric operation gathers data about dyadic relations, and these provide only partial measure of the group property *cohesiveness*. To illustrate, one experiment revealed that only 44 per cent of the variance in ratings by members of their own attraction-to-group could be attributed to attraction-to-members.[15] Operational difficulties also resulted because the variety of sociometric operations did not seem to have the same referent.[16] Thus inter-study findings tended to be inconsistent. In addition, the lack of specification of *intervening variables* (which affected the apparently general relations between cohesiveness and other variables) also plagued research. Hence, previously consistent findings have been contradicted by studies using the same conceptual and operational definitions.[17]

The resulting debate in the literature induced operational as well as conceptual changes. Consistent with conceptual changes, operational definitions of cohesiveness shifted from the earlier partial measures like the sociometric to more general "resultant" measures of attraction-to-group. Schachter for example, utilized this resultant set of questions to measure cohesiveness:[18]

1. Do you want to remain a member of this group?
2. How often do you think this group should meet?
3. If enough members decide not to stay so that it seems this group may discontinue, would you like the chance to persuade others to stay?

The resultant approach avoids the particularistic deficiencies of such operations as the sociometric. It also taps member attraction to a specific group, again in contrast to the sociometric operation which isolates relations between pairs of individuals. Finally, such resultant measures have proved effective in differentiating subjects exposed to high and low cohesiveness-inducing experimental treatments.[19] The use of such resultant operations, however, has been limited.

Despite such developments, important operational problems remain. First, in terms of Figure III.1, the translation of the resultant attraction-to-group scores of members (Step 3) into group cohesiveness (Step 4) presents a major difficulty. Thus far, the temporary expedient has been to average the several attraction-to-group scores. The expedient is not satisfactory. For such a mean may disguise within-group differences of a significant nature. Indeed, high intra-set differences may indicate that the entire group is not behaviorally relevant for all members. That is, such a group is categoric rather than psychological. Therefore, cohesiveness operations of substantial predictive utility must measure the spread of the data usually treated as aggregates.

Second, an even more elusive translational difficulty involves Steps 3 and 4 in Figure III.1. The equal weighting of member attraction-to-group scores in existing cohesiveness operations has a serious defect, for group status of individual members may be a crucial element in the weighting of these scores in total group cohesiveness. This position is a tenable one. But the unresolved conceptual and operational difficulties with the structural variable *status* inhibit its implementation.

Third, differences in cohesiveness sources seem important at Steps 2, 3, and 4 in Figure III.1. Relevant evidence, however, is thin. This evidence may be reviewed in terms of answers to three questions:

1. *What are the sources of attraction-to-group?* Three have been emphasized: (1) personal attractiveness of group members; (2) the attractiveness of the task with which the group mediates; and (3) the prestige of group membership. These sources of attraction are convenient. For they have been induced in experimental subjects by instructions (1) and (3) and planned assignment (2). But they also cover only a limited range. Ideally, however, cohesiveness should be related to a large number of sources in properties in the structural, style, and population panels.

2. *Do different sources of attraction have similar group consequences?* Research by Back presents mixed evidence.[20] Three batches of experimental collectivities were treated so as to expose each batch to one of these sources of attraction: personal attraction; task attraction; and membership prestige gains. Two-member groups were given the task of jointly preparing stories about several pictures. Each subject was given slightly different pictures to study alone in order to encourage the exertion of influence in the joint story-preparation. As expected, members of high cohesiveness (HiCo) groups exercised a greater and more equal

mutual influence. HiCo members also displayed more equal participation in the group discussion than members of low cohesiveness (LoCo) groups. This consistently reflects greater HiCo involvement in, or greater "felt importance" of, the discussion. Back thus concluded that "cohesiveness can indeed be considered as a unitary concept." But there also were quite distinctive inter-source effects on the group process between cohesiveness treatments. To illustrate:

> The Effect of Task Direction. The relationship created by setting up a goal which can be reached by the group activity tends to have somewhat opposite effects from those of the personal attraction relationship. Group activity is seen as a necessity which is to be completed as quickly and as efficiently as possible.
>
> . . . If cohesiveness was based on personal attraction, group members wanted to transform the discussion into a longish, pleasant conversation.

Thus, as expected, intervening variables must be specified if cohesiveness is to have high and consistent predictive utility. This complements common-sense expectations and some experimental work. Consider, for example, cohesiveness which is "leader-centered" (as in traditional organization theory) versus cohesiveness which is "member-centered" (as in much of the small-group literature). A priori, these types of cohesiveness would have markedly different group effects over a wide range. To illustrate, small-group style differences (e.g., directive versus permissive atmospheres) and population differences (e.g., more members who are high than low scorers on "authoritarianism") have been observed in groups with leader-centered cohesiveness and in groups with member-centered cohesiveness.[21]

3. *Does attraction-to-group from different sources yield increased total attractiveness?* The crucial experiment has not been performed, but its necessary design seems clear enough. A batch of groups could be treated so as to induce only one of the three sources of cohesiveness in any group, and a batch could be exposed to the three sources simultaneously. The test for between-treatment differences would answer this third question. Such an experiment might also reveal the sensitivity of existing resultant operations for measuring cohesiveness.

## IV. COHESIVENESS: DESIGNATING ITS LOCUS

A central problem—the unit to which these concepts and operations applied—was not raised directly in re-evaluating cohesiveness. Paradoxically, however, this problem contributed significantly to that re-evaluation.

Most early studies of cohesiveness analyzed formal groups, such as courts in a housing development, classrooms, and work units. But the problem, as Festinger, Schachter, and Back noted, was that mutual sociometric choices often seemed to reflect "a kind of subgroup development." They went on:

> It is, of course, impossible in the absence of more empirical data to decide just how much such *excess mutual choices* detract from the cohesiveness of the group as a whole. . . . We should not want to subtract the mutual choices completely since the fact that they are mutual certainly does not nullify their contribution to the cohesiveness of the group. As an approximation, we shall correct the proportion of "in-court" choices by subtracting . . . one half of the mutual choice pairs which occurred.[22]

Festinger, Schachter, and Back were interested in the relation between cohesiveness of the courts of a housing development and opinion of, and activity in, a tenants' association. They hypothesized that high cohesiveness would be associated with a low percentage of deviants from court patterns of opinion and activity. The modification for "excess mutual choices" resulted in appreciably higher negative correlations between cohesiveness and percentage of deviants in one case (Westgate courts). There the percentage of total variance accounted for by the correlation increased from 28 to 55 per cent. In another case (Westgate West courts) the change was in the same direction, but not so significantly. The adjustment was quite delicate, however, for mutual sociometric choice reflects a very strong friendship bond. Thus the position that "excess" choices decreased the attractiveness of the group was, without considerable clarification, quite peculiar. Such clarification was not offered.

The results of this doctoring may be explained, however, and the explanation suggests the dangers of attempts to extend existing cohesiveness concepts and operations to large aggregates. Consider the three general types of sociometric choice-patterns given in Figure III. 2. To the degree that formal groups approximate Type I, it seems unnecessary to compensate for "excess mutual choices." For Type I formal groups display a member choice "togetherness" which makes it reasonable to argue that the choice pattern is associated with an underlying opinional agreement. In Type III formal groups, by way of sharp contrast, the formal group is categoric only. Thus groups of this type are probably not characterized by any marked, group-induced opinional agreement. However, the case for two sets of opinional agreements is presumptively strong. Sociometrically defined cohesiveness of Type III formal groups would then probably yield results at odds with those predictable from the

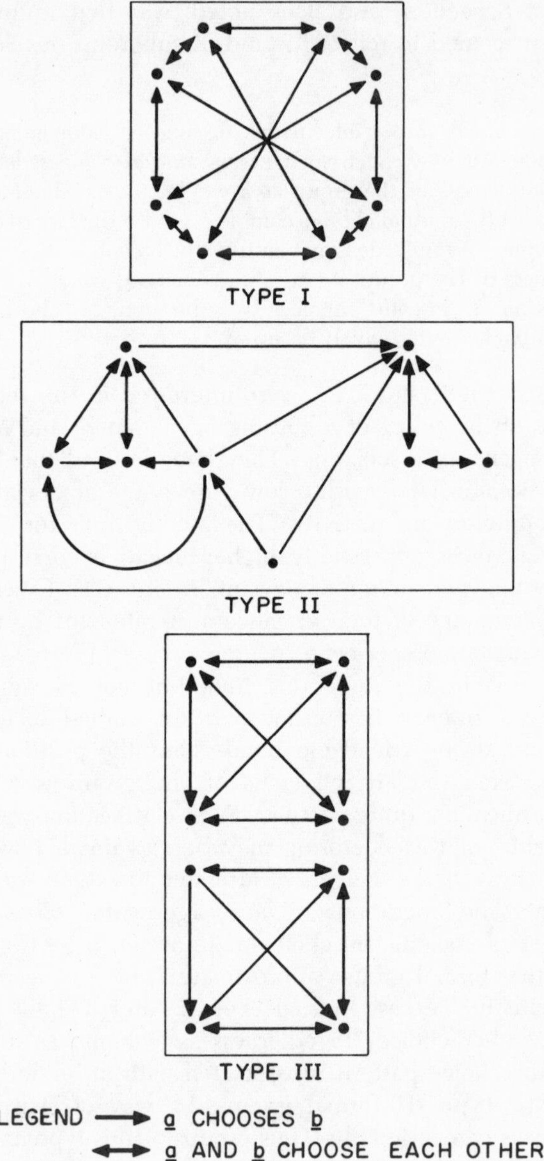


FIGURE III. 2 Hypothetical Patterns of Positive Sociometric Choices in Formal Groups.

general group-theory in which group cohesiveness is imbedded, for this theory presupposes that a group reflects substantial behavioral similarity. Type II formal groups, finally, are intermediate between Types I and III. This type is characterized by a moderately unified choice pattern and thus, reasonably, by a moderate tendency to share opinions.

Some distribution of these general types may be expected in any batch of small formal units. This permits an explanation of the higher correlation which resulted from the adjustment for mutual pairs. Westgate courts (hypothetically) tended toward Types II and especially III. To explain, the adjustment reduced the estimates of the cohesiveness of Type III groups significantly more than those of Type II groups. Type III groups (by definition) also would have a greater percentage of deviants. Hence the higher post-adjustment correlation between "per cent deviants" and court cohesiveness in Westgate. A similar argument can be developed to explain the less marked effect of the "adjustment" in Westgate West.

As in the housing study, concentrating on formally defined units always begs the basic question of group designation in behavioral terms. Any operational measure of cohesiveness, in turn, could have diverse co-variates as the behaviorally relevant part of the formal unit varies from respondent to respondent. These exhortations, of course, do not solve the designational difficulties. The point here is the more limited one of demonstrating how differences in group designations affect cohesiveness research. Incidentally, as attempts with matrix algebra and graph theory demonstrate, group designation (especially when large data batches are involved) is an effort in which the exact sciences will be indispensable.[23]

Raising the issue of how designational difficulties differ does not solve them, of course. We merely demonstrate here that the job requires doing, and why it requires doing.

## V. COHESIVENESS RESEARCH: FINDINGS RELEVANT TO THE MANAGEMENT SCIENCES AND POLITICAL SCIENCE

Shortcomings notwithstanding, cohesiveness has been valuable in the study of significant problems of group life relevant to management science and practice. On the broadest level, whether in experimental or natural-state situations, the small group may serve five functions:[24]

1. The group may be an agency through which members obtain and evaluate information about their environment;
2. The group may serve as the context within which are created some aspects of reality which are relevant for members;

3. The group may control some aspects of the physical and social environment of consequence to individual members;
4. The group may fill a need for affiliation and affect; and
5. The group may function as a defense against the extra-group environment.

### A. Cohesiveness Research: The Study of the Processes of Social and Political Control

Making too much of little is a disease of mankind, to be sure, but the five functions performed by small social groupings clearly imply very broad applications of research on cohesiveness within Political Science.[25] In the broad sense, Political Science deals with the crucial issues of social and political control. Hence political scientists cannot avoid the small group, whose very conceptualization is rooted in the notion of behavioral control. More discrete examples only heighten the sense of relevance. For example, every *allgemeinestaatslehre* worth its salt must face the problem of accounting for unified human action. One can argue that man is a social animal, as did Aristotle, and catch some of the essence of reality in the net of a tautology. The reality that escapes such assertions, of course, is the explanation of social fragmentation as well as social unity. Greater insight has been achieved intuitively. We have in mind the brilliant insights of a Chester I. Barnard about the "basic units" out of which large organizations are built,[26] and the various approaches to the social importance of the *gemeinschaft* community of a Rousseau, a Nisbet, a MacIver, or a Durkheim. Specifying differences in cohesiveness in small social units permits one to capture even more of reality in ways that are reproducible and subject to empirical test. Specifying such differences makes possible more pointed predictions about outcomes when cohesiveness is high and when it is low, that is, about social integration and social fragmentation. At another level of abstraction, in addition, cohesiveness can help in any political research dealing with small units, as, for example, the study of local boards of finance[27] or courts.[28] Finally, cohesiveness can be useful in studying such political processes as the exertion of power.[29]

The specific content of the predictions permitted by specifying levels of cohesiveness in Political Science and Public Administration can be suggested in terms of a kind of basic law of the social physics of small groupings. The more effective a group is in serving such functions, the greater its cohesiveness (and vice versa). And greater cohesiveness means that greater group demands may be placed upon members before their withdrawal is forced. Experimental studies have validated a number of logical derivations from this basic statement of relations. One class of such studies, for example, deals with the change of individual behavior. Such research has a patent relevance to management as well as to various political processes in which attitudes and communication are significant; that is, its relevance is all but universal.

The ubiquitous relevance of cohesiveness in behavioral change may be established directly. The general hypothesis underlying this research is that the "magnitude of the change which the group can induce (in its internal power) will be equal to or less than the magnitude of . . . its cohesiveness."[30] The main results of experiments confirming this hypothesis may be abstracted:[31]

1. *Amount and intensity of communications*: studies have generally shown that participation is more equal and more intense in HiCo than in LoCo groups, which is consistent with the prediction that participation in HiCo groups is more valued by members;
2. *Rejection of deviants*: HiCo groups tend to reject those who deviate from group opinion more than LoCo groups do; and communications directed toward deviants tend to be initially more frequent as well as finally less frequent in HiCo groups than in LoCo, which reflects more marked attempts in HiCo groups to preserve the psychological group first by conversion and then by rejecting him convincingly when conversion does not result;
3. *Willingness to accept influence:* HiCo members are more susceptible to group influence than LoCo members, a relation most interestingly reflected in experimental demonstrations that HiCo groups are more successful in maintaining high *or* low production levels than LoCo groups; and
4. *Reactions toward external threat or deprivation*: HiCo groups are more capable of producing and sustaining a hostile reaction against external threat than LoCo groups.

### B. Cohesiveness as Tridimensional: As Independent, Dependent, and Intervening Variable

The preceding brief catalog of findings may be framed in terms of a mini-vocabulary that is in widespread use in scientific research. Our vocabulary consists of three classes of variables: independent, dependent, and intervening. To explain, Finding 1 above implies that cohesiveness is an independent variable, measurable variations in which will have direct effects on measures of such dependent variables as the amount of communication directed at group members. The gross relation may be depicted as:

| | | Independent Variable | Dependent Variable |
|---|---|---|---|
| | | *Cohesiveness* | *Communication of Members* |
| Condition | | High → | High and Equal Rates, Intense Tone |
| | | Low → | Widely Asymmetric Rates, Less Intense Tone |

The flows of relations above cannot be brutishly interpreted. For example, the flows have complex undepicted feedback loops. Their interpretation is not that a (HiCo) experimental group always will make intensive efforts to communicate with all members of the collectivity, however. Finding 1 reflects only a gross regularity, and contradictory or inconsistent findings should be expected in nature.

Intervening variables help reduce the percentage of cases in which inconsistencies or contradictions occur. That is, for example, Finding 2 introduces one intervening variable in finer hypotheses about cohesiveness and communication rates, that of the "deviant" or the "non-deviant" role of the person communicated to. Specifically, Finding 1 holds only for non-deviants in a HiCo group over the long run. In the short run, a deviant member of a small group probably will receive a large volume of communications designed to induce him to respect group norms. And the more cohesive the group, the greater the initial volume is likely to be. These more complex flows of relations may be depicted in the following way:

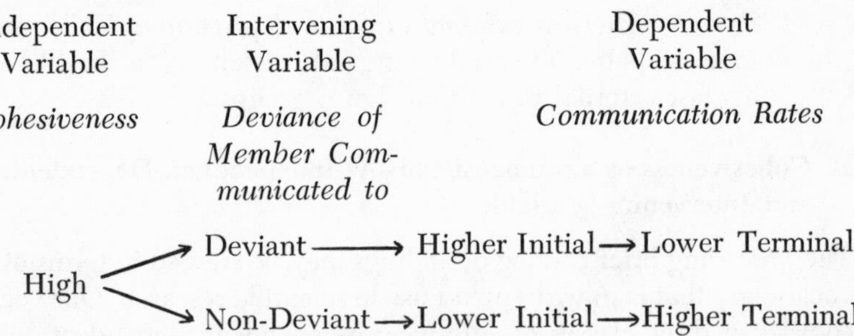


The intervening variable has a multiple usefulness in behavioral research, in sum. First, intervening variables help increase the specificity of theory fragments as they progress from natural-history regularities into middle-level theory. Second, intervening variables may help relate unconnected or even apparently contradictory findings. Hence also do increasingly comprehensive theoretical frameworks develop. Third, intervening variables can help in judging the usefulness of nominal and operational definitions. This strikes very near the heart of the scientific enterprise. Consider some hypothesis which has been validated and replicated. If that hypothesis cannot be extended to apparently related phenomena via intervening variables, one strong suspicion would be justified. The researcher reasonably could suspect that one or more of the nominal-operational pairs involved did not tap an orthogonal phenomenal area. The nominal and operational definitions of a purported dimension of reality must separate the analytical sheep and goats, of course. The process of specifying and testing for intervening relations therefore helps in judging the success of this crucial separation.

The line between the three types of variables should not be drawn too sharply, however. Thus what is an independent variable in one case may be an intervening variable in another hypothetical proposition. Cohesiveness (conceived as a gravitational field of positive and negative attractions and measured by a resultant operation) has been used successfully as an intervening variable, in fact. For example, groups exposed to substantial threat tend to "fight" or to "flee," as by disintegrating as a functioning unit. Cohesiveness seems a significant intervening variable between the independent variable "threat" and the dependent possible outcomes of fight/flight. HiCo groups can "fight"; LoCo groups can only "flee." Such uses of cohesiveness as intervening variable provide strong support for the theoretical underpinnings of cohesiveness.[32] A typical flow of relations using cohesiveness qua intervening variables takes such a form:

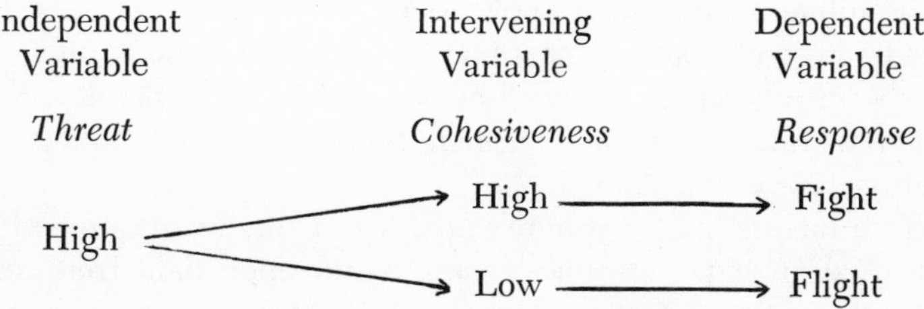


To complete the rounds with our mini-vocabulary, cohesiveness also can be considered a dependent variable. For example, the experimental instructions given to subjects can significantly influence the levels of cohesiveness that experimental collectivities develop, even if these instructions are deliberately false.[33] The relational flow may be given as:

| Independent Variable | Dependent Variable |
|---|---|
| *Experimental Instructions* (Bogus) | *Cohesiveness* |
| expect likeable group members ——→ | High |
| expect unlikeable group members ——→ | Low |

Such elemental illustrations may be made more complex so as to account for increased variation in nature, of course. For example, research shows, the independent variable Threat above must be differentiated to provide for at least two cases. Thus high Threat will co-vary with increased cohesiveness and fight, as provided above, but only in cases in which the threat does not overwhelm group members.[34] Where threat is so strong as to immobilize group members, the same effects are not likely. Thus Hamblin[35] demonstrated that cohesiveness did not increase under threat in the case in which group members did not have the resources for necessary problem-solving. Other details might be added to even this elaborated predictive chain,[36] but our illustrative purposes can be satisfied with gross rather than fine analysis.

### C. Cohesiveness Research: The Study of the Processes of Organizational Control

In whatever guise as a variable, research on cohesiveness implies many counterpart processes relevant to the management sciences generally and to Public Administration specifically. One could range widely across the discipline making such applications. The present focus will be on a limited range of counterpart processes in organizations only, however, and specifically upon the well-managed study by Stanley Seashore.[37] Seashore studied 228 relatively small, formal work-units in a plant manufacturing heavy machinery.

Two factors limit Seashore's analysis of these work-units. First, Seashore used an index of cohesiveness based upon data from answers to five fixed-response questions tapping these areas:

1. Are you really a part of the group?
2. Do you want to stay in the group?
3. How do the men get along?
4. Do the men stick together?
5. Do the men help each other?

There are sharp limits on the use of the combined data derived from answers to these questions. Thus only Questions 1 and 2, as Seashore noted, "appear to be relatively pure translations from the [resultant] definition of cohesiveness." Moreover, the low intercorrelations of data sets from Questions 1 and 2 with each other (.30) and with Questions 3–5 (tending toward the low end of the range .15–.38) also advise caution in interpreting the cohesiveness index.

Second, the high intercorrelations of the data sets from Questions 3–5 (.62, .64, and .70) also suggest that the choice-base was often narrower than the formal work-unit. Among other possibilities, Questions 3–5 may tap responses referring to psychologically relevant systems within the work-units, while Questions 1 and 2 may reflect judgments about the entire formal unit. The nature of the questions supports this surmise. In any case, Seashore realized that his research units were not necessarily psychological groups. But the analysis of variance of the cohesiveness scores by work-unit proved statistically significant. This provided some justification for treating the work teams as psychological groups.

Seashore's findings underscore the generality and importance of cohesiveness. His findings are consistent with laboratory research or are logically derivable from it. The findings are particularly noteworthy because the two reservations noted above would probably tend to dilute the strength of the relations in the data sample. Seashore's work tapped the covariation of cohesiveness and three classes of variables: (1) work-related anxiety, (2) productivity, and (3) situational characteristics of formal work-units and their members. His findings are consistent. The findings closely tie the several significant work-site variables to cohesiveness relations. Seashore's findings may be abstracted and commented upon briefly:[38]

1. The hypothesis that the "cohesive work group promotes effective support for the individual in his encounters with anxiety-producing aspects of his work environment" was generally and sometimes significantly supported. Such findings are consistent with the resultant conception of cohesiveness discussed above. Moreover, the tension-reduction associated with cohesiveness helps to explain group influence over member behavior. This finding also has a clear practical importance, for high tension has many dysfunctional consequences in organizations.[39]

2. The hypothesis that "the degree of cohesiveness . . . determines the power of the group to induce forces toward uniformity of work standards within the group and toward the formation of differential standards between groups" was demonstrated in two ways: (a) worker productivity was more uniform in HiCo than LoCo work units, and (b) productivity differences between work units were greater in HiCo

than LoCo units. These findings are consistent with outcomes of laboratory research. Cohesiveness, however, often has been associated with "good" (e.g., high productivity) group characteristics. Seashore's findings underscore the importance of the specification of intervening variables such as the style characteristics of groups. The centrality of cohesiveness —whether the style it supports is high or low productivity—is obvious for management.

3. Cohesiveness was related to two measures of the "opportunity for interaction": it was (a) related to the percentage of work-unit members with three or more years on their current job, and (b) curvilinearly related to work-unit size, i.e., both high and low cohesiveness were related to smaller size. Relevant situational characteristics should include structural, style, and population properties. Seashore's main emphasis thus was narrow. But his findings were consistent with cohesiveness theory. Length of service reasonably reflects attraction-to-group, for transfers out of hostile work-units would be expected. And small size—when length of service is not controlled—understandably encourages high (or low) cohesiveness because of the greater intimacy (or unfavorable reaction) possible in smaller units. These findings also suggest possible management techniques for manipulating cohesiveness.

## VI. CONCLUSION

This review of cohesiveness sketches a mixed picture of incomplete analytical development and demonstrated theoretical importance for the management sciences generally, and for Political Science and Public Administration as well. Despite the unsolved problems, therefore, six points seem tolerably clear.

First, research on cohesiveness is relevant to the study of administration. Existing organization theory (such as the principles of administration) does not provide for differences in cohesiveness. Indeed, the orthodox theory implies a mechanics rather than a psychology, as critics have long noted. Wide recognition of this theoretical bias induced the general emphasis on informal organization. But informal organization rephrased the research question. The development of concepts like cohesiveness is necessary to exploit such macroscopic insights. In an applied sense, cohesiveness also has important pay-offs. For organization is controlled behavior, and cohesiveness is related to the degree of behavioral control which may be exerted by a group. Thus the simple technique of allowing work-unit members to choose each other often results in higher output. This method is more likely to induce high work-unit cohesiveness than assignment by formal authority. For, *ceteris paribus*, the "personal attractiveness" source of cohesiveness is more likely to be induced when self-choice is permitted. In one case, to illustrate, self-selection versus selection by management of construction teams reveals that self-selected teams were more effective on four criteria: job satisfaction; turnover rate; an index of labor cost; and an index of materials cost.[40]

Second, cohesiveness research provides convenient conceptual and operational tools for natural-state empirical studies. The wide use of these analytical tools is necessary as well as convenient. For small-group analysis depends largely on the study of isolated, ad hoc groups in laboratory situations. The study of small groups in formal organizations, then, may validate and redirect laboratory research.

Third, such research will have important side effects. Thus the physical sciences have dealt with levels of organization (the atom, the molecule) and with their integration (e.g., "valence"). Analogously, the small group is a level of informal organization important in itself, but not capable of accounting for behavior at other levels.[41] In short, small-group theory must be integrated with the theory derived from other levels of formal and informal organization.[42] The contributions of students from disciplines concerned with management and organization will be valuable in this effort, for these disciplines have developed useful descriptive literatures dealing with macroscopic levels of organization. In any case, the research involvement of large numbers of researchers from a number of disciplines will at least acquaint them with a style of research that has paid significant dividends.

Fourth, cohesiveness research outlines the task of the application of the exact sciences to the problems of management. As in the physical sciences, empirical research demands the development of limited and general theoretical statements and of the mathematics such statements require.[43] The degree to which such demands are met and fed back into empirical research will influence substantially the pace of development of the management sciences and of Public Administration.

Fifth, cohesiveness has an apparently broad usefulness in Political Science. That is, the research products of the developmental history of the concept can be put to the service of disciplinary research needs outside of Public Administration. Moreover, the methodology supporting the development of these products has an application as wide as the empirical content of Political Science. The lack of similar work in the discipline oriented toward operational[44] and conceptual[45] clarification implies two conclusions. First, the void proclaims that political research needs the methodology circumscribed here. Second, the lack of conceptual-operational effort in Political Science suggests the value of appropriate methodological applications to spur the ongoing empirical revolution in the discipline.[46]

Sixth, a sophisticated technology for personal and organizational learning has evolved out of (in part) the work on cohesiveness reviewed here. "Laboratory education" or "sensitivity training," for example, is undoubtedly the fastest-growing contemporary approach to learning.[47] It rests solidly in group-related research such as that with cohesiveness. And the senior author has helped pioneer a related technique—the "confrontation design"—which has proved useful in a variety of situations.[48] Such applied uses reinforce the value of developing such theory-fragments as those sketched above; and these applications also suggest the valuable spin-offs that methodological concern often yields.

## NOTES

1. A large number of relevant studies reflecting the behavioral significance of small social groupings are analyzed in Muzafer and Carolyn Sherif, *An Integration of Studies on Intergroup Relations* (New York: Harper, 1953). Specifically, Clovis R. Shepherd notes of cohesiveness that it is the "key concept" in small group analysis. *Small Groups: Some Sociological Perspectives* (San Francisco: Chandler, 1964), pp. 25–26.

2. The point is potent in the series of studies beginning with Paul F. Lazarsfeld, Bernard Berelson, and Hazel Gaudet, *The People's Choice* (2nd ed.; New York: Columbia University Press, 1948).

3. Great strides have been made recently in this direction, however, as in Andrew W. Halpin and Don B. Croft, *The Organizational Climate of Schools* (Chicago: Midwest Administration Center, 1963).

4. As in Lazarsfeld, Berelson, and Gaudet, *op cit.*

5. For example, see the analysis in Robert T. Golembiewski, *The Small Group: An Analysis of Research Concepts and Operations* (Chicago: University of Chicago Press, 1962), especially pp. 104–10.

6. Robert T. Golembiewski, "The Small Group and Public Administration." *Public Administration Review,* 19 (Summer, 1959), 149–56.

7. This is the point of such work as that of Chris Argyris, *Personality and Organization: The Conflict Between System and the Individual* (New York: Harper, 1957).

8. Leon Festinger, Stanley Schachter, and Kurt Back, *Social Pressures in Informal Groups: A Study of Human Factors in Housing* (New York: Harper, 1950), pp. 164–65; and Warren O. Hagstrom and Hanon C. Selvin, "Two Dimensions of Cohesiveness in Small Groups," *Sociometry,* 26 March, 1965), 30–44.

9. Leon Festinger, Kurt Back, Stanley Schachter, H. H. Kelley, and J. W. Thibault, *Theory and Experiment in Social Communication* (Ann Arbor: Institute for Social Research, 1950), p. 21.

10. Dorwin Cartwright and Alvin Zander (eds.) *Group Dynamics: Research and Theory* (Evanston, Ill.: Row, Peterson, 1953), pp. 77–78. This nominal concept is similar to the "costs/benefits" approach of George C. Homans. He defines "cohesiveness" in terms of the "*values* of the different kinds of rewards available to members of the group: the more valuable to a group's members are the activities (or sentiments) they receive from other members or from the environment, the more cohesive it is." *Social Behavior: Its Elementary Forms* (New York: Harcourt, Brace, 1961), p. 88.

11. Lester M. Libo, *Measuring Group Cohesiveness* (Ann Arbor: Research Center for Group Dynamics, University of Michigan, 1953).

For example, individuals with high needs for affection could satisfy their mutual needs in a group and this satisfaction could be the basis of high cohesiveness. A. Paul Hare, *Handbook of Small Group Research* (New York: Free Press, 1962), 18; and Terence K. Hopkins, *The Exercise of Influence in Small Groups* (Totowa, N. J.: Bedminster Press, 1964), 76–78.

12. A similar schematization is utilized by Joachim Israel, *Self-Evaluation and Rejection in Groups: Three Experimental Studies and a Conceptual Outline* (Uppsala: Almqvist and Wiksells, 1956), p. 26.

13. See, for example, John G. Darley, Neal Gross, and W. E. Martin, "Studies of Group Behavior: The Stability, Change and Interrelations of Psychometric and Sociometric Variables," *Journal of Abnormal and Social Psychology,* 46 (1951), 565–76; and J. G. Darley, Neal Gross, and W. E. Martin, "Studies in Group Behavior: Factors Associated with the Productivity of Groups," *Journal of Applied Psychology,* 36 (December, 1952), 396–403.

14. Neal Gross and W. E. Martin, "On Group Cohesiveness," *American Journal of Sociology,* 57 (May, 1952), 547.

15. Everett W. Bovard, Jr., "Inter-

action to the Group," *Human Relations,* 9 (November, 1956), 482n.

16. This point was established by Bernice Eisman, "Some Operational Measures of Cohesiveness and Their Interrelations." *Human Relations,* 12 (April, 1959), 183–89.

17. See John Downing, "Cohesiveness, Perception, and Values," *Human Relations,* 11 (May, 1958), 157–66.

18. Stanley Schachter, "Deviation, Rejection, and Communication," *Journal of Abnormal and Social Psychology,* 46 (April, 1951), 190–207. See especially the reprint of the article in Cartwright and Zander, *op cit.,* p. 228.

19. Libo, *op. cit.,* especially pp. 30–31.

20. Kurt Back, "Influence Through Social Communication," *Journal of Abnormal and Social Psychology,* 46 (January, 1951), especially 19, 20, 23.

21. See the suggestive evidence in William Haythorn, Arthur Couch, Peter Langham, and Launor F. Carter, "The Behavior of Authoritarian and Equalitarian Personalities in Groups," *Human Relations,* 9 (February, 1956), 57–74. See also Victor H. Vroom, *Some Personality Determinants of the Effects of Participation* (Englewood Cliffs, N.J.: Prentice-Hall, 1960); and John R. P. French, Jr., E. Kay, and H. H. Meyer, "A Study of Threat and Participation in an Industrial Appraisal Program," *Behavioral Research Service Report,* General Electric Co., 1962, pp. 118–119. A rudimentary model encompassing these complex correlates of cohesiveness is presented in Robert T. Golembiewski, "Small Groups and Large Organizations," in James G. March (ed.), *Handbook of Organizations* (Chicago: Rand McNally, 1965), pp. 87–141.

22. Festinger, Schachter, and Back, *op. cit.,* p. 95. (Emphases added.)

23. Robert S. Weiss, and Eugene Jacobson, "A Method for the Analysis of the Structure of Complex Organizations," *American Sociological Review,* 20, (December, 1955), 661–68; Dorwin Cartwright, "The Potential Contribution of Graph Theory to Organization Theory," in Mason Haire (ed.), *Modern Organization Theory: A Symposium of the Foundation for Research on Human Behavior* (New York: Wiley, 1959), pp. 254–71.

24. See Festinger, Back, Schachter, Kelley, and Thibault, *op. cit.,* for the development of the underlying theory.

25. Sidney Verba, *Small Groups and Political Behavior* (Princeton, N.J.: Princeton University Press, 1961).

26. Chester I. Barnard, *The Functions of the Executive* (Cambridge, Mass.: Harvard University Press, 1938).

27. Research of such a design has been undertaken, for example, by James D. Barber of Yale University. *Power in Committees: An Experiment in the Governmental Process* (Chicago: Rand McNally, 1966).

28. Eloise Snyder, "The Supreme Court as A Small Group," *Social Forces,* 36 (March, 1958), 232–38; and S. Sidney Ulmer, "Toward A Theory of Sub-Group Formation in the United States Supreme Court," *Journal of Politics,* 27 (February, 1965), 132–52.

29. A particularly useful approach has been taken by James G. March, "Influence Measurement in Experimental and Semi-Experimental Groups," *Sociometry,* 19 (March, 1956), p. 260–71.

30. Festinger, Schachter, and Back, *op. cit.,* p. 166. Specifically, high cohesiveness should be associated with higher *or* lower performance. See Charles E. Warwick, "Relationship of Scholastic Aspiration and Group Cohesiveness to . . . Academic Achievement . . ., *Human Relations,* 17 (April, 1964), pp. 155–69.

31. Consult Schachter, *op. cit.;* and Leonard Berkowitz, "Group Standards, Cohesiveness, and Productivity," *Human Relations,* 7 (November, 1954), 509–19.

32. Lott and Lott, *op. cit.,* p. 288, for example, review several studies indicating a direct and positive relation between cohesiveness and the ability of group members to express aggression or hostility against the real or fancied offender.

33. The effects of such instructions tend to decay over time, be it noted. C. Backman and P. Secord, "The Effect of Perceived Liking on Interpersonal Attraction," *Human Relations,* 12 (1959), 379–84.

34. A. Meyers, "Team Competition,

Success, and the Adjustment of Group Members," *Journal of Abnormal and Social Psychology,* 65 (1962), 325–32.

35. R. L. Hamblin, "Group Integration During A Crisis," *Human Relations,* 11 (February, 1958), 67–76.

36. Lott and Lott, *op. cit.,* pp. 262–66.

37. Stanley E. Seashore, *Group Cohesiveness in the Industrial Work Group* (Ann Arbor: Survey Research Center, University of Michigan, 1954), especially pp. 39, 38, 36.

38. Seashore, *op. cit.,* p. 61 (I); pp. 63, 67, 69, 70 (II); and pp. 88–91 (III).

39. Some of the dysfunctional consequences of tension from budgets on first-line supervisors are isolated and analyzed in Chris Argyris, *The Impact of Budgets on People* (New York: Controllership Foundation, Inc., 1952), especially pp. 16–23. More comprehensively, see Robert L. Kahn, Daniel M. Wolfe, R. P. Quinn, J. D. Snoek, and R. A. Rosenthal, *Organizational Stress* (New York: Wiley, 1964). For one successful effort to reduce post-entry anxiety in organizations, see Earl R. Gomersall and M. Scott Myers, "Breakthrough in On-the-Job Training," Harvard Business Review, 44 (July-August, 1966), 67–72.

40. Raymond H. Van Zelst, "Validation of a Sociometric Regrouping Procedure," *Journal of Abnormal and Social Psychology,* 47 (April, 1952), 299–301.

41. A. B. Novikoff, "The Concept of Integrative Levels in Biology," *Science,* 101 (1945), 209–15.

42. Herbert A. Simon, "Comments on the Theory of Organizations." *American Political Science Review,* 46 (December, 1952), 1130–39.

43. Such a treatment of cohesiveness, for example, is provided by Herbert A. Simon and Harold C. Guetzkow, "A Model of Short and Long-Run Mechanisms Involved in Pressures Toward Uniformity in Groups," *Psychological Review,* 62 (1955), 56–68.

44. James G. March, "Influence Measurement in Experimental and Semi-Experimental Groups," *Sociometry,* 19 (March, 1956), 260–71.

45. James G. March, "The Power of Power," in David Easton (ed.) *Varieties of Political Power* (Englewood Cliffs, N. J.: Prentice-Hall, 1966), pp. 39–70; and Robert T. Golembiewski, "Personality and Organization Structure: Staff Models and Behavioral Patterns," *Journal of the Academy of Management,* 9 (September, 1966), 217–32.

46. Easton in two works—*Varieties of Political Power, op. cit.,* and *A Framework for Political Analysis* (Englewood Cliffs, N. J.: Prentice-Hall, 1965)—aptly outlines the scope and progress of this ongoing revolution.

47. Robert T. Golembiewski, "The Laboratory Approach to Organization Development: The Schema of A Method," *Public Administration Review* (September, 1967), 211–23.

48. Robert T. Golembiewski and Arthur Blumberg, "Training and Relational Learning: The Confrontation Design," *Training and Development Journal* (November, 1967), 35–43; and by the same authors, "Confrontation as a Training Design in Complex Organizations: Attitudinal Changes in a Diversified Population of Managers," *Journal of Applied Behavioral Science,* 3 (December, 1967), 525–48.

## iv

# Empirical Science at the Macro-Level: Authority as a Problem in Overlays

An empirical science of politics cannot endure at the micro-level of such dimensions as cohesiveness—which taps properties of small informal groups. But neither can it ignore the methodological lessons so conveniently learned at such manageable levels. That is, much of the subject matter of Political Science involves formally defined and massive aggregates; and their macroscopic analysis requires unique concepts and operations; but these concepts and operations must be developed in terms of the very methodological processes that were illustrated in the case of cohesiveness. Hence the present attempt to apply our notions of empirical methodology to the *authority* concept.

Motivation to focus on authority can be supplied easily. Relationally, stress on authority complements the analysis of cohesiveness in many senses. When linked, for example, the two concepts can provide powerful tools for description and prediction. Moreover, one concept relates to a micro-process and the other to a macro-process. And cohesiveness permits relatively controlled experimentation and replication of results, while the study of authority is considerably more untidy. Finally, many of the covariants of the latter concept have been explored experimentally while authority has been less favored in this regard.[1]

A methodological approach to authority also can generate its own motivation. Such an approach has several powerful attractions. First, it provides a specific illustration of the problems and possibilities of empirical analysis at a macro-level. Just as cohesiveness is imbedded in the small informal group, authority is at the heart of complex problems in man's life in large formal organizations. The twain do meet in practice, and must be made to meet in theory.

---

This chapter was originally published under the title "Authority as A Problem in Overlays: A Concept for Action and Analysis," *Administrative Science Quarterly*, Vol. 9 (June, 1964), pp. 23–49. Substantial modifications have been made to tailor the article for present purposes.

Second, authority is of across-the-board relevance to Political Science. Indeed, one astute commentator has argued that the emphasis upon authoritative relations is a key element linking organization theory and broader political theory.[2] The methodological analysis of authority, then, is a parsimonious way of coming to partial grips with a significant problem of the entire discipline. As a consequence, although the focus again will be on issues faced in the management sciences generally and in Public Administration specifically, the range of applications will be wide.

Nature exacts her toll in the case of authority, however, as she usually does. What will be gained in additional scope—as compared with the analysis of cohesiveness—in large part will be paid for by decreased sharpness of results and greater tentativeness in acting consistently with the empirical methodology. The developmental history of cohesiveness has generated useful nominal and operational definitions, but that standard is beyond the reach of the following methodological approach to authoritative relations. This realistic assessment hardly constitutes grounds for rejoicing, for plainly we cannot win for losing. However—although we do not subscribe to the philosophy as a general life-style—in this case it is how you play the game that counts in the long run.

## I. SIGNIFICANCE AND SOME SIGNPOSTS: CONCEPTUAL DEVELOPMENT AT A CROSSROAD

Authority is at once a conceptual keystone and a conundrum in the study of organizations. Authoritative relations obviously serve as the framework for much behavior in all forms of organized activity however one approaches the subject matter. On this point commentators agree. But this agreement does not extend to the several significantly different emphases in authority concepts, all of which seem relevant to understanding authoritative phenomena in organizations. Most commentators habitually weigh one emphasis to the exclusion of others.[3]

This mixed state of affairs sets two major tasks for this analysis. First, a number of conceptual emphases common in studies of authority will be represented as individual "overlays" of authoritative relations that exist in various combinations in all organized effort. The working concept of authoritative relations will be an integrative one, then, the several overlays being its major components. This approach follows the lead of Pfiffner and Sherwood. They introduced the useful notion of considering authoritative relations as an integration of the formal structure and several more or less potent modifying processes, all of which can be considered as overlays. As they explained:

> These modifying processes must be studied one at a time; a good way to do so without forgetting their "togetherness" is to consider each as a transparent "overlay" pattern superimposed on the basic formal organizational pattern. The totality of these overlays might be so complex as to be nearly opaque, but it will be a closer approach to reality than the bare organization chart so typically used to diagram a large . . . structure.[4]

Second, and a task far beyond conceptual description, this chapter seeks to orient the several overlays so that they will reinforce one another in accomplishing desired objectives. Some representative research relevant to this practical problem will be reviewed, with emphasis on ways of increasing the congruence of the several authoritative overlays.

The two major tasks of this chapter reflect a resolution-in-fact of a central dispute within Political Science. That is, the chapter will show how empirical analysis must be relatively value-free at one stage of processing, and this in order to permit effective attention to values at other stages. That is, the first task of this chapter involves developing a conceptual way to describe reality, an empirical task. The motivation is not empirical science for science's sake; and certainly that setting-aside of values is no sign of the "dogmatic atheism" sometimes attributed to science. The purpose, directly, is to put man in the service of man. Recall, that is, that the second task of this chapter is to suggest ways in which empirical knowledge can be put to the service of our values, to begin (in our terminology) to work toward the development of goal-based, empirical theories appropriate to our broad moral heritage.

## II. *AUTHORITY* AS CONCEPT: FOUR EMPHASES

*Authority* has not enjoyed conceptual unanimity, as four distinct emphases in its study illustrate. These emphases may be designated as the traditional, the functional, the behavioral, and the integrative, more or less following the typology suggested by Mandeville.[5]

1. The *traditional* concept of authority is reflected, for example, in Schell's observation that: "If we are to control, we must provide avenues through which it can function easily and directly. These avenues we speak of as paths of authority. They pass from administrators who determine policy, to the executives who are responsible for the performance of the policy, and then to the employees who perform the actual operations."[6] Proponents of this point of view are numerous, although there are serious difficulties with its formulation,[7] and particularly with

its placing a monopoly of authority in some one source. In Political Science, for example, concepts of this type often are labeled *legalistic.* The second Hoover Commission *Report,* by way of illustration, argued essentially that the President is the only elected official with a national constituency and that therefore he should exercise full and direct authority over all executive officers and departments.

2. The *functional* concept is less neat. It provides a real alternative to the *trickle down* traditional concept of authority by denying that the chief executive of an organization has a legitimate monopoly of authority which he may parcel out to subordinates. Proponents of the functional approach thus find authority only in the particular job to be done. Authority, therefore, is sharply limited and is certainly not monopolized by anyone. As Follett explained: "I do not think that a president should have any more authority than goes with his function. . . . Authority belongs to the job and stays with the job."[8] More contemporary statements of this point of view put matters in less personal terms than did Follett. Such a formulation might note that authority increasingly inheres in "the situation" and individuals respond as commonly to its demands as to an order of some formal superior.[9] The various formulations of the functional concept, however, all similarly imply a concept of authority as "bubbling up" from work.

3. The *behavioral* concept of authority stands somewhat apart. It seeks its data neither in legitimacy nor in function. The concept fixates on actual patterns of behavior of individuals as they influence others and are influenced. Simon is perhaps the foremost contemporary commentator of this persuasion,[10] acknowledgedly relying on Barnard's earlier argument that:

> Authority is the character of a communication (order) in a formal organization *by virtue of which it is accepted* by a contributor to or "member" of the organization as governing the action he contributes. . . . Therefore, under this definition the decision as to whether an order has authority or not lies with the persons of authority" or those who issue these orders.[11]

Standing apart as it does, however, the behavioral concept still bears a significant relation to the other concepts. Function helps determine who influences whom. Moreover, the behavioral concept is basically a strong reaction against the traditional concept.

4. An *integrative* concept, finally, includes all three emphases above under one conceptual tent. Fayol may be taken to represent this approach. He explained that: "Authority is the right to give orders and the power to exact obedience. Distinction must be made between a

manager's official authority deriving from office and personal authority, compounded of intelligence, experience, moral worth, ability to lead, past services, and so forth. . . . [Personal authority] is the indispensable complement of official authority."[12]

Fayol's conceptual approach has a patent integrative bias. For "official authority" has a meaning congenial to the traditional concept; "personal authority" overlaps significantly with the behavioral concept; and a significant measure of one's personal authority will derive from one's function and the style with which it is performed.

Fayol is no lonely voice in a conceptual wilderness, but few others join him in discord. Political scientists will find a similar notion in Neustadt's work, for example, albeit in few others.[13]

## III. AUTHORITY AS OVERLAYS: SOME DIRECTIONS FOR ANALYSIS

The preceding conceptual descriptions suggest a convenient accommodation in developing a nominal definition of authority. The first three concepts, *by themselves,* are not adequate to encompass all significant authoritative relations in organizations, but each taps an important aspect of such relations. The integrative concept suffers from an opposite fault. Its content is broad and unspecific. It therefore facilitates a survey of authoritative relations but it does not isolate those aspects that are descriptively significant. This analysis, then, will rely upon the integrative concept (the specific content of which is provided by the first three concepts), and will focus upon the several combinations of formal authority and (in Fayol's terminology) personal authority.

Using the integrative approach seems reasonable and necessary, as well as convenient. It is reasonable because experimental results demonstrate that consistent predictions require at least the threefold typology implied by the integrative concept. For example, work such as that of Thompson with "identical organizations" points up the explanatory inadequacy of the traditional, the functional, and behavioral concepts by themselves.[14] Research has been sufficient to establish once and for all the necessity of the integrative concept, however. Commonly, the several conceptual emphases tend toward mutual exclusiveness as a practical matter. Thus Hopkins noted that the approaches of Weber and Barnard are in "point of fact . . . seldom taken together." The consequence is pernicious: "Many studies of communication systems," Hopkins continued, "read as though the exercise of authority depended upon the good will and rationality of the participants, and many studies emphasizing power leave the impression that so far as the effectiveness of the system is concerned, the processes through which authority is exercised are of little consequence."[15] This condition, obviously, requires correction.

## IV. AUTHORITATIVE RELATIONS AS OVERLAYS: SOME EXAMPLES

The nominal definition of authoritative relations in terms of overlays permits correcting the bias of the literature. For example, Figures IV.1 through IV.4 sketch four simplified overlays. Figure IV.1, first, sketches a typical formal "line-staff" model based on the traditional theory of organization. IV.1, IV.2, and IV.3 refer to sequential lower-level processes in an industrial or administrative context; IV.4 can represent an inspection station. Although this first overlay is highly generalized, it has its analogs in the sub-literatures of Political Science. Public Administration and the literature on the American presidency, for example, generally reflect such a model of organization.

Whatever the extent of the analogs of the first overlay, its basic intent seems clear enough. And in that intent lies both the strength and the weakness of the traditional concept. Basically, the emphasis of the overlay is on the vertical relations of formal authority designed to tie (for example) $a_1$ to $M_{ABCD}$ through an intermediate supervisor. Figure IV.1 is faithful to the traditional concept of authority. Some, but certainly not all, authoritative relations in all organizations can be explained in terms of the structuring of superior and subordinate roles. This is both the strength and the weakness of the traditional concept.

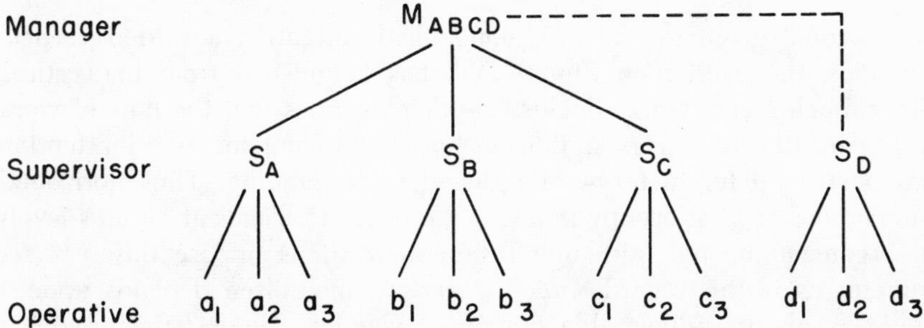


FIGURE IV.1 A Simplified Formal Structure Based on the Classical Theory of Organization.

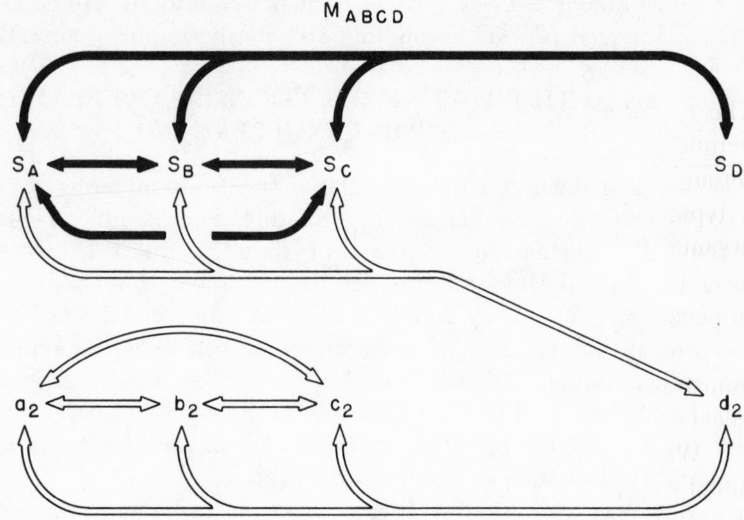


designates the major cooperative horizontal relations required for planning, scheduling, etc., of product ABCD in a flow of work

designates the major cooperative horizontal relations required for fabricating-inspecting product ABCD in a flow of work

FIGURE IV.2 The Flow of Work as an Overlay.

Second, given the all but monopolistic attention accorded vertical relations, the overlay in Figure IV.2 has languished from inattention. Since much recent work conclusively demonstrates that the flow of work in organizations has very significant horizontal components,[16] inattention has been paid for in terms of reduced understanding. Thus horizontal interactions at least occupy much of the time of officials at various levels of organization, and, although different positions impose different requirements in this regard, effective performance often depends upon a copious volume of favorable horizontal contacts "across" the organization. Moreover, such horizontal interactions have a particular significance because of the nature of the traditional theory of organization as shown in Figure IV.1 The theory has a very decided vertical bias, and in practice it encourages the separatism of units which it organizes in terms of particular functions or processes. This separatism often impedes the smooth flow of work from one work station to another.[17] Facilitative horizontal relations, then, can have a great relevance for effective performance. Many authoritative sequences in organizations also can be explained in terms of horizontal pressures induced by work, whether or not the formal structure legitimates these sequences.

Figure IV.2 sketches a hypothetical overlay of horizontal relations that would facilitate the flow of the set of "line" processes A, B, and C, and for the "staff" service D. Failure to tie the three "line" processes together horizontally with minimal conflict, and failure to bring in simultaneously and harmoniously service D at appropriate points in the horizontal sequence of work, both imply great mischief. Any such facilitative overlay is derived from the particular characteristics of the work itself and hence is consistent with the emphasis upon a functional concept of authority.

The flow-of-work overlay is simple and convenient, but it represents a family of more complex analogs relevant to Political Science. Relatively direct translations are possible to cases of jurisdictional disputes between federal executive departments, for example. Greater but surmountable difficulties inhere in transforming this analysis into terms comprehending the *Report* of the second Hoover Commission (as an example of the

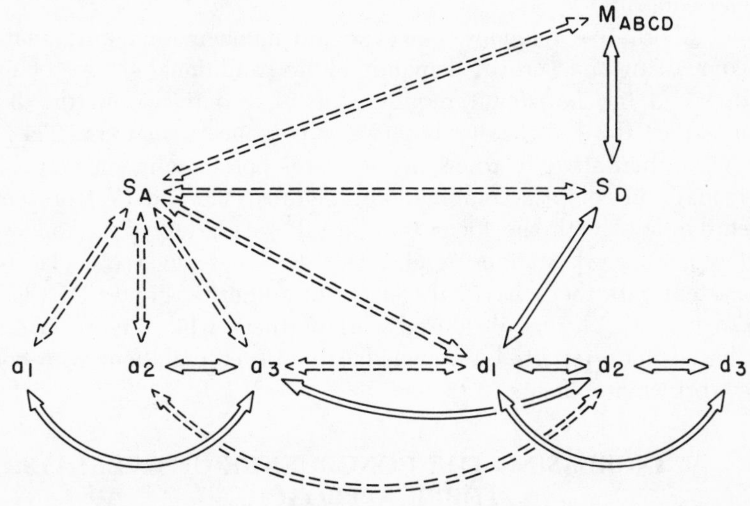


designates a mutual rejection on an affective-instrumental sociometric criterion

designates a mutual choice on an affective-instrumental sociometric criterion

FIGURE IV.3 Sociometric Choice Structures as an Overlay (Units A and D only).

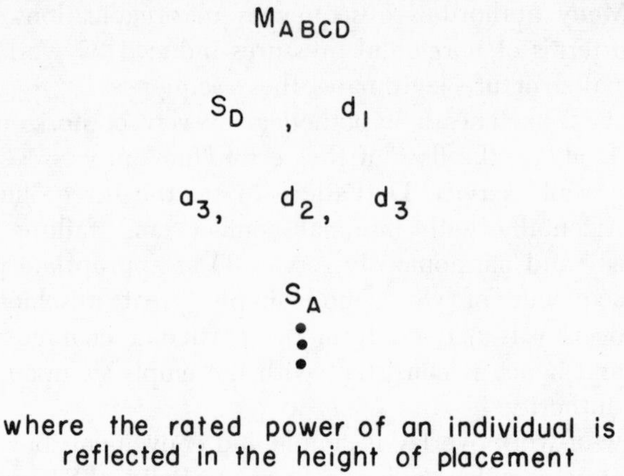

$M_{ABCD}$

$S_D$ , $d_1$

$a_3$, $d_2$, $d_3$

$S_A$

⋮

where the rated power of an individual is reflected in the height of placement

FIGURE IV.4 The Power Structure as an Overlay (Units A and D only).

traditional concept) and the flow of work institutionalized by the separation of powers and checks and balances (as an example of the functional concept).

Authoritative relations, however, are much more than a matter of encompassing the vertical demands of the traditional theory of organization and the horizontal requirements that derive from the flow of work. For, third, behavioral overlays complicate matters. They may orient authoritative relations, as it were, horizontally or vertically or diagonally in complex combinations. Figures IV.3 and IV.4 present two such overlays, with the focus for the sake of cartographic convenience being upon work stations A and D only. These overlays, clearly, are consistent with the behavioral concept of authority. Figure IV.3 is based on sociometric choices of desired work partners, while Figure IV.4 might be based upon reports by knowledgeable observers about who controls the work environment.

## V. INCREASING THE CONGRUENCE OF OVERLAYS: THREE APPROACHES

The four overlays usefully frame the complex problems facing the analysis of authoritative relations in organizations, as will be shown, but we cannot point by point act upon the full set of methodological guidelines developed in the preceding chapter. For example, we cannot solve here the detailed conceptual and operational problems of isolating the several overlays.[18]

Thus limiting this analysis does not signal an abandonment of empirical methodology. Rather, the limitation merely permits first things to happen first. Short of detailed tinkering with concepts and operations but consistent with methodological guidelines, the provisional usefulness of the approach to authoritative relations via overlays will be established in terms of the specific opportunities it provides for nominal and operational work. Second, the usefulness of the overlays will be judged in terms of their compatibility with existing and relatively firm empirical research. Third, the usefulness of the notion of integrative overlays also will be estimated. These three approaches to authority as a problem in overlays will be considered in turn.

### A. Opportunities for Empirical Research

The several overlays provide ample opportunities for methodologically relevant work. Consider but a few of the analytical possibilities presented by the overlays. Clearly, the behavioral patterns in Figures IV.3 and IV.4 hardly correspond to the requirements of Figures IV.1 and IV.2. Knowing "who chooses whom" on sociometric criteria often will aid in understanding who influences whom and why, for example. Highly chosen individuals, further, may or may not have a high rank on power in the organization, they may have high formal status or low, and they may or may not perform crucial roles in some horizontal flow of work. These distinctions permitted by the several overlays are not trivial, as will be shown. By implication, then, much must be learned about increasing the congruence of the several overlays.

It also seems likely that Figures IV.1 through IV.4 can help us work through the analysis of the congruence of authoritative overlays. Figures IV.1 and IV.2 seem representative enough of actual operating situations, even if they are simplifications of reality. There is, however, nothing absolute about the specific hypothetical patterns of sociometric choice and rank on power illustrated in Figures IV.3 and IV.4. There will be infinite variations. Moreover, it is not precisely clear how complex sociometric or power patterns might usefully be described.[19] However, as in Figure IV-3, an $M_{ABCD}$ often will lean heavily on an inspection unit D (or other "staff" unit) to aid in control. Further, members of an inspection unit such as D will commonly be rejected by members of "line" work stations.[20] Finally, as in Figure IV.4, there often will be great deviations of ranks on power and the formal status accorded individuals.[21] Consequently, the analysis is at least not blatantly improvised.

Note that we imply no neo-traditional argument about eliminating the incongruence between overlays. As a practical matter that would be impossible. It also may be unwise. For a certain degree of incongruence probably permits more facile adaptation to changed conditions. Rather, we contend that this "certain degree" of incongruence is often exceeded. The remedy, further, is not a brooding concern with uniformity. Indeed, increasing the congruence of the several authoritative overlays often requires heterogeneity, as in fitting structure and techniques to the diverse personality characteristics of members. This assures that innovation and adaptability need not be sacrificed in order to increase this congruence. The following two sections, then, suggest the ways in which the degree of incongruence can be held within tolerable limits. These sections also illustrate the advantages of so doing.

### B. Some Approaches for Action

The several authoritative overlays are compatible with significant themes of recent research. Indeed, a considerable volume of well-known research points to some clear approaches to increasing the congruence of the several authoritative overlays. This research demonstrates the importance of achieving increased congruence and also suggests techniques appropriate for effecting such an increase. Although space precludes anything approaching comprehensiveness here, two illustrations will prove instructive.

#### *1. Congruence of Formal and Power Overlays*

Available evidence implies that high congruence will exist, for example, when a formal supervisor is accorded high power over the work environment. Striving for high congruence seems worthwhile. For example, men in the high-producing units of one organization attributed far greater influence to three levels of supervision than did personnel from similar units with records of low production.[22] Similarly, Pelz could find no marked correlations of employee attitudes and effectiveness with fifty measures of supervisory practices. When the influence of a supervisor on his superiors was specified, however, sharp differences in attitudes and effectiveness were isolated.[23]

When power and formal status are congruent, in addition, employee satisfaction tends to be high. High congruence on these two overlays does not require the abject submission of employees to their supervisors. Indeed, members of the high-producing units mentioned above actually reported less "unreasonable pressure" for output than did members of low-producing units. They also attributed more power to themselves than did members of low-producing units. That is, high supervisory power did not make the men more vulnerable to control in the general case. Rather, high supervisory power was associated with the greater autonomy of subordinates. Likert has criticized the notion of a "constant pie" of influence, here challenged, with telling effect.[24] Basically, it seems, a high-power supervisor is more able to grant autonomy to his subordinates. A low-power supervisor might prove too weak to control his subordinates, but he would probably be too insecure to allow his subordinates greater autonomy.[25] In practice, the grant of autonomy in the former case tends to release emotional forces otherwise expended in ego-defense, thereby permitting (but not assuring) greater involvement in work. Efforts to wrest autonomy from an unwilling superior, in contrast, are likely to have less favorable consequences on the motivation to work and on employee satisfaction.

The existing research, scarcely tapped here, also does further service with respect to the formal and power overlays of authoritative relations. Not only does that research establish the efficacy of increasing the congruence of the two overlays; it also permits the listing of a wide variety of conditions that can be expected to covary with the high degree of power of a formal superior. Research shows that the power of a formal supervisor will tend to be high—and congruence of his formal and power ranks therefore great—as these conditions are approached:

1. His style of supervision is compatible with the personality characteristics of his subordinates; this implies, in general, a non-directive or supportive style;[26]

2. He reduces the degree of punitiveness characteristic of (for example) his reactions to error;[27]

3. The degree of "pressure" he exerts downward remains above the threshold that his subordinates consider reasonable;[28] and

4. The degree of autonomy available to him to plan his work, make decisions, and so on, is substantial.

These conditions must be interpreted carefully, of course. Their direct linkages with power have not all been established, though the inferential evidence is strong. Moreover, these conditions are generalizations of existing research, not inevitabilities.[29] Thus we should not be surprised, for example, to find that increased supervisory power in a particular case may be associated with a directive style of supervision.[30] Individuals with authoritarian personality characteristics predictably will tend to accord power to directive types. This is not to say that Condition 1 is inappropriate, however. Rather, Condition 1 implies that personality characteristics congenial to a directive style have not been dominant in the populations tested. When these personality characteristics are dominant in some particular sample, then, the generalization cannot be expected to hold.

These conditions, in turn, suggest applied techniques for increasing the congruence of the overlays of formal structure and rank on power. The training of supervisors, for example, could stress the efficacy of a supportive style. If the training "took," favorable effects on employee satisfaction and performance could be expected. However, the intensity of such effects would depend on (for example) the degree of reinforcement by the organization structure within which the trainee operates. The conditions above may also be induced by the assignment of superiors and subordinates in terms of personality characteristics. This, in turn, requires an organization structure capable of being adapted to such personality differences. More will be said under both headings at several points below.

### 2. *Congruence of Sociometric and Functional Overlays*

The usefulness of, and techniques for, increasing the congruence of overlays may be illustrated by considering the two other overlays. These are the sociometric and the functional overlays. Schutz's work with "compatibility," for example, demonstrates forcefully the significant pay-offs which result when individuals who must interact in a flow of work have complementary personality characteristics. Experimental groups composed of compatible subjects, for example, have favorable activity-profiles. They performed more effectively, were more satisfied with their experimental experiences and with their output, and in general outshone the incompatible groups.[31] Such "assignment effects" may also be induced in a far simpler (if incompletely understood) way. Van Zelst established the great benefit of allowing members of various building crafts—who perforce interacted in the same flows of work—to choose the individuals with whom they preferred to work. Self-choice crews proved more effective than crews assembled traditionally. In one case, for example, direct cost savings amounting to some 5 per cent were realized. In addition, employee satisfaction was higher and turnover lower for the self-choice crews.[32]

Lest such findings be interpreted incautiously, some reservations are in order. Such sanguine outcomes are not inevitable, of course. Increased group cohesiveness and thus increased group control of the work environment commonly will result from high compatibility, whether induced by self-choice or by more sophisticated testing devices like Schutz's FIRO-B. But groups can restrict as well as raise output. Many intervening variables influence which it will be. For example, applied techniques for inducing high compatibility will be most useful in organizations when relations are so structured that the facile measurement of performance is possible. This reduces the probability that any increase in cohesiveness will be employed to disrupt work. Notice also that compatibility is not required of all organization members. Participants in separate flows of work might be overtly hostile to one another with no damage, given appropriate structural arrangements.

Let us relate the present point directly to Figures IV.2 and IV.3. Assume, for example, that the flow of work requires Inspector $d_2$ to interact with Operatives $a_2$, $b_2$, $c_2$, as well as with the three supervisors. These interactions may occur under difficult conditions, such as the rejection of a batch of output. This being the case, the sociometric pattern in Figure IV.3 seems likely to make the worst of rather demanding circumstances.[33] Given effective controls over the work of Inspector $d_2$, he might be assigned to inspection at $a_3$ rather than $a_2$. Controls are necessary, of course, to guarantee that the favorable relations implicit in the mutual choice of $a_3$ and $d_2$ do not encourage the disregard of inspection standards. Quality control based upon sampling methods, for example, might provide the required control.

## C. Organization Structures as Intervening Variables

The preceding sketch of some research not only demonstrates the usefulness of the notion of integrative overlays, but it also demands and permits still broader research. Despite their usefulness, that is, the above-noted approaches to increasing the congruence of overlays must be found wanting. For example, it is generally appropriate to call for a supportive style from supervisors, but it is quite another matter to provide for the continuous reinforcement of such a style. Training certainly is not enough, especially if the environment is more or less hostile to its preachments. This implies pessimism about the efficacy of any technique for increasing the congruence of overlays as long as the traditional theory of organization is the benchmark overlay to which others are to be fitted. Figure IV.1, of course, sketches a structure based upon this theory.

Our position here may be framed in general terms. An important intervening variable in all hypotheses concerning authoritative relations in organizations is the specific structural framework within which behavior is observed. Attempts to increase the congruence of authoritative overlays *without changing structural relations* can anticipate difficulties. Our approach will contrast two analytical models to establish the centrality of structure as intervening variable, both in practice and in research.

Specifically, the inappropriateness of the traditional model for increasing the congruence of overlays is supported by three paired comparisons. Inherent in the Figure IV.1 structure are very great pressures for limiting the power of intermediate levels of formal supervisors. Congruence of the power and formal overlays, then, will tend to be low. Few non-trivial decisions, for example, can be made below the level of $M_{ABCD}$. For he alone oversees enough of the organizational elements to make reasonable decisions concerning the flow of work. The traditional structure encourages a directive style of supervision. That is, the activities of A, B, C, and D have to be delicately integrated, and this can be done only by $M_{ABCD}$. The latter will tend to exercise very close control over the several supervisors, therefore, and they in turn are likely to assume the same style in their relations with their own subordinates. Moreover, since the traditional structure is organized around discrete functions or processes, the autonomy of the several supervisors will tend to be inhibited by managerial action. The intended effect, of course, is to facilitate overhead control. "Staff" often will play an important role in thus reducing the power of lower-level supervisors.[34]

To summarize, the traditional theory of organization implies massive forces directly opposed to inducing a high degree of congruence of the formal and power overlays, at least at lower supervisory levels. The import of the point may be extended. To the degree that lower-level supervisors lose control over the work environment as a result of low congruence, and to the degree that lower productivity and lower satisfaction result, so also will upper levels of management find their power vitiated. Apparently reasonable behavior by upper levels of management, paradoxically, often fails as it succeeds.

Similar dynamics generated by the traditional theory of organization imply a low congruence of the formal and sociometric overlays. Consider only the matter of integrating the activities A, B, C, and D. $M_{ABCD}$ commonly will find it necessary to apply artificial pressure to force their integration. Thus he might resort to close supervision or create crises to induce a sense of urgency about total performance among the several organization units, each of which has responsibility for only a partial contribution.[35] The various supervisors, in turn, will tend strongly to pass on this pressure to the operatives,[36] with awkward consequences. Thus the supervisors and their punitive role will tend to be rejected sociometrically by the operatives.[37] This is a matter of some concern. For as both laboratory[38] and real-life experimentation[39] demonstrate, low congruence of the sociometric and formal overlays will tend to be associated with lower performance and satisfaction.

There is an alternative to the general relations sketched here which is no more attractive. This alternative seems relatively rare. Suitable organizational arrangements can reduce its incidence even further. For example, a supervisor can elect to resist pressure from above: he can identify closely with the operatives under his command while he supports their efforts to protect themselves against a punitive upper-level management. Employee satisfaction may be high under such conditions, but productivity will tend to be low.[40] Any organization structure designed to reduce the incidence of such cases must meet at least two tests. It must avoid forcing a choice between basic supervisory identification with management *or* employees only. And that structure must permit the facile measurement of performance so as to avoid (for example) the case in which the high congruence of the sociometric and formal overlays facilitates the restriction of output. The traditional structure fails both tests.

The complex senses in which the traditional structure fails the two tests above may be sampled. For example, the traditional theory of organization encourages low congruence of the sociometric and functional overlays of authoritative relations. Given a punitive environment, particularly, employees performing the several individual activities will tend to identify with their respective individual units of organization. Conflicts over programs, allocation of costs, budgets, and so on both require and reinforce such vertical identification.[41] Positive sociometric choices on affective-instrumental criteria, then, will tend to be directed toward those involved in the same functional activity. Very likely, in addition, negative choices will be exchanged between those performing different activities. Moreover, these patterns will be more marked as the individual organization units develop high morale. That is precisely that condition which many supervisors consider desirable and strive to cultivate.

The development of such sub-organization identifications in a Figure IV.1 structure implies unfortunate consequences of some magnitude. For the characterization above argues that positive sociometric choices will tend to be concentrated *among* those performing the same activity. The functional overlay, however—the flow of work being horizontal—requires favorable relations *between* those performing the several individual activities. Negative choices between such individuals are more probable, however. Evidence already cited strongly implies that productivity and satisfaction will tend to be low under conditions of such cross-pressures.

Of course, exceptions to these probabilities occur, but available evidence indicates they are rare. The traditional structure, in short, provides too little of that continuing reinforcement of the lessons implicit in existing research about ways to increase the congruence of overlays.

This brief analysis of the low congruence of the several overlays associated with the traditional theory of organization, then, may seem to hoist this analysis on its own petard. The dilemma can be shown to be only apparent, however, if an alternative pattern for organizing can be developed. Such an alternative pattern is now emerging from much

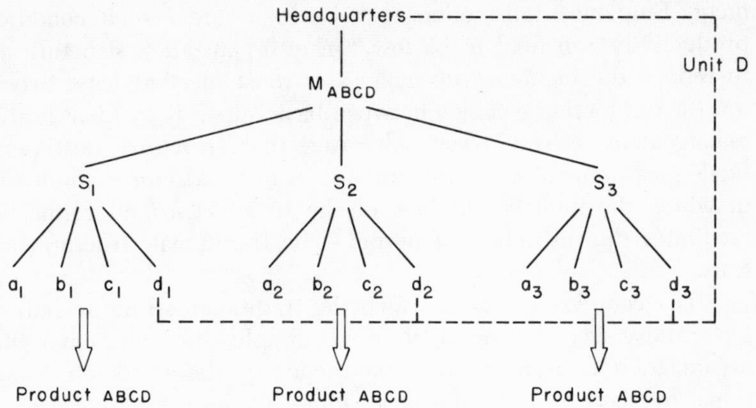


FIGURE IV.5 An Unorthodox Organization of a Simple Set of Task-Elements.

contemporary research, to which Worthy, Likert, and Argyris have contributed most significantly. The exact nature of the issue is yet to be determined, but the general properties of the emerging model are sketched in Figure IV.5 The figure organizes the same limited set of task-elements as does Figure IV.1, if in a very different way and with very different behavioral consequences.

The detailed analysis of the probable behavioral consequences of the structure in Figure IV.5 may be eschewed here. The necessary effort has been expended elsewhere to demonstrate the structure's efficacy, both in simplifying the general problems of management[42] and in alleviating the difficulties that typically beset such a functional specialty as accounting.[43] The usefulness of the structure in Figure IV.5 can be adumbrated economically here, given the background of the preceding analysis.

The Figure IV.5 structure may be analyzed briefly. Define an "administrative entity," following Worthy, as a unit of organization that controls all of the operations necessary for some complete flow of work. Figure IV.5 is built around smallish administrative entities at the level of the supervisors. The administrative entity in Figure IV.1, in contrast, is far larger. It includes $M_{ABCD}$, all three supervisors, and all their subordinates. One can generalize safely. Organizing around individual processes or functions requires larger administrative entities; organizing around discrete flows of work permits smaller administrative entities.

A chain of attractive behavioral consequences derives from this basic structural characteristic of Figure IV.5. These consequences, in general, facilitate the integration of authoritative overlays. Consider some of the ways this unorthodox formal structure induces congruent formal and power overlays. Figure IV.5 structures permit (if they do not require) that the several supervisors make non-trivial decisions relevant to the complete flow of work which each supervises. This should operate generally so as to increase their power. The structure also permits a "non-directive" style of supervision, at least down to the level of the supervisors. For $M_{ABCD}$ no longer will need to force the integration of the individual units of organization having separatist tendencies. The responsibility for that integration has been lowered to the level of $S_1$, $S_2$, and $S_3$. Acting upon this responsibility will be encouraged, in turn, by the facile comparative measurement of the performance of the several units, each of which handles a similar flow of work. Measures of performance in Figure IV.1 structures, in contrast, tend to be artificial in that they force such argumentative questions as: How many units of output at Work Station A are equal to *x* units at Station B? As a consequence, the separatist tendencies of the traditional theory of organization are often exaggerated.[44] Finally, the possibility of simple and meaningful measurement of comparative performance allows $M_{ABCD}$ to permit the several supervisors considerable autonomy. Giving such opportunities to formal supervisors to influence the work environment often would lead employees to accord high power to their supervisors.

The unorthodox structure in Figure IV.5 in many significant senses encourages a greater congruence of the formal and power overlays. Note the recurring paradox. In structuring the organization so as to increase the power of lower-level supervisors, given the safeguard of non-arbitrary measurement of performance, upper levels of management also enhance their own power. This is no play on words. Likert provides supporting data. He reports that higher productivity and higher satisfaction tend to be associated with the employees' perception that both they and all relevant levels of supervision exercise great influence over the work environment. Work units having low output and low satisfaction, in contrast, accord themselves and their superiors less influence than high-output and high-satisfaction groups.[45]

The structure sketched in Figure IV.5 also facilitates the congruence of the formal and sociometric overlays. Given that each organization unit now comprises all of the activities necessary for a complete flow of work, less supervisory pressure for the integration of operations will be required. Social and psychological identifications of individuals with their organizational unit support the integration of the several activities rather than oppose it. Moreover, what may be called "natural pressure" is built into the organization of work. Such pressure need not be induced by supervisors in specific subordinates, as for instance, by means of personal criticism. Natural pressure derives from the relative effectiveness of the work of the autonomous and (at least potentially) competitive teams. A contrived sense of urgency often is required in a Figure IV.1 structure, to put the matter baldly, if only because any one unit of organization can lower (but not increase) output. The pace of work at D, for example, could affect the entire sequence of operations.[46] In a Figure IV.5 structure, in contrast, any one unit of organization can independently raise (but not reduce) output.

There is a conclusion here for the taking. These rudimentary differences imply significantly less punitiveness of the supervisory role in Figure IV.5, which increases the chances that a formal supervisor also will be highly chosen sociometrically. No inevitability is implied, of course. But at the very least the Figure IV.5 structure creates no obstacles to the greater congruence of the formal and sociometric overlays. Figure IV.1 most definitely does create such obstacles.

The unorthodox model of organization sketched in Figure IV.5 also facilitates the greater congruence of the formal and sociometric overlays in a more subtle sense. Thus the unorthodox theory is adaptable to staffing the unit headed by $S_1$ with (let us say) high scorers on the Adorno *F* Scale, while staffing the unit of $S_2$ with low scorers. The two supervisors then could be chosen for compatible personality characteristics. The supervisors, in turn, could apply an appropriate style of supervision that is both natural to them and congenial to their subordinates. These capabilities of the structure in Figure IV.5 patently imply great potential for the creation of high congruence of the formal and sociometric overlays through the assignment of personnel, particularly in the light of growing sophistication with personality testing. Certainly there is no question but that awkward solutions of the assignment problem can significantly reduce productivity and satisfaction.[47]

Figure IV.1 structures provide less flexibility of this kind and pay the price for this reduced adaptability. Staffing the organization units headed by $S_A$ and $S_B$ with individuals of opposed personality characteristics, for example, could seriously hamper the flow of work.[48] Moreover, in implicitly recognizing this fact, the traditional theory of organization prescribes a uniform style of supervision. The difficulty, however, is dual: relevant personality characteristics of employees are more diverse; and most personnel (to judge from existing research, largely restricted to this country) do not have the personality constellations appropriate for the uniform style prescribed. Difficulties or no, however, there have been many massive attempts to act upon the monolithic prescriptions of the traditional theory, as in psychological testing. Hence come the significant criticisms of commentators like Whyte,[49] who noted that testing programs commonly have major inadequacies. They encourage a homogenized, conforming work force; such programs do not face the problem of what is to be done with the "throw-aways" who do not fit the desired personality profile; and the derived punitive bias of much testing encourages faking.

The congruence of sociometric and functional overlays, finally, is also enhanced by the unorthodox structure. Consider the common tension between the vertical and particularistic demands of the traditional theory and the horizontal and integrative demands of the flow of work. The unorthodox theory of organization attempts to make the best of matters by departmentalizing around autonomous flows of work. Individuals will still identify with their unit, of course, but their primary identification is with an autonomous flow of work rather than with some one function or process. The advantages are numerous. The concentration of positive sociometric choices within any unit of organization, for example, will serve to tie together the several activities required for some flow of work. Sociometric rejection of organizational "outsiders," on the other hand, will cause no particular difficulty. Indeed, it may buoy performance. A Figure IV.1 structure does not make good use of this clustering of sociometric choices. Moreover, the rejection of organizational "outsiders" could severely burden a flow of work in such a structure.

The Figure IV.5 structure goes with the grain of work; but Figure IV.1 imposes a structure on that flow of work which tends to fragment it vertically. Only the former approach facilitates the congruence of the sociometric and functional overlays. Thus the Figure IV.5 structure gives $d_2$ (for example) every organizational reason to cooperate closely with the individuals performing the three processes under $S_2$; $d_2$ thus is likely to choose sociometrically individuals in his own immediate work unit with whom he must interact in a common flow of work. The performance of $d_2$ will tend to blend with theirs into "our" performance. Figure IV.1, in contrast, merely requires close cooperation and integration between the several work stations, without reinforcing it continually. Indeed, given that the interests of the units headed by $S_A$, $S_B$, $S_C$, and $S_D$ commonly differ on significant issues, a Figure IV.1 structure may actually inhibit cooperation and integration.[50] Sociometric choices, then, are likely to be allocated in ways that do not reinforce the relations required by the flow of work.

Other evidence leads to the same conclusion: an unorthodox organization structure facilitates the greater congruence of the component overlays of authoritative relations. But let us not further postpone a basic issue. Are there but few opportunities in practice for increasing the congruence of overlays? Or, to put the matter in other terms, are technological and other constraints such that individuals must become increasingly estranged from their work, the unavoidable costs being a low congruence of authoritative overlays and those awkward consequences associated with it?

No conclusive answer to such questions is available. Some influential opinion leans toward a definite "yes" to the questions above,[51] and considerable industrial practice has been[52] and is[53] based upon the major premise that the work of most people can be only more or less dissatisfying and enervating. However, three considerations permit a qualified "no" to the two questions. First, opportunities for increasing the congruence of overlays do exist which require only the regrouping of existing tasks and equipment. Their number is impossible to specify, but the literature contains a fair number of cases in point.[54] Moreover, author Golembiewski's consulting experience leaves him impressed with the general opportunities available, although such experiences tend to be self-fulfilling in that one tends to see cases appropriate to one's interests.

Second, many additional opportunities for increasing the congruence of overlays can be created, given appropriate changes in job content or in equipment or in wage and salary programs. A job enlargement program, for example, can create such opportunities, and at least pay its own way by eliminating intermediate levels of supervision.[55] Or production bonuses for both line and staff might be tied to the effectiveness of their contributions to one of several similar flows of work. In a large assembly plant that approached the Figure IV.5 structure in this way, for example, there was virtually no supervision as conventionally understood. There was but one supervisory foreman for every 250 production workers, so effective were the self-regulating features of this unorthodox organizational arrangement.[56] One student estimated that some 500,000 industrial jobs could be enlarged,[57] and countless others could profit from arrangements such as those developed in the assembly plant. When allowance is made for administrative and clerical operations that could be handled similarly, the opportunities for approaching the Figure IV.5 structure and for increasing the congruence of overlays are numerous indeed.

Third, given the Western moral tradition, there is no real alternative to exploiting all existing opportunities and to creating additional opportunities to approach the structure in Figure IV.5, at least when no additional costs are generated or when actual cost savings can be achieved. That is, any *prescription* of what organization relations *should be* is a goal-based, empirical proposition. The values implicit or explicit in any such proposition, consequently, must be tested against the normative networks within which we operate. Chapter XIV specifies several components of our Western moral tradition and demonstrates how they can be built into a goal-based, empirical theory of organization. We can put ourselves directly in the service of our own values, however, only to the degree that we have available to us networks of empirical theory. Empirical theory, recall, has dual capabilities. It *describes* what is related to what; and empirical theory also permits us to *predict* how we can attain whatever it is that we value. In these terms, the ultimate immorality consequently would be to prohibit the development of such empirical theory.

There is no guarantee that the Figure IV.5 structure will induce the behavior necessary to increase the congruence of authoritative overlays, even if that structure is complemented (for example) by appropriate personality testing. Enmity between labor and management, for instance, might be so great as to destroy the efficacy of such structural arrangements. The existing research literature, however, demonstrates that under a wide range of conditions, individuals will probably react to different structural arrangements in the ways sketched. And life, over the long run, can be lived only in terms of the more probable.

There is another class of constraints on the congruence of overlays, those associated with the economic facts of life that people must be promoted, demoted, fired, disciplined, and so on because of recessions, changing market conditions, contractions of programs, or what have you. Changing such factors is largely beyond any mere tinkering with organization structures, but in their own way they make such tinkering all the more important. If this class of constraints will (more or less) always exist, all the more reason to develop compensating ways of facilitating the congruence of overlays. One may be pessimistic about the possibility of achieving very high levels of congruence of the several overlays. But there is ample reason for attempting to increase the level of congruence, whatever it is; and some appropriate applied techniques are available.

## VI. INVESTIGATING THE CONGRUENCE OF OVERLAYS: SOME DIRECTIONS FOR ANALYSIS

The notion of integrative overlays also implies the usefulness of research on micro-structures, to conclude our third point of approach to authority as a problem of overlays. Hence this chapter "builds up" into the larger formal organization, but it also "builds down" into micro-dimensions such as cohesiveness.

That is, this discussion is no unvarnished argument for resting contentedly with what seems probable in terms of today's research. The approach to authoritative relations via overlays, in addition to its uses in applied work, implies significant analytical opportunities. Indeed, this puts matters mildly. For in interpreting the existing literature, the preceding argument has generated a number of hypotheses that are consistent with existing research but still require independent verification.

Let the analytical opportunities of the approach via overlays be sampled most briefly. The overlays in Figures IV.2 through IV.4 were chosen because they fit closely with some exciting work in small-group analysis that has isolated a workable set of dimensions useful for analyzing leadership phenomena. Such work is not definitive, but it has a bulk and an internal consistency that cannot be ignored.[58] The overlays considered here each fit one of the dimensions that have proved useful in describing the several functional roles involved in the performance of leadership behaviors:

| *Overlay* | *Functional roles of Leadership* |
|---|---|
| Sociometric | Sociability |
| Functional | Aiding group attainment |
| Power | Individual prominence |

If the association here is not overly forced, there seem ample reasons to attempt to increase the congruence of the three overlays above with each other and with the formal overlay. The point may be established with economy. "Great Man Groups" have been defined as those in which the member most often identified as "leader" is also ranked highest on each of the three functional roles. Great Man Groups have distinct points of advantage over less well-endowed groups. In one experiment, for example, Great Man Groups proved: (1) to be more satisfactory in task performance, as implied by achieving greater consensus on proposed solutions to experimental problems; (2) to express a lower rate of tension, which seems an indicator of smoother group functioning and of high member satisfaction; and (3) to have a friendlier atmosphere.[59]

These results are convincing. Given a non-Great Man Group, for example, some conflict between the several individuals ranked highest on the three functional roles could be expected. The tendency toward status equilibration permits this generalization, and direct observation of groups confirms it.[60] Such conflict, in general, would disrupt task performance, if only because energy expended in conflict is not likely to aid performance. Tension rates would tend to be high and the atmosphere something less than friendly.

Many analytical possibilities suggest themselves. A significant volume of research could determine, for example, which mixes of personality characteristics, or which structural properties of groups, are associated with the development of Great Man Groups. Such information, then, could be used to generate a theory of organizing large-scale cooperative effort that permits far greater specificity than the monolithic model underlying Figure IV.1 That the approach to authoritative relations via overlays suggests such research says much about its usefulness.

## VII. CONCLUSION

This analysis, then, demonstrates the heuristic usefulness of an approach to authoritative relations in organizations through overlays. The integrative concept seems required to encompass the relevant aspects of reality. Also, it has the advantage of suggesting means of increasing the congruence of the several overlays, means that have substantial support in existing research. The approach has much to recommend it at this stage, and it seems capable of contributing significantly to future research.

Further, the approach to authority as integrative overlays serves our methodological purposes in two ways. First, although much of the reviewed literature is specialized, the approach illustrates the usefulness of methodological guidelines where much remains unknown, where much is unknowable, given our present research capabilities, and where guidance is particularly necessary. Second, the approach illustrates the way in which an empirical methodology encourages research into ever-widening spirals of comprehensiveness. Thus the dialectic forces one to build upon the established, and thereby to test it.

Although the basic emphasis here has been on empirical models, this analysis could easily be translated into a goal-based, empirical model of authoritative relations appropriate (for example) to approach values generally considered significant in the Judaeo-Christian tradition. As students of organization have long recognized, that is, the concept "authority" has important interfaces with value questions.[61] Evidence supporting the point is plentiful. As was widely recognized, for example, the research dealing with "styles of supervision" in small groups has both empirical and value components. An influential source of such research was the Lewin, Lippitt, and White work with "democracy" and "autocracy" in children's groups. At a macroscopic level, similarly, one eminent student—Warren G. Bennis—of planned change in large organizations reports that he is concerned necessarily with empirical data, but seeks to apply those data via a goal-based, empirical theory. The base-value of that goal-based, empirical theory is suggested by Bennis' dictum that "Democracy Is Inevitable."[62] The reader will be spared a full demonstration of the point here, but only because the concluding chapter of this volume specifically illustrates the integration[63] of empirical and normative elements in a goal-based, empirical theory. The significance of the demonstration inheres in a single datum: a developed Political Science will include many such goal-based, empirical models that detail how desired states can be achieved in terms of a knowledge of empirical regularities.[64]

## NOTES

1. A promising beginning has been made in Political Science by Robert L. Peabody, *Organizational Authority* (New York: Atherton Press, 1964). However, the study of authoritative relations in large organizations lags well behind the advances in small-group analysis sketched in Dorwin Cartwright (ed.), *Studies in Social Power* (Ann Arbor: Institute for Social Research, University of Michigan, 1959). The lag is not a given. For innovative prescriptions for reducing the lag, see Karl E. Weick, "Organizations in the Laboratory" and Louis B. Barnes, "Organizational Change and Field Experiment Methods," in Victor H. Vroom (ed.), *Methods of Organizational Research* (Pittsburgh: University of Pittsburgh Press, 1967), pp. 1–111.

2. Herbert Kaufman, "Organization Theory and Political Theory," *American Political Science Review,* 58 (March, 1964), 5–14.

3. For an exception, see Robert V. Presthus, "Authority in Organization," *Public Administration Review,* 20 (1960), 171–75.

4. John M. Pfiffner and Frank P. Sherwood, *Administrative Organization* (Englewood Cliffs, N.J.: Prentice-Hall, 1960), p. 19.

5. Merten J. Mandeville, "The Nature of Authority," *Journal of the Academy of Management,* 3 (August, 1960), 107–18.

6. Erwin Haskell Schell, *The Techniques of Executive Control* (6th ed.; New York: McGraw-Hill, 1946), p. 57.

7. Mason Haire (ed.), *Organization Theory in Industrial Practice* (New York: Wiley, 1962), pp. 5–6.

8. Mary P. Follett, "The Illusion of Final Authority," *Bulletin of the Taylor Society,* 11 (1926), 244.

9. Peter M. Blau and W. Richard Scott, *Formal Organizations* (San Francisco: Chandler, 1962), pp. 173–77.

10. Herbert A. Simon, *Administrative Behavior* (2nd ed.; New York: Macmillan, 1957), p. xxxiv.

11. Chester I. Barnard, *The Functions of the Executive* (Cambridge, Mass.: Harvard University Press, 1938), p. 163. Emphasis added.

12. Henri Fayol, *General and Industrial Management* (New York: Pitman, 1949), p. 21.

13. Richard E. Neustadt, *Presidential Power* (New York: Wiley [Science Editions], 1962).

14. O. J. Harvey, "Reciprocal Influence of the Group and Three Types of Leaders in an Unstructured Situation," *Sociometry,* 23 (March, 1960), 57–68; and James D. Thompson, "Authority and Power in 'Identical' Organizations," *American Journal of Sociology,* 60 (November, 1955), 290–301.

15. Terence K. Hopkins, "Bureaucratic Authority," in Amitai Etzioni (ed.), *Complex Organizations* (New York: Holt, Rinehart & Winston, 1961), p. 83.

16. See Robert Dubin, "Business Behavior Behaviorally Viewed," in George B. Strother (ed.), *Social Science Approaches to Business Behavior* (Homewood, Ill.: The Dorsey Press, 1962), pp. 11–25; and Henry A. Landsberger, "The Horizontal Dimension in Bureaucracy," *Administrative Science Quarterly,* 6 (December, 1961), 299–332.

17. Eliot D. Chapple and Leonard R. Sayles, *The Measure of Management* (New York: Macmillan, 1961), especially pp. 18–40; and Robert T. Golembiewski, *Organizing Men and Power: Patterns of Behavior and Line-Staff Models* (Chicago: Rand McNally, 1967), especially pp. 90–117.

18. A considerable volume of relevant research does exist, however. For example, the conceptual and operational problems associated with sociometric choice are analyzed in Robert T. Golembiewski, *The Small Group: An Analysis of Research Concepts and Operations* (Chicago: University of Chicago Press, 1962), pp. 56–66 and 110–28. A comprehensive treatment of the family of horizontal relations, moreover, has been provided by Leonard R. Sayles, *Managerial Behavior* (New York: McGraw-Hill, 1964). And we have some valuable evidence of convenient operations for estimating power in Melville Dalton's *Men Who Manage* (New York: Wiley, 1959), especially pp. 21–22.

19. For one approach to handling sociometric data, see Duncan MacRae, Jr., "Direct Factor Analysis of Socio-

metric Data," *Sociometry,* 23 (December, 1960), 360–71.

20. Robert H. Guest, *Organizational Change* (Homewood, Ill.: The Dorsey Press, 1962), especially pp. 66–81.

21. Dalton, *op. cit.,* pp. 20–27.

22. Rensis Likert, *New Patterns of Management* (New York: McGraw-Hill, 1961), pp. 56–57.

23. Donald C. Pelz, "Interaction and Attitudes Between Scientists and the Auxiliary Staff," *Administrative Science Quarterly,* 4 (December, 1959), 321–36, and 4 (March, 1960), 410–25.

24. Likert, *op. cit.,* pp. 57–58.

25. James G. March, "Influence Measurement in Experimental and Semi-Experimental Groups," *Sociometry,* 19 (March, 1956), 260–71.

26. Robert T. Golembiewski, "The Assignment Problem," *Journal of the Academy of Management,* 6 (March, 1963), 18–35.

27. Likert, *New Patterns of Management,* p. 11; and his *The Human Organization* (New York: McGraw-Hill, 1967), especially pp. 64–75.

28. Likert, *New Patterns of Management,* pp. 44–46.

29. For example, Robert F. M. Dubin has persuasively argued that task or technological differences can be crucial intervening variables in such propositional statements. *Leadership and Productivity* (San Francisco: Chandler, 1965), especially pp. 10–18. For support of this position, see Paul R. Lawrence and Jay W. Lorsch, *Organization and Environment* (Boston: Division of Research Graduate School of Business Administration Harvard University, 1967). Personality differences also can be major intervening variables.

30. Martin Patchen, "Supervisory Methods and Group Performance Norms," *Administrative Science Quarterly,* 7 (December, 1962), 275–94.

31. William C. Schutz, "What Makes Groups Productive?," *Human Relations,* 8 (November, 1955), 429–66.

32. Raymond H. Van Zelst, "Sociometrically Selected Work Teams Increase Productivity," *Personnel Psychology,* 5 (No. 3, 1952), 175–85.

33. For evidence of the importance of viable interaction patterns, see Charles R. Walker, *Toward the Automated Factory* (New Haven, Conn.: Yale University Press, 1957), especially p. 41. This study also more broadly suggests that the new technology implies both increased functional interdependence and increased problems of interaction as a normal feature of work. The matter of the congruence of functional and sociometric overlays, then, has a great and probably growing significance.

34. Dalton, *op. cit.,* especially pp. 72–109.

35. Chris Argyris, *Interpersonal Competence and Organizational Effectiveness* (Homewood, Ill.: The Dorsey Press, 1962), pp. 208–14.

36. Robert L. Kahn and Daniel Katz, "Leadership Practices in Relation to Productivity and Morale," in Dorwin Cartwright and Alvin Zander (eds.), *Group Dynamics: Research and Theory* (Evanston, Ill.: Row, Peterson, 1960), pp. 559–61.

37. Likert, *op. cit.,* p. 11.

38. William C. Schutz, *FIRO: A Three-Dimensional Theory of Interpersonal Behavior* (New York: Rinehart, 1958).

39. See the "low" and "medium" status congruency cases in Stuart Adams, "Status Congruency as a Variable in Small Group Performance," *Social Forces,* 32 (October, 1953), 18–21.

40. See the "high" cases in Adams, *op. cit.*

41. Dalton, *op. cit.,* pp. 58–68.

42. Robert T. Golembiewski, "Civil Service and Managing Work," *American Political Science Review,* 56 (December, 1962), 961–73.

43. Robert T. Golembiewski, "Organization Structure and the New Accountancy," *Quarterly Review of Economics and Business,* 3 (April, 1963), 29–40.

44. James C. Worthy, "Some Aspects of Organization Structure in Relation to Pressure on Company Decision-Making," in L. Reed Tripp (ed.), *Proceedings of the Fifth Annual Meeting of the Industrial Relations Research Association* (IRRA Publication No. 10; Madison, Wis., 1953).

45. Likert, *op. cit.,* pp. 56–57. Globally, see also Alfred J. Marrow, David G. Bowers and Stanley E. Seashore, (eds.), *Management by Participation* (New York: Harper & Row, 1967). They de-

tail an approach to wider sharing of influence in a complex organization.

46. Chapple and Sayles, *op. cit.*, pp. 92–93, for example, explain differences in the incidence of wildcatting in rubber tire and electrical goods manufacturing in these terms.

47. Golembiewski, "The Assignment Problem," *op. cit.*

48. Thus this analysis avoids the insightful criticisms directed against those students who argue that organizations must provide (for example) the same significant opportunities for participation and self-actualization for all workers. As Strauss argues, man is more diverse than that. The unorthodox structure (Figure IV. 5) is designed around that diversity. See George Strauss, "Some Notes on Power-Equalization," in Harold J. Leavitt (ed.), *The Social Science of Organizations* (Englewood Cliffs, N.J.: Prentice-Hall, 1963), pp. 41–84.

49. William Whyte, *The Organization Man* (Garden City, N.Y.: Doubleday Anchor Brooks, 1956), pp. 225–65.

50. James G. March and Herbert A. Simon, *Organizations* (New York: Wiley, 1958), pp. 36–47.

51. Strauss, *op. cit.*

52. The development of personnel administration "outside of work," for example, reflects the impact of this assumption. The solutions of problems induced at work, that is, were sought in rewards outside of work, whereas the organization of work was considered as fixed and invariable. Hence non-directive counseling of the Hawthorne variety was designed to provide catharsis for feelings but not to change work conditions inducing those feelings. See Robert T. Golembiewski, *Men, Management, and Morality* (New York: McGraw-Hill, 1965), Chapters 4 and 7.

53. Much programmed work, for example, is designed for minimal and fixed levels of performance from operators.

54. Guest, *op. cit.;* Chapple and Sayles, *op. cit.;* and Adolph Vleck, Jr., "Functional-Operational Organization Structure," in American Management Association, *Line-Staff Relationships in Production*, Special Report No. 18 (New York, 1957), pp. 39–52.

55. Douglas Elliott, "Increasing Office Productivity Through Job Enlargement," in *The Human Side of the Office Manager's Job,* Office Management Series, No. 134 (New York: American Management Association, 1953), pp. 1–13.

56. Seymour Melman, *Decision-Making and Productivity* (New York: Wiley, 1958), p. 176. A comparable plant, traditionally organized, would have at least 10 supervisors for each 250 employees.

57. Charles R. Walker, "The Problem of the Repetitive Job," *Harvard Business Review,* 28 (May, 1950), 57.

58. Golembiewski, *The Small Group,* especially pp. 117–44; and Robert T. Golembiewski, "Small Groups and Large Organizations," in James G. March (eds.), *Handbook of Organizations* (Chicago: Rand McNally, 1965), pp. 87–141.

59. Edgar F. Borgatta, Arthur S. Couch, and Robert F. Bales, "Some Findings Relevant to the Great Man Theory of Leadership," *American Sociological Review,* 19 (December, 1954), especially 755–58. Note, however, that some important qualifications of such findings are suggested by Fred E. Fiedler, *Leader Attitudes and Group Effectiveness* (Urbana, Ill.: University of Illinois Press, 1958), especially p. 29.

60. George Psathas, "Phase Movement and Equilibrium Tendencies in Interaction Process in Psychotherapy Groups," *Sociometry,* 23 (June, 1960), 177–94.

61. Daniel Katz and Robert L. Kahn, *The Sociology of Organizations* (New York: Wiley, 1966), especially pp. 211–15.

62. Warren G. Bennis, *Changing Organizations* (New York: McGraw-Hill, 1966), pp. 16–33.

63. The reader may also consult a more specific statement of organizational values which also summarizes some attempts to approach those values in organizations. See Robert T. Golembiewski, "The Laboratory Approach to Organization Development," *Public Administration Review,* 27 (September, 1967), 211–30.

64. For examples of such efforts in large organizations, see Frank Friedlander, "The Impact of Organizational Training Laboratories Upon the Effectiveness and Integration of Ongoing Work Groups," *Personnel Psychology,* 20 (Autumn, 1967), 289–307; and Marrow, Bowers, and Seashore, *op. cit.*

# PART TWO

## Some Methodological Tests: Three Pervasive Orientations to a Science of Politics

# V

# The Wages of Methodological Inelegance Is Circularity, I: The Group in a Science of Politics

This is an appropriate juncture for a retrospective glance as well as a look forward. Chapters I-IV develop and illustrate major *methodological guidelines* for empirical research in Political Science. These guidelines may be considered baseline minima, and they serve as the standards against which subsequent chapters will be measured. Further, Chapters V, VI, and VII attempt to illustrate within specific disciplinary contexts the awkward consequences of a failure to respect these methodological minima. These disciplinary contexts may be described as *pervasive major orientations* to the subject matter of a science of politics. Five following chapters will have a similar purpose, but their focus will be upon specific disciplinary *areas* rather than upon major orientations to data that tend to cut across these areas. The final two chapters of this volume outline the dual roles of a healthy Political Science: the generation and validation of empirical theory; and the blending of empirical and normative elements in goal-based, empirical theories.

The pervasive major orientation to the data of a science of politics which occupies this chapter is the place of *the group* in Political Science. The choice is not lightly made, for two basic reasons. First, emphasis on the group takes us right to the heart of the discipline. The concept has left clear evidence of its influence in diverse areas: in the study of political parties and interest groups; legislatures; behavior in public bureaucracies; political theory; and a far longer list as well. As Peter Loveday put it:

---

The basic argument of this chapter originally appeared as " 'The Group Basis of Politics': Notes on Analysis and Development," *American Political Science Review*, 54 (December, 1960), 962–71. Substantial modifications have been made for present purposes.

> In one sense, political theory has always been conducted partly in terms of "groups"—whether in terms of "classes," "estates," "sectional interests," "factions," "voluntary associations," or what have come to be called "pressure groups" since the 1920s. It is not difficult to trace such theories back to Plato and Aristotle, and they are implicit in such well-worn political concepts as "mixed government," "the separation of the powers," and the "balance of the constitution."[1]

Second, the analysis of the group demonstrates that Political Science must accept the challenge of nominal and operational definition. This point is made by detailing the consequences of a failure to accept the challenge. In sum, the group's disciplinary history may be written in terms of this circularity: a growing sense of the explanatory value of the concept, followed by a growing awareness of the research awkwardness of the terms in which the concept is formulated, and then by decreasing interest, which however has meant that it was only a matter of time before scholars became impressed anew with the concept and raised it to disciplinary prominence again. The characterization also applies to other common pervasive major orientations to a science of politics, as following chapters illustrate.

The need to break this circularity motivates this chapter and this volume. Some value derives from such circular sequences, but they certainly do not provide a desirable model for research progress. Only an empirical methodology can break the circularity and yield results that spiral outward toward greater comprehensiveness rather than inward toward rediscovery of the original insight.

## I. RATIONALE FOR A REVISIT

In late 1960, R. T. Golembiewski alerted academics who make scholarly book on trends in the literature to heed "the group theory of politics." For there was then much evidence that the approach was slipping into temporary obscurity for a third time. Arthur F. Bentley's *The Process of Government* was, of course, the most prominent of the contributions apparently headed for disciplinary oblivion.[2]

Even the brief intervening history has added perspective to the senior author's 1960 alert. Specifically, the "temporary obscurity" of Bentley's work was temporary indeed. And if recent signs are any indication, a fourth discovery of that seminal volume has gained considerable steam since the senior author of this volume sounded his original alert in 1960. As a revealing example, a fourth edition of *The Process of Government*, with an Introduction by Peter H. Odegard, has recently been published (Cambridge, Mass.: Belknap Press of Harvard University Press, 1967). The previous reprinting of the volume in 1949, recall preceded the last period of massive attention to Bentley, best represented by David Truman's central work of 1951, *The Governmental Process.*

Fourth discovery of Bentley or no, much remains to be done to achieve the broad intentions of the 1960 article. That is, the minor theme of that article was to encourage attention to Bentley's work. Such attention has been forthcoming. More essentially, however, the article sought to direct students to the unfinished (and largely untouched) business of scientifically exploiting the group approach. The prime vehicle for the effort was Bentley's *The Process of Government* rather than the corpus of his work or that of his interpreters. This broader intention remains essentially unfulfilled.[3]

Hence this chapter again attempts to buck the odds. Now, as then, a threefold rationale supports this analytical visit to the taproot of the group approach. Primarily, critics have avoided the issues posed by Bentley. Moreover, pleas for abandonment of his approach often reflect an important misconception. Consider Rothman's conclusion that "there is certainly room for studies of the kind which rely upon the mature judgment of their authors, rather than being bound by conceptual schemes which appear to be simple keys to reality, but which only serve to blind students to the obvious facts of politics."[4] No one, of course should be bound by inadequate conceptual schemes in the long run. But all empirical work must be based upon more or less adequate conceptual schemes in the short run. This implies the perfection of methodology, for which mature judgment is a necessity but not a substitute. Finally, the desire to disengage research from the group approach waxes strong, just as significant advances seem likely to accrue from modest analytical innovations.

## II. BENTLEY AS METHODOLOGIST: FOUR NEGLECTED EMPHASES

Four vital elements of Bentley's *The Process of Government* require detailing. These elements which outline Bentley's purposes as well as spotlight the methodological apparatus necessary to exploit his insights, include, in order: one of strategy, two of tactics, and one of the stuff of Bentley's approach. Moreover, the effects of these elements tend to be neglected, individually and collectively.

### A. Emphasis On Political Analysis

Bentley's basic strategy, at least, stands out starkly. His analytical ambition leaps from such statements of his strategic bias:

> If a statement of social facts . . . lends itself better to measurement . . . that characteristic entitles it to attention. Providing the statement does not otherwise distort the social facts, the capability of measurement will be decisive in its favor. The statement that takes us farthest along the road toward quantitative estimates will inevitably be the best statement.[5]

His approach thus called for a reorientation around "political analysis" rather than the traditional emphasis upon "political philosophy."[6] In terms of this analysis, Bentley thus issued a clear warning that it is empirical work that he is about. Consequently, his effort must be judged against appropriate methodological guidelines.

Bentley's strategic reorientation has prompted serious questions, which witnesses that many are unwilling to let Bentley call the tune to which he would dance. To illustrate, Odegard pithily wondered if "the group theory" does not "in effect defend the principle that Might is Right?"[7] He reflected the judgment of many scholars. Their concern is that political analysis will define its values in terms of its findings if the problem of values is not handled explicitly. This concern is felt sharply even by those who have a strong commitment to the approach for which Bentley argued.[8]

Such questions, however, are largely beside the point of disciplinary necessity or Bentley's intentions. Practically, the growing and successful poaching by students of other disciplines decisively establishes the necessity of Bentley's general approach. More basically, the three following elements of Bentley's contribution preclude such questions.

## B. Distinctions Between Types of Theory

The second major element of Bentley's work is his search for a theory applicable to the "material of the governmental process." Bentley was interested, without exception, in empirical theory. His meaning is modern. That is, briefly, theory for Bentley was a set of descriptive statements about the empirical world; and a theory was to be considered valid only as long as it was consistent with observations of relevant phenomena.

There were dangers in this approach, as Bentley realized, but his methodological guides had self-correcting features. A "bad" empirical theory, for example, would serve only the temporary (if vital) function of focusing research attention. A "mistaken" theory may of course distract that attention toward irrelevancies, but not for long. Moreover, whatever the dangers, the risks were well worth it. For a "good" empirical theory serves this quartet of purposes: it is

(1) *aggregative,* since theory indicates the set of

relations which are regarded as existing in some empirical universe;

(2) *suggestive,* since theory implies possible empirical relations other than those specifically provided for;

(3) *predictive,* since theory permits the prediction of relations in some empirical universe; and

(4) *corrective,* since theory permits continuous internal retesting by the comparison of empirical observations with derivations from the properties of the theory.

The general difficulty with this second element of Bentley's work stems, in large part, from a failure to distinguish purely empirical theory from goal-based, empirical theory. The latter is the theoretical statement of the empirical conditions necessary to achieve a particular set of values. Bentley is not at all interested in such theory, with substantial reason. For much progress can be made in empirical theory before any agreement on goals is reached. Moreover, empirical theory has a logical precedence. The *description* of the effects of groups with specific properties upon member behavior under specified conditions must precede the *prescription* of the conditions necessary to achieve a particular value-set, e.g., high productivity in industrial work units or high voter turnout in elections.

Critic and acclaimer alike tend to overlook Bentley's clear distinction. Thus both usually speak of *the* group theory in the singular. Moreover, many political scientists work both sides of the street of the two types of empirical theories, simultaneously and often unconsciously. For their work often assumes either that the normative *ought* is defined by the empirical *is*, or their *oughts* greatly influence reports of the existential. This contributes to the confusion of the two types of empirical theory. With similar effect, the critic (usually implicitly) approaches *the* group theory as if it were (or should be) a goal-based, empirical theory. Thus Odegard held that:

> If politics is a process for the *peaceful allocation of values* in society, political scientists must take account of the values no less than the process of allocation . . . . A theory of politics which excludes where it does not frankly reject a concern for values, which denies that reason has a significant role to play in the process of government, and which devalues the individual by its exaltation of the group is, I suggest, inadequate.[9]

The emphasis on *the* group theory is mischievous and unfortunate. *An* empirical theory of the group eventually may be developed, but there is literally no end to the possible goal-based, empirical theories that can be developed. One of the latter type might indeed rest on the value that Might is Right; but another could be developed around the goal of peaceful allocation of valued objects in society; and still other variants could be developed around other value-sets. Hence Bentley's proper reaction to a charge that the group approach "in effect defends the principle that Might is Right" would be some elementary methodological tutoring of the person making the charge. Or as Loveday put it, one can share the values of an Odegard while still noting that a purported empirical theory "... cannot be tested by its utility to reformers ... nor discredited because it leaves students to discover that there is a gap between the political norms and the political practices of a society."[10]

Bentley methodologically differentiates still further between kinds of social research. In addition, he left no doubt as to his position on the third theory-type, utopian theory. This is a type developed logically from an arbitrary set of goals, definitions, and axioms. As Bentley strikingly noted, the scholar utilizing the utopian approach settles "his whole study in advance by a whole mass of assumptions. . . . Such a study is merely a systematization and dignifying of [the student's] outlook on the world."[11] Utopian theory has its uses, of course. Even though there is no "space" corresponding to that of plane geometry, for example, its assumed properties correspond closely enough to empirical dimensions for some practical purposes. But reliance on utopian theory involves high risks of confusion, and especially in Political Science. As Bentley understood, empirical and utopian theories often were equated by students of politics: Much purportedly empirical theory reflected utopian assumptions consistent with the predilections of their formulators rather than with empirical reality. Hence Bentley took great pains to distinguish the two types of theory and doggedly stressed his preoccupation with empirical theory.

Despite Bentley's methodological strictures, however, he has been perceived unclearly in many cases by those who accept his guidance as well as by those who reject it. Generally, the utopian and the two empirical theory-types are equated, or at least they are not distinguished. Paradoxically, moreover, the existing group theory of politics remains essentially a utopian theory. Partly this is Bentley's fault, and partly it derives from the general failure of others to act upon his methodological directions. Both aspects are clear in the final two elements at the heart of *The Process of Government.*

### C. Polemics as a Tactic

The third element which characterizes Bentley's work is a tactic derived from his theoretical emphasis, and it may help explain many interpretive difficulties which scholars have had with Bentley. His book is in part a conscious polemic. Thus he repeatedly called attention to "certain exaggerations, or at least certain shades of overemphasis," and he warned that "if my line of criticism should be applied literally . . . there would be an exaggeration in its statement."[12] The tactic had negative effects. For it tended to obscure his basic issues in a sometimes vigorous counter-polemic. But the shock effect was intended. Its purpose was to pry students loose from their utopian theorizing, or at least to force them to recognize their method and its limitations. The goal was the encouragement of empirical theory. So his early chapters inveigh against utopian theorizing via a wide-ranging critique of the work of many leading scholars.

Such material may be read and interpreted as the outpourings of an angry young man of an earlier day. This is particularly the case since Bentley time and again referred to *The Process of Government* as "an anticipation of results" deriving from his empirical reorientation rather than as useful empirical theory.[13] This disclaimer reflects Bentley's sensitivity to the methodological requirements of empirical research, but its most common consequence is to leave him vulnerable to the charge that he added little substance to the work of the many leading scholars he took to task. Bentley's emphasis upon methodology rather than substance had its costs, then, costs of which he was aware and which he considered unavoidable. Indeed, he seems fascinated by this paradox: the common disregard of methodology at once motivated *The Process of Government* and all but doomed it to misinterpretation.

### D. The Locus of Political Data

*Activity,* the very stuff of his approach, is the fourth related element in Bentley's contribution. He desired to direct scholars from the fluff of utopian work toward the hard stuff of empirical reality. Hence his strong stand against utopian theory, the product of pure reasoning as a method. He regarded those "feelings" and "ideas" derived from utopian theory—and proffered as causes of behavior—as "soft." They were intangible, unmeasurable, and thus uncommunicable. In contrast, he conceived activity as "hard." It was objective, measurable, and communicable, and so capable of supporting his empirical ambitions. He stated his position emphatically:

> The "ideas" and "feelings" serve to give the individual man his orientation in the social activity in which he is involved; they serve, so to speak, to define him as an individual. There is no idea which is not a reflection of social activity . . . . He knows what he feels, and indeed even that he feels, only in terms of other men's lives.[14]

Critics have had a field day on this issue, with some seeing Bentley's treatment of ideas and feelings as excluding much of the material relevant for political analysis. Many critics, for example, cannot forgive Bentley for their interpretation of what he is supposed to have said about ideas or feelings. Hence such notices as "there is certainly room for studies of the kind which rely upon the mature judgment of their authors, rather than being bound by conceptual schemes which appear to be simple keys to reality . . . ."[15]

Although many cheap victories over Bentley are thus manufactured, he is not as simplistic as some imply. Principally, his position tends to be misunderstood. What he proposed is reasonable enough: The specification of empirical referents for purported empirical propositions. His approach was via method, although the products of a method (e.g., feelings) seem at first glance to have been his target. That is, Bentley set himself against utopian theorizing: e.g., an idea (*das Volk*) is attributed to an assumed subject (a race) and then is used to explain the subject's behavior. Bentley, in contrast, was convinced that many ideas and feelings—especially those relevant to politics—were products of groups whose properties could be specified. Such groups provided empirical referents to restrict the preoccupation with free-floating ideas. So he continually directed (or more accurately, over-directed) attention to the activity of an idea to prevent its mere assumption.

Bentley's strictures relevant to ideas and feelings, then, do not drum the latter out of the bailiwick of the political scientist. In sharpest contrast, he welcomed ideas and feelings to political analysis *if* they were isolated empirically. Ideas or feelings were major concerns of political philosophy, in addition. However, Bentley was concerned only with them as purported empirical statements or explanations and paid little attention to the normative realm. For example, he noted that the "habit background," or sub-culture of a specific group, may "usefully be taken into reckoning as summing up a lot of conditions under which the groups operate." But he cautioned that such reliance might inhibit investigation and encourage utopian theorizing. Consequently, he urged that the empirical properties of any habit background be established with care and he urged constant checks for change.[16]

Critics stress, about equally, Bentley's neglect of ideas or his illegitimate use of them.[17] The former critics reveal careless reading; the latter overlook Bentley's primary concern with method rather than with its products. Thus Bentley would not have criticized ideas or feelings had they been the empirical products of satisfactory polling techniques rather than variably acute—but typically conflicting—utopian speculations of scholars of his day.

Bentley's focus in *The Process of Government,* then, is upon the methodological conditions under which ideas and feelings can be admitted to empirical analysis. He certainly did not deny that they are part of the political scientist's legitimate concern.

In this case as in others, to be fair about the matter, Bentley provided sufficient provocation for his critics to become defensive. For example, two factors particularly encourage a simplistic characterization of *The Process of Government.* First, one senses a good deal of tongue-in-cheek in Bentley's analysis of the stuff of his approach. Indeed, he warns against too-literal an interpretation of his analysis. This warning seems to apply, for example, to his tortured treatment of activity,[18] which strongly suggests an attempt to bamboozle his readers with an extravagant example of the method he reproached them for using. But exactness does not trouble him.[19] "If any of these things lead us to interesting paths," he wrote, "we shall be prepared to follow them heedless of definitions. Who likes may snip verbal definitions in his old age, when his world has gone crackly and dry."[20] Second, he tends to be judged by his self-admitted "overemphases" (e.g., the sharp thrust above). This distracts attention from the balance of his argument, which is more delicate.

## III. BENTLEY'S METHODOLOGICAL ADVANCES

Nothing is gained by setting extreme criteria for evaluating Bentley's accomplishments, but this is what is normally done. *The Process of Government,* its acclaimers imply, is a monumental endpoint in the study of politics. Bentley's critics, in turn, assume that the work ought to be judged as a general theory. Both positions are grossly exaggerated. Arguments based upon them are thus unrewarding, being polemics on the one side and cheap victories on the other.

*The Process of Government* tends to elude the nets cast by critic and acclaimer alike. As Bentley saw it, the work was far more limited as an empirical statement than most people thought it was or felt it should be. But he claimed that the work also was more far-reaching in a methodological sense than is usually acknowledged. Thus the work was avowedly limited in that Bentley knew (and warned the reader) that he had at best sketched the rough outlines of an empirical theory, one based upon fragmentary and inadequate empirical research. Only the method he proposed to apply to his skeletal theory differentiated him from the utopian theorists against whom he railed. But this was an important *only.* As he noted in explaining his use of historical illustrations:

> I wish . . . to say frankly that I am writing without detailed verification [which] is, of course, an absolutely essential prerequisite

> [for empirical theory]. Here, however, I . . . use such rough knowledge of history as we have to throw light on the group method of interpretation. The group method is for its part only of value so far as it can be used in specific interpretations . . . . If there is any of the material of the governmental process which is not capable of statement by the method I propose, then I am open to serious criticism . . . .[21]

But Bentley also made far-reaching claims for his effort, particularly on methodological grounds. These claims may be outlined briefly: he believed the group was a useful focus for empirical theory; he believed he had presented useful methodological directions for the empirical effort required to develop that theory; and he felt that emphasis on the group facilitated early exploitation of those methodological directions. Thus Bentley described the book as a method or a tool, as opposed to a system or a theory. And he did not consider that his methodological suggestions were complete; rather, his efforts constituted "more of an anticipation of results than a statement of method." But he did hold that *his basic methodology was valid.*[22]

Realistically, then, any estimate or explanation of the degree to which he fulfilled his analytical ambitions faces two tasks. The adequacy of his focus for theory must be judged. And the long-run utility of his methodological suggestions in permitting the development of an empirical theory around this focus must be gauged.

Detailed attention to his claims and achievements is required to judge Bentley against his own standards. To begin, he straightforwardly asserted his claim for the greater adequacy of the group as a focus for empirical theory and as a vehicle for early exploitation of his methodological directions. The other possible foci isolated by Bentley were: ideas or feelings conjured up as explanations for everything under the sun without the bother of empirical verification, and similar utopian products; and a mechanistic and rational theory which Bentley called *the* theory of politics. These two foci for theory are descriptively inadequate, Bentley maintained, "even in the most deliberative acts of heads of governments." The group focus permits the required empirical description much more fully: it "points solidly to the social content, always in individuals [as in the traditional theoretical foci], *but never to be stated adequately in terms of individuals* [unlike the traditional foci]."[23]

This claim forces no denial out of hand. Indeed, it understates Bentley's contribution. For his core theoretical insights were far ahead of his time and constitute an important part of the century-long theoretical and methodological change which supports the modern study of social organization. So great was the impact of Marxian analysis during the early twentieth century, for example, that emphasis upon any level of social organization below that of macroscopic "class" was considered an evasion of *the* crucial social issue.[24] *The Process of Government* successfully swam into this flood tide.

Bentley must share credit with many others for certain elements of his contribution to the study of the group, but there is no question that credit is the proper word. Bentley's long list of indebtednesses to those who directed him toward the group as a theoretical focus reflects his acute awareness that he was building upon the work of others. But he could afford to be generous, for there is more than enough credit to go around. On the broadest level, he redrew attention to the crucial datum that much of what man is, is the product of men-in-relation. As Bentley explained: "The raw material we study is never . . . stated simply by adding man to man. It is a 'relation' between men, but not in the sense that the individual men are given to us first, and the relation erected between them. The 'relation' . . . is the given phenomenon . . . ."[25] In so arguing, Bentley does not necessarily deny to the human inherent and God-given prerogatives. But he does stress that the precise position on the immense range along which human beings have developed is significantly determined by the activities of men-in-relation. Feral children and others deprived of human contact over long periods provide dramatic proof of the point. Infra-human perhaps best describes their condition.[26] And while they do retain their humanity as a matter of principle, in practice they are very far down the developmental path that many men have traveled in community. The point may seem transparent today, but it was revolutionary in the context of the extreme emphasis on the isolated individual common to Bentley's day.[27]

More specifically, the focus on the group opened significant research avenues and permitted early action on Bentley's methodological imperatives. For example, the focus permitted the successful treatment of the previously awkward problem of the "inconsistency of behavior"—that is, the common observation that any individual exhibits apparently contradictory behaviors. Earlier theories emphasized the individual and some macroscopic social unit in explaining behavior. Such theories could explain apparent behavioral inconsistency only with some tortured utopian sleight-of-hand, unless students were willing to support the proposition that man was irrational and that therefore the empirical study of behavior was pointless.[28] Bentley, in contrast, preserved the notion of the consistency of behavior by shifting the explanatory focus (in many cases) to changes in the "reference groups" or "membership groups" influencing an individual's behavior. This explanatory focus has been validated many times.[29] Many social units, in effect, could do the explanatory job that often eluded the two research units of the individual and the macroscopic society.

Hence Bentley (with many others) helped evolve a complex notion of man's rationality via behavioral analysis. The shoe is usually put on quite another foot by those of the philosophic persuasion, but no matter. Behavioral analysis spotlighted the individual's delicate sensitivity to differing "social fields" and his tendency to vary his responses accordingly, both of which can only provoke wonder at what God hath wrought.

Let us attempt the point once more, this time in more measured terms. Bentley argued that specific groups with specific properties often serve as an important intervening and interacting variable between the individual's Self and his behavior. To a certain degree, the individual has limitations that are defined by his genes or his stage of evolution, and a man of action like Bentley would pause little to trouble over such inflexible limitations. He sought those factors which imposed variable limitations on man, those factors *about which someone could do something in humanoid periods of time.* And here the group must have seemed so central to Bentley that if it did not exist, he would have had to invent it. At least in extensive senses, that is, what an individual is and what he becomes are significantly influenced by his diverse group memberships and relations. Perhaps a few people test their genetic limits, but precious few. The multi-faceted group, then, is an intervening variable of fantastic significance between what man essentially and genetically is, and what he in fact becomes. Bentley urged that we become more clever in isolating groups and the specific dimensions along which they differ, all the better to act.

In these perceptions Bentley hardly stood alone, but many are the senses in which he far surpassed early students of man and his behavior.

The seminal nature of his work is illustrated strikingly by his accurate perceptions of the directions which fruitful research would take. Consider his treatment of the problem of definition. He is often chided for his neglect of a convincing definition of "group" or of "interest." This intended neglect was, primarily, a reflection of his opposition to utopian theory, whose starting point is definition. The neglect also reflects an important awareness that early social analysis involved more voluminous description than tidy definition. To put words in his mouth: "If I could define 'group' adequately," he would say, "there would be no point to writing *The Process of Government.*" Early definitions, indeed, would be likely to impede the development of the dimensions which would eventually permit precise designations.

More specifically, his core concepts also have proved useful foci for research in social organization. *Activity,* for example, has been particularly prominent, although Bentley does not always provide the inspiration for its use. At one extreme, the concept has been utilized in efforts to reorient entire disciplinary areas, as in John R. Commons' "collective economics." Commons meant to supplant traditional economic theory and the individualistic assumptions theory upon which much of it is based.[30] At the other extreme, activity has been the basis for sophisticated observer systems designed to permit the description of behavioral sequences in great detail.[31] A substantial empirical literature has been built upon such systems.

Bentley's preliminary development of the group focus also anticipated two other major, longer-run directions of research in social organization. First, he suggested a primitive but fruitful typology of groups, which he argued was necessary to permit the development of an empirical theory having high predictability. This typology included several varieties of political groups as well as racial and sectional groups. But he also isolated underlying groups. They were underlying in several senses: In them the individual developed his need for group affiliation and assimilated a style of group participation, which varied between cultures and was reflected in varying participation in political groups. Moreover, underlying groups were relatively permanent and intense affiliations, of which political groups were but transitory and surface reflections.[32] This typology thus previewed the emphasis of the research of a half-century later, sketching the clear outline and importance of the research unit—the small group—which has proved so useful in the early controlled studies of social organization. This feature of the typology also requires underscoring because of its general neglect. The group focus is not monolithic and certainly not restricted to *pressure groups*.

Second, Bentley also stressed the need to isolate the important *somethings* to describe groups and to validate the group as a focus for theory. This modern emphasis distinguishes him from many of his contemporary group theorists. For example, even the purported empirical theory of the extraordinarily influential LeBon was built upon an undifferentiated *crowd* concept and was self-fulfilling rather than self-correcting.[33] In contrast, Bentley explained his search for group dimensions in this way:

> . . . I am not so much attempting to get results as to indicate methods, and . . . I do not regard the extent of my study of the widely scattered facts of government as great enough to warrant me in being dogmatic about the exact *number or varieties* or even the typical *relationships of groupings*.[34]

His many suggestions of possible differentiating dimensions covered the broad spectrum from the personality characteristics of members to the specific habit background, or sub-culture, within which a group was situated.[35]

The scope of the description Bentley proposed can be suggested generally. It was nothing less than the isolation of the relevant dimensions of reality, and hardly the simplistic classification of farm groups, labor groups, and so on. "When the groups are adequately stated," he wrote in reflecting his broad empirical ambitions, "everything is stated. When I say everything, I mean everything. The complete description will be the complete science.... There will be no more room for animistic 'causes'...."[36]

This position has alienated many scholars. The easy interpretation of this position emphasizes Bentley's tiring monomania, but it is too facile. Bentley simply proposed to exorcise all the ghosts of utopian theory from empirical effort. The intent is particularly clear in the concluding nine words of the quotation above. Significantly, critics often omit just these nine words in citing this (in)famous passage.[37] Thus do the critics reflect their failure to distinguish types of theories.

Despite the hostile reaction, Bentley's ambitious statement that the complete description of the group will be the complete science requires little discounting. The complete empirical description of the groups of Bentley's broad typology would cover the immense analytical range from the properties of the groups to the ideas and feelings which comprise the behavioral rules-of-the-game for the many overlapping groups. The group concept is, in fact, a strategic one for precisely this reason. To illustrate specifically with but one type of group, the *internal analysis* of the small group requires three emphases: the description of microscopic cultures; the charting of small social structures; and the study of processes by which personality elements are developed and elaborated in the group experience. Such internal analysis permits quite discriminative prediction. But more precise prediction requires relational analysis. Thus confidence in predictions is increased by the specification of such environmental properties as the technology a group employs or the formal organization in which a group is located.[38] As three eminent students of the small group concluded, its study "does not 'belong' to any one of the recognized social sciences alone. It is the common property of all."[39]

The present illustrative use of the small group is consistent with Bentley's position, although the general point has known neglect. Thus Loveday perceptively stresses that critics usually "load the discussion in their favor at the outset by assuming a narrow interpretation of the group theory...." He concludes neatly that: "They then have no difficulty demonstrating that [the theory] cannot deal with all admitted facts. Their conclusion, that the theory should be confined to the area of pressure groups, or that it is not a general theory of political processes, is *simply* their first premise restated."[40] In contrast, Bentley took the full range of activity as his analytical range.

Interestingly, Bentley's critics sometimes want to have their critical cake and eat it too. Thus his assertion that "everything is stated" with adequate group description is often parodied. Concurrently, the attempt is made to isolate group study from the very phenomena whose systematic examination Bentley urged to flesh out his theoretical skeleton. That is, the undifferentiated group concept itself is required to explain "everything." This, in turn, is precisely (and correctly) the position for which Bentley's followers are chastised. For example, Rothman scored Truman's use of the "status-role" concepts. He noted that status-role and group are on different analytical levels. The latter is an "abstraction from action"; the former, a "type of actor." In addition, the traditional definition of the dual concept requires: (1) its application throughout any social system, and (2) its use as a variable which is "at least as important if not more important than group membership for explaining individual attitudes."[41]

The position is curious. For the group is an "abstraction from action," as are all concepts. By the same reasoning, Rothman would preclude the existence in the same theory of electron and valence, which are in his terminology an "actor" and an "abstraction from action," respectively. In addition, status-role is defined only in terms of group membership. Weighing the importance of status-role and group membership, then, is fatuous. Finally, the concepts are inextricably of the group approach. They have proved useful, for example, in the study of small groups as well as of the broader social system. Indeed, Bentley himself emphasized the importance of status and role in specifying the properties of various groups in his typology.[42]

## IV. BENTLEY SEEN AS "REDUCTIONIST" AND "MECHANISTIC"

Despite the magnitude of the theoretical breakthrough to which Bentley contributed, its follow-up in the group theory leaves much to be desired. If one asks why, our emphasis in answer is upon a single explanatory factor: Bentley's inadequate methodology hindered, if it did not preclude, the exploitation of his core theoretical insights. More specifically, this section will demonstrate the lack of methodological development of the group approach. The two following sections will explain, why this methodological impasse occurred and how it can be overcome.

That Bentley's methodological ambitions have not been realized can be demonstrated in terms of four themes. First, most of his followers presume that he stressed a subject matter. But he was interested primarily in how a subject matter should be exploited, whatever it was.[43] He was deeply involved with the problems of the isolation and transmission of knowledge about empirical reality.[44] But, although he himself knew better, his lot has been to legitimate a subject matter rather than to inspire methodological innovation.

Second, consistently and perversely, scholars taking his lead have rewritten the frontispiece of *The Process of Government* to read: "This Book is a Complete Statement of a Comprehensive Theory." Bentley's frontispiece, however, more accurately says: "This Book is an Attempt to Fashion a Tool."

Third, elaborations of Bentley's effort strongly tend to be new versions of the ghosts of utopian theory which he sought to banish from empirical analysis. There are a few dissenters,[45] but in general, students rushed upward to dizzying theoretical heights. Witness the postulation of *group equilibrium.* As Latham articulated the notion: "What may be called public policy is actually the equilibrium reached in the group struggle at any given moment."[46]

The giddiness was bound to pass. Without the development of the social counterparts of entropy or blood pressure, and the like, attempts like Latham's were pitched at a mystical level. That is, no testing is possible without such empirical dimensions. Thus the acute scholars who have contributed to such formulations encouraged utopian theorizing by the less gifted in assuming that methodological problems had been solved—rather than merely posed—by Bentley.

Fourth, partly because of his own cuteness and occasional gross inconsistencies, Bentley abetted generations of scholars in obscuring crucial methodological issues. Consider two critical themes: that Bentley's argument is reductionist, and that it is mechanistic.

Bentley commonly is accused of reductionism, which Loveday tells us is the characterization of a theory "that explains away what its exponents claim it explains." The things explained away by the group approach, claim the critics, are said to include this range: "The individual, his personality, his ideas and beliefs, his reason and intelligence; the state, its public interest and important features of its institutions."[47]

True to form, Bentley provides particular fuel for this critical fire in his references to "fundamental groups." Thus he instructs us that political processes—including the processes of government and of pressure groups—are "built up out of, or better said, upon" groups that are "underlying" and "more fundamental." One thus must pass from the legislative, executive, and judicial branches, spiraling downward (as it were) "to phenomena which show us public opinion and leadership, the discussion and organization of governmental activity, in closer contact than we have at any time seen them." Underlying groups are still some distance removed. The "bottom of the analysis of their relationship," Bentley warns us, has not been reached. We have taken but "one more step on the way."[48]

If by *fundamental* Bentley really means fundamental, his argument is reductionist. Loveday's conclusion then would hold:

> [Bentley's argument] is reductionist because [he] and his followers are convinced that the political process can only be explained if a fundamental basis is found for it. This alone is sufficient to destroy the generality of the theory. The actual basis chosen is immaterial: *any* search for a basis, for something underlying the political process, is certain to be reductionist if it is carried through consistently."[49]

Everything—institutions, individuals, and all—collapses into fundamental groups on this reading of the word.

Ample grounds for doubt exist about Bentley's actual meaning, however. He interchangably uses the terms "underlying groups" and "fundamental groups." Moreover, he seems to have more fully intended the sense of the former term. "Fundamental" in this sense must be translated as "at a different level of social organization than," or "different from," rather than as somehow "more basic." In this meaning of the term, Bentley can be taken to say something to this general effect:

> Now, to really understand politics you must above all understand that several levels of organizations must be considered. I am going to stress one of these levels, for two reasons. First, too much attention has been given the most obvious level, as to the three branches of government. There are complex groupings underlying these macroscopic institutions; the institutions represent these groupings in complex ways; and both levels must be looked at. This summarizes much of what my argument is about. Second, and more important to me at this stage of development of Political Science, I also tell you that these underlying groups permit us to develop an empirical methodology which may then be extended to macroscopic groups. I don't have firm evidence on the point, but it seems reasonable enough that smaller units have definite research advantages at the beginning. Anyhow, I believe it to be true, and that is enough for me.
>
> Let me warn you, then. I intend to make the very strongest argument I can, to get you to accept my position. And I will deliberately neglect some issues, although I recognize that some people

> will argue that (for example) the legislature is nothing but a pale reflection of its underlying groups. But that is *their* problem. My problem is to get you to see the substantive and methodological relevance of the group. Like Rousseau, I am content to note that I have not mastered the art of making myself clear to people who will not read me closely and who will not take me at my word, even when I tell them I will be thundering away for particular emphasis.

Bentley himself provides support for this flight of fancy, although he is infinitely more prolix and indirect. Thus he repeatedly draws attention to his "exaggerations" in emphasizing the "underlying pressures," explaining that it was by way of over-correction for the bias in the literature toward the more visible groups in politics. And he clearly accords the representing groups, finally, all of the attributes of the underlying groups. For example, Bentley writes that representing groups are "forms of the organization of social life in a wider sense of the word organization . . . [with leadership, with set, habitual phases, and with their own interest]."[50]

Representing groups, then, are no less basic than fundamental groups. This demolishes one of the crudities of interpretations of *The Process of Government.* For example, a legislature need not merely respond to underlying pressures. It has its own complex personality, its own corporateness, and its own counter-pressures. In short, Bentley has been wronged by many, both friend and foe alike, although he did much to try the former and to alienate the latter.

The contention that Bentley can be scientific only as long as he is mechanistic similarly dissolves, although he again helped his critics. The emphasis upon activity is usually seized upon as particularly doing Bentley in, as demonstrating that there is no place for the individual in the group theory, and so on.[51] But Bentley is anything but mechanistic in developing his concept of *interest.* Thus he argued that: "If we try to take the group without the interest, we have simply nothing at all. . . . The group is activity and the activity is only known to us through its particular type, its value in terms of other activities. . . ."[52] Consequently, one cannot consider "activity as complete in itself." The enterprise is doomed from the start. One is left with "a fragment of a corpse. . . . We have one great moving process to study, and of this great moving process it is impossible to state any part except as valued in terms of the other parts."[53]

Bentley's general orientation was methodologically sound, as can be inferred from its consistency with developments of substance and technique that have taken place outside of Political Science. Thus Bentley's insistence that activities cannot be considered apart from the valuational or cultural field in which they occur directly implies a modern scientific concept. Rather than being mechanistic in the Newtonian sense, Bentley reflected the "field" orientation presently so respectable in modern science. For his day, the field notion was revolutionary.[54] The individual has a definite place in such a field orientation as he helps create or support this valuational context, or as he is a deviant from specific valuational contexts. In the latter sense, for example, Bentley's formulation is compatible with recent research on the role of the deviant from group norms in achieving social change.[55] Bentley's field orientation, similarly, is adequate as general grounding for the work on complicated observational systems that has attracted so much attention in the last decade or so.[56]

That Bentley can be read in such modern terms, of course, starkly implies the enormity of the failure to accept his urgings toward methodological change. He provided the "shoulders," in short, over which useful leaps could be made toward increasingly comprehensive descriptions of reality and the development of appropriate techniques for the task.

## V. SOME OPEN ISSUES EXPLORED

Time has seen relatively little use of Bentley's "shoulders" in Political Science, however, and this general failure to methodologically reorient a discipline should not provoke wonder. For, on balance, he failed to draw clear attention to a research medium convenient for early exploration. Moreover, in important particulars, Bentley's methodological directions could not be consistently useful at any stage of empirical study. Two major emphases help support this point.

His research medium, first, imposed enormous practical difficulties which overwhelmed early researchers. For example, the "laboratory experimentation in society" which he prescribed for the study of "interests" was (and is) a formidable proposition.[57] The history of the application of a natural-science approach to the conceptual breakthrough to which he contributed documents the point. The most startling research advances in the study of social organization have come but recently in small-group analysis, after a half-century's search for a manageable research medium. The small group is an important—but hardly exclusive—research medium for the controlled study of behavior. However, the small group has research advantages—especially limited size—which encourage early methodological progress via testing and retesting. Moreover, such study provides an object lesson in the methodology necessary to develop an empirical theory for less amenable research units.

Ironically, Bentley did recognize the existence of underlying groups. But, in a few revealing passages, he chose "political groups" as his first subject for study. He explained:

> It would seem at first sight that the political process could not be studied till the process of the underlying groups had been studied, for political groups are built up out of, or, better said, upon, the other groups. Political groups are highly differentiated groups reflecting, or representing, other groups, which latter can easily, and I believe for most purposes properly, be regarded as more fundamental in society. The political process goes on, so to speak, well up toward the surface of society. . . .
>
> Nevertheless, it is my conviction that political groups, highly differentiated as they are, can well be studied before the other groups . . . .[58]

His conviction seemed to rest upon the importance of such political groups, rather than upon methodological grounds. Sympathy with his ambitions comes easily. But the complexity of his subject matter encouraged the tangled regrowth of the very utopian theory which provoked his effort.

Second, his methodological suggestions were inappropriate. Consider his analytical goals: some means for the accurate perception of reality, and some means for the clear and consistent reporting of such perceptions. Only thus, he correctly argued, could empirical theory be developed and order be made out of the confusion of utopian theories, each offered as the key to reality but none subjected to the tests which would validate its claim. His solution was the postulation of a "universal base"—"activity"—to measure social phenomena. This did not succeed in measuring social life, he sometimes realized. But he felt it did provide "a foundation upon which a coherent system of measurements can be built up."[59]

However, Bentley fell into a trap which has ensnared other scientific pioneers.[60] Basically, he encouraged a sharp distinction between "things" and "relations between things." Things are hard and real; relations between things are abstractions, as one student articulated it, "phases of our experience with which we can deal only by thinking or talking about them. They cannot be heard, seen, or pointed to with any part of our bodies . . . ."[61] In dealing with activity, Bentley often implied, one is dealing with things, hard reality. All other concepts are ghosts, non-empirical constructs of the imagination.

Bentley's distinction did not seem to help his own analysis, and it certainly has been no boon to his followers. And no wonder. Straightforwardly, there could be no empirical science without relations between things such as atomic structure of electrical field. The implied hard concept of reality is thus inadequate and misleading. As Horowitz and Perlmutter explained:

> To ask the question of whether [a conceptualized dimension of reality] "exists" is really to ask "what are the scientific criteria for reality and existence?" . . . existence is tentative, or relative, at any stage of a science and any concept which has explanatory power, is defined in relation to other concepts, in subject to experimental test, and has not yet been "disproved," can be said to have this tentative existence.[62]

Thus Bentley's professed aim was the use of natural-science methods in the study of politics but his separation of things and relations between things discouraged the application of these methods.

Relatedly, Bentley gave ample encouragement to students to succumb to what has been called The Fallacy of Misplaced Concreteness. This is the common belief that, in the words of one student, "for anything to be real it must have 'simple location' in physical spacetime."[63] Bentley's emphases upon activity suggest such a simple location for behavior. Meaningful empirical description, however, does not require simple location. Many useful *somethings* in the empirical sciences, to illustrate, are ratios between several component elements which have no physical space-time locus. Thus any description limited to simple location would be incomplete, at best.

Bentley's emphasis in these two particulars is not monolithic. On many occasions, for example, he argued that it was necessary only to catalog as much activity as possible to understand political behavior.[64] This again reflects his conception of reality as hard and with simple location. On the other hand, Bentley often displayed great sensitivity to the subtler character of empirical investigation. His brief analysis of multiple group-memberships, conceived as a large number of planes passing through the individual's lifespace, suggests the enormously complicated problem of workably defining a group, let alone restricting it to a simple location.[65] And he also cautioned that the analysis of the formal structure and overt activities of a group is inadequate for scientifically useful description.[66]

The grosser aspects of Bentley's argument have prevailed, however. The conception of a hard reality with simple location patently underlies the generally low-level description in the literature. This triumph of the gross over the subtle must be attributed to his inadequate methodological directions. Tersely, he provided a devastating critique of then-existing research. The ghosts of feelings and ideas typified for him the results of a pliable methodology which could be stretched to cover lack of empirical knowledge. He also offered the attractive goal of an empirical theory. But he provided no adequate route from the critique to the goal. His emphasis upon hard, simply-located reality was a methodological cul-de-sac.

## VI. SOME OPEN ISSUES ACTED UPON

The methodologically appropriate means to attain Bentley's objectives without forcing reality into a restrictive mold, however, are within reach. In fact, the methodological knowledge is available. In addition, some disciplinary work points in the direction of the required innovations.[67] The following brief analysis, then, will try to capitalize on these opportunities for easing the developmental work in the discipline. It will also spotlight Bentley's methodological inadequacies.

The required innovations in method constitute the ground rules of, or the general limits for problem-solving in, empirical research. The innovations are implicit in the discussion of the two empirical theory-types above, and differentiate them from utopian theory. And these innovations permit the solution of the two problems of research at the middle-range theoretical level: the isolation of the important *somethings* in any problem area (the problem of *nominal definition*, or conceptualization); and the development of procedures and techniques for the valid and reliable measurement of the degree to which these important somethings exist at any point in space-time (the problem of *operational definition*, or operationalization).[68]

Nominal definition is vital, for it concerns the isolation of those properties necessary to describe a problem area. Beginning efforts are seldom very precise. Consequently, finer prediction usually requires the substantial modification of early conceptions and the theory to which they led. Early conceptions of crime, for example, suggested its relations to poverty and slums. Modifications of the concept to include white-collar crimes—as well as the traditional crimes against property and person—induced marked theoretical changes.

Bentley displayed a definite respect for the problems of nominal definition. Thus he avoided premature definitions which might be permanent as well as procrustean. For example, activity was conceived tentatively as broad and highly differentiated.[69] In addition, he began the isolation of the dimensions necessary to describe the chaos of activity parsimoniously. He warned against the exclusive use of such measures of activity as legislative roll calls. They may be helpful, but the underlying dimensions of voting process, paramountly, must be isolated. He advised students, then, "to measure the measure, to go far back and examine the quantities that have been in play to produce the given results."[70] Bentley's habit background was one of these background dimensions which give different meanings to the same activity in different societies.[71]

He discouraged a similar sensitivity to nominal definition in his followers by his emphasis upon reality as hard and with simple location. His contribution need not be denigrated because of such difficulties, however, for the processes of concept-formation are ineluctably subtle.[72]

The problems associated with operational definition were beyond Bentley in *The Process of Government* and still elude his followers. It would be anachronistic to argue that the 1908 Bentley ought to have been aware of such problems. For natural scientists were yet to formulate firm notions about operational definition. But, as a matter of fact, his lack of awareness had a determinant influence on the failure to develop the empirical dimensions necessary to provide specificity for the group approach. This is one of the responsibilities that Bentley must bear for having had other people pay attention to him. Bentley poorly bore this responsibility. For example, the very process of developing appropriate operational definitions is an important guide in the development of useful nominal definitions. In sum, general directions of *how* to measure (operations) are helpful guides to *what* to measure (conceptualizations). Moreover, operational definition permits the transmissibility of results and consistent retesting which Bentley sought.

The goal of operational definition suggests its utility: the development of valid and reliable measures of phenomena as nominally defined. There are no easy answers to either validity or reliability: operations are mere conventions whose only test is consistent predictive utility. When a specific operation does not permit consistent prediction, there are three analytical possibilities. First, the nominal definition underlying the operation does not in fact identify a unidimensional and important (i.e., predictively useful) aspect of reality. Second, the operation does not validly measure the empirical phenomena marked out by the nominal definition. Thus an operation may indiscriminately tap two or more dimensions of reality. Application of this operation would result in mixed results over replicatory studies, since (because of their independent character) two or more dimensions would not always co-vary. Third, the operation does not permit reliable observations of the same phenomena by the same observer at different times or by different observers at the same time. More than one of these possibilities may apply to any specific case of inconsistent prediction.

Much room for developmental work is implicit in these complex analytical possibilities. And all of them will be investigated many times in any problem area as its empirical theory moves toward greater comprehensiveness and fineness of prediction. This subtle process of intellectual advance stands in marked contrast to the hard concept of reality which Bentley often reflected. Moreover, polemics are not necessary to establish the point.

The appropriate dialectic may be begun here to suggest the possible. Consider the commonplace proposition that where party competition is vigorous, pressure groups have less influence. Given a rough operational definition of the latter notion in terms of judgments by "knowledgeable" persons in the several states, and given a more reliable measure of party competition the proposition can be tested. Table V.1

**TABLE V.1 Patterns of Relations of Party Competition and Pressure Politics**

| | | % States With S, M, or W, Pressure Politics | | |
|---|---|---|---|---|
| | | *One-Party States* | *Weak Minority Party States* | *Two-Party States* |
| Pressure Politics | Strong | 86 | 58 | 18 |
| | Moderate | 14 | 42 | 41 |
| | Weak | 0 | 0 | 41 |

Source: Robert T. Golembiewski, "A Taxonomic Approach to Political Party Strength," *Western Political Quarterly*, 11 (December, 1958), 503.

supplies some relevant data which support the general usefulness of the proposition above. Moreover, independent replications using different nominal and operational definitions yield a similar pattern.[73]

The available results imply that a dominant set of regularities in nature is being explored, but they merely set the stage for empirical analysis having more exalted aims than rudimentary description. For example, the problems of relying on panels of experts for data are well known. Hence the need for the comparative study of alternative operations for measuring pressure politics. Similar intensive analysis is appropriate for party strength operations. Other research might strike out on a factor-analytic search for a parsimonious set of dimensions in terms of which states could be compared. Such dimensions then might be put to use in exploring questions like: In terms of which specific dimensions did the 18 per cent of the two-party states having "strong pressure politics" differ from the 41 per cent who were reported to have "weak pressure politics"? Explanations might cover the full range of the influence of socio-economic variables, the traditions of different states, some pressing policy issues, the nature of the party organization, and the personality characteristics of influentials. Complex answers to the leading question above might then permit longitudinal studies to determine whether specific changes over time within particular states on specified dimensions had the predicted effect on pressure politics. The increasingly fine research would in turn require more precise nominal and operational definitions, and their validation in replicatory studies. And so empirical research goes on.

## VII. CONCLUSION

The skeleton of this chapter is simple, then. A number of important components of Bentley's contribution have been isolated; the neglect of these components in the research literature has been stressed; and an avenue for future development has been outlined.

Not much more can be said without being repetitious. Two points, however, require emphasis. First, Political Science and the social sciences generally are characterized by fantastic discontinuity—one of the unfortunate consequences (and causes) of the research fads which periodically sweep across them. The lack of a viable empirical methodology seems a major cause. Hence the title of this chapter.

Both the patent circularity and the assumed importance of methodology motivate the attempt here to build upon the work of Bentley and the many valuable (if limited) descriptive studies his work induced. These studies comprise the natural-history stage of the discipline. It is time to move along to the development of empirical theory, deriving from and improving upon the data and insights of this literature. The experience of other areas of scientific inquiry—suggested in the brief review of nominal and operational definition—certainly gives hope and direction for such an effort.

Second, there can be no methodological revolution. Like Newton, one can see only a little further. This is the sense of Bentley's position that the methodology of establishing reliable statements of the group facts must be developed "out of materials which in cruder forms are now available." Thus Bentley himself could go only part of the way toward inducing the theoretical and methodological innovations to which he aspired. Fortunately, however, only small further innovations in method (if they imply much effort) are required to achieve a major research breakthrough in the group theory, to push beyond what Bentley cannot be expected to have known and beyond his incomplete break with the restraints of the leading ideas of his time.

The time is ripe, in short, to leap to Bentley's shoulders with newly available knowledge. It is not a time to nip at his heels because he did not do what he did not intend to do.

# NOTES

1. Peter Loveday, "Group Theory and Its Critics," in Peter Loveday and Ian Campbell, *Groups in Theory and Practice* (Sydney: F. W. Cheshire, 1962), p. 3.

2. The history of the first two discovery-reaction sequences is reviewed in the Introduction to Arthur F. Bentley, *The Process of Government* (Bloomington, Ind.: Principia Press, 1949), especially pp. xvii–xviii. The volume was published more than a half-century ago (1908) and reprinted some years later (1935). All quotations below from Bentley are from the 1949 reissue. The recent critical literature is large. Selected references cited below are: Peter H. Odegard, "A Group Basis of Politics: A New Name for an Old Myth," *Western Political Quarterly,* 11 (September, 1958), 689–702; Bernard Crick, *The American Science of Politics* (Berkeley: University of California Press, 1959), pp. 118–30; Joseph La Palombara, "The Utility and Limitations of Interest Group Theory in Non-American Field Situations," *Journal of Politics,* 22 (February, 1960), 29–49; and Stanley Rothman, "Systematic Political Theory: Observations on the Group Approach," *American Political Science Review,* 54 (March, 1960), 15–33.

3. The promise of a far better future is clear in such titles as Joseph La Palombara, *Interest Groups in Italian Politics* (Princeton, N.J.: Princeton University Press, 1964); and Lewis A. Froman, Jr., "Some Effects of Interest Group Strength in State Politics," *American Political Science Review,* 60 (December, 1966), 952–62. Hope for research advances also is stimulated by the recent appearance of such teaching aids as that by H. R. Mahood, editor, *Pressure Groups In American Politics* (New York: Scribner's, 1967).

4. Rothman, *op. cit.,* p. 33.

5. *Op cit.,* p. 20.

6. Ernest Barker, *The Study of Political Science and Its Relation to Cognate Studies* (Cambridge: Cambridge University Press, 1928), p. 42.

7. Odegard, *op. cit.,* p. 701.

8. Oliver Garceau, for example, stressed the conflict of the study of behavioral uniformities and the "liberal, democratic faith" in man's capacities as an individual. See his "Research in the Political Process," *American Political Science Review,* 45 (March, 1951), 69.

9. Odegard, *op. cit.,* p. 701.

10. Loveday, *op. cit.,* p. 10.

11. *Op. cit.,* p. 195.

12. *Ibid.,* p. 443.

13. *Ibid.,* p. 484.

14. *Ibid.,* p. 177.

15. Rothman, *op. cit.,* p. 33.

16. Bentley, *op. cit.,* pp. 218–19.

17. Crick, *op. cit.,* for example, stresses the former position; and Odegard, *op. cit.,* pp. 694–95, emphasizes the latter.

18. Bentley distinguished: "activity"; "tendencies toward activity"; and "tendencies which have no clearly evident action following after them" because they are "suppressed, blocked, postponed, or inhibited." The latter two types are necessary, e.g., to explain the emergence of new groups. But the necessity had its price. Thus "tendencies to activity" were proffered as a "stage of activity" and the same as, although different from "activity." "Suppressed tendencies," as Bentley acknowledged, defied even such audacity. *The Process of Government,* pp. 186–89.

19. As Loveday, *op. cit.,* p. 8, observes.

20. Bentley, *op. cit.,* p. 199. On the apparent pointlessness of his ire, see the discussion of definition below.

21. *Ibid.,* pp. 330–31n.

22. *Ibid.,* p. 482.

23. *Ibid.,* pp. 197, 447. (Emphases added.)

24. Edward A. Shils, "The Study of the Primary Group," in Daniel Lerner and Harold D. Lasswell (eds.), *The Policy Sciences* (Stanford, Calif.: Stanford University Press, 1951), p. 45.

25. Bentley, *op. cit.,* p. 176.

26. J. A. L. Singh and R. M. Zingg, *Wolf Children and Feral Man* (New York: Harper, 1943).

27. As in Gustav LeBon, *The Crowd*

(London: T. F. Unwin, 16th impression, 1926).

28. For ample evidence of the state of the literature, see Gordon W. Allport, "The Historical Background of Modern Social Psychology," in Gardner Lindzey (ed.), *Handbook of Social Psychology* (Cambridge, Mass.: Addison-Wesley, 1954), I, 3–56.

29. For one of the early experiments, see Leon Festinger, "The Role of Group Belongingness in a Voting Situation," *Human Relations,* I (1947), 154–80.

30. *The Economics of Collective Action* (New York: Macmillan, 1950).

31. Robert F. Bales, *Interaction Process Analysis* (Cambridge, Mass.: Addison-Wesley, 1951).

32. *The Process of Government,* pp. 434–36. The "underlying group" is patently similar to the "primary group" concept developed at about the same time by Charles H. Cooley in his *Social Organization: A Study of the Larger Social Mind* (New York: Scribner's 1909). Cooley's seminal role in the development of the modern study of social organization is often stressed.

33. Allport, *op. cit.,* p. 26, notes that: "Perhaps the most influential book ever written in social psychology is LeBon's *The Crowd* (1895)." LeBon's "crowd" concept, however, was applied indiscriminately to juries, legislatures, electorates, and so on (that is, when they behaved in the inelegant way LeBon said crowds behaved). Moreover, the "crowd" was a "condition" for LeBon rather than a conceptual entity whose properties required description.

34. *The Process of Government,* p. 434. (Emphases added.)

35. *Ibid.,* pp. 218–22.

36. *Ibid.,* pp. 208–9.

37. Rothman, *op. cit.,* p. 15, for example, does so.

38. See the development of this position in Robert T. Golembiewski, "The Small Group and Public Administration," *Public Administration Review,* 19 (Summer, 1959), 149–56.

39. A. Paul Hare, Edgar F. Borgatta, and Robert F. Bales, *Small Groups: Studies in Social Interaction* (New York: Knopf, 1955), pp. v–vi.

40. Loveday, *op. cit.,* p. 8.

41. Rothman, *op. cit.,* p. 19.

42. *The Process of Government,* p. 228.

43. For Bentley's vigorous denial of paternity of the "pressure group" literature, see his "Kennetic Inquiry," *Science,* 112 (December 29, 1950), 775–83.

44. *The Process of Government,* p. 202.

45. Phillip Monypenny, "Political Science and the Study of Groups: Notes to Guide a Research Project," *Western Political Quarterly,* 7 (June, 1954), 184–85.

46. Earl Latham, *The Group Basis of Politics* (Ithaca, N.Y.: Cornell University Press, 1952), p. 36.

47. Loveday, *op. cit.,* p. 6.

48. *The Process of Government,* p. 400.

49. Loveday, *op. cit.,* p. 17.

50. *The Process of Government,* p. 441.

51. Merle Fainsod, "Some Reflections on the Nature of the Regulatory Process," in *Public Policy* (Cambridge, Mass.: Harvard University Press, 1940), pp. 297ff.

52. *The Process of Government,* p. 213.

53. *Ibid.,* p. 178.

54. The compliment that Einstein gave to a physical scientist for recognizing that "it was not the charges nor the particles but the (electro-magnetic) *field* in the space between the charges and particles which is essential for the description of physical phenomena" may be extended to Bentley for a similar insight about social phenomena. The quotation is from Albert Einstein and L. Infeld, *The Evolution of Physics* (New York: Simon and Schuster, 1938), p. 259. Emphasis added.

55. For an early study, see Stanley Schachter, "Deviation, Rejection, and Communication," *Journal of Abnormal and Social Psychology,* 46 (April, 1951), 190–207.

56. See Robert T. Golembiewski, *The Small Group: An Analysis of Research Concepts and Operations* (Chicago: University of Chicago Press, 1962), pp. 208–23.

57. *The Process of Government,* p. 482.

58. *Ibid.*, pp. 209–11.

59. *Ibid.*, p. 202.

60. See, for example, Floyd H. Allport, *Institutional Behavior: Essays Toward a Reorienting of Contemporary Social Organization* (Chapel Hill, N.C.: University of North Carolina Press, 1933).

61. *Ibid.*, p. 15.

62. Milton W. Horowitz and Howard V. Perlmutter, "The Concept of the Social Group," *Journal of Social Psychology*, 37 (February, 1953), 80.

63. Quoted, *ibid.*, p. 80.

64. *The Process of Government*, p. 188.

65. *Ibid.* pp. 204–5, 207.

66. *Ibid.*, pp. 210–11.

67. La Palombara, *op. cit.*, p. 30, has proposed the comparative examination of some middle-range propositions to determine whether or not the "interest group" focus is a useful one in the "construction of a general [empirical?] theory of politics."

68. In general, see William J. Goode and Paul K. Hatt, *Methods in Social Research* (New York: McGraw-Hill, 1952), especially pp. 41–53. Bentley's later work also bears on these problems, particularly his *Inquiry into Inquiries: Essays in Social Theory* (Boston: Beacon Press, 1954), pp. 113–40.

69. *The Process of Government*, p. 194.

70. *Ibid.*, p. 202.

71. He was interested in "certain special activities of men, which can be stated, environment and all. That is our raw material. Our . . . fertile land ready for immediate use . . . is a good illustration. Given no increasing population, no improving transportation, that land would have little meaning . . . . Given a population of *different activities*, it would have a *different meaning*." *Ibid.*, p. 202. Emphases added.

72. Generally, consult Carl G. Hempel, *Fundamentals of Concept Formation*, Vol. II, No. 7, of the *International Encyclopedia of Unified Science* (Chicago: University of Chicago Press, 1952).

73. Harmon Zeigler, for example, found much the same pattern in an unpublished study. See also the useful attention given to conceptual and operational clarification by David G. Pfeiffer in his "The Measurement of Inter-Party Competition and Systemic Stability," *American Political Science Review*, 61 (June, 1967), 457–67.

## vi

# The Wages of Methodological Inelegance Is Circularity, II: Elitists and Pluralists

Perhaps the hottest track in all Political Science (to use the houndsman's terminology) has been the analytical pursuit of influence and the influential. The chase is both ancient and modern. Thus Plato's Thrasymachus and the Machiavelli of *The Discourses* share a common orientation across the centuries which links them with the most recent thinking in our professional literature. Only a few names need be mentioned to illustrate the range of those who forged these connections over the last few decades: Merriam,[1] Lasswell,[2] March,[3] Dahl,[4] and Presthus.[5]

The sheer volume and diversity of work exploring influence and the influential are intimidating, but (as with Everest) the challenge of that complex mass cannot be neglected, simply because it is so ponderously there. We shall do the expedient thing here, however, and concentrate on one approach[6] to the phenomenal area of influence and the influential—the contemporary test of strength between "elitists" or "stratificationists" on the one hand and "pluralists" on the other. Moreover, only very limited methodological aspects of even that one approach will be investigated with thoroughness.

The underlying rationale is uncomplicated. We cannot neglect the attention given to influence and the influential in Political Science, nor can we exhaust that attention. While we cannot presume to present an *Allgemeinemachtslehre* in this chapter, we can use significant aspects of the literature in ways that give substance to the methodological guidelines sketched in the introductory chapters of this volume, as well as in ways that promise to help advance the very literature that permits our methodological illustrations.

The point of this chapter may seem to be repetition for its own sake. Much of the analytical pattern of this chapter will be familiar. As was the case with the group basis of politics, for example, the study of influence and the influential clearly reflects indecision or confusion about types of theories. These studies also evidence an inadequate appreciation of the roles of conceptual and operational definition, and they are generally insensitive to other methodological limits. Moreover, the familiar analytical circularity so clear in the disciplinary history of the group also can be distinguished in the study of influence. Fortunately, recent work seems to have broken that circularity. But given the discovery-rediscovery sequences associated with the names of Merriam, Lasswell, March, and Dahl—to mention only a few—perhaps cautious optimism is appropriate about what seems to be happening in the discipline.

But we do not stake this chapter on the caveat that there is virtue in repeating things so that their significance will not be forgotten. In it there are patent and significant differences from what has gone before. The context, first and foremost, *is* different. Merit inheres, then, in the very demonstration that distinct areas of subject matter can be approached usefully in terms of common methodological criteria. Avoiding methodological strictures has proved all too easy, and using them only against the other guy too convenient. These tendencies should be curbed in as many disciplinary areas as possible. Landau has put the point directly and succinctly:

> . . . discussions . . . of methodology . . . are often received with irritation and impatience, and frequently minimized, if not as fad, then as esoteric ventures that serve only to divert from, and even confuse, the ongoing study of important problems. Yet methodology, in its basic sense, has to do with organizing assumptions, the concepts and definitions that underlie any systematic inquiry. . . . Hence, it is most unfortunate that methodological discussion often takes place in a charged atmosphere; that exchanges are more a matter of combat than communication; that epithet and invective explode; that more is defended than clarified.[7]

Second, the purpose here is not to rehash the existing critical literature. That literature will be referred to and exploited, but only very selectively, for our purpose is to add to that literature methodologically oriented issues that generally get short shrift. Finally, certain aspects of the debate between elitists and pluralists have yielded scientific gains beyond those of many areas of Political Science, and the implied methodological lessons deserve explicit treatment. In this sense, that is, this chapter reflects increasingly successful resort to the methodological paths required to break analytical circularity. Thus the chapter transcends mere illustration that methodological inelegance is paid for in terms of analytical spirals that tend to collapse into their starting points.

## I. THE STRATIFICATION THEORY OF COMMUNITY POWER: METAPHYSICAL PATHOS AS A METHODOLOGY

Baptizing and describing the immediate object of attention—the elitist or stratification elaboration of community power—will not detain us long. We need not be lengthy or too precise here in designating our specific target for several weighty reasons. A considerable volume of contemporary literature provides content for our general category for study, first, and footnotes will permit even greater specificity. Second, stratification theorists of community power reflect a homogeneity that permits sharp differentiation.[8] Consequently, third, only a general definition of *community power* is required for present purposes. Given the context of some organized political entity, following Polsby, we "can conceive of 'power'—'influence' and 'control' are serviceable synonyms—as the capacity of one actor to do something affecting another actor, which changes the probable pattern of specified future events."[9]

Stratification theory, however, does require some specification. That theory basically assumes that a community's "power structure" correlates highly with its "social structure," if, indeed, the power structure is not a mere reflection of the underlying social structure. "The political organization of Jonesville," William Lloyd Warner points out, "fits the rest of the social structure .... [Indeed, one can observe it] curving or bulging with the class outlines of the body politic."[10]

The sense in which Warner wrote as representative of the stratificationist position may be established. Polsby has done us the kindness[11] of reducing a sizable body of stratification studies[12] to five propositions about patterns of power in American communities. Polsby is a committed combatant in the contemporary debate-war between elitists and pluralists, but his summary propositions seem appropriate enough. His five propositions about stratification theory provide that:

1. The "upper class," usually defined operationally in economic terms, rules in any community;[13]
2. The upper class is, or controls, the single "power elite" that sits at the top of the pyramid of "all-purpose" community power; thus the upper class authoritatively rules any community over a wide range of issues and over all significant issues;
3. Political and civic leaders are subordinate to the upper-class power elite; that is, the overt community leaders possess less power than the upper class, and do their bidding;
4. The upper-class power elite rules in its own interests; and
5. Consequently, social conflict basically is rooted in the inter-class dynamics of the upper-class power elite consistently serving its own interests and increasingly alienating the broader community.[14]

The five propositions of stratification theory have been treated circumspectly by the very students who swear by them, and this is methodologically significant. Although each of the propositions can be formulated in terms of a hypothesis that could be verified or rejected by empirical tests, to illustrate, these potentials have not been exploited. For example, Polsby provides substantial evidence that the propositions (or, better, "assertions") of stratification theory have been held substantially above and beyond empirical scrutiny. His evidence of the neglect of empirical testing of the assertions is of three kinds:

1. Stratification studies do report data that contradict all five propositions, but these data do not prompt reformulation or rejection of the propositions;
2. The methodology of stratification studies does not provide for the testing of hypotheses; it permits pseudo confirmation of the five assertions by the very avoidance of empirical tests; and it sanctions the use of major concepts that are conceptually and operationally elusive;
3. Authors of stratification studies do recognize cases in their own data that contradict the five propositions above, but the contradictions are handled in such ways as developing ad hoc explanations that do not require rejection of the propositions.[15]

The pathfinding study of Middletown by the Lynds permits parsimonious illustration of empirical neglect. Summarily, Polsby concludes that:

> This oldest of the stratification studies of community life is in many ways the best, since all five generalizations which seem to characterize stratification analyses . . . are set forth and accompanied by a wealth of circumstantial detail. Indeed, one of the Lynds' greatest contributions is the care and responsibility with which they recorded data that disprove each of the propositions of stratification theory in spite of the fact that they themselves adhere to these propositions. This is, of course, the ultimate tribute to their skill as reporters.[16]

Or consider the Lynds' treatment of the awkward (to them) datum that Middletown's workers seldom expressed class antagonism, despite the fact that they should have if stratification theory held in their case. The Lynds' explanation is contrived but revealing.[17] Middletown's workers, it was alleged, were burdened by a "false class consciousness" that perverted the responses "objectively" expected of them. This reflects a "Heads I win, tails you lose" methodology. Polsby put the point more formally. "If we presume that the class is always wrong and the analyst invariably right when the two disagree," he noted, "then there seems to be no way to disprove the analyst's empirical propositions by referring them to the data his propositions are supposed to describe."

How did stratification theory come to such an end? Many factors contributed,[18] but the emphasis here will be on methodological factors. To put it tersely, given its methodological tethers, nothing better could be expected of stratification theory. Two methodological features illustrate the total argument: (1) the stratification model is too little disciplined by an appreciation of the uses and limits of empirical theory; and (2) stratification theory has given little attention to operational definition. Only this neglect made possible the long-standing acceptance by many students of the major propositions of the theory. Attempts to make the major concepts of the theory operational would have been their own undoing. But operational definition has been neglected in stratification analyses.

The two major methodological inadequacies of stratification theory can be considered in turn. To begin, the stratification model does not respect the role of empirical theory. This may seem surprising. For, if nothing else, the position that communities are organized—after the fashion of layer cakes—into strata or classes, and that class standing is a crucial determinant of the community power possessed by individuals, should have very firm roots in that which exists. Surprising or not, however, this is how things are: stratification theory is unrestrained by the guidelines for empirical research.

Let us briefly sketch the role of empirical theory, the more solidly to make this point. The sketch, of course, derives from the introductory chapters of this volume. Empirical theory should at once guide research and feed upon it. A useful empirical model will parsimoniously describe a set of relations existing in nature, and that model will generate hypotheses that spiral out toward greater comprehensiveness in accounting for increasingly broad relations in nature. And whether useful or not, no orderly empirical observation is possible except in terms of some model—however rudimentary—of what is thought to exist. The relation is subtle but powerful. As Suzanne Langer noted: "The way a question is asked limits and disposes the way in which any answer of it—*right or wrong*—may be given."[19]

We may hazard a summary. A useful empirical model is self-correcting in that it sets in motion the dynamics of its own rejection. Models that guide observation, however, also are self-fulfilling. That is, over a considerable range any model focuses attention on confirming events. Scrupulosity is in order, then, lest the self-fulfilling proclivities of any model get out of hand. But get out of hand they often have. Many well-intentioned empirical efforts basically if inadvertently developed into what have been utopian theories.

Abundant evidence implies that stratification theory is a stranger to the methodological scrupulosity necessary to guard against its own self-fulfilling proclivities. That is, stratification theory has many of the characteristics of utopian theory.

The evidence confirming the utopian properties of stratification theory may only be sampled. Consider the sophistry brought to bear on the wide range of findings at odds with the propositions of stratification theory. For example, two authors felt no inhibitions about concluding that a certain Negro sub-community "has no genuine power structure"[20] even though Negroes "have been remarkably successful"[21] in gaining their own ends on a variety of issues. Why no "genuine power structure" in the face of such successes? "Their sub-community lacked large-scale business and industrial organizations," Barth and Abu-Laban concluded, "and, consequently, no genuine power structure had developed."[22]

Utopian characteristics thrust themselves at the reader. The proof of a "genuine power structure" lies in consistency with definitions rather than in actual ability to influence the environment. Acknowledging a genuine power structure among Negroes, would have required at least some modification of the propositions of stratification theory. Protection of these propositions, however, seems to have had the highest priority. For "big businessmen" are clearly "upper class," and the Negroes in question were not big businessmen. Hence the Negroes had their successes, but they could not have a "genuine power structure."

Abundant examples reinforce this view of the self-fulfilling bias of stratification theory. Indeed, a whole family of gambits have served stratification theorists intent on safeguarding the inviolability of their own theory. Among them are:

1. Explanation by infinite regression: "If the overt leaders of a community do not appear to constitute a ruling elite," Dahl explained, "then the theory can be saved by arguing that behind the overt leaders exist a covert group who do. If subsequent evidence shows that this covert group does not make a ruling elite, then the theory can be saved by arguing that behind the first covert group there is another, and so on."[23]

2. Explanation by inadequate motivation: If a power elite does not in fact seem to determine community decisions, it is often argued that they could do so if they really wanted to. This assumes that "assumed potential for control" is equivalent to "actual political

effectiveness."[24] Or if it is not, it can be, and perhaps should be!

3. Explanation by "false consciousness": When a "class" violates a researcher's expectations, that class may be said to be behaving "irrationally."[25]
4. "And also" explanations: This approach suggests (or states) that the cases in which the expectations of stratification theory are not met are trivial, or irrelevant, or due to temporary factors that will soon pass.[26]
5. Explanation by generalization: This argument has dual applications. If inequalities of power existed in Cases A and B, researchers generalize that similar inequalities exist over all significant cases and that a power elite PE—which exercised control in Cases A and B—also exists. If in Case C, PE did not seem to control events, this can be explained as: the exception that proves the rule; lack of motivation of PE; or as a mere apparency, with PE actually controlling events through other overt actors.

These gambits do not exhaust those employed, but they do (clearly) illustrate that stratification theory has very strong self-fulfilling tendencies. As Polsby's summary analysis of eight stratification studies concluded, for example, stratification theory approximates an unknowing exercise in utopian theory.[27] Polsby explained the unanimity in the results of stratification analyses that flew in the face of much contradictory data in these terms: the propositions of stratification theory derive from an underlying model of assumptions that are widely (if implicitly) held and from which the propositions were derived. These assumptions are only gross approximations of existential states,[28] if in fact the assumptions are not at direct odds with reality. Polsby details four such assumptions:[29]

1. The community is stratified horizontally into layers of ranks, with a single layer on top;
2. Power is closely correlated with class, as determined by economic status criteria;
3. Classes maximize their own interests over the long run; and
4. The total supply of community values is more or less chronically short of the demands of all classes.

Given such assumptions, Polsby noted, it is "improbable that propositions different from those given would appear as findings in stratification studies. . . ."

The approach to stratification theory as a derivation had a further value, Polsby noted. Viewing the propositions of stratification theory as a derivation from assumptions rather than as a pattern existing in nature "may explain why stratification writers have advanced similar propositions about community power despite the fact that the propositions were not justified by the facts in the communities they studied." Again, the characteristics of utopian theory are prominent in stratification analysis.

In sum, a set of assumptions about reality was so widely accepted by stratificationists that pictures of reality were drawn after the image of the assumptions; even in the face of compelling contradictory evidence. This is the disciplinary condition Gouldner characterized as "metaphysical pathos." Under its heady influence, researchers had trouble seeing the real world for the artificial world of assumptions that they brought to their observation.

Our argument cannot be allowed to become a bloated caricature. Every observer has his own metaphysical pathos, that is, and each observational system must be false to reality to some degree. The point here is that the metaphysical pathos of the stratificationists did not provide the self-checking features that scientific man has learned to use to compensate for the observational frame he so desperately needs but which may also imprison his senses. Chapter II details some of the self-checking technology of science.

The lack of self-checking features in the stratificationist position has patent reflections, such as the lack of concern with operational definition, which clearly reflects their methodological insensitivity. For example, the concept *power elite* is bandied about with paltry attention to what it means even in rough terms. And even less attention is accorded ways of measuring that conceptual *something*. That early stratification studies were reportorial—if sometimes monumentally so—helps explain the reliance on intuitive and imprecise major concepts and the general lack of concern with operational matters. But explanation does not reduce one whit the grave scientific liabilities of the reportorial approach. And the reportorial tradition of stratification theory has been hard to live down. Specifically, operational difficulties plague even Hunter's study of Regional City, which is perhaps the most methodologically self-conscious of stratification studies.

The operational difficulties in Hunter's work suggest that the problems with work that is less methodologically concerned are monumental. Hunter leaves little doubt of his allegiance to the stratificationist approach. Two explicit propositions reveal this allegiance most clearly. First, the structural relations of community power as conceived by Hunter were marked and stable. As he noted, "power is a relatively constant factor in social relationships with policies as variables."[30] Moreover, second, Hunter informs us that: "Wealth, social status, and prestige are [major] factors in the 'power constant.' "[31]

That Hunter's work had significant methodological inelegancies re-

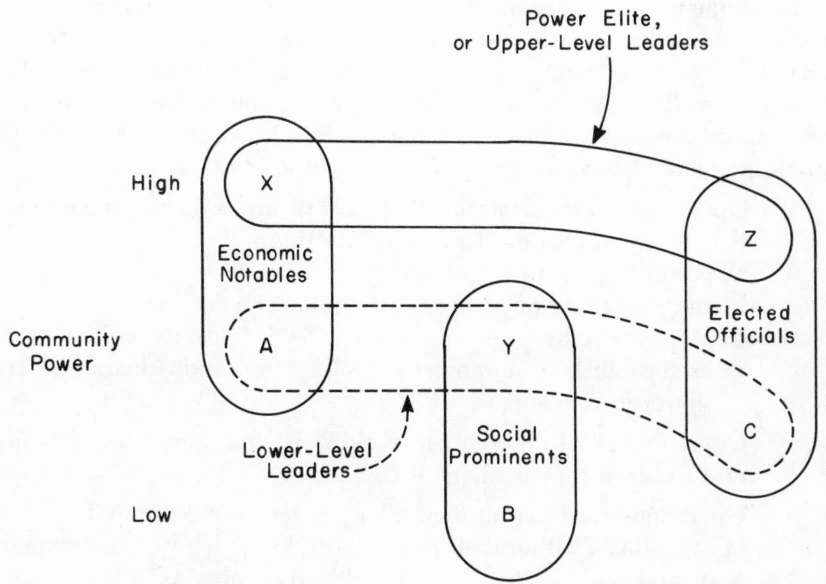


FIGURE VI.1 A Simplified Stratificationist View of the World.

mains to be established. The general strategy here is to sketch and analyze Hunter's attempts at nominal and operational definition of community power. Nominally, to set the stage for our basic emphasis on Hunter's operations, he conceived of community power as "the ability of men to command the services of other men."[32] And he firmly rooted his concept in the macro-organizations that constitute a "community," that is, a set of recurring relations between people. These relations for Hunter (after the elitist fashion) are "pyramidal," and they comprise the structural vitals of an identifiable social system. Without denying that individuals can exert personal power, Hunter argued that individuals have *community* power only as they participate effectively in the sets of relations that are community-relevant. These relations are supra-individual: effective community power "must be structured into associational, clique, or institutional patterns."[33] Community power, in short, refers to a structural description of persistent asymmetries in social processes relevant to the development of policy.

These straightforward nominal definitions imply many challenges for operational resolution. Figure VI.1, albeit crudely, helps spotlight some of these challenges. To simplify matters, our hypothetical community includes only three "associational, clique, or institutional patterns" (ACIPs). Since community power inheres in the recurring relations between these three ACIPs, a suitable set of operations for measurement faces multi-dimensional tasks of eliciting data necessary to confirm the propositions of stratification theory. Among these tasks are:

1. Operations must permit the direct test of stratification propositions, that is, operations must demonstrate that
   a. power is pyramidally structured;
   b. the patterning of power is a "constant factor"; and
   c. a "power elite" can be distinguished from individuals who exercise little or no power as well as from individuals who are "lower-level leaders";
2. Operations must differentiate each ACIP and permit the drawing of a roster of the members of each;
3. Operations must permit the ranking in terms of community power of individuals within their own ACIP (in Figure VI.1, individuals X, Y, and Z are all top-ranked within their own ACIP);
4. Operations must differentiate the range of community power over which members of each ACIP operate (in Figure VI.1, Y as the highest-ranked Social Prominent will exercise only as much influence over major policy as the lowest-ranked Economic Notable);
5. Operations must differentiate "personal power" from the community power" which derives from an individual's ACIP;
6. Operations must distinguish patterns of integration between the several ACIPs, such as mutual members, coalitions, and so on; and
7. Decision rules must specify when a single power elite drawn from the several ACIPs can be said to exist.

Hunter's *Community Power Structure* at best partially meets this selected list of operational challenges, although different criteria of adequacy can make more or less of this datum. Some observers consider the performance damning. "Hunter has tried to deal with a phenomenon before adequate tools are at hand to handle it," two early critics put it, "and his findings must therefore be regarded as intuitive . . . rather than scientific."[34]

Such a strict criterion is not appropriate, however. Scientific progress is not an all-or-nothing matter. Moreover, if everyone were to wait for adequate tools to be developed, they never would be. A more appropriate test, therefore, is whether Hunter's operations permit others to replicate his results, whether they permit others to leapfrog over his efforts toward greater comprehensiveness.

Even with this less demanding criterion, we must view Hunter's operations with pessimism, for they but weakly encourage and support replication. A few factors must suffice to illustrate this argument. First, Hunter's operations tend to be self-fulfilling. Basically, that is, many of Hunter's central operations are variations of this question: Which individuals on this list constitute the power elite in Regional City? The form of the question, that is, assures what should have been a central focus for analysis. A more appropriate guiding question for operations would have been: Is community power structured in any recurring patterns in Regional City, and what are these patterns if they exist? The basic research design, in sum, severely limited any real operational response to Challenge 1.

Second, because of his prior and overt nominal conception of community power as a "constant factor," Hunter's operations emphasized what might be called "general power." On the showing of Hunter's own data, this emphasis proved awkward. Thus one George Delbert was ranked highest on one set of responses to a "general power" criterion[35] but not on another.[36] Among other possibilities,[37] this result might reflect the importance of "specific power" rankings that varied as issues or situations changed. This possibility, indeed, was accepted by Hunter. Despite his general fascination with *a* pyramid dubbed "Policy Making Structure," that is, Hunter momentarily deviated from the monolithic model presumed by his research:

> Only a rudimentary "power pyramid" of Regional City will be presented. . . . I doubt seriously that power forms a single pyramid with any nicety in a community [this] size. . . . There are *pyramids* of power in this community which seem more important to the present discussion than *a* pyramid.[38]

But this excerpt must be considered a lapse; his general emphasis is a pole apart.

Whatever its other virtues, consequently, Hunter's approach via "general power" begged important questions raised by Challenges 4 and 5 to operational definition. Moreover, it avoided significant questions raised by his own data. The emphasis on "general power" also may have foreclosed questions about possible differences between communities that might favor "specialized power." As Hunter himself observes, for example, smaller cities might be characterized by the former pattern. Larger cities might tend toward influentials specialized by issue-area, if only because of greater resources and greater workload.

Third, significant difficulties inhere in Hunter's basic "operation" for selecting his power elite. He used 14 judges, of whom we know little.[39] The judges selected "by mutual choice" 40 individuals from lists of some 200 presumed influentials submitted to them. The original lists had been compiled from diverse sources, with individual lists developed for these "associational, clique, or institutional patterns": officers of civic, fraternal, and professional organizations; government officials; business leaders; and persons of social prominence and affluence.

Hunter's "reputational" operation for isolating his power elite, as many have noted,[40] raises serious questions. We can allow the original sources to make the full argument. Following our rule of parsimony, we will but illustrate their argument and attempt to move beyond it in methodological terms. For example, the "reputation for exerting power" may be correlated only slightly with actual influence, as the pluralists correctly note. Thus the use of judges—even if we knew more about who they were, about their qualifications, and about the criteria they utilized—is not a direct approach to community power.

Emphasizing the indirectness of the reputational operation is valuable, but critics often follow a false trail. Commonly, that is, they denigrate Hunter's approach because it ". . . is not the way one would try to decide who the wealthiest people in the community are or what the city's average temperature is,"[41] or because "... asking about reputations is asking, at a remove, about behavior [and any] researcher should . . . make it his business to study the requisite behavior directly, and not depend on second-hand opinions."[42] In point of fact, however, many scientifically useful data are gathered in just this way.[43]

The major weakness with Hunter's reputational operation, in contrast, is that opportunities to internally test stratification theory were neglected. For example, 27 individuals on the final list of 40 responded to a follow-up questionnaire. But the questionnaire was biased in such a way that the validity of the final list was assumed rather then tested. And this is *the* crucial datum. For example, respondents were asked: "If a project were before the community that required *decision* by a group of leaders—leaders that nearly everyone would accept—which *ten* on the list of forty would you choose?"[44] The self-fulfilling bias is patent. Any clustering of choices, at least in substantial measure, is an artifact of the question asked. Presumably, most respondents would be motivated to make the best use of even a bad list.

These and similar inelegancies support an unequivocal conclusion. Hunter's operations do little to meet Challenges 2 and 3 above. Moreover, the self-fulfilling bias of questionnaire items used by Hunter also raises serious doubts about the meaning of otherwise well-designed operations to test for the cohesiveness of big power elite.[45] These operations, in effect, provided some answer to Challenge 6.

Failure to specify decision rules further obfuscates Hunter's results, while it also avoids Challenge 7 above. For example, the responses reported for the "top ten" question quoted above are puzzling. Hunter concludes that the responses showed "considerable unanimity of opinion":[46] one individual received 21 of 27 possible choices; and 13 of the remaining 39 individuals received 10 or more choices. Hunter's interpretation may be incautious, for fully 15 individuals received two votes or less. Given that the respondent's universe was limited to 40 names, one can probably make any convenient guess as to what the results mean. And Hunter's interpretation certainly was based on a very loose decision rule. Statistical techniques like Kendall's coefficient of concordance," for example, could have been employed to provide a reproducible decision rule.[47]

The interpretation of these "top ten" responses is further troubled, and this in ways that characterize Hunter's data. Thus of the 270 possible "top ten" votes, only 174 choices are accounted for in the table reporting the relevant data.[48] This averages out to some 6.4 choices per respondent, each of whom was given 10 choices. Whether this suggests a pyramid of power, or several more or less exclusive choice-clusters, is problematic. Even more puzzling, the "mutual choices" among the final list of 140 were used to distinguish the "power leaders" into "upper-limits leaders" and "lower-limits leaders." This seems an approach to Challenges 1 and 6 to operational development, but only very restrained enthusiasm is possible about the effort. We are told only that the "group receiving the largest number of votes will be designated an upper-limits . . . group."[49] The decision rule and its interpretation are unclear. "Fewer votes" in most cases apparently meant no mutual choices. This is an interesting way of choosing "lower-limits leaders." Furthermore, one individual who received one mutual choice made the "upper-limits leaders," while six others who also apparently received one choice were relegated to the "lower-limits leaders." Finally, two individuals who apparently received no mutual choices are classified as "upper-limits leaders."[50]

One clear conclusion emerges from such ambiguities about decision rules. They do not encourage replicating—indeed, they preclude understanding—Hunter's results. Specifically, these difficulties permit little confidence that Challenges 1, 3, 4, 6, or 7 were substantially answered.

From a variety of points of view, then, *Community Power Structure* reveals significant methodological inadequacies. What is more, it suggests the more severe methodological inadequacies of other stratification efforts. Basically, considerable evidence supports a characterization of stratification theory as utopian theory. That is, stratification theory seems derived from assumptions about reality that coincide today but imprecisely with empirical regularities. Hence the empty circularity of stratification theory. More specifically, stratification theory also may be characterized as utopian because of two methodological weaknesses: its inadequate concept of the requirements and limitations of empirical theory; and, relatedly, its insufficient attention to questions of operational definition.

## II. THE PLURALIST ALTERNATIVE WHO (IF ANYONE) *DOES* GOVERN?

The "pluralist alternative" to stratification theory in significant senses developed under conditions approaching disciplinary self-defense. Political scientists increasingly felt themselves being eased out of their own domain following World War II. Psychologists had begun important studies of voting,[51] an area of some interest to the student of politics. And the 1953 publication of Hunter's *Community Power Structure* threatened a far greater encroachment on their disciplinary preserve. Prominent sociologists and psychologists openly acknowledged that this was indeed poaching but—how the barb struck!—they steadfastly maintained that it was necessary poaching.[52]

There being no gentleman's agreement about not working the other discipline's side of the street, political scientists girded their loins for the fray. The necessity of so doing, was perhaps the dominant theme of the leading (and often angry) review of Hunter's *Community Power Structure* by Kaufman and Jones.[53] A similar battle cry resounded along many of the research frontiers of the discipline.[54] And gird their loins political scientists did, particularly in the area of community power, one of long-standing interest to them. Much of the research in the area can be traced to the Kaufman and Jones review, and the most massive early effort was accomplished within the very department which Kaufman and Jones both served when they wrote their review. Moreover, the counter-attack by political scientists came along a broad front.

The disciplinary boosterism surrounding the pluralist alternative encourages caution in evaluating claim and counter-claim, and this section will be cautious. Two of its major themes are set down here as evidence of its character. Stratification analysis and the pluralist alternative have different emphases, but they are not so starkly opposed as some of the more vocal proponents of each would have us believe. Moreover, the pluralist approach does avoid some of the pitfalls of the stratificationists, but only by creating substantial difficulties of its own. The implied moral is direct. It is one thing to have an insight about a major patterning of reality, but it is quite another to support that insight with research utilizing nominal and operational definitions that permit replication. The methodology of the pluralists does not provide the required support.

Exhaustive support of the summary conclusion above cannot be given here, nor is it necessary. The plan of approach, rather, is first to describe the pluralist alternative broadly and then to focus upon the common methodological difficulties plaguing research inspired by the alternative. Dahl's leading *Who Governs?* will be of especial interest in the latter task. Nothing like a comprehensive review of that complex and wide-ranging book is attempted. But the volume does serve to spotlight the methodological difficulties in even insightful and well-financed pluralist analyses.

Let us therefore get on with sketching the outlines of the political scientist's response to the stratificationists. What, more specifically, is the pluralist alternative? Five emphases will provide us with enough of the substance of the approach for present purposes. First, the pluralist position on community power usually is presented as open-ended. For example, Dahl spoke for the pluralists when he explained that "there is no more *a priori* reason to assume that a ruling elite does exist than to assume that one does not exist."[55] Polsby made the same point at more revealing length. He observed that

> . . . nothing categorical can be assumed about power in any community. It rejects the stratification thesis that *some* group necessarily dominates a community. If anything, there seems to be an unspoken notion among pluralist researchers that at bottom *nobody* dominates in a town so that their first question to a local informant is not likely to be, "Who runs this community?" but rather, "does anyone at all run this community?"[56]

Second, Polsby's "unspoken notion" often appears quite explicitly. Briefly, although some pluralists act consistently with the dictum that nothing categorical can be assumed about their approach, many other pluralists in practice have great difficulty acknowledging that community power can be anything but pluralistic. That is, they say nothing categorical about community power, nothing except that it cannot be monolithic. This world-view of the pluralists is admirably described by Sayre and Kaufman in their study of New York City.[57] Note particularly this vivid description of the influence dynamics they perceived:

> Decisions of the municipal government do not emanate from any single source, but from many centers; conflicts and clashes are referred to no single authority, but are settled at many levels and

> at many points in the system: no single group can guarantee the success of any proposal it supports, the defeat of every idea it objects to. Not even the central governmental organs of the city—the Mayor, the Board of Estimate, the council—individually or in combination, even approach mastery in this sense.
>
> Each separate decision center consists of a cluster of interested contestants, with a "core group" in the middle, invested by the rules with the formal authority to legitimize decisions (that is to promulgate them in binding form) and a constellation of related "satellite groups" seeking to influence the authoritative issuances of the core group.[58]

Third, while stratification theory focuses on the various elite groups as holders of socially structured power, pluralists seek to identify influence as it becomes manifest in decision-making. Too simply perhaps, the former emphasizes these relative statics: Which individuals as representatives of which class or group have how much reputation for power in general? Pluralists stress the dynamics of specialized influence in particular decisions on specific issues. We may rely on the major proponent of the *issue orientation* to community power to provide its rationale. Although he acknowledged the difficulty of the demonstration, Robert A. Dahl confessed inability to "... see how anyone can suppose that he has established the dominance of a specified group in a community ... without basing his analysis on the careful examination of a series of concrete decisions. And these decisions must either constitute the universe or a fair sample from the universe of key political decisions taken in the political system."[59] In these terms, Hunter did not bring off his advertised demonstration. In fact—and Dahl considered this "remarkable and indeed astounding"—Hunter was said to have made only "improper tests" of the major hypothesis of stratification theory. In the first place, Hunter had equated a "ruling elite" with categories of individuals who at best had only a reputation for high *potential* in exerting influence. Moreover, Hunter had fallaciously assumed "that the absence of political equality proves the existence of a ruling elite."[60] Political inequality is certainly the normal condition of man, Dahl agreed, but this condition hardly supports the full weight of stratification theory.

Fourth, the pluralist assumes that community power varies over time and as issues change. Stratification theory argues to the contrary that the distribution of power is a quite permanent aspect of social structure. Changes come for the elitist in the distribution of community power, but they come but ponderously and on a system-wide basis.[61] Pluralists see significant advantages in their fluid concept. As Polsby summarizes their prevailing opinion:

> Pluralists held that power may be tied to issues, and issues can be fleeting or persistent, provoking coalitions among interested groups and citizens ranging in their duration from momentary to semipermanent. There is a clear gain in descriptive accuracy in formulating power distributions so as to take account of the dimension of time. . . . For it is easily demonstrated that coalitions *do* vary in their permanence, and to presume that the set of coalitions which exists in the community at any given time is a timelessly stable aspect of social structure is to introduce systematic inaccuracies into one's description of social reality.[62]

Fifth, it is often smoothly announced that pluralists emphasize roles while stratificationists fixate on status or "social position."[63] The two approaches do differ, but the antithesis above is too facile. The literatures on status and roles are tortuously complex,[64] and perhaps the only safe generalization they permit is that generalizations are hazardous in the extreme. But we need not completely abandon the distinction. Thus roles imply the performance of specific behaviors, and pluralists do stress their concern with influence behaviors as they manifest themselves. Stratification theorists have been generally content to consider purported status as having a 1 : 1 correspondence with influence exercised, thus reflecting their preoccupation with the relatively static structural nexus from which community power is alleged to derive.

Even given these differences between pluralists and stratificationists —and they often are sharper in principle than in practice—choosing a victor is not possible, as can be seen by comparing Hunter's work with that of Dahl and his associates. We have argued that Hunter did not demonstrate the existence of an elite in Regional City. Dahl, in contrast, failed to establish that an elite did not exist in New Haven. The basic limiting factor in both cases is identical: no decision rule is specified which defines when an elite group does in fact exist and when it does not. This basic limiting factor at once compounds and rests upon conceptual and operational difficulties.

Evidence drawn from Hunter and Dahl adds spirit and blood to the bare bones of the position sketched directly above. Recall that Hunter argued for an elite interpretation by demonstrating who-chose-whom on power-relevant criteria among (for example) the upper-limits leaders drawn from a large pool of the wealthy, the socially prominent, high-placed business and public executives, educators, and so on. The derived pattern of mutual choices did reveal some internal unity. But the basic question is: How much choice-unity is required on which criteria before one can speak with tolerable precision about the existence of an elite? Hunter required, but did not supply, a decision rule. The neglected problem is an analog of the need for group designation raised in Chapter III's discussion of suitable operations for measuring cohesiveness. As that chapter demonstrates, the price of continued neglect will be contradictory results and a circular analytical going-nowhereness.

Dahl shares similar unsatisfied needs for decision rules, conceptual clarification, and testing of operations. He utilized three issue-areas—redevelopment, party nominations, and public education—and attempted by intensive analysis to determine which specific individuals influenced particular decisions within them. Dahl then showed to his own satisfaction that: basically different sets of individuals seemed to be influential in different issue-areas;[65] relatively few individuals could be classified in more than one of these categories, Social Notables, Economic Notables, or public officials;[66] and public officials were more influential than Social Notables or Economic Notables.[67]

These and other findings presented by Dahl are significant, but their interpretation must be tentative in at least three major senses. Clearly, the absence of decision rules makes their interpretation chancy. Moreover, conceptual problems in the pluralist alternative also exact their toll in interpretive ambiguity. Finally, significant questions about many of the operations utilized by Dahl compound the difficulties of interpretation.

The significance and neglect of decision rules in Dahl will be handled first. Like Hunter's data, and indeed data from all of nature, Dahl's did not conform to an all-or-nothing pattern. The question implied was neglected: How low (or high) an incidence of specific outcomes is necessary to support or reject the study's major hypotheses? The neglect is troublesome. For example, few Social Notables held "selected offices" in the issue-areas studied by Dahl. In percentage terms, however, the Social Notables did quite well: they had twice their proportionate share of party offices; seven times their relative weighting in public education; and twenty-seven times their relative share of offices in urban development.[68] Other factors in Dahl's operations,[69] moreover, also imply that the 2700 per cent relative over-representation of the Social Notables in urban development is the truest measure of the influence of Social Notables. Perhaps, alternatively, Dahl is correct in noting that the proportions of Social Elites holding offices in all three issue-areas are "indeed small." In any case, some explicit decision rule is necessary. This is particularly the case because the holding of office need have no direct relation to being "in control" in the stratificationist's sense.

Several other features of Dahl's effort relating to the imprecision of decision rules further inhibit a choice between the findings of the pluralists and the elitists. Thus Dahl implies too strict a test for stratification theory, and ungraciously considers the failure to meet this test to be a proof of the validity of the pluralist position. His basic tests for the existence of an elite in New Haven seem to be: whether the *same individuals* are influential in different issue-areas; and whether the *same individuals* rank high on the same several economic and social criteria.

Although we are not told how much generality is considered sufficient to support stratification theory, all signs indicate that the standards the pluralists set for the elitists are very demanding.[70] Wildavsky provides perhaps the most unequivocal example of such definitional winning-of-the-day. "There is an enormous difference ... between influence by many small groups who compete with one another," he noted in support of the pluralist's emphasis upon substantially different sets of influentials in different issue-areas, "and influence by a single group (a power elite) *which can enforce its desires without considering the preferences of others*."[71] Wildavsky made no bones about the rarity of the latter extreme condition. "It is difficult to think of a community," Wildavsky acknowledged, "which does not have its share of disagreements."[72] The test for a pluralist distribution of power, then, is the failure of a community to meet the standard for an elite group which "is difficult [even] to think of."

Dahl and the pluralists seem more stratificationist than the stratificationists, on this issue. Hunter selects his upper-level leaders or power elite from among (for example) both the wealthy and government officials. Moreover, he does not require a commonality of rosters on various status criteria. Indeed, he requires no overlap at all. What Hunter does require (if not rigorously) is that upper-level leaders constitute a self-perceived elite, whether they are Economic Notables, government officials, or what have you, and whether or not each of them influenced any specific decision. Hunter is as clear on this issue as any other.[73]

In these terms, Dahl's results may be viewed from two perspectives. That is, he stressed a basis for stratification that stratificationists tended to neglect, or which they undervalued, and he produced a picture of community power in New Haven similar to that sketched by Hunter. Concerning the first factor, Dahl found that government officials had a decided advantage in exerting community power in the issue-areas he studied. Dahl thus provides at least an important amplification of stratification theory, which characteristically has viewed government officials as pawns of the power elite. But stratification theory is basically at home with any criterion for status, and Dahl's finding adds to rather than destroys stratification theory in this sense. Certainly a rationale supporting the recent coming into power of local government officials could be developed easily.

With qualifications, Dahl's analysis and that of Hunter have some strong parallels. Indeed, the trans-issue influence of New Haven's Mayor Lee, Edward Logue, and a handful of others suggests the dim outline of a new elite heavily influenced by government officialdom. Anton is even more expansive on this point. He explained that

> . . . in New Haven, a largely different group dominates each of the three issue areas, that within each issue-area only a small group of persons actually wield much influence, and that, for the period [Dahl] studied, this relatively small group of power wielders was relatively stable in membership. . . .
>
> [The] kind of "structure" I have just outlined differs very little from the kind of structure discovered by Hunter in Atlanta. The principal difference is that Hunter reported the existence of policy co-ordination among the top leaders of several issue areas, while Dahl rejects this idea. . . .[74]

In addition to these inelegancies associated with decision rules, Dahl's *Who Governs?* also raises significant issues related to conceptual development. Consider certain biases implicit in the pluralist's espousal of the issue-orientation. At this stage of the game, these biases raise serious questions about any pluralist findings. Scoble has summarized some of these biases, and we will paraphase his list.[75] (1) The pluralist focus on major public decisions emphasizes the amount of conflict in the community being studied. Since amount of conflict and degree of pluralism tend to be equated, the issue-orientation of the pluralist has a self-fulfilling tendency. "Tendency" is perhaps a milktoast term, for not even a totalitarian elite can be expected to "win them all" in matters of major policy. And if a major issue of public policy is conceived as one which an elite by definition cannot control well or at all—because that is what makes it a "major issue"—studying who influences such issues is not likely to reveal an elite even if one exists.

(2) The issue-orientation avoids those issues that never get raised (and are settled only in that sense), and (3) it also neglects those issues that are settled with little fanfare but which individually or cumulatively may be very significant. Many of the phenomena in these two categories are encompassed by what Bachrach and Baratz called the "nondecision-making process."[76]

Biases (2) and (3) of the pluralist approach raise significant issues. For example, what Bentley called the "habit background" of a community will play a crucial role in the nondecision-making process.[77] Various levels of values and value-laden institutions, in short, often will define which issues become "public" and which issues do not reach that threshold or which reach it only in exceptional cases. Clearly, on this point, the very broad framework of our federal government is so designed as to place a low probability on certain types of decisions entering the arena of public policy. Federalist 10, for example, may be consulted with profit on this head.[78] More broadly, Schattschneider explains that: "All forms of political organization have a bias in favor of the exploitation of some kinds of conflict and the suppression of others, *because organization is the mobilization of bias*. Some issues are organized into politics while others are organized out."[79] At a microscopic level, it is often impossible to assign to specific actors influence for the maintenance or change of such going rules of the game. Some actors may successfully change a habit background, or bend it to their own purposes. As longitudinal studies in small groups tend to demonstrate, however, central actors most often find their behavioral range circumscribed by such norms.[80] The pluralists face great problems, by implication. For if a policy dispute is one in which the prevailing habit background is somehow considered inappropriate, the issue-orientation encourages neglect of that variable but often formidable volume of decisions quietly made within the confines of some habit background.

Conceptually, then, the pluralist faces a cruel dilemma in handling the "issue-area" notion. The "more significant" are the issue-area and the decisions within it that he chooses—"significant" here defined in terms of high actual or potential conflict about policy—the more likely the pluralist is to generate self-fulfilling data. That is, the pluralist skates very close to defining *elite rule* in terms of the absence of conflict. This seems a ham-stringing decision rule. On the other hand, choosing "less significant" issue-areas and decisions hardly suits the pluralist rationale.

The conceptual problems raised by Dahl's approach may be honed even finer. Todd Gitlin puts his finger on an important conceptual problem for students like Dahl. "Local pluralism," Gitlin explains in *A Political Politics* (p. 133), "exorcises the concept of co-optation, so that all power is above-board, intended, and non-reciprocal." Gitlin refers to a number of properties of Dahl's "power" concept, among them that "someone has it only to the extent that someone else does not." This property eliminates many analytical problems, but it may over-simplify reality. For example, on his own conceptual grounds, Dahl is justified in concluding that differences in the names on the rosters of influentials in different issue-areas signify more or less exclusive power elites. Given other conceptual grounds, the justification is weakened or dissolves. Conceivably, for example, those in one issue-area might exercise power only while respecting their interests *and* the interests of individuals operating in other issue-areas. Any long-run violations of external interests would bring their day of harsh reckoning. In this concept, some actors with basic shared needs and interests recognize the complexity of the decision-making arena and in effect parcel out operating primacy among themselves and co-opt others, while still retaining sovereignty. This brief caricature is consistent with much of the reality reported by Dahl in *Who Governs?*, as in the case of the New Haven Board of finance. The associated subtle processes are not elitist in the extreme sense of that term; but neither are they patently pluralist, except by permissive definition.

(4) The pluralist issue-orientation assumes that "public decisions" are more important indicators of community power than "private decisions." This is a very significant conceptual exclusion—however understandable it is in professional terms—and it is at least a potentially troublesome exclusion. In any case, little imagination is required to develop the potentially serious difficulties with fixating on public decisions. For example, Scoble provides a telling example of derivative empirical and theoretical difficulties with the pluralist's exclusion. Consider two identical cities, he notes, as determined by their size, growth rate, and similar factors.[81] Assume also that Dahl's findings are replicated in both cities: that there is little overlap of influentials from one issue-area to another; that only the mayors participate in decision-making in more than one issue-area; and that influentials come from different ethnic backgrounds. The neglect of "private decisions" may be crucial. As Scoble illustrates:

> But one city's public decisions (especially those determining tax collections and public expenditures) are contingent on decisions made collectively in Detroit which set the level of operations of the dominant local automobile plant, while the other city is not so dependent. The fact that present methods would lead to classifying both systems as equally pluralistic tells us more about methods than it does about systems.

Finally, there are many significant operational difficulties and ambiguities in Dahl's study which—since they also characterize other pluralist studies—pose considerable interpretive obstacles to dealing with the pluralist literature. For example, determining who influenced specific decisions in various issue-areas is the crucial task in *Who Governs?* However, Dahl gives only very sketchy details about the operational ground rules used for isolating those who influenced public policy.[82] Indeed, apparently no efforts were made to test for inter-observer reliability, as by comparing the decisions of the author with those of outside judges on the same data, and consequently replicating Dahl's findings would be difficult. Kellstedt's broadside about pluralists and their use of the decisional approach thus applies in this case: "... the theoretical criteria utilized for the inclusion and exclusion of data are never clear."[83]

The two observations above about unclarities in Dahl's operations for assigning influence need not be artificially puffed up to significance. They have been made significant by Dahl and his associates, who present very few cases and yet place tremendous interpretive weight upon them. Even trifling operational difficulties, consequently, can distort results. The point holds despite the acknowledged difficulties in the natural-science study of influence at the community level.[84]

Compounding the lack of information concerning the operations for according influence, is Dahl's vagueness as to what constitutes a "decision." Symptomatically, the index of *Who Governs?* contains no entries under "decisions" or "decision-making." The omission seems significant. For the decision-making process is complex, and selective emphasis upon its various stages can be crucial in determining who is considered influential. Consider Table VI.I, which (in part) details the phases in the decision-making processes employed by Agger, Goldrich, and Swanson.[85] The most likely locus of dominant involvement (crudely, "public" or "private") in each of the phases is also hazarded. Even at this general level, it seems reasonable that emphasizing different phases of the complex processes of decision-making may thrust different actors to prominence. Dahl's emphasis is not clear, and his findings are consequently difficult to interpret.

Despite the complexities associated with specifying phases of the decision-making process, several conclusions seem there for the making. First, for all their stress upon decisions, the pluralists reflect an uncomplicated view of the decision-making process in their research design. No doubt this is due to the complexities of treating the full process. Complexity, however, does not reduce the derived interpretive difficulties in the least.

One major interpretive difficulty implied by Dahl's uncomplicated view of decision-making illustrates the broader family. At best, Dahl's research design concentrates on one *structural* aspect of the *processes* by which decisions are made. Even if his description of the power structure was unquestionable, therefore, interpretation would be limited. Roughly, in contrast, empirical theory can be built only as differences in *structure* or *processes* are related to differences in *outcomes*, as the interacting effects of "independent variables" on "dependent variables" are encompassed in wider and wider sets of theoretical propositions. Robinson and Majik summarize the point aptly [*op. cit.*, p. 188]:

> But process analysis alone neither constitutes nor builds theory. Theory-building hinges upon our ability to relate the growing store

> of descriptive knowledge about *how* decisions are made to the *outcomes* and *effects* of those decisions. The immediate challenge is to search for the process data for patterns and characteristics that make a difference for outcomes. Further efforts in this direction promise to inspire propositions upon which to build from the decision-making approach a *theory* of political decision-making that will enhance our understanding of "who gets what, when, how."

In this sense, the debate between pluralists and elitists has some unfortunate aspects. Perhaps a little uncharitably, it is as if two botanists were describing two unspecified kinds of trees at two unspecified locations. "It is fully-leafed," one might report. "It has no leaves," the second botanist might report. Both reporters could be accurate, of course, but botanical science does not advance very far until such sequences are investigated and the critical effects of the one on the other are established:

| *Independent Variable* | | *Dependent Variable* |
|---|---|---|
| Differences in Temperature | → | Degree in Leafiness of Various Varieties of Trees |

The debate between pluralists and elitists, similarly, will begin to bear scientific fruit as such outcome cluster sequences are investigated. [See the valuable development of the notion of an "outcome cluster" in Robinson and Majik, *op. cit.*, pp. 184–88.]

| | *Independent Variable* | | *Dependent Outcome Variable* |
|---|---|---|---|
| A. | Differences in Community Ecology, History, Form of Government, etc. | → | Differences in Community Power Structures |
| B. | Differences in Community Power Structures | → | Differences in "Outcome Clusters," e.g., in voter turnout, in political efficacy felt by voters, etc. |

Interestingly enough, indeed, Dahl in an earlier work himself provides a solid theoretical take-off point for such an effort. That is, "four basic social control processes" are distinguished: hierarchy; polyarchy; bargaining; and price mechanism. The decision-making in any social unit could be characterized by a profile of the degree to which these four processes were operative. Various profiles then could be compared in terms of the outcome clusters associated with them. Indeed, just this was done at a general level by Dahl and Lindblom for economic choices. [See Robert A. Dahl and Charles E. Lindblom, *Politics, Economics, and Welfare* (New York: Harper, 1953), especially pp. 369–412. The typology has been expanded and refined by Lindblom, *The Intelligence of Democracy: Decision-Making Through Mutual Adjustment* (New York: Free Press, 1965).]

The neglect of phases in the decision-making process, second, gives the lie to the claims of pluralists that they stress roles of leadership rather than status. To explain, stressing the phases of decision-making would permit the isolation of role-types of specialized behaviors, such as those suggested in Table VI.1. Any or all of these role-types might be

**TABLE VI.1 Phases of Decision Making, Dominant Loci of Involvement, and Provisional Role-Types**

| *Phases of Decision-Making* | *Probable Dominant Locus of Involvement* | *Provisional Role-Types* |
|---|---|---|
| 1. Policy Formulation | Public or Private | Idea Man |
| 2. Policy Deliberation | Public or Private | Negotiator |
| 3. Organizing Political Support | Public | Leg-man |
| 4. Authoritative Consideration | Public | Solon |
| Event: Decisional Outcome | Public | Solon |
| 5. Promulgation of the Decisional Outcome | Public | Leg-man |
| 6. Policy Effectuation | Public or Private | Administrator |

considered "influential" in a particular decision sequence. Such roles could be operationally defined with relative ease. They also could serve various analytical uses, as in differentiating influentials, determining whether specific decisions or issue-areas depend more upon one role-type than another, and so on. In contrast, pluralist studies in practice emphasize the *leader qua person*[86] rather than *leadership as a function to which many individuals may contribute*. The leader-person concept simplifies the research problem in all areas, but (at least in the massive "leadership" literature) the concept did so only by obscuring and distorting reality.[87]

The leader-person reference deserves close attention. For it reflects an operational difficulty that obscures the meaning of Dahl's reported findings and those of other pluralists as well. Dahl's operations and analysis neglect the group as a relevant unit of observation. The group level of analysis is consequently given little attention. The present point is a limited variant of Anton's salvo, which does catch some of the essence of Dahl's work but is lacking in specificity. "It is clear that in thinking of power," Anton explained, "Dahl was thinking primarily in terms of the individual. His basic unit of study is the actor and . . . his suggestions for research work are specifically aimed at precise measurements of the power of individuals."[88] How is our variant limited? To be sure, as he has vigorously insisted,[89] Dahl always defines influence as an *interpersonal* phenomenon. But to be equally sure, interpersonal relations differ in important particulars from group relations.[90] The point may seem exotic, but failure to recognize it has resulted in massive mischief.[91]

The present point could easily spiral out to a footnoted vagueness, so let us tether it to a recurring example from *Who Governs?* Dahl rejects the existence of an elite in New Haven by observing that different influential individuals tended to specialize in different issue areas. Now perhaps there is no elite in New Haven—however *elite* is defined operationally—but the evidence of non-commonalities between rosters of the influentials on various decisions does not establish that point or any other. If an elite is conceived as a behavioral group, an elite could exist with no commonality at all between such rosters. Oppositely, such a behavioral elite need not exist even given perfect commonality of the names on several rosters of influentials in different issue-areas.

Third, the very use of the decisional approach also raises serious questions concerning the self-fulfilling nature of pluralist research. That is, the distribution of power in the stratification model is both markedly asymmetric and stable. The decisional operation of the pluralist, however, provides the sharpest possible contrast with the "general power" reputational operation used by many stratificationists. For a decisional approach makes it improbable that power will be seen as stable or asymmetric. As Thomas Dye notes in an unpublished paper "Values and the Study of Community Power":

> . . . the case study approach to which the pluralists are committed is notorious for its inability to produce generalizations about anything. By definition the case study treats each decision as *sui generis.* By examining power in relation to a particular decision, one's findings about power are likely to be tied to particular decisional situations. It is not surprising that the pluralist researcher after compiling a series of separate case studies concludes that the exercise of power is situational, and that generalizations about power exercised in different issue areas are unwarranted. The case study method predisposes the researcher to see power in situational terms.

In addition, the pluralist also may thereby condemn himself to pessimism about the scientific study of community power. Indeed, Dye sees signs of just this uncomely consequence. "Dahl himself," Dye stresses, "is very pessimistic about the comparability of power studies and the likelihood of developing generalizations about power."

Several conclusions derive from the ways pluralists generally and Dahl specifically develop their focus on *role*. Thus the data gathered by Dahl—deriving from a research design that does not probe for group influence or group characteristics—are unlikely to establish the existence of any group, elite or not. Moreover, the underlying and largely pluralist conceptions of *group* and *leadership* seem entirely too wooden. The available literature is vague on the matter, which may say it all. However, the pluralists apparently lean heavily on concepts that have been discarded in other behavioral sciences. For example, the pluralists (as noted above) never do exploit their avowed view of leadership as a function. Rather they seem preoccupied in practice with leaders as individuals. Similarly, pluralist operations imply that a group is a collection of persons. Replicatory failures have driven such notions out of currency in other areas, as in small-group analysis.[92] In this case, some of Hunter's operations are clearly superior. Thus his sociometric questions about who-chooses-whom permit some test of the "groupness" or cohesiveness of a purported elite. No comparable, group-oriented operations are utilized by Dahl. Consequently, group-relevant regularities would have difficulty emerging from the data gathered by Dahl.

Operational difficulties of omission as well as commission further challenge interpretations of all studies of community power. That is, both stratification theory and the pluralist alternative have avoided these related problems: the definition of *community* in more than formal terms, and the determination of dimensions to differentiate communities. Each approach to community power has avoided these problems in its own way, but with the same effect. Stratification theory practices avoidance by assuming that a highly structured monolith constitutes the universal community prototype. This makes differentiation pointless, of course.

Pluralists walk a narrower line in their failure to differentiate community. Perhaps as an over-reaction to the concreteness of stratification theory, pluralists often come close to losing an image of the community as a conceptual entity. Of course, immense conceptual and operational problems incredibly complicate the behavioral differentiation of community dimensions. A promising start has been made, however.[93] Moreover, no matter how onerous the prospects, there is no long-run alternative to facing up to the task. Certainly the avoidance of community dimensions seems potentially very significant. Perhaps, for example, there are cities that may with tolerable precision be considered communities and that exhibit patterns of influence not unlike those called for by the stratification model. And some formally defined cities may be considered only as congeries of communities—or of some other still undefined behavioral entity—with strong tendencies toward that distribution of power whose picture is the pluralist model.

If the latter is avowedly vague supposing, two points are definite enough. First, the convenient assumption that a legally defined entity is a viable unit for discovering empirical regularities about community power is not likely to prove tenable. Chapters III and IV suggest the point at both the micro-level and the macro-level.

Second, pluralists give little sign of anything constructive under the head of isolating community dimensions, although the debate has been sharp on occasion. For example, Anton's critique of both the elitist and pluralist models emphasized the necessity of dealing with the "unsolved problem of defining 'community.'"[94] Dahl reacted pointedly. Anton's references to a "notion of community," he noted, amounted to "nothing more than a kind of *mystique,* with footnotes."[95] And there the entire matter was left.

The preceding is a substantial catalog of difficulties in the pluralist approach, and particularly in Dahl's *Who Governs?*. The absence of decision rules, the persistence of operational inelegancies and conceptual difficulties: these outline substantial barriers to considering the pluralist literature as an empirical theory in the process of building.

That such wide-ranging difficulties in interpreting pluralist findings exist cheek by jowl with ardent verbalizations of the superiority of that approach to community power suggests a further conclusion. Without denying the usefulness of the basic pluralist orientation, one could nonetheless note that pluralists have, to varying degrees of severity, been victims of their own brand of metaphysical pathos. Some evidence supporting this position seems unequivocal, in fact. Several self-fulfilling features of the pluralist approach have been noted, for example.

That the pluralist alternative has been a vehicle of political scientists, and political scientists under some pressure to produce and elaborate a distinct approach to a phenomenal area they considered as solidly within their own area of expertise, also encourages caution. The implied protection of disciplinary "turf" probably encourages sharper differences with stratificationists—who are largely sociologists—than results call for. Such a disciplinary inducement to overdrawing differences may explain some otherwise baffling elements in the pluralist-elitist controversy. For example, Dahl comes down hard on Hunter for his reputational approach to community power. "I do not see how anyone can suppose that he has established the dominance of a specific group in a community,"

Dahl noted, "without basing his analysis on the careful examination of a series of concrete decisions."[96] Hunter's failure in this regard is cited as "remarkable and indeed astounding." The punishment does not seem to fit the crime in this case. For examine his elite's impact on "concrete decisions" is just what Hunter did, albeit not always prominently.[97] Similarly, however valid their basic concept, pluralists have leaned very hard on fragile data. Indeed, they doth protest too much about how their data differentiate them from the stratificationists.

Anton would extend such cues beyond our own tastes, finally, but his position cannot be rejected out of hand. He notes that several studies by political scientists "have substantiated the bold assertion of Kaufman and Jones" in their leading critical review of Hunter's *Community Power Structure* "that local power systems are pluralistic rather than monolithic." Anton also cites the increasing prominence of the issue-orientation to influence, as opposed to Hunter's reputational approach. He concludes, as they say, without hiding his feelings:

> It would not be exaggerating, then, to assert that Kaufman and Jones did more in their book review than summarize a reaction of political scientists and point the way to further research; their review actually presented, in advance, a summary of the *results* of later research!
>
> It should be emphasized that this rejection of Hunter's sociological work was not based on the nature of the empirical world. Hunter's report was dismissed primarily because what he wrote was inconsistent with the pluralist interpretation of that world.[98]

## III. SOME HOPEFUL SIGNS

Despite the soft spots, one need not conclude that naught availeth in the analytical struggle over community power. The contraposition of elitist and pluralist has had mixed by-products: light as well as heat; clarification as well as conflict; and reconciliation of diverse findings as well as differences set at irreconcilable odds. Moreover, the by-product "mix" of late increasingly favors the empirical investigation of a complex phenomenal area. Polemically tinged efforts by romantic pluralists and by avowedly realistic elitists should find a narrowing audience.

This hopeful convergence in methodology and results may be sketched broadly, with the focus upon specific conceptual and operational developments. In turn, these developments reflect a general and growing commitment to, and an understanding in practice of, the methodological requirements of empirical research. Both specific and general developments require substantial modification of the "state of phenomenal area" sketched by Dahl, who argued that

> . . . we are not likely to produce—certainly not for some considerable time to come—anything like a single, consistent, coherent "Theory of Power." We are much more likely to produce a variety of theories of limited scope, each of which employs some definition of power that is useful in the context of the particular piece of research or theory but different in important respects from the definitions of other studies. Thus we may never get through the swamp. But it looks as if we might someday get around it.[99]

What modifications of Dahl's position seem appropriate? To put it summarily, a viable empirical methodology is oriented toward the development of a consistent and coherent "theory of power." That methodology encourages the choice between "definitions of power" in terms of their usefulness in replicatory studies, as opposed to the looser test of their usefulness "in the context of the particular piece of research or theory." And that methodology tests a "variety of theories of limited scope" for their ability to account for what is known and at the same time to predict continually what is as yet unknown, as opposed to a kind of implicit and extended co-existence on something like equal terms.

Recent conceptual developments in community power seem promising carriers indeed of an empirical approach. These developments center around "pluralism" as defined by a Dahl in loose operational terms. Dahl, of course, holds that pluralism exists where it cannot be shown that a single roster of decision-makers dominates all significant issue-areas in a community. And these conceptual developments consciously seek to improve on what Presthus perceived as "a curious reluctance on the part of scholars precisely to define 'pluralism.' "[100]

Students increasingly see significant problems in the prevailing pluralism concept. For economy's sake, two such problems will be discussed here from various points of view. First, critics note that Dahl's concept of pluralism departs widely from traditional usage which (Presthus tells us) "historically . . . included as a necessary condition active participation in local and national affairs and a reasonable equity of bargaining power among interested groups."[101]

There may seem to be no great methodological crime in this designational innovation. But the conceptual departure has in fact been mischievous, and sometimes powerfully so. One can give nominal concepts the precise designation one sees fit, of course, but historical connotations can persist and cloud meaning. These connotations can prove a liability to scientific effort. Indeed, some evidence implies that pluralists have themselves succumbed to their own conceptual rhetoric. They often confuse their modern designation of pluralism with the concept's historical connotations, thereby insisting on a purported empirical state of affairs that is unverified and perhaps unverifiable. To explain, Dahl argues (as the historical connotation requires) that "average" citizens of New Haven exercise "very great"[102] or a "good deal of"[103] indirect influence in policy questions, and especially over elected political officials.

Dahl's motivation in claiming "very great" indirect citizen influence on New Haven's policy is conjectural, but obviously, powerful. It is only clear that Dahl's insistence on popular influence is consistent with his major conclusion that a pluralist system existed in New Haven. But was the latter a conclusion based on the former? Or was the popular influence a mere logical derivative of the basic decision that New Haven was pluralistic? The difference is significant, if beyond our abilities to judge. Dahl's evidence is not convincing, in any case, for it leans heavily on fragmentary data[104] and on the interpretation of ambiguous cues.[105] At the very least, Dahl's insistence overcame some of his own contrary evidence. For example, although Dahl reports little commonality in the rosters of influentials in the three issue-areas, he notes that *within* each issue-area very few individuals are represented. He finds that: "urban development has been the direct product of a small handful of leaders";[106] few citizens "participate directly in important decisions bearing on public schools";[107] and the "bulk of the voters had virtually no direct influence on [party] nomination."[108]

Even Dahl seems uncomfortable with his insistence on significant indirect citizen influence in the face of such evidence in opposition. Indeed, when the chips are down, Dahl is all tentativeness on the evidence while he everywhere else still urges the conclusion. He explains that

> . . . in each of a number of key sectors of public policy a few persons have great *direct* influence on the choices that are made; most citizens, by contrast, seem to have rather little direct influence. *Yet it would be unwise* to underestimate the extent to which voters *may exert indirect* influence on the decisions of leaders by means of elections.[109]

These words do not seem to constitute two links in this chain: that citizens of New Haven do in fact exert considerable indirect influence on public policy; and that for this and other reasons one may describe the distribution of community power in New Haven as "pluralist."

The mischief of designational-connotational confusion is considerable. To those who favor traditional pluralism, Dahl's findings may seem comforting despite their radically different designational base. This exemplifies one of the "conservative" biases in behavioral research against which students like Bay[110] have warned. The warning seems appropriate in this case. For contemporary pluralist findings give little actual comfort to traditional pluralists. In a Syracuse study of 39 decisions, for example, Freeman found that "... in fact, the doctrines of local democracy are incorporated into the pieties rather than the practices of the Syracuse municipal and metropolitan communities. Less than three-tenths of one per cent of the adult citizens participated in the making of these 39 community decisions."[111]

Confusion of designations—connotations is exacerbated by methodological carelessness about types of theories. For example, consider two responses to findings such as those illustrated above. First one can extend such empirical data into a resolutely-held statement of what should be and/or of what must of necessity be. Jack L. Walker criticizes the "elite theory of democracy" on just such grounds of methodological blurring of empirical theory and goal-based, empirical theory.[112] Oppositely, one can start with the same empirical data about limited popular participation but attempt thereafter to fashion goal-based, empirical theories adequate to the complex job of changing the existing state of affairs.[113] Thus Peter Bachrach gives attention to the empirical data concerning low popular political participation, as well as to action programs designed to change what is for him an undesirable existential tendency. Bachrach's focus is on some of the major research findings of studies of community power, which findings are inconsistent with his own values. His reaction, in largest part, is to think in programmatic terms of ways to improve the empirical state of affairs by reinvigorating "political participation." His slim volume thus constitutes a mini-model of the healthy interaction between the empirical and the normative which this volume has been supporting.[114]

Students also more clearly recognize the pre-emptive characteristics of contemporary pluralist concepts and operations, to stress another hopeful feature of recent research. Elites literally cannot exist, by definition, in some pluralist research designs. And if an elite does not exist, goes the facile argument, then the distribution of power must be pluralistic. The sense one gets is that of pluralism and elitism as discontinuous variables rather than as points on a continuum. *Elitism* is defined by very limited boundary-conditions; and *pluralism* is defined as everything else.

Much of the pluralist literature has been content with such a cheap victory of the pluralist alternative over stratification theory, and this contentment has its price. Consider one set of questions whose neglect is encouraged by narrow pluralism concepts. Are there degrees of pluralism that can be usefully distinguished, e.g., from 0 to 100 per cent? And if such degrees do exist, is it not reasonable to define (e.g.) the range 0–25 per cent as "elite distribution of power" and the range 75–100 per cent as "pluralist distribution of power"? The range 25–75 per cent might be labeled an "oligarchic distribution of power."

Affirmative answers to such questions seem reasonable and probably necessary. For example, available findings are sprinkled across a range wide enough to encourage both elitists[115] and pluralists[116] to conclude that they have truth by the tail. Nor is a discontinuous, bi-model pattern apparently appropriate. The more complex somewhere-in-betweenness often encountered is well illustrated by Jennings' summary of his restudy of Regional City, or Atlanta, Georgia. He observed that ". . . the findings do not warrant a picture of a homogenous, generalized elite. . . . Nevertheless some actors . . . do have extremely extensive role-scopes."[117] These findings do not unequivocally support stratification theory. But neither do they imply anything but an attenuated pluralism.

The usefulness of a continuous concept of community power is established more firmly at two levels—that of the "leaders" and the "led"—by Presthus' development of operations for estimating the degree of pluralism-elitism in a community. That is, Presthus calculated an "index of elitism," operationally defined as the proportion of commonality of names on the rosters of influentials participating in several decisions. The index has some interesting uses. For example, the index permits a natural-history classification of existing studies, as in Table VI.2.

Such a classification of studies of community power as in Table VI.2, in turn, suggests further steps in the dialectic toward the develop-

**TABLE VI.2 Differences in "Index of Elitism," Population, and Relative Proportion of "Influentials" in Selected Cities**

| *Community* | *Index of Elitism in Percentages* | *Population* | *Proportion of "Influentials," as percentage of Community Size*[a] |
|---|---|---|---|
| New Haven | 6 | >100,000 | 0.2 |
| Madison | 19 | >100,000 | |
| Syracuse | 36 | >100,000 | 0.3 |
| Racine | 29 | 75-100,000 | |
| Kenosha | 52 | 50-75,000 | |
| Green Bay | 11 | 50-75,000 | |
| Riverview | 32 | <10,000 | 0.4 |
| Edgewood | 39 | <10,000 | 0.6 |
| Bennington | 39 | <10,000 | 0.7 |

[a]These are rough calculations derived or estimated roughly from the several original studies.
Source: Based on Robert V. Presthus, *Men At the Top* (New York: Oxford University Press, 1964), p. 95.

ment of increasingly comprehensive empirical research. Presthus himself suggests the following two hypothetical propositions about distributions of community power:

1. that an inverse relation exists between size of city and "degree of elitism"; and
2. that the influential—or power elite, if you will—comprise perhaps one per cent of the total populations, independent of community size.[118]

These hypotheses are fair game for subsequent studies, which could attempt to explain both the "general rule" and the "exceptions" (such as Green Bay and Kenosha in Table VI.2, and also Atlanta with its substantial population and its high index of elitism).[119] Such follow-up studies might conceivably show that while size accounts for much of the variance in patterns of community power, more refined predictions will require the specification of such intervening variables as the degree to which various research units approximate an "organic community" as opposed to a "formal community."[120] And such intervening variables, in turn, require nominal and operational definition, testing, recasting, and extension into increasingly broader theoretical statements, ad infinitum. Presthus' index, that is, contributes to the dynamics of empirical research.

Pluralism-elitism conceived as a continuum then has twin powerful attractions. First, it forces empirically relevant investigation, as demonstrated above. And this is the crucial test of any concept. A concept of elitism and pluralism as sharply differentiated discontinua fails this test. It discourages all but a narrow range of empirically relevant questions.

Second, the reconceptualization promises operational developments that at once further empirical investigation and are tested by it.[121] Thus a concept of power-as-continuum can help generate operations without the self-fulfilling features of reputational and decisional operations. That is, elitists resonably enough chose an operation tapping "general power" that is biased toward isolating a stable pattern of power consistent with stratification theory. Pluralists similarly, if oppositely, tend to choose a decisional operation that emphasizes congenial discontinuities in patterns of power on different decisions in different issue-areas. And never the twain shall meet. As was the case with cohesiveness, conceptual refinement in the study of community power can encourage less self-fulfilling operations.

With similar possible applications, Presthus also developed an "index of pluralism."[122] It is oriented, as it were, toward community "Indians" rather than "chiefs." His operations for the index were based upon:

organizational memberships of individuals; individual participation of various kinds in policy decisions; and participation by private organizations qua organizations in policy development. His findings give no comfort to the traditional pluralist concept. And these findings seem to point up useful differences between the two communities studied by Presthus.

If Presthus' two indexes require the specification of inter-community differences, moreover, there is some hope that researchers can rely on something more than (in Dahl's strong terms) "a mystique with footnotes." Agger, Goldrich, and Swanson, for example, usefully distinguished four types of power structures; consensual mass, competitive mass, consensual elite, and competitive elite. Dichotomizing these two variables generates the four types of power structure: the broad or narrow distribution of political power; and competition or consensus about political ideology. Two variables also generate four types of regimes: high versus low sense of potency by the electorate; and high versus low probability that citizens' efforts to intervene in government actions will be met by illegitimate sanctions.[123] The four types of regimes are: developed democracy (high–low); underdeveloped democracy (low–low); guided democracy (high–high); and oligarchy (low–high). Figure VI.2 depicts the implicit $4 \times 4$ matrix of these four variables.

Although conceptual and operational problems abound, the $4 \times 4$

TYPES OF REGIMES

| TYPES OF POWER STRUCTURES | (1) Developed Democracy | (2) Underdeveloped Democracy | (3) Guided Democracy | (4) Oligarchy |
|---|---|---|---|---|
| (A) Consensual Mass | | | | |
| (B) Competitive Mass | | | | |
| (C) Consensual Elite | | | | |
| (D) Competitive Elite | | | | |

FIGURE VI.2 A Paradigm of Community Types Relevant to Distributions of Power. (Based upon Robert E. Agger, Daniel Goldrich, and Bert E. Swanson, *The Rulers and the Ruled* (New York: Wiley, 1964), pp. 69–90.)

approach to community power has much to recommend it initially. Consider but two advantages. First, the approach breaks out of the narrow pluralist-elitist debate, which is posed in awkward either-or terms. Second, the approach encourages longitudinal study, that is, the study of communities as they develop over time. Indeed, some very interesting analysis was encouraged by the longitudinal thrust of the 4 × 4 matrix. More generally, static or correlational studies have their real value. But the development of empirical theory basically rests upon its ability to predict dynamically as well as to describe episodically. As a further attraction, focusing on the change-process requires the nominal and operational specification of dimensions necessary to account for the dynamics of change. "Snapshot" analyses do not so pointedly direct attention to these dimensions.

All this implies significant advantages over both early pluralist and stratification models. Stratification theory could hardly have been less encouraging to longitudinal studies, for example, although the Lynds did return to Middletown. Early pluralist studies improved on this record, and particularly in Dahl's major study. Although pluralists did acknowledge change in patterns of community power, however, it was only in the direction of pluralism and particularly as cities grew in size.[124] Relatively bold summary about the 4 × 4 approach seems appropriate, therefore. As Kellstedt concluded:[125] "Such a classification of political systems is a major step beyond the elitist and pluralist alternatives usually advanced by community power researches."

In addition to conceptually oriented advances, recent studies have contributed considerable operational clarification. The reputational and decisional approaches to community power have received particularly useful attention, for example. Adherents of the one operational approach or the other have tended to react strongly and negatively to the other; and some still count themselves definitely in one camp or the other.[126] An integrative consensus seems to be emerging, however. Thus Jennings reports that Hunter's reputational approach is "neither so infallible as its supporters claim nor so misleading as its attackers insist."[127] And Presthus, despite a greater initial faith in the decisional operation, concluded that the "two methods are better conceived as mutually supportive means of ascertaining power."[128]

A sketch of the complementary strengths and weaknesses of the two major operational approaches to community power suggests the nature of the emerging consensus. Among other operational consequences, for example, Presthus found that the decisional approach overweighted the formal positions of individuals. These individuals may or may not actually influence public policy. They may have only been spokesmen or "leg men" for groups or individuals which they served as "weak representatives."[129] On the other hand, reputational operations face a problem familiar in the analysis of sociometric choices in small-group analysis. Sociometric choices may have bases that are affective and/or instrumental.[130] Some of Presthus' respondents named persons they "would like to work with," for example, as opposed to those with "real influence to get the job done."[131] The task for operational clarification is thus set, and the experience in small-group analysis suggests both the difficulty and the value of such a posing of operational issues.

Operationally, also, recent research attempts to be more sensitive to community power in its group or institutional aspects. Freeman illustrates this hard-won and difficult-to-act-upon sensitivity from direct research experience in these terms:

> For example, when John Jones is named as a top leader, he may not be named as John Jones, participant in public affairs, but as John Jones, head of the Ace Corporation, *and that the corporation* is active in the resolution of community issues. In other words, the individual would not be the proper unit of study.[132]

Similar sensitivity to group phenomena is similarly crucial in interpreting the findings of pluralists and stratificationists alike, and that sensitivity is commonly lacking. The proof of the pluralist position hinges on two conditions, for example: that total commonality does not exist on the rosters of influentials in several issue-areas; and that influentials in the several issue-areas do not comprise a group or an integrated set of groups. The proof of the second condition—in Dahl's version of the pluralist approach as in others—is basically to note that if the influentials in the several issue-areas in fact were members of an integrated group, that fact would have become patent to pluralist investigators.[133] Maybe yes, and maybe no. Dahl's research design does not seek group-level data, and consequently "maybe no" seems the better guess. Thus the non-group orientation of the design is reflected variously. For example, Dahl explains that: "Of the fifty different [influential] actors, fifteen were agencies, groups, or corporations; they acted in situations *where it was impossible to ascribe* the initiation or veto of policy to a particular person."[134] Group analysis, derivatively, seems a residual category. More directly, Dahl notes that ". . . leaders in different issue-areas do not seem drawn from a single homogeneous stratum of the community."[135] There is multiple irony in these words. First, the fact that influentials isolated by Dahl were Yankee, Irish, Italian, Jewish—and thus were said not to be "drawn from a single homogeneous stratum"—creates only the very barest presumption that they were not members of an integrated group. Second, Dahl interestingly borrows his explanatory terminology from stratification theory. Thus consorting with the conceptual enemy does not settle matters, for a behavioral group need not be drawn from a "homogeneous stratum."

These conceptual and operational advances sketch successful approaches to the phenomenal area of community power, and disciplinary successes at that. As Kellstedt concluded: "Should it not be considered a victory ... that political scientists are now using and refining techniques that were formerly the almost exclusive bailiwick of sociologists?"[136]

## NOTES

1. Charles W. Merriam, *Political Power* (New York: McGraw-Hill, 1934), and *Systematic Politics* (Chicago: University of Chicago Press, 1945).

2. Harold D. Lasswell, *Politics: The Study of Who Gets What, When, How* (New York: McGraw-Hill, 1936); and with Abraham Kaplan, *Power and Society* (New Haven, Conn.: Yale University Press, 1950).

3. James G. March developed his approach to power in a number of valuable articles, including "Influence Measurement in Experimental and Semi-Experimental Groups," *Sociometry,* 19 (March, 1956), 260–71.

4. Robert A. Dahl, *Who Governs?* (New Haven, Conn.: Yale University Press, 1961).

5. Robert Presthus, *Men at the Top* (New York: Oxford University Press, 1964).

6. We shall neglect, for example, the sizable literature on various political and business elites. See Harold D. Lasswell, et al., *The Comparative Study of Elites* (Stanford, Calif.: Stanford University Press, 1952).

7. Martin Landau, "The Concept of Decision-Making in the 'Field' of Public Administration," in Sidney Mailick and Edward H. Van Ness (eds.), *Concepts and Issues in Administrative Behavior* (Englewood Cliffs, N.J.: Prentice-Hall, 1962), pp. 1–2.

8. For example Nelson Polsby retrospectively framed in these revealing terms the difficulties he faced in his review study *Community Power and Political Theory* (New Haven, Conn.: Yale University Press, 1963), p. 1: "These problems did not come about because the works I chose to study failed to agree among themselves. The major difficulty was, rather, to account for the extraordinary unanimity that scholars displayed in upholding propositions . . . which . . . seemed quite wrong."

9. *Ibid.,* p. 1.

10. William Lloyd Warner, et al., *Democracy in Jonesville* (New York: Harper, 1949), p. xviii.

11. Polsby, *Community Power and Political Theory.*

12. *Ibid.,* pp. 3–13, lists a wide range of such studies.

13. The specific economic indicators utilized have been diverse. They include such indicators as: occupation and patterns of consumption.

14. Polsby, *Community Power and Political Theory,* pp. 7–14.

15. *Ibid.,* p. 14.

16. *Ibid.,* p. 15.

17. The emphasis appears, for example, in Robert and Helen Lynd, *Middletown in Transition* (New York: Harcourt, Brace, 1937), pp. 41, 367.

18. Among these many factors that contributed to the bias of stratification theory, the enormous impact of Marxism must be accorded a primary place. One might also approach stratification theory from other standpoints, with much the same results as those to be unfolded in this chapter. For example, stratification theory can be looked upon as a product of its underlying concept of power as an attribute of social structure. This concept, in turn, could be shown to affect the methodology of stratificationists and also their findings.

19. Suzanne K. Langer, *Philosophy in a New Key* (New York: New American Library, 1948), p. 1.

20. Ernest A. T. Barth and Baha Abu-Laban, "Power Structure and the Negro Subcommunity," *American Sociological Review,* 24 (February, 1959), 76.

21. *Ibid.,* pp. 71, 76.

22. *Ibid.,* p. 69.

23. Robert A. Dahl, "A Critique of the Ruling Elite Model," *American Political Science Review,* 52 (June, 1958), 463.

24. *Ibid.,* p. 465.

25. Polsby, *Community Power and Political Theory,* pp. 67–68.

26. *Ibid.*

27. Our conclusion is also supported, for example, by Raymond E. Wolfinger, "Reputation and Reality in the Study of Community Power," *American Sociological Review,* 25 (October, 1960), 636–44. More broadly, but relatedly, some have argued persuasively that elitist formulations basically are ideological critiques of Marxist Socialism and De-

mocracy and consequently should not be approached as an empirical theory. In this sense, they are arguments against rather than descriptions of. For example, see T. B. Bottomore, *Elites and Society* (New York: Basic Books, 1964).

28. Thus it is possible that the propositions were closer to reality during the Great Depression, when stratification theory began emerging.

29. Polsby, *Community Power and Political Theory,* pp. 110–11.

30. Floyd Hunter, *Community Power Structure* (Chapel Hill: University of North Carolina Press, 1953), p. 6.

31. *Ibid.*

32. *Ibid.,* pp. 2–3.

33. *Ibid.,* p. 6.

34. Herbert Kaufman and Victor Jones, "The Mystery of Power," *Public Administration Review,* 14 (Summer, 1954), 208.

35. Hunter, *op. cit.,* p. 62.

36. *Ibid.*

37. A wide range of other possibilities is detailed in Chapter II. For example, the concept in this case might not correspond to a dimension of reality. Or its operational definition might be invalid or unreliable.

38. Hunter, *op. cit.,* p. 62.

39. *Ibid.,* p. 61.

40. E.g., Wolfinger, *op. cit.;* and Nelson Polsby, "Three Problems in the Analysis of Community Power," *American Sociological Review,* 24 (1959), 796–803.

41. Kaufman and Jones, *op. cit.,* p. 208.

42. Polsby, "Three Problems in the Analysis of Community Power," p. 797.

43. In a strict sense, of course, no phenomena are ever studied "directly." Chapter II develops the point in some of its diversity. In any case, the question is not whether the approach is "direct" or "indirect." Rather, *the* test is the ability to make accurate predictions about reality.

44. Hunter, *op. cit.,* p. 62.

45. *Ibid.,* pp. 70–71, 77.

46. *Ibid.,* p. 62.

47. The technique has been used with advantage, for example, in small-group analysis to determine the communality between several rosters of status ranks of the same individuals on several criteria.

48. Hunter, *op. cit.,* p. 63.

49. *Ibid.,* pp. 67–68.

50. This conclusion rests upon a comparison of Table 2 on p. 63 and Table 3 on p. 67 in Hunter. Our conclusion is tentative, for the treatment is very unclear.

51. Paul F. Lazarsfeld, Bernard Berelson, and Hazel Gaudet, *The People's Choice* (New York: Duell, Sloan, and Pearce, 1944).

52. William F. Whyte, "Small Groups and Large Organizations," in John H. Rohrer and Muzafer Sherif (eds.), *Social Psychology at the Crossroads* (New York: Harper, 1951), p. 311.

53. *Op. cit.*

54. The call was loud and clear, for example, in *Research Frontiers in Politics and Government,* 1955 Brookings Lectures (Washington, D.C.: Brookings Institution, 1955).

55. Dahl, "A Critique of the Ruling Elite Model," p. 467.

56. Polsby, *Community Power and Political Theory,* p. 113.

57. Wallace Sayre and Herbert Kaufman, *Governing New York City* (New York: Norton, 1965).

58. Herbert Kaufman, "Metropolitan Leadership: The Snark of the Social Sciences," p. 5. Paper presented at Social Science Research Council Conference on Metropolitan Leadership, Evanston, Ill., April, 1960.

59. Dahl, "A Critique of the Ruling Elite Model," p. 466.

60. *Ibid.,* p. 465.

61. Hunter, *op. cit.,* pp. 6–7.

62. Polsby, *Community Power and Political Theory,* pp. 115–16.

63. *Ibid.,* p. 118.

64. Robert T. Golembiewski, *The Small Group: An Analysis of Research Concepts and Operations* (Chicago: University of Chicago Press, 1962), pp. 117–44.

65. Dahl, *Who Governs?,* p. 131.

66. *Ibid.,* pp. 65–75, for example.

67. *Ibid.,* p. 182.

68. *Ibid.,* p. 65.

69. "Social Notables" were defined operationally by appearance on a certain list that included residents of the "great-

er New Haven area." We are not told, but it is very likely that many (most?) Social Notables lived outside of New Haven proper. Thus their participation in (for example) city partisan activities would be limited by residence requirements and the like. And "everyone who is anyone" in New Haven sends their children to private schools. Therefore, even the Social Notables who lived in the city would be less likely to participate in matters relating to public education.

70. Dahl, for example, usually implies that complete or very substantial commonality of individuals on lists of influentials in various issue-areas is required.

71. Aaron Wildavsky, *Leadership in a Small Town* (Totowa, N.J.: Bedminster Press, 1964), p. 322.

72. *Ibid.*, p. 340.

73. Hunter, *op. cit.*, pp. 95–96.

74. Thomas Anton, Letter to the Editor, *Administrative Science Quarterly*, 7 (May, 1963), 262–63.

75. Harry S. Scoble, book review, *Administrative Science Quarterly*, 9 (December, 1964), 314–315.

76. Peter Bachrach and Morton S. Baratz, "Two Faces of Power," *American Political Science Review*, 51 (December, 1962), 947–52. See also Charles A. McCoy and John Playford (eds.), *A Political Politics: A Critique of Behavioralism* (New York: Crowell, 1967), p. 108.

77. See Chapter V above.

78. Students such as Willmoore Kendall also have argued that our institutions are so oriented as to organize such issues as race out of politics.

79. E. E. Schattschneider, *The Semi-Sovereign People* (New York: Holt, Rinehart & Winston, 1960), p. 71.

80. A classic demonstration is provided by Ferenc Merei, "Group Leadership and Institutionalization," *Human Relations*, 2 (January, 1949), especially 23–35.

81. Scoble, *op. cit.*, pp. 314–15.

82. Dahl, *Who Governs?*, pp. 332–33.

83. Lyman Kellstedt, "Atlanta to 'Oretown–Identifying Community Elites," *Public Administration Review*, 25 (June, 1965), 163.

84. The proof of this point is the major burden of Golembiewski, *The Small Group*.

85. Robert E. Agger, Daniel Goldrich, and Bert E. Swanson, *The Rulers and the Ruled* (New York: Wiley, 1964), pp. 40–51. The value of differentiation is strongly suggested by such early microscopic work on public decision-making as that of Morris Davis, "Aspects of Detroit's Decisional Profile," *Administrative Science Quarterly*, 12 (September, 1967), 209–24. More broadly, the usefulness of differentiating phases in decision-making is massively demonstrated in James O. Robinson and A. Roger Majik, "The Theory of Decision-Making," in James C. Charlesworth (ed.), *Contemporary Political Analysis* (New York: Free Press, 1967), pp. 176–79.

86. The bias is clear in Dahl's lists of specific influential actors, which do not differentiate functions of leadership or roles of leadership.

87. Golembiewski, *The Small Group*, especially pp. 128–44.

88. Thomas Anton, "Power, Pluralism, and Local Politics," *Administrative Science Quarterly*, 7 (March, 1963), 444.

89. Robert A. Dahl, Letters to the Editor, *Administrative Science Quarterly*, 8 (December, 1963), 251–52.

90. Robert T. Golembiewski, "Small Groups and Large Organizations," in James G. March (ed.), *Handbook of Organizations* (Chicago: Rand McNally, 1965), pp. 131–33.

91. Golembiewski, *The Small Group*, especially pp. 34–68.

92. *Ibid.*, especially pp. 104–17.

93. See the sources cited in footnote 94 in Anton, "Power, Pluralism, and Local Politics," p. 451.

94. *Ibid.*, p. 456.

95. Dahl, "Letters to the Editor," pp. 254–55.

96. Dahl, "A Critique of the Ruling Elite Model," p. 466.

97. Hunter, *op. cit.*, pp. 94–97.

98. Anton, "Power, Pluralism, and Local Politics," p. 430.

99. Robert A. Dahl, "The Concept of Power," *Behavioral Science*, 2 (July, 1957), 202.

100. Presthus, *Men at the Top*, p. 10.

101. *Ibid.*, p. 40.
102. Dahl, *Who Governs?*, p. 106.
103. *Ibid.*, p. 159.
104. *Ibid.*, p. 106.
105. *Ibid.*, p. 159.
106. *Ibid.*, p. 115.
107. *Ibid.*, p. 151.
108. *Ibid.*, p. 106.
109. *Ibid.*, p. 101.
110. Christian Bay, "Politics and Pseudopolitics: A Critical Evaluation of Some Behavioral Literature," *American Political Science Review*, 59 (March 1965), 39–40.
111. L. Freeman, et al., *Local Community Leadership* (Syracuse, N. Y.: University College, 1960), p. 26.
112. Jack L. Walker, "A Critique of the Elitist Theory of Democracy," *American Political Science Review*, 60 (June, 1966), 289–90.
113. This is Robert A. Dahl's position in response to Walker's classification of the former as a "democratic elitist." "Further Reflections on 'The Elitist Theory of Democracy,'" *American Political Science Review*, 60 (June, 1966), 301.
114. Peter Bachrach, *The Theory of Democratic Elitism: A Critique* (Boston: Little, Brown, 1967).
115. See, for example, the several sources cited in Presthus, *Men at the Top*, pp. 42–43, fn. 22.
116. Pluralists seem intent on finding such evidence everywhere. Thus Aaron Wildavsky, *Leadership in a Small Town*, p. 346, notes that: "The various reputation and stratification studies . . . do come up with different conclusions. But the evidence presented in them suggests that the communities . . . were probably pluralist." Only two pages are devoted to supporting this broad conclusion.
117. Kent Jennings, *Community Influentials* (New York: The Free Press of Glencoe, 1964), p. 105. A similar lack of conceptual rigidity also characterizes such research designs as that of William V. D'Antonio and William H. Form, *Influentials in Two Border Cities* (South Bend, Ind.: University of Notre Dame Press, 1965), pp. 14–16.
118. Presthus, *Men at the Top*, p. 95.
119. We infer a high index from Hunter's data.
120. Presthus, *Men at the Top*, pp. 45–46.
121. Essentially, it is just such effort that was prescribed some years ago as necessary in the study of community power by Morris Janowitz, "Community Power and 'Policy Science,'" *Public Opinion Quarterly*, 26 (Fall, 1962), 398–410.
122. Presthus, *Men at the Top*, Chapter 3.
123. Agger, Goldrich, and Swanson, *op. cit.*
124. Presthus, *Men at the Top*.
125. Kellstedt, *op. cit.*, p. 166.
126. E.g., Wildavsky, *op. cit.*
127. Jennings, *op. cit.*, p. 164.
128. Presthus, *Men at the Top*, p. 59.
129. *Ibid.*, p. 413.
130. Golembiewski, *The Small Group*.
131. Presthus, *Men at the Top*, pp. 59–68.
132. Quoted in *ibid.*, p. 424.
133. Dahl, *Who Governs?*, p. 62.
134. *Ibid.*, pp. 182–83.
135. *Ibid.*, p. 183.
136. Kellstedt, *op. cit.*, p. 163.

# vii

# The Wages of Methodological Inelegance Is Circularity, III: Simon's "Decision-Making" as Intent and Content

Any observation involves looking at phenomena through a knothole, as it were. Epigramatically, in order to see any of the game one must pay the price of missing some of the action. This is certainly the case with our methodological knothole for looking at scholarly contributions in various areas. What we miss is missed painfully: that is, for example, we cannot dwell upon the valuable insights in work that might have significant methodological inadequacies.

We can avoid being common scolds, then, only as what we have "seen" makes bearable the costs of our narrow focus. And in the two preceding chapters we have seen significant variations on the general theme of this part of our investigations: that methodological inelegance in Political Science as in all other fields is paid for in terms of circular discovery-neglect-rediscovery sequences that re-cycle more than they build cumulatively. That is, the group approach to politics and the study of community power both derived from unpretentious methodological backgrounds. They did differ, however, in another significant respect. The study of the group is still locked in tightly to its history of circular re-cycling, but present approaches to community power seem to have broken out of the circularity that earlier characterized research in the area.

Decision-making provides still another and more complex variation on the circularity theme. And again this chapter will pay the price of neglecting significant features of relevant research because of its methodological orientation. And again, the price will be worth the return, for the emphasis below on decision-making will differ from that in the preceding two chapters in several significant senses. First, decision-making historically has been the most methodologically concerned of the three approaches. Indeed, much of its modern history is rooted in

Herbert Simon's *Administrative Behavior*, which clearly advertised its grounding in methodological issues, and which stands as one of the most cited books of recent memory. These two data, in fact, explain the focus in this book on Simon's seminal contribution. Of course, Simon has not remained stock-still over the years. But the following analysis is appropriate for the body of his work on the behavioral (as sharply distinguished from the mathematical) aspects of management.[1] In addition, significant withdrawals from his early position in *Administrative Behavior* will be emphasized.

Second, various areas of decision-making have seen significant additions to the store of human knowledge about administration. But these successes do not establish the adequacy of Simon's methodological guidelines. Hence our methodological focus below. Analytical re-cycling, does not characterize the whole of decision-making as an area of study. Breakthroughs after World War II in computational and mathematical-statistical approaches relevant to decision-making, for example, have been breathtaking.[2] *Administrative Behavior* postdated many of these developments, but it pays little attention to any of them. Indeed, the Introduction to the 1957 re-issue of that volume deliberately sets itself apart[3] from a (perhaps, *the*) major postwar advance in the application of mathematical and proto-mathematical models and techniques.[4] Decision-making also has served as a focus for much valuable work in business and public administration. The contemporary slew of case studies, for example, falls in this category. Case studies have great value, to be sure, but the case literature has hardly been preoccupied with methodological questions.[5] Indeed, at best, they have used *Administrative Behavior* to give a surface legitimacy to their efforts.

Third, major developments by Simon himself of his original model tend to destroy or replace major elements of that model. This is true, for example, of the contemporary emphasis on "satisficing versus maximizing," as well as of the current disenchantment about the possibility of using means-ends analysis at more than allegorical levels. This history suggests the value of a methodological overview of Simon's contribution.

The twin foci here for the methodological review of the decision-making schema are "intent" and "content." By way of preview, Simon's intent was the global one of providing new direction and vocabulary for approaching administrative study. That Simon achieved his intention in significant ways could hardly be in doubt. Massive bibliographies testify to the incredible industry devoted to manifold aspects of decision-making,[6] and much of that industry either has been supplied by Simon[7] or was in some measure motivated by his seminal contribution. Moreover, the decision-making approach has significantly influenced this diverse range of disciplines and research areas: Public Administration; international relations;[8] community power, as in the issue-orientation of a Dahl; and diverse mathematical and statistical specialties.[9] Dill appropriately notes that: "Decision-making is one of the major functions that administrators (or managers or executives) perform. It is accepted by many, in fact, as *the* central activity in management and as a key subject for attention in management training."[10]

The approach to *Administrative Behavior* as "intent" may be summarized in a revealing way. Even his harshest critics acknowledge Simon's important role—if they usually accord primacy to Chester I. Barnard—in establishing the centrality of decision-making as a focus for the study of administration. For example, Storing allows that:

> The most significant recent contributions to the study of administration have undoubtedly been made by Herbert A. Simon. He was one of the first to popularize the vocabulary of decision-making which, it is scarcely an exaggeration to say, is the native tongue of a growing body of students. If the approach to administrative problems which this vocabulary is intended to facilitate has not yet replaced the traditional one, it seems likely to dominate the field for many years.[11]

The position here, in addition, is that in crucial senses Simon's decision-making schema did not realize its "intent" because of significant problems with its methodological "content." Two variations of our orientation can be distinguished here briefly. One variation emphasizes that while (and perhaps, because) it strives so hard to achieve its comprehensive intent, the content of Simon's approach is general and unspecific and diffuse. Thus William Gore—certainly no unreconstructed critic of Simon, he—suggests the difficulties with the overly wide sweep of the typical formulation of the decision-making approach. To this effect, for example, he notes that: "Research indicates that decision-making is an ubiquitous concept, referring variously to change, to a choice, to a climate of opinion, to a condition of agreement, to communication, or to a vaguely-felt state of affairs which—like ice—melts in the hands of anyone who stops to examine it."[12] A second variation of decision-making as "content" goes even further. It grants something to *Administrative Behavior,* but not much. This variation agrees only with one of Simon's own evaluations of the volume. "I suppose that I might claim some sort of prophetic gift," he noted, "in having incorporated in the title and subtitle three of the currently most fashionable words in social science—'behavior,' 'decision-making,' and 'organization.' "[13]

Our complex approach to *Administrative Behavior* as intent and content deals only with the methodological issues raised but not resolved by the volume. Our rationale is straightforward. First, that volume is a major historical source of the emphasis upon decision-making, and the usefulness of its methodological dicta consequently assumes enormous significance.

Second, the present methodological emphasis will complement earlier notices of the problems generic to uses of decision-making. The issue of "non-decisions," for example, was raised in the chapter on community power. Other problems with decision-making as an analytical focus will be raised later in the context of specific substantive areas of Political Science. The methodological discussion here should add depth to these other issues-in-context, both past and future.

Third, we shall eschew textual analysis here. That job has already been done in exhaustive fashion.[14] Moreover, Simon's forte is not careful analytical development.

Fourth, despite many major shifts in his opinion,[15] Simon has allowed the basic methodology of *Administrative Behavior* to stand. Thus he has noted that he had enough of the methodological debate about "facts and values in decision-making" which has been emphasized "all out of proportion to its importance in the book as a whole." But a central chapter on the issue stands without change in a re-issue of the volume, and its emphasis is still acknowledged in context "to be a very fundamental one."[16]

## I. ADMINISTRATIVE BEHAVIOR AS INTENT: DEFINING A "CENTER" FOR THE DISCIPLINE OF PUBLIC ADMINISTRATION

The sweep of *Administrative Behavior* qua intent might be illustrated variously, but we shall do the expedient thing and concentrate on the volume's re-definition of the scope of Public Administration. No complex supporting rationale will be supplied. The matter has a patent relevance for all of Political Science, however, as will be demonstrated. The argument has seldom been made at length, in part because Simon almost casually tosses off his re-definition of the scope of Public Administration. Finally, Landau has developed a detailed argument of the nature and value of Simon's effort at re-definition.[17] Landau's argument will be relied on heavily in this section, although neither the insight about the disciplinary implications of Simon's position[18] nor a positive evaluation of that position[19] is unique to Landau.

Simon's effort at re-defining the scope of Public Administration came as a consequence of a concern that the disciplinary area, "that lusty young giant of a decade ago" in Landau's words, "may now 'evaporate' as a field."[20] The prime difficulty was widely perceived as the lack of an organizing focus for research. Its major consequences are a lack of coherence and a lack of cumulative relevance. If a healthy discipline "has a solid center as well as an active circumference," following Waldo, the state of Public Administration was disturbing. "I have a nagging worry of late," Waldo confessed, "a fear that all is not as healthy as it should be at the center of the discipline."[21]

Simon's *Administrative Behavior* in a major sense was a sharp reaction to the spiraling out from definiteness to vagueness of the scope of Public Administration. But the reaction was too late and too little. That spiraling out predated Simon's emergence as an influential in Political Science; and it continued after Simon—not unrelatedly—began to seek his vision of the good research life in the applied social sciences under the organization tent of Industrial Administration. Simon's volume, that is, attempted to stop the progression of Public Administration through four major stages that led to the contemporary condition. The four stages differed both in scope and content, and sometimes radically so. They are:

1. The *analytic* distinction of "politics" from "administration," interpreted as ideal categories or functions of governance;
2. The *concrete* distinction of "politics" from "administration," interpreted as having a real locus in the legislative and executive and in the "neutral civil service," respectively;[22]
3. The internal differentiation and analysis of the components of "administration," based upon the concrete distinction of "politics" and "administration,"[23] as represented by such efforts as early work in "human relations" on the behavioral side and scientific management on the mechanical;
4. The orientation toward "public policy," in which "politics" and "administration" are said to commingle in the real world, which commingling has a real locus in the executive and in the civil service.[24]

The definition of Public Administration's disciplinary province progressively became less precise as the discipline moved historically through these four major stages. The point may be approached by defining Phase 1 in some detail to serve as our bench mark. Frank Goodnow's *Politics and Administration* (New York: Macmillan, 1900) provides our basic source. The analytical province of Public Administration is clear in Phase 1, although the real locus of the appropriate phenomena is not specified. That is, wherever they occur, the phenomena of concern in Public Administration are defined as those activities of governance that possess "internal" criteria of correctness. In Goodnow's words, these activities include "semi-scientific, quasi-judicial and quasi-business or commercial activity." These activities have "little if any influence on the [political] expression of the true state will," and consequently require little if any "external" control as (for example) by representative legislatures. "External" means of control are appropriate only when no "internal" criteria of success exist, that is, when some measure of the consensus about the degree of correctness must perforce suffice.

Goodnow's distinction is analytically clear, even though students respecting it still face the universal problem of determining which specific phenomena fall within that analytical province. That is, Administration might be found anywhere and everywhere. And anywhere and everywhere students of Public Administration would seek out their phenomena and cope with them: in the executive or legislative or judicial branches; at state or local or federal levels; in matters both great and small. Not that all real loci were equally likely to produce phenomena of Politics or of Administration. Goodnow's obscure terminology sometimes gets in the way of his argument on the matter of concrete locus. But if we give him the benefit of an inept usage or two, he consistently conceives of the three branches of federal government as having different loadings of Politics and Administration. The legislative branch qua concrete locus is mostly Politics, for example; and the lower bureaucratic levels are largely Administration. Whatever the loading in a real locus, however, Public Administration is concerned with the Administration component wherever it appears.

Because it was analytically clear, Goodnow's two concepts permitted easy differentiation of the provinces of Public Administration and Political Science. Their focus, that is, was on different classes of behaviors. As Landau noted, Goodnow's two major distinctions "referred to a different class of behavior and each presented a different set of problems." The total operations of government, however, cannot be assigned completely to different agencies of government which perform them. Landau put the matter in these terms: ". . . the empirical processes of politics were far too complex to be discharged by any single governmental body and, similarly, administrative functions could not be deemed exclusive to any specific agency."[25]

Goodnow's analytical distinction is a difficult one with which to live, a conclusion irrefutably supported by the plain fact that few scholars (including Goodnow) ever did so consistently. The magnitude of these difficulties may be indicated economically. For example, any discipline with a "generalist" orientation to its real locus faces acute practical difficulties. And it is just such a generalist orientation which Goodnow urged for Public Administration. In terms of their real locus, most disciplines are "specialist"-oriented. Goodnow's definition of Public Administration, consequently, would require that students of administration confront specialists in (for example) legislatures in a competition to claim the latter's real locus. This implies a simple thing: a subtle analytical distinction is no match for a distinction based on concrete locus, for a variety of reasons. In addition, Goodnow's distinction certainly would cut off students of Public Administration from significant issues of governance. Some students identified with Public Administration—particularly given its intimate connections with Political Science—would resist thus being separated from phenomena of learned concern to them. Analytical distinctions are fragile barriers indeed against such resistance. This is an acute practical consideration, even though the purpose of any analytical distinction is to cut off some phenomenal areas from others.

Such perceived difficulties set the consensus in Public Administration moving, and that movement did not stop until the field was defined so as to swallow virtually the whole of Political Science. Of course, this did not happen in one fell swoop. But it happened quickly. The eyes of students of Public Administration were bigger than their stomachs, and these were bullish days indeed among disciplinary adherents. This characterization helps us understand important components of the disciplinary history which we will summarize in thumbnail fashion: why ambitions were so expansive; why the pace of pushing forward the scope of the discipline was so rapid; and why a kind of dyspepsia persists after scholars forced their specialty to attempt to swallow too much too quickly.

Phase 2 of the moving consensus about the boundaries of Public Administration is at once definite about the locus of relevant phenomena and indiscriminate about its focus. Thus the locus of Public Administration is restricted to the executive and the governmental bureaucracy. But within that real locus the discipline knows no analytical limits in Phase 2. Everything is its meat. Administrative case-law and administrative behavior, for example, are put cheek by jowl at a common trough in Phase 2. In contrast, Phase 1 has a sharp analytical focus, but its locus is unspecified.

The difficulties with Phase 2 are manifold and significant, both practically and conceptually. First, a real locus is given to the analytical distinction between Politics and Administration. This left proponents of this definition of the field with no defense against the correct charge—and it was leveled time after interminable time—that "things are not that way" within the executive and its bureaucracy. That Politics and Administration in fact were really intermixed in this real locus thus became a datum to be "discovered" in the post-World War II period. Second, Phase 2 cuts off the field of specialization from relevant phenomena in other real loci. The rapidly obsolescing—but still very real—isolation of Business Administration from Public Administration stands as perhaps the most unfortunate of the products of Phase 2's defining the discipline in terms of a specific locus. This left many scholars out of intimate touch with the revolutionary developments that have taken place of late in our many schools of business.[26] Third, in its very emphasis upon locus rather than focus, Phase 2 assumes that where phenomena occur is more significant than what the phenomena are. This seems a procrustean basis for differentiation.

The gross magnitude of the disciplinary expanionist tendencies became manifest in Phase 3, in a negative sort of way. In sum, Phase 3 had a short reign as king-of-the-mountain, although it was glorious while it lasted. Both the briefness and the brilliance of Phase 3 had a similar root: the narrow scope of the definition of the area of concern. Indeed, Phase 3 may be characterized as concerned largely with the "internal" analysis of the components of Administration. As such, Phase 3 was sharply honed. It gave Goodnow's basic distinction a concrete locus; and it dealt with but a narrow spectrum of phenomena within its locus.

Phase 3's simultaneous restriction of locus and narrowing of focus provoked mixed reactions. On the one hand, when Gulick proposed his famous mnemonic word POSDCORB[27] derived from the first letters of purported administrative functions, Public Administration was by consensus at the top of the heap in terms of competence in handling the problems of large-scale organizations. A rash of published and unpublished work spanning the period between the Great Depression and World War II established this superiority definitely, for example, over what was going on in business administration.[28] One of the most lasting monuments of Phase 3, in this sense, is Gulick and Urwick's *Papers on the Science of Administration.*[29] Some of the work in this symposium was so much fancy embroidery, but the foundations have withstood the test of time. Early work on human relations also was part of Phase 3's behaviorally-oriented work, as was the more established and technically-oriented "scientific management" that had such a major impact on Public Administration between the two World Wars.

Success in the limited disciplinary area prescribed by Phase 3 proved no match for the allures of a far broader scope for Public Administration. In part, this was due to a common feeling among students that they had "gone about as far as they could go" with Phase 3. The senses in which this work was merely a solid introduction for what could be done became clear only in the late fifties, and then largely outside of Public Administration. That is, guardianship of Phase 3 passed essentially into the hands of researchers in our numerous schools of business and departments of industrial administration, where fantastic advances have been made in mathematical and behavioral extensions of Administration differentiated "internally." Public Administration—which started it all—became largely a bastard child at a family outing featuring a feast of managerial research. An increasing number of students trained in Political Science and Public Administration, but with particular interests in administration, did the reasonable if difficult thing.

Rather than running out of track in exploiting "internal" administration, however, students chafed at the narrow confines of Phase 3. And perhaps the state of Political Science—as then a very junior member of the social sciences, still professionally delicate, and threatened by the secession of such fields as Public Administration and International Relations[29a]—placed a premium on the solidarity implied in a congruent definition of the scope of Political Science and Public Administration. Consensus moved rapidly to Phase 4, whatever the explanation, to what is generally called the *public policy approach.* The emphasis can be dated accurately enough as a post-World War II phenomenon.[30]

Students of Public Administration may have made a gross mistake in leaving the narrow definition of their field in Phase 3. But at least they made that mistake almost unanimously; they made it in high spirits and in delicious awareness of their past successes; and their re-definition of their field was consistent with their training and affiliations in Political Science. The public-policy approach of Phase 4 builds around variations on this theme: ". . . as a study, public administration examines every aspect of government's efforts to discharge the laws and to give effect to public policy. . . ."[31] There is no mistaking the change, certainly. In surveying changes in the concepts of the scope of the field of Public Administration, for example, Landau concludes that ". . . the sharpest change to be seen, of course, [is] between the definitions of the 1930's and those of the 1950's."[32] Indeed, except for trans-disciplinary ambitions, Phase 4 is the end of the line. Landau put the point sharply: "The field of public administration is left with an imprecise and shifting base, indistinguishable from political science. [In Phase 4], public administration is neither a subfield of political science, nor does it comprehend it; it simply becomes a synonym."[33]

Like most revolutions, however, the public-policy approach had roots firmly (if unconsciously) in the past. All limits of real locus and analytical focus were swept aside by some of the more exuberant versions of Phase 4's definition of the scope of the discipline, that is. In most cases, however, parallelisms with Phases 2 and 3 seem clear. Thus both orthodoxy and neo-orthodoxy emphasize the same real locus—the executive as an institution. And both distinguish internal (administrative) and external (political) areas within the executive, although public policyers argue that if Politics and Administration really are separable in any real locus, it is only at lower bureaucratic levels than most orthodox adherents assumed.[34] Public policy advocates rushed into the future, as it were, with both feet solidly planted in the past.

Disciplinary ambition had its clear costs, in any case. Landau stresses that the public-policy definition of the scope of Public Administration "challenges the integrity of the 'field.'" The "rigidities of the politics-administration dichotomy" needed correction, he observed, but the public policyers provided the correction only by defining away the problem. Their definition of scope, Landau continues, is "so extensive as to provide little meaning." Indeed, he notes, the public policyers "make it virtually impossible to specify an area of [governmental] activity that cannot be considered within [their] scope." The public-policy re-definition of the field, that is, fails a primary test: it does not designate clearly the phenomenal field of interest, and its locus is as wide as all Political Science. Landau pushes the point even farther. "In the effort to define the field," he concludes, "the field evaporates."[35]

Recent disciplinary history provides ample support for Landau's position. With but a scattering of notable exceptions that seek to define scope and method for Public Administration,[36] the matter tends to be shrugged off. Consider Mosher's response to these central questions: Is Public Administration a field? Is Public Administration a discipline? Mosher clearly carried the public-policy banner into battle, although he ostensibly refrained from the definitional fray:

> Public administration cannot debark any subcontinent as its exclusive province—unless it consists of such mundane matters as classifying budget expenditures, drawing organization charts, and mapping procedures. In fact, it would appear that any definition of this field would be either so encompassing as to call forth the wrath or ridicule of others, or so limiting as to stultify its own disciples. Perhaps it is best that it not be defined. It is more an area of interest than a discipline, more a focus than a separate science.[37]

If directly given, this response implied significant costs for Public Administration as a distinct area of inquiry. Rather than being a proud area of specialization, Public Administration must somehow find its "chief satisfaction in providing a way of looking at government."[38] This offers but a niggardly and vague opportunity, if indeed it is not the death-rattle of a once-virile area of specialization.

A younger Herbert Simon was not disposed to give up the discipline's ghost so easily. *Administrative Behavior* was published just as the mass of specialists in public administration were gathering momentum for their rush into Phase 4. And Simon left no doubt as to his hunches and feelings about what was happening around him. He opted for Phase 3, as specifically defined in terms of his descision-making schema.

Simon clearly foresaw that the public-policy re-definition of the scope of Public Administration implied the end of the golden days of Phase 3, whose fuller flowering he correctly perceived as being just around the disciplinary corner.[39] Unfortunately for Simon, at least, he was a little too far ahead of the research that would substantiate his hopes. As it was, his argument was an easy target.[40] And he also correctly but ineffectually warned that the public-policy orientation set scholars in pursuit of multiple analytical will-of-the-wisps, thereby destroying that "center" so vital to a healthy discipline. Simon held out little promise for the success of the effort, but he thought he knew what success in public-policy terms required: ". . . nor can it stop when it has swallowed the whole of political science; it must attempt to absorb economics and sociology, as well."[41] The maw of the public-policy approach, that is, was cavernous.

Simon did more than point with alarm, however; he provided an alternative definition of the scope of Public Administration in terms of focus. As Landau observed, Simon's contribution was ". . . all the more significant in the face of the general disorganization which has occurred. Simon was trying to redefine public administration so as to give it a 'solid center,' a standard of relevance, a set of operating concepts—to make it, in short, a 'field' of inquiry. This was the function of the decision-making scheme."[42]

A brief description of Simon's decision-making schema will serve dual ends. The description will sketch the scope of Public Administration he proposed as an alternative to the public-policy orientation; and it will outline the senses in which Simon attempted to sharpen Goodnow's analytical distinction between Politics and Administration. Simon saw "deciding" rather than "doing" as the heart of administration, and decision-making involves both factual and ethical elements. "Facts" and "values" differ fundamentally; the former may be validated by empirical tests, and the latter are imperatives beyond empirical proof or disproof. In Simon's terms, "different criteria of 'correctness' . . . must be applied to the ethical and factual elements in a decision."[43]

The basic distinction between factual and ethical elements is analytic, as Simon recognizes. Reality does not always divide so neatly. Given that behavior in organizations is purposive at multiple levels, an "end" in some immediate means-end linkage may be a "means" in some more distinct means-end linkage. Simon's decision rule for applying his analytical distinction is this then: As far as decisions lead to the selection of "fine goals," they are considered to be "value judgments" beyond empirical validation. When decisions implement any final goals, they are "factual judgments."[44]

Major parallels were drawn by Simon between his schema and Goodnow's analytical distinction of Politics and Administration. Basically, Simon argued that Goodnow's development of his two central concepts was too ragged to support inquiry. When Goodnow was written and read, one still faced the challenge of distinguishing a policy decision from an administrative decision. "Apparently it has been assumed that the distinction is self-evident," Simon observed, "so self-evident as hardly to require discussion."[45]

Simon took advantage of the open opportunity to provide the required discussion of Politics and Administration in terms of his decision-making schema. Goodnow had proposed that Politics and Administration be distinguished analytically in terms of different criteria of correctness. Administrative issues are beyond politics in that they "do not require external control because they possess an internal criterion of correctness," embracing as they do the "fields of semi-scientific, quasi-judicial, quasi-business or commercial activity" which all have "little if any influence on the expression of the state will."[46] Political issues, in contrast, are value-loaded and beyond scientific standards. Simon sees a transparent parallel here with his decision-making schema. "The epistemological position of [*Administrative Behavior*] leads us to identify [Goodnow's] internal criterion with the criterion of factual correctness," he spelled out the matter, "and the group of decisions possessing this criterion with those that are factual in nature."[47] "If it is desired to retain the terms 'politics' and 'administration,' " Simon concluded, "they can best be applied to a division of the decisional functions that follow these suggested lines. While not identical with the separation of "value" from "fact," such a division would clearly be dependent upon the fundamental distinction."[48] Significantly, Simon also carefully and consciously preserves the analytical flavor of Goodnow while recognizing the problems of application to any real locus. He notes:

> Democratic institutions find their principal justification as a procedure for the validation of value judgments. There is no "scientific" or "expert" way of making such judgments, hence expertise of whatever kind is no qualification for the performance of this function. If the factual elements in decision could be strictly separated, in practice, from the ethical, the proper roles of representative and expert in a democratic decision-making process

> would be simple. For two reasons this is not possible. First, as has already been noted, most value judgments are made in terms of intermediate values, which themselves involve factual questions. Second, if factual decisions are entrusted to the experts, sanctions must be available to guarantee that the experts will conform, in good faith, to the value judgments that have been democratically formulated.[49]

## II. ADMINISTRATIVE BEHAVIOR AS CONTENT: SOME METHODOLOGICAL DIFFICULTIES WITH SIMON'S DECISION-MAKING SCHEMA

Why Simon's attempt at the re-definition of the scope of Public Administration should be such a neglected portion of so prominent a volume as *Administrative Behavior* cannot be explained simply, and we shall not attempt the full, complex demonstration. Rather, our economical analysis will stress a few major methodological difficulties with Simon's decision-making schema. Some of these difficulties do in fact explain the general neglect of Simon's re-definition of disciplinary scope, and all of them would have bedeviled any students of Public Administration who accepted the schema as their jumping-off point for empirical analysis. Broadly, content inadequacies implied limits on achieving Simon's intent.

These methodological difficulties illustrate the inadequacies of *Administrative Behavior* as "content." In sum, that volume ill equipped students of Public Administration for empirical inquiry. Four methodological problem-areas will receive attention here. We shall stress: the confusion of types of theory in *Administrative Behavior;* its inadequate and ambiguous attention to operational definition; the significance of the phenomena neglected by the decision-making schema; and the narrow definition of decision-making implicit in *Administrative Behavior.*

The following may seem a particularly academic exercise, but it does not lack a firm rationale. True enough, Simon's specification of Politics and Administration in terms of types of decisions was not generally accepted as a re-definition of the scope of Public Administration, even when it was perceived as such. Thus Sayre writes caustically of "prophets" such as Simon who have "presented a new administrative science" but whose "claims . . . have not been widely accepted" in Public Administration or Political Science.[50] But this hardly destroys Simon's great impact, even upon his sworn disciplinary enemies. For Simon must bear the massive responsibility of all those who contribute a major book for any age. They help form the language, and thus the patterns of thought, of the reading masses. Indeed, Simon consciously expressed just such a central goal. His desire in *Administrative Behavior* was to develop "adequate linguistic and conceptual tools," thereby striking for the analytical jugular. For such linguistic and conceptual tools can become "the shaper of ideas, the program and guide for the individual's mental activity, for his analysis of impressions, for his synthesis of his mental stock in trade."[51]

There is a grave responsibility for writer and reader in all of this subtle business; and that responsiblity provides rationale aplenty for us. For once they are out and achieve any vogue at all, such linguistic and conceptual tools can be called back only with enormous difficulty by even the most careful author. Less reserved polemicists riding in the wake of an analytical dreadnought like Simon, as they inevitably do, have less motivation and less power to do the job. Alice in *Through the Looking Glass* had to face the implicit responsibility more squarely and immediately than most, but she illustrates the present point:

> "The cause of lightning," Alice said very decidedly, for she felt quite sure about this, "is the thunder—no, no!" she hastily corrected herself, "I meant the other way."
>
> "It's too late to correct it," said the Red Queen; "When you've once said a thing, that fixes it, and you must take the consequences."

Ample evidence demonstrates that Simon has long since left far behind all but the vestiges of *Administrative Behavior*. But once he said the thing, that fixed it, and the consequences must be faced.

**A. Confusion of Types of Theory**

Herbert Simon proposed a science of administration divorced from values, but his approach leans heavily for its support on what is purportedly excluded. Or at least many observers in Public Administration saw this unseemly dependence. These observers consequently rejected Simon's argument as analytical sleight-of-hand, and rather unpolished sleight-of-hand at that. And with the rejection of his argument, many observers also rejected out of hand the possibility of a science of administration.

The paradox of the forceful rejection of, and the abject dependence upon, values requires illustration and amplification. The only possible "science of administration" is absolutely value-free, according to Simon, and that can be our starting point. "Propositions about administrative processes will be scientific in so far as truth and falsehood, in the factual sense," he notes, "can be predicated of them." Nor does Simon take any chance that the point will escape even the most casual reader. "Conversely," he notes, "if truth or falsehood can be predicated of a proposition concerning administrative processes, then that proposition is scientific."[52] Consistently, Simon denies that the "science of administration contains an essential ethical element." Indeed, given his framework, it logically cannot contain any ethical element. "If this were true," he instructs, "a science of administration would be impossible, for it is impossible to choose, on an empirical basis, between ethical alternatives."[53]

Many were willing to take Simon at his word, and conclude that a science of administration was impossible. For they saw no way of excluding "an essential ethical element" from the study of administration. And Simon left them no alternative but to deny—as he said they must—the possibility of a science of administration.

That Simon's methodological position rather than a science of administration was impossible may be established by backing into the demonstration. That is, given the inevitable imprecision of any argument, Simon's position is defensible under (but only under) three conditions. Let us describe these conditions, demonstrate that they are very restrictive, and describe how they were violated even by Simon.

First, Simon's prescription for science of administration applies tolerably well to what we have in Chapter III designated as the progress toward, and the development of, conclusions in *empirical theories*. In this phase of scientific effort, clearly, no values but the values of the scientific process itself ought intrude. This phase should be value-free, in short. But scientific effort has other significant phases and—although Simon neglects them—they are in significant respects value-loaded. The choice of a subject for study, for example, is value-loaded. We do not deal with trifles. A major inelegancy of Simon's adumbration of a science of administration rejects the crucial relevance of values to these phases of the scientific process: the choice of research problems; the treatment of materials and experimental subjects; the application of the canons of scientific procedure, which are "values" rather than "facts"; and the use of results.

The exclusion of values from a science of administration is awkward, then. Research could never begin in their absence, that is, nor could it proceed, nor could anything be done with the results of empirical research.[54]

Second, Simon's description of a science of administration is more tolerable if nothing is ever to be done with the results of empirical investigations. This is a faint concession, indeed, and unacceptable even to Simon. For any specific empirical datum might be put to many uses, depending on the values of the user. In our terms, several *goal-based, empirical* theories might be developed within a "science of administration." The neglect of this point is of some moment, since Simon's "science" is clearly meant to be put to "practical" use. But logic wins out in this case. Since a science of administration must be value-free, according to Simon, there patently can be no room in it for goal-based, empirical theories whose bases are in preferential goals or values. Many students of Public Administration found logic in this case difficult to square with what they felt was one unavoidable emphasis in *their* discipline.

Third, Simon's position is defensible if and only if he can and does abide by his own limits for a science of administration. That is, recall that his science of administration is restricted to those propositions whose truth or falsity may be established empirically. There will be many administratively relevant propositions that fit this definitional mold. But many will not, and not all of these are trivial cases.

Ample evidence indicates Simon's unwillingness and inability to respect his own boundaries. It is difficult to judge what proportion of relevant phenomena fall inside or outside of Simon's boundaries for a science of administration. Substantial considerations suggest, however, that Simon's science will be considerably less extensive than the phenomena we normally think of as "administrative." Indeed, some observers go so far as to suggest that Simon's decision-making schema excludes all but low-level phenomena, and does not include all low-level phenomena at that. Moreover, even Simon seemed to chafe within his own confines. Thus a trick with means-ends analysis—which Simon has abandoned of late—is necessary to give *Administrative Behavior* even the reduced analytical room it has. Simon attributes a greater "factual component" to some proximate ends as they mediate "higher-level" goals, thereby admitting more data to his science of administration.[55] Indeed, Simon implies that the process can be extended indefinitely by recognizing "more final goals" and then "still-more final goals." And all this without admitting values to his science of administration! Dwight Waldo's complaint is appropriate: "In reply to any question concerning [values], the logical positivist [like Simon] points to an escalator that ascends and ascends but never arrives anywhere."[56]

There are fragile elements indeed in Simon's treatment of values. But let us accept Simon's own condition for the relative appropriateness of that treatment, and add one condition of our own. His decision-making schema must be restricted to non-valuational data, as he notes, and in the process must encompass a broad enough range of phenomena to permit speaking of a science of administration. In addition—and Simon is not very insistent on the point—the decision-making schema must at once encourage and permit the incorporation of a range of "factual data" beyond those explicitly treated by Simon.

Even Simon does not respect these variably restrictive conditions which define the relative appropriateness of his science of administration. The point is clearest in his original emphasis on "the structure of human rational choice" and on "a theory of rational choice in order to be able to understand the influences that come to bear upon decision-making in an organizational environment."[57] In its most unencumbered form, then, Simon is interested not in an empirical theory of what-is-related-to-what in organizations. Rather, from the start, his focus is upon one of the innumerable goal-based, empirical theories, relevant for administration, specifically that one whose focus is "human rational choice." That is, Simon's basic argument is not of this form: *X* is related to *Y* under conditions *a, b,* and *c.* Simon's basic underlying formulation is this:

> If increased rationality in decision-making is the goal—and it is so obvious to me that I can conceive of a science of administration in no other terms—then a, b, c . . . are some of the factors that foster intended rationality and d, e, f . . . are some factors which must be eliminated or whose incidence must be reduced because they limit the rationality of organizational actors.[58]

This unacknowledged but basic emphasis on goal-based, empirical theory particularly prompted the earlier observation that Simon at once rejected and was dependent upon values in his science of administration. For the maximization of "human rational choice" is the value toward which Simon's attention is directed.

For an author as complex as Simon, every position has its multiple qualifications and exceptions. But we need shrink little if any from the bold position sketched above. Simon's preoccupation with a base-value—and certainly not the only conceivable base-value, nor even a clearly defined one—may be established directly. Thus Storing notes with interest that Simon uses the "term 'efficiency' . . . most commonly . . . in connection with the values and opportunity costs as viewed by the managerial group in an organization, rather than the values and opportunity costs as assessed by employees or some other group."[59] This orientation is reasonable, but it squares poorly with the dictum that in adopting that orientation, one is free of values.

But we are not content with debater's points. Consider a broader range of evidence supporting Simon's monolithic drive to gain the best of all possible worlds in relation to values. He clearly and often enough says that his heart is with intended rationality, and he implies that the rest of administrative reality can take care of itself. As one major consequence, the "limits of rationality were defined . . . largely as residual categories"[60] in *Administrative Behavior,* as Simon notes in the Introduction to the re-issue of the volume, although he does little with this product of ten years of perspective. The omission is a truly remarkable one in any purportedly empirical theory. To a similar point, Simon in the same place acknowledges that during "the past several years"—in sharp contrast with *Administrative Behavior*—he attempted "to construct a model of rational choice that would incorporate the actual properties of human beings [as well as] some of the formal clarity of the economic model."[61] This is truly notice of a monumental neglect in a purported science of administration.

Such omissions of mountainous realities in *Administrative Behavior,* in addition, were not likely to be spotlighted by Simon's methodology. Indeed, Simon's clear bias is to deny to Nature the phenomena omitted from his model. This is a curious posture for a scientist, but curious or not, Simon often assumes that posture. More or less consistently, his basic press is articulated in such terms:

> An important fact to be kept in mind is that the limits of rationality are variable limits. Most important of all, consciousness of the limits may in itself alter them. Suppose it were discovered in a particular organization, for example, that organizational loyalties attached to small units had frequently led to a harmful degree of intra-organizational competition. Then, a program which trained members of the organization . . . to subordinate loyalties toward the smaller group to those toward the larger, might lead to a very considerable alteration of the limits [of rationality] . . . .[62]

That Simon pushes this position to unreasonable extremes is made clear in his explanation that "propositions about behavior, in so far as it is rational, do not involve propositions about the psychology of the person who is behaving." He acknowledges the apparent paradox, but dismisses it. Given a system of values, that is, Simon argues that "there is only one course of action which an individual can rationally pursue." And that one course is the one which permits maximum attainment of the applicable system of values. "Psychological propositions," Simon concludes, therefore are "needed only to explain why . . . behavior, in any given instance, departs from the norm of rationality."[63] With the implicit assumption that the science of administration deals only with rational behavior, "psychological propositions" have a narrow province indeed in Simon's science.

Here again Simon succumbs to his own vocabulary and chooses to impose it on reality. His rationale may be sketched. Simon's decision-making schema is to deal with data without dependence on values. He claims the emphasis on "rational choice" meets this condition. That is, the individual rational actor in behaving makes no value choices, for "there is only one course of action which an individual can rationally pursue." The individual, in sum, acts out of logical necessity, not preferential choice. Neglecting the question of what this line of argument means in any but very simple choice-decisions, its motivation seems clear enough. It avoids some embarrassing questions about values, but only at the expense of throwing out "propositions about the psychology of the person who is behaving." An empirical theory, needless to note, could not be so cavalier.

That Simon cannot live with the three conditions above also may be suggested indirectly, thereby demonstrating the methodological weaknesses of *Administrative Behavior* from another point of view. For example, the more Simon attempts to inject reality-based elements into the original model of *Administrative Behavior,* the less integral and meaningful is the model. This is curious indeed, given that the decision-making model is tied so tightly to the "facts." The opposite effect is the expected one.

The inability of Simon's model to increasingly absorb reality will be illustrated here and at a number of points. Consider only the case of "satisficing" versus "maximizing" man. *Administrative Behavior* leans heavily on the latter, and for a necessary reason. Since maximizing man weighs *all* factors and compares *all* alternative outcomes in decision-making, the relevance of value elements is sharply reduced. Such a reduction is crucial for Simon's argument. Indeed, there may be "only one course of action" which maximizing man can rationally pursue, which case is the one particularly dear to Simon. Maximizing man need not puzzle greatly about what he values, that is, because he has the computational skills to compare any alternative against every other alternative.

But maximizing man is a rare bird indeed, as Simon's Introduction to his second edition notes. Thus it is not really possible for Simon to whistle his way through what is, for his argument, the graveyard of values. Although the body of *Administrative Behavior* remains undisturbed by the note, Simon's introduction of "satisficing man" who does "not have the wits to maximize"[64] vitally undercuts the argument of that volume. Note just a few of the difficulties that satisficing man implies for Simon's treatment of values. If administrative man seeks the alternative that is "good enough" rather than a one-best alternative, this patently and enormously increases the importance of those values which Simon has defined out of his science of administration. A train of problems cries for attention. Simon, consistently enough, does not recognize them. And his science must be poorer for that fact. Storing puts one of the questions incisively. He noted that:

> "Satisficing" is a new name for an old idea. It is sensible to say that a rational man seeks a course of action that is good enough; and that is surely preferable to saying that he seeks the unique

> best way. But Simon gives scarcely any systematic consideration to what would seem to be the next question, the one that points to the basis on which we distinguish more or less rational behavior in ordinary life: good enough for what?[65]

In brief, the admission of satisficing man has two crucial consequences for the place of values in Simon's analysis. One consequence is direct; the other implied. Admitting valuational man qua satisficer sharply narrows the real locus to which, on Simon's own accounting, his science of administration can apply. For example, Simon acknowledges[66] that satisficing man will depend in major ways on the institutional values of his organization in choosing a decision that is good enough. But these "ethical elements" have been defined out of a science of administration. Moreover, indirectly, if satisficing man utilizes a drastically simplified model of an incredibly diverse real world, what of the canons of "internal correctness" which might serve to discipline the decision-making of maximizing man? Storing pithily expresses the challenge to value analysis spotlighted by Simon's admission of satisficing man, the challenge that faced even maximizing man but less dramatically. Satisficing determines by fiat what is "good enough." Here is revealed "with a startling clarity what was always implicit in Simon's conception of rationality—the absolute subservience of 'rationality' to nonrational preferences,"[67] or to values. Strong though Storing's statement is, it does not lack firm support. The fascination in contemporary discussions with "levels of aspiration" provides a case in point. Decision-making is commonly rooted in the differential levels of aspiration of relevant actors and—although the point does not receive great emphasis—this ties decision-making firmly into considerations of value.

These and other considerations establish that Simon cannot operate consistently within his own boundaries for a science of administration; and they also imply the inappropriateness of the decision-making schema as a methodologically viable definition of a disciplinary core for Public Administration. As Chapter II establishes, a viable discipline of Public Administration should provide for active research in: empirical theory; goal-based, empirical theory; and value analysis. *Administrative Behavior* provides guidance only for the first of these necessary emphases, and at best does so only in clumsy ways. Other specific examples of the methodological clumsiness of Simon's schema even for empirical theory will be of immediate concern.

### B. Awkward Approaches to Operational Definition

Commonly, and unfairly, the decision-making schema is criticized because of its incompleteness or its generality. These criticisms impose standards on Simon other than his own, however. Clearly enough, Simon has described his own ambitions in more limited terms. Thus he is predisposed "to construct tools" for the study of administration, "adequate linguistic and conceptual tools for realistically and significantly describing . . . administrative organization—describing it, that is, in a way that will provide the basis for scientific analysis of the effectiveness of its structure and operation."[68] He prefaced the original edition of *Administrative Behavior* with this disclaimer:

> These conclusions do not constitute a "theory" of administration, for except for a few dicta offered by way of hypothesis, no principles of administration are laid down. If any "theory" is involved, it is that decision-making is the heart of administration, and that the vocabulary of administrative theory must be derived from the logic and psychology of human choice.[69]

If Simon cannot reasonably be taken to task for incompleteness, however, raising the question of the probability that his "linguistic and conceptual tools" will generate an empirical theory is appropriate. Simon's confusion of types of theory, adumbrated above, does not encourage optimistic estimates of this probability. The attention given to operational definition in *Administrative Behavior* further deepens this pessimism.

Operational definition is at the heart of empirical research, but operational definition is at best of only surface interest to Simon. Early on, Simon does acknowledge that the "first task of administrative theory is to develop a set of concepts that will permit . . . description." And he affirms that these concepts "to be scientifically useful, must be operational."[70] Beyond this early point, however, reservations about Simon's handling of the matter of operational definition are in order. Several factors particularly encourage caution.

First, Simon gives but meager attention to operational definition. This is suggestive, but certainly not damning. Second, the attention actually accorded operational definition presents significant ambiguities that permit little optimism about their successfully sustaining empirical inquiry. Thus Simon explains that concepts "must be operational," which he explains requires that "their meanings must correspond to empirically observable facts or situations."[71] This implies a concreteness that is inappropriate, if indeed the explanation has any meaning at all. Moreover, it sets up an awkward criterion for judging whether concepts are operational. Chapters II and III, particularly, should make the point with a considerable margin to spare. But we will develop some supporting argument below.

That we should expect the worst of the ambiguities in Simon's treatment of operational definition can be established directly. Matters only get more confused when Simon notes that his "definition of 'authority' . . . is an example of an operational definition." Referring to that definition (15 pages earlier, which is suggestive) helps only to establish the fugitive character of Simon's meaning. "A subordinate may be said to accept authority," we are told, "whenever he permits his behavior to be guided by a decision reached by another, irrespective of his own judgment as to the merits of that decision."[72] The example permits no definite construction, however. Thus if the criterion for an operational definition is whether the phenomenon referred to has empirical counterparts, then Simon's definition of authority is operational. But this is a very permissive criterion indeed. It also has multiple additional liabilities: it excludes few or no concepts; it gives no hint of how one scientifically chooses between two operational definitions, as Simon conceives them; and it is innocent of the complications attending operational definition in empirical inquiry.

Let us be more specific. If we conceive of an operational definition as one providing predictively useful measurements, for example, one can at least entertain doubts about Simon's approach. Thus Simon's example implies no specific ways in which measurements of "acceptance of authority" can be made. Indeed, that problem is not raised. Apparently, "acceptance of authority" is assumed to be an easily defined condition. Even if Simon could measure the phenomenon, moreover, there is every reason to believe that attempts to verify predictions based on Simon's notion of authority would yield mixed results.[73] That is, at least three combinations can be formed of the two components of Simon's approach to authority: acceptance of authoritative orders; judgment by the acceptance of authoritative orders; and judgment by the acceptor of the merits of the order. These three combinations are:

1. Acceptance, irrespective of judgment
2. Acceptance, judgment supporting
3. Acceptance, judgment rejecting.

That these three combinations will yield homogeneous consequences is an extreme presumption, as Chapter IV establishes. That only the first of them is useful for describing reality is similarly presumptuous.

### C. Significance of the Phenomena Neglected

Such inattention to matters of operational definition seems a mere symptom of the pervasive orientation of *Administrative Behavior* toward the data it will admit to analysis. Hence there is little hope that a clarification of operational issues, even were it brought off, would remedy matters. Tersely, Simon is quite selective of the data admitted to his study-universe. This picking and choosing on non-empirical grounds stands in marked contrast to the bias toward comprehensiveness in empirical theory and goal-based, empirical theory.

A brief comparison of two approaches to decision-making helps make the present point. Students of group dynamics, for example, have had a strong interest in decision-making in a variety of applied areas. In accordance with their empirical bias, variations in decision-making were explained in terms of a network of theory that was comprehensively extended to such levels of phenomena as: the demands of specific kinds of decisions; the specific properties of the large organizations within which specific decisions were made; the properties of decision-makers; the characteristics of the social atmosphere within which decisions were made; and so on. The dynamics of the process may be chained to a few words. This was the dialetic of the group dynamicists: to achieve increasingly accurate prediction, and this by specifying an increasingly wide range of conditions which reduce the amount of unpredictable variance in tests of hypotheses.

Simon works in an opposed direction, apparently from contrary assumptions. His dialectic in *Administrative Behavior* is to increase the clarity and the simplicity of his model by a priori exclusion of major classes of phenomena of significance in any organization. Given his definition of a science of administration, of course, Simon is justified in excluding whatever phenomena he wishes. The plain fact is this, however. As he excludes phenomena, so does the content of his science of administration dwindle.

The danger of starving his science of administration does not deter Simon from really phenomenal exclusions of phenomena. Rationales vary in Simon, but the consequence is uniform. In the Introduction to his 1957 re-issue, that is, Simon notes that he treats very wide phenomenal areas as "residual categories." Because the "model of economic man was far more completely and formally developed," he informs us, treatment by *Administrative Behavior* of "the actual properties of human beings" was "very incomplete." The explanation makes some sense, up to a point. But some massive omissions by Simon are truly puzzling. For example, much of Lewin's pioneering work with choice—certainly an area of relevance for any approach to human decision-making—was available to Simon. Indeed, that work had roots in studies published long before Simon began his work on *Administrative Behavior*. No matter how compelling any rationale for exclusion might be, it does nothing to enhance the decision-making schema. At best, any rationale helps make the volume's inadequacies understandable.

The inadequacies of omission of the two editions of *Administrative Behavior,* however, tend to be interpreted by Simon as virtues. Thus "unavailable" behavioral data are excluded, as a methodological rule rather than as an unfortunate necessity. Thus Simon defends the "paradoxical statement" that "propositions about human behavior, in so far as it is rational, do not ordinarily involve propositions about the psychology of the person who is behaving." Paradoxical the statement is for someone dealing with a science of administration. But it could not be avoided, given Simon's emphasis on rational behavior, his professed preoccupation with empirical theory, and his patent neglect of actual behavioral properties. No good case could be made for the "paradoxical statement," given these conflicting elements in Simon. And no good case is made: Simon's argument limps badly. He notes correctly that: "In any given situation, and with a given system of values, there is only one course of action which an individual can rationally pursue."[74] But winning a point by logical definition was paid for by the narrowing of the scope of *Administrative Behavior* to a veritable phenomenal pinpoint. For the obvious next question is: Just how much behavior anywhere is rational in this sense? And the answer is: Precious little. Indeed, Simon himself acknowledges the point when he introduces "satisficing man," which concept does not even make a pretense that "there is only one course of action which an individual can rationally pursue."

### D. Decision-Making$_1$, Decision-Making$_2$, . . . Decision-Making$_3$

This section builds toward three conclusions. Simon's emphasis on rational decision-making, first, has the effect of shrinking drastically the scope of his science of administration. Second, Simon's methodology is such as to inhibit forceful efforts designed to remedy this condition. Third, the act of deciding tends to be seen by Simon as too definite, if not too dramatic, and as discontinuous.

Considerable detail is necessary to flesh out these three conclusions. In terms now fashionable, to approach the task of detailing our argument from one point of view, Simon emphasized a "closed system." In a closed system, individual actors have more or less full factual and value inputs which can be exhaustively manipulated and in which all alternative outcomes can be compared. Lindblom has generically classified closed systems as examples of the Rational-Comprehensive Model of decision-making.[75] Table VII.1 summarizes the properties of the Rational-Comprehensive Model.

An alternative "open system" of decision-making contrasts sharply with closed systems. Some of the particular points of contrast are ex-pressed by Wilson and Alexis in these terms:

> (1) predetermined goals are replaced by some unidentified structure which is approximated by an aspiration level.

(2) all alternatives and outcomes are not predetermined; neither are the relationships between specific alternatives and outcomes always defined.
(3) the ordering of all alternatives is replaced by a search routine which considers fewer than all alternatives.
(4) the individual does not maximize but seeks to find a solution to "satisfy" an aspiration level.[76]

More broadly, open-system analysis stresses the subtle and continuous character of decision-making. In this sense, Barnard epitomized open-system analysis when he observed that: "most executive decisions produce no direct evidence of themselves and . . . knowledge of them can only be derived from the accumulation of indirect evidence."[77] Such a notion is foreign to Simon, which only spotlights his preoccupation with low-level decision-making and the apparently "firm" facts associated with it. Lindblom has designated an open model as a Successive Limited Approximations Model of decision-making. Table VII.1 details the major properties of that model.

Closed system analysis is increasingly seen as analytically sterile. As two students conclude:[78] "There is a growing disenchantment with 'closed'

**TABLE VII.1 Two Contrasting Models of Decision-Making**

| *Rational-Comprehensive Model* | *Successive Limited Comparisons Model* |
|---|---|
| 1a. Clarification of values or objectives distinct from and usually prerequisite to empirical analysis of alternative policies. | 1b. Selection of value goals and empirical analysis of the needed action are not distinct from one another but are closely intertwined. |
| 2a. Policy-formulation is therefore approached through means-end analysis: First the ends are isolated, then the means to achieve them are sought. | 2b. Since means and ends are not distinct, means-end analysis is often inappropriate or limited. |
| 3a. The test of a "good" policy is that it can be shown to be the most appropriate means to desired ends. | 3b. The test of a "good policy" is typically that various analysts find themselves directly agreeing on a policy (without their agreeing that it is the most appropriate means to an agreed objective). |
| 4a. Analysis is comprehensive; every important relevant factor is taken into account. | 4b. Analysis is drastically limited: (i) Important possible outcomes are neglected. (ii) Important alternative potential policies are neglected. (iii) Important affected values are neglected. |
| 5a. Theory is often heavily relied upon. | 5b. A succession of comparisons greatly reduces or eliminates reliance on theory. |

Source: Based on Charles E. Lindblom, "The Science of 'Muddling Through,'" *Public Administration Review*, 19 (Spring, 1959), 81.

decision models in economic and management science circles." One supporting datum must suffice to explain this change of taste. Closed-system analysis is appropriate largely for "programmed" ( = simple and recurring) decisions. Even Simon seems convinced. He has argued that heuristic problem-solving—the muddling through characteristic of open-system analysis—is not susceptible to resolution through logic. Moreover, heuristic problem-solving is said to characterize much—if not most—problem-solving by managers. Appropriately, Wilson and Alexis conclude that "... most vital decisions are non-recurring. 'Search' is required to find feasible alternatives," they continue. "And often this search must not be constrained by the bounds of some preferred solution. Problem-solving requires a flexible and dynamic framework. Organizations grow and thus have growing aspirations; and changes occur in definition of what are organizational problems and of what constitute acceptable solutions. The future of 'open' decision models, in light of these straws in the wind, seems highly promising."[79] Finally, Simon's recent emphasis on "satisficing man" reflects his own movement toward open-system analysis.[80]

The methodology of *Administrative Behavior* but weakly supports Simon's new emphasis on open-system analysis. For open-system analysis requires the empirical investigation of "a complex mixture of many elements—[man's] culture, his personality, and his aspirations ... the limitations of human cognition and the complexity of man's total environment."[81] In our terms, that is, open-system analysis requires the development of a comprehensive empirical theory. And this effort, in turn, rests upon a supporting methodology. That methodology's role is multiple. It enforces an appreciation of the complexity of man's total environment; it provides the framework for cumulative work through nominal and operational definitions; and it requires a clarity about types of theories and about their uses and limitations.

The methodological press of *Administrative Behavior,* however, is ill suited to meet these requirements of open-system analysis. It serves only a narrowly construed science of administration. Given these properties, patently, that volume and its methodology could hardly serve either as a vehicle for exploiting open-system analysis or as a viable definition of the scope and method of Public Administration.

## III. ADMINISTRATIVE BEHAVIOR AS CONTENT: TECHNICAL PREOCCUPATION AND INSTITUTIONAL NEGLECT

The issues raised by *Administrative Behavior* also can be painted on a broader canvas of contrasting approaches to administrative reality. That volume and its methodology tend toward one extreme, and in doing so that volume reflects a special case of the neglect of relevant phenomena. Two consequences of this neglect are particularly noteworthy for our purposes. The volume's extreme approach to administrative reality severely limits its usefulness, both generally as a primer for the scientific study of administration and specifically as a definition of scope for Public Administration.

Philip Selznick's *Leadership in Administration* poses a view of administrative reality sharply opposed to Simon's, and his treatment will provide a contrast with *Administrative Behavior.* Selznick basically distinguishes two contrasting views of administrative life: organization engineering, and institutional leadership. At best, *Administrative Behavior* qualifies as a treatise on the former. This is clear from Selznick's description of organizing engineering:

> When the goals of the organization are clear-cut, and when most choices can be made on the basis of known and objective technical criteria, the engineer rather than the leader is called for. His work may include human engineering to smooth personal relations, improve morale, or reduce absenteeism. But his problem remains one of adapting known qualities through known techniques to predetermined ends.
>
> From the engineering perspective, the organization is made up of standardized building blocks. These elements, and the ways of putting them together, are the stock-in-trade of the organization engineer.[82]

Organization engineering has a range of limitations in comprehending administrative reality that have clear analogs in *Administrative Behavior.* The basic bond is the highly programmed nature of organization engineering and the closed-system analysis of that volume. More specific similarities are illustrated by Simon's description of the ultimate in science. "What is a scientifically-relevant description of an organization?" he asks. "It is a description that, so far as possible, designates for each person in the organization *what* decisions that person makes, and the influences to which he is subject in making each of these decisions."[83]

Organization engineering has its value, but it has significant limitations in both practice and analysis. In practice, some—but only some—administrative activities approach a closed system. To them, of course—but only to them—organization engineering is an appropriate approach. However, and here is the greater mischief, extending such a limited approach into a methodological guide for the analysis of administrative phenomena has substantial costs. Radical separation of fact and value in practice—based upon the useful analytical distinction between what is desired and what exists—causes particular grief. As Selznick explained:

> Like other forms of positivism, this position in administrative theory raises too bright a halo over linguistic purity. Pressing a complex world into easy dichotomies, it induces a *premature* abandonment of wide areas of experience to the world of the aesthetic, the metaphysical, the moral. Let us grant the premise that there is an ultimately irreducible nonrational (responsive) element in valuation, inaccessible to scientific appraisal. This cannot justify the judgment in a particular case that the anticipated irreducible element has actually been reached.[84]

Selznick's point is not one of delicate logic. Its point is often boldly (if not grossly) reflected in work ostensibly dedicated to exploring the real world. For example, Simon hastily discarded vast areas of experiential data in the process of developing his science of administration. Moreover, he felt it necessary to develop rationales to exclude those experiential data forevermore.

We may summarize the present point by using our methodological terms. Science *inter alia* requires hypothetical statements of co-varying factors, of the effects of nominal independent variables on dependent variables. An important part of validating such hypotheses involves attempting their extension to increasingly wider phenomenal areas by specifying intervening variables and testing for their effects. Terseness and accuracy go hand in hand in Simon's case. He neglected to specify and to provide for the test of intervening variables, in the overwhelming majority of cases. Moreover, he also commonly defined out of existence potentially significant intervening variables that could have helped in estimating the usefulness of his model.

Simon's methodological inelegance may be demonstrated easily. We rely on Selznick to sketch one vast phenomenal area neglected by Simon, saving for later the demonstration of how Simon in fact excluded that area from his analysis. Selznick has left a slim volume reflecting his concerns with "institutional leadership," which he sees as necessary in all but completely programmed organizations and as particularly vital when "we must create a structure uniquely adapted to the mission and role of the enterprise. This adaptation goes beyond a tailored combination of uniform elements; it is an adaptation in depth, affecting the nature of the parts themselves."[85] To create such a structure, in effect, is to infuse technical structures with value, to make social organizations out of technical structures. Organization engineering must give way to institutional leadership in the process. Products of this process are familiar to all students, as illustrated by technically identical units of organization that have distinctive commitments to program, method, or clientele. These pervasive commitments become so intimate a part of organizational life that they influence if not determine a wide range of decisions at many levels. They give "organizational character" to technical operations, and they reflect an organization's "distinctive competence." As Selznick concluded:

> The terms "institution," "organization character," and "distinctive competence" all refer to the same basic process—the transformation of an engineered, technical arrangement of building blocks into a social organism. This transition goes on unconsciously and inevitably wherever leeway for evolution and *adaptation* is allowed by the system of technical controls; and at least some such leeway exists in all but the most narrowly circumscribed organizations.[86]

If such processes of institutionalization are significant in organizations—and that cannot be disputed—*Administrative Behavior* has significant liabilities in its presentation both of a framework for administration and of a definition of scope and method for Public Administration. To be sure, Simon may not completely disregard institutional leadership. But he could hardly give it less attention. We may parsimoniously rest our case on two pieces of evidence. First, as Stark correctly notes, "the word leadership itself cannot be found in the heading of a single chapter, chapter section, chapter subsection, or anywhere in the index" of *Administrative Behavior.*[87] Given the vast dimensions of the then-existing literature on leadership—and it was overwhelming in 1957 if it was only mountainous in 1947—the omission is truly startling. Here, again, is an example of the premature exclusion of data about which Selznick wrote. Within Simon's framework, the exclusion may be due to the fact that leadership patently implies valuational elements. But so much the worse for that framework. As the still burgeoning literature on leadership demonstrates, much empirical work can be done with leadership even though many aspects of relevant phenomena are value-loaded.[88]

Second, the press of Simon's *Administrative Behavior* permits little confidence that the processes of institutionalization will receive attention. Recall Simon's position that a "scientifically relevant description of an organization" is one that "designates for each person in the organization what decisions that person makes, and the influences to which he is subject in making each of these decisions." Such "influences" might include leadership and its diverse forms, but *Administrative Behavior* does not urge that inclusion.

Properly construed, then, any science of administration must encompass institutional leadership. We may outline briefly how our own methodological guidelines could do the job. Any empirical theory, first, would have to attempt to treat empirically the total fact-value mix associated with leadership. For example, specific styles of supervision can be shown generally to produce specific existential outcomes.[89] This is clearly an empirical task, and cannot be shunned simply because both specific styles of supervision and specific outcomes raise issues of value. Briefly, our methodology avoids two dangers: (1) it does not encourage or require the premature exclusion of phenomenal areas like leadership that are value-loaded; and (2) our methodological guidelines—involving operational definition and so on—restrain observers anxious to report seeing what they prefer.

Any science of administration also must generate diverse goal-based, empirical theories. One goal-based, empirical theory would have such components, among others:

Goal: to increase the amount of "supportive" supervision

Required Empirical Conditions:

(1) to select supervisors who are low scorers on the Adorno *F* Scale and who are not "authoritarians of the left"[90]

(2) to select subordinates with appropriate personality predispositions for such supervisory style, as above

(3) to departmentalize around "flows of work" rather than functions or processes.

The list might be extended significantly, as it has been elsewhere.[91] Such goal-based empirical theories are necessary for practical applications. Moreover, such theories help sharpen many evaluative issues. For example, one might highly value the goal of fostering a "supportive" supervisory style. The specification of necessary empirical conditions and ways of achieving them might well modify such clear preferences. For example, even from the brief list above, some individuals may be concerned with what happens to subordinates who do not have personality characteristics appropriate for a supportive supervisory style. And one's valuation of likely ways of handling deviant cases may encourage modification of the original goal of increasing the amount of supportive supervision. And these are but simplistic examples of the universe relevant to the fact-value mix in administrative reality that any science of administration must encompass.

## IV. SIMON'S "DECISION-MAKING" AS INTENT AND CONTENT: A SUMMARY STATEMENT

There is no completely satisfactory methodological summary of Simon's complex effort, but like his new administrative man we shall be satisfied with less than a whole loaf. Our straightforward strategy is to focus on the classification of Simon's effort in *Administrative Behavior.* Is it a major step toward an empirical theory? Or a goal-based, empirical theory? Or is it a variant of utopian theory dealing with a phenomenal area of contemporary popularity?

The preceding analysis permits some boldness in approaching one aspect of this classification. Very definite reservations prevent us from regarding the decision-making schema as a success in developing method or results appropriate for empirical theory or goal-based, empirical theory. The evidence will not be re-marshaled, but no other position squares with Simon's exclusion of vast phenomenal areas. Further, the exclusion was not only analytically convenient—which is reasonable—but it was made in terms which preclude or hinder the subsequent admission of those phenomena.

The same point can be usefully made in a different way. Consider Meehan's trio of standards for evaluating empirical theory. Any such theory must be evaluated in terms of:

1. its explanatory power, which depends on the range of data it includes, on the comprehensiveness of the phenomena it seeks to explain, and on the significance of those phenomena;
2. the esthetic and psychological satisfaction the theory affords; and
3. its usefulness to a particular discipline at a particular point in time.[92]

Simon's decision-making schema scores low on Standard 1 for, even using the loosest criteria, it explains little. Indeed, Simon has stressed his emphasis on developing a vocabulary and a method rather than on enumerating theoretical propositions of predictive and explanatory power. As for Standard 2, the present analysis should reflect some of the significant senses in which the decision-making schema provides little aesthetic or psychological satisfaction, that is, if one's base line for judgment is defined in terms of the methodology of empirical science. The decision-making schema has proved useful to a variety of disciplines, at their present level of development; that is, it scores highest on Standard 3.

A second aspect of the classification of Simon's work permits less boldness. That is, the fact that the decision-making schema falls short of standards for an empirical theory does not establish that it is an exercise in utopian theory. The schema does have some resemblance to a utopian model. The schema's formal and deductive character, for example, suggests that it was logically developed from a (presumably) poorly articulated set of assumptions and goals. And the deductions often triumph over reality. On the other hand, the schema is rooted in some significant phenomenal data, and it does assert a claim to its usefulness for scientific purposes as a picture of the administrative world. Those data and that claim must be honored.

A specific choice need not be really made in classifying *Administrative Behavior*, however. For the volume is complex enough and inconsistent enough to reflect significant strains of all three types of theory distinguished above. Meehan expresses the sense of this "yes, but" kind of theory in appropriate terms. He calls such a theory a "quasi-theory." It does not reflect the conscious rigor and verbal precision of what we have called utopian theory; neither does it respect the methodology of empirical theory; and all the while it tends rather more toward the former than toward the latter. As Meehan described a quasi-theory, it

> . . . refers to any intellectual construction that is a useful tool for the . . . theorist, though it cannot meet the standards [relevant for empirical theory.] In particular, quasi-theories serve as aids to classification, exploration, and discovery . . . . Actually, constructions of this sort are widely used in political science, though more often than not they are simply referred to as "theories." Max Weber's "Ideal Types," the postulational structures suggested by Talcott Parsons, the mathematical theory of games . . . and so on all fall into this category. The structures range from a fairly simple classification system to complex mathematical networks . . . . They do not "explain," in the strict sense of the term, but they can be very useful indeed in theory.[93]

## NOTES

1. Significantly enough, Simon's popular introduction to the computer and its prospects was titled *The New Science of Management Decision* (New York: Harper and Row, 1960).

2. For example, such techniques as linear programming and computer methods for the required calculations.

3. Herbert A. Simon, *Administrative Behavior: A Study of Decision-Making Processes in Administrative Organization* (2nd ed.; New York: Macmillan, 1957), pp. xxvii–xxix.

4. John von Neumann and Oskar Morgenstern, *Theory of Games and Economic Behavior* (Princeton, N.J.: Princeton University Press, 1944).

5. For one exception, see Kenneth R. Andrews (ed.), *The Case Method of Teaching Human Relations and Administration: An Interim Statement* (Cambridge, Mass.: Harvard University Press, 1953).

6. For one example, see William J. Gore and Fred S. Silander, "A Bibliographical Essay on Decision Making," *Administrative Science Quarterly,* 4 (June, 1959), 97–121.

7. Herbert Storing tells us, on this point, that Simon's bibliography contains an article, book review, or comment for every two months of his professional career. Simon also has averaged a book every two years. "The Science of Administration," in Herbert Storing (ed.), *Essays on the Scientific Study of Politics* (New York: Holt, Rinehart & Winston, 1962), p. 123n.

8. Richard C. Snyder, H. W. Bruck, and Burton M. Sapin (eds.), *Foreign Policy Decision Making* (Glencoe, Ill.: The Free Press, 1962).

9. By way of ultimate selectivity, see Robert Schlaifer, *Probability and Statistics for Business Decisions* (New York: McGraw-Hill, 1959); and *A Comprehensive Bibliography on Operations Research* (New York: Wiley, 1958).

10. William R. Dill, "Administrative Decision-Making," in Sidney Mailick and Edward H. Van Ness (eds.), *Concepts and Issues in Administrative Behavior* (Englewood Cliffs, N.J.: Prentice-Hall, 1962), p. 29.

11. Storing, *op. cit.,* p. 65.

12. Gore, *op. cit.,* p. 50.

13. Simon, *Administrative Behavior,* p. ix.

14. Storing, *op. cit.*

15. For example, Simon's major shift from Administrative Man as "maximizing" to him as "satisficing" is one of these changes. Herbert A. Simon and Peter Simon, "Trial and Error Search in Solving Difficult Problems," *Behavioral Science* 7 (October, 1962), 425–29. Samuel Krislov expressed the consequence pithily. Speaking of Charles Lindblom's "incrementalism," Krislov noted that: "Simon . . . is in the interesting position of being both Lindblom's chief opponent and his John the Baptist." "Organizational Theory: Freedom and Constraint in a Large-Scale Bureaucracy," in Charles Press and Alan Arian (eds.), *Empathy and Ideology: Aspects of Administrative Innovation* (Chicago: Rand McNally, 1967), p. 50.

16. Simon, *Administrative Behavior,* pp. xxxiv, 45.

17. Martin Landau, "The Concept of Decision-Making in the Field of Public Administration," in Mailick and Van Ness, *op. cit.,* pp. 1–28.

18. Much of the reaction against Simon by "public policyers," for example, was motivated by a correct view of what it was that Simon's argument implied.

19. Robert T. Golembiewski, "The Small Group, Public Administration, and Organization," Ph.D. dissertation, Yale University, 1958.

20. Landau, *op. cit.,* p. 2.

21. Dwight Waldo, *Perspectives on Administration* (University, Ala.: University of Alabama Press, 1956).

22. William F. Willoughby, *Government of Modern States* (New York: Appleton-Century, 1936), pp. 219–21.

23. Marshall E. Dimock, "The Study of Administration," *American Political Science Review,* 30 (February, 1937), 28–40.

24. John Pfiffner and R. Vance Presthus, *Public Administration* (3rd. ed.; New York: Ronald Press, 1953), p. 5.

25. Landau, *op. cit.,* p. 17.

26. Unfortunately for Public Administration, the estrangement was near its peak during the period when Business

Administration was well along in attempting to set its own house in order. As massive evidence of this self-scrutiny, see Robert Aaron Gordon and James E. Howell, *Higher Education for Business* (New York: Columbia University Press, 1959); and Frank Pierson, *The Education of American Businessmen: A Study of University-College Programs in Business Administration* (New York: Carnegie Corporation, 1959). Relatedly and in sharpest contrast, the Committee for the Advancement of Teaching of the American Political Science Association took a more casual approach to their disciplinary state of affairs in the report *Goals for Political Science* (1951). James W. Fesler—as moderate and fair a reviewer as might be found—concluded that the report had "little more than distinguished authorship to recommend it." "Goals for Political Science: A Discussion," *American Political Science Review*, 45 (1951), 1000. Other observers are more direct, if anything. Albert Somit and Joseph Tanenhaus, *The Development of American Political Science: From Burgess to Behavioralism* (Boston: Allyn and Bacon, 1967), p. 188, for example, conclude that "the very triteness and superficiality of the volume made it important."

27. The mnemonic word represents Planning, Organizing, Staffing, Directing, Coordinating, Reporting, and Budgeting. Luther Gulick, "Notes On the Theory of Organization," in Gulick and Lundall Urwick (eds.), *Papers on the Science of Administration* (New York: Institute of Public Administration, 1937), p. 13.

28. The most prominent mass of such materials may be attributed to the President's Committee on Administrative Management, including its *Report with Special Studies* (Washington, D. C.: Government Printing Office, 1937). On this crucial part of our administrative history, including its major and minor actors, see Barry Dean Karl, *Executive Reorganization and Reform in the New Deal* (Cambridge, Mass.; Harvard University Press, 1963). Acknowledgement of the superiority of this work over that in Business Administration, for example, is a dominant theme of Gordon and Howell, *op. cit.*

29. Gulick and Urick, *op. cit.*

29a. Albert Somit and Joseph Tanenhaus, *The Development of Political Science: From Burgess to Behavioralism* (Boston: Allyn and Bacon, 1967), pp. 147–48.

30. A prominent dating-point is provided by Paul Appleby's *Policy and Administration* (University, Ala.: University of Alabama Press, 1949).

31. Marshall E. Dimock, Gladys O. Dimock, and Louis W. Koenig, *Public Administration* (New York: Rinehart, 1953), p. 12.

32. Landau, *op. cit.*, p. 9.

33. *Ibid.*, p. 9.

34. Harold Stein, "Preparation of Case Studies," *American Political Science Review*, 45 (June, 1951), 479–87.

35. Landau, *op. cit.*, p. 9.

36. Dwight Waldo, *The Study of Administration* (Garden City, N.Y.: Doubleday, 1955), especially pp. 1–14.

37. Frederick C. Mosher, "Research in Public Administration," *Public Administration Review*, 16 (Summer, 1956), 177.

38. Roscoe Martin, "Political Science and Public Administration," *American Political Science Review*, 46 (September, 1952), 672.

39. Herbert A. Simon, "A Comment on 'The Science of Public Administration,'" *Public Administration Review*, 7 (Summer, 1947), 200–203. Most of this "flowering" has occurred in the behavioral sciences and in schools of business and industrial administration, not the least of which is the Carnegie Institute of Technology, with which Simon has been associated since 1949. Within Public Administration, work consistent with Phase 3 has been more rare and less noted. One exception is John D. Millett's *Management in the Public Service* (New York: McGraw-Hill, 1954). Waldo notes that it "is somewhat narrower in focus than the customary textbook, concentrating on management," (*op. cit.*, p. 71). Most students would evaluate that "narrowness" as undesirable.

40. Robert A. Dahl, "The Science of Public Administration: Three Problems," *Public Administration Review*, 7 (Winter, 1947), 1–11.

41. Simon, "A Comment on 'The Science of Public Administration,'" p. 202.

42. Landau, *op. cit.*, p. 15.

43. Simon, *Administrative Behavior*, p. 53.

44. *Ibid.*, p. 21

45. *Ibid.*, p. 54.

46. Frank J. Goodnow, *Politics and Administration* (New York: Macmillan, 1900), p. 85.

47. Simon, *Administrative Behavior*, p. 55.

48. *Ibid.*, p. 58.

49. *Ibid.*, pp. 56–57.

50. Wallace S. Sayre, "Premises of Public Administration," *Public Administration Review*, 17 (Spring, 1958), 194.

51. Benjamin Lee Whorf, "Science and Linguistics," in John B. Carroll (ed.), *Language, Thought, and Reality* (New York: Wiley, 1956), p. 212.

52. Simon, *Administrative Behavior*, p. 249.

53. *Ibid.*

54. See especially Chapter II above.

55. Simon, *Administrative Behavior*, p. 21.

56. Dwight Waldo, "Replies and Comment," *American Political Science Review*, 46 (June, 1952), 503.

57. Simon, *Administrative Behavior*, p. xiii.

58. The bias becomes more explicit in James G. March and Herbert A. Simon, *Organizations* (New York: Wiley, 1958), in their chapter on the limits of cognitive rationality.

59. Storing, *op. cit.*, p. 104.

60. Simon, *Administrative Behavior*, pp. xxiv–xxv.

61. *Ibid.*, p. xxv.

62. *Ibid.*, p. 41.

63. *Ibid.*, p. 149.

64. *Ibid.*, p. xxiv.

65. Storing, *op. cit.*, pp. 115–16.

66. Simon, *Administrative Behavior*, p. 198.

67. Storing, *op. cit.*, p. 71.

68. Simon, *Administrative Behavior*, p. xlv.

69. *Ibid.*, p. xlvi.

70. *Ibid.*, p. 37.

71. *Ibid.*, p. 37.

72. *Ibid.*, p. 22.

73. Robert T. Golembiewski, *The Small Group: An Analysis of Research Concepts and Operations* (Chicago: University of Chicago Press, 1962), especially pp. 97–104.

74. Simon, *Administrative Behavior*, p. 149.

75. Charles E. Lindblom, "The Science of 'Muddling Through,'" *Public Administration Review*, 19 (Spring, 1959), 79–88.

76. Charles Z. Wilson and Marcus Alexis, "Basic Frameworks for Decisions," *Journal of the Academy of Management*, 5 (August, 1962), 162.

77. Chester I. Barnard, *The Functions of the Executive* (Cambridge, Mass.: Harvard University Press, 1938), p.193.

78. Wilson and Alexis, *op. cit.*, p. 164.

79. *Ibid.*

80. Simon, *The New Science of Management Decision*, p. 21.

81. Wilson and Alexis, *op. cit.*, p. 160.

82. Philip Selznick, *Leadership in Administration* (Evanston, Ill.: Row, Peterson, 1957), p. 137.

83. Simon, *Administrative Behavior*, p. 37.

84. Selznick, *op. cit.*, p. 81.

85. *Ibid.*, pp. 138–39.

86. *Ibid.*, p. 139.

87. Stanley Stark, "Creative Leadership," *Journal of the Academy of Management*, 6 (June, 1963), 166–67.

88. Golembiewski, *The Small Group*, especially pp. 128–44.

89. Robert T. Golembiewski, *Men, Management, and Morality* (New York: McGraw-Hill, 1965).

90. The test apparently does not discriminate "authoritarians of the left" from "authoritarians of the right." See Edward A. Shils, "Authoritarianism: 'Right' and 'Left,'" especially pp. 24–49, in Richard Christie and Marie Jahoda (eds.), *Studies in the Scope and Method of "The Authoritarian Personality"* (Glencoe, Ill.: The Free Press, 1954).

91. Golembiewski, *Men, Management, and Morality*, especially pp. 161–202.

92. Eugene J. Meehan, *The Theory and Method of Political Analysis* (Homewood, Ill.: The Dorsey Press, 1965), p. 157.

93. Meehan, *op. cit.*, p. 161. For a related view, see James N. Rosenau, "The Premises and Promises of Decision-Making Analysis," in James C. Charlesworth (ed.), *Contemporary Political Analysis* (New York: Free Press, 1967), pp. 189–92.

# PART THREE

## Some Methodological Tests: Five Specific Fields In a Science of Politics

viii

# Some Leading Approaches Methodologically Viewed, I: The Comparative Study of Political Systems

Methodologically speaking, comparative politics knows much of the best and some of the worst of it. We emphasize the former for a straightforward reason. Despite the continuing dominance of inelegant research and of even less sophisticated writing, the field of comparative politics has experienced important advances toward the construction of broad-gauged empirical models. Foremost among the signposts of a better research tomorrow are: (1) a recognition of the often-dominant significance of "informal" political processes; (2) a blending of institutional studies with functional approaches; (3) more systematic utilization of existing historical studies, particularly by conceptually relating discrete case studies through the drawing of analogies at higher levels of generalization; (4) identification of political concepts with significance in all political systems; (5) more vigorous concern with the process of change, as opposed to purely static description; and (6) great and growing interest in quantification and/or mathematization designed to facilitate the comparability of comparative studies.

While we feast essentially on meaty dishes, we do not overlook the real signs of famine in comparative politics. In fact, briefly, comparative politics can claim the dubious distinction of being more unfaithful to its self-defined methodological goals than perhaps any other segment of the discipline. What now is called the "comparative analysis of political systems" has in the past been non-comparative and non-analytical, and has failed to focus on *systems*. Indeed, some observers even accuse it of being "non-political" in accounting for political events.

Further, like most analytical menus, ours must necessarily exclude some tasty dishes. This chapter does not examine, for example, the growing body of cross-national survey research[1] despite the fact that a number of the methodological problems we discuss are reflected in comparative survey research. Our neglect of cross-national survey research reflects its newness and tentativeness only, as well as the arbitrariness of any selection process.

## I. COMPARATIVE POLITICS METHODOLOGICALLY VIEWED: FOCUS, LOCUS, AND ECOLOGY

Students of comparative politics have never really agreed upon their place in the discipline of Political Science, nor have they come to a common position concerning what comparative analysis qua method is supposed to be. These problems of disciplinary and methodological self-definition demand attention for two reasons. First, what comparative politics specialists are doing is conditioned by their own view of their place in the academic enterprise. Second, much of the methodological inelegance of the field results from the multi-directional orientation of comparative politics.

### A. Conceptual Focus and Locus: What (and Where) is Comparative Politics?

The methodological confusion extant in comparative analysis may be sketched via six major approaches to this focal question: "What *is* comparative analysis?" Borrowing from political sociologists, some make comparative analysis a single, broad-gauged approach which by definition represents the basis of all theory-building. Martindale supports this view, for example, contending that comparative analysis is one of three acceptable kinds of systematic procedure by which theories may be constructed or verified. His triumvirate includes comparative analysis, experimental method, and statistical method. The "logic of the method" remains constant in all three cases: "these sub-distinctions arise only in terms of the degree of precision of the theory and the amount and kind of control possible over the data to which a theory is addressed."[2] Of the three, comparative analysis presumably has the smallest degree of theoretical precision and the smallest amount of data control.

Most political scientists and anthropologists, by contrast, have opted for a second position. They generally hold that there are numerous comparative methods that differ too much to be grouped together meaningfully. The various approaches and techniques used in a comparative manner also are alleged to have substantially different implications for theory-building. Lewis argues that various comparative methods differ sharply, and that the procedures and implications of any method are largely determined by the nature of the problem.[3] In particular, Lewis stresses the distinctness of cross-cultural and longitudinal comparisons.

Their objectives are different; the content of the hoped for theories will differ; and the data obtained will be meaningfully different. Similarly, according to Lewis, the comparative uses of quantitative and qualitative techniques must be distinguished.

A third position with numerous adherents denies any sense to speaking of comparative method or comparative analysis. This paradoxical position reflects an intellectual nationalism, rather than a prolegomena to intellectual surrender by comparative politics specialists. In sum, comparative analysis is viewed as pervasive in all areas of inquiry. In this view, comparison is not part of science. It *is* science.

The rationale for the third position has merit, and we shall stress four points here in support of it. First, comparison is the basis of concept formation. That is, we give similar labels to phenomena which seem similar in certain ways, and we determine similarity by comparing. Second, the process of classification, or typing, must rely on the identification of similarities and differences among relevant sets of phenomena. Third, comparison is a crucial concomitant of induction. The fruitfulness of any generalization for future investigations is closely related to the breadth of the parent sample of observations and to the degree to which these observations are couched in comparable terms. Fourth, after observable propositions have been deduced from general statements, the process of verification must make use of comparative replications. In short, comparative analysis is a crucial component at every step in the process of theory-building.

Several of our *avant-garde* colleagues assume a fourth posture, that comparative methodology essentially constitutes the behavioral approach that underlies all quantification and mathematization. The perception of comparative method as a prerequisite for increasing quantitative sophistication developed first among anthropologists. For example, Nadel *defines* comparative analysis in terms of its application of the techniques of correlational analysis and co-variation.[4] Naroll's data quality-control technique similarly rests fundamentally on comparative method.[5] In more general terms, applications of scaling or measurement theory involve implicit comparison. Moreover, almost all statistical methods are based on the presumption that systematic comparison is both desirable and possible. In fact, statistics may be considered the most highly systematized form of comparative analysis.

Some students of politics view comparative analysis as the social sciences' answer to controlled experimentation, a fifth variation. Ackerknecht put the matter directly: "One of the great advantages of the comparative method," he noted, "will be that in a field where the controlled experiment is impossible it provides at least some kind of control."[6] Since political scientists cannot yet widely use laboratory research techniques,[7] comparative analysis has a patent value in the discipline.

Finally, a significant number of contemporary scholars argue that systematic comparative analysis simply is not possible. This sixth position has several major variants. For example, some argue that "Historical and other factors give nations characteristics that are unique, that is to say, cannot be duplicated." The conclusion is direct, despite many such variations as: "In fact, we shall find it virtually impossible to verify any hypothesis or to develop any generalization that is valid for *all* political systems."[8] Macridis and Brown are joined in a similar position by Almond and Coleman.[9]

Confusion over the methodological focus of comparative politics begets or at least co-exists with debate over physical locus. That is, specialists in this field are unsure about where, if anywhere, they stand in the discipline of Political Science. Some argue that comparative politics is an identifiable sub-field within the discipline; others urge that comparative politics *is* Political Science.

Paradoxically, the questions about the disciplinary position have become increasingly insistent with the growing respect for comparative method (or methods) in Political Science. In their earlier years of blissful inadequacy, specialists in "comparative government" felt secure in precisely what they were studying and how it was related to the rest of Political Science. Since the field excluded the United States as a focus of study, it might have been called "foreign governments." Further, as Macridis has indicated, the traditional approach in comparative government focused primarily on the governmental process within the larger Western democracies. Other governments, more or less, were deviations from the norms of these Western systems. The traditional limits were confining. They permitted description, but not analysis or explanation.

This state of blissful unawareness was first jolted by the Social Science Research Council's Committee on Comparative Politics.[10] As the recognition of past inadequacies was driven home to specialists in comparative politics, the field began painfully (although not always painstakingly) to re-evaluate itself. One of the early by-products of the new introspection was disciplinary insecurity for foreign/comparative government specialists. Older specialists, particularly, could not help but recognize that they and analysts of American politics would increasingly need to pool their efforts in developing a genuinely comparative mode of analysis. Going into business with a clearly more powerful partner is never a comforting prospect. Moreover, as Almond, Cole, and Macridis suggest, "If one compares the literature on American government and politics with that which concerns continental Europe, it is quite evident that the two fields of study in the last decades have proceeded on somewhat different assumptions as to the scope and methods of political science."[11] Specialists in comparative politics, vis-à-vis their colleagues specializing in the American system, obviously went to the post with a substantial handicap in their race toward increased methodological sophistication. Precisely where a genuine merger will leave the more traditional comparative politics scholars is unclear. The traditional legalistic, historical posture in this field patently has been dealt a telling blow.

## B. How Comparative Politics Got That Way Methodologically: A Brief Chronology of Comparative Political Studies

How matters come to such a difficult decision point may be sketched broadly. Commonly, students trace the origins of comparative politics to Machiavelli and the Renaissance. Let us also acknowledge the debt owed by specialists in the comparative area to the classics, especially to Aristotle. For many purposes, the efforts of these two men constitute the termini of a continuum across which the bulk of comparative analysis has ranged.

For our purposes, two characteristics of Aristotelian thought are most significant. First, Aristotle contended that the essence of a political relationship was the presence of authority, rule, or power, striking a chord that is still heard. Second, Aristotle advanced one of the first, and one of the most durable, classification schemes for governments. In Dahl's words, "Aristotle's classification has . . . proved so useful for so many different purposes that it has survived the political vicissitudes and transformations of twenty-five centuries. Indeed, it or something like it is as much a part of the habitual thinking of the student of politics today as it was to the observant Greek in Aristotle's day."[12]

Aristotle's concerns with power and classification blend as one. He proposed that states, or political systems, be distinguished according to two criteria. First, the taxonomist must ask the nature of the goals toward which a state or a political system might be moving. Second, differentiations may be made on the basis of "the various kinds of authority to which men and their associations are subject." Obviously, Aristotle was combining empirical and normative criteria in his scheme of classification. He was concerned not only with the description of current states of affairs; he was also deeply interested in assessing the congruence of reality with his conception of what *ought* to be. Thus, for Aristotle, the comparison of states or political systems consisted of carefully combining empirical observations with value judgments, while respecting the integrity of each.

Aristotle proved a better molder than a model. That is, Aristotle himself—in the company of scores of comparative political theorists over the years—argued that the intermingling of empirical and philosophic considerations was dangerous. However, many over-extensions of this element of Aristotelian thinking survive. Given periods of decline and reassertion, the essentials of his posture and exaggerations thereof can still be found in some contemporary comparative works. In this sense, Aristotle's approach is a forerunner of the less inhibited "ideal-types" approach which has found some currency in political sociology.

Machiavelli made a determined effort to guard against that contamination of fact and value into which guileless extensions of Aristotle led. Machiavelli's emphasis might be described as an effort "to discover directly techniques of statecraft."[13] Machiavelli was the student par excellence of the art of political manipulation. He was interested in the examination of experience; this he viewed as a kind of "record of trial and error." In Machiavelli's perspective, human experience in politics represented a kind of "thoughtless experimentation in which some procedures are revealed to be conducive and others not conducive to certain ends."[14] In a sense, Machiavelli was a forerunner of what we now call policy-oriented studies. Our terminology describes his work in *The Prince* as a goal-based, empirical effort. Methodologically unpretentious though it was, his research focused on constructing a medium-range prescriptive theory about the art of statecraft.

Machiavelli served as a model for some comparative analysts, but Aristotelian variants have inspired many more. That is, the lure of broad worlds to conquer encouraged many students to grapple methodologically with combining elements of fact and of value in analysis of large political aggregates. Thus it was with the political philosophers of the Enlightenment. For example, Montesquieu was interested in using induction primarily for purposes of statecraft. But his emphasis was less on the micro-prescription of leadership behavior and more on the macro-prescription of how governments should be legally constituted. His approach to the proper construction of a constitutional order is what has guaranteed him a permanent place in the chronology of comparative politics.

Montesquieu cut a wide swath, and in many senses did so with an insight whose acuteness is reflected in the contemporary rediscovery of its manifold usefulness. *The Spirit of the Laws* emphasizes the importance of the congruence of government structure and constitutional arrangements with the sociological and ecological milieux which constitute the environmental setting of political activity. That is, Montesquieu engaged a variety of central problems facing comparative specialists. For example, there is more than a little in Montesquieu of the relationship of the structure of government to the kinds of functions which it is called upon to undertake. Some commentators also have seen "scattered, but suggestive, hints,"[15] at process analysis, at social dynamics no less than social statics. Finally, Montesquieu was at least a little concerned with what we now label a systems approach. That is, he was interested in describing societies as entities having a finite number of interrelated parts, each of which responded in some way to changes or fluctuations in the nature of the others. As Eckstein has put the matter:

> In Montesquieu . . . and in the writings of lesser men of the Enlightenment we can see emerging a comparative science of politics not so very different from that which present political scientists seem to want: a "science" aiming at the construction of a structural-functional analysis of political systems, sophisticated typology of such systems, a set of broad generalization about the links between polity, society, economy, and environment and a set of mechanistic theories of political dynamics—all in embryo, of course, but in many cases in surprisingly sophisticated form.[16]

Neither Montesquieu's insight nor acuteness was complemented by methodological guidelines, however, and comparative analysis easily over-extended itself. Scholarship historically slipped the implicit methodological moorings provided by Machiavelli, who was assuredly a prophet with little honor in his own time. Social thought for the period following Montesquieu proceeded from, and proceeded to, very different kinds of ideas. In the manner of Condorcet, Hegel, Comte, and Marx, the dominant style became unbridled historicism replete with grand developmental theories, usually deterministic, utopian, and broadly speculative as to the first causes of momentous historical events.[17] This historicist period was principally characterized by two concerns: an interest in the construction of extremely broad-gauged theories; and a growing obsession with "detailed and formless political history, a sort of political ethnography."[18]

We may sketch some of the specific senses in which rejection of Machiavelli did not imply respect for Montesquieu. At least in Political Science, historicism's importance derives not so much from what it was, as from the reactions to which it led. Generally speaking there were three kinds of reactions against historicism: (1) the retreat of some scholars into almost totally abstract logical expositions in deductive philosophizing; (2) the initiation of institutional studies of formal governmental structures; and (3) what we may call configurative studies, those inquiries describing the characteristics of a single national entity, often in laborious detail.

First, some scholars rejected almost all tenets of empiricism, losing themselves in deductive logical expositions. They thought about thought, not about any behavioral manifestations of ideas. Some analysts—such as Rousseau in his *Social Contract*—did so consciously, skillfully, and with full awareness of the limitations of their efforts. Many others went on building theories even if that "was so much the worse for the facts."

Second, in sharp contrast, some students of politics rejected exercises in abstract theory and chose a path which ultimately became something close to a polar opposite. The "institutionalists" almost completely ignored the significance of ideas, as well as the possible importance of what we now call the "informal" aspect of politics. Their focus also neglected the environmental setting of governmental activity, which Montesquieu had so painstakingly insisted was of great significance. These institutionalists increasingly concentrated on the constitutional and legal structures of major governments. Thus developed what Eckstein considers a "natural outgrowth of the positivistic reaction to historicism," the study of formal-legal arrangements. And thus also developed the approach which has characterized so much of the comparative government literature until very recently.

The development of configuration studies as a third anti-historicist reaction may legitimately be viewed as the forerunner of "non-comparative comparison." Configurative studies were simply descriptions of specific societies, treated either explicitly or implicitly as unique entities. In their pure form, these inquiries were much ado about virtually nothing.[19] They provided extensive, often indiscriminate, coverage of a relatively small number of phenomena.

Like all of life, these three unfortunate products of methodological inelegance affected the future and were shaped by it. The nineteenth and early twentieth centuries saw the emergence of two new schools of thought in the social sciences which had important impact on contemporary comparative politics. Some social scientists began to develop evolutionary constructs purporting to explain the origins of the state. These evolutionary approaches were based on theories then in currency in the physical and life sciences. And "informal politics" received rapidly increasing attention from a group of political sociologists whose work reflects a conscious disgust with the legalistic, formalistic studies then dominant in the field.

Evolutionary theories, as applied to politics, emphasized the specification of prerequisites for the modernization of political systems. These models usually were based on an hypothesized set of stages of political development through which all societies supposedly must pass.[20] Evolutionary theories thus tended to be deterministic. Yet if they were unidirectional, they were not correspondingly uni-causal in their assumptions. Evolutionary theories were indeed concerned with causal factors underlying sequential changes, but evolutionary theorists substantially disagreed as to the nature of these causal factors. Current opinion in comparative politics has argued both yes[21] and no[22] concerning the long-run influence of evolutionary approaches. In any case, the recent expansion of the scope of study of comparative politics has at least raised the question of the utility of evolutionary theories, since they seem to have at least a surface relevance to the politics of the developing areas.

The scholars who may be called the early political sociologists cannot be separated easily from those whose contributions might be considered contemporary. For our purposes Mosca, Durkheim, Pareto, Michels, and Ostrogorski are prototypes of the political sociologists who first put effective emphasis on the informal side of political activity.[23] Principally, the early sociologically oriented students of politics branched out from studies of the state into studies of a wide variety of other phenomena. They discussed the structure and functioning of political parties, as well as various categories of interest groups. They made extensive and often impressive efforts to relate politics to its environmental setting. Of great significance were the efforts by these forerunners to develop new concepts and novel techniques for the comparative study of politics. The chapter below dealing with research on political parties excuses the broad brush with which we paint here.

What comparative analysis represents, then, is basically a changing but recognizable resultant of such multi-directional approaches. Our chronology emphasizes how some early patterns of thought and investigation have influenced trends of recent decades in the comparative study of politics, as filtered by an intervening history of excess. First, early research implied a broad focus for comparative research. Parochialism lives on, but in reduced circumstances. Second, these earlier trends prodded the development of scientific rigor, particularly by adopting concepts and operations from other segments of Political Science and from other social sciences. Third, embryonic political sociology contributed much to a more systematic concern with informal political processes. In particular, the development of group approaches, the growing concern with political socialization and motivations toward political participation, studies of leadership recruitment, and investigations of the decision-making and policy-making processes have been especially important in advancing the scientific study of politics. Finally, the importance of the variegated social settings of political activity also may be traced back to theorists and researchers of earlier periods.

## II. METHODOLOGICAL CAMEOS OF THREE TYPES OF COMPARATIVE ANALYSIS

The attention to focus, locus, and ecology helps frame more specific analysis. Our approach to specificity proceeds through representatives of three approaches to comparative analysis: the philosophic traditionalists, the model-builders, and the mathematizers/quantifiers. We stress convenience, but, it is hoped, with no neglect of comprehensiveness. And we stress simplification, but not to excuse drawing caricatures. There is at least a little of the philosophic posture in most contributions to the comparative politics literature. We ask Heckscher[24] to speak for the legions, therefore. The model-builders discussed will be Aberle, et al.,[25] Almond,[26] Apter,[27] Easton,[28] and Spiro.[29] Deutsch,[30] Lipset,[31] and Cutright[32] will represent the mathematization-quantification approach.

### A. Philosophic Traditionalists in Comparative Politics: Denial as an Anti-Methodology

The philosophic traditionalists proceed from a valid and significant charge against those who would transform the study of politics into a purely scientific enterprise. In its most reasonable and meaningful form, traditionalism urges that the discipline has suffered from numerous uncritical extensions of method that were kidnapped from the natural and life sciences and impressed as awkward servants in the study of politics. Unfortunately, the philosophic traditionalist is frequently observed in unrestrained, unbridled form. In this variant, he asserts that *none* of the subject matter of comparative politics is in fact amenable to scientific techniques.

If the philosophic traditionalists have achieved "neo-eminence" in other areas of Political Science,[33] they apparently have failed to hold their own in comparative politics. The comparative field is not methodologically sophisticated or theoretically advanced, but it has few exponents who fit comfortably into the philosophic traditionalist category. However, we can safely detail some major tenets of the philosophic persuasion and demonstrate where they remain as vestigial survivals of an earlier era. As summarized by Heckscher, the philosophic anti-science school in comparative politics holds the following basic propositions.[34] First, the comparative study of political systems can never be objective, or value-free. The supporting evidence can only be sampled. Thus the initial act of scholarly inquiry, that of selecting problems for research, is shown to be a subjective matter. Criteria of relevance for problem selection cannot be devised, since no universal categories of significance exist.[35] Similarly, approaches, techniques, and units and levels of analysis also must be subjectively chosen. The philosophic argument occasionally goes even further. It sometimes asserts that even if objective criteria for problem selection, focus, and method could be devised, there still could not be objective research.[36] Human beings, it is contended, simply cannot exclude what they value and believe from the collection and analysis of data.

Second, the philosophic traditionalists argue that the social sciences are quite distinct from the "exact" or natural sciences. Scientific exactitude in the comparative study of political phenomena is precluded because human beings behave in unfathomable ways. Consistently, Heckscher contends that the social and especially the behavioral sciences—focusing as they do on the actions of human beings—offer even less hope of scientific precision than the "older humanistic sciences." For example, Law has more scientific potential than does Psychology. In Political Science, as in its sister disciplines, "scientificness is hardly more than an attitude of mind."[37]

Third, while philosophic traditionalists acknowledge that at least rudimentary explanation is now possible in comparative politics, they insist that prediction is quite another matter.[38] Thus, the traditionalist declines to accept what is now generally acknowledged in the natural sciences and, indeed, in Sociology and Psychology: that adequate explanation automatically yields some predictive power. Consequently, political scientists may well explain given phenomena. But to project these narrow explanations into the future would allegedly be foolhardy. The course of human events is unpredictable, the universe is essentially unknowable, and even those social scientists with methodological seven-league boots would find it impossible to traverse enough of the terrain of reality to encompass the diverse factors which influence individual behaviors.

Fourth, Heckscher suggests that quantification is of little value in Political Science. Since quantification is inescapable in empirical theory, this means that Political *Science* is out of reach. The senselessness of quantification is particularly applicable to comparative politics, suggests Heckscher. For the comparative field must deal with comparisons of data obtained from a number of varying national settings. Just as one "can't combine apples and oranges," so is it also inappropriate to combine conceptually similar observations made in different settings. For example, some argue that we cannot measure intensities of preference,[39] since the subjective psychological cost of maintaining a given preference may be substantially different between political systems, or even among different individuals in the same political setting.[40]

A fifth philosophic contention is that genuinely systematic hypothesizing, especially that projected across national boundaries, is impossible. Roughly, the argument is this. If we had reasonably sound information on the political phenomena with which we were concerned, we really would not need to hypothesize. In the absence of information, on the other hand, hypotheses "are apt to be somewhat uninteresting."[41] As a matter of fact, without substantial information to guide the process of hypothesizing, these tentative constructs are little more than intuitive hunches.

Much of the argument of the philosophic traditionalists demands attention. For example, Heckscher opines that "attempts made so far [to re-work the terminology of Political Science] have frequently proved more ridiculous than precise."[42] The underlying concern has two components. First, the philosophic school is opposed in principle to the adoption of *terminology* from other social sciences—as it should be—when it appears to them as if the *treatment* of that concept within the other disciplines has been somehow inconsistent with the ways in which it might be validly handled in Political Science. Second, the philosophic traditionalists are very concerned with communicating to a broad audience.[43] Model-builders and mathematizers/quantifiers, in contrast, seem essentially unconcerned with the ability of the political practitioner or educated layman to read and understand their material.

Relatedly, the philosophic traditionalists have facilitated reform as they attempted to obstruct it. For example, perhaps the principal contribution of the philosophic school has been the strengthening of the movement ("behavioral," "systematic," or whatever) which seeks scientific rigor in political research. We intend no backhanded slur on the philosophers. They have not strengthened the opposition by being inept antagonists. Indeed, they have bloodied many behavioral heads with weighty arguments well-put. The philosophic traditionalists have aided the discipline immeasurably by performing a time-honored function of the mature generation: they have caused the young Turks to temper their own exuberance, to become increasingly willing to acknowledge that its Rome will require more than a day to build, and to recognize that such building often can make good use of earlier foundations.

But the position of the philosophic traditionalists invites critical comment as well. Consider their fundamental and frequent objection that a "value-free" science of politics is impossible. Broadly speaking, the philosophic argument about subjectivity is so obviously true that it is meaningless. The application of any criteria for any purpose implies valuation, by definition. The notion of subjectivity at once encompasses everything and nothing. *To say that an act is value-laden is to say nothing empirically significant about that act.* All human behaviors are at least implicitly concerned with the selection of some phenomena from among others for attention, and such selection is patently value-based. If we conceive of subjectivity as broadly as the philosophic traditionalists uniformly do, consequently, every act through which a human being relates to his environment is subjective. Subjectivity then becomes a useless concept. But there will be some selections—e.g., separating elephants and fleas—that are useful descriptively and predictively. Science seeks such selections, and in doing so reflects the meta-values in which all science must rest. The philosophic traditionalists are correct in a trivial sense, that is to say, but their position is monumentally irrelevant.

Further, granting the philosophic premise does not necessarily require that comparative political *research* be inextricably tied to normative preferences. No necessary connection exists between the role of values in problem selection and such other phases as the determination of conclusions, identification of facts, and the assessment of evidence.[44] The point has been suggested elsewhere, especially by Nagel,[45] Kemeny,[46] Popper,[47] and Van Dyke.[48] Simply put, there is no necessary link between our choice of where to go and what we see when we get there.

But is a hard-headed filtering of substantive values *really* possible? The ability to predict behavior in many areas suggests a "yes" answer. At the very least, there is only one way to ascertain whether an empirical science of politics can be devised, and that is to try to devise it. If insight on the road to wisdom is to triumph over observation on the road to knowledge, both cases must be heard. Reliance need not be placed on faith in science or anti-science. Faith here can be—and must be—confronted with hard evidence.

**B. Model-Builders in Comparative Politics**

We have chosen to focus on a handful of models attempting the comparative study of political systems. Generally, a handful suffices for two reasons. First, explicit models constitute better targets for methodological evaluation. Since comparative politics continues to be plagued by a plethora of vaguely articulated approaches, there are few suitable targets. Second, marked similarities do exist among the explicit models in widest use in the field. Similarity facilitates summary comment, and it also simplifies our selection. The models receiving attention here will be the formuations of Aberle, et al., Almond, Apter, Easton, and Spiro.[49] Commonalities of method and substance characterize these models.

Constructive criticism of the common features of model-building efforts will occupy us, but our necessarily brief observations will strike at least some readers as doing substantial violence to the often complex analytic structures with which we are dealing. Certainly there are important differences among these models, and our analytic difficulties are complicated by the necessity of analyzing these models without providing full summary of them. We acknowledge and lament these difficulties. Yet selectivity and simplification are necessary. We have tried to plug the dikes somewhere short of distortion. Relatedly, for pedagogic reasons we focus on one or two offerings of each model-builder. Intellectual creativity seems rather centralized, and these seminal thinkers in comparative politics continue to elaborate and refine their efforts. Our comments deal with frequently-cited versions of these models, and thus occasionally overlook minor modifications subsequently made by the authors. Apter's work in particular has undergone noticeable re-orientation since he developed his social stratification model of politics.

The comparative model-builders share at least two elements of methodological commitment. First, they seek universal concepts, that is, concepts which have similar (if not identical) empirical referments in all political systems. This search clearly is a prerequisite of general theory. Second, the model-builders are methodologically committed to broad, verifiable generalization. Higher levels of generality naturally call for an increasing degree of abstraction from empirical observations. If it is true that historical situations are unique, then general theorists may face a temporary need to emphasize differentially the explanatory and predictive functions of theory. Ignoring relatively specific characteristics of the political process in a given setting may have little or no effect on the ability of a theory to predict outcomes of the process, for example. The explanatory value of the theory might be considerably diminished, however. Our emphasis thus should be made clear. We seek general theory and consequently inquire how far existing efforts take us toward that goal. However, any analytic structure which is not on the doorstep of general theory should not be summarily rejected. Models of limited applicability may be quite useful, provided we recognize the limitations of each model.

The approaches of the comparative model-builders selected here have numerous substantive characteristics in common. We stress seven of them here. The usual model-building enterprise tends to:

1. focus on the environmental context of political activity;
2. utilize action-oriented concepts, generally culled from Parsonian thinking;
3. conceptualize political activity in a systemic way, with a particular concern for the goals of political system functioning;

4. deal, explicitly or implicitly, with the requisites (or prerequisites) for effective system operation;
5. imply the difficulties of "structural/functional" analysis;
6. emphasize a "group perspective" in viewing the political process; and
7. imply the model's universal applicability.

Because the characteristics above are interdependent, their analytic separation is merely convenient. Indeed, all of them point toward one general question: Are the models closing on the goal of a general, empirical theory?

A negative response seems appropriate. Each model has certain specific shortcomings, but we shall raise several consistent objections to the group as a whole. Typically, the models are:

1. terminologically quite careless, a fact which results in substantial ambiguity;
2. not operational, and some have doubtful operational promise;
3. dependent on a level of quantifiability of political concepts which has not yet been achieved; and
4. of narrower applicability than their authors would like to believe.

### *1. Focus on the Environmental Context of Political Activity*

Happily, model-builders are aware that political activity does not take place in a vacuum. Political actors behave partially in response to economic, social, cultural, religious, geographic, and other kinds of stimuli. We need but sample this conceptual agreement. In Easton's model of the political system, for example, demands from the essentially non-political environment are seen as major inputs into the political process. And Apter's model focuses on the concept of social stratification. He assumes that

> the dominant motive of social behavior [is] increased mobility toward the higher end of the stratification hierarchy. Members of the public join in political groups in order to expand mobility opportunities and, in this respect, make representations to government or to influence or control government in some manner. Government policy must then in part be responsive to the interests of political groups.[50]

There is little but compliment to offer the model-builders on the present point. Generally, they seem to have avoided the tendency of nineteenth-century political analysts to view politics as *entirely* dependent upon, for example, economic factors. At the same time, the model-builders

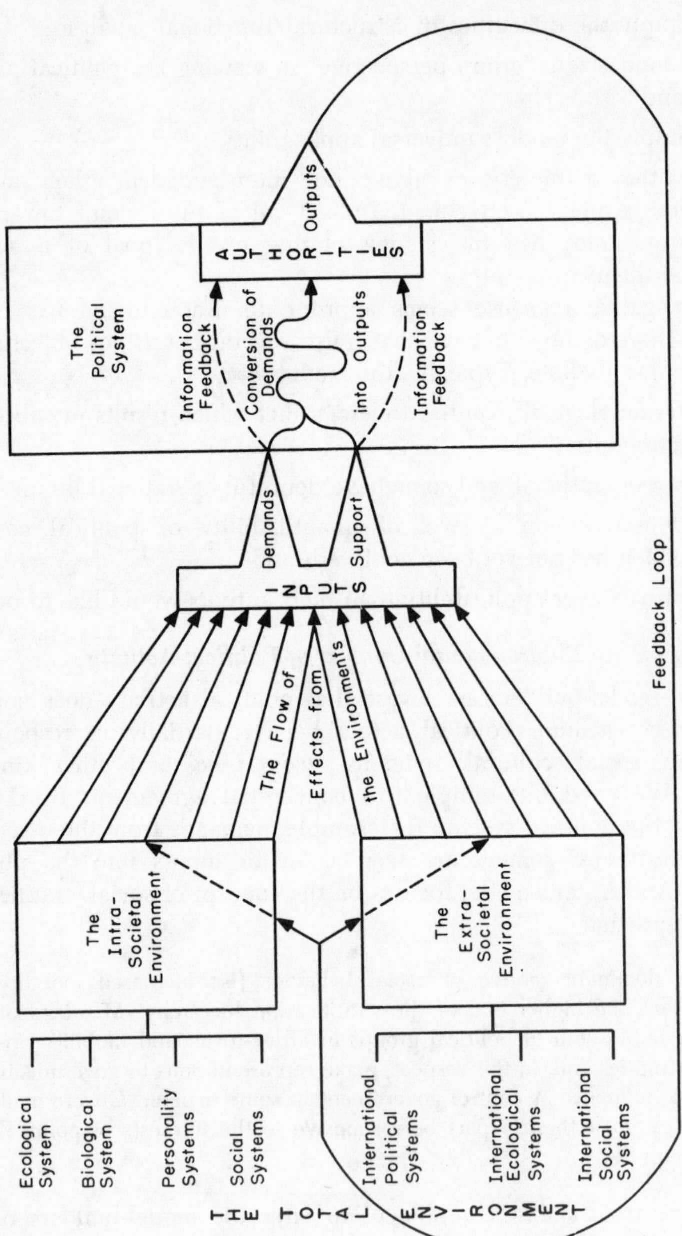


FIGURE VIII.1 Easton's "Dynamic Response" Model of a Political System. (From *A Framework for Political Analysis* (Englewood Cliffs, N.J.: Prentice-Hall, 1965), p. 110.)

occasionally do ignore the extent to which feedback from outputs of the political system may be channeled directly back into politics, rather than being carried indirectly through social groups in the environment. Examine Easton's model (Figure VIII.1), for example. Directly, making a decision influences the *way in which* one will make decisions in the future. In common-sense terms, experience matters. Little society-wide feedback occurs about the procedures by which authorities make decisions, since these procedures are often unknown outside a limited circle of elites. In such cases, feedback goes back into the political system, rather than through non-political agencies in the environment.

Handling this procedural feedback could be a simple matter for Easton. His model needs only a re-definition of one of its variables to incorporate all significant non-environmental inputs. For Easton does recognize that "we might search in vain for an explanation of the emergence of a given set of internal demands if we turned only to the environment."[51] There are, he says, "withinputs" or demands which do not have their "major locus" in the environment. Easton's "withinputs," however, seem overly narrow in definition. Furthermore, "withinputs" lack explicit conceptual definition; we must infer their nature from a handful of examples. These examples have two distressing attributes. First, they consistently involve actions by members of the political system who are motivated by their perceptions of the environment. Commonly, these perceptions involve growing inconsistency between cultural norms and extant political practices. Second, the "withinputs" mentioned by Easton seem to be system-wide in origin, involving the transmission of aggregated demands *to* decision-makers. The possibility that a societal sub-system could initiate and internally process self-demands without significant external influence is ignored.

### 2. *The Action Approach: Parsons and the Model-Builders*

In a laudatory effect to avoid the multiple pitfalls of static description, some comparative model-builders have sought to develop dynamic pictures of political processes. These pictures deal more with how things are changing than with what they are like at the moment. More specifically, action-oriented analysts are interested in how political systems are getting where they have decided to go. That is, their focus is on how systems utilize different means, different processes, to reach specified goals.

In much of their treatment of political processes, comparative model-builders reveal a substantial intellectual debt to Parsons.[52] Sometimes the linkage is made overt. For example, Almond acknowledges that his concepts have "emerged out of the Weber-Parsons tradition in social theory."[53] For Almond, a political system is a system of action. The basic unit of analysis in studying politics is the role. The system approach replaces the process approach, which is deemed inadequate because of the vagueness of the concept of *process*. Consequently, Almond views "political institutions or persons performing political roles . . . in terms of what it is that they do, why they do it, and how what they do is related to and affects what others do."[54] More microscopically, Almond stresses the concept of orientation to political action. This orientation may be expressed in three modes—cognition, cathexis, and evaluation—which are culled directly from Parsons.

The debt to Parsons also appears less explicitly. Thus Aberle and his associates do not trace their Parsonian heritage in any detail. But the action-oriented approach is central in their model. They observe only that "neither the nature of the dependence of our formulation on this theory of action nor the theory of action itself can be further elaborated here."[55] Yet they specify that the theory of action is at "the heart of the definition" of society. Further, they suggest that the "full significance [of the theory of action] will be developed in the exposition of the functional prerequisites" of society.[56] The theory of action indeed emerges as crucial, for "functional prerequisites" constitute the core of the model. Specifically, in any society there are *activities* which must be regularly performed if the society is to persist.[57] When the regularity of these activities—or "functional prerequisites"—is interrupted, the society collapses.

Other variations on the action approach have less clear, but still identifiable, Parsonian roots. Consider social stratification—one form of role differentiation—which has a special significance in Apter's model as well as in Aberle's scheme. Social stratification is hypothesized to result from the differential allocation of scarce resources. From this stratification follows much of what is significant about political activity, according to Apter. Hoping "to create a framework for the treatment of governments in diverse social settings in order to make possible some generalization about how the presence, absence, or clustering of certain combinations of variables affect politics,"[58] Apter proceeds from a model of politics in which "the dominant motive of social behavior is assumed (whether rightly or wrongly) to be the increased mobility toward the higher ends of the stratification hierarchy."[59] The derived behaviors, in turn, are conditioned by the nature of the political groups which spring up around particular goal-orientations, as well as by the nature of government and its degree of representativeness.

### *3. Goals and "Functional Requisites"*

Generally speaking, the comparative model-builders consider meaningful only those behaviors directed toward the attainment of specific systemic goals. It is not that the model-builders ignore the existence of non-purposive political behavior. Nor do they assume that all purposive behavior is consciously aimed at a political goal. The model-builders acknowledge that human beings act in specific ways for reasons unclear even to themselves. But for purposes of analysis, the model-builders tend to dismiss behavior which is not goal-oriented, as they define goals in functional requisites, for example. Two elements of their rationale seem most prominent. First, non-purposive behaviors are assumed to be insignificant in determining political outcomes, particularly at the system level. Second, apparently non-purposive behaviors may actually reflect conscious but empirically indeterminable motivation patterns. Intellectual discretion is considered the better part of valor, and speculation on personal motivations is thus avoided by the model-builders.

The significance of system goals is perhaps strongest in Spiro's model for comparative analysis. In his view, the existence of "community" is dependent upon the presence of persons who consciously pursue a finite set of goals. One type of community is a political system, which has one broad prerequisite: dissensus on the means by which a set of common goals should be achieved. According to Spiro, all political systems pursue four basic goals: stability, flexibility, efficiency, and effectiveness. (See Figure VIII.2.)

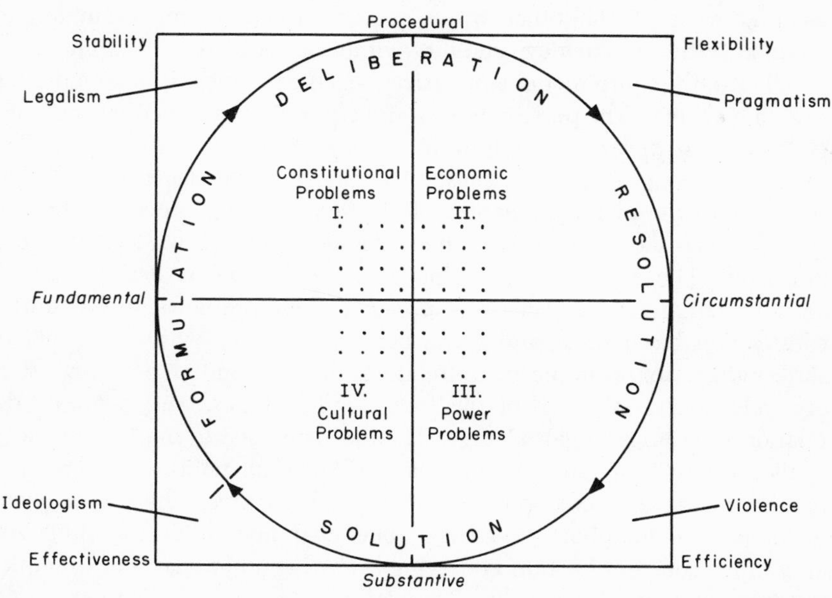


FIGURE VIII.2 A Diagrammatic Representation of Spiro's Model for the Comparative Analysis of Political Systems. (Adapted from *American Political Science Review,* LVI (September, 1962), 580.)

Spiro's use of systemic goal-orientation differs significantly from that of many model-builders. He admits the possibility that a system may fail to realize fully one or more of its basic goals without disintegrating, or at least undergoing "drastic modification."[60] Rather, Spiro chooses to evaluate the "relative success of political systems . . . by the degree to which they manage to sustain a dynamic equilibrium among the four basic goals."[61]

Methodologically speaking, the last phrase is a microcosm of the Spiro model, and bears elaboration here. First, Spiro implicitly views all characteristics of political systems on continua. Systems will more or less achieve what they are trying to do, for example. The existence of "subsystem distortion," too, is always a matter of degree. A system may be somewhat legalistic, or somewhat violent, or somewhat pragmatic, or somewhat ideological. In short, Spiro is not an "either-or" theorist. He explicitly avoids a methodological pitfall into which other model-builders, especially Apter, seem implicitly to have stepped.

Second, Spiro is very much concerned with the interrelation of system goals. As he explains: "none of the four basic goals [stability, flexibility, efficiency, effectiveness] by itself is sufficient for the success of a political system."[62] Further, the probable success of a system in meeting any one of the goals is at least partially dependent upon its success in meeting each of the other three goals. Ultimately, for example, no political system can achieve stability without a measure of flexibility.

Third, the Spiro model emphasizes social dynamics. It is a model for studying change. The possibility of static equilibrium is ruled out because systems seek *dynamic* equilibrium among the four basic goals. The relations among goals are constantly changing, at least partially in response to the changing nature of the issues being processed by the system. Then too, a given issue may change in nature while it is being processed. The model suggests four types of problems which may be encountered as basic goals are pursued. The problems are cultural, constitutional, economic, and power problems. We may visualize conflicts surrounding, for example, race relations in the United States as successively generating each of the four problem types. And not only do relationships among goals change. The means chosen to implement these goals are also in a state of constant flux. Since all political systems (to one degree or another) operate with limited resources, the use of given techniques in an effort to achieve one goal may limit the range of alternative courses of action in striving toward another goal. For example, the commitment of extensive financial resources to maintain a large military establishment may limit the funds available for domestic social welfare programs.

Concern with the goals of systems is critical not only for Spiro, but for most of the other model-builders as well. Apter equates the structural *requisites* of government, the *structure* of government, and the *goals* which governments must meet. In discussing the structural requisites of government, he identifies a "tentative set of goals," including "1) the structure of authoritative decision-making, 2) the structure of accountability and consent, 3) the structure of coercion and punishment, 4) the structure of resource determination and allocation, and 5) the structure of political recruitment and role assignment."[63] Unfortunately, Apter does not inform us just how requisite these structural requisites are. They are held to be "vitally necessary"; we are left with the impression that they cannot be done without. In short, Apter appears not to be concerned with the *degree* of attainment of these requisites. Either they are achieved or they are not. There seems to be no middle ground.

Aberle assumes a position somewhere between Spiro and Apter in definitiveness. All societies, he and his associates tell us, must avoid the *complete* realization of four conditions: the biological extinction or dispersion of its members, apathy of its members, "the war of all against all," and the absorption of the society into another society. The third condition is translated (perhaps questionably) into "a society based solely on force."[64] Completely avoiding these four conditions, of course, is not the same as fully achieving the opposite situation, viz., everyone in the society living forever, the interest and motivation levels of all citizens remaining high at all times, the total absence of force being applied within the society, and the unqualified self-sufficiency of the system. Indeed, achieving each of these conditions might destroy society. In any event, while we are told that certain conditions cannot be achieved fully, precisely how far a society could go toward the realization of one of these sets of circumstances is never spelled out. Thus, "every society needs *enough* adult members to insure reproduction and to man the essential status positions."[65] Obviously, we cannot expect precise mathematical formulae telling us how many virile specimens are needed to maintain a society under given environmental conditions. But it remains true that some kind of operational hint as to, for example, what status positions are essential is needed before much use could be made of the Aberle scheme.

As it now stands, the Aberle model stands open to charges of triviality as well as lack of operationality. The model provides no a priori basis for determining the adequacy of a system's efforts at goal attainment. The only way to tell how close a society may come to complete apathy of its members, for example, is to wait until a society ceases to exist. We could then attempt to discover how apathetic the citizenry was when the end came. Further, it might be extremely difficult to tell whether apathy was actually the catalytic agent in the system's disintegration. Stress along one or more of the other three dimensions could have been involved, and the tolerance level could be different for each dimension. This reduces us to dealing in tautologies. As long as a society exists, the tolerance level has not been reached on any of its requisite dimensions. When the society ceases to exist, we may presume that one or more of the critical terminating conditions was reached. Such a trivial conclusion hardly advances the cause of theory-building.

While Easton does not include the concept of *goals* as an element of his model, he is most concerned with the kinds of behaviors which others treat as goal-oriented, or goal-related. The goals of political actors are viewed by Easton as inputs (in this case, demands) into the political system. In a general sense, the basic goal of the political system is the resolution of conflicts among these demands, that is, the authoritative allocation of values for the whole society.[66] The system's outputs—"decisions or policies"[67]—must generate another type of input—"support"—"to keep [the political system] going."[68] In the grossest sense, then, self-preservation is the goal of the political system.

The wispy agreement on "goals" and "requisites" does break down in some senses, even while their essential similarity is preserved. For example, Apter demands that "the minimal requirements for the maintenance of government must be related to society in such a way that both can exist."[69] Easton is ambiguous on the point, however. At "least for analytical purposes," he conceptualizes the political system as a "self-contained entity surrounded by, but clearly distinguishable from, the environment or setting in which it operates."[70] By definition, political systems have "important outputs (decisions/policies) for society."[71] At the same time, Easton implicitly subscribes to the notion that some elements of the environment are essentially unrelated to the political system. Whether the converse is true is not clearly indicated. We are not told if *all* outputs of the political system affect the environment. In any case, Easton seems uninterested in whether the goals of the political system are either partially or completely congruent with those of the society (or broader social system) as a whole.

Seldom is the marked but imprecise agreement on "goals" and "requisites" violated, but it does happen. In fact, Almond alone among the prominent model-builders shows little concern with systemic goals in defining a political system as "the patterned interaction of roles affecting decisions backed up by the threat of physical compulsion."[72] Of course, the interactions of various political roles do involve demands upon descision-makers and these demands might well be viewed as goals of particular individuals or groups. But there is no concern in the Almond model for system-level goals. Indeed, even inferring the perhaps implied goal of self-preservation requires taking considerable liberty with the language of Almond's presentation.[73]

### *4. Structural/Functional Analysis as a Mother Theory*

In various forms, structural/functional analysis is a crucial component of contemporary models for comparative political study. Indeed, the similarities between functionalism and the central elements of these models are compelling enough to warrant reference to that product of anthropologists and sociologists as a "mother theory" of most models in comparative analysis. Illustratively, Flanigan and Fogelman serviceably characterize the models above in their list of central emphases in structural/functional analysis. Their central emphases include:

1. a conceptual focus on whole systems as the unit of analysis;
2. the postulation of requisite functions for system maintenance; and
3. a concern to demonstrate the functional interdependence of diverse structures within the system.[74]

If our reference to a mother theory is appropriate, maternity has not been given its full due. Flanigan and Fogelman suggest the point in noting that: "At no time has functionalism been a prevalent mode of analysis in political science, and political scientists have never borrowed extensively from the functionalists in anthropology and sociology."[75] The two observers conclude on an even flatter note. "Functional analysis," they observe, "has come to political science only recently and relatively few major works in the discipline have explicitly developed a functional analytic scheme." Specifically, the critical literature about the mother theory has been neglected—although that is fortunately changing[76]—while acceptance of the mother theory is facile and widespread. Functionalism can be observed in at least three discernible forms—eclectic functionalism, empirical functionalism, and structural-functional analysis—and Flanigan and Fogelman go so far as to insist that really "we are all functionalists now."[77] Further, they note that "it is obvious . . . that structural functionalism has attracted some of the ablest political scientists."[78]

We attempt here both to acknowledge the impact of functional analysis and to give it critical attention. Functionalism has come under considerable fire on logical, conceptual, and operational grounds. We summarize some of the critical emphases below, complementing the treatment in Chapter I and sharpening its focus to comparative analysis.

The logical difficulties with functional analysis—five of which we stress—are especially troublesome. First, functional approaches usually assume that all actions are either functional or dysfunctional for system maintenance. Consequently, these approaches ignore "vestigial survivals"—social patterns which do not seem to have adapted to a given social order.[79] This is more than a debater's point. Significantly, on the level of theory, some social theorists have argued that these survivals may provide the bases for social change.[80] Moreover, practically, it is too convenient to designate as a "vestigial survival" any element that does not fit one's model.

Second, functional approaches frequently embody the *post hoc, ergo propter hoc* fallacy. As Hempel notes, "temporal precedence does not in itself make an event relevant to the genesis of the item under consideration." A criterion of relevance is needed for historic-genetic explanation. Relevance here must consist in causal or probabilistic determination.[81] However, only a few political studies generate empirical data of sufficient strength to support these kinds of explanation.

Third, most functional explanations are formally inadequate, since they ignore what Gouldner has called the principle of reciprocal functionality. In his words: "The formal adequacy of a functional explanation of the persistence of a social pattern would seem to require that the analyst demonstrate not merely the consequences of A for B, but also, the reciprocal consequences of B for A."[82] For example, Apter holds that one of the structural requisites of government is providing means for making authoritative decisions. However, a formally adequate support of that requisite demands that we explain the persistence of authoritative decision-making, as well as the maintenance of equilibrium in the system for which these authoritative decisions are made. That is, the impact of equilibrium on decision-making must be specified, along with the significance of decision-making for equilibrium.

Some critics of functional analysis allege that the approach is largely tautological, a fourth criticism. Thus Flanigan and Fogelman note that structural-functional analysis does not point the researcher to *specific* relationships between given functions and given structures. Hempel sees the defect as fatal. He concludes that:

> . . . In most, if not all, concrete cases it would be impossible to specify with any precision the range of alternative behavior patterns, institutions, customs, or the like that would suffice to meet a given functional prerequisite or need. And if that range could be characterized, there is no satisfactory method in sight for dividing it into some finite number of cases and assigning a probability to each of these.[83]

A fifth logical shortcoming of functional analysis notes that specifying functional requisites helps little in explaining processes of change. Any set of prerequisites for system initiation, or requisites for system maintenance, is no more than a minimum specification of the "necessary and sufficient" conditions for system operation.[84] Thus such formulations may be useful in explaining the *origins* of systems, and they may help in *describing* the critical *components* of an extant system. But they do not explain the *processes* by which the system sustains (or fails to sustain) dynamic equilibrium.[85]

A series of conceptual problems adumbrates the broader case against functional approaches. First, functional analysis lacks explicit theoretical underpinnings. Put otherwise, functionalism as theory is inadequate. Criticism often focuses on three facets of the inadequacy of the theoretical structure of functionalism:

1. Reciprocal relations among functions are rarely spelled out. Despite the assumption that requisite system functions influence one another, few functional models address themselves to these intra-function linkages.

2. There have been few efforts to ascertain the relative significance of different functions for system maintenance, especially over time and in different systems. And the conditions under which the weighting of these requisites might change have been ignored. Functions generally are treated as undifferentiated attributes rather than as dimensions capable of significant variation along a continuum. The dichotomous treatment of functions does enhance operationality in a general sense, but only at the risk of sacrificing validity.

3. The processes through which relations between given structures and functions may change have been given passing consideration, at best.

A second conceptual problem concerns the functional autonomy of sub-systems in complex social systems. Functional analysis consistently omits a requirement of patent importance in complex societies: the need to *inhibit* systemic integration, wherever integration would impair the functional autonomy of sub-systems. For example, Parsons' model focuses concern largely on the "needs" of social system as a whole.[86] The stability of the system is viewed as dependent on the satisfaction of four system-wide functional requisites—pattern maintenance and tension management, goal attainment, adaptation, and integration. Yet the very striving of the total system to satisfy its "needs" may generate tension for the system, insofar as this goal-oriented behavior impairs the functional autonomy of sub-systems. Easton makes the most commendable attempt to cope with the functional autonomy of sub-systems in complex systems, but he is an exception.[87]

A third conceptual difficulty concerns tendencies toward mixing analytic and normative criteria. Functional-requisite approaches suffer from diverse conceptions of the essential characteristics of genuine survival for a system. In the absence of specific criteria for evaluating the adaptation of a system to environmental changes, for example, the student may project his own ethical standards into *his* functional requisites. That is, the analyst may see as necessary those features which constitute for him a "proper" or "good" system adjustment.[88] The danger is particularly prominent because any "requisite" is difficult to test, if indeed it does not defy testing. Most functionalists shrug off the task of supporting their list of functions, with lesser[89] or greater[90] concern about consequent reduction in explanatory and predictive power.

Fourth, the common functional requisites lack cross-cultural validity. For example, Almond and Coleman advance a set of functions allegedly applicable to the study of the "developing areas," and acknowledge that they "derived our functional categories from the political systems in which structural specialization and functional differentiation have taken place to the greatest extent."[91] No doubt, the search for universal concepts might well proceed by tentative extension of concepts describing one class of phenomena to test their fit with other phenomenal sets. But the Almond-Coleman strategy, as typical of the approach of functional theorists, is distressing. They choose not to begin with relatively "simple" traditional societies, and thus foreclose the possibility that alternative differentiation patterns might develop outside the Anglo-American democracies.

These several logical and conceptual problems generate a host of operational difficulties. We can only sample the latter. Functionalism has been criticized on empirical grounds in the following particulars:

1. No theorist has as yet provided a systematic rationale for any given set of functional requisites. Generally, functional requisite analysis hardly suggests definitive guidelines for empirical research. More specifically, the mother theory provides little guidance for the delicate job of developing increasingly useful operational definitions.
2. The hypothetical functional requisites generally lack operational definitions. This sharply limits their value as bases for empirical theory.
3. Functional approaches offer little counsel on where or how to look for answers to several critical questions. For example:
   (a) At what levels of generality do we find social patterns for which "requisites" may be specified?

(b) Must the analytic level of the requisites correspond with that of the pattern to be explained?
(c) How do we identify the *means by which* a system ceases to maintain itself, that is, the processes by which dynamic equilibrium is transformed into progressive disintegration?
(d) How can we establish criteria for limiting the range of activities which *may* or *do* fulfill requisite functions?

This list of operational challenges is hardly exhaustive. But it does establish that the operationalization of functional approaches to comparative political research raises numerous critical problems.

### 5. *The Group Approach to Comparative Politics*

While most disciplinary model-builders would explicitly disavow the label of group theorist, all are convinced of the critical significance of various types of groups in the political process. At the same time, they seem convinced that excessive reliance on the group concept could be fatal. Unfortunately, however, neither conviction overcomes the real methodological difficulties which accompany the group approach. We will attempt to demonstrate the point generally and briefly at first, and then at some length, by reference to Apter's social stratification model, whose heavy reliance on the group exposes the model to the concept's methodological shortcomings.

An earlier chapter surveys the methodological issues raised by the group approach to politics, and we here reinforce its conclusion that the wages of reliance on a methodologically inadequate approach is methodological inadequacy. And the probability is greater as the group is conceived in such terms as those employed by Macridis:

> . . . Group analysis is . . . a crude form of determinism. Interest is the primary propelling force and every action is based upon sharing of interest. Power configuration is basically the configuration of competing and struggling interests organized into groups. Ideology, values, the state, the formal organization of political decision-making, and the content of decisions are determined by the parallelogram of group forces. Perhaps this may be an oversimplification, but I do not think it does violence to the scheme of group analysis.[92]

Narrow concept or broad, however, the group is something that model-builders in comparative politics usually cannot do without. The most enthusiastic proponent of the group approach among the model-builders is Almond. Witness his announcement that

> The kinds of interest groups which are present in a society, the specificity or diffuseness of their demands, their conceptions of the political arena and of the "rules of the game," the ethos which they bring with them into the political process—these are the "raw materials" of politics—the unaggregated demands—which some set of mechanisms must transform into political personnel and public policy.[93]

Reliance on the group concept occurs even in cases of studied attempts to do without it. For example, Easton and Spiro might appear to slight the role of groups in political activity. In neither scheme does the concept appear with any frequency, and calculatedly so in one case.[94] In point of fact, however, Easton and Spiro are quite aware of the importance of political groups. For example, the issues which provide the foci of the Spiro model are frequently formulated by interest groups, as he explicitly acknowledges.[95] In a more general sense, groups are crucial to the existence of community, without which a political system cannot survive, for communities and interest groups alike require a certain amount of goal consensus. In this way, groups are microcosms of communities. Similarly, groups are an integral component of the Easton model, albeit a largely implicit component.[96] Other examples might be cited.[97]

Less tentative reliance on the "group" often leads to difficulty while it also reflects the centrality of the concept in comparative analysis. For example, Apter's model slips clearly into determinism. For Apter, political groups are *the* vehicles through which the "dominant motive of social behavior"—the desire for "increased mobility toward the higher ends of the stratification hierarchy"—is expressed. Logically, then, "government policy must . . . in part be responsive to the interests of political groups."[98] Indeed, government is not responsive to anything else, although it obviously need not be completely responsive to the demands of any given groups. Moreover, in Apter's scheme, government is a "maximizer, sending out streams of satisfactions."[99] These streams flow to only two types of outlets: political group leaders and political group followers. These actors reflect, en masse, the extant system of social stratification. Thus, no one outside a group helps determine social stratification. Nor do these "outsiders" (if they indeed exist) receive satisfactions from the government.

Apter's treatment of political groups illustrates well the most significant methodological traps faced by comparative model-builders. Apter's model is (in his own words) "inelegant, not parsimonious." In our words, he has attempted two difficult things which most of the model-builders have shied away from: (1) a full-blown effect to interrelate all the variables in a somewhat complex scheme; and (2) the formulation of general hypotheses about which specific observations might be made. The complexities far overreach our present capabilities.

A second objection concerns Apter's conceptualization of *group*. To begin with, nowhere does Apter specifically define group. Despite the central importance of this concept to his model, Apter gives it cavalier definitional treatment. His nominal concept *group* seems to be at once amorphous and inexhaustive. Derivatively, his categorization of political groups is logically unclear in that the categories substantially overlap. Although Apter proposes to structure his model around "sets of variables in each of three main dimensions,"[100] for example, he quickly demonstrates that his "dimensions" are not even analytically discrete. Apter's "dimensions" are social stratification, political groups, and government. But the concept of government, we are told, "refers to a concrete group." More specifically, "in a system 'government' is the most generalized membership unit possessing (a) defined responsibilities for the maintenance of the system of which it is a part and (b) a practical monopoly of coercive powers."[101] Hence one "variable dimension" (government) becomes a sub-type of another (group). Worse still, since labor unions and churches (among many other institutions or groups) assertedly have coercive powers,[102] a great number of groups with "generalized" membership fall within his definition of *government*. At best, the proposed distinction between government and group seems in severe danger of evaporating.

Apter's typology of political groups is even more troublesome methodologically than his distinction of government and group. According to the Apter model,

> Modification in the stratification system can be brought about by the two major groups of entrepreneurs:
> (a) those who use the factors of production and are primarily *economic* and (b) those whose entrepreneurial activities are essentially devoted to the recruitment of followers who attempt to modify the system either by participation in the government or by directing their actions against it. These latter will be regarded as *political*.[103]

Apter goes on to distinguish three types of political groups: associations, parties, and movements.

Apter's typology of groups raises myriad questions. First, what defines the existence of a group? We know only that we are looking for a *something* which, for example, uses the factors of production and is primarily economic. Second, every such something must be distinguished in terms of some empirical dimensions, none of which Apter provides. A *group,* then, is a group. Third, the Apter typology seems to indicate that "primarily economic" groups do not attempt to modify the system by participating in government or by directing actions against government. It seems indefensible to exclude the National Association of Manufacturers, the United States Chamber of Commerce, or the Committee for Economic Development from the category of "political" groups. Yet they clearly are "primarily economic." Fourth, precisely what does "participation" in government connote? Its conception is critical but troublesome in Apter. If the only attributes setting political parties apart from other political groups are the maintenance of prescribed and observed membership rules and the support of candidates for government positions, then we must substantially adjust our concept *political party.* Fifth, the difficulties with the typology of groups spill over into other areas. For example, Apter's leadership typology[104] has myriad methodological inadequacies. The model offers no specific definitions, either conceptual or operational. This is awkward. Moreover, Apter treats leadership characteristics as undifferentiated attributes. The familiarity of the first problem does not diminish the significance of its neglect by Apter. The latter problem suggests conceptual carelessness.

Further, Apter tends to dichotomize his variables, such as his leadership dimensions. There is no reference to a middle ground between bureaucratic and personal leadership, for example, or between durable and fragile leadership. It is either one or the other—analytically, at least. Whether nature conceptually has the same attribute seems gravely doubtful,[105] even if Apter gave any hints of the operations capable of distinguishing one polar type of leadership structure from its opposite. Apter treats types of groups similarly. Political groups may be elite *or* mass, urban- *or* rural-dominated, territorial *or* supra-territorial in recruitment, and ethnic *or* regional in scope. Indeed, this "either-or" posture permeates Apter's scheme.

Other objections might be raised to the Apter model,[106] but we can let him speak for himself. Although Apter began by presenting a "method," he judiciously concluded that the analytic structure in question might better be considered a "prolegomena" to a comparative method. He concluded that

> . . . the scheme is very inelegant. It does not have precision. Much of it would be difficult, though hopefully not impossible, to opertionalize for fine treatment. A wide variety of research techniques would be appropriate to its use. Refinements in comparative criteria would be essential.[107]

Methodologically speaking, Apter's self-evaluation of his social stratification model is appropriate. But however tentative, the model represents a step in the right direction. Moreover, the model's breadth, extensive structure, and potential for hypothesis-generation argue strongly that refinements should in fact be undertaken.

### *6. Universality of Models in Comparative Politics*

The traditional parochialism of research and writing in the comparative government field has been much remarked. Yet the comparative model-builders generally claim or strongly imply that their models are applicable to whatever political systems the researcher may wish to study. Hence our interest here in determining just how "universally" some of the models may be applicable. For our purpose, universality is the highest level of generality. In turn, generality refers to the number of contexts in which a given statement is *relevant* or *accurate.*

Our judgment of the models must be gentle. First, a concept cannot be "accurate." Concepts are arbitrary labels having no truth value. They cannot be verified. However, given the necessary evidence, we can assess *empirically* the usefulness of a given concept in a particular situation. Specifically, we evaluate the fit of the *definitions* of concepts in the several models with the phenomena in question. Second, hypotheses may be checked for accuracy or validity. Any comments made here on the validity of an hypothesis or the relevance of a concept, however, must be based on impressionistic evidence. Generally, we prefer to await the research which commonly is lacking.

We argue here that, among those models which we have been discussing, only the Spiro scheme is of general utility. At least two of the models, those of Easton and Apter, are unambiguously limited in applicability. Specifically, neither the Easton nor the Apter model seems fully relevant to totalitarian political systems, especially dictatorships.[108] Basically, the two models are burdened with the properties of Western political systems, e.g., "legitimacy," "peaceful action in common," and popular "support."[109]

Let us focus initially on Easton. He tells us that "it is a familiar axiom of political science that a government based on force alone is not long for this world."[110] Regimes must induce a "favorable state of mind" among the citizenry. They must have not mere acquiescence, but "support resting on a sense of legitimacy." Members of a political system must be "willing to support the existence of a group that seeks to settle differences or promote decisions through peaceful action in common."[111] This position implies real limits on Easton's analysis. Obviously, systems have survived for significant periods of time without possessing all, or any, of the above-noted characteristics. Among these examples we may number the Stalinist regime in the Soviet Union during the *Yezhovshchina,* Hitler's National Socialist regime, and the mainland Chinese system during the mid-1950's. Violence may well be modal in the settlement of disputes without destroying the system. Similarly, regime sustenance does not necessarily depend upon support or perceptions of legitimacy among significant segments of the citizenry.[112]

Apter's model seems equally inapplicable to totalitarian systems. Apter defines the "format of government" in terms of "the degree of representativeness of government." While acknowledging that "oligarchical governments and totalitarianism are common,"[113] Apter calls for the comparative analysis of *democracies* so that "we can learn something about their potentialities and ultimate compatibility with drastic social change." These efforts eventually should "produce a genuine theory of democratic government—a theory having practical as well as ethical implications for our times."[114]

In short, Apter's concern for an empirical theory of politics gives way to his "practical" and "ethical" concerns for the development of democracy. Normative theories clearly are important, as are goal-based, empirical theories. Thus we do not flee from explicit concern with values. But we do not support the elaboration of models based on explicit values, focusing on a limited range of phenomena, and buttressed by scant empirical data. We submit that such models provide a less than ideal base for the construction of general theory in comparative politics.

The Spiro model escapes the two problems—violence and legitimacy—which limit the general applicability of the Easton and Apter approaches by stressing reality more than reflecting preferential values. For example, Spiro rejects defining the existence of political community in terms of the "absence or presence of violence as a means to settle disputes."[115] Empirically, he suggests numerous political systems in which violence was the predominant mode of conflict resolution, at least periodically. These systems cannot be excluded from analysis, especially when they share similarities with political systems which do not utilize violent means in resolving conflicts. Further, argues Spiro, the idea of an *international* community or *international* system is precluded if violence as a technique for conflict resolution is excluded in the definition of system or community. As Spiro properly points out, the existence of armed conflict between two nations does not necessarily mean that these two parties have no sense of community. That is, they may still share a common awareness of shared problems on which collective action may be necessary.[116] The current cold war is an excellent example.

Spiro also dismisses legitimacy as a useful concept in general comparative models. Basically, legitimacy has been burdened with such a diverse collection of implicit and explicit definitions that it has lost most of its communicative utility. Further, the concept frequently has carried a normative connotation. It has generally been assumed that achieving legitimacy was "good" for any regime. Or, alternatively, regime legitimacy was assumed to be a functional condition for the maintenance of a political system. On the contrary, Spiro suggests that a systemic preoccupation with legitimacy might well be dysfunctional. There can be "too much of a good thing"—flexibility, stability, efficiency, effectiveness, and legitimacy clearly included.

### C. Quantifiers and Mathematizers in Comparative Politics: Numbers and Abstractions and Tentativeness

Quantification and mathematization are *au courant* in comparative politics today. Their recent emergence demands some explication, which requires some distinctions between *measurement, quantification,* and *mathematization.* Generally, measurement involves assigning numbers to observations. Contrary to popular assumption, however, all measurement is not quantitative. Quantitative measurement involves the use of *measurement theory,* which includes the theories of interval and ratio scales. Qualitative measurement involves the use of *scaling theory,* on the other hand, which includes the theories of the ordered matrix and less powerful scales (i.e., nominal, partially ordered, and ordered scales). Consequently, we may view quantification as a more sophisticated form of measurement. Mathematics may have nothing to do with numbers. Mathematization involves the formalization of relations which have been abstracted from their empirical referents. The process of mathematization focuses on the logical explication and elaboration of these relationships.[117] Mathematics thus may be seen as advanced logic. In Kemeny's words, "all scientific theories—numerical or other—are mathematical. . . . When a scientist states a theory precisely and is interested in knowing just exactly what his theory involves, he is practicing mathematics."[118]

The antecedents of the increasing concern with mathematization among Political Scientists seem obvious. To be sure, the coming of mathematics to the behavioral sciences has not been without its tense moments.[119] As Massarik notes, the broadening intrusion of mathematics into the social sciences has occasioned considerable intellectual combat, not infrequently accompanied by an exaggerated oppositeness of viewpoints.[120] And as Benson recognized, the use of mathematics has developed especially slowly in comparative politics, largely because of the highly-traditional nature of this field.[121] There are still many comparative government specialists who have barricaded themselves behind verbally ornate, reassuring anti-mathematical fortifications.

Broadly speaking, mathematics has come to Political Science as a carrier of precision. Not surprisingly, the traditional language of the social sciences has been words. The limitations of verbal discourse for scientific theory-building are both transparent and well-cataloged. Words are ambiguous; they permit multiple interpretations of a given term by reasonable men. Further, our conventional verbal languages are frequently value-laden, and differentially so. That is, many of the central concepts used in describing political phenomena not only carry affective connotations, but they also induce different affect in different observers. In addition, if words often are descriptively inadequate for discrete phenomena, they are even less useful in describing complex relations among a large number of variables. At advanced stages, mathematical precision is the heart of theory-building.

Guetzkow thus finds three central contributions of mathematics to Political Science. First, mathematics can provide a symbolic handle by which a verbal concept may be made manipulable. Second, mathematics may supply the basis for making a qualitative concept somewhat more quantitative. And, third, mathematics provides a means by which a large number of variables may be set in complex but precise relation to one another.[122]

Quantification has come to comparative politics for similar kinds of reasons. We quantify because we desire an objective, manipulable language which will facilitate the comparison and interrelation of superficially diverse phenomena. As we shall suggest, the comparison of a large number of political systems is extremely difficult unless we possess a considerable range of quantifiable data on each system. Further, as Kemeny points out, theoretical convenience best explains the desire to quantify variables. The more sophisticated the techniques which we apply to conceptual development, the simpler will be the theoretical apparatus with which we interrelate them. Concepts with loose nominal or operational definitions can be tied together only by a highly intricate series of propositions.

There are at least three other more specific reasons why aggregate, quantitative data are of growing significance in research on comparative politics. First, the level of analysis at which comparative studies operate demands aggregate numerical data. That is, comparative politics increasingly compares areal units or nation-states; and numerous concepts useful in comparative analysis cannot be readily expressed in terms of individual attributes.[123] These concepts include political competitiveness, industrialization, urbanization, and political socialization, to name only a few. Second, aggregate quantitative data recommend themselves because of their availability. The coverage of our aggregate statistical data generally is much better than that of survey data, or any other type of information which we have for a broad range of political systems. Further, these aggregate quantitative data usually cover relatively long periods of time. Thus they facilitate research on the processes by which political systems change. Third, aggregate quantitative data are susceptible to a greater variety of statistical manipulations than other types of data. For example, "since aggregated data are generally descriptive of total populations, they are not subject to sampling error."[124]

Not that mathematization and quantification have had it all their own way. There are several frequent objections to the mathematization of concepts in comparative politics, as well as to the quantification of variables in comparative research. We address ourselves briefly to three such general criticisms. First, some question the motivation for, and the applications of, mathematical-quantitative analysis. The adoption of more rigorous procedures from the "harder" sciences amounts to no more than intellectual gamesmanship to some.[125] This motivation may be consequential. Lusting for intellectual status encourages careless use of the status symbols, which in this case are mathematical and numerical.

The philosophic traditionalists raise a second objection. They argue that the essence of the political component is drained from human behavior when numbers or other symbols are used to characterize and relate political variables. Further, we are sometimes urged that any political truth that can be discovered by mathematical rigor is equally susceptible to intuitive or subjective analysis.[126] But if such criticisms often seem over-expansive, they are also shared by a consequential number of colleagues.

A third argument against quantification in comparative politics concerns the effect of quantification on the data being manipulated. Some argue that assigning numbers to essentially qualitative data renders meaningless any subsequent statistical manipulations with these data. We have already outlined Heckscher's position to the effect that combining and comparing votes across national boundaries is akin to adding and attempting to compare apples and oranges. Since the motivational factors undergirding different sets of votes probably differ significantly, it is held that treating such votes as aggregate quantities means that the political scientist will be dealing with corrupted data.

### *1. Karl W. Deutsch: The Comparative Analysis of National Profiles*

Attempts to quantify and to mathematize in comparative politics have reflected some of the best of the preceding paragraphs, not a little of the worst, and much of the in-between. For example, Deutsch suggests in two frequently-cited articles that students compare nations through the use of quantitative national profiles.[127] Roughly, the technique has these features. First, the analyst selects what he believes to be the most important variables characterizing political systems. Some of these characteristics will be quantitative in raw form, e.g., gross national product, work force in non-agricultural occupations, and literacy rate. Such characteristics can be included in measurement profiles. It will also be necessary, says Deutsch, to construct rating profiles. These are sets of numerical values for national characteristics which are qualitative in the sense that they are assigned by expert raters.

Having selected his critical variables, the student proceeds to assign one digit in his numerical profile to each variable. He then obtains the full-sample frequency distribution for each variable. This permits the ranking of each country on each variable, using a five-class ranking scheme. Class numbers are then entered for each variable into the corresponding digit of each nation's country profile. The analyst may then match the country profiles for any number of nations that he may wish to compare.

Deutsch argues that these country profiles should be useful not only for comparing one nation with another but also for constructing typologies of political systems, but we find several problems with either application. These difficulties have been cogently summarized by Retzlaff,[128] and bear elaboration here. First, the usefulness of country profiles diminishes as the breadth and complexity of analysis increases. That is, Deutsch's illustrative use of a ten-digit measurement profile does not seem unduly cumbersome. Recent efforts at quantification in comparative politics, however, imply that many times that number of variables may be needed to characterize adequately the nature of political systems. For example, Banks and Textor base their *Cross Polity Survey*[129] on 57 characteristics. Russett and his associates[130] include more than 70 variables in their compendium. Manipulating country profiles of this size, especially for a large number of nations, would be extremely awkward.

Not that we lack the hardware with which to sort out and interrelate large volumes of data. Indeed, electronic data-processing has moved several strides ahead of the demands of most social scientists. Rather, the increasing complexity of the country profiles would make it much more difficult to control the independent effect of any given variable on whatever political outcomes we might be interested in studying.

Second, and perhaps more significant, Deutsch provides no specific clues as to how country profiles could actually be used to *compare*. Retzlaff thrusts our question directly:

> Even on a more modest level, if one were to limit oneself to the analysis of characteristics relating to some restricted clustering of phenomena, the precise manner of how such comparisons would be carried out through the use of the country profile approach is left unspecified. Is it to be done merely by visual inspection of two or more sets of country profiles? If so, what can be said if a given number of country profiles, located in a similar cell of a given table, display common rankings on only five of the ten variables listed in the profiles, whereas in two other cells they agree on three and eight variables respectively?[131]

That is, the issue concerns the absence of guidelines indicating what is to be done with country profiles once they have been constructed. Numerous questions are involved. How do we go about delineating the extent of any similarity? Should similarities or differences on each variable within the profiles be assigned relative weights? And if so, how might these weights be determined?

Third, Deutsch's country profiles are basically quantitative in nature, but they actually preclude the use of more sophisticated statistical-quantitative techniques. At best, non-parametric tests of association might be used, along with rank-order correlations for a sub-set of the variables. The inclusion of partially qualitative indices on the rating profile segment of the country profile would preclude most other statistical manipulations.

Yet all is not lost, statistically speaking. At least two reasonably sophisticated techniques might be used with the Deutsch country profiles to facilitate comparison. These techniques are factor analysis and hierarchical decomposition. Integrating the country profiles into these techniques, especially factor analysis, would involve some transformation of the profiles from their raw form. In particular, it would be necessary to convert non-parametric association values (such as chi square) into contingency coefficients.[132] Doing this would permit the use of these two techniques with the Deutsch profiles.

Essentially, factor analysis is based on the assumption that, if two or more variables indicate a correlation, some more general factor or factors can explain the common variance.[133] Thus analysis is projected to a higher level of generalization, and involves a rigorous search for broad behavioral antecedents. North and his associates summarily posit two primary functions for factor analysis: reducing voluminous and complex materials to manageable proportions, and simplifying the interpretation of co-variance.[134]

The use of factor analysis in Political Science is increasing very rapidly, a fact which accents its obvious virtues. We emphasize two basic limitations here.[135] First, there are several types of factorial solutions which may yield substantially different results when applied to a given set of data; there is no sure way to determine which is "best." Some factorial procedures are somewhat more appropriate than others for specific sets of data, but it is difficult to argue that some other approach might not have provided equally valid analysis. Second, any interpretation of any factorial solution is *essentially* indeterminate. That is, given the correlations of a set of variables, the coefficients of a factor pattern are not uniquely determined.

Indeterminacy does not imply uselessness, however, and fortunately so. For almost all analyses—regardless of the techniques used—are essentially indeterminate. As Moulton has argued,

> Every set of phenomena can be interpreted consistently in various ways, in infinitely many ways. It is our privilege to choose among the possible interpretations the ones that appear to us most satisfactory, whatever may be the reasons for our choice. If scientists would remember that various equally consistent interpretations of every set of observational data can be made, they would be much less dogmatic than they often are, and their beliefs in a possible ultimate finality of scientific theory would vanish.[136]

Factor analysis also carries a more general liability. Statistically significant associations among variables, no matter what the underlying computational procedures, do not necessarily indicate relationships of importance.[137] The analytic efficacy of any given set of observations based on statistical tests depends not only upon research design, but also upon the adequacy and appropriateness of the tests used, as well as upon the meaningfulness of the substantive conclusions at which one arrives.

Broadly, factor analysis seeks economy of description through a relatively powerful mathematical apparatus.[138] From a matrix of intercorrelations among any universe of variables, factor-analytic programs seek to extract a set of generic components of the data system represented by the interrelations. The extracted factors are assigned a factor score, or loading, for each variable in the matrix. A loading is a statistical measure of the degree to which a given factor explains the common variance of a set of variables. Hence the factoring of a matrix of correlations places a pattern of variables within an interpretative frame of reference defined by the axes of a factorial structure. Once factor loadings have been determined, vectors which represent the set of variables may be plotted within two-factor orthogonal space. The location of each variable is defined within this two-factor space by its loading on the two factors. The factor structure may be rotated, and single-factor and aggregate-factor saliency may be calculated. In short, factor analysis is a technique which permits sophisticated probing of a set of interrelations in search of common factors explaining the variance of a large number of variables.

Any social scientist who has used both contingency tests and more powerful techniques such as factor analysis with collections of polychotomous data has longed for some procedure which might combine the features of the two types of techniques. For example, we might hope for a technique in which all of the variables usable with chi-square tests could be used; in which linear relationships among indices were not assumed; and which suggested more general antecedents accounting for variations in the behaviors of variables in the analytic scheme.

Fortunately, such a technique is available, one based on the mathematics of graph theory. This is the Hierarchical Decomposition computer program developed by Alexander and Manheim in the Civil Engineering Laboratory at M.I.T.[139] The variation of the program—HIDECS 2—which has been used in the only social science applications of which we know accepts as input data a matrix indicating absence or presence of statistically significant relationships among variables. On the bases of this matrix, a graph isomorphic to the matrix is constructed on the assumption that each link of the graph represents a statistical correlation among variables. The program iteratively seeks out that partition of the graph's vertex set for which the strength is minimal, decomposing hierarchically the total configuration of linkages into the most independent sub-sets of variables; i.e., those with the most dense internal interactions and those with the least dense external interactions. The successive decompositions form a tree in which all linkages among variables are arranged hierarchically. Thus, at the bottom level of the tree one finds clustered together only those sub-groups of variables most closely linked statistically. At successively higher levels of the tree more general clusterings of variables are encountered. A variable set hierarchically decomposed by HIDECS 2 is presented in Figure VIII.3.

As with any relatively complex technique, there are difficulties with HIDECS. Three related problems may be cited briefly. First, a few linked variables usually are separated in the branching process carried out by the program. Two mutually linked variables might adhere so strongly to two different sub-groups that they would split, even though related to one another at a statistically significant level. A modification of the original HIDECS program, however, makes it possible to verify all direct linkages, including those which have separated by branching. Still, the last level of the created hierarchy does not provide a complete picture of all mutual ties among variables.

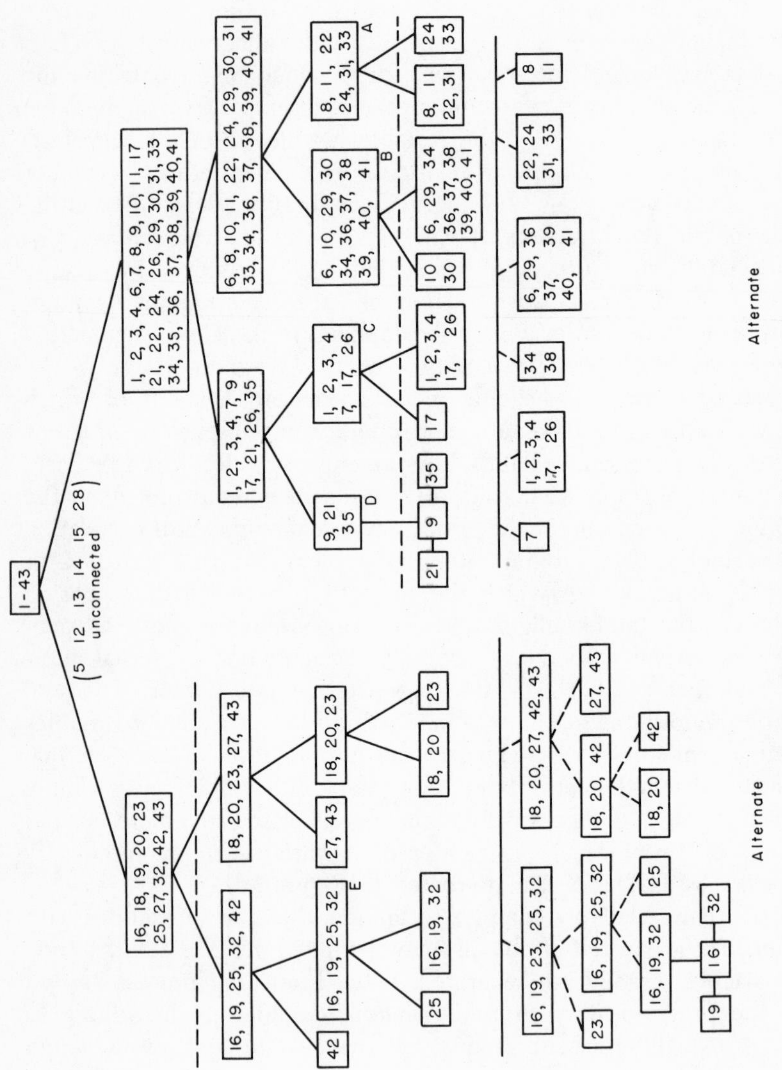

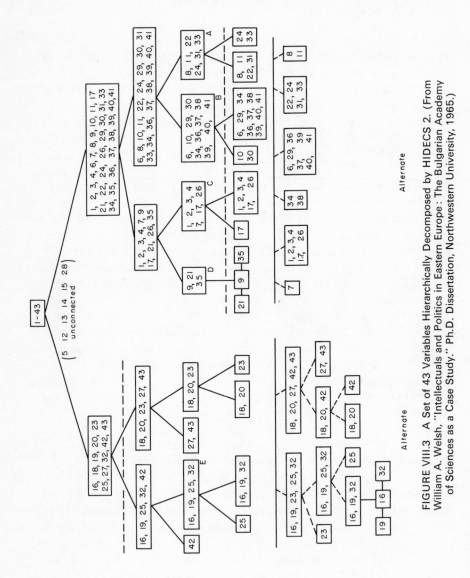

FIGURE VIII.3 A Set of 43 Variables Hierarchically Decomposed by HIDECS 2. (From William A. Welsh, "Intellectuals and Politics in Eastern Europe: The Bulgarian Academy of Sciences as a Case Study." Ph.D. Dissertation, Northwestern University, 1965.)

Second, the biparous breakdown of sub-groups is arbitrary. There is no logical reason to assume that a group of variables can optimally be split into two sub-groups or any other number. Further, HIDECS 2 contains a built-in bias which seeks approximately to equalize the number of variables grouped into each of the sub-sets into which the variables are divided at each stage in the branching process.

Third, the division of any sub-group containing a small number of variables is nearly always arbitrary to a degree. This is true because of the greater likelihood that a small number of variables may have two or more equally good partitions when compared with this probability for a large configuration of variables. This problem is considerably less significant if one is dealing with a large number of variables, and can direct his analysis at a point above the final level of the hierarchy.

Again, indicating some of the problems encountered in using such a technique does not seriously argue against its utility. On the contrary, hierarchical decomposition has impressive advantages. They include its susceptibility to use with a broad range of data, and its capacity to cluster variables after inspecting a very large number of interrelations. Indeed, when used in conjunction with other techniques, HIDECS can be a most useful tool.

But we have digressed at length to outline some of the advantages and problems involved in the use of two reasonably sophisticated techniques in comparison. We must return to our original task, the evaluation of Deutsch's country profile approach. A fourth, and most significant, question raised by Retzlaff concerns the use of these profiles for purposes of theory construction. It is unclear how the country profiles might contribute to testing hypotheses, or to the measurement of trends over time. Indeed, although Deutsch's later article focuses on a seemingly specific relationship between social mobilization and political development, his profiles and indices do not seem to have generated hypotheses relating these two variables. Implicitly, Deutsch's position seems to be that hypotheses should be generated through statistical analysis. Still, although he mentions the use of correlation, he at no time specifies what forms of multivariate analysis might be most appropriate. Nor does he indicate the ways in which, nor the purposes for which, the statistical techniques might be applied.

Broadly speaking, then, the principal limitation of Deutsch's approach rests in his lack of explicitness. Our discussion of factor analysis and hierarchical decomposition suggests that there are statistical techniques which could be used to bring some order and utility to the country profile approach. But the dependence of Deutsch's procedures on other techniques is patent.

## 2. *Seymour M. Lipset: Economic Bases for Democracy*

Another pioneer in the use of quantitative analysis in comparative politics is Seymour Martin Lipset. In an often-cited article,[140] Lipset addresses himself to the hypothesized relationship between economic development and democracy. The suggestion, of course, is that "the more well-to-do a nation, the better the chances it will sustain democracy."[141] To begin coping with the operational problems, Lipset devised "quantitative" indices of both economic development and political democracy. The democracy indices, as we shall see, were not fully quantitative.

Fifteen variables were used to index economic development. These variables were grouped under four general characteristics—wealth, industrialization, education, and urbanization. For each variable, data were gathered on a total of 48 European, English-speaking, and Latin American nations. Lipset then classified the nations into one of four categories: European and English-speaking stable democracies ($N = 13$); European and English-speaking unstable democracies and dictatorships ($N = 15$); Latin American democracies and unstable dictatorships ($N = 7$); and Latin American stable dictatorships ($N = 13$). The *mean* and the *range* for each variable in the four political categories were computed, and these calculations constitute the political data used in the analysis.

There are numerous objections to Lipset's approach. First, Lipset provides no hint of the operational procedures used in dividing the political systems in question into his four political categories. Indeed, his classificatory scheme seems to have a subjective, intuitive base. This in turn gives a self-confirming aura to the entire presentation. For example, "democracy" and "stability" seem to be tied together in Lipset's mind in terms of the social requisites, especially economic development, which he purports to be studying. That he finds significant association between economic development and legitimacy on one hand, and the existence of democracy on the other, appears prompted in part by the operational overlap of the major variables in the Lipset scheme.

Second, Lipset makes no effort to ascertain if the indices used under each general economic category are in fact closely related to one another. That is, he does not attempt to combine, for example, the six variables presented as indices of wealth into a composite index. Information on each of the 15 economic variables is presented separately. Similarly Lipset was not persuaded to devise any over-all index or scale of either economic development or democracy on which all countries studied could be simultaneously examined and evaluated.[142]

Third, there is some reason to doubt Lipset's facile contention that the data are not really open to conflicting interpretations. As Cutright has suggested, ". . . the spread in the values on almost every indicator is so extreme" that the association between democracy and economic development is uncertain.[143]

### 3. *Cutright's Quantitative Analysis of National Political Development*

Cutright has advanced a considerably more sophisticated and useful approach[144] which follows the path blazed by Lipset. Cutright's concern is to demonstrate the interdependence of political institutions, educational systems, communications systems, urbanization, labor force distribution, and economic development. For each of these variables he devises a quantitative index. The composition of the political development index is of particular concern to us. This index is based on a summation of point scores awarded annually to a country over a 21-year period according to the characteristics of party representation in the legislature and the method of executive selection.[145] The total value obtained for each country on this political development index was then *T*-scored.[146]

Three kinds of analyses link Cutright's variables. First, Cutright calculated a multiple correlation coefficient for a matrix including the political development, communication, urbanization, education, and agricultural indices. This matrix also served as the basis for determining the degree of co-variation in each pair of variables. Second, Cutright plotted a scattergram of the relationship between the communications and political development indices. Regression analysis was done on this relationship. Third, the residual error of prediction of the actual and expected values of political development by continent and by nation were determined.[147]

The Cutright article, while representing a considerable refinement of Lipset's earlier work, succumbs to two difficulties which are commonly found in quantitative approaches in comparative politics. First, Cutright's variables lack explicit *verbal* definitions. Their subsequent dependence upon quantitative indexing for definition occasions some conceptual fuzziness, despite operational precision. Second, like Lipset, Cutright sometimes flirts with the tautological. These two problems are closely intertwined.

As Retzlaff indicates, apart from suggesting measurement criteria, Cutright does not explicitly define the concept of political development.[148] We know that political development refers to the characteristics of party representation in the legislature, and to the methods by which executive leadership is selected. We are not told, however, precisely what is *developmental* about changes along these two political dimensions. Implicitly, Cutright suggests that the evolution of "stable, democratic government" is the controlling measure of political development. We hardly need to underscore the parochialism inherent in such a position. Indeed, "the extent to which determinist or teleological characteristics are being imported into the term political development through the implicit positing of a terminal model based upon a synthesis of the British and American systems"[149] is one of the principal concerns of comparative politics specialists who study the developing areas. It certainly remains problematic whether many political systems are indeed tending in the direction of democracy. In the absence of substantiating empirical evidence there would seem to be no valid theoretical basis for positing a combination of political democracy and stability as the terminal point in a developmental model of political change.

## III. CONCLUSION

We began this chapter with a broad description of promising recent advances in the comparative study of political systems. Nevertheless, a good many of our intervening thoughts have centered on the shortcomings of several comparative approaches. Our thrust has been toward refinement of these promising models. The needed refinements vary considerably. But they do share relevance to a critical and as yet unrealized requisite for scientific theory: the marriage of empirical research and systematic conceptualization.

It is frustrating and regrettable that the analytic frameworks of the model-builders have excited so few researchers. The perplexing bifurcation of theoretical and research leadership in comparative politics is a major stumbling-block on the road to intellectual maturity. Those who devise grandiose schemes often leave their operationalization and use to others—who sometimes do not fully understand the model, especially given the initial absence of empirical referents. Conversely, the political scientists who gather, amalgamate, and analyze data commonly do so without the guidance of explicit analytic models.

Division of labor is generally considered a hallmark of progressive development. The separation of theorists and researchers in Political Science has been similarly functional, at least in the past. But the time is at hand for a re-blending of the two enterprises. The new mix should be expected to provide significant impetus to both its constitutent elements. Frequent repetition does not dull the argument that intellectual intercourse between theory and data is a prerequisite for scientific offspring.

## NOTES

1. Cross-national survey research is indeed a burgeoning enterprise. For a sampling of recent efforts, and analysis thereof, see: Gabriel Almond and Sidney Verba, *The Civic Culture* (Princeton, N.J.: Princeton University Press, 1963); Angus Campbell and Henry Valen, "Party Identification in Norway and the United States," *Public Opinion Quarterly,* XXV (Winter, 1961), 505–25; Davis Bobrow, "International Interactions, Surveys, and Computers." Paper presented to Computers and the Policy-Making Community Institute, Livermore, California, April, 1966; Philip Converse and G. Depeux, "Politicization of the Electorate in France and the United States," *Public Opinion Quarterly,* XXVI (Spring, 1962), 1–24; Stein Rokkan, "Party Preferences and Opinion Patterns in Western Europe: A Comparative Analysis," *International Social Science Bulletin,* VII, 4 (1955), 575–96; Robert E. Ward, et al., *Studying Politics Abroad* (Boston: Little, Brown, 1964); Morton Gorden and Daniel Lerner, "The Setting for European Arms Control: Political and Strategic Choices of European Elites," *Journal of Conflict Resolution,* 9, 4 (December, 1965), 419–33.

2. Don Martindale, "Sociological Theory and the Ideal Type," in Llewelyn Gross (ed.), *Symposium on Sociological Theory* (New York: Harper and Row, 1959), p. 58.

3. Oscar Lewis, "Comparisons in Cultural Anthropology," in Frank W. Moore (ed.), *Readings in Cross-Cultural Methodology* (New Haven, Conn.: Human Relations Area Files, 1961), especially pp. 55–58.

4. Quoted in Oscar Lewis, *op. cit.,* p. 58.

5. See Raoul Naroll, *Data Quality Control* (New York: The Free Press of Glencoe, 1961).

6. E. H. Ackerknecht, "On the Comparative Method in Anthropology," in Robert F. Spencer (ed.), *Method and Perspective in Anthropology* (Minneapolis: University of Minnesota Press, 1964), p. 5.

7. For a recent exception, see James D. Barber, *Power in Committees: An Experiment in the Government Process* (Chicago: Rand McNally, 1966).

8. Roy C. Macridis and Bernard Brown, "Introductory Essay," in Macridis and Brown (eds.), *Comparative Politics: Notes and Readings* (rev. ed.; Homewood, Ill.: The Dorsey Press, 1964), p. 5.

9. Gabriel Almond and James S. Coleman, *The Politics of the Developing Areas* (Princeton, N.J.: Princeton University Press, 1960), p. 16. The approach used in the Almond and Coleman volume has been refined somewhat in Almond and G. Bingham Powell, Jr., *Comparative Politics: A Developmental Approach* (Boston: Little, Brown, 1966).

10. See Karl Loewenstein, "Report of the Research Panel on Comparative Government," *American Political Science Review,* XXXVIII (June, 1944), 540–48; Roy C. Macridis and Richard Cox, "Research in Comparative Politics," *American Political Science Review,* XLVII (September, 1953), 641–75. The latter summarized the 1953 deliberations of the Social Science Research Council Inter-university Research Seminar on Comparative Politics.

11. Gabriel A. Almond, Taylor Cole, and Roy C. Macridis, "A Suggested Research Strategy in Western European Government and Politics," *American Political Science Review,* XLIX, 4 (December, 1955), 1042. Reprinted in Harry Eckstein and David E. Apter (eds.), *Comparative Politics: A Reader* (New York: The Free Press of Glencoe, 1963), pp. 52–57.

12. Robert A. Dahl, *Modern Political Analysis* (Englewood Cliffs, N.J.: Prentice-Hall, 1963), p. 26.

13. Harry Eckstein, "A Perspective on Comparative Politics, Past and Present," in Eckstein and Apter, *op. cit.,* p. 6. The outline of our historical sketch of comparative political studies is drawn from Eckstein's excellent essay.

14. *Ibid.*

15. *Ibid.,* p. 7.

16. *Ibid.,* p. 8.

17. See Gordon W. Allport, "The Historical Background of Modern Social Psychology," in Gardner Lindzey (ed.), *Handbook of Social Psychology*

(Cambridge, Mass.: Addison-Wesley, 1954), I, 3–56.

18. *Ibid.*, p. 9.

19. "National character" studies represent a contemporary variant of these configurative studies. For an excellent summary of national character writings and research, and an extensive bibliography, see H. C. J. Duijker and N. H. Frijda, *National Character and National Stereotypes* (Amsterdam: UNESCO 1960).

20. Eckstein cites numerous examples of these evolutionary formulations including Sir Henry Maine's *Ancient Law* (1861) and *Early History of Institutions* (1874), Edward Jenks' *The State and the Nation* (1919), Karl Marx's *Communist Manifesto* (1848), and Sir John Seeley's *Introduction to Political Science* (1896). Perhaps the best-known recent statement of evolutionary theory by a social scientist is in Walt W. Rostow, *The Stages of Economic Growth* (Cambridge: Cambridge University Press, 1960).

21. Affirmative views are reflected in several of the papers presented at the conference on Social Science and the Under-Developed Areas: A Revival of Evolutionary Theory? held in 1961 at Northwestern University. Especially Donald T. Campbell, "Evolutionary Theory in Social Science: A Reappraisal;" C. C. Moskos, "The Social Transformation of the Albanian Elite;" and Joseph J. Spengler, "Social Evolution and the Theory of Economic Development."

22. Eckstein, "A Perspective on Comparative Politics, Past and Present," in Eckstein and Apter, *op. cit.*, p. 15. In Eckstein's opinion, "developmental theories . . . have gone out of style."

23. See: Gaetano Mosca, *The Ruling Class*, translated by Hannah D. Kahn, edited by Arthur Livingston (New York: McGraw-Hill 1939); James H. Meisel, *The Myth of the Ruling Class: Gaetano Mosca and the Elite* (Ann Arbor: University of Michigan Press, 1958); Vilfredo Pareto, *The Mind and Society*, 4 vols. (New York: Harcourt, Brace, and Co., 1935); George C. Homans and Charles P. Curtis, Jr., *An Introduction to Pareto: His Sociology* (New York: A. A. Knopf, 1934); M. I. Ostrogorski, *Democracy and the Organization of Political Parties*, 2 vols. (New York: Macmillan, 1902); M. I. Ostrogorski, *Democracy and the Party System in the United States* (New York: Macmillan, 1910); Robert Michels, *Political Parties* (New York: Dover, 1959); Robert Michels, *First Lectures in Political Sociology* (Minneapolis: University of Minnesota Press, 1949); James H. Meisel, *Pareto and Mosca* (Englewood Cliffs, N.J.: Prentice-Hall, 1965); Robert A. Nisbet, *Emile Durkheim* (Englewood Cliffs, N.J.: Prentice-Hall, 1964).

24. Gunnar Heckscher, "General Methodological Problems," in Harry Eckstein and David E. Apter (eds.), *Comparative Politics: A Reader* (New York: The Free Press of Glencoe, 1963), pp. 35–42.

25. D. F. Aberle, et al., "The Functional Prerequisites of a Society," *Ethics*, 60 (January, 1950), 100–111.

26. Gabriel Almond, "Comparative Political Systems," *Journal of Politics*, 18 (August, 1956), 391–409.

27. David E. Apter, "A Comparative Method for the Study of Politics," *American Journal of Sociology*, LXIV (November, 1958), 221–37.

28. David Easton, "An Approach to the Analysis of Political Systems," *World Politics*, IX, 3 (April, 1957), 383–400.

29. Herbert J. Spiro, "Comparative Politics: A Comprehensive Approach," *American Political Science Review*, 56, 3 (September, 1962), 577–95.

30. Karl W. Deutsch, "Toward an Inventory of Basic Trends and Patterns in Comparative and International Politics," *American Political Science Review*, LIV, 1 (1960), 34–57; "Social Mobilization and Political Development," *American Political Science Review*, LV, 3 (1961), 493–614. Two other outstanding contributions by Deutsch are not discussed in this volume, but demand attention by specialists in comparative politics. See his *The Nerves of Government: Models of Political Communication and Control* (New York: The Free Press, 1966), and *Nationalism and Social Communication: An Inquiry into the Foundations of Nationality*, second ed. (Cambridge, Mass.: M. I. T. Press, 1966).

31. Seymour M. Lipset, "Some Social Requisites of Democracy: Economic Development and Political Legitimacy," *American Political Science Review,* LIII, 1 (1959), 69–105. A revised version appears in his *Political Man* (New York: Doubleday, 1960), Chapters 2 and 3.

32. Phillips Cutright, "National Political Development: Measurement and Analysis," *American Sociological Review,* 28, 2 (1963), 253–64.

33. See Chapter I in this volume.

34. Heckscher, *op. cit.*

35. For an effort to devise standardized criteria for problem selection, see James A. Robinson, "The Major Problems of Political Science," in Lynton K. Caldwell (ed.), *Politics and Public Affairs* (Bloomington: Indiana University Press, 1962), pp. 161–88.

36. A convenient summary of the argument may be found in Ernest Nagel, *The Structure of Science* (New York: Harcourt, Brace and World, 1961), pp. 487–96. Nagel, of course, finds the argument less than compelling.

37. Heckscher, *op. cit.,* pp. 36, 37. The philosophic contention seems particularly striking, since it is sometimes argued that the other social sciences could be "reduced" to Psychology. For a general discussion of reductionism in the philosophy of science, see: Gustav Bergmann, "Reduction," in John T. Wilson, et al., *Current Trends in Psychology and the Behavioral Sciences* (Pittsburgh: University of Pittsburgh Press, 1954), pp. 59–81; Abraham Edel, "The Concept of Levels in Social Theory," in Llewellyn Gross (ed.), *Symposium on Sociological Theory* (New York: Harper and Row, 1959), pp. 167–95; John G. Kemeny, *A Philosopher Looks at Science* (Princeton, N.J.: Van Nostrand, 1959), pp. 207–11; Nagel, *The Structure of Science,* pp. 336–97.

38. *Ibid.,* p. 37.

39. *Ibid.,* p. 37.

40. See Dahl, *op. cit.,* pp. 43–44. Dahl discusses the problem, but generally disagrees with Heckscher's conclusion.

41. Heckscher, *op. cit.,* p. 37.

42. *Ibid.,* p. 42.

43. For example, see Wladyslaw W. Kulski, *International Politics in a Revolutionary Age* (New York: Lippincott, 1964), pp. vii–viii.

44. This general characterization of scientific activity is from *The Structure of Science,* Nagel, p. 385.

45. *Ibid.,* pp. 485–502.

46. Kemeny, *op. cit.,* especially pp. 230–43.

47. Karl R. Popper, *The Logic of Scientific Discovery* (New York: Science Editions, 1961), especially pp. 27–48.

48. Vernon Van Dyke, *Political Science: A Philosophical Analysis* (Stanford, Calif.: Stanford University Press, 1960), pp. 8–13, 192–93.

49. See the citations in footnotes 25 through 29 for this chapter.

50. Apter, *op. cit.,* p. 221.

51. David Easton, "An Approach to the Analysis of Political Systems," p. 398.

52. For a convenient summary of Parsonian social theory, see Talcott Parsons and Edward A. Shils (eds.), *Toward a General Theory of Action* (New York: Harper and Row, 1962), pp. 3–275.

53. Almond, "Comparative Political Systems," p. 393.

54. *Ibid.*

55. D. F. Aberle, et al., *op. cit.,* p. 100, footnote 3.

56. *Ibid.,* p. 101.

57. *Ibid.,* see pp. 100, 101.

58. Apter, *op. cit.,* p. 221.

59. *Ibid.*

60. Aberle and his associates and Apter seem convinced that the realization of basic system goals is an invariant requisite for system sustenance. Spiro, by contrast, asserts that "perfect equilibrium among the four basic goals is hard if not impossible to achieve and would not be desirable to insure success except under very rare conditions" (*op. cit.,* p. 584).

61. Spiro, *op. cit.,* p. 578.

62. *Ibid.*

63. Apter, *op. cit.,* p. 225.

64. Aberle, et al., *op. cit.,* pp. 103–4.

65. *Ibid.,* p. 104.

66. For a convenient summary of Easton's thinking on this central theoretical notion, see *The Political System* (New York: Knopf, 1960), pp. 129–43.

67. David Easton, "An Approach to the Analysis of Political Systems," pp. 395, 384. Easton's tendency to use the concepts *decision* and *policy* interchangeably is distressing. Decisions are more appropriately viewed as selections of a single alternative from among several by authoritative decision-makers. Policies then would result from the interaction of decisions and the environment in which the decisions are to be enforced. It is by now a truism that all political systems experience "slippage" between the point of authoritative decision and the point of policy enforcement. Spiro alone among the comparative model-builders handles this difference between decision and policy explicitly. He contrasts "resolution" (authoritative prescription) with "solution," the policy resulting from efforts to put the resolution into effect in the real world.

68. Easton, "An Approach to the Analysis of Political Systems," p. 385.

69. Apter, *op. cit.*, p. 225.

70. Easton, "An Approach to the Analysis of Political Systems," p. 384.

71. *Ibid.*, p. 385.

72. Almond, "Comparative Political Systems," p. 395.

73. See *ibid.*, p. 394.

74. William Flanigan and Edwin Fogelman, "Functionalism in Political Science," in Don Martindale (ed.), *Functionalism in the Social Sciences* (Philadelphia: American Academy of Political and Social Science, 1965), pp. 111–26.

75. *Ibid.*, p. 111.

76. The best examples are Martindale, *op. cit.;* Llewelyn Gross, pp. 241–307; Robert K. Merton, *Social Theory and Social Structure* (rev. ed.; Glencoe, Ill.: The Free Press, 1957), especially pp. 19–84; Ernest Nagel, *Logic Without Metaphysics* (Glencoe, Ill.: The Free Press, 1957), pp. 247–83.

77. Flanigan and Fogelman, *op. cit.*, p. 112.

78. *Ibid.*, p. 124.

79. Alvin W. Gouldner, "Reciprocity and Autonomy in Functional Theory," in Llewelyn Gross (ed.), *Symposium on Sociological Theory* (Evanston, Ill.: Harper and Row, 1959), p. 251; also see R. C. Sheldon, "Some Observations on Theory in Social Science," in Talcott Parsons and Edward A. Shils (eds.), *Toward a General Theory of Action* (Cambridge, Mass.: Harvard University Press, 1951), p. 35.

80. Gouldner, *op. cit.* The argument has been advanced particularly in Anthropology.

81. Carl G. Hempel, "The Logic of Functional Analysis," in Gross, *op. cit.*, p. 282.

82. Gouldner, *op. cit.*, p. 249.

83. Hempel, *op. cit.*, p. 286.

84. Marion J. Levy, Jr., "Some Aspects of 'Structural-Functional' Analysis and Political Science," in Roland Young (ed.), *Approaches to the Study of Politics* (Evanston, Ill.: Northwestern University Press, 1958), p. 53; Hempel, *op. cit.*, p. 284.

85. At the root of the problem is the teleological basis of functional explanation. See Hempel, *op. cit.*, especially pp. 279–301. Also instructive is Robert T. Holt, "A Proposed Structural-Functional Framework for Political Science," in James C. Charlesworth (ed.), *Functionalism in the Social Sciences,* pp. 84–110. Especially note his distinction between functions as *dependent* variables, and processes as *intervening* variables, at pp. 89–91.

86. Gouldner, *op. cit.*, p. 257.

87. Easton, "An Approach to the Analysis of Political Systems," p. 386.

88. Hempel, *op. cit.*, pp. 294–95.

89. Almond and Coleman, *op. cit.*, p. 16.

90. Hempel, *op. cit.*, p. 296.

91. Almond and Coleman, *op. cit.*, p. 16.

92. Roy C. Macridis, "Groups and Group Theory," *Journal of Politics*, 23, 1 (February, 1961); reprinted in part in Macridis and Bernard Brown, *Comparative Politics: Notes and Readings* (rev. ed.; Homewood, Ill.: The Dorsey Press, 1964) p. 139.

93. Gabriel Almond, "Interest Groups and the Political Process," in Macridis and Brown, *op. cit.*, p. 131. The article originally appeared as "Research Note: A Comparative Study of Interest Groups and the Political Process," *American Political Science Review*, LII 1 (March, 1958). This is a summary of the work

of the Committee on Comparative Politics of the Social Science Research Council.

94. Spiro (*op. cit.*, p. 590), notes that he avoids conventional terminology because it "easily leads to erroneous universilization of the familiar."

95. *Ibid.*

96. Easton, "An approach to the Analysis of Political Systems," p. 385.

97. Indeed, the "group" seems to have found a permanent home in Political Science. Among the numerous prominent contributions which rely to one degree or another on the concept "group" are David Easton, *The Political System* (New York: A. A. Knopf, 1953); Bertram Gross, *The Legislative Struggle: A Study in Social Combat* (Hightstown, N. J.: McGraw-Hill, 1953); and David Truman, *The Governmental Process* (New York: A. A. Knopf, 1951). In addition to the analyses of the group approach cited elsewhere in this chapter, see Earl Latham, "The Group Basis of Politics, Notes for a Theory," *American Policital Science Review*, LIV (1960), 15–33.

98. Apter, *op. cit.*, pp. 221.

99. *Ibid.*

100. *Ibid.*, p. 222.

101. *Ibid.*, p. 224.

102. *Ibid.*

103. *Ibid.*, p. 227.

104. *Ibid.*, p. 222.

105. The unwillingness of comparative politics specialists to conceptualize variables as continua, rather than as undifferentiated attributes, is distressing. Even the best efforts at comparative political analysis shy away from this needed development, presumably because viewing variables on continua implies at least a higher order of qualitative measurement. See the subsequent section in this chapter on quantification in comparative politics.

106. For example, Apter tends to use historical and contemporary cases to illustrate phenomena with which they are not usually grouped. Illustrative is his classification of Napoleon as the first modern "radical totalitarian" (Apter, *op. cit.*, p. 232), despite general agreement in comparative politics that totalitarianism is a twentieth-century phenomenon made possible by the rapid advance of technology. See Carl J. Friedrich and Zbigniew K. Brzezinski, *Totalitarian Dictatorship and Autocracy* (rev. ed; New York: Praeger, 1966), especially pp. 15–27.

107. Apter, *op. cit.*, p. 221 and p. 236.

108. Contrary to popular usage, not all totalitarian systems are dictatorial. See J. L. Talmon, *The Origins of Totalitarian Democracy* (New York: Praeger, 1960).

109. Especially see Easton, "An Approach to the Analysis of Political Systems," pp. 390, 391, 399.

110. *Ibid.*, p. 393

111. *Ibid.*, p. 391.

112. See Spiro, *op. cit.*, p. 589.

113. Apter, *op. cit.*, p. 237.

114. *Ibid.*

115. Spiro, *op. cit.*, p. 589.

116. *Ibid.*

117. See Kemeny, *op. cit.*, especially pp. 14–35, 141.

118. *Ibid.*, p. 33.

119. Fred Massarik, "Magic, Models, Man, and the Cultures of Mathematics," in Massarik and Philburn Ratoosh (eds.), *Mathematical Explorations in Behavioral Science* (Homewood, Ill.: The Dorsey Press, 1965), pp. 7–8.

120. *Ibid.*, p. 8.

121. Oliver Benson, "The Use of Mathematics in the Study of Political Science," in James C. Charlesworth (ed.), *Mathematics and the Social Sciences* (Philadelphia: The American Academy of Political and Social Science, 1965), p. 34.

122. Harold Guetzkow, "Some Uses of Mathematics in Simulation of International Relations," in John M. Claunch (ed.), *Mathematical Applications in Political Science* (Dallas: The Arnold Foundation, Southern Methodist University, 1965), p. 25.

123. Ralph H. Retzlaff, "The Use of Aggregate Data in Comparative Political Analysis," *Journal of Politics*, 27, 4 (1965), 799.

124. *Ibid.*, p. 800.

125. Massarik and Ratoosh, *op. cit.*, p. 22.

126. Andrew Hacker, "Mathematics and Political Science," in James C.

Charlesworth (ed.), *Mathematics and the Social Sciences,* (Philadelphia: The American Academy of Political and Social Science, 1965), p. 75.

127. Deutsch, "Toward an Inventory of Basic Trends and Patterns in Comparative and International Politics," pp. 34–57 and "Social Mobilization and Political Development," pp. 493–514.

128. Retzlaff, *op. cit.,* pp. 797–817.

129. Arthur S. Banks and Robert B. Textor, *A Cross-Polity Survey* (Cambridge, Mass.: M. I. T. Press, 1963).

130. Bruce M. Russett, *et al., World Handbook of Political and Social Indicators* (New Haven, Conn.: Yale University Press, 1964).

131. Retzlaff, *op. cit.,* p. 802.

132. See Sidney Siegel, *Nonparametric Statistics for the Behavioral Sciences* (New York: McGraw-Hill, 1956), pp. 196–202; Quinn McNemar, *Psychological Statistics,* (2nd ed.; New York: Wiley, 1955), pp. 203–7.

133. Robert C. North, et al., *Content Analysis* (Evanston, Ill.: Northwestern University Press, 1963), p. 118. An excellent introduction to factor analysis may be found in Harry Harman, *Modern Factor Analysis* (Chicago: University of Chicago Press, 1960). Also see Rudolph J. Rummel, *Applied Factor Analysis* (forthcoming). Rummel has pioneered in the application of factor analysis and related techniques to data in International Relations.

134. North, et al., *op. cit.,* p. 118.

135. E. P. Cureton, "The Principal Compulsions of Factor Analysis," *Harvard Educational Review,* 9 (1939), 187.

136. F. R. Moulton, quoted in Harman, *op. cit.,* p. 21.

137. J. W. Tukey, "Statistical and Quantitative Methodology," in Donald P. Ray (ed.), *Trends in Social Science* (New York: Philosophical Library, 1961), p. 85.

138. This summary of the structure of factor analysis is drawn from R. C. North, et al., *op. cit.,* pp. 118–20.

139. Christopher Alexander and Marvin L. Manheim, *HIDECS 2: A Computer Program for the Hierarchical Decomposition of a Set Which Has an Associated Linear Graph.* (Cambridge, Mass.: M. I. T. Civil Engineering Systems Laboratory, 1962). A later version, HIDECS 3, is described in M. I. T. Department of Civil Engineering Publication R63-27 (June, 1963). The authors are grateful to Steven J. Brams for an introduction to the use of hierarchical decomposition programs. For an application of HIDECS 2, see William A. Welsh, "Intellectuals and Politics in Eastern Europe: The Bulgarian Academy of Sciences as a Case Study," Ph.D. dissertation, Northwestern University, 1965.

140. Lipset, "Some Social Requisites of Democracy: Economic Development and Political Legitimacy," pp. 69–105.

141. *Ibid.,* p. 75.

142. Retzlaff, *op. cit.,* p. 806

143. Cutright, *op. cit.,* p. 254.

144. *Ibid.,* pp. 253–264.

145. Retzlaff, *op. cit.,* p. 808.

146. Cutright used the T-scoring method suggested by Edwards. See Allen E. Edwards, *Statistical Methods for the Behavioral Sciences* (New York: Holt, Rinehart & Winston, 1954).

147. Retzlaff, *op. cit.,* p. 810. See Cutright, *op. cit.,* p. 259.

148. Retzlaff, *op. cit.,* pp. 811–812.

149. *Ibid.,* p. 811. Also see F. W. Frey, "Political Development, Power and Communications in Turkey," in Lucian Pye (ed.), *Communications and Political Development* (Princeton, N.J.: Princeton University Press, 1963), pp. 298–301.

# ix

# Some Leading Approaches Methodologically Viewed, II: Inter-Nation Simulation as Approach and Avoidance

Perhaps no field within the discipline of Political Science has experienced as much post-World War II agony in its pursuit of methodological rigor as the study of international politics. The pain is only in part a function of the development of techniques and skills with which to confront its research problems. Indeed, the tool kits of specialists in international relations are prodigiously well stocked. Rather, the difficulties were primarily a function of the breadth and depth of the endeavor. The inelegance of some of the literature in international politics mostly reflects the herculean efforts necessary to achieve a great leap forward into empirical theory. Perceiving a longer road to travel, theory-oriented students of international relations have set out with heavier packs and an added measure of determination.

*Simulation* is one of the difficult but more promising roads down which these empirical theorists-to-be have traveled. Like all *au courant* vocabulary, simulation has been used variously. Following Brody, simulations here are considered to be "physical and/or biological representations of systems which attempt to replicate socio-political processes. They are models which yield information about unit and variable changes over time."[1] As a kind of model—or perhaps, as an operating representation of other models—simulations share the common characteristic of being "extensions of experimental techniques."

Specifically, simulation has three major features of experimental techniques.[2] First, simulations are rooted in the analog foundations of science. The development of scientific inquiry generally has depended upon the construction or observation of analogs. They include laboratory analogs of real-world circumstances and analogous properties common to two or more classes of empirical phenomena. Second, simulations are based on something of a sampling procedure. "Of all the aspects or properties of something 'out there' only selected ones are used," one student noted.[3] The need to make reality more manageable dictates the dependence of science on simplifying procedures. Third, simulations employ substitute mechanisms or surrogate functions. Laboratory control of environmental factors often involves the use of *equivalent* rather than *identical* procedures. Thus "the experimenter or simulator replaces the natural forces, random factors, and accidents assumed to operate in the real world."[4]

In sum, simulations are selective abstractions from reality. Their manipulability and relative simplicity facilitate better understanding of a complex and essentially unmanageable reality.

## I. SIMULATION IN RESEARCH AND TRAINING: METHODOLOGICAL ADVANTAGES IN POLITICAL SCIENCE

The burgeoning of simulation enterprises accents their important research and teaching advantages. Indeed, the rapidly growing fascination with simulation stems substantially from the breadth of advantages it seems to provide for Political Science. Once limited to management research and war gaming, simulation has spread to international relations, small-group-research, and studies of voting behavior. And these are only the more prominent applications. The commitment of human and material resources to simulation projects in international politics research has been especially heavy. Pay-offs already permit at least cautious optimism regarding the pedagogic and theory-building contributions of simulation.

Principal among the research advantages of simulations are the manipulative opportunities they provide. Simulation facilitates theory-building in three major senses. First, researchers ordinarily encounter very substantial difficulties in attempting to conduct experiments on natural systems. Access is commonly limited, costs are often high, and most important, there are usually a myriad of confounding variables that cannot be controlled. While canceling, irrelevant, or additive factors usually can be identified through existing field-study techniques, confounding factors cannot. When properly designed, simulation models can facilitate such identification. As Zelditch and Evan explain:

> The classic *ex post facto* method of dealing with contamination is to hold constant the contaminating factor, *c*. But where *a* and *c*, or *b* and *c*, are highly correlated in natural settings, obtaining a sufficient number of the necessary contrasts may be costly or even impossible. In such a case it may be necessary to create the required contrasts artificially. The contaminant may be a *cancelling* factor, the

> effects of which run counter to the effect of *a;* an *additive* factor, independent of *a* but obscuring the relative importance of *a;* an *irrelevant* factor, unrelated to *b* but highly correlated with *a* so that the package *ac* requires purification; or a *confounding* factor, spuriously generating the correlation between *a* and *b.* . . . The effects of confounding are never entirely controlled by investigations in natural settings, since randomization is the only (relative) safeguard against the indefinitely large number of relevant factors of which we are, at any moment, quite ignorant.[5]

Second, simulation also offers advantages in generating hypotheses, whether they be predictive or verificatory. The "re-creation" of past events in the simulate may yield new insights into previously unexplained phenomena. And the ability to move forward in time in a controlled fashion from a set of circumstances abstracted from the contemporary real world may provide important information on future states of affairs.

Third, simulations as *operating* models may help refine existing verbal models. Particularly in the case of complex verbal formulations, implicit assumptions often limit efforts to apply models to reality. Indeed, as we note in Chapter I, some of our more complex verbal models are so constructed that they defy the ordeal by testing. Their failure to generate operating models in simulations would make patent their inadequacy. Likewise, illogical (e.g., intransitive) relationships among variables may be unknowingly posited and hidden in complex verbal models. Simulation can aid both in identifying and in correcting these omissions or covert insertions.

Formidable research advantages notwithstanding, simulation's greatest advantages *today* be may pedagogic. Alger reports that undergraduate students generally responded more favorably to instructional programs in international relations utilizing inter-nation simulation (INS) than to classes using more traditional methods. The students emerged with a keener appreciation of the informal side of diplomacy and international affairs.[6] Alger more broadly summarizes his students' impressions of INS. Simulation

1. provides vividness and understanding beyond what one gets from a textbook;
2. gives one a realization of the complexities and the lack of simple solutions to international relations problems;
3. indicates the importance of having reliable knowledge and the importance of communication in international relations;
4. develops better understanding of the problems and goals of nations not like the United States;

5. gives experience in decision-making which enables one to better understand the problems of the decision-maker; and
6. demonstrates the difficulties of balancing the requirements of internal and external affairs.

Not that the issue of pedagogic usefulness can be taken for granted. Indeed, the pedagogic value of simulation has come under question of late. For example, four scholars associated with the Northwestern Inter-Nation Simulation reported a complex comparison of the effects of simulation and case-study methods in undergraduate international relations courses. They concluded that "the claims and expectations we had for simulation were not borne out."[7]

The Northwestern evaluation project deserves emphasis here, for two reasons. First, it is a reasonably systematic example of a relatively rare bird, the objective self-evaluation. Second, its conclusions have challenged broadly accepted presuppositions concerning the pedagogic value of simulation. Three upper-division undergraduate courses in Political Science at Northwestern were selected as settings for the research. Each class was divided into two student groups, one using the case-study method, the other utilizing simulation. All students attended two one-hour lectures weekly. Both groups engaged in interim evaluations of their respective methods (case studies and simulation) during the course of the quarter.

Significantly, there were efforts to control, at least roughly, the distorting effects on the experiment of differences among students. Students were assigned to sections based on intelligence (as questionably measured by SAT scores), grade-point average, and selected personality data. The latter included motivation toward achievement, affiliation, and power, as well as cognitive style. The research then attempted to ascertain any variations in impact of case–study and simulation methods. Only shortrun effects (e.g., classroom behavior and over-all course learning) could be calculated, although the experimenters evidenced concern for longer-run considerations (e.g., impacts on career choices, reading interests, and political behavior).

Addressing themselves to the "most frequently cited claim for simulation . . . that it heightens student interest," Robinson and his colleagues noted that simulation "is not uniformly superior to the case study as a supplementary teaching activity." One of the few consistent patterns of student response to simulation was clearly unexpected: "The case method succeeds more than simulation in eliciting student interest as measured by students' *perceptions,* but measures of students' *behavior* indicate that simulation succeeds more than case in affecting student interest and involvement."[8] Similarly, other gaming applications in the classroom have met with mixed student response. Business management games at the Carnegie Institute of Technology, as well as a foreign policy game at the University of Wisconsin, have encountered "dislike" and "boredom" resulting in "absenteeism."[9]

The complexities of evaluating INS also are compounded by interpretive puzzles. For example, "boredom" is not a particularly happy pedagogic by-product. But neither is "boredom" easily interpreted. Thus Robinson and his associates suggest that simulation's most important pedagogic benefits may derive from the technique's ability to "penetrate the firm 'set' that college students bring to courses on politics and international relations." The data gathered in the Northwestern simulation-versus-case evaluation project do seem to support this possibility, in fact. And boredom is one way of protecting one's "set," or organized biases, from examination.

The possible research and teaching advantages of simulation notwithstanding, the reader may ask why a technique such as this should be accorded relatively detailed treatment in this volume. One cannot say that simulation is in general use in the discipline. The extent of its application assuredly is less than, say, Simon's decision-making scheme or elitist or pluralist approaches to community power. Nor is the approach fully developed. To hear the simulation designers themselves describe the situation, their technique is perhaps still in its infancy, and definitely not yet into the throes of adolescence. Further, there seems little likelihood that simulation will proliferate. The resources required—men, money, materials—are that massive.

Anyone concerned with the methodological revolution in Political Science, however, ignores simulation at substantial peril. Three reasons may be cited. First, social science simulations originally emerged from concern with basic methodological difficulties plaguing other approaches. In particular, social (especially, political) scientists could not manipulate the environment in ways analogous to laboratory experiments in the "hard" sciences. This inability became increasingly frustrating as the calls for empirical theory grew more strident. Similarly, builders of explanatory models of political processes became disenchanted with static verbal structures because of their inability to handle complex, dynamic real-world relationships. Manipulable operating models were needed. Simulation was one response to this need. And it has a range that includes the use of relatively naive college undergraduates as well as the experienced government officials that James D. Barber used in his *Power in Committees* (Chicago: Rand McNally, 1966).

Second, the complexity of most simulation enterprises almost from the beginning nurtured the image of methodological sophistication, the protection of which image in turn encouraged critical neglect. For example, perhaps the best-known simulation now in use in Political Science is the Northwestern Inter-Nation Simulation. The godfather of this enterprise, Harold Guetzkow, deservedly enjoys the reputation of being one of the best "methods men" in the business; and the Northwestern department has for some time been a hotbed of methodological rigor. Consequently, the products of this shop generally reflect sophisticated concern for questions of method. At the same time, however, reactions to simulation follow the general rule that areas which seem highly involved or inaccessible are given a wide critical berth. Evaluations of simulations in Political Science have been highly general, therefore, and many have been content to ascribe precision as a "logical" result of complexity. Hence our emphasis here.

Third, simulation assumes importance because of its constantly changing nature. The INS model, for example, has undergone frequent modifications, sometimes of substantial importance. The fluidity of applications of the technique generates both problems and promise for us. Problems exist because it is difficult to be sure that one is not evaluating a non-current phase of the project's development. Promise also exists, for it is likely that significant methodological questions will continue to be unearthed and examined.

### A. INS in the Simulation World

Although we attribute to simulation a special importance, we question rather than assume the methodological soundness of applications of this technique. Specifically, we focus here on a particular simulation project, the Northwestern Inter-Nation Simulation (INS). We may rely on Guetzkow to describe our quarry. He offers this general description of INS:[10]

> Actions within the inter-nation simulation originate through individuals and groups. The human beings participating in the simulation represent the decision-makers within national political systems. A group of 2 or 3 to 5 or 6 decision-makers along with their resources and capabilities operate as the nation. Some or all of these nations in turn may combine to form supra-groups, such as regional and universal organizations . . . . The simulation thus consists of components at three levels: individuals (decision-makers); groups (nations); and supra-groups (alliances or international organizations).

Not that INS is typical or representative of the several types of simulation now used in the social sciences. On the contrary, three principal sub-types have been identified: (1) machine or computer simulations; (2) "mixed" or man-machine simulations; and (3) all-man simulations, or games.[11] Variations among these types principally depend upon the degree to which human actors are involved in the operation of the model as "units" or "sub-units." The most important of each of these types of simulations have been summarized elsewhere,[12] so no re-summarization will be attempted here.

The INS typifies only "mixed" simulations, and this only with reservations. Mixed simulations range between "much man, little machine" and "little man, much machine" systems. The Northwestern project falls somewhere within these boundaries. It has been described as "partly man and partly machine."[13]

The Northwestern INS rests upon a series of posited core variables and their specified interrelations. Included among the core variables which have been operative in recent INS runs are such items as authority, office-holding, decision latitude, national capabilities, and validator satisfaction. Relations among these core variables are specified prior to the beginning of an inter-nation simulation run. But these relations can be and have been varied between runs, a capability deriving from the fact that these relationships are specified in precise mathematical formulae. For example, the relation of outcome of revolution to internal controls is given by the formula

$$p(SR) = 1 - k' \ (FCic/FC)$$

where $k = 2$, $p(SR)$ is the probability of success of revolution, and $(FCic/FC)$ designates the percentage of total national Force Capability allocated to the maintenance of internal control.[14]

A most important dimension differentiating political simulations is the nature of programmed variables and inter-variable relationships. In particular, some simulations program only intra-nation characteristics, while others prescribe international system circumstances as well.

Most of the closely programmed variables and the specified inter-variable relationships in INS are concerned with the internal structure of the simulated nations. As we shall suggest subsequently, this fact has important implications. The values of the variables describing the internal circumstances of the nation—economic growth and stability, military capacity, the degree of decisional latitude enjoyed by authoritative decision-makers, and the satisfaction level of its citizens—are programmed variables whose initial values are set by the researchers, and which vary according to fixed rules. In contrast, however, relations among the variables connected with the international system—the closeness of alliances, the amount of trade entered into, the nature of international conferences—are *not* programmed by the experimenters. Thus, in INS the relations between nations seem to be heavily influenced by pre-ordained conditions within individual nations prescribed by the researchers. Much of what emerges as interesting or theoretically fruitful in INS involves the effects of these intra-national patterns on the international system, consequently. This outcome tendency of the Northwestern Inter-Nation Simulation contrasts sharply, for example, with the Kaplan, Burns, and Quandt "balance of power" game. In it, the actions of players are largely responses to an international situation which has been pre-ordained, relatively speaking.

INS and "balance of power" games are not the Scylla and Charybdis of simulation, however. Some simulations do not formally prescribe either intra- or extra-national behaviors. For example, an approach involving minimal formalization has been embodied in the RAND "role-playing—crisis-playing" game described by Goldhamer and Speier.[15] Here participants were professional area specialists. They were constrained only by their own preconceptions of what "their" assigned countries might "realistically" do, either in terms of domestic or foreign policies. Attention was focused on the team representing the United States. Consequently, that team was encouraged to be inventive in exploring foreign policy strategies. Both internal characteristics and international relations were "prescribed," that is, but the prescription was highly informal.

## II. SOME PRELIMINARY CRITERIA OF PERFORMANCE

The evaluation of any approach or technique in the study of politics must proceed on the basis of a set of explicit criteria. "Must proceed" must be qualified, of course, for little agreement exists about appropriate, scientifically relevant criteria. Perhaps the social sciences reflect the implicit persuasion that the task is not feasible, given the broad mix of pedagogic and research orientations we collectively bring to our work. In any event, the underlying subjectivity of any set of criteria must be acknowledged. But we are unwilling to fixate on qualifications. Not all criteria are equally appropriate for specific purposes, for example. For our specific purpose, that is, we believe we can select criteria that permit a rough judgment of the relative progress toward, and the avoidance of, methodological adequacy of specific approaches to politics.

Let us work toward refining our criteria of methodological approach/avoidance. We postulated at the outset of this volume that contemporary approaches to the study of politics, at a minimum, should be evaluated in terms of three criteria. First, any approach should be methodologically compatible with existing work in other fields. That is, minimally, no approach should peremptorily reject or exclude that which has proved methodologically useful in other areas of study. Second, any approach should seek its confirmation or disconfirmation in events external to the theoretical systems being developed. Our major concern here was that no approach be "self-sealing." And third, we argued that any approach should contribute to the isolation of dimensions of reality useful for descriptive and predictive purposes.

Inter-nation simulation meets the first test clearly. INS seems susceptible to a broad range of relatively sophisticated methodological innovations. Two examples among many of interdisciplinary borrowing are the conceptual application of game-theoretic considerations in simulation and the use of experimental laboratory techniques adopted in substantial part from research in Social Psychology.

With regard to the other two criteria, however, no better than very cautious optimism is justified. INS only inadequately meets our second and third desiderata. We do acknowledge, however, that the picture might be brighter if evaluation were made according to criteria considered more relevant by the simulators themselves. The problem is not so much whose criteria are more appropriate from the perspective of scientific precision. Rather, the issue is whether any specific criteria of methodological adequacy across the social sciences can be devised.[16] The question thus goes to the appropriateness of holding a still-embryonic project to criteria perhaps not given similar consideration by its architects. For example, Dawson suggests that simulation must be evaluated against possible alternative techniques, and this in terms of three criteria:

1. Applicability: Will the technique adequately solve the problems involved in the research or training exercise?
2. Cost: Are the costs in terms of time, money, equipment, and effort less than those for any other technique yielding comparable results?
3. Simplicity and communicability: Is it the least complex and most comprehensive technique, considering the persons who might be using it and those to whom the results might be communicated?[17]

The first of Dawson's criteria dovetails with our third criterion suggested above. The solution of research problems is at least substantially dependent upon isolating dimensions of reality. Dawson's other points stress criteria of evaluation apparently more congenial to INS people, as contrasted with the more absolute nature of the present approach.

This difference in the bases for evaluation is consequential. Simulation researchers consistently have adhered primarily not to criteria of methodological adequacy, but rather to considerations of convenience. Rather than asking if the enterprise meets rigorous tests of scientific adequacy, they inquire whether its operation seems practicable, given available resources.[18] This is not the kiss of death it seems. For projects chosen for feasibility may be tailored to meet more demanding and methodologically relevant criteria. Indeed, this is precisely the present course of INS, and the scientific pay-off of simulation should increase commensurately as this goal is realized.

## III. METHODOLOGICAL INELEGANCE IN THE INTER-NATION SIMULATION: "AVOIDANCE" AS A MODALITY

While we recognize that the strategy underlying INS reflects "approach" to methodological development, "avoidance" seems more characteristic. Two conclusions undergird this judgment. First, we reject convenience as a criterion, although we recognize its usual attractions and its common necessity. Second, in terms of the three criteria applied in this volume, the Inter-Nation Simulation has substantial methodological inadequacies.

We do not make demands on the reader's faith alone. The bulk of this chapter supports the two conclusions above. Even so, however, we must enter two caveats here. First, the architects of INS can hardly be accused of failing to recognize that their technique has faults. The tenor of their descriptions of the project is ever-tentative, eminently reasonable. Acknowledging a host of "pressing" problems, Guetzkow opines that "the task ahead . . . is a large one.[19] Consequently, our evaluative comments, it is hoped, contribute to an on-going concern. We certainly do not criticize a terminal project. But comments there must be. Recognizing problems is a crucial first step, but the road to empirical theory is a long one, indeed.[20] That is, we need to ask not only if problems are significant and whether they *might be* overcome. We must also ask whether, given the methodology of the project, these problems *are likely to be solved.*

Second, the thrust of this volume bypasses strawmen. That simulation finds its way into these pages testifies to its achievement and its promise. The possible pedagogic benefits of simulation are probably substantial, and its research applications seem to hold considerable promise. In short, we evaluate simulation here because it is worth evaluating.

The two preceding qualifications aside, our purpose is not merely to skirt the edges of substantive areas of concern. We move now to what this chapter advertises as simulation's dual character: as "approach" and as "avoidance." Social scientists have demonstrated well their lack of concern with the congruence of labels and content. But we must develop the approach and avoidance theme more explicitly. In short, we need to ask: "Approach to and avoidance of what?"

Kemeny has outlined this "what." He describes the genesis of a science in these terms. Empirical observations inductively beget models (or theories, or conceptual schemes); these models deductively beget hypotheses interrelating increasingly broad sets of empirical phenomena; and these hypotheses must be susceptible to replicable verificatory procedures.[21] While inference from particularistic statements to those at a higher level of generality is a never-ending process in evolving any tentative theoretical scheme, the inductive process should decline in significance as the Inter-Nation Simulation model develops. Emphasis should shift to the refinement of the simulation model into empirical propositions of the middle range, with the goal of developing a deductive system. In short, INS should be moving toward the specification and testing of the empirical implications of given propositions.

Approach and avoidance are thus conceived in terms of the success with which simulation is in process of becoming at least a prolegomena to empirical theory. In broad terms, the entire present chapter is concerned with assessing the success of the simulators. We see both positive and negative entries on the balance sheet. In some ways, INS seems to be almost uniquely close (among social science models) to a marriage with empirical theory. Hence we stress approach. Yet in other ways the abyss seems disappointingly wide and deep. Therefore, we also stress avoidance.

Brief illustrations of both approach and avoidance are in order. On the credit side, the manipulability of simulation—its ability to re-create elements of the real world in a laboratory situation—greatly facilitates verification of hypotheses, especially replicated verification. In Political Science, simulation is all but alone at this advanced point along the path to empirical theory.

At the same time, the laboratory setting of simulation implies dangers. The abstracted, simplified nature of all simulations calls into some question the relation of the laboratory exercise to reality. Conversely, the greater the efforts of the simulation designers to close with reality, the greater the likelihood that the model will become self-confirming. Much of the remainder of the chapter will be devoted to elaborating this argument.

### A. Circularity and the Place of "Free Variables"

Methodological avoidance in INS may be illumined more fully by considering the related issues of validation and the place of "free variables." Validation is a particularly sore spot. Several impressive attempts to validate the Inter-Nation Simulation runs are now underway; we catalog them subsequently in this chapter. On balance, however, there is a real danger that the INS model will never evolve into empirical theory. In particular, the methodology of simulation tends to militate against full use of validation studies, as we indicate below. Indeed, the likelihood that a model such as the Inter-Nation Simulation will become a self-sealing system seems to be borne out by the project's performance to date. This is true despite the "open-ended" nature of most INS runs so far conducted. That is, the simulation has attempted to generate hypotheses (indeed, to generate new variables) concerning the interrelation of political systems. While the simulation model has proceeded from a set of prior (often implicit) hypotheses, it has generated a host of potential modifications. But what has been generated rarely has been used. A certain amount of restructuring of the basic simulation model has taken place. But as we document below, the simulators are unwilling or unable to program generated hypotheses and variables into their basic model.

The role of free variables adds detail to the charge of methodological avoidance in INS. Free variables are recurrent behavior patterns generated by the interrelations of core variables in the simulation model. For example, *authority* and *decision latitude* are core variables. Their interaction—produced by the need for persons in positions of authority to make decisions within given constraints—may yield a free variable such as *delegation of authority* or *division of labor* among decision-makers.[22] Variables generated in this way by the operation of the simulation include *decisions on external affairs, office-holding needs, national goals, stability of behavior expectations,* and *alliance patterns,* to name only a few.

Simulators are careful to acknowledge the possible significance of the free variables generated by the model's functioning. Recognizing that important factors may have been omitted in the original structuring of the model, the INS researchers propose to retain a dynamic model capable of incorporating its own self-correcting virtues.[23] That is, if specific free variables consistently influence the outcomes of simulations, these variables supposedly would be built into the core of the model in future runs. The obvious importance of building significant variables into the model derives from the need for the experimenters to maintain at least rough control over the values of the variables.

But generating free variables and new inter-variable relationships does not preclude circularity. While the INS model is not fully self-confirming, that is, it is partially so. The model is not so constructed that *specified* outcomes *shall* occur, but it does provide that a certain *range* of outcomes probably *cannot* be generated. The kinds of inter-nation relations emerging from the simulation logically are substantially dependent on the nature of the programmed variables, and of the assumptions relating these variables, which are built into the model. If the simulate does not include one or more variables which are significant in determining a class of real outcomes, those outcomes cannot be generated by the model. To put the point more formally: the greater the amount of statistical variance in real-world events accounted for by a given variable, the more significant its omission from the simulation model.

In this sense, realism is the key to both the second and the third criteria submitted by the present authors. The criterion of self-fulfillment and that of isolating dimensions of reality both hinge on the congruence of the INS model with the natural international environment. And here reality treats simulation harshly. Head articulated the point sharply in discussing the relatively simpler simulation of "real-time systems," such as a computerized airline reservation system. Simulated runs certainly could help isolate the "bugs" in such a program, but there was one major hitch. "It is a dismaying paradox," Head observed, "that all the data needed for simulation are not available until the system to be simulated has been designed and put into operation.[24] Similarly, nature must be well understood to support an inter-nation simulation.

The issue of the congruence of reality and simulated outcomes is paramount. That is, the congruence becomes critical especially in developing theoretical propositions of the middle range and beyond. In a heuristic sense, simulation may be useful pedagogically. Perhaps even low-level theory about a restricted set of phenomena may be developed, regardless of the number of programmed variables or the ways in which these variables are operationalized. More sophisticated theoretical undertakings, however, demand from the model a higher degree of structural and elemental isomorphism.[25]

Not only does the exclusion of numerous variables from the basic simulation model preclude the generation of given outcomes but, perhaps even more important, the unprogrammed free variables apparently influence the interrelation of the real-world counterparts of the simulate's core variables. By and large, for example, the core variables in INS concern only domestic states of affairs. Many of the free variables have to do with inter-nation behavior. The generated variables are viewed in the simulation largely as outputs, and not as inputs, of the decision-making process. In the real world they doubtless are also inputs. Thus "nationalism" (which we view as an ideological component) may well be nurtured by inter-nation behaviors, but it also contributes to the intra-nation decisions from which these nurturing interactions follow. In short, the absence of programmed relationships between the inter-nation behaviors (generally treated in INS as free variables) and domestic core variables renders questionable the programmed relations among the core variables themselves. There has been insufficient effort in past INS runs to treat the generated factors as intervening or independent variables influencing the decision-making process.

To stress our point: generating unprogrammed relevant variables does not guarantee self-correction. It is further necessary to program these feedbacks from the international system into the posited relationships among core variables in subsequent runs. And the designer must also maintain all the while the congruence with reality which is so essential. Again, the simulation planners certainly are aware of this need. They simply are unsuccessful (and perhaps sometimes uninterested) in attempting to meet it. For example, Noel reports that the only two major efforts to introduce feedback from "national prestige" ratings into calculations for "validator satisfaction" proved fruitless.[26]

More specifically, these failures in feedback-programming relate to two of the most important elements of the simulation structure: participant decision-making and calculations of validator satisfaction. Decision-making and validator satisfaction are closely intertwined, since a given participant's position is determined by the acceptability of his program to those researchers or other participants who have the power to authenticate his office-holding.

Here is one example of the bind in which simulators find themselves. In response to the emergence of "ideological overtones" in unprogrammed inter-nation relations, the simulators have attempted to program ideological struggles between nations by relating each nation's validator satisfaction to the extent to which other nations had similar decision latitudes.[27] (The assumption is that "democratic" versus "non-democratic" ideological positions can be operationalized by controlling the extent of decision latitude enjoyed by the officeholders of simulate nations. We shall quarrel with this assumption directly.) The effort to program inter-nation ideological struggles was "considerably less than effective." Only one nation evidenced any response to this newly programmed situation, and "it was decided that the small contribution of similarity in decision latitude to the political aspect of the system did not warrant the complications involved in its retention."[28] Similarly, efforts to program national prestige into the simulation as a new source of validator satisfaction were unsatisfactory in two separate runs. The simulation directors found that participants attempted to falsify national prestige ratings, and tried to use these concocted ratings as manipulative tools in both intranational and international conflicts. The attempt to program national prestige was disruptive of the simulation runs, the simulators decided. Consequently they dropped the variable completely,[29] despite the strong smell of realism in the sly behavior of their experimental subjects.

INS is hoist with its own petard on the issue of free variables. The wholesale incorporation of such variables—assuming its feasibility—would be inconsistent with one of the basic premises of the simulators' enterprise. For the simulation model initially rests on a desire to allow participants to "freely develop relations between their states"[30] on the basis of purely domestic programmed restrictions. The fundamental premise doubtless follows in part from the research interests of the designers of INS, viz., the study of behavior in the *international* political system. That is, the simulators manipulate and simplify domestic variables in order to allow inter-nation behaviors to vary. The premise also reflects the simulators' stress on convenience in structuring the simulation model. Moreover, any programmed feedback may *not be possible,* given the present structure of the model. Consider the question: "Is it possible to program a free variable into a core variable by making an appropriate assumption? For example, could one formally link the esteem variable into the probability of office holding . . .?" The director of INS thinks "the answer is negative." He explains that although "one can speculate about the impact of core variables on free variables (and vice versa) by means of unprogrammed hypotheses, one cannot program one's hunches into the simulation unless one already has defined core variables for incorporation into the near assumptions."[31]

The inter-nation simulators thus find themselves on the horns of a dilemma. They may continue to treat international system variables as outputs alone, thereby making partial self-correction possible. That is, free variables of relevance could be observed. This approach, however, leaves grave doubts concerning anything but accidental congruence of the model with reality. Or simulators may attempt to incorporate these inter-nation behaviors into the programmed structure of the model, thereby reducing the likelihood that important inputs are omitted. This sharply increases the possibility that the model would become self-sealing, however. Specifying in advance the nature of national goals and strategies or the impact of nationalism or the shape of international organizations, to illustrate briefly, probably would produce a simulated international system reflecting the same set of characteristics. In short, one of the principal concerns of the INS designers—the desire to keep the simulation runs innovative by minimizing their formal structuring—would have to be sacrificed. Outcomes of a given simulation run would tend to be pre-ordained by the postures toward international affairs of the simulation supervisors and previous simulation participants, whose behavioral interactions would influence the emergence of free variables.

A prescriptive model could still retain a modicum of usefulness, of course, in that it might be used to project contemporary circumstances into the future. This use would naturally assume that the simulate operated in close congruence with the real international system, however. Thus the critical question: just how realistic can INS be?

These pages are hardly the first to raise doubts concerning the relation of inter-nation simulation to "reality." With admirable cogency, Verba had summarized the problem for the inter-nation simulators:

> If the variables selected are those that are significant for the process under study, if no significant variables are left out, if no additional distorting variables exist in the simulation, and if the variables are properly replicated within the simulation—they do not have to *look like* the variables in the real world as long as they *operate* like them—the simulation model will be isomorphic to the real situation and it will operate like the real-world phenomenon that is being modeled. Thus, the major problems in simulation research are selecting the aspects of the real world to simulate, replicating them in the model, making the model "work" and, above all, connecting the model back again with the real world.[32]

Verba has outlined a task of substantial proportions. It certainly is a monumental undertaking to abstract from an incredibly complicated real world its salient characteristics, and to manipulate them in a quasi-laboratory situation. Even more demanding is the validation of observed interrelations by referring them back to the real world. For the simulator did not really understand that world in the first place—hence his resort to simulation.

Perhaps we overstate the dilemma facing simulators, but we believe otherwise. Consider only Dawson's modest acknowledgment that "the simulator must know a great deal about the real system before he can presume to simulate it."[33] This pre-simulation knowledge, it is hoped, is less comprehensive than that contributed by the simulation itself. Otherwise, the simulation would add little and its substantial costs could hardly be justified. But even if simulation can generate meaningful hypotheses which aid in conceptually simplifying reality without distorting it, this does not guarantee that simulators can avoid their dilemma, or resolve it. Take the relation of any generated hypotheses to the concepts and operations which are part of the simulation model. Clearly, hypothesis generation does not guarantee conceptual clarification or operational simplification of the dimensions of reality. There is reason to expect the worst from INS in this regard. For the simulators frankly acknowledge the intuitive basis for the inclusion of most of the model's core variables. As Guetzkow observes:

> As yet, no formalized criteria have emerged to provide guidance for our exploitation of the work of others. For instance, no sampling technique seemed appropriate to guide our selection of core variables. Sometimes detailed rationalizations of the choices must be provided . . . an almost total reliance upon an intuitive grasp of this literature [must] be circumvented.[34]

Likewise, little effort has gone into establishing the validity of the mathematical formulae which serve to specify relations among the core variables. Implicit efforts in this direction in recent validation studies of simulation results must be acknowledged, however. We note some of these validation attempts subsequently.

## B. Exclusions, Distortions, and Prospects for Self-Correction in the INS Model

Several specific factors imply a methodologically awkward resolution of the general issue of circularity. We direct attention to: (1) the question of whether significant variables have been partially or entirely omitted from the structure of the simulation; (2) the nature of the operating controls designed to minimize distortion, especially that distortion induced by the "unrealistic" motivational setting of the simulation; and (3) whether existing methodological controls permit an optimism that dimensions of reality necessarily neglected in early simulation runs will find their way into subsequent runs, and whether these same controls also maintain a defense against the tendencies of the simulation model toward self-confirmation.

Among the relevant exclusions we may single out the failure to treat ideology and geography as inputs in the decision-making process. Perhaps the most significant distorting factor is participant personality, which is linked in turn to the motivational setting of the simulation. The model's empirical promise also is limited by the operational convergence of units at different levels of analysis, by the limited number of countries acting in the simulated international environment, by an apparently culture-bound treatment of the variable of domestic revolution, and by difficulties associated with efforts to validate the simulation. And perhaps of paramount importance are the self-sealing tendencies of the simulation. It is to this collection of problems that we now turn.

### *1. Exclusions in the INS Model: Ideology and Geography as Case Studies*

The architects of the INS project seem to have inadequately handled the possible impact of national or supra-national ideological doctrines on participant decision-making. National goals and strategies have been treated as free variables in INS runs. That is, they have been formulated by the participant decision-makers without direct influence, for example, from the prescriptive ideologies which are of substantial importance in the real international environment.

Ideology is programmed into INS primarily via the variable of decisional latitude, although national histories have recently been introduced. Those states with high decision latitudes represent totalitarian ideologies, while low decision latitude is associated with "democratic" states.[35] This formulation raises all sorts of difficulties. First, it confuses internal and external decision-making latitude. While the two are operationally fused in the INS model, the real world abounds with nations whose regimes appear to have a free hand internally but have little latitude in relations with other countries. Paraguay comes to mind, for example. Second, the usual approach ignores the fact that essentially "democratic" or "totalitarian" states may differ very substantially among themselves in the degree of decisional latitude enjoyed. Of course, if one empirically observed that no democratic nation ever had greater decisional latitude than any totalitarian country, the problem might not be critical. The required relationship between decision latitude (internal and/or external) and ideology does not always obtain in the real world, however. For example, political administrations in the United States have substantially greater internal and external decision latitude than the regime in Hungary.

The characterization of ideological neglect in INS holds except for one case, in which participants overwhelmingly failed to respond to efforts to program ideological conflict into the simulation model. The simulation supervisors concluded that the "complications" far outweighed the potential improvements.[36] The unpleasant experience of INS with ideological conflict as a variable highlights two arguments central to our evaluation of simulation. First, it underscores the principal concern of INS researchers with convenience, rather than with methodological adequacy. Second, the lack of participant response to efforts to insert ideological conflict might well reflect the inadequacy of the model's representation of ideology via differences in decisional latitude. That only one simulate nation "responded" to the insertion of this variable may simply indicate that the variable was improperly operationalized. The assumed relationship between decision latitude and ideology seems dubious in any case.

The handling of ideology in the INS model also confuses elite and mass ideological preferences. Or, alternatively, INS makes no effort to differentiate them. Allowing the goals and strategies formulated by decision-makers to represent an operating index of ideology denies significance to mass ideology in influencing political outcomes. Some degree of congruence between elite and mass values exists in the United States, for example. There appears to be much less congruence in Poland or Hungary. This fact in itself assuredly does not condemn the INS model. The point is that in some nations (e.g., Hungary), the elite-mass ideological preference gap is an important constraint on policy-formulation, while in other states, apparently it is not (e.g., mainland China, or perhaps the U.S.S.R.). By failing to treat mass ideology explicitly, the Inter-Nation Simulation loses the opportunity to incorporate these meaningful differences. At the same time, mass ideological values could be handled more directly in the INS validator satisfaction calculations. Assuming a willingness to introduce more extensive structuring, the simulators might introduce mass and elite ideologies as discrete core variables. As long as this degree of over-simplification exists, in any case, simulation research into the influence of ideological factors on inter-nation behaviors must be somewhat artificial, if not misleading.

The extensive over-simplification in handling ideology in INS still might be defensible, given the critical assumption that ideology accounts for little variance in real-world outcomes. That assumption seems inappropriate, however. For example, one might assume that Soviet decision-makers attribute to ideology nothing more than a rationalizing function. Perhaps decisions are made in Communist systems in spite of the ideology, rather than because of it. This is not the place to labor a reply. Ideology undeniably has declined in importance in the Soviet Union (if not in mainland China) in recent years. But there seems precious little reason to presume that the end of ideology, as forecast by Bell, is upon us.[37]

More telling support for our position inheres in the fact that simulators themselves do not defend neglect of ideology. For example, ideology recently has been introduced in simulations through national histories or scenarios for participants. Western, Soviet, and "neutralist" interpretations of recent history have been written, with principal events partially masked in an effort to avoid nurturing an overly prescriptive aura for the runs. These histories do not, however, spell out strategic or tactical alternative courses of actions which have been considered previously by decision-makers from simulate countries. Unfortunately, research on decision-making under crises suggests that these "histories of alternatives" are often among the most critical determinants of decision-making behavior. Indeed, two political scientists who were for several years close to the Northwestern simulation project have convincingly argued this point: decision-making behavior is often conditioned substantially by the nature of choices which have been made in past situations perceived to be roughly analogous by contemporary decision-makers.[38]

Our thrust is a simple call for continued open-mindedness. The INS researchers should more seriously consider the possible significance of ideological doctrines for the content of decisions or policies which are effected in the real world. Renewed efforts are needed to correct the superficiality of the present INS handling of ideology. The barely perceptible nod toward ideology embodied in the current INS model amounts to operationalizing the variable into irrelevance. This treatment represents a significant and harmful omission in the simulation model.

While the INS model makes some effort to handle ideological considerations, it ignores completely the variable of geography. To be sure, geo-political theorists such as Fox, Kissinger, and Kennan have been forced to modify their postures of immediate post-World-War II vintage. One hears much less talk today of the impact of naked geography on inter-nation behaviors. But as the Sprouts have demonstrated,[39] students of international affairs have long delighted in asserting causal relationships between environmental factors—especially geography—and the international political behaviors of states. That these causal assertions as such are often methodologically injudicious is now well established. At the same time—as the Sprouts again suggest—environmental factors such as geography may well influence the "operational results of decisions," if not the decisions themselves.

Nor does the evidence come only from those whose bread is geographically buttered. The call for incorporation of geography as an input recently has been sounded by someone close to the simulation operation. In comparing Wolfers' alliance theories with underlying postulates of the simulation, Gottheil has contended that greater isomorphism might be obtained between verbal and simulate theories if geography were introduced as a core variable.[40] Viewed as one variable in the "capability analysis" approach, then, geography is an important factor worthy of attention from specialists in international relations.

### 2. *Controls for Distortion in INS: Personality and Group Properties*

The inadequacy of the controls for distortion in INS is diversely reflected. Consider the undeveloped state-of-the art in handling the variable of participant personality in simulation. Participants infrequently have been selected on the basis of systematic personality evaluations, and personality structures have not been related to role performances in the simulation.

The neglect of personality factors is significant, beyond any doubt.[41] Social scientists have amassed experimental and observational data which demonstrate the effects of personality characteristics over an impressive range of behavior. Consider only one student's testimony. "Fundamental psychological research has overwhelmingly documented the influence of personality variables, attitudes, opinions, values and social experience on a variety of behaviors."[42]

Both neglect and significance are real enough to simulators. Indeed, the principal exception of the failure of INS to attempt to control distortions due to personality differences—the 17 runs of INS-8, held at Northwestern during the summer of 1960—itself provides strong proof of the significance of the general neglect. Participants were selected on the basis of their general tendencies to think "concretely" or "abstractly." Comparisons then were made of the simulation behaviors of the two basic personality types. Significant differences were found. For example, Driver reports significant curvilinear relationships between cognitive complexity and reactions to stress in the simulation participants.[43] The Hermanns also have attempted to match personalities of student participants and world leaders in a simulation of the outbreak of World War I.[44] In addition, a rough stratified occupation/personality control has been exercised through comparison of simulation behaviors of professional diplomats and those of university undergraduates. The latter, of course, have constituted the pool from which the vast majority of participants have been drawn.

Other evidence of the inelegance in controlling for actor differences may be sampled. The clearly greater participant motivation of career diplomats and professional journalists in one of the INS runs supports the thesis that personality interaction *quite distinct from the substantive nature of the simulation exercise* may have decided effects on outcomes. Apparently, keener involvement of the professionals reflected their desire to maintain peer-group prestige.[45] Hence group properties as well as personality properties are involved. Likewise, the present authors' observation of college students participating in simulations strongly suggests that they are influenced by desires to perform better than, for example, members of competing fraternal organizations. Little attempt has been made to control for the effect of inter-personal rivalries among undergraduate students on decisional outcomes, however. Of course, the simulation structure might be defended on the ground that such inter-personal rivalries could be roughly analogous to personal status rivalries among real-world decision-makers. In the broadest sense, no one can quarrel with the asserted analog, for human beings are involved in both cases. The critical questions, however, concern (a) the nature of the analogy and (b) whether any efforts are being made to isolate significant environmental differences between the simulation and the real world which may catalyze personality and experimental variations between the two groups of subjects involved. Unfortunately, the INS researchers have been able to sustain few efforts to answer these questions systematically.

Significantly, a recent application of the INS model strongly supports the notion that characteristics of participants may have a very substantial impact on the functioning of the system. Crow and Noel, proceeding from the position that "the inescapable 'human element' in simulation is the major source of uncertainty of the information gained,"[46] have attempted to ascertain "whether decision outcomes, in a simulation, are affected (a) by individual psychological characteristics of the participants, (b) by the social (organizational) context in which they are functioning, and (c) by the nature of the situation they confront."[47] Our concern primarily is with variations in the first two elements. These simulation runs, undertaken primarily through the facilities of the Western Behavioral Science Institute (WBSI), selected subjects with high/low scores on three attitudinal dimensions—militarism, nationalism, and risk-taking preference. Differentiation of organizational context came in the separation of individual judgments of participants from those judgments arrived at through group discussion culminating in mandatory (but not substantively prescribed) consensus.

The results of the WBSI runs clearly emphasize and support our concern with personality variables and organization context, for these variables affected decision outcomes with statistically significant regularity. Crow and Noel conclude that "any decision-making model claiming completeness must include all three variables,"[48] that is, personality, organizational context, and situational elements.

In addition, logic and a great deal of external evidence can be focused on the omission of personality dimensions. These approaches also lead us to the proposition that personality variables are of importance in choice-taking. We now acknowledge that nations, being social abstractions, do not act. Rather, human beings commit the resources of nations by making decisions. Thus any identifiable and salient elements of personality which influence decision-making must be studied if inter-nation behaviors are to be understood.

We do not urge an extreme position here. No one concerned with feasibility proposes that the simulation model attempt to include the myriad idiosyncrasies of all decision-makers acting in the inter-national arena. But it does seem a reasonable task to include personality variables hypothesized to be characteristic of large numbers of decision-makers. And at the very least one might expect some kind of control over the personalities of subjects recruited to act as participant decision-makers.

Once again the perceived difficulty of the task, not any naiveté of the experimenters, has inhibited work with personality variables in the simulation. Guetzkow acknowledges that numerous implicit variables—such as those of personality and organizational expectation—are carried into the simulation by participants.[49] Further, these variables are admittedly of importance:

> The lack of prescribed structure among the decision-makers, except for the allocation of prime authority to the central decision-makers, allows freedom for the participants in the evolution of their decision-making roles. . . . But the utilization which is made of this "programmed" authority by the decision-makers depends upon such unprogrammed features of the simulation as their personality characteristics and developments within their situation.[50]

The difficulty created by the uncontrolled presence of these factors is twofold. First, the insertion of these masked variables severely restricts the degree to which programmed relationships are actually pre-ordained. Second, the impact of personality and related factors on outcomes (especially on unprogrammed inter-nation behaviors) is very difficult to pinpoint. The researchers in turn must remain uncertain of the precise genesis of any "generated" hypothesis. Ultimately, efforts to program in feedbacks from the generated relationships would have to rest at least in part on intuition and hunch.[51] The possible presence of contamination from uncontrolled factors would be exceedingly difficult to ferret out.

We have emphasized in the last few paragraphs the importance of personality variables for simulation outcomes. Yet much of the supportive evidence we have cited is broader in thrust. Specifically, it also emphasizes the significance of specifying group properties, particularly structure and organizational styles as determinants of simulate behavior. Recent small-group research renders a truism the observation that the behavior of the whole reflects more than the sum of its individual parts. Further, the salience of group characteristics for decisional outcomes may be magnified in experimental situations such as simulation. As Verba concludes:

> This special situation will affect the way in which the experimental group operates. The artificiality of the situation reduces the chances that affect and tension will develop in the group. The lack of past relations among the group members also influences the group behavior. Groups will have to solve a whole series of problems of internal structure that groups with a history will already have solved. The process of group formation will have to take place simultaneously with the solution of the particular problem that the experimenter presents to the group. And the lack of expectations

> of continuing relationship after the group meetings allows the group members to behave differently from the way in which they would have behaved had they to consider the effects of their behavior on future relationships to which they were committed.[52]

In sum, participant-centered problems in simulation extend beyond the complex realm of personality. Uncontrolled variations in group properties may have similarly deleterious effects. That we have stressed personality distortions in these pages should not detract from the importance of group variables. The latter, too, must be controlled more effectively in the Inter-Nation Simulation.

### *3. Controls for Distortion in INS: Inter-Level Convergence*

A perplexing problem which applies to simulation (as well as to other approaches used in the study of international politics) concerns the overlap of different levels of analysis. In INS, this difficulty is especially critical. The simultaneous behaviors of simulate components at three levels—individual, group, and supra-group—are often determined by a very small number of participants. Indeed, the spectacle of one participant dictating to the rest of the simulate system is frequent in INS runs. This may well conform to occasional real-world circumstances, *at least in terms of outcomes.* That is, the preferences of a leading decision-maker in a given country may be faithfully reflected in his country's behavior, in the actions of groups of nations, and perhaps even in the means chosen to handle collectively a conflict in the international system. In the real world, however, policy agreements among nations infrequently are determined by the overriding influence of a single person.

Whether this element of the simulation is "realistic" is of secondary importance. The crux of the matter is that inter-level uncertainties severly limit the ability of the model to generate hypotheses interrelating individual, group, and supra-group variables. Variables at all three levels may overlap to such an extent that their conceptual separation becomes meaningless. More important, even if the variables in question do co-vary empirically, they must still be isolated by appropriate nominal concepts and operational definitions. Predictive and descriptive failures are inevitable in other studies in the absence of such conceptual and operational attention.

The isomorphism between simulate model and international system is at the root of the present problem. The internal decision-making process in INS is far from being an analog of the highly complex procedures by which decisions are made in many real-world systems. This fact, coupled with the unrealistic simplicity (especially in terms of the number of decisional units) of the simulate's international environment, understandably limits the hypothesis-generating capabilities of the model.

Again, the INS researchers are aware of the possible impact of oversimplifying decision processes in the model. Further, they assertedly are interested in developing hypotheses relating variables at the three levels of analysis.[53] Unfortunately, this interest has been neglected in the dominant concern of the INS directors for inter-nation behaviors. In the past, the former interest has been sacrificed to the latter, as another reflection of the pre-eminence given the criterion of convenience.

### *4. Controls for Distortion in INS: The Relation Between Quantity and Quality of Interaction*

Another important but neglected problem area in INS deals with the intimate relation between quantity and quality of interaction in simulations. Again our focus is dual: on the present state of affairs, and on the probability that INS is so methodologically rooted as to be self-correcting. Again, evidence supports substantial pessimism about what exists now and what probably will exist.

There have been few efforts to program into the INS model characteristics or behaviors of additional nations (beyond those actively represented by participants in the simulation) as factors influencing simulated international relations. A more populated international system probably would bring about meaningful changes in the behaviors of the INS participants. For example, alliance patterns might evolve partly in response to the number and type of potential partners. The internal dynamics of international organizations probably would vary significantly as their size increased. And the more complex feedback from the simulated international system should in turn alter the internal decision-making behaviors of participants. Consequently, the number and nature of feasible alternative courses of action would be affected.

#### *a. Self-Correction in INS: Number of Nations*

Fortunately, some steps are now being taken to manipulate "quantity" in simulations, although these steps fall short of expanding the number of nations in the model. Further, there are increased efforts to ascertain the qualitative implications of this extension. Hermann reports the use of confederates (i.e., experimenters acting as participant decision-makers) to introduce certain behaviors into INS runs, behaviors which were not generated by the functioning of the model itself.[54] Plans are underway to extend such interventions in forthcoming runs.

The use of confederates is not really analogous, however, to an expansion of the absolute number of nations represented in the simulation, for two reasons. First, confederates precipitate circumstances selected by the researchers for experimental reasons. The antecedents of confederate behaviors are largely extra-system in nature. Presumably, the same is not true when additional nations are added. Second, the use of confederates in INS thus far has not been coupled with any effort to increase appreciably the total number of decisional units acting in the system. That is, confederates generally have been used instead of other participants, rather than in addition to them. The total number of nations involved in a given INS series has not exceeded nine. The INS rests on the assumption that the division of participants into reasonably discrete decisional units is useful for research purposes. Alternatively, simulators at least assume that $n$ decision-makers acting as $N$ "countries" will behave differently from $n$ participants assigned in some other way. And, one would think, simulators must assume that those $n$ subjects will act more consistently than $n + 2$ subjects with whatever reality is being simulated. Beyond these points, however, little has been done to investigate the effects of varying the total number of countries and observing differences in decisional outcomes.

There is more than hunch underlying our argument. The size of $N$ has been manipulated in experimental groups with significant consequences.[55] The size of task-oriented groups appears to have considerable impact on their internal operation, and on their output,[56] for example. Beyond the confines of the laboratory, the behaviors evidenced by major nations in the United Nations are influenced by the number and types of nations newly admitted to the organization.[57]

Allegations of unfairness may follow our charges about sins of omission in a continually evolving approach to politics, for there remains at least the possibility that these sins may be rectified. We are too concerned with the likelihood that repentance will in fact occur. In the immediate case, the convenience-oriented criteria emphasized by simulators seem to discourage any sweeping extension of the number of participants. The INS does not promise self-correction in this regard, that is. We stress the heavy importance accorded convenience (especially manipulability) and low cost by the architects of INS. As the Northwestern researchers have discovered, large numbers of undergraduate students are not easily enticed into courses structured around simulation —and college students are the most "captive" subjects available, with the possible exception of low-ranking military personnel at non-strategic bases. And the more restricted the pool of participants, the lesser the probability of isolating the ways in which personality background variables may be distorting the products of the model.

### *b. Self-Correction in INS: Cultural Bias*

Any comparative analysis of nations could hardly avoid another challenge to INS self-correction, "culture-boundedness." Social science texts fashionably charge that any theoretical approach is culture-bound; that it is inextricably linked to the values represented by the culture in which the theorist is operating. Hence the frequent charge that our attempts to build low-level or medium-range theory about politics in the "developing areas" are doomed to failure. We are leery of being fashionable in the present sense. On balance, the INS seems to reflect neither a value bias, nor a bias of intellectual approach, which might preclude the integration of this work with other major efforts to understand the international political system.

But perhaps we have not looked closely enough, for there is some evidence of culture-boundedness in INS. Consider that the Validator Satisfaction calculations made in the simulation are based in part on the assumption that revolution is not an institutionalized (or "normal") mode of change. The probability of revolution does vary in the INS model. However, the average probability of revolution over time for any nation included in recent INS runs has been substantially lower than the probability of revolution in, say, certain Latin American countries. In the operation of the simulation there has been nothing approaching the rate of elite turnover which one observes in a country such as Ecuador or even Brazil.[58] The INS handling of revolution is in turn related to the number of nations included in the simulation runs. Naturally, few "national types" may be represented if one has only five or six nation-state units with which to work. The resources available to the simulators are controlling here. That the problems facing simulators are understandable, however, does not diminish their significant consequences.

In a more subtle sense, in addition, the entire simulation *is* culture-bound. It reflects what we may call *laboratory culture.* The INS researchers have acknowledged that "motivational setting" is one of the more important and distressing characteristics of the experimental situation. Snyder asks,

> Can one duplicate the requirements of actual situations or the moral properties of momentous political decisions in simulation? Do participants ever escape the realization that 'it does not really count'? What effect does the fact that the experience is vicarious have upon its values for learning? We do not have satisfactory answers to these questions, nor is it clear that the problem itself is fully understood. The critical question is whether the artificiality of the contrived exercise eliminates an indispensable counterpart of reality, namely a full sense of responsibility—of having to live with decision consequences.[59]

Snyder understandably responds in an optimistic vein, but we hesitate to join him. First, he argues, abundant evidence exists that participants take simulation very seriously indeed and are capable of complete absorption.[60] The data presented by Alger do, indeed, seem to support this statement (assuming, of course, that students were willing to express their full range of responses to the simulation experience when asked to by INS directors). However, there is no necessary relationship between *intensity* or *depth* of involvement on one hand, and the *antecedents* or *directions* of involvement on the other. Nor is intensity of involvement necessarily a crucial determinant of the behavior which follows. That is, the international environment has not been realistically simulated simply by inducing a student to take his role in the simulation exercise "seriously." Thus, the student who commented that he "[felt] like an Omnian!" and had "developed a nationalistic patriotism . . . which in many ways is just as strong as my American patriotism"[61] might have been motivated by a desire to outshine or impress some other student, or to obtain a satisfactory grade in the course. These reasons may be admirable and even functional in that they keep motivation at a reasonably high pitch, but they most clearly are complex "realisms." That is, they have a doubtful correspondence with motivations of political decision-makers and diplomats in the real world. At best, we may say that the connection remains unestablished.

Second, Snyder suggests that selection by motivational states is possible. And again we hesitate. Thus, he notes that "throwing one's self into a dramatic role" aids one in transcending the laboratory world. In his words,

> . . . a connection between play-acting and hypnosis has been noted for a long time. Throwing one's self into a dramatic role apparently creates a psychic state not unlike the trance, except that the former is usually self-induced. Individuals differ widely in their susceptibility to hypnosis. It does not seem far-fetched to suggest that as a . . . technique, participants in simulation exercises could be tested for susceptibility—in this case to the demands of the particular form of role assumption demanded by gaming. Getting so caught up in a contrived situation that one *does* behave in accordance with system rules or constants and in response to unfolding interactions, rather than in accordance with personal whim may be analogous to the inability of a hypnotized subject to lower his outstretched arm even when he feels he is quite free to do so. Though simulation participants are aware that they are not actually making decisions in a real foreign office, their behavior produces effects which in turn cause a "shock of recognition" of real-world likenesses.[62]

Only two responses to this argument seem necessary. First, while the connection between "play-acting" and hypnosis has been tentatively established in other contexts, the linkage remains unclear in the Inter-Nation Simulation. And second—and most important—the fact that the simulation designers feel they must search for ways to *escape* the possible dangers of an untranscended laboratory environment underlines our main point. There *is* a laboratory culture. And it *does* have pitfalls for those whose ultimate focus rests in the less-rarefied air of reality.

To reflect tentativeness about coping with the laboratory culture does not imply defeatism, however. If the modal posture of the discipline is skepticism, it is at least skepticism tinged with hope. Learning to transcend the experimental laboratory culture would be a gigantic step forward toward Political *Science*. Further, Snyder's implicit suggestion that participants be selected through a battery of personality inventories is worthy of test. Indeed, such a procedure seems a prerequisite for controlling actor-related distortions in INS.

Specifically, Snyder further suggests that the absence of the real world's impressive sanctions may not always alter significantly the behavior of experimental subjects. Similarly, he cautions against assuming any particular relationship between role structures and personal values among real-world decision-makers. That is, we are urged that personal values may enter into the natural environment quite as frequently as they seem to in laboratory situations. Again, we can only join in the collective (and breathless, given its cruciality to simulation) hope that Snyder is right. For, as he gingerly submits, "judgment should be suspended until a more adequate empirical basis has been established."[63] This is a reasonable position, provided one recognizes that until such time as the hoped-for evidence comes in, undertakings based on the unestablished hypotheses are open to substantial methodological challenge.

## IV. THE VALIDATION PROBLEM IN INS: SELF-CORRECTION ON MAJOR TRIAL

Validation is related to, but looms above, questions of self-correction. Although few efforts to validate the inter-nation simulation have been undertaken, validation is fast becoming the most consuming interest of the simulation researchers. The growing concern with validation stems in part from the desire to use simulation for verification and for prediction. That concern also results from the fact that the most vigorous criticism of simulation is that it is so "artificial" as to be grossly "unrealistic."

Criticisms of INS are often severely overstated, especially because of misunderstanding and confusion of the different ways in which a simulate may be "artificial" or "unrealistic." As Zelditch and Evan have noted, a simulation may be artificial in any of three senses:

> (1) Its independent variables are given unreal values, although they are the same variables that operate in the natural world and, if left to themselves, would yield descriptively natural results. Ex-

> ample: "free communication" permitted in a bureaucratic organization. (2) Its correlated properties, those describing the setting of the experiment, motivation of the subjects, etc., may differ from those which the simulation represents. Example: college students as subjects where executive board committee meetings of business corporations are represented. (3) Its properties do not behave like real properties. Example: puzzles to represent the tasks of a bureaucratic organization.[64]

The various artificialities rate differential concern. Zelditch and Evan correctly argue that the first form of artificiality is unlikely to hinder the theoretical applications of simulation (although it may well diminish its instructional value). In fact, this kind of artificiality is probably beneficial for theory-building because it focuses attention on "relations among a system of variables, more than on their actually descriptive states."[65]

The second kind of artificiality may be more serious. It points up the difficulties associated with the use of college students in most INS runs. Zelditch and Evan believe that simulation's research pay-off is inherently limited by the background of its participants. As they explain, "Guetzkow's simulated international diplomacy is excellent for teaching, but less adequate for experimental purposes because the college students probably differ from diplomats in ways relevant to the results desired of the simulate."[66]

Although it may be less than meaningful to accuse simulation of operating from "unrealistic" states of affairs, it is still necessary to isolate unreal relationships among variables which may be generated through these artificial states. What has been called the rule of genotypic similarity stipulates that, at least for research purposes, the variables in a simulated system need not *look* like the phenomena they purport to represent: they need only obey the same laws.[67] The key problem, of course, is to be able to recognize when real-world laws and simulate laws are congruent. After all, one simulates because he does not know the nature of laws governing reality. Hence the crucial nature of validation.

The concept of genotypic similarity begs for explication. We have urged more than once in this volume that the social science antidote for the disease of "black-box" methodology seems to be most ineffective. The "black-box" approach involves the treatment of a complex structure as a single, essentially undifferentiated entity. The behavior of the total system is then observed under varying stimuli. Generally, one's observations are restricted to the outputs of the "black box." We and many others doubt the possibility of establishing genotypic similarities merely by comparing outcomes in natural and simulate systems.

If our appraisal of the "black-box" is appropriate, simulation pays the implied costs. In terms only slightly simplified, INS efforts reflect a meta-model that is essentially a black box. In general, for example, the INS simulators are preoccupied with decisional products or outputs, as opposed to inputs and to processes. Hence the otherwise puzzling neglect of such inputs as ideology or personality in simulation designs. In the usual .INS approach to validation, similarly, genotypic similarities are established by comparing decisional outcomes in the natural state and in simulations.

The present important point, then, may be framed in terms of a sharp contrast between what is commonly designed into simulation exercises, and what is methodologically appropriate. Simulators strongly tend to act as if they were unable to gain invitations to a phenomenal feast. Nonetheless, they perch on the back doorstep of the festive house, hoping to judge the menu from the shadows on the windowshades, the sound of the garbage disposal, and some few scraps in the garbage can. Empirical methodology prescribes an apposite approach. It is scientifically more useful to treat *laws* as generalized descriptions of *processes* which tie variations in specific *inputs* to specific variations in specific *outputs*. To focus on outcomes, that is, cuts the heart out of the scientific enterprise. That is, focusing on outputs implies a primitive Stimulus-Response chain. We mean this in two senses. First, the output orientation does not spotlight the role of various independent and intervening variables. Only the dependent variable of differential outputs gets strong attention. This is patently awkward. Second, and by far more significant, the output orientation encourages the neglect of the central scientific task of isolating dimensions of reality necessary to describe processes that link various inputs to various outputs. That is to say, the output orientation discourages the long, hard look at the complexities of developing suitable nominal and operational definitions of dimensions of reality, of testing them, and of tying them into increasingly comprehensive theoretical networks. In still other words, the output orientation of simulation encourages a neglect of that which is most intimately the scientific process.

The slippage in INS between what is and what should be supports a clear conclusion. If our argument applies even remotely, a very long and very hard look at the simulation enterprise and its validation efforts is called for.

We do not argue that the "black-box" technique is without value. Meehan suggests the contrary. "By subjecting a single black box to a variety of inputs," he notes, "much can be learned about that particular box, and by comparing the response of many similar boxes to identical inputs, further useful information can be gathered." At the same time, any information obtained about the contents of the "black box" (in this case, the decisional units) will be strictly inferential. With Meehan, we submit that the researcher "cannot fully specify the contents of the system" with this technique. "Yet when all that can be done has been done, the technique remains imperfect and the interpretation of results problematic."[68]

Some conclusions need stating. In short, the present structure of INS has relatively little explanatory value. It may, however, be of help in predicting future states of affairs. But any predictive value would rest on pragmatic, not logical, grounds. No approach embodying the "black-box" technique can evolve into a formal theoretical system from which empirically testable propositions logically follow. This again confronts us with the fact that the utility of simulation in theory-building must rest upon its congruence with reality.

Simulators are struggling with their "black-box," to be sure. The simulation researchers subscribe to the notion that validation efforts may be of two types. First, past events can be re-created in the simulation runs, with the intention of comparing the outcomes of these runs with the real-world outcomes associated with the events which are being simulated. One objection to this procedure is that, unless the simulation participants are completely unaware of what the real-world outcomes actually were, they are likely to attempt to make the simulation emerge as valid so as to make the simulation a "success." Or, given a simulation participant biased against the undertaking, "unrealistic" behavior might be expected. Moreover, even if the outcomes do happen to coincide, this goes only a short way toward establishing the congruence of the simulate system and of the real world. And even if that congruence were established, the researcher would be little closer to isolating the dimensions of reality required by scientific effort. Indeed, he might be so conditioned as to neglect the conceptual and operational problems of empirical science.

Second, validation of the simulation could be undertaken through a "predictive" use of the INS runs, with some gain. That is, future circumstances—such as the behaviors of nations in an international system in which nuclear weapons technology has been more widely dispersed—could be simulated. Here the goal would be to produce a set of predictions which might be tested against a future state of affairs, should the future state of affairs in fact come to pass. While this approach to validation avoids some objections to the first approach, it has its own difficulties. As Verba had inquired, with what events does one compare the simulation? In what respects do the real-world event and the simulated event have to match before one can conclude that the simulation has been validated? And how does one interpret a success or a failure in matching the real political world?[69] And suppose one observes that the simulated and real world outcomes are not the same? A bevy of explanations still might be entertained. The two systems may not be isomorphic. Or simulate variables may have been given inaccurate initial values. Or psychological or social psychological variables, such as participant expectations, may contaminate the simulation environment (for example, participants may act as they believe the experimenters want them to act). Or the probabilistic nature of outcomes in the simulation and in the real world may occasion incongruity in outcomes despite total isomorphism of relationships, variables, and processes.

Two points concerning these approaches to INS validation also support our recommendation for a process-orientation. First, both types of validation are product-oriented, not process-oriented. Indeed, the concern to date of INS researchers with outputs raises a most serious question: Precisely what is being "validated"? Certainly hypotheses about the dynamics of intra-nation decision-making are not being validated. Rather, these two common approaches to validation can confirm nothing more than the *credibility* of simulate *outcomes,* when they are compared with a range of observed real-world occurrences. Second, these validation efforts only tentatively approach our third methodological criterion, the need to isolate dimensions of reality. Descriptive and explanatory purposes cannot be served well by comparing simulation outputs with past or hypothesized future states of affairs, even given no difficulties with such comparisons.

And difficulties aplenty do exist. We can only suggest their magnitude and number. Note only that during one of the major efforts to validate an inter-nation simulation (in this case simulation of past states of affairs), the real-world outbreak of war did not occur in the simulation.[70] Further, while the major future-oriented simulation, that by Brody,[71] does seem to have predicted some trends in international relations, the failure of alliance systems to develop in close congruence with the predictions of the simulation model encourages some caution. Only detailed concern with processes encourages developing the conceptual and operational definitions of the dimensions of reality underlying some decision-product. Again, in this regard, INS gives no great hope of self-correction.

The conclusion is patent. As Verba expressed it: "It may be that the most fruitful simulation will involve comparisons with the real world in terms of the micro-processes that are involved in international relations."[72]

Tentativeness on the matter of validation probably will be less necessary soon. Numerous simulation-validation efforts have been recently completed, or are well underway.[73] Two studies comparing historical and research data with outcomes deriving from simulations are now finished.

Zinnes has observed that hostility processes extant in the immediate pre-World War I period paralleled those noted by Brody in the 1960 Brody-Driver simulations of the bi-polar period preceding the spread of nuclear weapons technology. And Druckman reports that the "nationalistic" tendencies of the decision-makers in simulation runs conducted by the Western Behavioral Sciences Institute for Project Michelson were similar to those described by other researchers in both field and laboratory work.[74] Chadwick also has compared the dimensions obtained from a factor analysis of the Brody-Driver runs with those obtained on data supplied by Rummel from his Dimensionality of Nations Project.[75] Plans are underway to conduct simulation runs of disarmament negotiations, with an eye to validating them with empirical data from post-World War II East-West disarmament debates. Meier and Jensen are conducting separate studies aimed at systematically comparing predictions made by foreign service personnel with inter-nation simulations involving high school, college, and diplomatic corps participants.[76]

No one can predict the resultant thrust of this in-process research, but substantial revisions of INS seem in the offing. Chadwick's work[77] deserves special mention, for two reasons. First, his dissertation is the initial effort to subject a significant part of the INS model to comprehensive empirical testing. Other validation work has centered on very limited segments of the simulation model. Second, Chadwick raises substantial doubts about the validity of the INS model in its present form. Chadwick chose 10 variables from the INS model, each representing domestic conditions presumed to be relevant for international behavior. These variables were indexed by empirical data collected through the Dimensionality of Nations project.[78] The assumptions linking these variables in the model then were subjected to statistical test, especially by correlation and factor analysis. Approximately one-half of the relationships assumed in the simulation model appear to be disconfirmed by Chadwick's analysis.

Some of Chadwick's other findings encourage even greater caution. When he compared correlations among 7 international system variables and 10 domestic variables, with correlations generated among these variables in the simulation, he discovered that only 8 of 68 correlations were statistically significant in both sets of data. Eleven correlations were significant in the simulation, but not in the empirical data, and 49 were significant in the empirical data but not in the simulation.[79]

## V. CONCLUSION

The construction of empirical theory is a hand-in-glove partner of the search for Political *Science*. Simulation heralds identifiable advance toward empirical theory in several particulars. The operationality of simulation demands explication of assumptions underlying the model. This explicitness, unfortunately, is often missing from verbal models. Further, simulation deals with an abstracted and scaled-down version of reality. From this fact derive the manipulability, clarity, and relative simplicity which characterize INS. The INS model also has generated a substantial body of quantifiable data which are subject to relatively rigorous manipulation and analysis.

Yet simulation has its clear-cut limitations as well. We have argued that these principally include tendencies toward self-confirmation, over-simplification of the international environment, an absence of controls over the distorting effects of participant personalities, and a "laboratory culture" which considerably limits the researcher's ability to generalize findings.

These criticisms of simulation reflect its patent methodological inadequacies, but they also may be unfair, speaking relatively. As Verba suggests, "the same dilemmas that affect simulation studies can be found in verbal models of international relations, and with the same consequences." Verba elaborates:

> One can think of studies of international relations that use only a few quantifiable variables and others that use many variables and little quantification. In the former case, the difficulty is that one is not sure what it is that one can and ought to measure. One ends up measuring that which is measurable, often without regard for its significance and relevance. On the other hand, without measurement, statements as to the relationship among variables become difficult, if not impossible, for there is no clear and precise way of describing changes in the values of the variables.[80]

In short, international relations theorists often are forced to choose between the two contrasting kinds of approaches, a rather unenviable choice shared by simulators and non-simulators alike. And the possible advantages of simulation, both as a research technique and as a teaching device in the study of international relations, have been well cataloged.

Unfair or not, our criticisms imply accelerated change in INS. For example, only very recently have the simulators begun to address themselves to one of the most significant untapped resources of their technique: its ability to generate hypotheses *about itself*. That is, the study of simulations should yield understanding of the simulation technique. As Verba indicates, a knowledge of the dynamics of simulation itself may be of substantial value to social scientists, perhaps especially social psychologists and political scientists. After all, "the participants in the simulation are real people, and their behavior is real behavior."[81]

## NOTES

1. Richard A. Brody, "Some Systemic Effects of the Spread of Nuclear Weapons Technology: A Study Through Simulation of a Multi-Nuclear Future," *Journal of Conflict Resolution,* 7, No. 4 (December, 1963), 671.

2. Richard C. Snyder, "Some Perspectives on the Use of Experimental Techniques in the Study of International Relations," in Harold Guetzkow, Chadwick F. Alger, Richard A. Brody, Robert C. Noel, and Richard C. Snyder, *Simulation in International Relations: Developments for Research and Teaching* (Englewood Cliffs, N.J.: Prentice-Hall, 1963), p. 4.

3. *Ibid.*

4. *Ibid.,* p. 5.

5. Morris Zelditch, Jr. and William M. Evan, "Simulated Bureaucracies: A Methodological Analysis," in Harold Guetzkow (ed.), *Simulation in Social Science: Readings* (Englewood Cliffs, N.J.: Prentice-Hall, 1962), p. 50.

6. Chadwick F. Alger, "Use of the Inter-Nation Simulation in Under-graduate Teaching," in Guetzkow, et al. *Simulation in International Relations,* pp. 150–89, especially at pp. 178–79.

7. James A. Robinson, Lee G. Anderson, Margaret G. Hermann, and Richard C. Snyder, "Teaching with Inter-Nation Simulation and Case Studies," *American Political Science Review,* LX, No. 1 (March, 1966), 64.

8. *Ibid.,* p. 57.

9. See William R. Dill, "The Educational Effects of Management Games," in William R. Dill, James R. Jackson, James W. Sweeney, *Proceedings of the Conference on Business Games* (New Orleans: Tulane University School of Business Administration, 1961), pp. 61–72; and Bernard C. Cohen, "Political Gaming in the Classroom," *Journal of Politics,* 24 (1962), 367–81.

10. Guetzkow, et al., *Simulation in International Relations,* p. 106.

11. Brody, *op. cit.,* p. 672.

12. *Ibid., especially* pp. 671–79.

13. *Ibid.,* p. 679.

14. Guetzkow, et al., *Simulation in International Relations,* p. 131.

15. H. Goldhamer and H. Speier, "Some Observations on Political Gaming," *World Politics,* 12 (1959), 71–83.

16. Chapter 14 of this volume suggests six criteria for the evaluation of social science models, viz., validity, generality, flexibility, measurement sophistication, significance, and internal logic. These in turn comprise the most important general criterion, predictive capacity. One of the few efforts at suggesting criteria for problem-selection in political science research is James A. Robinson, "The Major Problems of Political Science," in Lynton K. Caldwell (ed.), *Politics and Public Affairs* (Bloomington: Indiana University Press, 1962), pp. 161–88.

17. Richard E. Dawson, "Simulation in the Social Sciences," in Guetzkow (ed.), *Simulation in Social Science: Readings,* p. 12. A different approach to evaluating INS is reflected in William D. Coplin, "Inter-Nation Simulation and Contemporary Theories of International Relations," *American Political Science Review,* 60 (September, 1966), 562–578.

18. *Ibid.,* p. 14.

19. Harold Guetzkow, "Structured Programs and Their Relation to Free Activity Within the Inter-Nation Simulation," in Guetzkow, et al., *Simulation in International Relations,* pp. 147–48.

20. See Stanley H. Hoffmann, "International Relations: The Long Road to Theory," *World Politics,* 11 (1959), 346–77.

21. John G. Kemeny, *A Philosopher Looks at Science* (Princeton, N.J.: Van Nostrand, 1959), especially pp. 85–104.

22. Guetzkow, "Structured Programs . . . ," in Guetzkow, et al., *Simulation in International Relations,* pp. 107–8.

23. *Ibid.,* especially pp. 105–6.

24. Robert V. Head, *Real-Time Business Systems* (New York: Holt, Rinehart, & Winston, 1965), p. 56.

25. For an explication of structural and elemental isomorphism in model-building see Chapter 14.

26. See Robert C. Noel, "Evolution of the Inter-Nation Simulation," in Guetzkow, et al., *Simulation in International Relations,* pp. 69–102.

27. *Ibid.,* p. 84.

28. *Ibid.*

29. *Ibid.*, p. 99.

30. Guetzkow, "Structured Programs . . . ," in Guetzkow, et al; *Simulation in International Relations*, p. 104.

31. *Ibid.*, pp. 134–35.

32. Sidney Verba, "Simulation, Reality, and Theory in International Relations," *World Politics*, XVI, No. 36 (April, 1964), 490–519.

33. Dawson, *op. cit.*, p. 14.

34. Guetzkow, "Structured Programs . . . ," in Guetzkow et al, *Simulation in International Relations*, p. 147.

35. Professor Lloyd Jensen (former Associate Director, Simulated International Processes Project, Northwestern University), personal communication, August 26, 1965.

36. Noel, *op. cit.*, p. 99.

37. See Daniel Bell, *The End of Ideology: On the Exhaustion of Political Ideas in the Fifties* (New York: Collier Books, 1962). Attacking the problem from a somewhat different perspective are Joseph La Palombara, "Decline of Ideology: A Dissent and Interpretation," pp. 5–16; and S. M. Lipset, "Some Further Comments on 'The End of Ideology,' " pp. 17–18, both in *American Political Science Review*, LX, No. 1 (March, 1966).

38. See Richard C. Snyder, "The Korean Decision (1950) and the Analysis of Crises Decision-Making," paper presented at the Stanford University Conference on Decision-Making in Crises (January 12–13, 1962); and James A. Robinson, "Decision-Making in International Crises," paper presented at American Association for the Advancement of Science, Denver, 1961.

39. Harold and Margaret Sprout, "Environmental Factors in the Study of International Politics," *Journal of Conflict Resolution*, 1, No. 2 (December, 1957), 309–28.

40. Dianne L. Gottheil, "An Approach to a Comparison of Propositions from Verbal Theories of International Relations with Propositions from the Inter-Nation Simulation," cited in Lloyd Jensen, "Outline of Activities, Simulated International Processes Project," (Northwestern University: International Relations Program, May, 1965).

41. For a discussion of the importance of personality variables in the functioning of small groups, see Robert T. Golembiewski, *The Small Group: An Analysis of Research Concepts and Operations* (Chicago: University of Chicago Press, 1962), especially pp. 243–82.

42. Wayman J. Crow and Robert C. Noel, *The Valid Use of Simulation Results* (La Jolla, Calif.: Western Behavioral Sciences Institute, June, 1965), p. 2.

43. See Michael J. Driver, *Conceptual Structure and Group Processes in an Inter-Nation Simulation. Part One: The Perception of Simulated Nations.* (Princeton, N.J.: Educational Testing Service, April, 1962).

44. Charles F. and Margaret G. Hermann, "Possible Use of Historical Data for Validation Study of the Inter-Nation Simulation," Naval Ordnance Test Station, China Lake, California, 1962. Also see the Hermanns' *Studies in Deterrence. X. Studies of the Inter-Nation Simulation.* Naval Ordnance Test Station, China Lake, California, 1963.

45. See Noel, *op. cit.*, p. 99.

46. Crow and Noel, *op. cit.*, p. 2.

47. *Ibid.*

48. *Ibid.*, p. 24.

49. Guetzkow, "Structured Programs . . .," in Guetzkow, et al., *Simulation in International Relations*, p. 105.

50. *Ibid.*, p. 108.

51. *Ibid.*, pp. 134–35; and Noel, *op. cit.*, pp. 84–85.

52. See Sidney Verba, *Small Groups and Political Behavior: A Study of Leadership* (Princeton, N.J.: Princeton University Press, 1961), pp. 61–109.

53. See Guetzkow, "Structured Programs . . . ," in Guetzkow, et al., *Simulation in International Relations*, pp. 106–7.

54. Charles F. Hermann, *Crisis in Foreign Policy Making: A Simulation of International Politics* (Ph.D. dissertation, Northwestern University, 1965).

55. See R. T. Golembiewski, *Behavior and Organization: O and M and the Small Group* (Chicago: Rand McNally, 1962), *passim.*

56. *Ibid.*

57. See Alexander Dallin, *The Soviet Union at the United Nations* (New

York: Praeger, 1962), especially pp. 152–213.

58. For a comprehensive analysis of elite change in seven Latin American countries between 1935 and 1960, see William A. Welsh, *Political Leadership in Latin America* (Columbus: Charles E. Merrill, 1969).

59. Richard C. Snyder, "Perspectives on the Use of Experimental Techniques," in Guetzkow, et al., *Simulation in International Relations,* p. 12.

60. *Ibid.*, p. 13.

61. Alger, *op. cit.*, pp. 177–78.

62. Snyder, *op. cit.*, p. 13.

63. *Ibid.*, p. 14.

64. Zelditch and Evan, *op. cit.*, p. 58.

65. *Ibid.*

66. *Ibid.*, p. 59.

67. *Ibid.*, p. 60.

68. Eugene J. Meehan, *The Theory and Method of Political Analysis* (Homewood, Ill.: The Dorsey Press, 1965), p. 202.

69. Verba, "Simulation, Reality, and Theory in International Relations," p. 505.

70. *Ibid.*, p. 513.

71. Brody, *loc. cit.*

72. Verba, "Simulation, Reality, and Theory in International Relations," p. 511.

73. These validation projects are summarized in Lloyd Jensen, "Outline of Activities, Simulated International Processes Project" (Northwestern University: International Relations Program, May, 1965), (mimeographed).

74. Daniel Druckman, "Ethnocentric Bias in the Inter-National Simulation," unpublished M.S. thesis, Department of Psychology, Northwestern University, June, 1965.

75. Richard W. Chadwick, *The Development of a Partial Theory of International Behavior: A Test, Revision, and Extension of the Inter-Nation Simulation Theory* (Ph.D. dissertation, Northwestern University, 1966).

76. See Jensen, "Outline of Activities, Simulated International Processes Project," p. 3.

77. Chadwick, *op. cit.*

78. This project was initiated at Northwestern University under Harold Guetzkow in 1961. It was transferred to Yale University in 1964. The principal investigator, Rudolf Rummel, is now at the University of Hawaii. For examples of the kinds of work being done under the aegis of DON, see R. J. Rummel, "Dimensions of Conflict Behavior Within and Between Nations," *General Systems: Yearbook of the Society for General Systems Research,* VIII (1963), pp. 1–50; and Raymond Tanter, "Dimensions of Conflict Behavior Within and Between Nations, 1955–60," *Journal of Conflict Resolution,* X, No. 1 (March, 1966), pp. 41–73.

79. Chadwick, *op. cit.*

80. Verba, "Simulation, Reality and Theory in International Relations," p. 497.

81. *Ibid.*, p. 502.

# X

# Some Leading Approaches Methodologically Viewed, III: The Study of the International Political System

International Relations is a relative fledgling in the nest of Political Science, but it has developed rapidly in a methodological sense. Students of international affairs were late in awakening to the methodological inadequacies of their work but, once perceived, they have acted on these inadequacies more directly than has been the case in other areas of Political Science. Specialists in international politics of late have been deeply, sometimes painfully, introspective about their own efforts. In Sondermann's words:

> Presumably, no social scientist is ever fully satisfied with the progress of his discipline. Yet few seem to be more self-conscious about the state of their studies, to be searching more keenly for newer and better foci, concepts, data and methods than those who specialize in the area of international relations. It is painfully obvious to most of them that there is need for a clearer sense of purpose, for greater clarity of concepts, and for progress toward the development of more specific propositions, hypotheses and theories which will unify a field of inquiry whose boundaries are vague and whose content is diffuse.[1]

The period of change may be dated rather precisely: it began after World War II. International Relations during the period between the two great wars was only a little advanced beyond the humanities, and especially History, in its search for system and rigor. In the past twenty years, however, striking successes have firmed up its methodological basis. Much remains to be done, but specialists in the study of international relations deserve plaudits for the distance they have come in a relatively short period of time.

## I. INTERNATIONAL RELATIONS AS AN AREA OF STUDY: BY WHOM? OF WHAT? WHERE? HOW?

Defining our intellectual quarry is more difficult than appraising it. International Relations as an area of study cannot be bounded easily or definitely. Even the casual attempt to do so raises subtle and unanswerable questions of who does the research, what they study, where they study it, and how they do it.

We shall not attempt to disentangle these questions related to the broad conceptualization of what International Relations is. Rather, we treat these questions here as they occur in nature, ineluctably interrelated. Consider the issues of the *where,* the *what,* and the *how* of International Relations. As Snyder[2] has demonstrated, the very selection of a subject will render some methods inappropriate. That choice will suggest at least an informal hierarchy of preferences among those approaches and techniques which superficially appear to be relevant. So it was with International Relations. The strong historical tendency for area teaching and research to occur within the framework of Political Science had a profound impact on the *what* and the *how* of International Relations.

The influence of the *where* of International Relations can be traced briefly. The area of concentration is not merely a branch of Political Science. The study of international relations specifically excludes certain political phenomena (especially some aspects of domestic political activity), except insofar as they affect relations among national or supranational groups. Further, and perhaps less obvious, International Relations includes multifarious phenomena beyond the political. That is, the political foci of the field are not merely influenced by economic, sociological, demographic, and other factors. Rather, these extra-political factors *are part of the field.*

However inadequate the traditional definition of Political Science to encompass the phenomena of International Relations, that locus had its major effects. We describe but one. Despite the presence within it of phenomena usually considered to be within Sociology, Psychology, Economics, or other specialties, International Relations has in the past benefited surprisingly little from these fields. To be sure, economists and sociologists have studied specific aspects of international behavior. But they have tended to view the international system simply as another field-setting in which relatively narrow-gauged economic or sociological theories could be examined. Consequently, these specialties have contributed only indirectly to the construction of general theory in International Relations. The failure resulted in large part from the traditional unwillingness or inability of political scientists to adopt approaches and techniques from the other social sciences. That failure was only partly a function of the relative disinterest of these other social scientists in devising theory about relations among nations.

The *where* of International Relations is less significant today, for two reasons. The intellectual broadening of Political Science has heralded important advances in the study of international affairs. Adoption of terminology, approaches, and techniques from other fields has sensitized students of International Relations to the narrowness of their focus. Perhaps more important, the increased concern of social scientists outside Political Science with the development of theory in International Relations has pushed this field ahead noticeably in a short time. Many signs of this new interest exist.[3] For example, many of the models now enjoying currency in the International Relations literature were adopted from disciplines and fields other than Political Science. These models include systems theory, equilibrium analysis, and decision-making analysis.

The less parochial circumscription of the *where* of International Relations had demonstrable effects on the *how* and on the *what* as well as on the *who*. For example, the imprecise use of terms such as *international relations, international affairs, foreign policy,* and *foreign affairs* was rampant until after 1945. Efforts at terminological clarification of *what* accompanied post-war attempts to systematize the field.[4] With this clarification came the increasing use of the term *international politics* to separate out the "political core" of international affairs. At the same time, International Relations specialists hesitated to foster any development which might tend to diminish newly found interdisciplinary cooperation via a narrow definition of *who*. In turn, this concern has still unsettled implications for *where*. For example, some observers urge an autonomous, self-contained International Relations, perhaps one "subdivided along political, social, economic, demographic, psychological and technological lines."[5] Others maintain that the area of specialization lacks the most important characteristics of intellectual autonomy—it has neither a distinct methodology nor a discrete set of organizing concepts and theoretical propositions.[6] One may challenge these "criteria for autonomy," but that does not settle matters. The criteria do however reflect the traditional juxtaposing of the "hard" and "soft" sciences. In contrast, most of those interested in empirical theory-building believe that the several behavioral disciplines ultimately will have fully complementary and perhaps congruent methodologies, as well as compatible and perhaps overlapping concepts and deductive theories.

The question of disciplinary autonomy for International Relations no longer seems methodologically pressing. The locus of International

Relations in Political Science did methodologically inhibit its development in the past. But we believe (perhaps too wishfully) that Political Science has matured into a more congenial home for interdisciplinary research. It is enough if, as Sondermann says, "the student of international relations investigates a set of special problems in a particular way; no other specialist investigates quite the same problems in quite the same manner."[7] There are, after all, relations—including political ones—among nations. Consequently, worrying over the character of International Relations as a "fully independent discipline, as an evolving separate discipline as a subdivision of one of the older established disciplines, or as an exercise in synthesis,"[8] may direct attention away from currently more significant methodological questions of *how*. *Where* International Relations is located probably always will remain a political issue, of course.

This brief review of the dimensions of International Relations should help emphasize one point. The interdisciplinary nature of the field demands intelligent integration of the methodology, approaches, and techniques, from many sources. This integration is underway, and we hope to accelerate it; remarkably little of it was attempted until the last few years.

## II. INTERNATIONAL RELATIONS AS CHRONOLOGY: EVIDENCES OF HOW PAST IS PROLOGUE

Where any field is now is determined in part by where it has been in the past. Hence we review briefly the history of International Relations. The changing subject-matter foci and methodology of the field should be made clear. They provide the foundations, as it were, from which we propose to launch methodological advances.

Traditionally, the end of World War I is considered the approximate starting point of the field. The studies of the intervening years have been categorized in different and conflicting ways.[9] The following pages lay claim neither to originality nor to an explicit rationale for categorization. Indeed, strictly speaking, this chronology of International Relations studies is not chronological. Several distinct sets of approaches will be discussed in the order of their emergence in the field, to be sure. But, since some analytic foci have had greater longevity than others, it is difficult to argue that any given period of time was dominated by any relatively homogeneous approach.

Initially, International Relations fixated on diplomatic history. The focus was on formal governmental interactions between the major nation-states. The methodology of this period was unbridled historicism. There was great concern for objectivity coupled with an explicit deprecation of generalizing. These studies of diplomatic history were largely descriptive, and presumed a uniqueness for all human events.[10]

The stress on diplomatic history had substantial momentum, extending in several disciplines beyond the end of World War II. Witness the 1950 address of the retiring president[11] of the American Historical Association. He declared that "the sole aim of any objective and scientific historian ought to be the full and complete reconstruction of a selected incident in history." Nor was there any doubt of how this was to be done. "The historian," we learn,

> should avoid every temptation to generalize or dabble in universal principles in recording a story which it was his duty to portray in all its essential simplicity. Every effort to connect an event with what had gone before or to draw up lofty and ambitious principles could only weaken this first paramount undertaking.[12]

The dominance of extreme historicism did not continue in International Relations through 1950, although much work still reflects the bias. Moreover, the imprint of history is clear in the developmental struggles within the area of study. Shortly after World War I, specifically, two trends developed in the study of international relations. The first trend was an apparent reaction to the backward-looking, narrowly focused orientation of diplomatic history. This trend may be characterized as a *current-events* approach. It stressed a day-to-day orientation, but also encompassed a vast subject matter. One leading student of the interwar period circumscribed his field as including "all experiences and events which involved peoples of many lands."[13]

We should assess the current-events approach. Students of international relations did not really know what they were supposed to be studying; consequently, they were generally unconscious of any methodological problems. The current-events approach was most often normative, in that analysts of international affairs were constantly called upon to judge the character of foreign policies, or to assess the morality of state behavior. Even if not called upon, these analysts usually were willing to offer such judgments.

The current-events orientation made at least two contributions to recent International Relations work, problems of scope and focus notwithstanding. First, despite the normative and episodic character of the current-events approach, its exponents were inclined to generalize. It was a special kind of generalization, to be sure, a speculative effort to predict the future course of international affairs on the basis of a limited number of contemporary cases. Like so many movements of strong reaction, the current-events approach explicitly rejected what had gone before it. And what had gone before was anti-science, in short. In abreacting from it, the current-events approach made its contribution to the methodological development of International Relations.

Second, the current-events approach paid heed—if sometimes only by lip service—to the interdisciplinary character of International Relations. This concern fed on the extremely broad phenomenal area encompassed by the current-events approach. That the approach knew few limits is clear in Sir Alfred Zimmern's 1935 assertion that the "study of international relations extends from the *natural sciences* at one end to moral philosophy or even further at the other."[14] Zimmern was concerned only with the *subject matter* of the natural sciences as a focus for the study of international affairs and not with their methodology. At least by indirection, however, others in the field voiced concern about the possible relevance of intellectual policy (especially methodology) borrowed from the other social sciences, if not from the "hard" sciences.

Growing concern with international law and international organizations constituted a second parallel interwar trend. The emphasis reflected then-strong views (or hopes, perhaps) of the impact which the League of Nations, and the increasingly codified and ostensibly accepted tenets of international law, would have on international peace and stability. The public purpose of this variant of International Relations research was unabashedly to stimulate "advancement of a spirit of international co-operation and good will among the world's people."[15] Less charitably, the approach can be characterized as "aimless humanitarianism,"[16] more interested in "international understanding" than in science or in understanding international affairs. The methodology of this approach reflected strong normative overtones consequently. Moreover, effort was guided by a broad set of underlying assumptions, especially an optimism concerning the development of International Relations in a particular direction. Only an absence of conscious concern with methodology, needless to say, can explain this well-intentioned but awkward approach.

By the mid-1940's, new trends in International Relations could be identified. In particular, the "underlying forces and trends" in international politics became central. The behaviors of nation-states, especially in their foreign policies, constituted the point of departure. The over-riding concern was in one way or another with "power relations" among nations.

The new trends of the 1940's could lay claim to developmental novelty even with one foot firmly planted on the foundations of the work preceding them. The behavior-oriented research was concerned with the distinction between values and observational data; it was consciously explanatory; it sought generalizations about inter-nation relations at a relatively high level of abstraction; and it evidenced some methodological concern.[17] At the same time, however, studies of this period were still very much concerned with "the great issues facing mankind."[18] Consequently, much of the real desire for objective research was diluted by the pressing need to serve meta-ends, and this long before empirical research had developed sufficiently to support any but the most rudimentary fragments of goal-based, empirical theories. Methodological considerations paled before the hope for a science of international relations which would contribute to a philosophy of international affairs. The point still holds. There has been a growing tendency to change analytical postures, but the literature still reflects the work of some important theorists who pursue their research with very much these same normative interests.[19]

Sharpening methodological concern did not sweep all before it. In the early 1950's, indeed, Thompson could identify three competing "theories" of international political behavior.[20] He identified political realism, political idealism, and eclecticism. We shall be concerned later with the first two, at least indirectly. Thus the contribution of Hans J. Morgenthau, the godfather of "political realism" against whom "political idealists" abreacted, will be analyzed later. The eclectic approach has three principal components: thoroughgoing empiricism; a conscious concern for the systematic conduct of research; and the absence of a priori assumptions about what the nature of international affairs was or should be.

While "eclectic" suggests a multitude of foci, techniques, and approaches more or less coherently tied together, Thompson sees its International Relations variant of the 1950's as rather narrow. As he observes: "the eclectic point of view has shown a preference for a sociological approach to the problems of world politics."[21] He notes that sociology: (1) is empirical; (2) draws a distinction between facts and values; (3) is inclusive and broad in scope; and (4) is

> alone capable of providing tests of clues by which to separate subject matter that is clearly international in character from what is essentially domestic in nature. It finds this test in the general principle of whether or not a given issue or episode affects the growth or disintegration of international society.[22]

Eclecticism reflects problems and potentials. The balance seems favorable, and particularly so if one does not insistently raise the issue of specifying the "international society" whose "reactions" are the standard for judging "clearly international" issues. Specifically, eclecticism in International Relations was significant for three major reasons. First, it implied the need for utilizing resources outside the traditional bounds of Political Science in the study of international affairs. Second, the eclectic approach tended to center around concepts other than power, which had been dominant. For example, the eclectic perspective might focus on development, or on disintegration, of the international system. Third, the eclectic approach raised the "generalist-specialist dilemma" as a critical problem in the methodological advance of the field. Implicit in the emergence of the eclectic approach was the problem of finding generalists capable of integrating diverse approaches into a general theory, generalists who also possessed the competencies necessary to make intelligent use of the sometimes complicated research available from the social sciences.

This chronology supports a firm summary. In the relatively short time since the First World War, International Relations has made important progress on a number of fronts. We list them briefly under seven heads:

1. International Relations has largely freed itself from a historicist tradition.
2. The subject matter of the field has stabilized, following a swing from a very narrow to an excessively broad perspective.
3. The legalistic bias of the field has slowly lessened, with a correspondingly increased concern for describing and explaining the informal aspects of international political activity.
4. The separation of empirical and normative elements is more conscious and consistent.
5. Similarly, methodological concern and sophistication have increased.
6. Deterministic or quasi-deterministic thinking is being increasingly rejected.
7. Recent years have seen a great increase in conscious concern about theory-building, proceeding from the comparison of a large number of case studies as well as from inductive generalization from individual observations.

## III. INTERNATIONAL RELATIONS AS A CONTEMPORARY SPECIALTY: TRENDS AND PATTERNS

All is not yet well in the international relations/international politics field, despite impressive and important signs of progress. Our few words here depict the large and complex phenomenal area of International Relations as in motion from pre-scientific to scientific states. And the direction now appears irreversible, although it assuredly has been late in coming.

Singer[23] suggests three reasons why the field has tended to lag in its evolution toward the status of a scientific discipline. First, there is the subject matter of international relations. In coping with nature, as a general principle, man finds it especially difficult to observe, hard to classify, and difficult to measure. Scientific progress, of course, depends upon the development of concepts and operations which are at once reasonably easy to apply and which also abstract the essence of complex relations. Further, building verifiable theory requires at least a meaningful classification of phenomena. And progress toward a deductive theory will require increasingly precise measurement and the use of advanced techniques for gathering and manipulating data. Nature helps little. The field most assuredly is no laboratory, however. Nor does the real world of international affairs seem amenable to large-scale laboratory manipulation, at least in the near future.[24]

Second, according to Singer, the academic recruitment process has hindered the scientific development of International Relations. He explains that "scientifically-oriented people tend to gravitate toward those fields which are already more or less scientific and in which the norms encourage the scientific spirit."[25] The scientific rich get richer, in this view, and the poor get poorer. Precisely why this lack of attraction has been overcome in the last few years defies explanation. But overcome it has been. More and more professionals interested in constructing a science of international relations are moving into the field.

Third, the extra-disciplinary roles of political scientists, perhaps especially those specializing in international politics, have slowed its scientific development. In particular, the consultant role of numerous specialists in international affairs serving various government agencies often leads to stress on pragmatic considerations in research, as opposed to scientific-theoretical concerns. Participation in the value-oriented world of politics also often has led to an injudicious blending of normative and empirical procedures in the execution or interpretation of research. Paradoxically, those deprived of such practical experience in the real world of international politics are no better off. Commonly, they are somewhat hesitant and unsure about understanding the processes about which they write. For other social scientists, this problem is substantially less significant. As Singer explains: "Psychologists have unlimited opportunity to experience their own and others' attitudes, beliefs, and behavior, nor do sociologists lack the opportunity to participate in the activities of families, ethnic groups, professions, or even social strata."[26]

Given such barriers, *uneven* best characterizes the state of development of International Relations. For example, recent years have seen a growing, explicit concern among International Relations specialists about what science actually is. Hence the implications of the philosophy of science literature for the study of international politics are being sampled.[27] More than simple differentiation of normative and empirical theory is involved, however. As Rosenau comments, "neither a readiness to be more systematic nor a sensitivity to conceptual problems can guarantee the correct application of the methods of science."[28] As a similar sign of development, political scientists certainly are acquiring a new language. One expression of the point notes that specialists "talk of quantifying data, of building models, of testing hypotheses, of verifying constructs, of comparing abstract and empirical formulations."[29] But the language of science is hardly a substitute for intelligent application of its methodology, and still less it is a substitute for the theoretical products of that methodology.

This volume hopes to foster greater *evenness*. Hence our emphasis on the construction, utilization, and limitations of scientific devices. Hence also the attempted sensitization to the *operational* as well as *conceptual* differences between proposed dimensions of reality. And our hopes also explain our emphases—in specific contexts—on differences between dependent, independent, and intervening variables, between analytic and concrete structures.

Fortunately, others have long labored to achieve such an evenness. In the last five or six years, students of international politics have become methodologically introspective about their own theoretical orientations. Moreover, they have asked for, and received, help from professionals in other fields in attempting to understand the implications of their quest for theory. Indeed, perhaps the most significant trend in the study of international politics today is that toward increasing utilization of the methodology and the products of the other social sciences, as well as the natural sciences. These intellectual borrowings fall generally into three categories: (1) concepts and models; (2) methods; and (3) findings.

Students of international affairs increasingly adopt concepts and models from the other social sciences. For example, sociological inputs have been particularly prominent in the recent development of International Relations through such concepts as *role, stratification, integration, conflict,* and *mobility*. Anthropology has offered *diffusion*. From Psychology, especially Social Psychology, have come the concepts of *crisis* and *stress*. And from mathematical economics have come the terminology of game theory, the theory of bargaining, and the theory of coalitions.

The borrowings of methodology and techniques also are being

directed toward operationalization or quantification. Among the more prominent techniques now being grafted on to the fabric of international relations research from other disciplines are scale analysis (from Social Psychology),[30] laboratory simulation (largely adapted from Social Psychology),[31] elaborate statistical techniques such as factor analysis and multiple regression analysis (from Statistics and Mathematics),[32] "eclectic" statistical procedures such as hierarchical decomposition (from civil engineering),[33] and quasi-quantitative methods for partial data control in field situations (e.g., data quality control, from Anthropology).[34]

The findings of other disciplines—the empirical data and the generalizations which summarize those data—are also increasingly perceived as relevant to the study of international politics. Some of these findings are directly applicable; others must be applied indirectly, or perhaps only suggestively. As Singer has emphasized, for example, Social Psychology has accumulated an impressive body of data relevant to international affairs. These data particularly concern public attitudes toward foreign nations, as well as the patterns of events, experiences, and conditions which shape these attitudes.[35] Similarly, small-group researchers in Social Psychology and Sociology have learned a great deal about the speed and accuracy of problem-solving when the size of a group, its leadership, organization, or communication patterns are varied.[36]

Such extra-field borrowing is not pure profit, of course. Numerous problems inhere in generalizing from the laboratory to the real world, for example. Similar problems also exist in the reverse direction, in moving back from the real world into the laboratory for elaboration or verification of observed phenomena.[37]We resist cataloging the problems attendant on bridging the gap between experimental situations and non-manipulable social reality. However, efforts at inter-disciplinary integration have not always been undertaken with appropriate caution.[38] In such cases, the consequence may be more frustrating, and perhaps more misleading, than the intellectual vacuum which these efforts were intended to fill.

Extra-area borrowing, however, has proved a general boon. Witness the marked trend toward greater coherence and more explicit conceptualization. Traditional terminology is at last being re-examined in the light of recent findings and of new concepts from other fields. Rapidly, if belatedly, International Relations specialists are realizing that the precision and clarity of their terminology does influence the likelihood that the study of international relations will become scientific. For science is based on cumulative knowledge. Without reasonably standardized conceptual and operational definitions of critical terms, the upward spiral toward scientific attainment will be exceedingly slow and difficult. Similarly, more and more conscious efforts are being made to link one's *research* (as opposed merely to one's intellectual or personal goals, or his conclusions) with the work of others, both in the field of international politics and in related areas of inquiry.[39]

There is even more expansive evidence of the "internal" results of external borrowing. Perhaps the dominant characteristic of International Relations today is the tremendously broad variety of approaches and techniques which are in use. One recently formulated typology of at least partially distinct approaches includes 24 entries.[40] They include numerous traditional approaches, including those which may be labeled historical, philosophical, legalistic, sociological, economic, geopolitical, and psychological. There are "single explanatory concept" approaches, including power theories, capability analysis, ideological theories, equilibrium analysis, challenge and response approaches, the game theory approach, and communications theory. A number of "partial explanatory concept" approaches also may be identified. They include behavioral, institutional, conflict and bargaining, and integration-disintegration perspectives. Finally, there are several broad, integrative theories, including decision-making, general systems theory, and the actor-means-ends approach.

The dual thrust of this diversity in IR is inescapable. A tremendous amount of intellectual energy is being directed toward the construction and application of a very broad range of conceptual schemes. And this expenditure of energy raises the issue of its conservation. The point has gained attention, especially in the growing concern with general systems theory. The need for, and impending development of, general theories of international politics was signaled in 1950 by Harold Guetzkow. His characterization of the process of theory construction is an excellent and concise statement of what is happening, or appears to be about to happen, in International Relations. He described that process in these terms.

> First, using the nation as the primary unit, propositions would be developed to explain how national behaviors in the international scene originate within the state. Then, a general theory of the relations between any two states might be erected. Later, as one becomes more sure of his footing, this artificially-restricted binary theory might be elaborated into a multi-nation theory. This latter development would undoubtedly be accompanied by research on the functioning of international agencies as dynamic supra-national organizations.[41]

To be sure, Guetzkow is not a general systems theorist. His emphases, however, are consistent with systems approaches, and Guetzkow may be broadly depicted as a forerunner of systems theory applications in International Relations. Subsequently, general systems theory will be characterized as one of the more promising theoretical developments in International Relations.

## IV. INTERNATIONAL RELATIONS AS A CONTEMPORARY SPECIALTY: GENERAL METHODOLOGICAL INADEQUACIES

We have treated in detail only the more promising developments of recent years. Let us begin to correct this imbalance. Numerous general methodological problems do exist, most of which are receiving some attention but none of which appears to be close to solution. We begin via general comments which apply to most current efforts in the field. Later, more will be said by way of direct methodological evaluation, as we look at several specific approaches and techniques.

Numerous important problems characterize the existing literature in International Relations. First, few conceptual schemes or models appear to be based on any coherent effort to define the most important theoretical and empirical questions which are to be studied. Snyder has stressed the need for a thoroughgoing intellectual inventory directed toward specifying what it is we wish to know, and where we wish our knowledge to carry us.[42] But neglect is more characteristic than attention. Generally, extant approaches to International Relations seem to have been constructed either in an effort to avoid the shortcomings of existing models or conceptual schemes, or from a set of grossly simplified assumptions about what the nature of inter-nation behavior *is*, or what it *ought* to be. In short, these approaches reflect what we assume to be true, rather than any reasonably coherent, explicit picture of what we *need* to know.

Second, the organizing concepts of the dominant approaches in the study of international politics tend to be inadequately defined and loosely used in research. There are still a few cases in which *no* specific nominal definitions of concepts are given. In other cases, the nominal definitions are imprecise, or so broad as to defy their application in any specific research situation. Operational definitions are seldom even attempted. As Snyder illustrated the point:

> To say that the study of international relations includes *all* the actions, interactions and relationships between societies does not tell us what is to be meant *analytically* by "action," "interaction," and "relationship," and does not specify for us what the distinguishing characteristic of the empirical events is for the political analyst—in other words it does not specify what is *political* and what is *politically relevant.*[43]

Similarly, third, the literature abounds with failures to recognize that while classificatory categories are linked to concepts, the two are not identical. Categories sometimes become independent of their original assignment criteria, and the criteria often are ambiguous to begin with. Consequently, categories usually become mere labels. As Snyder argues, "the danger lies in the illusion that by labeling something we have either said something significant about it or explained it." Danger and usefulness go hand in hand, however. As Snyder explains: "By classifying we hope to separate phenomena and aspects of phenomena for some useful purpose. Concepts help explain what we have classified. Slipshod categorization hinders analysis because it confronts the investigator with multiple choices of interpretation without any clear guide to selection."[44]

Fourth, students commonly confuse observer and phenomenological perspectives in both nominal and operational definitions. To take but one prominent example, examine the use of the term *national interest* in the literature.[45] Precisely how we determine the *predominant interest* of a given nation, or of a sub-system of the international system, is a question rarely treated with precision either nominally or operationally. *National interest* is sometimes implicitly conceived as something which is "good for all the people." A similar definition, and one which is somewhat more realistic, stresses perceptions by some majority of the articulate segment of the population of their own interest, which is then taken as the national interest. On the other hand, recognizing that the operationalization of such conceptual definitions would be extremely difficult, some theorists have viewed national interest as the preferential expression of governmental decision-makers. All of the foregoing definitions would be phenomenological. That is, they are operationally defined in terms of the perceptions of political actors. By contrast, national interest may be the student's assessment of what course of action would seem to be most consistent with the broad goals toward which a nation-state is moving. The operation in this case is within the observer. What is most unfortunate from a methodological perspective, observer and phenomenological perspectives are often mixed within the same conceptual scheme or model. And few students get around to gathering data consistent with their nominal and operational definitions, even if they keep their perspectives straight.

Fifth, scholars uninhibitedly and all but unanimously assume the significance of certain factors in the international environment as determinants of political outcomes. In particular, the literature treats the concept of *power* in this way. The power explanation is a postulate—an assumption which is taken for granted, rather than being subjected to verification or testing. Power theorists are quite certain that power is there, somewhere. Consequently, whatever evidence of relevance is available must be interpreted in such a way as to demonstrate that which has already been rendered extant by definition. In short, assumptions become translated into self-fulfilling prophecies about the behavior of actors in the international system. Neglect of operational definition, particularly, explains the persistence of the approach.

Our point does not lack support. Consider Morgenthau, the power theorist *par excellence*. Morgenthau's power formulation, which hinges around the notion of *control,* suffers from numerous shortcomings. His nominal concept *power* is quite ambiguous, for *control* is never explicitly defined. Moreover, he does not make it conceptually clear whether power refers to a symmetrical or to an asymmetrical relationship, or both. Power may refer to a *quantity* of something, a *capacity*, or a *relationship*. Most significantly, operational indices of power are not provided. Generally, as a consequence, most theorists whose models give importance to the concept simply assume that the presence of a *power factor* is sufficient to constitute proof of its role in explaining patterns of behavior.[46] And the lack of a methodological conscience concerning nominal and operational definition encourages considering the convenient to be correct.

Sixth, the linkages between political and non-political factors which influence the nature of the international system receive inadequate or uneven treatment in extant models. Some earlier approaches were deterministic or quasi-deterministic,[47] asserting that political relations were entirely or largely determined by non-political factors, such as geography or economics. While recent models generally do not make such gross assertions, they usually make little effort to outline systematically the impact of broad social behavior patterns on a country's foreign policy,[48] for example. Snyder found that in five standard international relations/international politics textbooks only some 130 out of more than 4,000 pages in the five books were devoted to possible relations between the social differentiae of nations and their external behavior.[49] In a similar vein, most of the current models give inadequate attention to the relationships between intra-national and extra-national political variables.

Finally, seventh, the literature neglects developmental or process models.[50] Static description of the international environment at a given point in time absorbs too much of the scholar's attention. We have come beyond the point where students of international affairs ignore the tremendous significance of change as a basic feature of their subject matter. Yet there have been few efforts to develop comprehensive models of the policy-making process, for example, in national decision-making units or in supra-national groups. Nor has there been sufficient concern with models which might account for changes in interaction flows of various kinds in the international system.

This is hardly an exhaustive cataloging of the problems which students of international relations must overcome if they are to build meaningful theory. It does purport to be at least suggestive, and we hope to cover more significant shortcomings of specific models in the following section.

## V. SELECTED APPROACHES IN INTERNATIONAL RELATIONS: SPECIFIC METHODOLOGICAL ADVANCES AND ISSUES

This section covers a brief span of years and substantial methodological development. Less than 30 years ago the philosophic traditionalists occupied the center of the stage in International Relations. Sir Alfred Zimmern—whose approach has been characterized as vague, unsystematic, and normative—is generally acknowledged to have been the most influential specialist of the inter-war period. "His opinions concerning the nature of the science of international relations . . . were rarely questioned by his colleagues,"[51] we are told. Yet barely more than a decade later the traditionalists had been effectively nudged into the wings. And today they have all but moved down into the audience to watch the unfolding panorama of systematic approaches to the study of international politics.

Four selected approaches encompass the few years of International Relations history and its substantial methodological development. They include:

1. an adumbration of the philosophic traditionalist position through Kulski;
2. the description of a transitional phase anticipating deliberate model-building, via looks at Morgenthau and Hoffmann;
3. a look at micro-model building which focuses on specific processes, as reflected in Snyder's approach to decision-making, and
4. an analysis of macro-model building as exemplified by general systems theory.

### A. Kulski as Representative of the Classical Tradition

The rapid demise of traditionalists in International Relations encourages their brief treatment here, but it does not permit their neglect. Wladyslaw W. Kulski remains one of the few prominent students of international affairs who can be comfortably designated a philosophic traditionalist. His *International Politics in a Revolutionary Age*[52] reflects the posture quite well. Kulski proceeds from a self-consciously non-theoretical approach. His book is "not woven around any of the current theories of international relations," for "these theories are new, . . . not yet fully and convincingly tested."[53] Indeed, says Kulski, "they do not yet offer a foolproof and all-embracing explanation of international phenomena and cannot provide total guidance for an examination of international politics."[54]

Having thus set unattainable criteria for evaluation, Kulski predictably finds the available products wanting and rejects them. The formulation of a "comprehensive theory of international relations" faces at least three problems which, Kulski feels certain, stand little chance of being overcome. First, human beings do not always act rationally. In Kulski's opinion, non-rational behavior probably cannot be predicted. Hence we cannot predict the behavior of actors in the international arena. Second, "freedom of choice introduces a considerable factor of chance which cannot be defined in advance."[55] That is, human beings exercise "free will."[56] There is no way to specify when an individual is free of the many external limitations on the exercise of this free will, or to specify how he will act when free of these restraints. Hence Kulski observes that "the fact remains that any two individuals faced with identical circumstances do not necessarily choose the same course of action."[57] This makes Political *Science* impossible, in Kulski's view. Third, the calculus of probabilities, upon which science must be built, is held to be inapplicable to international affairs. This is true, says Kulski, because "international phenomena of a similar kind, those which may be grouped together in one class, do not amount to large numbers."[58] Since the calculation of probabilities must proceed with large numbers of phenomena, the international system must necessarily be a poor host to statistical analysis and, hence, to science.

We have elsewhere set down our reactions to some central propositions of traditionalists in other areas of study. Here we emphasize only three points which are especially appropriate to Kulski. First, it must remain an open question whether human behavior can be predicted in the international arena. To assert flatly that it cannot in politics seems singularly suspect, particularly in view of the numerous predictive successes in some of the behavioral sciences. The only way to ascertain whether scientific theories can be devised is to attempt to devise them.

Second, the philosophic traditionalist misunderstands the role of theory and the nature of prediction in *any* science. The thrust of predictive theory is not to foresee specific events, but rather to specify the probabilities associated with several classes of outcomes, given a range of identifiable situational parameters. The model-builders in International Relations seek to isolate the factors which probabilistically determine certain types of outcomes. For example, no responsible theorist will predict the date, leadership, and instrumentalities of the next public uprising in a dictatorial system. It is hoped, however, that we might be able to specify the probability of revolt in a given *class* of political systems, assuming different varieties of situational determinants. For that matter, we know no responsible physicist who will predict with certainty the time it takes a cannonball to drop ten feet, or even whether it will drop. All physicists will hazard a probability estimate therefore, of course, and an estimated time. International Relations theorists properly propose nothing more.

Third, the traditionalist over-extends the notion of the uniqueness of individuals and events. To be sure, no two human beings are exactly alike and no two happenings are precisely similar. Yet many classes of events and many individuals in some situations are *enough* alike that we would be foolish to neglect their likeness. Further, the fact that "times change" does not preclude the possibility of analogous circumstances developing in time-space.

### B. The Transition to Model-Building via Morgenthau and Hoffmann

Times did change in International Relations, and one pervasive way they changed is reflected by the pervasive and growing influence of model-building. Yet the significance of theorists such as Richard C. Snyder, Thomas C. Schelling, Charles McClelland, Kenneth Boulding, Robert C. North, Morton Kaplan, J. David Singer, and George Liska did not develop overnight. Rather, their coming has been heralded by a number of transitionalists who have significantly altered the map of their area of study.

To the transitionalists we now turn, and to their methodological contributions. Broadly, the transitionalists make two methodologically notable contributions to International Relations. First, the transitionalists generally recognize the need for systematic theory, and they are explicitly concerned with prediction. Many of the elementary outward signs of the scientific enterprise consequently appear in their publications. These signs include reasonably explicit conceptualization, generalization and construction of hypotheses, some concern for the quality of evidence, and attention to the processes of verification. Second, the transitionalists have highlighted the informal political forces of relevance in determining outcomes in the international system. That the key to relations between states might not be found in formal diplomatic communications exchanged between accredited ambassadors was widely acknowledged only when the transitionalists came to the fore.

These two contributions to the study of international relations were most significant. Indeed, the transitionalists not only cleared a path for the model-builders, but they made considerable advances along that path toward empirical theory.

The transitionalists had their methodological problems, however, both conceptual and operational. First, they projected a cloudy picture of the relationship between international politics and international relations. For example, Morgenthau saw no meaningful distinction between the two.[59] Second, the transitionalists knew the difference between empirical and normative theory, but they frequently failed to respect the distinction. At best, their empirical theory-building was ultimately directed toward highly normative ends. At worst, normative considerations overpowered the supposedly empirical segments of their theories. Third, transitionalist approaches commonly are uni-dimensional and narrow in scope, or they are so broad that they lose theoretical articulation and coherence.

Let us resort to some analytical fine-tuning. Although we count many scholars among the transitionalists—including Quincy Wright, Ernst Haas, A. F. K. Organski, Arnold Wolfers, and Harold and Margaret Sprout—we can only sample their efforts. We turn our attention primarily to Morgenthau, whose selection implies the continuing importance of his "realist" theory of power. We also give attention to Stanley Hoffmann. He has been far less influential, but he merits attention for at least two reasons. He is the most self-consciously transitionalist theorist of the group. That is, Hoffmann explicitly assumes a position somewhere between the anti-science and scientific schools of thought in the study of international politics. Moreover, perhaps more than any of the other transitionalists, Hoffmann has been concerned with critical evaluation of the efforts of his contemporaries, and with building upon those efforts.

### *1. Morgenthau's Realist Theory of Power Politics*

For perhaps a decade the realist perspective of Hans Morgenthau was dominant in International Relations. Central to this theory are the concepts of *interest* and *power*. The former is defined in terms of the latter. In turn, *power* is defined fuzzily in terms of *control,* as we noted above. The essential flavor of the realist approach is easily suggested, if the specifics are another breed entirely. Thus from one perspective, Morgenthau

> succeeds in focusing attention on the principal actors in world affairs: the states, and on the factors that account for the autonomy of international relations: the difference between domestic and world politics which thwart the operation in the latter of ideas and institutions that flourish in the former, the drastic imperatives of survival, self-preservation and self-help which are both the causes and the product of such differences.[60]

Morgenthau's theory has taken considerable intellectual pummeling in recent years.[61] Yet the significance of his approach demands an excursion into its methodological shortcomings. First, Morgenthau's use of the concept *power* begets a bevy of problems. For example, the realist approach fails to distinguish between nominal concepts of power as political outcomes, as an instrumentality, and as motivation. To Morgenthau, these conceptions blend into one. Most political scientists see finer distinctions.[62] That is, power may be nominally defined as an actual outcome —the observed phenomenon of bringing about modifications in the behavior of others. Alternatively, power may be seen as an instrumentality, a latent means which may be utilized toward any of a large number of ends, including the preservation of power itself. Finally, power may be nominally conceived in terms of more or less invariant levels of personal motivation. Morgenthau's tendency to emphasize the last nominal definition creates one of the principal limitations on his theory. For Morgenthau, politics is shaped almost exclusively by "man's lust for power."[63] Implicitly, power is an inherent and instinctive motivator of human behavior. Significantly, Morgenthau fails to distinguish between the perhaps inherent aspects of the "power drive" and the situational or accidental aspects thereof.[64] More centrally, Morgenthau cannot understand or explain by baptizing, by merely giving names.

The inelegance of Morgenthau's nominal definition is reflected in the neglect of concern about operational definition, and both significantly limit the explanatory utility of his theory. Contrary to Morganthau's assumption, as Hoffmann notes, power is a "most complex product of other variables."[65] The complexity Morgenthau neglects may be suggested briefly. For example, a wide range of both domestic and supra-national factors appears to be relevant in the operational definition of power at any given point in time. This is true regardless of whether one views power as outcome, instrumentality, or motivation. Consequently, operational definitions are likely to change with changes in locus of analysis. In contrast, a few aspects of power tend to be singled out for undue emphasis in operational definitions. As Organski and Hoffmann suggest, the over-emphasized elements tend to be military force and economic strength.[66] But this is too simple. Power—however defined nominally and operationally—clearly acts through and on multiple variables in addition to "man's lust" for it.

Another concept of central importance in Morgenthau's theory, *national interest,* is also poorly handled. Morgenthau blithely treats *national interest* as an objective, easily identifiable factor. Such a view seems too uncomplicated today. At best, it might be applicable in the study of eighteenth- and nineteenth-century international affairs. Indeed, Hoffmann argues that Morgenthau takes just this golden age as a norm for both empirical analysis and evaluation. The inappropriateness of this conceptualization seems patent. As Hoffmann explains:

> The conception of an objective and easily recognizable national interest is one which makes sense only in a stable period in which the participants play for limited ends, with limited means and without domestic kibitzers to disrupt the players' moves. . . . An attempt at using the theory as a key to the understanding of contemporary realities puts one in the position of a Tiresias who recognizes interests which the parties refuse to see, who diagnoses permanence where the parties find confusing change, and whose *ex post facto* omniscience is both irritating and irrelevant.[67]

Morgenthau also seems guilty of confusing observer and phenomenological perspectives. Rather than asking if political actors actually hold a simplistic view of national interest, Morgenthau assumes that he and the world wear the same glasses. Perhaps there was a time when almost everyone agreed on desirable states in international affairs. But it seems hardly necessary to demonstrate that, empirically, "national interest" may vary considerably when nominally defined in alternative ways. Three such alternatives define the concept as: (1) goals having system-wide consensus; (2) formally articulated expressions of preference by some sub-set of the population (e.g., interest groups or voters); or (3) decisions of governmental officials considered responsible for the authoritative allocation of values for the whole society.[68]

Morgenthau's handling of the concepts of power and interest hardly exhausts the list of shortcomings of his approach. A third problem rests in his generally static view of international affairs. Morgenthau's "international system" is an essentially unchanging one. Man's "lust for power" is here to stay. Consequently, the heart of international relations will always be power politics among nations. As Hoffmann says, "the postulate of the permanence of power politics among nations as the core of international relations tends to become a goal. The static qualities of the theory lead to confusion between the phenomenon of power conflicts and the transitory forms and institutions in which such conflicts have been taking place in recent centuries."[69] Morgenthau thus projects his opinion that power is here to stay into a conviction that the shape of international politics must continue in an essentially unaltered form.

A fourth objection to Morgenthau's approach concerns his view of the foreign policy decision-making process. For Morgenthau, foreign policy is rationally made. We are led to believe that, as it was allegedly in the time of cabinet diplomacy, the foreign-policy process is little more than the "simple adjustment of means to stable and generally recognized ends."[70] Yet detailed analysis traces much international political conflict to the dynamics of decision-makers seeking to determine their own ends.[71] The goals of the major nation-states seem substantially ambiguous, and consequently, little consistency exists in their selection of means.[72]

Fifth, despite his concern with the informal side of diplomacy, Morgenthau insufficiently acknowledges the importance of non-political variables as determinants of international outcomes. He does not ignore factors such as economic strength or military capacity. On the contrary, these are among the "perennial forces" which may affect the shape of international politics. But beyond these commonly recognized factors, Morgenthau has little time for extra-political variables. For example, the long-run impacts of attitudes toward authority, or of levels of the influence on citizens on their government, remain unattended. Indeed, Morgenthau's preoccupation with power aggravates this problem. Since power explains nearly everything, Morgenthau need not concern himself with other independent or even intervening variables which might have explanatory significance. Power is *the* independent variable for him, in short.

### 2. *Hoffmann's "Systematic Historical Sociology"*

Hoffmann illustrates that criticism and construction differ markedly. He engaged in a self-defined "wrecking operation."[73] Having decimated to his satisfaction Morgenthau's realist theory, Kaplan's systems approach, Liska's equilibrium theory, and Snyder's decision-making approach, Hoffmann sets out to reconstruct order out of the ruins. He provides some suggestions "for a far more modest and slow way of proceeding toward theory."[74]

Hoffmann's call is for "systematic historical sociology." Rejecting as disappointing the search for "timeless propositions" through the deductive method, Hoffmann argues for an inductive, historical approach. His technique begins with a study of "diplomatic constellations," or historical situations. He proposes to study historical systems of international relations in an effort to identify the main variables of each system, and to discover the dynamics of change from one system to another.[75] Second, he would systematically compare these historical systems, perhaps generating types of systems, "each type being characterized by a feature or combination of features which determine its originality."[76] Third, Hoffmann would study the linkages between these historical international systems and the domestic political systems which existed alongside them.

Hoffmann's conceptual scheme embraces four sets of data, which he offers as adequate bases for defining an international system. Hoffmann wants to study the *structure* of the international system, the *forces* which cut across or operate within the units of the international system, the *relations* between the domestic and foreign policies of the basic units, and the precise *pattern* of relations among nation-states. This last is conceived of as the outcome of some process of combining the other three sets of data.

Hoffmann's "methodical and gradual"[77] approach constitutes an exercise in futility. Basically, he does much of what he has criticized so severely in the work of others. Globally, he acknowledges that his own suggestions "are based on postulates which are certainly as debatable as those I have discussed."[78] We focus on three particulars in which Hoffmann knowingly sins. First, he borrows from here and there, and yet criticizes Kaplan for doing precisely the same, and commits a dual impropriety thereby. Thus Hoffmann complains that:

> Mr. Kaplan grafts concepts torn from sociology, economics, cybernetics, biology, and astronomy onto a very different subject—a strange method for a believer in "systems." The previous question, whether these questions fit our field, has not been asked. Consequently, this inter-disciplinary arsenal serves a pointless invasion of our field by uprooted foreign methods, rather than a guided raid into neighboring fields by a rigorous method of our own.[79]

Hoffmann essentially misses the point. That is, at a macroscopic level, systems theory is a reasonably coherent, explicit mode of analysis. Its basic form has been corrupted very little by applications to a considerable range of empirical phenomena, although some of these applications go little beyond the metaphorical. Hoffmann appears to make the mistake of assuming that applicability of a conceptual framework to several sets of data automatically devalues it.

Second, Hoffmann is a self-admitted creature of our normative and perception-distorting environment. His approach to the study of international politics reflects this, although he attacks Morgenthau in part for succumbing to the same influences. For example, Hoffmann chastised Morgenthau for the latter's static conceptualization of the international system. Yet Hoffmann is straightforward in saying that his own approach is strongly affected by the nature of the international system which he perceives today. Further, he is similarly influenced by a vision of the international system he *wants* to see tomorrow.[80] In Hoffmann's opinion, "the broader the area the social scientist wants to understand, the more he is guided by his own values."[81] We interpret these words as encouraging caution in research designs. But Hoffmann senses some license therein: the student should "pronounce on value problems." We must merge "systematic empirical analysis and a philosophy of international relations. We must try to build relevant utopias."[82]

Third, while Hoffmann acknowledges that systems analysis tends in the right direction—that of systematic empirical analysis—he perceives systems theory as "a huge misstep" in that direction.[83] Clearly, much of Hoffmann's attack on systems theory concerns the central significance of the concept of *system*. Yet throughout Hoffmann's own approach he holds that "an understanding of international politics or any aspect thereof presupposes an understanding of the characteristics of the international *system*."[84] Or the freedom of action of the basic units in international affairs "is limited and their choices are conditioned by the nature of the *system*."[85] Clearly, a reading of Hoffmann's "suggestions" underscores his dependence on a systems perspective. Of course, Hoffmann may argue that his approach relies little on the concept of *systems*. In any case, Hoffmann never specifically defines system.

We do not rush to a conclusion. Hoffmann asserts that "historical sociology" is both "systematic" and "predominantly . . . empirical."[86] We believe that it is neither. Basically, Hoffmann's approach is necessarily non-systematic and non-empirical because of the nature of available data with which he works. Then too, Hoffmann ignores the problem of establishing standards for the acceptance of historical evidence. Needless to say, these criteria are critical for Hoffmann's enterprise, especially given the data necessary to give meaningful answers to such questions. Consider the questions he would answer:

> What are the basic units . . . how many are there, how is power distributed, and what is the hierarchy among them? . . . What are the "objective factors" for the unit considered (geography, technological level, economic resources, population, military potential)? . . . How does the unit's pattern of power affect the making of foreign policy? . . . How does the unit's political culture affect the making of foreign policy? Here I refer both to the judgements, beliefs, and emotions toward outside units of those domestic groups which try to influence foreign policy, and to the origin, education, and ideas of the decision-makers themselves: what are their views about the ends of their policies, and about the means to be employed? [87]

We seriously doubt the ability of political scientists *systematically* to gather *empirical* data adequate to answer these questions for many historical periods. And if he could obtain the necessary data, Hoffmann provides no key as to how he would systematically interrelate the variables in the international system. He refers more than once to "correlation" of sets of data. For example, he wishes to "correlate" the "structure of the world," the forces which cut across or operate within many of the units, the relations between domestic and foreign policies of the basic units, and the political outcomes occasioned by the interrelation of these first three factors.[88] Correlation is a specific statistical technique, and not one patently applicable to the relationships which Hoffmann describes. The situation does not improve under detailed analysis, as when he confuses mathematization, quantification, and measurement.[89]

But we resist analytical overkill here. Hoffmann may supply the final evidence of his own analytical mishap. That is, he does provide a fleeting glimpse at the kinds of data he might accumulate and attempt to "correlate," but that glimpse does not inspire. He explains that "among the materials to be used for such research, none have been more neglected than the writings of philosophers, theorists, and statesmen."[90] From these, Hoffmann hopes to cull not only "insights" but "models of international politics." These source materials do not seem promising, except as indicators of the diverse notions of the nature of international politics. And these exist already in ample supply.

### C. Micro-Models: Snyder's Approach to Decision-Making

Sometimes with more exuberance than effect, transitionalists encouraged extensive attention to model-building in International Relations. There are models and models, of course, but we shall inspect only two examples. The present emphasis is on a *micro-model,* a model focusing on one process. Later, the focus will be upon one *macro-model,* which designation here only suggests a *systemic* (as roughly opposed to *processual*) concern.

Snyder's decision-making approach is one of the pioneering efforts at systematic conceptualization in the study of international affairs. His approach may be summarized broadly, although his emphasis has changed over time.[91] He sees decision-making as a process of sequential stages involving interacting actors in a decisional setting. This setting principally includes a unit (or units) of decision. The actors are influenced by spheres of competence, motivations, and constraints associated with communication and information-processing.[92] Snyder's approach, like other forms of social action-analysis,[93] focuses attention on actors, goals, means, and situations. This general focus will be elaborated by looking at some of the specifics of Snyder's approach.

Broadly, Snyder's model reflects methodological problems because he has been willing to confront conceptual issues which were sidestepped by earlier International Relations theorists. Specifically, first, Snyder's model directly reflects operational shortcomings. In particular, his nominal definitions of two crucial variables—"potential decision-makers" and "attitudes of decision-makers"—are so broad as to defy practical investigation. For example, potential decision-makers include

> Those who are empowered to make or carry out decisions, who are held responsible for official acts; those whose duties require them to formulate policies and to plan for the execution of policies on behalf of those who are held responsible; and those who function directly or indirectly to influence the other two groups.[94]

Similarly, Snyder's nominal definition of attitudes is insufficiently explicit. Attitudes are viewed in terms of the "readiness of individual decision-makers to be motivated."[95] Precisely how this "readiness" might be ascertained operationally is left by Snyder to speculation.

Snyder does not avoid crucial conceptual problems. His handling of motivations is broadly troublesome. To be sure, he attempts to come directly to grips with the impact of individual personalities and motivations on the decision-making process. Hence he deals conceptually only with "acquired motives," which he defines as "acceptable justifications for programs of action."[96] Thus motives primarily have a rationalizing, after-the-fact, function for decision-making. This formulation raises questions about the reliability and validity of verbal statements of motivations by political actors, as well as about the congruence of self-reports and behavior. With Hoffmann, we suggest that the acceptance of these verbal expressions as evidence of motivation "implies that (operationally) politics is . . . made of highly conscious moves and choices that can be analyzed in terms of neat categories."[97] That is, Snyder may have made a dangerous over-simplification of reality. Without question, moreover, it implies and neglects massive issues related to operational definition.

Second, Snyder has been accused of leaving inexplicit the relationships among major variables in his scheme.[98] His model does not permit even loose predictions of which variables will be most relevant for any given decision, for example. Furthermore, the ties between the individual and organizational levels of analysis in Snyder's model are quite indistinct. The theoretical coherence of the scheme, especially its hypothesis-generating ability, is understandably limited by such ambiguities and vacuities. Thus the model seems capable of predicting that, given particular circumstances, *some* decision will be made, *some* policy will be acted upon. Beyond that, the predictive capacity of the model seems questionable. That is, Snyder's model does spotlight one important perspective for *post-hoc* analysis and evaluation of the policy-making processes. It has largely *a posteriori* use in bringing conceptual clarity to the process of choice-taking. This could be an important redeeming feature, but only at very early stages of empirical analysis.

Third, the choice of *decisions* as a central focus may have been unfortunate, for two reasons. It remains problematic whether those who formally participate in the "authoritative allocation of values" are always, or even commonly, decision-makers. The issue has been treated earlier in Chapter VII, but the associated methodological dilemma may be illustrated. For example, if one conveniently focuses on *formal* officials in decision-making, one ignores the possible significance of "non-decisions." Bachrach and Baratz have cogently summarized this argument.[99] They hold that the most powerful individuals in a system may well be those who can define the parameters of the decision-making process, rather than those who participate directly in the choice of one from among a number of accessible alternatives. In short, those who can prevent decisions from being made are the most influential decision-makers. On the other hand, if one focuses on *actual* decision-makers, the conceptual and operational issue is how they are identified. Here Snyder's model provides little direction.

Moreover, Snyder's focus on decisions also may be troublesome because looking at choice-taking may imply that the stuff of international relations is largely conscious, goal-oriented behavior. In point of fact, values *may* be informally allocated even in the absence of such explicitness. Indeed, we are reasonably certain that conflicts will be resolved in some manner, regardless of the intervention of formal "authoritative decision-makers."[100]

This over-emphasis on conscious, goal-oriented behavior leads to a further objection to the Snyder scheme as a basis for International Relations theory, that is, taking the decision-making approach brings emphasis on intra-national factors. Its strength may rest in the analysis of foreign policy *formulation,* as opposed to *application.* The model's strong concern for intra-national considerations implies an inappropriate narrowness for the study of international affairs.

Snyder's use of the phenomenological approach also raises methodological issues relevant to concepts, operations, and validity of data. Phenomenologically, operational definitions favor perceptions of actors as data-sources. Thus devaluing observer-oriented data raises issues of validity. Assume that political actors view reality through a variety of differently tinted glasses. Their perceptions of the world may differ considerably from the objective state of affairs. Of course, as Snyder argues, even unreal perceptions on the part of actors are critical determinants of their decision-making behavior. People do not act on the basis of what "really is"; they proceed on the basis of whatever perceptions they have, right or wrong. However accurately Snyder's version of the phenomenological approach mirrors reality, in any case, it does raise operational problems. Empirical investigations based on this model depend on the researcher's ability to "recreate the mental universe of the decision-makers,"[101] we are told, a task of some substance.

Snyder's focus on *authoritative* decision-making creates further difficulties. Snyder wishes to study only those decisions which are made by public officials. Yet political scientists have long recognized significant non-governmental, but clearly political, organizations which substantially influence the shape of a nation's foreign policy. Snyder recognizes that "all politically important decisions are not made within the governmental structure."[102] He does contend, however, that only "decisions actually made by public officials are politically *authoritative*."[103] And he argues that the impact of non-governmental, politically relevant groups can be ascertained by focusing on the behavior of official decision-makers. After all, argues Snyder, these non-governmental groups must work through authoritative public structures. Perhaps. Winning the day by definition, however, must be suspect. Indeed, much data at least restrict applications of Snyder's position. In the Soviet Union, for example, authoritative prescriptions may be promulgated through decree by the Supreme Soviet, or by the Council of Ministers. Unfortunately for the decision-making analyst, the actual allocation of values for the system is usually made by sometimes unidentified Party functionaries, whose decisions may be conveyed in *Pravda* editorials. In short, the decision-making approach may make a good deal of sense when studying foreign-policy formulation in some systems, but as a basis for theory in the study of international politics, the scheme is unambiguously lacking.

Snyder is not unconscious of such conceptual and operational problems. Indeed, he has suggested modifications of his decision-making model. We mention them here in part because of their intrinsic worth, as well as to underscore Snyder's recognition of the need for improvements in his scheme. First, Snyder suggests the development of a typology of political objectives, and the construction of hypotheses linking different decisional procedures with different objectives. Second, the model usefully could incorporate a typology of decisional units, along with some specification of procedural variations which may be peculiar (in kind or in degree) to each type. Third, Snyder recognizes the need for more attention to nominal and operational definition in handling the personality characteristics of decision-makers. Fourth, he calls for applications of the model in a series of case studies of decision-making under varying environmental conditions. Beyond the work of Snyder and Paige, Robinson, and Hermann, however, little of this has been done to date under any of these heads.[104]

### D. Macro-Models: General Systems Theory

The transitionalists also encouraged the building of macro-models, of which general systems theory is probably the most useful in the study of international politics. Two of the most cogent proponents of a systems approach are Morton Kaplan and Charles McClelland.[105] They have developed their approach in response to the perceived needs for a "synthetic discipline," a "large neutral framework which would accommodate modes, foci, subjects and topics along with numerous conceptual schemes and islands of theory."[106]

Systems theory proceeds from the common-sense notion that, despite their complexity, relationships in the international arena have some orderliness and regularity. Events unfold in patterns, and these patterns are not beyond human capacities of identification and analysis. Thus systems theory addresses itself to three central questions:[107]

(1) What are the operating parts of the system (these parts are usually called *components*)?—what do they do, how are they arranged, how are they coordinated, how do they fluctuate, how do they change or grow, and how are they replaced?

(2) What are the boundaries between the system and its environment—what functions do the boundaries serve, how are they structured, maintained, and changed?

(3) What is the character of the influence of the environment on the system and of the system on the environment—how do these two hypothecated complexes interact?

Less certainty about general systems theory is possible as we become more specific, however. Systems theory in international politics research is undergirded by "collections of *ad hoc* concepts and propositions."[108] This does not, however, imply a lack of theoretical coherence. The synthetic nature of such a theoretical amalgam does not preclude specificity or operationality, in principle. In McClelland's words, one of the principal contributions of the general systems approach is "to help to clarify and rationalize the theory we already have."[109] The incorporation of concepts and methodologies from other approaches does not obscure the fact that the general systems perspective utilizes a single, identifiable vocabulary and a fully consistent set of concepts.[110] In practice, however, the systems approach has not penetrated International Relations as deeply as (for example) Cybernetics. International Relations applications are still largely metaphorical.

We can be more explicit. Numerous objections have been raised to general systems theory. To begin with, general systems theory is criticized as prematurely pitched at a high level of generality. The point has merit. The systems perspective is hardly a behavioral approach, despite its common association with the "young Turks" in International Relations. Systems theory is criticized further because it cannot easily be linked to real-world phenomena. For example, Kaplan's formulation—certainly the most extensive statement of the systems approach—provides few specific guidelines for nominal definitions and fewer for operational definitions suitable for testing hypotheses derived from the model.[111] In this sense, the methodological difficulty with systems theory is that it is metaphorical, a new way of saying old things. Discoveries often come in just this form, of course. But the lack of explicit concern in systems theory for operational definition does not promise an easy or early movement beyond the metaphorical.

Other features of systems theory also imply its fixation on the metaphorical. For example, the *analytic* characteristics of the theory tend to be projected into the *empirical* picture of the international arena. That is, the pervasive orderliness of systems theory encourages projecting a biased picture of the international system by ignoring its complex character. Many of the variables which Kaplan discusses—the objectives of the international system, the roles of the actors in that system, the structure of the system—are extremely hard to identify in the real world. Kaplan seems to assume that because the logical relations among these variables *must* be reasonably orderly if the international system qua model is to survive, then empirically we will find these relationships to be just that structured.

In addition, general systems theory is a variant of structural-functional analysis. As such, it fixates on behaviors clearly related to system preservation. As one observer complained: "Purposes and values other than preservation of the system are left out . . . the only processes discussed are processes of maintenance, integration, and disintegration; for the implied supreme value is . . . mechanical stability."[112] We find this objection more compelling empirically than logically. That is, it may not be particularly mischievous to exclude analytically those factors which do not influence the preservation of the international system. The perplexing issue remains, however. How does one determine if any set of behaviors *is* related to system preservation?

The perplexing question of system preservation usually is ducked. Not being able to isolate the specific behaviors that "preserve a system," systems theorists generally are content to make do with some basic assumptions. Systems theorists tend to build their models on an implicit base of two troublesome concepts—equilibrium and stability. Equilibrium analysis has its own shortcomings.[113] And these are aggravated when one confuses equilibrium and stability—as systems theorists often do. For example, Kaplan seems to assume that a state of equilibrium in the international system must always refer to a stable condition.[114] Easton thinks otherwise.[115] He recognizes that "although the equilibrium approach is seldom explicitly elaborated, it has permeated a good part of political research, especially . . . international relations." It is thus "customary to analyze the system, if only implicitly, in terms of a tendency to return to a presumed pre-existing point of stability. . . . A careful scrutiny of the language used reveals that *equilibrium* and *stability* are usually assumed to mean the same thing."[116]

The assumption of stability is hardly defensible, for it projects a picture of a system whose "normal" state is static. In contrast, the components of a system may remain in a roughly similar relation to one another, while undergoing rapid and unpatterned change. Such a system would be in *dynamic* equilibrium; in Easton's terms, *unstable* equilibrium.[117] Again, the analytic orderliness of systems approaches may breed theoretical over-simplification.

Further, equilibrium-stability assumptions leave the impression that one goal dwarfs all others for members of a system: the re-establishment of equilibrium, or the realization of stability. Such an impression is particularly troublesome. Consider only that it obscures the critical differences between equilibrium as a convenient point of analytic reference in describing the international system, and between equilibrium as a goal-object which saturates human motivations. There can be no logical objection to viewing human behavior in terms of its functionality in maintaining system stability. Empirically, however, this hardly establishes that system stability motivates the behavior being described. Thus Hoffmann observes that since the international system is constantly engaged in an effort to preserve itself, in concept, "the status quo becomes an empirical . . . pivot."[118] To be sure, systems theorists address themselves to processes of disintegration. But they do seem to assume that such trends are aberrations from the systemic norm.[119] The systems theorists do not consider it problematic whether the international system will initiate compensatory responses to any disequilibrating tendencies. On balance, then, the assumed tendency in international politics would seem to be toward evolutionary rather than revolutionary change.

The usual assumptions in systems theory seem too broad. Systems may well have numerous other goals besides equilibrium-maintenance. Indeed, members in a system "may . . . wish . . . to destroy a previous equilibrium or even to achieve some new point of continuing disequilibrium."[120] Further, many political actors (including nation-states) undertake a broad range of behaviors with no apparent concern for their possible system-wide impacts. Equilibrium or stability seem not to be over-riding factors influencing international decision-making, except perhaps *in extremis*.

Finally, the systems approach to the study of international politics over-emphasizes the role of inter-nation behaviors and circumstances. This liability underscores a common limitation on macro-approaches. Intra-national factors—which clearly influence inter-nation interactions—are usually slighted, and as a result, general systems theory seems to lose a good deal of the hoped-for predictive utility. It addresses itself to intra-national factors only after these conditions have been demonstrated to be of relevance to system-related inter-nation conditions.[121] This hardly seems an adequate base for predicting changes in the international system.

## VI. CONCLUSION

International Relations carries an aura of uniqueness among the scholarly disciplines in several particulars. Even its own professionals are unsure of the *what* and of the *who* of the field. Only recently has marginal consensus on *how* and *why* been reached. The distinction between student and practitioner has often been blurred in International Relations. Efforts at theory-building have been diverse, uncoordinated, and frequently inelegant. In sum, the field has been overwhelmed by itself: by the real-world significance of its subject-matter foci; by the almost infinite range of approaches and techniques which seem superficially relevant; by the difficulties involved in bringing system and rigor to a fledgling and uncertain field of study.

That these problems are not insurmountable has been demonstrated. This in turn implies the vigor of the theory-oriented, methodologically sensitive scholarly leadership which has emerged in International Relations since 1950. Patently, the study of International Relations still begs for increased methodological concern. But credit must be given where credit is due. Recent methodological advances have indeed been significant.

We may subsume the needed refinements in International Relations under three general requisites. Scientific maturity in this field first demands the systematic, judicious blending of concepts, methods, and research findings from several established disciplines, especially Sociology, Psychology, Political Science, Economics, and History. This inter-disciplinary co-ordination cannot come merely through the mails. Permitting social psychologists to describe their research in International Relations-oriented journals is but a small step forward. Needed are explicit theory-building and data-collecting efforts jointly conducted by supra-disciplinary teams of scholars.

Second, we stress Snyder's call for a thoroughgoing intellectual inventory of International Relations. Few agree on what we really *know* about international affairs. Further, we are even uncertain of what we *need* to know to build a science of International Relations.

Third, International Relations specialists must follow the foot they have thrust in the door of the philosophy of science reading room. We must be further sensitized to the nature of definition, concept-formation, hypothesis-construction and testing, mathematization of relationships and measurement of variables. It is now fashionable to be "systematic." Eventually, it must be second nature.

## NOTES

1. Fred A. Sondermann, "The Linkage Between Foreign Policy and International Politics," in James N. Rosenau (ed.), *International Politics and Foreign Policy* (New York: The Free Press of Glencoe, 1961), p. 8.

2. Richard C. Snyder, "Toward Greater Order in the Study of International Politics", *World Politics,* VII (1955), 461–78. Reprinted in James N. Rosenau (ed.), *International Politics and Foreign Policy, ibid.*

3. We can only sample this growing interest. For example, decision-making analysis was initially developed in Public Administration, and has been carried to International Relations primarily by Richard C. Snyder. A convenient summary of Snyder's approach may be found in Roland Young (ed.), *Approaches to the Study of Politics* (Evanston, Ill.: Northwestern University Press, 1958), pp. 3–38. Equilibrium analysis, originally little used outside Economics, has been propounded in International Relations by George Liska. See his *International Equilibrium: A Theoretical Essay on the Politics and Organization of Security* (Cambridge, Mass.: Harvard University Press, 1957). General systems theory also is finding support among International Relations theorists. Morton Kaplan's *System and Process in International Politics* (New York: Wiley, 1957) is the principal work on the subject. Psychological and social-psychological approaches have been developed by Harold Guetzkow. See his "Isolation and Collaboration: A Partial Theory of Inter-Nation Relations," *Journal of Conflict Resolution,* I (March, 1957), 48–68, and *Multiple Loyalties: Theoretical Approach to a Problem in International Organization* (Princeton, N.J.: Princeton University Press, 1955). Guetzkow also has fathered the use of simulation techniques in International Relations teaching and research. These techniques are discussed in Chapter IX of this volume. Mathematical economics has given International Relations game theory. See Richard C. Snyder, "Game Theory and the Analysis of Political Behavior," in James N. Rosenau (ed.), *International Politics and Foreign Policy, op. cit.,* pp. 381–90. Related sociological theories of bargaining, conflict, and strategy have been applied in International Relations by Thomas C. Schelling, Kenneth Boulding, and Robert C. North. See Schelling, *The Strategy of Conflict* (New York: Oxford University Press, 1963); Boulding, *Conflict and Defense: A General Theory* (New York: Harper, 1962); Robert C. North, et al., "The Integrative Functions of Conflict," *Journal of Conflict Resolution,* IV (September, 1960), 355–74. This listing is barely suggestive of the many theoretical borrowings gaining currency in International Relations.

4. James N. Rosenau, *International Politics and Foreign Policy, op. cit.,* p. 5 Also see Kenneth W. Thompson, "The Study of International Politics: A Survey of Trends and Developments," *Review of Politics,* 14 (October, 1952), especially pp. 439–40; Sondermann, *op. cit.,* especially pp. 9–12.

5. Rosenau, *ibid.,* p. 6.

6. *Ibid.* The first section (pp. 5–43) of the Rosenau reader provides an excellent summary of boundary problems in International Relations.

7. Sondermann, *op. cit.,* p. 8.

8. *Ibid.*

9. The best summary of the interwar period in International Relations may be found in William T. R. Fox, "Interwar International Relations Research: The American Experience," *World Politics,* II, 1 (October, 1949), 67–79. Kenneth W. Thompson synthesizes Fox's article, and extends it to cover early post-World War II developments in "The Study of International Politics: A Survey of Trends and Developments," *Review of Politics,* 14 (October, 1952), 433–67. We substantially accept Thompson's perspective in this section.

10. Thompson, *op. cit.,* pp. 434–35.

11. Samuel Eliot Morison.

12. Morison, quoted in Thompson, *op. cit.,* p. 435.

13. *Ibid.,* p. 436.

14. Sir Alfred Zimmern, "Introductory Report to the Discussions in 1935," in Zimmern (ed.), *University Teaching of International Relations* (Paris: Inter-

national Institute of Intellectual Cooperation, League of Nations, 1939), p. 8.

15. Thompson, *op. cit.*, p. 437.

16. Hans J. Morgenthau and Kenneth W. Thompson (eds.), *Principles and Problems of International Politics* (New York: Knopf, 1950), p. 19.

17. Thompson, *op. cit.*, pp. 439–40.

18. *Ibid.*, pp. 441–42.

19. One of the most prominent examples is Harold Guetzkow. His numerous theoretical efforts in International Relations have been directed toward finding the "surest and quickest way to world peace." He argues that the most efficacious procedure toward this end is the construction of basic theory about international affairs: "No other approach . . . holds any promise of enabling men of good will to understand and control the present system of international relations, whose breakdown now threatens the world with utter devastation." See "Long Range Research in International Relations," *American Perspective*, IV (1950), 421–40. Reprinted in Rosenau, *op. cit.*, pp. 53–59.

20. Thompson, *op. cit.*, pp. 443–50.

21. *Ibid.*, p. 449.

22. *Ibid.*

23. J. David Singer, "Introduction," in Singer (ed.), *Human Behavior and International Politics* (Chicago: Rand McNally, 1965), pp. 1–20.

24. Of course, areas of International Relations can be approached via laboratory analysis. Chapter IX of this volume deals with the use of simulation in studying the international system. To cite another example, Robert T. Golembiewski was involved in PROJECT ACCORD for the United States Department of State. The project's general purpose is to build into administrative operations in the Department of State a large if unruly body of knowledge concerning individual and group behavior in organizations. On the general approach, see Edgar Schein and Warren G. Bennis, *Personal and Organizational Change Through Group Methods* (New York: Wiley, 1965). The Singer compendium, *op. cit.*, contains several contributions to International Relations research which were developed in the laboratory by social psychologists. On the microscopic level, a good deal of suggestive research has been done. For example, see Leon Gordenker, *The United Nations and the Peaceful Unification of Korea: The Politics of Field Operations.* (The Hague: M. Nijhoff, 1959).

25. Singer, *op. cit.*, pp. 2–3.

26. *Ibid.*, p. 3.

27. Two excellent articles reflecting such an explicit concern are Charles A. McClelland, "The Function of Theory in International Relations," *Journal of Conflict Resolution*, IV, 1 (September, 1960), 303–36; and Anatol Rapoport, "Various Meanings of 'Theory,'" *American Political Science Review*, LII (1958), 972–88.

28. Rosenau, *op. cit.*, pp. 6–7.

29. *Ibid.*, p. 7.

30. The term *scale* is being used here to connote not only the general use of attitude scales, but also the application of more specific techniques such as Guttman scaling. See Louis Guttman, "The Principal Components of Scale Analysis," Chapter 9 in Samuel A. Stouffer (ed.), *Measurement and Prediction* (Princeton, N.J.: Princeton University Press, 1950), and "The Principal Components of Scalable Attitudes," Chapter 5 in Paul F. Lazarsfeld (ed.), *Mathematical Thinking in the Social Sciences* (Glencoe, Ill.: The Free Press, 1954). An application in International Relations research is Bernard Fensterwald, Jr., "American 'Isolationism' and Expansionism," *Journal of Conflict Resolution*, II (1958), 280–307.

31. See Chapter IX of this volume.

32. The principal applications in International Relations of factor analysis have been made by Rudolph J. Rummel, Raymond B. Cattell, and Raymond Tanter. See: Cattell, "The Dimensions of Culture Patterns by Factorization of National Characters," *Journal of Abnormal and Social Psychology*, 44 (1949), 443–69; Cattell, "The Principal Culture Patterns Discoverable in the Syntal Dimensions of Existing Nations," *Journal of Social Psychology*, 32 (1950), 215–53; Cattell, H. Bruel, and H. Parker Hartman, "An Attempt at More Refined Definition of the Cultural Dimension of Syntality of Modern Nations," *American Sociological Review*, 17 (1952), 408–21;

Rummel, "Dimensions of Conflict Behavior Within and Between Nations," *General Systems: Yearbook of the Society for General Systems Research,* 8 (1963), pp. 1–50; Tanter, "Dimensions of Conflict Behavior Within and Between Nations, 1958–1960" (Ph.D. dissertation, Indiana University, 1964). Rummel has completed two similar studies using regression analysis. See Rummel, "Dimensions of Foreign and Domestic Conflict Behavior: A Review of Empirical Findings," in Dean Pruitt and Richard C. Snyder, *Readings on Conflict* (forthcoming): and Rummel, "Testing Some Possible Predictors of Conflict Behavior Within and Between Nations," *Papers* I (Philadelphia: Peace Research Society, 1964), pp. 79–111.

33. The HIDECS family of computer programs was developed in the Civil Engineering Systems Laboratory at M.I.T. See Christopher Alexander and Marvin L. Manheim, *HIDECS 2: A Computer Program for the Hierarchical Decomposition of a Set with an Associated Linear Graph* (Cambridge, Mass.: Department of Civil Engineering, Massachusetts Institute of Technology 1962). A later version, HIDECS 3, is described by Alexander in M.I.T. Department of Civil Engineering Publication Number R63–27 (June, 1963). Steven J. Brams has pioneered the use of HIDECS in the social sciences. See his "Transaction Flows in the International System," *American Political Science Review,* LX, 4 (December, 1966), 880–98. William A. Welsh used HIDECS 2 in his dissertation, "Intellectuals and Politics in Eastern Europe: The Bulgarian Academy of Sciences as a Case Study" (Ph.D. dissertation, Northwestern University, 1965). HIDECS is described in some detail in Chapter VIII of this volume.

34. See Raoul Naroll, *Data Quality Control* (New York: The Free Press of Glencoe, 1961).

35. Singer, *op. cit.,* p. 4.

36. *Ibid.,* p. 5.

37. We have dealt with some of these validation problems in the chapter of this volume dealing with simulation in the study of International Relations.

38. For an excellent summary of the problems encountered in bridging both laboratory-field and inter-disciplinary gaps, see Sidney Verba, *Small Groups and Political Behavior: A Study of Leadership* (Princeton, N.J.: Princeton University Press, 1961), especially pp. 61–109.

39. This tendency perhaps is best exhibited by Harold Guetzkow. (See his work noted in footnotes 3 and 41). Despite the growing concern for integrating theory and empirical research, however, International Relations continues to suffer from a clearly definable gap between "thinkers" and "doers." Analytic models and data-gathering efforts rarely exhibit congruence.

40. This typology was suggested by Dr. Willard E. A. Range of the Department of Political Science, University of Georgia. The present authors would take occasional exception to Professor Range's classifications, e.g., with his description of decision-making approaches as "broad, integrative theories," but the typology is serviceable and suggestive.

41. Guetzkow, "Long Range Research in International Relations," in Rosenau, *op. cit.,* p. 56.

42. Snyder, "Toward Greater Order in the Study of International Politics," in Rosenau, *op. cit.,* p. 38.

43. *Ibid.*

44. *Ibid.,* p. 39.

45. For one of the best discussions of the concept *national interest* and the methodological problems its use presents for specialists in International Relations, see Morton A. Kaplan, *System and Process in International Relations* (New York: Wiley, 1957), pp. 151–61.

46. Snyder, "Toward Greater Order in the Study of International Politics," in Rosenau, *op. cit.,* p. 40.

47. Examples of determinist geographic postures are presented in Harold and Margaret Sprout, "Environment Factors in the Study of International Politics," *Journal of Conflict Resolution,* I (1957), 309–28.

48. Snyder, "Toward Greater Order in the Study of International Politics," in Rosenau, *op. cit.,* p. 41.

49. *Ibid.*

50. *Ibid.,* pp. 42–43. General systems

theory is a usual exception to this criticism. At the same time, some critics of systems approaches contend that this perspective projects a status-quo–oriented picture of the international arena. See our comments on general systems approaches below.

51. Hans J. Morgenthau and Kenneth W. Thompson (eds.), *Principles and Problems of International Politics* (New York: Knopf, 1950), p. 18.

52. New York: Lippincott, 1964.

53. *Ibid.*, p. vii.

54. *Ibid.*

55. *Ibid.*

56. *Ibid.*, p. 3.

57. *Ibid.*

58. *Ibid.*, p. vii.

59. In a sense, Morgenthau's rough equation of the two terms was functional for specialists in the field. That is, equating international relations and international politics helped narrow the exceedingly broad subject-matter focus which lingered from the Zimmern school of the inter-war period. At the same time, failing to distinguish the two terms tended to obscure the important and often-neglected relationships between primarily political and primarily non-political factors which influence inter-nation behaviors.

60. Stanley H. Hoffmann, "International Relations: The Long Road to Theory," *World Politics*, XI (April, 1959), 349–50.

61. Hoffmann (see footnote 60 above) certainly has provided one of the most vigorous critiques of Morgenthau's work. Also see John H. Herz, *Political Realism and Political Idealism* (Chicago: University of Chicago Press, 1951); Robert W. Tucker, "Professor Morgenthau's Theory of Political 'Realism,'" *American Political Science Review*, XLVI, 1 (March, 1952), 214–24; Herbert Butterfield, "The Scientific Versus the Moralistic Approach," *International Affairs*, XXVII, 4 (October, 1951), 411–22; Harold Sprout, "In Defense of Diplomacy," *World Politics*, I, 3 (April, 1949), 404–13.

62. See Snyder, "Toward Greater Order in the Study of International Politics," in Rosenau, *op. cit.*, pp. 39–41; Hoffmann, "International Relations: The Long Road to Theory," p. 350.

63. Hoffman, *op. cit.*, p. 350. See Hans J. Morgenthau, *Scientific Man versus Power Politics* (Chicago: University of Chicago Press, 1946), pp. 50–51 and 188–202.

64. Hoffmann, "International Relations: The Long Road to Theory," p. 350.

65. *Ibid.*

66. *Ibid.*, p. 351. Also see A. F. K. Organski, *World Politics* (New York: Knopf, 1958).

67. Hoffmann, "International Relations: The Long Road to Theory," p. 351.

68. The third definitional alternative for the concept *national interest* is implicitly posed by David Easton, *The Political System* (New York: Knopf, 1960), pp. 129–31. For other conceptions of *national interest,* see Thomas I. Cook and Malcolm Moos, "Foreign Policy: The Realism of Idealism," *American Political Science Review,* XLVI, 2 (June, 1952), 342–56.

69. Hoffmann, "International Relations: The Long Road to Theory," pp. 352–53.

70. *Ibid.*, p. 352.

71. *Ibid.* Also see Henry A. Kissinger, *A World Restored* (Boston: Houghton Mifflin, 1957).

72. Inconsistency over time in the selection of appropriate means to be directed toward given ends may be concisely illustrated by reference to Soviet foreign policy. In the Soviet case, means-ends ambiguities have manifested themselves in (a) conflicting intra-bloc, extra-bloc, and domestic programs, (b) changes over time in each of these three spheres, and (c) an apparent modification of desired ends, at least for the foreseeable future.

73. Hoffmann, "International Relations: The Long Road to Theory," p. 365. Although McClelland comments on only a small part of Hoffmann's "wrecking operation," he seems to agree with the present authors that Hoffmann's analytic sledge hammers were not always on target. See Charles McClelland, "The Function of Theory in International Re-

lations," *Journal of Conflict Resolution,* IV, 1 (September, 1960), 313.

74. Hoffmann, "International Relations: The Long Road to Theory," p. 365.

75. *Ibid.,* p. 367.

76. *Ibid.*

77. *Ibid.,* p. 370.

78. *Ibid.,* p. 365. Hoffmann does suggest that "there is a difference" between the "debatable postulates" he has criticized and the "debatable postulates" upon which his own approach rests. That difference is that Hoffmann does not "claim that it is possible to squeeze the whole camel of international relations through the eye of one needle" (p. 365). We might well disagree as to the presumptuousness of some of the approaches criticized by Hoffmann. Caution in theory-building is, of course, admirable; it does not reduce the tenuousness of underlying postulates, however.

79. Hoffmann, "International Relations: The Long Road to Theory," pp. 358–59.

80. In Hoffmann's words: "Our first problem is the clarification of the values we would like to see promoted in the world ... the problems of peace and of a world order command all others" (pp. 375, 374).

81. *Ibid.,* p. 365.

82. *Ibid.,* p. 376.

83. *Ibid.,* p. 356.

84. *Ibid.,* p. 368. Emphasis added.

85. *Ibid.* Emphasis added.

86. *Ibid.,* p. 366.

87. *Ibid.,* pp. 371–72.

88. *Ibid.* Hoffmann also refers on p. 369 to discovering "factors" and "correlations."

89. Initially, Hoffmann implicitly confuses quantitative and qualitative measurement when he asserts that he will "correlate" the nominal data described above. Since he would be working in part with qualitative data, he could use statistical tests of association, such as chi square. Correlation techniques, however, would seem to be inapplicable to the sorts of data mentioned by Hoffmann. Hoffmann's "historical sociology" could achieve qualitative measurement (using the ordered metric or less powerful scales), but not quantification. More specifically, Hoffmann details his apparent confusion in the following passage: "... the model-builders try to *measure* all the important variables, but this involves some fantastic assumptions, such as the postulate that in our discipline *quantification* always entails a gain in precision rather than a possible loss, or that *quantities measured* independently can be added or combined meaningfully. The result is *always* a timeless and closed *mathematical* universe" (p. 359; emphasis added). Not only does Hoffmann apparently assume that all measurement is quantitative; he further seems to feel that measurement and mathematics are necessarily related. Chapter XIV of this volume outlines the commonly accepted position that quantification, measurement, and mathematization bear no necessary relation to one another.

90. Hoffmann "International Relations: The Long Road to Theory," p. 374.

91. The early statements of the decision-making approach came in Edgar S. Furniss, Jr. and Richard C. Snyder, *American Foreign Policy* (New York: Rinehart, 1954), pp. 89–134; and Snyder, H. W. Bruck, and Burton Sapin, *Decision-making as an Approach to the Study of International Politics* (Princeton, N. J.: Princeton University Press, 1954). The approach was developed in Snyder, "A Decision-Making Approach to the Study of Political Phenomena," in Young (ed.), *Approaches to the Study of Politics, op. cit.,* pp. 3–38; and Snyder and Glenn D. Paige, "The United States Decision to Resist Aggression in Korea: The Application of an Analytical Scheme," *Administrative Science Quarterly,* III, 3 (December, 1958), 341–78.

92. Snyder, "A Decision-Making Approach to the Study of Political Phenomena," especially pp. 15–27, 36–37.

93. Snyder's model again underscores the pervasive influence of social action theories among model-builders in Political Science. An earlier chapter in this volume emphasized the significance of the *action approach* for theory-oriented

students of comparative politics. For a general exposition of *social action* analysis, see Talcott Parsons and Edward A. Shils (eds.), *Toward a General Theory of Action* (Cambridge, Mass.: Harvard University Press, 1951). Snyder also acknowledges a considerable intellectual debt to Alfred Schuetz. See the latter's "Choosing Among Projects of Action," *Philosophy and Phenomenological Research,* XII (1951), 161–84.

94. Furniss and Snyder, *op. cit.*, p. 92. The notion of "potential decision-makers" is handled less explicitly in subsequent writings by Snyder.

95. Snyder, "A Decision-Making Approach to the Study of Political Phenomena," p. 33.

96. *Ibid.*, p. 31.

97. Stanley Hoffman, *Contemporary Theory in International Relations* (Englewood Cliffs, N.J.: Prentice-Hall, 1960), p. 52.

98. *Ibid.*

99. Peter Bachrach and Morton S. Baratz, "Two Faces of Power," *American Political Science Review,* LVI, 4 (December, 1962), 948.

100. On the dynamics of conflict, see E. E. Schattschneider, *The Semi-Sovereign People* (New York: Holt, Rinehart & Winston, 1960).

101. Hoffmann, *Contemporary Theory in International Relations,* p. 52.

102. Snyder, "A Decision-Making Approach to the Study of Political Phenomena," p. 16.

103. *Ibid.*

104. See Snyder and Paige, *op. cit.*, p. 16, James A. Robinson, "Decision-Making in International Political Crises." Paper presented at American Association for the Advancement of Science, December 27, 1961, and *Congress and Foreign Policy-Making* (Homewood, Ill.: The Dorsey Press, 1962); Charles F. Hermann, "Crises in Foreign Policy Making: A Simulation of International Politics" (Ph.D. dissertation, Northwestern University, 1965). Also see William A. Welsh, "The Analysis of Crisis: A Comparison of Five Cases," MS, International Relations Program, Northwestern University, 1961. Unfortunately, only the Snyder-Paige application involves the use of anything approaching the full decision-making model being described here.

105. See Morton A. Kaplan, *System and Process in International Politics* (New York: Wiley, 1957); Charles A. McClelland, "Systems and History in International Relations: Some Perspectives for Empirical Research and Theory," *General Systems Yearbook,* III (1958), 221–47; "Applications of General Systems Theory in International Relations," in James N. Rosenau (ed.), *International Politics and Foreign Policy, op. cit.*, p. 412–20; and "The Function of Theory in International Relations," *op. cit.*, pp. 303–36, especially pp. 327–34.

106. McClelland, "The Function of Theory in International Relations," p. 326.

107. *Ibid.*, p. 328.

108. *Ibid.*, p. 331.

109. *Ibid.*

110. For a general statement of systems theory, demonstrating its theoretical cohesion, see Ludwig von Bertalanffy, "General System Theory," *General Systems,* I (1965), pp. 1–10. Reprinted in part in Singer (ed.), *Human Behavior and International Politics, op. cit.*, pp. 20–31.

111. See Hoffmann, "International Relations: The Long Road to Theory," p. 359; also, McClelland, "The Function of Theory in International Relations," p. 315: ". . . there are no facts to which a large part of the theory might correspond. There is no way to determine the worth of such a symmetrical theory against the yardstick of common sense or surface plausibility."

112. Hoffmann, "International Relations: The Long Road to Theory," p. 360.

113. The principal exponent of equilibrium theory in International Relations has been George Liska. See his *International Equilibrium: A Theoretical Essay on the Politics and Organization of Security* (Cambridge, Mass.: Harvard University Press, 1957). See Hoffmann's critique in *Contemporary Theory in International Relations,* pp. 50–52.

114. See Hoffmann, *Contemporary*

*Theory in International Relations,* pp. 50–51 (re: Liska) and 47–48 (re: Kaplan).

115. David Easton, "Categories for the Systems Analysis of Politics," in Easton (ed.), *Varieties of Political Theory* (Englewood Cliffs, N.J.: Prentice-Hall, 1966), pp. 143–54, especially pp. 145–47. Also see his "Limits of the Equilibrium Model in Social Research," *Behavioral Science,* I (1956), 96–104.

116. Easton, "Categories for the Systems Analysis of Politics," p. 145.

117. Easton, "Limits of the Equilibrium Model in Social Research," pp. 96–98.

118. Hoffmann, "International Relations: The Long Road to Theory," p. 360.

119. Kaplan and Liska both make this assumption. The problem for analysis is presumed to be *how* the international system will counteract disintegrative forces, rather than *if* it will—or, if any units in the system are *interested in* arresting disintegration. For most systems theorists, the very existence of a system implies the presence of self-preserving tendencies within that system.

120. Easton, "Categories for the Systems Analysis of Politics," p. 146.

121. Hoffmann, "International Relations: The Long Road to Theory," p. 360.

# xi

# Some Leading Approaches Methodologically Viewed, IV: The Quest for Scientific Meaning in Analyses of Political Parties

Examining the research on political parties qua scientific effort is at once discouraging and encouraging. On the one hand, generally speaking, the canons of scientific investigation have not been respected in research on political parties. For example, few studies successfully approach even the primitive criteria offered in Chapter I. These first-sort criteria require: methodological compatibility with existing sciences; (dis)confirmation in events external to any theoretical systems developed; and a prime emphasis on definition of dimensions of reality. This methodological barrenness of research on parties is most evident in its failure to produce scientific fruit, that is, theoretical constructs able to support cumulative research. The importance of theory in scientific work cannot be overestimated.[1]

On the other hand, research on parties generates a substantial optimism. Whatever its present state, that is, important trends going back more than a half-century testify that the movement toward an empirical methodology has deep roots. Analogies can be troublesome. But these deep roots imply that a harvest of scientific work on parties is increasingly probable.

Documenting both pessimism and optimism is the concern of this chapter. The work of four writers—M. Ostrogorski, Robert Michels, Maurice Duverger, and Samuel Eldersveld—has been chosen to exemplify the grounds for pessimism and the trends that support optimism. These four scholars share a concern about advancing the scientific investigation of political parties by contributing to a concept of the party organization capable of supporting empirical research. The chief purpose here is not to measure their work against the methodological yardsticks developed above. Such measurement will not be neglected. But our prime purpose is to chart the developmental impact of these four scholars in inducing empirical research on political parties. Basically, the four scholars chosen labored with success to develop a useful focus for research. And—if with less effect—they struggled to produce concepts adequate to generate cumulative research. These dual ends they achieved by sharpening their focus on the party organization, and by imbedding that concept in a theoretical nexus congenial to diverse scholarly efforts.

## I. THE PRESENT STATE OF RESEARCH ON PARTIES: SOME FACTORS SUPPORTING PESSIMISM

Establishing the case for pessimism about research on parties is a relatively simple task. First, we will briefly and broadly characterize the parties literature. Second, we shall try our hand at developing a likely rationale for the characteristics of that literature.

Let us boldly characterize the parties literature first, reserving for later direct support of the characterization. Three properties strike us as most salient in this characterization.

1. *Research on political parties lacks any identifiable, commonly accepted focus.* Studies exist in superabundance, but they also exist in splendid isolation. Let us hazard a metaphor. Parties research is to voting behavior—a younger but scientifically more advanced field—as a detonated fragmentation grenade is to a rifle shot. One is sure the fragments fit together into some whole—at least the feeling is that they should—but how they do is something else again. Lack of any clear focus among researchers on parties has led to another problem. Some sub-areas stimulate great investments of time and energy. If anything, these areas suffer from an abundance of riches. For example, the amount of descriptive material available on such topics as campaigns, individual candidates, and the urban boss of yesteryear is virtually unlimited. Other sub-areas of parties are almost ignored. The paucity of studies on the structural organization and operation of the party characterizes this imbalance. Studies of the social and psychological characteristics of party adherents also are under-represented.

2. *There has been a serious shortage of works attempting to theoretically conceptualize parties* and their role in such a manner as to provide a framework for cumulative research. Such efforts are necessary for a scientific approach to parties research. Theoretical studies of any nature are uncommon in the field.[2] The types of research that predominate are the descriptive-historical, the anecdotal and inside-dopester, and the normative.[3]

3. *The major deficiency in the field is theoretical and methodological,*

and not one involving the applicability of specific techniques or approaches to party phenomena. That is, the field is susceptible to analysis by virtually any scientifically reputable investigative approach or technique. Such approaches as game theory, simulation, historical reconstruction, or participant-observer all can be useful. And such techniques as content analysis, field surveys, factor analysis, and stratification analysis also are all appropriate for research on parties. Specific approaches or techniques then represent no barrier to research on parties, but lack of methodological sophistication is a formidable barrier.

There are many ways of supporting our characterization of research on parties. We will rely on Maurice Duverger's justification of his own attempt at filling the theoretical lacunae in empirical research on parties. Revealingly, Duverger felt it necessary to urge his readers not to be "astonished" by the attempt to categorize, systematize, and theorize in a work on political parties![4] In more detail, Duverger in 1951 saw research in the area starting from this basic contradiction: "*It is at the present time impossible to give a valid description of the comparative functioning of political parties; yet it is essential to do so.*"[5] Duverger pinpointed the vicious circularity. A comprehensive empirical theory must rest on a multitude of research projects that strike to the heart of party phenomena. Without a general theory of parties, however, that multitude of studies probably will not be additive. For Nature answers only when questioned appropriately, and nothing but a general theory generates such questions.

Duverger's analytical strategy also supports our characterization of research on political parties. That is, what he considered necessary reflects what he considered lacking. His emphases are three. First, he attempted to stress practical methods of investigation so as "to introduce objectivity into a field where high feeling and special pleading are the general rule . . . ." Second, Duverger attempted to classify existing research findings and questions. As he explained: ". . . political science will make no true progress so long as its investigations are scattered and individual, empirical rather than scientific." Third, despite the unevenness of the data, Duverger pressed toward formulating "hypotheses capable of guiding the future research which will one day permit the formulation of authentic sociological laws."

Accepting Duverger's characterization of the state of research as essentially applicable today, we must ask: Why? What explains the spotty performance of party researchers? Ironically, one major contributor may be the over-accessibility of certain materials and the ease with which certain data can be procured. The scholar interested in analyzing socialization processes in Iran or the information networks in a large corporation is faced with patent methodological problems as to research design and execution. He must also theoretically justify the relevance of his undertaking within some broader framework. In contrast, the student of parties only infrequently employs elaborate research designs, or seriously weighs advantageous alternative approaches. He assumes that others recognize the importance of party analysis. The result is a relaxation of methodological rigor in collecting materials and an apparent unwillingness, or inability, to attempt to conceptualize a set of relations that are seemingly quite ordinary.

Another problem in party analysis is the general feeling that the study of political parties remains—more than most academic areas—the province of any interested student or layman. In effect, Everyman has presumptions of expertise about political parties. Sorauf makes the point effectively.

> The study of political parties . . . operates . . . under the disadvantage of unrecognized expertise. We are too much the prisoners of a widely held conventional wisdom about American politics, and conventional wisdom is by definition unsystematic, non-rigorous, popular wisdom. It is the wisdom of the non-specialist, the dilettante, and the scholarly amateur. . . . In a democracy all men and women are by definition political scientists, perfectly capable (they think) of reaching the sorts of knowledge the political scientists reach . . . And no field within political science suffers more from the rejection of its specialty in the invasion of a non-specialist than this one. . . . If political science is everyone's science, then the study of parties and politics is every political scientist's political science.[6]

Simple and sovereign explanations always must be suspect. But vulnerability to the self-proclaimed expertise of the vagabond scholar or the interested amateur at least partially explains the unscientific and uncoordinated nature of parties research. That vulnerability also helps explain the field's notable resistance to methodological innovation.

The preceding remarks are not meant cavalierly. Any research on political parties that aims to be of more than passing interest is deceptively difficult to execute, for reasons that are subtler than those sketched above. For example, party behavior comprises something more than a completely unstructured, random series of interrelationships, and yet something less than a conventionally ordered, neatly categorized pattern of behavior. This implies grave difficulties. That is, the most obvious vehicle for coordinating diffuse research and for providing some order for diverse behavior patterns stresses the organization of the party. But this vehicle travels no glory road to methodological sophistication and theoretical development. One could assume that the party organization approximated a conventional bureaucratic organization with a functional division of labor, discernible lines of authority and control, specified role functions, and an incentive system to reward performance, that is, that party structure corresponds in some manner to the classical theory of organization overlay noted in Chapter IV. The notion is naïve. Commonly, the party does not evidence even the minimal characteristics of a conventional organization. The dangers of riding one's assumption about the party qua formal organization too far are sketched by Eldersveld. He observes that:

> In attempting to spell out the relevant structural dimensions of parties as tentative theoretical positions for subsequent analysis, it must be recognized that parties do not possess many of the conventional attributes of the bureaucratic system. In particular, the bureaucratic prerequisites of impermeability, depersonalized human regulations and rule enforcement, precise allocation of obligations, duties, and roles, discipline, and sanctions, even low circulation of personnel, are found wanting in most party structures. We sense that the Republican and Democratic parties are structurally different from General Motors, the Catholic church, the AFL-CIO, or the Farm Bureau; how they differ is the task of empirical theory and research.[7]

We claim only two things for the preceding pages. They help to describe and to explain the current state of research in the field. They also introduce the basic problems a student of political parties must contend with in his research.

## II. DEVELOPMENTAL TRENDS IN METHODOLOGY VIA EMPHASIS ON PARTY ORGANIZATION

We do not wish to paint a static picture of research on parties. The dynamic focus here is upon four men whose work signaled significant methodological progress, therefore. These four individuals and many of their followers, in effect, helped to integrate the disparateness and to overcome the particularism of party research. The impetus each provided differs in kind and degree, as we shall show. In several significant senses, however, the four students shared a common orientation toward empirical research. And these students—if with varying sharpness—shared a common major focus for their attention. That focus is upon the party organization.

The implied skeletal outline for this section may be made explicit. The usefulness of an increasingly sharp focus on party organization will be suggested briefly. And more elaborate schematic efforts will be made to indicate the developmental trends in research on parties which may be discerned from Ostrogorski to Michels to Duverger through Eldersveld, as each exploited his approach to the party organization and its properties.

Despite grave problems, the focus on the party organization in formulating a theory of parties has a number of advantages.[8] Organizational modifications can reflect changes in environmental forces. For example, party organizations changed as they struggled to cope with an increased electorate resulting from the expansion of suffrage. The focus on organization also provides an orientation for the analysis of such diverse topics as ideology, policy formulation, individual motivation, characteristics of activitists, and party properties. Moreover, the party at once reflects and helps shape its cultural environment. By focusing on organization, the researcher can analyze the party within a broader setting and evaluate the degree to which the party helps realize societal goals. And finally, the schematic and logical difficulties implicit in many studies can be clarified by relating the structural characteristics of the party to those of the society. In short, a focus on organization can comfortably include the types of data important in any general theory of politics.[9] That focus also can provide a coherent framework for analysis.

The broad sweep of the progression Ostrogorski-through-Eldersveld constitutes a search-discovery sequence for a manageable area of inquiry that is meaningful. Table XI.1 conveniently presents background infor-

**TABLE XI.1 Basic Information about Four Authors**

| Author | Major Work | Year Published | Emphasis on: Environmental Conditions | Emphasis on: Structural Attributes | |
|---|---|---|---|---|---|
| 1. M. Ostrogorski | *Democracy and the Organization of Political Parties* (2 vols.) | 1902[a] | + | − | "Organismic," or "Holistic," analysis of "external" conditions that give rise to parties |
| 2. R. Michels | *Political Parties* | 1915[b] | − | + | Analysis of one allegedly universal "internal" tendency |
| 3. M. Duverger | *Political Parties* | 1951 | − | + | Comparative analysis of many "internal" properties |
| 4. S. Eldersveld | *Political Parties: A Behavioral Analysis* | 1964 | + | + | Model of operationally defined "external" and "internal" properties |

[a]A revised edition appeared in 1910 and is important for its more extended exposition of Ostrogorski's proposed reforms.
[b]This is the date of the first English-language edition. The original appeared in 1911.

mation on the works of each of the authors and indicates some of the distinguishing attributes of their contributions. The broad *holistic* approach of Ostrogorski certainly reflected his desire to encompass the meaningful. The search for manageability, however, required the narrowing of focus to *internal* party properties in Michels and Duverger. And Eldersveld was in a position to begin to spin out a theoretical structure relating *internal* party properties with some of the very *external* social-cultural-institutional properties that had preoccupied Ostrogorski.

Table XI.1 sketches that sequence characteristic of scientific work—a narrowing of focus in search of the manageable, then a reaching-out in search of increasing comprehensiveness. In sum, systematic attempts to conceptualize party organization and to develop an empirical theory began with Ostrogorski. After important contributions by Michels and Duverger, the moment has momentarily culminated some sixty years later in the work of Eldersveld. But let us underscore *momentarily*. For table XI.1 reflects but one sequence of a far more complex scientific process reaching toward deductively formulated theory.

The progressive contributions of the four students of parties reflect a diversity of lights concerning a shared belief. The authors not only share a concern with essentially the same problems—the manner in which

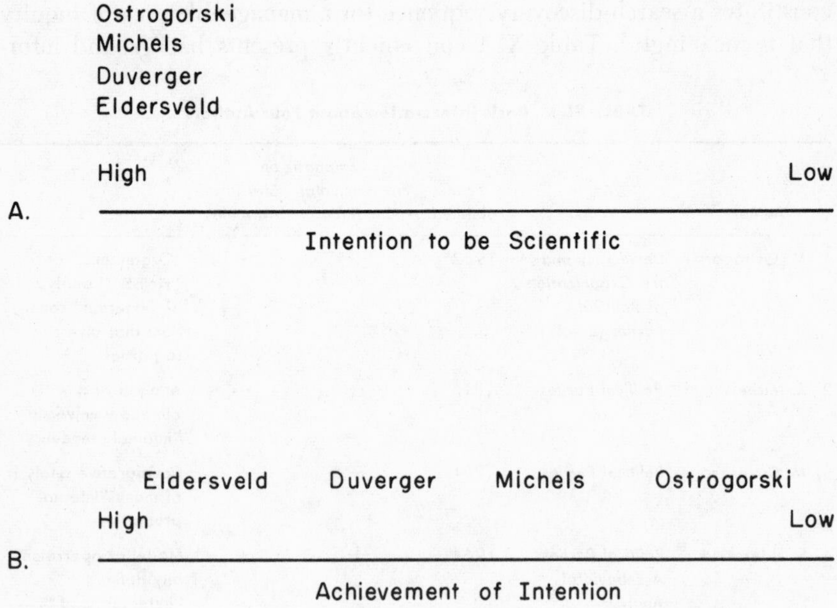

Ostrogorski
Michels
Duverger
Eldersveld

High — Low

A. Intention to be Scientific

Eldersveld — Duverger — Michels — Ostrogorski

High — Low

B. Achievement of Intention

FIGURE XI.1 Methodological Intent and Achievement of Four Leading Scholars in the Study of Political Parties.

political parties are organized, the consequences that this has for their performance, and the ways in which appropriate dimensions of reality can be isolated—but, more significantly for our tastes, the four also pay homage to the canons of scientific investigation. Even Ostrogorski—in a manner most unusual for his era—self-consciously states his methodological intentions and emphasizes the comparative uniformities that he is seeking in his data.[10] Not that all acted comparably on their shared belief. Eldersveld, the most recent of the theorists, is by far the most successful in structuring his problem and in operationalizing his concepts. An ordering of the four scholars in terms of methodological intent and fulfillment is hazarded in Figure XI.1.

A methodological lesson requires noting. In an area in which there is little reliable data, "fishing expeditions" or the mere indiscriminate collection of facts is justifiable and even potentially useful. If there is a backlog of information, a more promising approach would call for the design of a tightly knit project that draws extensively on what is known, organizes this information into a coherent framework, establishes some theoretical focus for the investigation, and then empirically tests the theory. The latter approach is exemplified by the work of Eldersveld, and it requires the methodology described and illustrated throughout this volume. Failure to employ that methodology must be paid for in terms of the analytical recycling characteristic of so much of Political Science.

Although we hope to make more ambitious use of our panel of scholars, we will not hesitate to reinforce the relatively apparent. The dynamic trade-offs of manageability and meaningfulness characterize the process of developing empirical theory, just as they characterize the study of parties. Being too preoccupied with either manageability or meaningfulness can be troublesome at any stage of research. And being captivated by a broadly conceived meaningfulness at early stages is just the concern most likely to inhibit the scholar's movement into stages in which greater meaningfulness can be attained.

Let us venture beyond reinforcing the apparent, as is our general wont. The vocabulary developed in Chapters I and II helps refine the gross methodological lesson reflected in Table XI.1 and Figure XI.2. Two microscopic views of the general progression sketched thus far do the job. Figure XI.2 focuses on the four major stages of empirical inquiry. Roughly, the figure fits our panel of authors to these four stages. Figure XI.2 focuses on types of theories and classifies our panel of authors accordingly.

Figure XI.2 sketches the progression of a universe of scientific discourse that can successfully broaden only as it first narrows in scope.

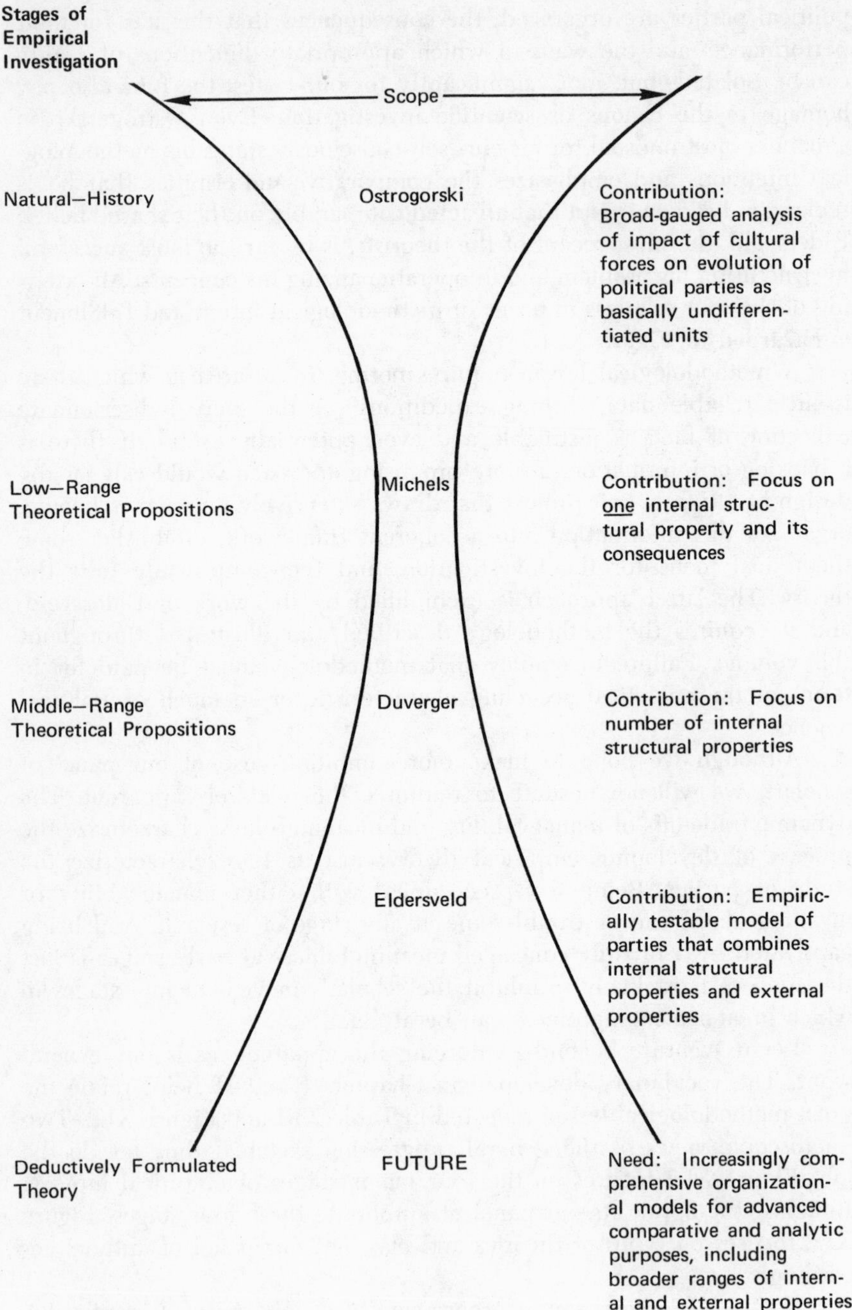


FIGURE XI.2 Research on Political Parties and Stages of Empirical Investigation.

For example, Ostrogorski wrote when little was known in the social sciences about scientific methodology, and when a good deal less was known about political parties. Ostrogorski reacted typically. His approach was *organismic* or *holistic*. He speculated about the broad environmental conditions out of which political parties evolved. To simplify his task, for Ostrogorski a political party was essentially a political party. "Internal" differentiation was too subtle an enterprise for the early phases of natural-history classification and description reflected in Ostrogorski's effort. Increasing theoretic power, up to a point, had to be paid for in terms of the narrowed scope of inquiry of a Michels or a Duverger. But the derived low-range theoretical propositions were perforce highly generalized. Increased predictive power could be gained only by selectively enlarging the scope of inquiry, as in Eldersveld, while respecting methodological guidelines capable of preventing the enlarged scope from overwhelming inquiry and the inquirer. The product of this selective enlargement of focus is a deductively formulated theory of great and growing scope and power for prediction and description.

Figure XI.3 permits yet another important approach to the Ostrogorski-through-Eldersveld progression. For example, Ostrogorski's work often implicitly contained unreconciled and unreconcilable traces of all three types of theories. Thus his choice of a holistic focus implied a necessary frustration of his announced passion to develop an empirical theory. Indeed, Ostrogorski took on three demonstrations, small parts of any one of which would have been test enough of any scholar's talent. Moreover, each of the demonstrations was beyond the supporting resources on which Ostrogorski could call. The three demonstrations included: a historical recounting of the dynamics of party development; a description of party anatomy at one point in time; and an elaboration of the relations of a political party and its environment.

Not that Ostrogorski was willing to state only these sybarite empirical passions. He was not, most definitely. Empirical knowledge, for Ostrogorski as for so many Western students of parties, was only as good as the supports it provided for liberal democratic institutions. In our terms, Ostrogorski was clearly concerned with *a* goal-based, empirical theory. Much of his analysis, as will be shown in detail, deals with what political parties should be. Reality he roundly damned and disregarded. However, spotty knowledge of empirical regularities left Ostrogorski filling in very broad gaps indeed.

Hence Ostrogorski's legacy was essentially a utopian theory—despite his concern with reality—and this legacy was disowned for the most part only by students like Duverger and Eldersveld. They, unlike Ostrogorski, more successfully safeguarded their analysis from their desires by in-

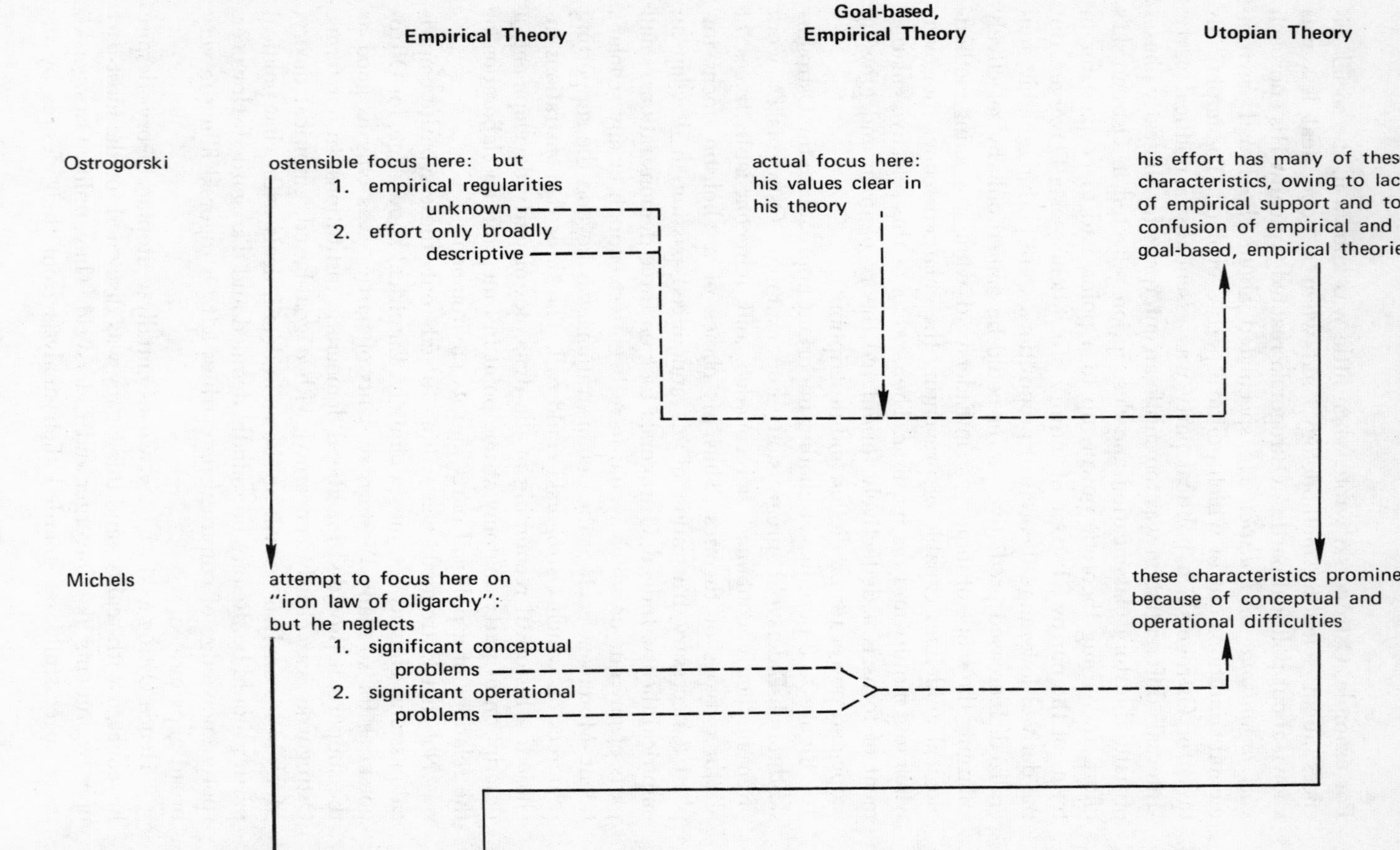
Empirical Theory
Goal-based, Empirical Theory
Utopian Theory
Ostrogorski
ostensible focus here: but
1. empirical regularities unknown
2. effort only broadly descriptive
actual focus here: his values clear in his theory
his effort has many of these characteristics, owing to lack of empirical support and to confusion of empirical and goal-based, empirical theories
Michels
attempt to focus here on "iron law of oligarchy": but he neglects
1. significant conceptual problems
2. significant operational problems
these characteristics prominent, because of conceptual and operational difficulties

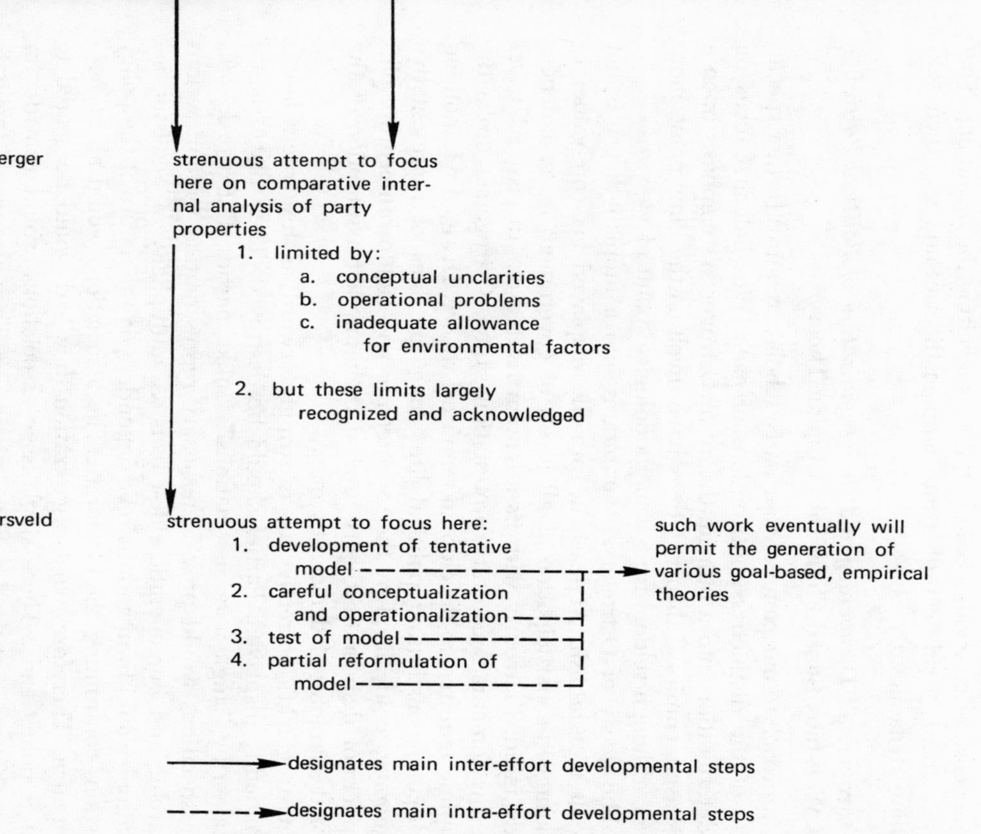


FIGURE XI.3 Research on Political Parties and Types of Theories.

creasing their concern for nominal and operational definition within a delimited study-universe.

Figure XI.3 is worth looking at closely from one other vantage point. Note that only Eldersveld's attention to empirical theory will eventually permit the development of goal-based, empirical theories. And no doubt of it, goal-based, empirical theories have a compelling attractiveness and significance. All the more reason to absorb the methodological moral implied by Figure XI.3. As that figure reflects, failure to respect the crucial role of empirical theory and its underlying methodology has an onerous cost, often enough paid but always awaiting the incautious. That onerous cost is a subtle sliding into utopian theories and into their self-fulfilling dynamics.

### A. Ostrogorski's *Democracy and the Organization of Political Parties:* A Well-Intentioned Flight Into Utopian Theory

Our approach to our panel of four party scholars requires further specification of the distinctive contributions of each. We shall first focus on the deterioration into a utopian theory of Ostrogorski's emphasis upon a goal-based, empirical theory. Others have dwelt on the same point, more or less, although seldom from a methodological point of view.

The decay of Ostrogorski's ambitions into a utopian theory is not difficult to establish. At least, he proudly displayed his core-value: to encourage the participation at all levels of government of an independently minded citizenry with its attention riveted on "the issues."[11] Despite his sometimes contrary protestations, then, Ostrogorski broke the discipline required to develop an empirical theory. His goal was nothing less than reconstituting political life along the lines of representative democracy, as idealized by the seventeenth- and eighteenth-century philosophers of democratic theory around their implicit assumption of the rational character of democratic man.

Ostrogorski's corrective is as straightforward as his core-value is prominently displayed. Parties should be destroyed. Their place should be taken by "single-issue associations." Unlike parties, Ostrogorski tells us, associations would provide necessary representation without serious oligarchic and bureaucratic side-effects. A multiplicity of one-issue associations would form and dissolve depending on the nature of the policy questions confronting the electorate. The associations would all be non-permanent. Therefore, what organization they had would be geared to limited policy ends. These single-issue associations would provide for policy-oriented, "rational" political discussion. They also would facilitate the rise to positions of power of a "natural elite," i.e., those most knowledgeable concerning policy questions and most willing to actively champion specific issues. If such changes were adopted, Ostrogorski contended, corruption and tyrannical control of party organizations over governmental leaders and over an unwary and overburdened citizenry all would be eliminated. No small clique could control the party machinery, that is, because of the impermanence of associations. Political man could therefore focus on "the issues."

Detail can be added to Ostrogorski's prescription without essentially changing the outline above. Table XI.2 conveniently does the job. His

**TABLE XI.2 Ostrogorski's Views of Parties, Existing and Proposed**

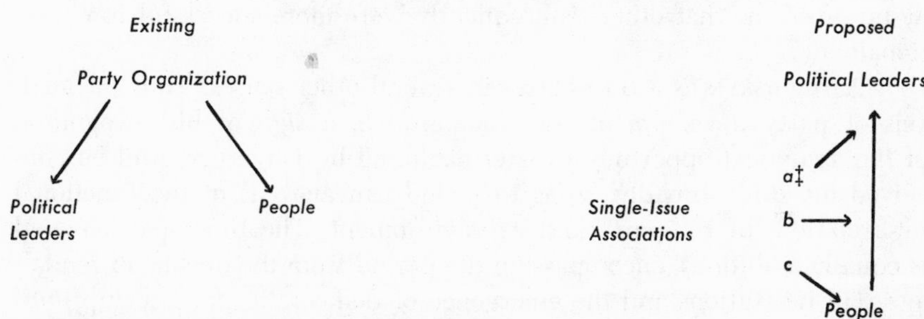


N. B. Arrows denote influence channels.
‡a, b, and c are single issue associations, or spontaneous, temporary uprisings led by the most interested and most knowledgeable citizens. Resolution of issue signifies death of association.

*Background Setting*

1. Party organizations rose to meet needs of an expanding electorate to serve as linkage *between* mass and political leadership.
2. Political and economic demands emanating from industrial revolution and extension of suffrage beyond citizen's capacity to master.

*The Problem*

1. Party organization superimposed its control over an indifferent citizenry; government leaders are also dependent on the party organization for election and are therefore subservient to it.
2. Party organization seeks only profit; the common good suffers.
3. Independence and quality of public office-holders declines; although democratic formalities still are observed, their substance is increasingly eroded.

*The Solution*

1. Eliminate political parties.
2. Transfer functions of parties to temporary associations concerned with *a* policy issue; associations are non-permanent and dissolve when an issue is decided.

*Anticipated Results*

1. Corrupting influence of party is neutralized.
2. Participation in public decision-making by an informed citizenry is stimulated.
3. "A natural elite," i.e., one characterized by interest and ability, rises to power through leadership on policy issues.
4. Democracy is returned to pursuing twin goals of "Reason" and "Liberty."

utopian bias is patent in his neglect of the question of how political parties are to be wiped out, and how single-issue associations are to be restrained from parlaying success on one issue into attempts to exert influence on other issues.

Despite its methodological centrality, Ostrogorski's utopian approach must be balanced off against other features of his work. Although his utopian preoccupation inhibited subsequent work, his contribution still formed an important link in the chain of progress in the empirical study of parties over the years. For example, Ostrogorski's volume notably describes party evolution and stresses the pathology of party anatomy. In these two areas he is representative of the natural-history stage of inquiry on parties. His prime contribution, then, was in isolating analytic problems that others subsequently were more successful in operationalizing.

Ostrogorski was a trail-blazer in several other senses. Thus his analysis of party development was comparative, a sign of his recognition of the analytical opportunities later exploited by Duverger. And he conceived his study broadly, so as to include an analysis of the functional interrelations of the party and its environment. The time span covered is equally ambitious, encompassing the period from the decline of feudal-agrarian institutions and the emergence of democratic practices up until the end of the nineteenth century. The countries chosen for analysis, England and the United States, represented the most advanced of democratic societies. And finally, although his focus is on party organization, Ostrogorski gives extended treatment to social and economic changes such as industrialization that parallel the growth of parties. This inclusive approach accounts for the characterization of Ostrogorski's work as *holistic*.

Such factors suggest Ostrogorski's methodologically scrupulous conscience. There is some evidence, indeed, that Ostrogorski wished to keep separate his comparative research on party structures and his policy recommendations. The portions of Ostrogorski's analysis dealing with party evolution and anatomy are intended by him to be empirical. His explicitly goal-based emphasis comes in the later stages of his presentation when he articulates a theory of democracy, and when he details the standards that the citizens and the institutions of the society must meet in order to make the democracy viable. He concludes that the party organization, the key agency in linking the people with the government and in achieving long-run democratic goals, is demeaning the level of public conduct and corrupting the fibre of the society. At this point, he introduces his "single-issue associations."

That Ostrogorski's methodological conscience failed him in the end reflects the formidable challenge facing any scholar in the natural-history stage of analysis. When little is known about a topic, the researcher may take on the impossible task of developing all aspects of the subject matter. Or he may elect to focus on one aspect of the topic without being able to place it within any broader and more meaningful framework. Ostrogorski chose the more ambitious line of inquiry. His experience constitutes a warning. Regardless of how impressive or extensive his scholarly groundwork, moreover, Ostrogorski has the misfortune to be best remembered for the speculative note on which he ended his study. This suggests that the methodological consciences of Ostrogorski's fellow professionals were less scrupulous than his own.

### B. Michels' Political Parties: An Exercise in a Universal Particularism

Ostrogorski basically struggled to clarify the relations between party organization and environmental forces. Michels, on the other hand, was primarily concerned with the effect of one structural variable on the operation of the organization. Hence our reference to a "universal particularism." He abstracted *party* as a concept, assigned it certain structural and ideological qualities, and then defined it out of existence when it failed to meet these criteria. As the party adjusted to its cultural setting and the forces within the society, its programmatic and associative purity were sacrificed and its very nature was transformed.

We hazard an introductory summary. Michels had little sympathy with empirically studying the functional role of the party in society. He was more concerned with analyzing the extent to which organizational arrangements facilitated the realization of the functions he had ascribed to it.[12]

Michels followed his particularistic orientation strictly. He confined the empirical phase of his study to the examination of one political party, the Social Democrats of Germany—reputedly one of the most democratically organized and most ideologically aggressive of the socialist parties on the European continent. And Michels enunciated one "iron law of oligarchy," a vague generalization identifying the conditions that made inevitable the emergence of a powerful autocratic elite within an organization. He advanced the "iron law" as a fact of organizational life with which any bureaucracy, or political party, must contend. Here he generalized universally one structural particularism.

We may build toward Michels' conclusion in his own terms. Michels made a number of value and empirical assumptions about parties. First, on the value level, he believed the party should be the embodiment of democratic practices. He argued that the institutions in any democratic society—*and in particular the political parties*—should be more democratic than the system of which they are a part. In practice, he found this not to be the case.

Second, on an empirical level, he assumed the party-as-an-organization was very similar to a military command unit. The latter, of course, has a standard characterization. It includes a well-articulated hierarchy, unity of command, strict discipline, quick decision-making, and precise execution of orders.

Third, again empirically, Michels assumed that the party was an association of like-minded men committed to a common purpose. This assumption has two consequences. If broad segments of the electorate were to be wooed, then the ideology of the party would have to take on a secondary importance. Combining heterogeneous group interests into the coalition necessary for winning public office would be emphasized, and the required vehicle would be no more than an ersatz consensus on a jerry-built policy. Consequently, such a party would soon enough become committed to seeking power, not advancing principle. Then, Michels announces, the party would be transformed from a "party" into an "organization."

Michels reflected but did not reconcile a schizophrenia of the real and the desirable; and even less did he discipline the assumedly real with an empirical methodology. He believed that the leadership of an ideologically oriented party was duty-bound to seek fulfillment of the party's principles regardless of the cost to them or the group. Yet in the case of socialist parties, parliamentary caution had replaced revolutionary fervor. The objectives of the organization—i.e., expansion of its base, augmentation of its resources, and a strengthened position among a broader electorate—had come to over-ride the ideological principles of the party. These survival tendencies of The Organization induced a change from a party to an organization. If Ostrogorski sought to eliminate parties, then, Michels' goal was to prevent parties from becoming "organizations."

Michels did not hesitate to identify the fly in the ointment of party ideology. Figure XI.4 visualizes in simplified terms the emergence of an oligarchic elite within a party organization. Michaels argued that the size and complexity of modern societies imply a functional division of labor. Specialization in turn requires structure. Since the mass of the membership cannot exercise equal authority within that structure, specialists must be called upon to provide technical knowledge and expert direction. Once in power, party functionaries can use their expertise to gain growing control over communications, advancement, and other resources. The emergent leadership cadre, within broad limits, then becomes independent of its base. Psychologically, the masses more and more come to depend upon their leaders. Leaders thus may be seen as indispensable; at least they portray themselves as such. Instead of resent-

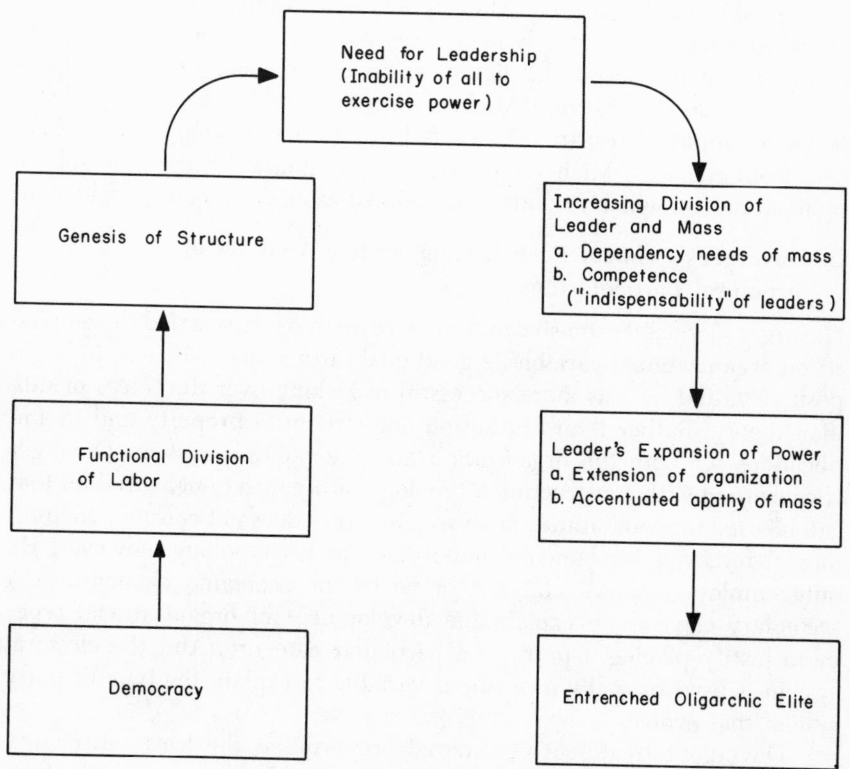


FIGURE XI.4 The Iron Law of Oligarchy.

ing the elite's self-aggrandizement, consequently, the mass bestow gratitude on the leaders in recognition of their superior abilities and their ostensible attempts to advance the interests of followers.

There are many deficiencies in Michels' seemingly plausible presentation. For example, his conceptualizations lack precision and his arguments permit numerous interpretations.[13] Chapter VI on community power suggests many of the difficulties with Michels' work. Thus: Is one of Michels' "elites" always an elite in the stratificationist's sense? And do "pluralist elites," if such there are, induce different organization styles and policies?

With all these deficiencies however, Michels substantially advanced the study of political parties. Unlike Ostrogorski, for example, he resisted giving his heart control over his head. Despite sharing Ostrogorski's essential goals, that is, Michels tenaciously clung to his empirical analysis. One of the factors supporting his resolve, no doubt, was his sharpened focus on the party organization. His analytical tether was shorter than

Ostrogorski's, and this gave Michels less opportunity to roam speculatively. And his focus certainly helped set a style for important subsequent research. Finally, despite his limited focus on the emergence of an independent leadership cadre,[14] Michels also suggested broader hypotheses to guide empirical research.[15] In this lusting after the more comprehensive from the less, Michels also provided a guide for the research on political parties which essentially developed after the Second World War.

## C. Duverger's *Political Parties:* Comparative Analyses of Structural Particularisms

Duverger sacrificed extensive for intensive analysis. He carried the emphasis on organizational variables a good deal further than Michels, to begin positively, and he was more successful in kicking over the traces of utopian theory. Rather than fixating on one structural property and its implications for both the organization and the political system, Duverger is concerned with constructing a typology of organizational variables that can be used for comparative analysis. Duverger does not consider environmental forces of fundamental importance to his typology, however. He only employs external cultural, or social, or economic elements in a secondary capacity to explain the development of organizational types or to justify placing a party in a particular category. And the electoral system is used basically as a causal variable to explain the type of party system that evolves.

Duverger's treatment of external properties is the least satisfactory component of *Political Parties.* This treatment deserves brief attention, because its inadequacy has aroused much controversy,[16] so much indeed as to obfuscate his more useful emphasis on organizational properties.

Duverger's treatment of external properties may be sketched briefly.[17] He argues that the formal electoral conditions under which the parties operate do much to define their character. He stresses the common co-existence of single-member districts, plurality elections, and two-party systems. He finds a similar co-existence of proportional representation and multi-party systems. Two general rules are hypothesized: (1) the simple-majority (plurality) single-ballot system favors the two-party system;[18] and (2) the simple-majority system with second ballot or proportional representation favors multi-partyism.[19] Building on this base, Duverger engages in a general and discursive treatment of the causal factors in party proliferation, develops some rudimentary measures of party strength,[20] enumerates the alliances into which parties can enter, and investigates the relation of the party to the governmental system.

Duverger's analysis of external factors is broad-ranging and unfocused. There is a lack of conceptual precision, clearly enough. Moreover, some of the interpretations presented are unsubstantiated, some naïve, and others simply dated. The exposition is plagued by many of the problems in terminology and development evidenced in his initial failure to provide a vehicle for distinguishing the cultural norms under which the party labors, as well as for distinguishing the function that the party serves within a regime.[21] The stage of social or political evolution of a country as well as the value commitments of the society also are neglected as variables of importance in organizational analysis. Such neglect complicates attempts to operationalize his concepts.

Duverger's construction of a comparative organizational typology, to move on, is a good deal more promising than his analysis of electoral factors. Duverger takes an unconventional approach to comparative analysis. He distinguishes among three constructs adaptable to the comparative analysis of bureaucratic institutions: the presence or absence of intermediate and independent groupings interposed between the party base and its apex; the organizational elements that characterize the local levels of the party bureaucracy; and the linkages, or articulation, among the component units in the party hierarchy. Table XI.3 details these distinctions.

**TABLE XI.3 An Outline of Selected Structural Properties in Duverger's Comparative Analysis of Organizations**

| *Party Structure* | *Party Membership* |
|---|---|
| *Structure: General* | *Inclusiveness* |
| 1. Direct | 1. Cadre |
| 2. Indirect | 1a. "Devotee" |
| *Structural Units: Local Level* | 1b. "Semi-mass" |
| 1. Caucus | 2. Mass |
| 2. Branch | *Intensity of Commitment* |
| 3. Cell | 1. Electors |
| 4. Militia | 2. Supporters |
| *Structural Cohesion: Articulation* | 3. Militants |
| 1. Party Linkages | *Nature of Participation* |
| a. Weak | 1. Community |
| b. Strong | 2. Association |
| 2. Direction of Linkages | 3. Order |
| a. Vertical | |
| b. Horizontal | |
| 3. Power Distribution | |
| a. Centralized | |
| b. Decentralized | |

The first differentiating property of party organization is the unitary or confederate nature of the structure. In parties with "direct structure," the membership constitutes the limits of the party, and no groupings are superimposed over this base. In other political parties, membership participation is filtered through other groups, e.g., trade unions. And these filtering groups constitute the actual components of a party of "indirect structure."

Second, Duverger also distinguishes parties in terms of the characteristics of local units. He describes four basic types of local organization:

1. the *caucus* is composed of a small, seasoned, nucleus of professionals who fulfill primarily electoral functions for the middle-class constituents they serve;
2. the *branch,* symptomatic of socialist parties, is characterized by a highly bureaucratized although democratic structure, a clear division of duties and responsibilities among its sub-units, a wide range of activities available to its membership, and a permanent organization;
3. the *cell,* found mostly in working-class Communist parties, is built around a selectively chosen, highly motivated, and ideologically committed nucleus of people drawn from an occupational base and is more adapted to the role of agitator and provocateur than that of electoral agent;
4. the *militia,* a Facist invention modeled after military units, employs militaristic symbols, strict training procedures, rigid discipline, an emphasis on obedience and strength, and a veneration of the physical in general.

Duverger's third basic property—"articulation"—focuses attention on the manner in which the units of the party are bound together. Usually there is some form of hierarchical structuring, quite frequently paralleling the structure of the state. An incoherent collection of groupings, factional rivalry, and the presence of indistinct and fluid organizational ties are all indicative of "weak" articulation. "Strong" articulation is characterized by progressive levels of organization, clear differentiation of membership, and acknowledged channels of communication and control. Articulation also has *direction.* It may be vertical, that is, relevant to the subordination of one unit to another. Or articulation may be horizontal, as when units at the same level are joined. Virtually all party organizations combine the two in some measure, although Communist and Fascist parties discourage horizontal articulation. Organizational analysis should be designed to indicate the degree to which one or the other prevails. Centralization and decentralization are distinguished from, and related to, articulation. These two concepts refer to the extent to which power is distributed among the various levels of the party hierarchy and among its component units.

Duverger complements these structural properties by emphasizing differences in party membership. One major difference focuses on polar extremes. The "cadre" party is composed of small groups of individuals concerned with supervising elections and campaigns and maintaining contact with candidates; the "mass" membership parties are dominated by the idea of "inclusiveness." The mass parties incorporate into the organization as much of the electorate as is willing to join, even if such broadening dilutes doctrinal education. Beyond such all-inclusive mass parties, Duverger distinguishes "semi-mass," "devotee," and "cadre" parties. The devotee party is more open to members than the cadre party, but it is less inclusive than the mass party. The semi-mass party is akin to the American experience of cadre-directed extensions of the party base (for example) through primaries.

The intensity of individual involvement in organizational affairs, further, can be employed to distinguish between "party identifiers." Duverger distinguishes three types. There are "electors," or those who merely vote for the party for a variety of reasons; "supporters," or those whose allegiance to the party goes beyond voting to include such things as financial contributions and membership in auxiliary organizations; and "militants," or those who command the party organizational apparatus and direct its activities.[22] The analytic challenge comes in defining the boundaries of each category, isolating the membership within the groupings, and developing the subtle relations between the three types.

In addition to the intensity of participation, Duverger raises some interesting possibilities for analyzing further the nature of participation within an organization. Three classifications, based on the links of solidarity within the party, are differentiated—the "community," the "association," and the "order." "Community" refers to a natural and spontaneous social group, well established, and with a strong traditional basis of support. An "association" is a voluntary group made cohesive by the moral or ideological beliefs of its members and committed to political action. An "order" (or "bund") is also a voluntary group characterized by a passion for involvement, a communion of feeling, and a dedication that exceeds any normal sense of membership. Duverger indicates that most organizations exhibit an overlapping of membership types. The researcher's problem is to determine which forms of social linkage predominate between member and institution.

These several differentiating properties represent a selective presentation of some of the more promising aspects of Duverger's conceptualizations. His typologies need refinement,[23] to be sure, and many problems are evident in his analysis.[24] But he advances his ideas as "provisional and hypothetical."[25] Accepted on this basis, they can prove useful. His approach is unconventional, and it can force a rethinking of organizational analysis.[26] At the very least, his categorizations are an advance over the less rigorous work of Michels and Ostrogorski. And his theoretical outline does provide a base line for scientific dialogue over party organizational analysis. In part, Duverger is responsible for stimulating a renewed interest in the systematic analysis of party organization within a comparative conceptual framework that presents opportunities for operational development and, consequently, testing.

### D. Eldersveld's *Political Parties:* Toward an Empirical Theory

Eldersveld builds upon the ideas of his predecessors, and begins the squaring of the apparent circle in their work. That is, he retains a narrow focus on structural properties of political parties, *a la* Michels and Duverger. And he complements that focus with an orientation toward the holistic approach of an Ostrogorski. That is, Eldersveld concentrates on describing the structural properties that constitute a model for empirical inquiry, but he makes adequate allowance for the interaction of the "organism" with its environment. Eldersveld's first structural property, for example, is the "adaptive," "clientele-oriented" nature of

**TABLE XI.4 Eldersveld's "Working Model" of Party Organization**

| *Structural Properties* | *Identifying Conditions* |
|---|---|
| I. Adaptive, Clientele-Oriented Organization | 1. Parties' "open" recruitment practices are dictated by power drives |
| | 2. Permissive recruiting leads to sensitivity to sub-group needs |
| | 3. Permeable, flexible organization |
| II. Coalitional Balance; Institutionalized Conflict | 1. Identifiable social, economic, and ideological sub-groups in party |
| | 2. Conflict among sub-group goals; sub-group and total party loyalties |
| | 3. Party emphasis on maximizing avoidance of conflict |
| III. Stratarchy | 1. Entropic communication |
| | 2. Authority and control formally separated; "strata commands" share power and responsibility |
| | 3. Reciprocal deference; emphasis on local unit importance |
| IV. Party Elites | 1. Plural career groups which are products of coalitional balances in party |
| | 2. Multiple career origins |
| | 3. Multiple career patterns |
| | 4. "Replacement," not "circulation" of elites |

the party organization (see Table XI.4). By this he means that the party organization does not restrict its membership. That is, it attempts to adapt its policies to the pressures exerted by the coalitions in the electorate it hopes to attract in order to win elections. In empirically testing his model, Eldersveld explicitly considers the characteristics of the population and the interaction of environmental forces as they affect the organization.

Many other feedback loops exist between our panel of scholars. Eldersveld aims at the same level of middle-range propositions that Duverger sought. While his work is the most methodologically impressive of the four analyzed, that is, it is far from a deductively formulated theory of party behavior. His work is impressive in its concern to define his concepts operationally and to test their validity. From his research, Eldersveld is able not only to assess the organizational vitality of the party, but also to identify empirically the functions performed by the organization. Like Michels, that is, he seeks the broader implications of structural properties. In his conclusion, he assesses the contribution of the organization to the democratic system of which it is a part. He thus explicitly returns within a different frame of reference to the implicit objective of Ostrogorski—a goal-based, empirical theory of parties.

The four structural properties of party organizations identified by Eldersveld relate to: (1) the strains on the organization produced by the needs of maintaining group solidarity in concert with the policy of broad social representation; (2) the pressure to achieve group goals and simultaneously accommodate sub-coalitional demands; (3) the bureaucratic ordering of sub-units; and (4) the profusion of party elites.

We will consider the four themes in turn. First, the need to adapt to group demands in order to achieve the party's ultimate goal—control of the resources of government—helps account for the frustration among organizational theorists with party analysis. As explained by Eldersveld:

> The party is a mutually exploitative relationship—it is joined by those who would use it; it mobilizes for the sake of power those who would join it. This porous nature of the party—at its base, sides, and apex—has tremendous consequences for individual perspectives and organizational relationships. Where adaptation is maximal, internal managerial control is difficult, factional pluralism multiplied, operational efficiency likely to be impaired, and goal orientations and ideological consensus highly non-congruent; where adaptation is minimal, such consequences for internal control and perspective will doubtless be less severe.[27]

Eldersveld's second structural property is related to the first. The adaptive nature of the party induces diverse and often contradictory pressures within the party organization. For example, sub-unit objectives may clash with those of the total organization. Such internal conflict must be handled with tolerance and flexibility for the arbitrary or divisive resolution of tensions would only weaken the party's attempt to maximize its appeal to the electorate.

Eldersveld borrows a concept—*stratarchy*—from Lasswell and Kaplan[28] to clarify the hierarchical structuring of subdivisions within the organization. This is his third distinctive property of the party. The diversity of structured sub-units, social groupings, and member orientations within the party organization is continually being weighed against a tendency toward a concentration of power in a self-sustaining elite. The resolution of the problem balances autocratic control of the party's resources against complete intra-party democracy. Power is diffused within the party organization according to "strata commands," i.e., the sub-coalitional units within the party hierarchy or discrete units outside the hierarchy that retain substantial independence. These strata commands remain as centers of responsibility and of conflict adjustment within the total organization. Moreover, the absence of effective sanctions in the hands of party leaders, the relaxed recruitment procedures, and loose membership criteria also contribute to a system of "downward deference" in the stratarchy. Higher-echelon units often defer to those at the local level, since the latter represent the real basis of the party's strength.

The fourth structural property of the party is the distinctive nature of the party *elites*. Eldersveld hypothesizes that the party leadership is plural, consisting of a series of distinct career groups. These elites do not form an integrated managerial class as feared by Michels. The career classes are a product of the sub-coalitional balance within the party. They can be analyzed in relation to their motivational, ideological, and social similarities, as well as in terms of their awareness of themselves as distinctive entities. Furthermore, movement within any given strata-command into leadership positions is not sponsored by those in power. The career classes are characterized by a "replacement" rather than by a "circulation" of elites, which contrasts with Michels' elitist ideas. That is, those in power can be dislodged by individuals with totally unsympathetic ideological perspectives. In identifying these career classes, data on comparative career origins, intra-organizational advancement, future objectives, socialization practices, individual motivations, and the representativeness of the multiple elites are relevant.

Eldersveld contends that these four factors form structural properties that—together with the goal of controlling the government—identify the distinctive nature of the political party as a social group. He tests these assumptions in an analysis of county, district, and precinct organizations in Wayne County (Detroit), Michigan. The basic analytic unit is the precinct, of which 87 out of a possible 2,007 were chosen by a random, stratified sampling procedure. In each precinct the leaders (147 in all) and a cross-sectional sample of the electorate (a total *N* of 596 were interviewed). In addition, socio-economic data and materials gathered in lengthy interviews with 70 upper-echelon party leaders—county chairmen, congressional district chairmen, congressional candidates, and a sample of executive board members in each congressional distict—were employed. This field work was executed in late 1956 and early 1957.

We cannot detail the wealth of Eldersveld's research design or his data, for he cuts a wide swath. His analysis has these four major components: (1) an elaboration of his model and its structural properties; (2) a survey of the "political perspectives" of party leaders; (3) an evaluation of the effectiveness of the party organization, as gauged through the introduction of several performance criteria; and (4) the tracing of relations between the party organization and the public it serves, which reflects a functional definition of the role of the party within the political system.

Settling for less than the whole analytical loaf in this case, however, will still prove useful. Let us focus on Eldersveld's treatment of the "political perspectives" of party leaders. Even a very small-bore illustration can suggest the family of methodological advances represented by Eldersveld's effort and thus reinforce the value of a focus on structural properties of the party. Moreover, Eldersveld's concern for conceptual and operational definition will be evident. Finally, the integrative potential of Eldersveld's approach for weaving together disparate research on parties also will be highlighted.

Conceptually, Eldersveld reflects his analytic concern in a strategic network of relations. He establishes his focus on diverse perceptions and values of party leaders, particularly as they relate to organizational effectiveness. The connection is commonly neglected in empirical research. To employ his own terminology, Eldersveld is ". . . primarily interested in the competition-maximization problem, and [in] seek[ing] to interpret the data in terms of the probabilities and actualities of the success of the party as an action group."[29] His analytical framework is defined by the structural properties of the conceptual model that introduces the study. In particular, Eldersveld stresses the efficiency of the organization as an integrative and adaptive structure within the community of beliefs with which it must contend.

Not that Eldersveld is content with the global insight. The political perceptions and values he stresses fall into five categories: (1) The leader's perceptions of the goals of his party, the relative priorities of these goals, and his commitment to them; (2) the leader's ideological perspectives and the degree to which they are compatible with follower views; (3) the leader's motivation for continuing in politics, including the needs thereby satisfied and the rewards being sought; (4) the leader's role-perception, or the manner in which political leaders characterize the demands implied by their office; and (5) the leader's perceptions of the complex interplay between the party and its total environment.

Eldersveld's *Political Parties* also reflects a concern with operational definition that helps restrain his analytical ambitions from overtaxing his data. Although the details cannot be set down here, the public nature of Eldersveld's operations are clear (for example) in his treatment of "ideology."[30] He is primarily concerned with the *direction* (liberalism or conservatism) of policy views, the *intensity* of commitment to policy stands, and the *congruence* of ideological perspectives of the different organizational groupings within the party. Respondents in Eldersveld's cross-sectional survey were asked to indicate the extent of their interest in the happenings at the local level, the national level, and the international level *per se* and also in various areas of foreign and domestic policy. Specific issues were presented to the respondents to test the intensity with which they held their opinions, their perceptions of the government's involvement in the issue, and their perceptions of the extent to which the two political parties agreed with their own position. The questions asked of the party leaders were similar.[31]

The public nature of Eldersveld's operations implies some important advantages. Consider only two points. First, such operations permit various approaches to checking apparent regularities in the data. These approaches include: specifying intervening variables to determine the consistency of relations; establishing the ability of specified "laws" to account for increasingly comprehensive sets of relations; and so on. Appropriate intervening variables in Eldersveld's study include: the hierarchical level of the organization; party affiliation; indices of policy agreement; leaders' and followers' opinions; saliency of ideology; socio-economic characteristics; and career aspirations. These variables are used singly and in various combinations to bring into sharper relief the implications of the data. Second, the public nature of Eldersveld's operational definitions permits integration of his results and those of others, to note but one positive feature. Thus related topics have been explored in research designs by, among others, Stouffer in his nationwide study,[32] McClosky in his analyses of convention delegates,[33] and the Survey Research Center in their samplings of presidential electorates.[34]

The fruits of Eldersveld's approach to nominal and operational development may be illustrated briefly. For example, McCloskey had urged earlier the proposition that lower levels of Republican party leaders held attitudes on political issues that were similar to those of the lowest levels of political leaders among the Democrats.[35] Persons in top party positions in the Republican party differed most sharply on the same issues from the low-level Democratic leaders, he also reported. Eldersveld's results demand a close comparative analysis of his and McClosky's concepts and operations. That is, Eldersveld reports more ideological diversity among party leaders. Figure XI.5 crudely depicts Eldersveld's ranking of officials

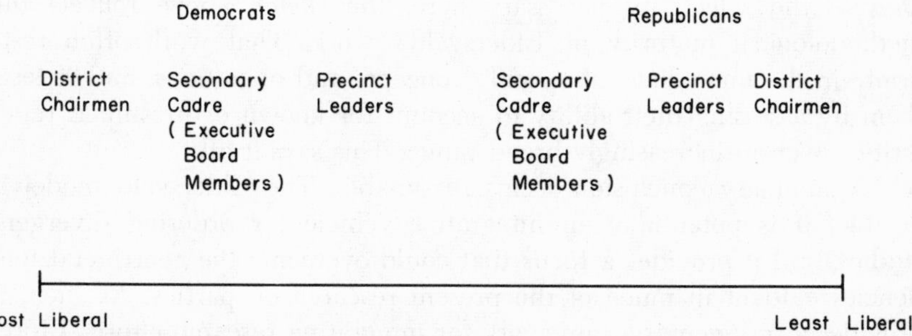

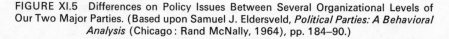

FIGURE XI.5 Differences on Policy Issues Between Several Organizational Levels of Our Two Major Parties. (Based upon Samuel J. Eldersveld, *Political Parties: A Behavioral Analysis* (Chicago: Rand McNally, 1964), pp. 184–90.)

of political parties at three distinct levels, utilizing a continuum of most-least liberal on policy issues. Eldersveld's data do not directly refute McClosky. They do add a dimension to the ideological analysis of party elites that bears further investigation. Only public operational definitions will facilitate that investigation.

Such findings cast a large interpretive shadow. For example, the data sharply reflect the "serious limits to ideological control," particularly in the slippage between upper and lower levels of organization. Large minorities of party officials at all levels did not know or did not follow the "party line." Consequently, for example, many precinct leaders retained their posts even though their ideological positions were different from those of the top leadership. Eldersveld concludes typically, supporting a major conclusion with much detail. He notes:

> . . . though conformity to the party line may seem to have some value, the 'deviants' were tolerated and nonconformists promoted. . . . Apparently, the top elite nucleus could not obstruct their mobility aspirations despite ideological nonconformity. Above all,

> the sub-coalitional diversity in ideology which the party must and did tolerate is obvious. We have here, then, concomitant with evidence that ideology is influenced by party associations, evidence also of great ideological diversity, autonomy, nonsocialization, dilution, and dissent. The party machine is no monolith, co-opting and coercing a homogeneous and unique ideological leadership. Pressure to conform exists. But the party gladly embraces, and freely associates with, a most ideologically conglomerate set of potential supporters and activists. From the bottom to the top, the party welcomes, and rewards, the ideological deviant.[36]

Despite the selectivity necessary here, the sketch above reflects the methodological maturity of Eldersveld's work. That work often rests firmly in the immediacy of specific concepts and operations, and it tests them by assessing their ability to account for known or presumed regularities over an increasingly broad range. This says it all.

A summary conclusion seems reasonable. The Eldersveld model is flexible, it is potentially an integrative vehicle for ordering divergent studies, and it provides a focus that could overcome the centripetal tendencies evident in much of the present research on parties. As such, it provides a rudimentary framework for integrating research efforts. Moreover, along with the previously presented works (especially Duverger's), it can serve to trigger ventures in theorizing in an area otherwise marked by conceptual torpor.

## III. CONCLUSION

There have been some encouraging indications in recent years of a more sustained and sophisticated methodological attack on the phenomena of parties. Given a conceptual schema and a common focus to guide research efforts, the next decade or so may witness the systematic accumulation of an integrated body of knowledge sound enough to meet the standards of scientific relevance. The value of a conceptual focus on party organization allows for the accumulation of a coherent body of systematic and variable data; it permits asking the "proper question;" and it provides the focus necessary for the methodological developments that will take the study of parties out of the province of the amateur and the dilettante and into the realm of the scientist. This chapter details the progress toward just such a focus, sketches some of its research fruits, and waits for more abundant harvests.

Possibilities along these lines have already been illustrated by party researchers who have adapted problems of relevance in broadly conceptualizing the organization techniques and methodology appropriate to empirical research. As noted, McClosky and his associates have surveyed the ideological perspectives of that "party elite" who became convention delegates.[37] He has also utilized a nationwide survey to probe for ideological differences between party leaders and the electorate.[38] And Lester Milbrath has approached levels of affiliation in terms of psychological attributes, with results suggesting that much can be done on the psychology of party affiliation.[39] Moreover, Renate Mayntz has used participant-observation to study internal party operations in Germany.[40] And Schlesinger has propounded an "ambition theory" that does serve to focus on the availability of offices, in addition to procedures in recruitment for elective and organizational positions.[41] Finally, for our purposes, others have attempted to develop indices of achievement to judge the impact of the party organization at the local level.[42] These studies do indicate exploratory veins that can be profitably developed. Basically, however, they exist in conceptual isolation from one another and from previous work. Consequently, they, as is the case with most of the research in the area, represent uneven contributions to empirical knowledge.

## NOTES

1. *Theory* here is used in a general sense. The term includes deductive and non-deductive theories, quasi-theories, typologies, and models. All impose some order on observations and at least suggest relations that need to be explored.

2. One piece of work that does attempt to draw the common assumptions out of some of the major works in the field and place them within a logical framework is David Braybrooke's "Some Steps Toward a Formal Theory of Political Science" (New Haven, Conn.: Yale Univ. mimeographed, 1955). Other noteworthy contributions to a broad analysis of approaches to the study of political parties include Avery Leiserson, *Parties and Politics* (New York: Knopf, 1958); and Neil A. McDonald, *The Study of Political Parties* (Garden City, N.Y.: Doubleday, 1955).

3. The normative debate over party responsibility in the late 1940's and early 1950's demonstrated the negligible amount of "hard" empirical data available about the party organization and its actual performance. The basis for the controversy was the Report of the Committee on Political Parties of the American Political Science Association, *Toward a More Responsible Two-Party System* (New York: Rinehart, 1950).

4. Maurice Duverger, *Political Parties* (New York: Wiley, 1963), p. xiv.

5. *Ibid.*, pp. xiii–xiv.

6. Frank J. Sorauf, "American Parties and the Scholar: The Last 30 Years," Paper presented at Meeting of American Political Science Association, September 4–7, 1963, p. 3. Revealingly also, discussions of political parties are conscientiously avoided in assessments of the impact of the scientific method on the discipline. Such books as Herbert J. Strong (ed.), *Essays on the Scientific Study of Politics* (New York: Holt, Rinehart & Winston, 1962), and Austin Ranney (ed.), *Essays on the Behavioral Study of Politics* (Urbana: University of Illinois Press, 1962) illustrate this omission.

7. Samuel J. Eldersveld, *Political Parties: A Behavioral Analysis* (Chicago: Rand McNally, 1964), p. 4.

8. These points are developed in Leiserson, *op. cit.*, pp. 48–50.

9. Consult Frank J. Sorauf, *Political Parties in the American System* (Boston: Little, Brown, 1964), pp. 154–55 and especially his general discussion in Chapter 9.

10. M. I. Ostrogorski, *Democracy in the Organization of Political Parties,* 2 vols. (New York: Macmillan, 1902).

11. Ostrogorski's proposed reforms are more explicitly developed in a somewhat revised work: M. I. Ostrogorski, *Democracy and the Party System in the United States* (New York: Macmillan, 1910). Interpretative essays on Ostrogorski can be found in: Max Weber, "Politics as a Vocation," in H. H. Gerth and C. Wright Mills (eds.), *From Max Weber: Essays in Sociology* (New York: Oxford University Press, 1958), pp. 105–11; Austin Ranney, *Doctrine of Responsible Party Government* (Urbana: University of Illinois Press, 1962), pp. 113–33; and S. M. Lipset, "Introduction" in M. I. Ostrogorski, *Democracy and the Organization of Political Parties,* 2 vols., edited and abridged by S. M. Lipset (Garden City, N.Y.: Doubleday Anchor Books, 1964), pp. ix–lxviii.

12. Robert Michels, *Political Parties* (New York: Dover, 1959). Interpretative analyses of Michels are available in: C. W. Cassinelli, "The Law of Oligarchy," *American Political Science Review,* 47 (September, 1953), 773–84; John D. May, "Democracy, Organization, Michels," *American Political Science Review,* 59 (June, 1965), 417–29; Philip Selznick, "The Iron Law of Bureaucracy," *Modern Review,* 3 (January, 1950), 157–65; James Burnham, *The Machiavellians* (New York: John Day, 1943), 135–70; and S. M. Lipset, "Introduction" in Robert Michels, *Political Parties* (New York: Collier, 1962), pp. 15–39.

13. Cassinelli, *op. cit.*, pp. 778–79.

14. Michels showed a preference for the writings of Pareto and Mosca and some of his most provocative ideas are in elite theory. For an introduction to his later thinking, consult Robert Mi-

chels, *First Lectures in Political Sociology* (Minneapolis: University of Minnesota Press, 1949). Some of his contributions have been clarified and their operational significance developed by Harold D. Lasswell, Daniel Lerner, and C. Easton Rothwell, *The Comparative Study of Elites* (Stanford, Calif.: Stanford University Press, 1952); Donald R. Matthews, *The Social Background of Political Decision-Makers* (Garden City, N.Y.: Doubleday, 1954); and Joseph A. Schlesinger, *How They Became Governor* (East Lansing: Michigan State University Press, 1957). The best analysis of the application of elite theory to the study of party organizations can be found in: Dwaine Marvick, "The Middlemen of Politics," in William J. Crotty (ed.) *Approaches to the Study of Party Organization* (Boston: Allyn and Bacon, 1968), pp. 341–74.

15. Michels' ideas have provided a fruitful frame of reference for many investigators. In general, the "iron law" has proved resilient. Serious research illustrates what can be done using Michels' approach. For a description of the conditions under which oligarchic leadership does not emerge, see Seymour M. Lipset, Martin Trow, and James Coleman's investigation of the competitive two-party politics of the International Typographical Union, *Union Democracy* (Garden City, N.Y.: Doubleday Anchor Books, 1962). For one example of an organization in which the "iron law" is operative, consult Oliver Garceau, *The Political Life of the American Medical Association* (Cambridge, Mass.: Harvard University Press, 1941). Michels' arguments, besides their obvious value in elite analysis, can be profitably incorporated into the theoretical developments of others. See Philip Selznick, "An Approach to a Theory of Bureaucracy," *American Sociological Review*, 8 (February, 1943), 47–54; and Alvin W. Gouldner, "Metaphysical Pathos and the Theory of Bureaucracy," *American Political Science Review*, 49 (June, 1955), 496–507.

16. Consult Alfred Diamant, "*Les Partiques Politiques*," *Journal of Politics*, 14 (November, 1952), 731–34; and Aaron Wildavsky, "A Methodological Critique of Duverger's *Political Parties*," *Journal of Politics*, 21 (May, 1959), 303–18.

17. Another important attempt to devise a conceptual schema for comparative party analysis has been made by Sigmund Neumann, "Toward a Comparative Study of Political Parties," in Neumann (ed.), *Modern Political Parties* (Chicago: University of Chicago Press, 1956), pp. 395–421.

18. Duverger, *Political Parties*, p. 217.

19. *Ibid.*, p. 239.

20. One of the more interesting of these descriptive categorizations distinguishes parties on the basis of a scalar dimension of party strength. In order, the classifications are: parties characterized by a "majority bent," that is, those that either command a majority or are capable of acquiring one in the normal swing of the electoral cycle; "major parties," or those unable under ordinary circumstances to obtain the power to rule but those who are *always* important factors in coalitions; "medium" parties, a hybrid classification consisting of parties more influential than the impotent minor parties and displaying some bargaining impact in coalitions; and "minor" parties, that is, those personality-dominated or permanent minority parties that have a negligible following and that operate on the fringes of all competitive electoral systems. *Ibid.*, pp. 281–99.

21. In other writings, Duverger makes adequate allowance for a diversity of environmental forces. See his analysis of political parties in France during the period 1947–1952, "Public Opinion and Political Parties in France," *American Political Science Review*, 46 (December, 1952), 1069–78.

22. Duverger suggests that provisions should be made for a fourth group intermediate between supporters and militants. These are the "cadre-men" who constitute a circle wider than the militants and who are more intensely involved than the sympathetic supporters. *Ibid.*, pp. 90–1.

23. Aaron Wildavsky imposes some ordering on Duverger's ideas in "A Methodological Critique of Duverger's *Political Parties*," *op. cit.*, pp. 313–14.

24. Alfred Diamant, "*Les Partiques Politiques*" pp. 731–34. Others disagree

in principle with Duverger's attempt to formulate a theory of parties. The critics include G. E. Lavau, *Partis Politiques et Realites Sociales* (Paris: A. Conlin, 1953).

25. Duverger, *Political Parties,* pp. 422, xiv.

26. Much work on party organization has relevance to Duverger, although not all of it is attributable to his influence. Frederick C. Englemann, "A Critique of Recent Writings on Political Parties," *Journal of Politics,* 19 (August, 1957), 423–40.

27. Eldersveld, *op. cit.,* pp. 5–6.

28. Harold Lasswell and Abraham Kaplan, *Power and Society* (New Haven, Conn.: Yale University Press, 1950), pp. 219–20.

29. Eldersveld, *op. cit.,* p. 180.

30. *Ibid.,* especially Chapter 8.

31. *Ibid.,* Appendices A and B, pp. 547–602.

32. Samuel A. Stouffer, *Communism, Conformity, and Civil Liberties* (Garden City, N.Y.: Doubleday, 1957).

33. Herbert McClosky, Paul J. Hoffman, and Rosemary O'Hara, "Issue Conflict and Consensus Among Party Leaders and Followers," *American Political Science Review,* 54 (June, 1960), 406–27; and Herbert McClosky, "Consensus and Ideology in American Politics," *American Political Science Review,* 58 (June, 1964), 361–79.

34. Angus Campbell, Philip E. Converse, Warren E. Miller, and Donald E. Stokes, *The American Voter* (New York: Wiley, 1960), and Converse," The Nature of Belief Systems in Mass Publics," in David Apter (ed.), *Ideology and Discontent* (New York: The Free Press, 1964), pp. 206–61.

35. McClosky, Hoffman, and O'Hara, *op. cit.*

36. Eldersveld, *op. cit.,* pp. 218–19.

37. McClosky, Hoffman, and O'Hara, *op. cit.* For a related study at the state level, see Thomas A. Flinn and Frederick M. Wirt, "Local Party Leaders: Groups of Like Minded Men," *Midwest Journal of Political Science,* 9 (February, 1965), pp. 77–98.

38. McClosky, *op. cit.*

39. Lester W. Milbrath, *Political Participation* (Chicago: Rand McNally, 1965).

40. Renate Mayntz, "Oligarchic Problems in a German Party District," in Dwaine Marvick (ed.), *Political Decision-Makers* (Glencoe, Ill.: The Free Press, 1961), pp. 138–92.

41. Joseph A. Schlesinger, *Ambition and Politics* (Chicago: Rand McNally, 1966), and Schlesinger, "Political Party Organization," in James G. March (ed.), *Handbook of Organizations* (Chicago: Rand McNally, 1965), pp. 764–801.

42. Peter H. Rossi and Phillips Cutright, "The Impact of Party Organization in an Industrial Setting," in Morris Janowitz, (ed.), *Community Political Systems* (Glencoe, Ill.: The Free Press, 1961), pp. 81–116; and Cutright, "Activities of Precinct Committeemen in Partisan and Non-partisan Communities," *Western Political Quarterly,* 17 (March, 1964), 93–108 and Daniel Katz and Samuel J. Eldersveld, "The Impact of Local Party Activity upon the Electorate," *Public Opinion Quarterly,* 25 (Spring, 1961), 1–24. See also William J. Crotty, "The Political Party and its Activities," in Crotty, (ed.), *Approaches to the Study of Party Organization, op. cit.,* pp. 247–306.

## xii

# Some Leading Approaches Methodologically Viewed, V: Re-Orienting Voting Studies Around "Sciencing" and away from "Counting"

The analysis of voting behavior has come to symbolize in Political Science the prototype of scientific research, and as such it has become both deity and demon. Proponents may acknowledge the problems and difficulties of making the effort, but they see research on voter decision-making as the first large-scale and serious approach to "sciencing" political phenomena. And no one can deny that the phenomenal area has experienced a remarkably swift and cumulative development. In the relatively short period of two decades, four major works on voting behavior—*The People's Choice* (1944, 1948), *Voting* (1954), *The Voter Decides* (1954), and *The American Voter* (1960)—each a logical extension of that which preceded it, were published. The four studies constitute major methodological and substantive extensions of our knowledge.

Critics, on the other hand, see voting studies as mere "counting," as a kind of barefoot empiricism. The massive but uneven additions to the literature of the voter's decision-making process at least provide an eminently visible target for any critic. And the very scope and swiftness of research developments provide the critic with ample opportunities to point with scorn.

This chapter acknowledges both the deity and the demon in the study of voting, and it focuses directly on how we may maximize the former and diminish the latter. Our immediate purpose is to illustrate the case of the critics. The longer-run goal is to integrate their criticisms of value into specific directions for the scientific development of the study of voting.

## I. CONTRA "SCIENCING" THE BEHAVIOR OF VOTERS: A REACTION DIRECTED AGAINST "COUNTING"

Illustrating the critical case against the analysis of voting behavior should sharpen our evaluative senses before we take a chapter-and-verse approach to the literature. In the round, voting studies represent to some the evils inherent in adapting empirical procedures to an eminently normative sphere, the guidance of democratic government. Directly or indirectly, voting research represents a foray into the very heartland of political philosophy. At least, the research has been accepted as such by the "philosophic know-nothings"—those primarily concerned with restricting major topics of governance to the insights of the traditionally oriented political philosopher.

Walter Berns well represents the critical school of thought in taking vigorous exception to voting studies pretty much *sui generis* in *Essays on the Scientific Study of Politics.*[1] A few vignettes from Berns' assessment of voting research illustrate both the argument and the argumentativeness of many normatively oriented political scientists. Generously, Berns allows that the "study of voting behavior is altogether proper, provided the purpose of voting is not forgotten in the formulations of the questions asked in the study." But beyond this point, Berns' allowable science takes on arbitrary form. That is, he has very definite notions of that "purpose of voting" which alone is capable of making "altogether proper" the study of voting qua behavior. "Democratic elections are one way of deciding the political question of who should rule and of what should be the character of that rule," he begins. Derivative conditions tumble forth. One "test of an electoral system" becomes the extent to which it is "democratic, that is, the extent to which everyone is permitted to participate in the choice." Another test—"perhaps the decisive one"—becomes "the quality of the men elected to office," since their selection is the "primary purpose" of elections. And this requires inexorably that voting studies be concerned with the "quality" of individual voters, on which "the quality of the men chosen depends, in part."[2]

"Altogether proper" voting studies consequently must meet strict conditions. "Proper" electoral research must deal with the "character" of democratic government, the "quality" of participants and representatives, as well as the factors influencing the outcome.

Berns evidences a minimal appreciation of empirical methodology and a distorted impression of its application. Only minimal appreciation of methodological requirements, for example, can explain Berns' restriction of his science of voting behavior. For he restricts his "altogether proper" study to one goal-based, empirical theory, and that developed around the core-value of maximizing the "quality" of elected officials. In this he is his own worst enemy. For such a restriction is just the one likely to preclude the development of the empirical theory of voting upon which any goal-based, empirical theory must be based.

In addition, Berns has a rigid view of the limits of the applicability of empirical methodology. He approaches the position that the very nature of scientific research confines it to superficial questions in politics. More expansively, that is, he observes that a scientific approach to political phenomena has neglected the more fundamental concerns of individual motivation and the functional relevance of the voting act for the society. At least inferentially, he also accuses the researcher of being incapable of investigating such questions. Why people vote as they do, Berns sees as a question "related to the purpose of voting." But voting studies do (and perhaps, must) neglect the derivative issues that Berns considers crucial: "the extent to which voters act with view to the common good and the extent to which they act intelligently." But these are the very issues which Berns sees as the bête noire of the science of voting. Avoiding these issues relegates the study of voting to mere counting, and not particularly useful counting at that. Berns characterizes the response of the "modern political scientist" in revealing terms. He notes that:

> His response is to ask questions the respondents can, and perhaps do, answer accurately (such as their age, sex, education, religion, and voting choice) and to report their answers with statistical exactitude. The result is the sacrifice of political relevance on the altar of methodology. The questions asked and pursued are determined by the limit of the scientific method rather than by the subject matter, which is voting or, more specifically, the purpose of voting. They prefer exact, statistical answers to less exact, politically relevant answers.[3]

Berns confuses methodological rigor with substantive sterility in an analytically disarming way. That available research reflects little concern with identifying the "common good" or with isolating the factors that distinguish a genuine from a spurious interest in the common good is undeniable. These are concerns of the nominalist in political science, of course, on which much effort has been lavished. Moreover, the early fixation on demographic variables in voting research reflects convenience rather than some methodological desideratum. But there is evidence that voting researchers could not win the day, whatever they did. Curiously, that is, Berns would have it both ways. When broader questions of democratic theory are related by the researcher to his empirical findings,

Berns rejects this breach of ethics as a naïve and unworthy intrusion into a complex area. In discussing Berelson's chapter on "Democratic Practice and Democratic Theory," in *Voting* for example, Berns writes:

> The authors' [Berelson, Lazarsfeld, McPhee] failure to take classical democratic theories seriously in their haste to suggest its "revision . . . by empirical sociology" . . . is only an aspect of their failure even to begin a penetrating consideration of problems of modern democracy. Ignoring these older thinkers [J. S. Mill, Rousseau] and the questions they raise, the authors of *Voting* confine their discussion to *trivialities* and present conclusions that might very well be wholly false.[4]

Interpreting the attempt by the authors of *Voting* to place their findings within the context of classical theory and democracy as a return to the "outmoded notion of political health,"[5] Berns asks rhetorically whether it is possible to refute the Great Thinkers of antiquity without giving serious attention to what they had to say. And why should the notion of "political health" be superior to other teachings?[6]

The differences in perspectives between the utopian philosopher and the empirical scientist shimmer through Berns' criticisms. The one poses the great problems associated with man's attempt to rule himself; the other attempts to piece together a picture of the identifiable forces that lead to a discrete act; and the slightest neglect of one by the other makes it unlikely that the two perspectives will reinforce one another as they ought.

Given his frame of reference, Berns' assessment of the voting studies comes as no surprise. He rejects as rigid constrictions the operational and conceptual restraints laboriously developed in such major works as *Voting* and *The Voter Decides*.[7] He is further exercised by the lack of concern in voting behavior research with the "political," the implicit rejection of traditional philosophic concerns, the failure to examine the quality of decision-making, and the inability to specify standards of citizenship.[8] Worse still, Berns charges, the bare empirical findings deny the rationality of man.[9] Thus does Berns run the risk of rejecting the data gleaned from research on voting behavior because it conflicts with his values, and thereby endangers the achievement of that which he values. Unflattering as any findings about the nature of democratic man may be in the light of traditional philosophic assumptions, in short, congruence with one's preferences hardly is the criterion of scientific validity. Moreover, such illegitimate rejection of empirical findings may inhibit the eventual development of a goal-based, empirical theory that would serve Berns' needs. This theory would be rooted in man's contemporary condition, but it also would be oriented toward achieving a loftier state.

Like many political scientists, Berns is angered because he sees voting studies as intruding into an area of classical concern and also as contributing little to *the* important questions.[10] Because the voting studies operate on scientific assumptions, their value for his purposes he believes to be very limited. "Thou shall not sit with statisticians, or commit a social science."[11] Berns and the school of thought which he represents accept this dictum.

To be sure, some of Berns' vehemence is well-founded. The methodological criteria outlined at the beginning of this book, for example, support significant criticisms of current research on voting behavior. When Berns stresses vague conceptualization, methodological rigor mortis, and the inability or unwillingness of many researchers to place their findings in a framework of broader theoretical relevance, he can often count this chapter as friend. Voting research has fallen prey on many occasions to counting, the indiscriminate reporting of observations. Moreover, the research often has failed to respect the methodological qualities associated with science.

But our ambitions here are broader still. While joining Berns in censure when the study of voters methodologically lapses into mere counting, this chapter also will indicate the ways in which "sciencing" can be advanced. The major studies and the types of voting analyses will be discussed, and the theoretical foundations of the four principal works will be analyzed. Our special concern will be the demands of developing a middle-range theory with predictive and descriptive capabilities. Finally, some potentially useful avenues for future research will be explored.

## II. THE SEQUENTIAL DEVELOPMENT OF VOTING RESEARCH

Like all of Gaul, research on voting behavior can be divided into three parts.[12] Each category in Table XII.1 represents a progressive methodological advance in voting research. The studies in Category I—exemplified by the exploratory work of Rice and the more sophisticated analyses of Key—seek measures of change within gross electoral units. The goals are to determine the direction in which events are moving or to isolate forces beyond the immediately observable data that will assist in describing and explaining. Available aggregate data are generally utilized, which restricts analysis to large categoric or areal units. Such restriction has advantages. Field research costs are minimized, time demands are less severe, and important macro-level problems can receive attention. V. O. Key's work, particularly—especially when used with techniques of data collection such as personal interviews—illustrates the valuable contributions that can be made to understanding political topics.

**TABLE XII.1 Three Categories of Voting Research: Summary Comparisons of Characteristics of Representative Studies**

| Category | Type of Study (Examples) | Analytic Emphasis | Data Base | Year of Field Research | Theoretical Perspective |
|---|---|---|---|---|---|
| I | *Aggregate Analysis* | | | | |
| | Rice, *Quantitative Methods in Politics* (1928) | Macro-Level: Gross Analysis | Census data, roll-call votes, election statistics, Dartmouth College students, Grange members | Mid-1920's[a] | Discrete models, e.g., Spatial Distribution of Attitudes, Group Theory of Representation |
| | Key, *Southern Politics* (1949) | | U.S. South-election, socio-economic data, interviews political influentials | 1946–1949 | Pattern Model: Dynamics of One-partyism in American South |
| II | *Community Panel Studies* | | | | |
| | Lazarsfeld, Berelson, Gaudet, *The People's Choice* (1944, 1948) | Micro-Level: Restricted Analysis (Sociological, focus on SES, characteristics of categoric groups, etc.) | Probability sample, panel design, Erie County (Sandusky), Ohio | 1940 | Consumer Model: (Rational Democratic Man) |
| | Berelson, Lazarsfeld, McPhee, *Voting* (1954) | | Probability sample, panel design, Elmira, N.Y. | 1948 | Cleavage and Consensus in Democratic Society |
| III | *Nationwide Surveys* | | | | |
| | Campbell, Gurin, Miller, *The Voter Decides* | Micro-Level: Comprehensive Analysis (Social-psychological focus on perceptions and attudinal development in relation to group memberships, SES, etc.) | Probability sample, U.S. electorate | 1952[b] (1948) | Three-factor Theory of Voter Motivation (Candidate Appeal, Issue Orientation, and Party Identification) |
| | Campbell, Converse, Miller, Stokes, *The American Voter* | | Probability sample, U.S. electorate | 1956[b] (1952, 1948) | "The Funnel of Causality" |

[a]Series of studies over different time periods, including trend analysis of election data.
[b]Study employs data from previous election(s).

Work in Category I implies significant problems, however. Most important are the severe limitations on what can be done with the data. Unskilled analysts can produce tediously repetitive and even misleading pieces of work, given these limitations and the rigidities and simplifications they encourage. A sample of the minor voting works available in any journal in the field reveals a plethora of just such studies. They reflect the "counting" approach to electoral research.

Category II studies reflect a bittersweet combination of advances and disadvantages. These studies constitute a distinct advance over those in Category I in major senses. Their research designs encourage a flexibility with techniques and analysis not permitted by aggregate analysis. Consequently, the analyst may extend the gross uniformities of behavior made manifest in Category I studies and relate them to co-variants at the micro-level. That is, improvements in techniques of data collection—specifically via the panel study—make it possible to say something reasonably certain about the complex relations tying together the voter, his group affiliations, and his voting decision. Category II studies have their significant liabilities too. They generally fail to relate respondent behavior to specific group memberships. This is a failure of conceptual design. Moreover, virtually no attention is paid to the individual's perceptions of his environment or to the extent to which he psychologically interrelates external events to his voting decision. Psychological variables as they affect the respondent's electoral behavior then are obviously and significantly lacking. Finally, the Category II studies restrict their data-base to one community, and consequently, the conclusions of the analysis are problematic for any broader population.[13]

The studies in Category III constitute a breakthrough in methodology almost as dramatic as that between the studies in Categories I and II, difficulties notwithstanding. Four emphases characterize that breakthrough. First, Category III studies employ psychological variables in their conceptual designs to help explain voting decisions. Second, the data base is extended from the community to a probability sample of a national presidential electorate. Third, concerted attempts are made to establish the co-variation of the voting decision and group memberships of voters. Fourth, the research design breaks through the bounds of the conventional with important implications for the future realization of a true science. The search for dimensions of reality in Category III studies seems particularly significant, although caution is necessary. The conceptualization and operationalization of such aspects of reality as "obligation" ("sense of citizen duty"), ego strength ("sense of political efficacy"), and emotional commitment to politics (intensity of party identification) are cases in point.

We do not wish to prejudge the matter. Replicatory studies may establish that these conceptual-operational efforts do constitute actual dimensions of reality, in the sense of permitting the development of middle-range theoretical propositions and, eventually, of a deductive theory. Or replicatory studies may establish that different conceptual-operational pairs are necessary to account for the co-variations in nature. Whatever the outcome, the immediate significance is that Category III studies earnestly began the search for appropriate dimensions. This signaled a movement beyond reliance on merely available aggregate data, categoric groups, and psychologically undifferentiated voters. Much of Berns' criticisms, recall, assumed that such reliance was unprofitable although perhaps unavoidable in any "science of politics."

A summary conclusion may be made safely. The work of Campbell and his associates in Category III has not only incorporated the methodological advances perfected in the other approaches but gone well beyond them as well. The differences are evident in the sophistication of the research design, the more thorough conceptualization of the problem, and the type of variables emphasized in the analysis.

To some degree, of course, we have exaggerated tendencies toward differences in roughly describing the three categories. Distinctions between the categories are usually matters of degree. For example, Stuart Rice and V. O. Key utilized sociological variables—such as membership in categoric groups—in analyzing ideological perspectives or voting patterns in the American South. More complicated similarities also exist between research in the three categories. Lazarsfeld and his colleagues, like Rice and Key, employ aggregate data. And at least in *Voting*—like Campbell, Miller, et al.—Lazarsfeld and Berelson acknowledge that psychological considerations are important co-variants in voter choice. Campbell and others at the Survey Research Center mix all these approaches thoroughly. They even use what Rossi calls a "truncated panel design,"[14] roughly reminiscent of the panel techniques pioneered in the Category II studies by the sociologists at the Bureau of Applied Social Research at Columbia University.

## III. SOME CHARACTERISTICS OF VOTING RESEARCH

Our strategy of elaborating the four studies in Categories II and III—the core of this chapter—will be served by detailing several more characteristics of the research reflected in Table XII.1. Three characteristics receive particular attention. They include: the aggregate emphasis in studies of voting, particularly characteristic of Category I studies; the emphasis on the individual voter and his decision within a group environment that typified research in Category II; and the more comprehensive study of the voter-in-context that characterizes studies in Category III.

To begin, studies in Category I have left a clear and lasting legacy. The earliest—and still the most common—approach to electoral analysis employs aggregate data.[15] This came as no accident. Voting statistics, census materials, and other aggregate data are relatively easy to obtain and to apply. Moreover, such data may well be "harder" than comparable information obtained from surveys. That is, the reliability of the data is not subject to the same vagaries of schedule design, sampling, interview bias, respondent set, integrity of responses, and coding which present very real problems in survey research. The cost in time and money is also minimized.

Social scientists were quick to capitalize on such advantages of aggregate data. Stuart Rice's *Quantitative Methods in Politics* (1928) remains one of the better representations of the earlier efforts with aggregate data.[16] Rice's contribution lies in isolating topics of political importance and in adapting statistical techniques to them. V. O. Key also exemplifies the best of the aggregative approach. Key focused on major issues of political relevance and then molded the materials at his command so as to reveal the forces underlying the phenomena he was examining. The products—like his *Southern Politics* (1949)—often constitute milestones in political analysis.[17]

Aggregate data can be valuable, particularly in the natural-history stage of empirical inquiry. For example, aggregate data have proven useful in isolating major regional and social divisions in the voting population.[18] These data also have been skillfully employed in the analysis of specific elections or campaigns in various localities.[19] The primary complementary values of aggregate analysis are two. First, it can indicate differences among analytic units, e.g., categoric groupings or areal units. Second, aggregate analysis can indicate changes over a period of time, e.g., the important differences in the Democratic vote in the pre-1932 period and the post-1932 period. The two approaches are complementary, but more in principle than in practice. Trend analysis in various jurisdictions to reveal shifts in the electoral cycle over long periods of time is promising, for example, but it has not been fully exploited.[20]

But aggregate analysis also has significant liabilities, particularly in the development of theoretical propositions of the middle range and beyond. The explanation for any observed differences in aggregate analysis must be supplied by the analyst. This permits a good deal of discretion that can prejudice the results. For example, historical interpretations, shrewd guesses, or evaluations of differences must be employed to connect observations of aggregate tendencies to one of the potential alternative descriptions and explanations of the relations underlying the phenomena. What is more limiting, the analysis of large units can only indirectly reveal or explain the behavior of individuals.[21] Lest the point be over-extended, we acknowledge that aggregate data may prove useful in developing empirical theory. For example, cross-cultural analysis can help indicate the major relations among variables and thus provide the framework for more intensive investigations.[22]

Category II studies are particularly noteworthy for boring through gross uniformities in aggregate data. They focus microscopically on the individual. Rather than employing categoric groupings or general trends, that is, the analytic unit becomes the individual and, to a degree, the individual in relation to his group memberships. The data were gathered by a panel design—i.e., a repeated interviewing of the same respondents[23] —which utilized a probability sample of the electorate within a limited geographical locale. Data analysis was primarily within a sociological frame of reference. The sharpening of focus and scientific advantages permitted by the panel design were purchased by sharply increased costs of time and money, as compared with those of aggregate analysis.

*The People's Choice* marked the initial departure from the limitations of aggregate analysis. Its authors envisioned the study as an extension into voter decision-making of many of the findings and techniques of consumer research. Their assumed voter was a relatively rational individual advancing his own self-interest by voting for the candidate or party most likely to realize the goals he considered important. Consequently, the research design conceived the mass media as conduits of information and the campaign period as a time span within which the decision was formulated. The underlying expectation was that the voter would weigh the various sales campaigns of the parties and the candidates. Sometime late in the campaign, he would decide where to invest his vote. To test their assumptions, Lazarsfeld and his associates innovated the panel design. They interviewed the same 600 or so respondents during the 1940 presidential campaign on seven different occasions from the end of May until just after election day in November.

The most important substantive contributions made by *The People's Choice* refuted the assumptions that guided the research, mute testimony of the self-correcting nature of the design. The voting decision is *not* analogous to consumer decision-making, basically as Table XII.2 indicates. Three points of refutation are most central.

1. "Brand-name loyalty" in politics—the reaction of the voter to the party label—is a very powerful force. In fact, the study suggested the important role of the emotional, or the non-rational, in politics. "Suggested" must be emphasized. For the implications of the position were

**TABLE XII.2 The Relative Contributions of Four Major Voting Studies**

| Works | Emphasis: *Sociological* | Emphasis: *Social-Psychological* |
|---|---|---|
| Exploratory (Initial Venture) | *The People's Choice*<br>1A. three functions of campaign<br>2A. unintentional focus on "non-rationality" of voting decision<br>3A. "two-step" flow of communication via opinion leaders<br>4A. de-emphasis of role of mass media<br>5A. index of political predisposition<br>6A. theory of "cross-pressures"<br>7A. use of panel technique | *The Voter Decides*<br>1C. emphasis on values of respondent<br>2C. attention to perception, attitude development, within politically relevant frame of reference<br>3C. identification of three prime elements in vote analysis (party identification, candidate appeal, issue orientation)<br>4C. psychological theory of attitudinal conflict ("cross-pressures")<br>5C. development of analytic tools, scales of political efficacy, civic duty<br>6C. use of probability sample, nation-wide electorate |
| Developmental (Systematic Extensions of Earlier Work) | *Voting*<br>1B. broad attempt to relate empirical findings to democratic theory<br>2B. informal communications channels emphasized<br>3B. SES and group considerations in voting clarified<br>4B. roles of "hereditary vote," and party allegiance sketched<br>5B. community influence ("breakage effect"), political institutions treated<br>6B. "position issues," "style issues" dichotomy<br>7B. "life-history" of political issues developed ("political gateway" concept) | *The American Voter*<br>1D. "funnel of causality"<br>2D. elaboration, weighing of three prime elements (3C) influencing vote<br>3D. partisanship, choice, and timing of vote decision<br>4D. comparative political involvement, turnout, non-voting<br>5D. party identification: development, importance, influencing conditions<br>6D. ideology and attitude structure<br>7D. status polarization<br>8D. social, economic, group influences and the vote<br>9D. categorizations of elections (maintaining, deviating, realigning) |

not elaborated until *Voting;* and the forces underlying the decision awaited a clearer identification in *The American Voter.* Correspondingly, the attention lavished on the mass media demonstrated only that they were of marginal importance. The study did identify what it referred to as a "two-step flow" of communication.[24] That is, as a first step, some individuals on *all* socio-economic levels were interested in politics and consumed campaign information from the mass media, the candidates' statements, and party releases. These "opinion leaders" digested information and restructured it within their own frame of values. As a second step in the flow of communication, central persons passed on processed-information to those with whom they came in contact. In this manner, opinion leaders served as intermediaries for disseminating information.

The interpretive transmission of election events identify these individuals as pivotal "opinion leaders" in the electorate.

2. The political campaign did not fulfill the functions envisioned by the authors. Three possible effects of the campaign could be distinguished. Campaigns could "activate," or "reinforce," or "convert." In practice, the campaign did activate and partly reinforce latent predispositions favoring one party or the other. The 1940 campaign induced little conversion, however. Only about 8 per cent of the electorate changed their minds during the course of the campaign. The campaign, then, was clearly not a period during which the voter, relatively unencumbered by previous loyalties, made an "independent" decision on the candidates. Indeed, roughly 50 per cent of the voters "knew" in May for whom they were going to vote in November.[25] A selective attention to campaign propaganda simply served to convince many voters of the correctness of their original decision.

3. Few individuals delayed their decision until late in the campaign. The individuals who did fit this pattern of behavior fell into two groupings: the apathetic, who constituted the largest portion of the eventual non-voters; and the "cross-pressured." In developing their theory of the "cross-pressured" voter, the authors devised an Index of Political Predisposition intended to distinguish individuals disposed to support each of the two parties. The Index distinguishes categoric groupings based on three criteria, socio-economic status (SES), religion, and urban-rural residence. For example, a Catholic of high SES status would be a cross-pressured individual.[26] That is, individuals in the categoric grouping "Catholic" tend to be attracted to the Democratic party; but individuals in the categoric grouping "high SES status" tend to support Republicans.

Despite its inability to induce positive results, the conceptual focus on the individual qua political consumer absorbed the attention of the research team contributing to *The People's Choice*. Thus a "party machine" in the subject city went unrecognized until too late to influence research design or data collection. Only a compelling focus on the individual can explain this monumental neglect of a significant macro-factor relevant to the voting decision.

Category II studies are not like peas in a pod, however. *Voting*—a study of the 1948 election—indirectly extended the ideas and techniques of *The People's Choice*. The latter was a provocative but rudimentary work; and the analysis of the data in the former is much more thorough. For example, *Voting* admirably exploits some of the interesting but crudely developed findings in *The People's Choice*. Table XII.1 suggests the point. Less attention is paid to the media of communication and more to behavioral processes; and less attention is given to the individual and more to group phenomena. One particular stress is upon peer-group interaction, which signals the new emphasis on social processes and on the group. Other evidence exists of the attempt to emphasize the individual-in-context. Thus *Voting* included an analysis of community influence on the vote, via the notion of a "breakage effect." That is, a predominantly one-party climate in a community influences the "undecideds" to vote for the majority party in a greater proportion than chance expectation. In addition, the authors of *Voting* extended their conceptual design to account for such variables as policy issues, candidate personalities, and party organizational efforts as they affected the electorate. The distinction introduced in *Voting* between "style" issues and "position"[27] issues also has proved of analytic value.[28] Moreover, the volume gives attention to the hereditary nature of party affiliations and its effect on the vote. Finally, *Voting* concludes with two chapters—one on the psychology of the voting decision, and a second chapter by Berelson on the relationship between the findings of the two voting studies and classical democratic theory.

*Voting* extended a sociological analysis of electoral behavior during a *short time-interval* about as far as it could go. And although psychological variables are acknowledged to be important, the common assumption underlying both studies in Category II is unvarnished. As *The People's Choice* puts it, "a person thinks, politically, as he is socially."[29]

The analysis of the data in *Voting* does not recognize the limits of the design, however. Indeed, one of the prime criticisms directed against *Voting* holds that the analytic extrapolations go well beyond the data. Also, discussions such as that of party organization are by authors other than the principals, and are poorly integrated into the presentation.

Category III studies cast a larger and finer net than their predecessors, while retaining substantial similarities. *The Voter Decides* by Campbell, Gurin, and Miller, like *Voting,* was published in 1954, and similarly it helps usher in a new stage of the analysis of voting behavior. *The Voter Decides,* a brief monograph, is also similar to *The People's Choice.* It primarily indicates a new avenue of research, and it serves as a base for a later and more elaborate work. Both characteristics are understandable in terms of its dual ambitions: to enlarge the focus of research, and to increase the data base. First, a dissatisfaction with the sociological nature of the primary works in the field led to an emphasis in *The Voter Decides* on social-psychological variables during the 1952 election. For example, the authors introduced two measures—"political efficacy," nominally defined as a sense of mastery of and control over the political environment, and "civic duty," nominally defined as a feeling of obligation to participate in elections—as variables of importance in describing voter intent.[30] The authors also emphasized individual perception of candidates, issues, and political parties in structuring the political information received by individuals. Second, the design also extended the data base from the community level—with its restricted implications for broader electorates—to a nationwide probability sample, interviewed before and after the national election.

Drawing on their experience in 1948 and 1952, the Survey Research Center team conducted a more extensive analysis of the 1956 presidential election. The results appeared in *The American Voter* (1960). The volume is easily the most sophisticated and substantively valuable of the voting studies to date. That is, methodologically this work comes closest to meeting the three methodological criteria outlined at the beginning of this monograph. Substantively, it makes the greatest contribution of the voting studies. It provides much of the data needed for formulating the deductive theories that will help advance electoral research toward that shifting ultimate-product of an empirical science.

The debts of *The American Voter* to earlier research are patent, but so are its extensions of that research and its own innovations. Again, a nationwide probability sample of one campaign period—the 1956 presidential election—provided the data for the analysis. However, the data were treated within an inclusive frame of reference that encompassed (for example) election laws and formal vote requirements, regional and urban-rural population shifts, personality characteristics,[31] social groupings and social class, and agrarian political movements. The primary emphasis remained on the individual's perception of political stimuli. The study was conceptualized within a theoretical framework based on Kurt Lewin's "field theory,"[32] a vehicle for incorporating past political influences as they affected contemporary events. In addition, the volume developed analytic schema for categorizing future types of presidential elections and placed them within their over-all theoretical framework.[33]

The flavor and imagination of *The American Voter* can be gleaned from a few examples of its contributions to a meaningful framework for continued analytic efforts. The chapter on "membership and social groupings" is an exemplary model for original analysis and lucid development. The authors detail the theoretical parameters of the study; the potential influence of groups in political life is weighed; a series of specified groups are isolated for intensive analysis, including union members and their households, Catholics, Jews, and southern and non-southern Negroes; an index of group cohesion is devised and applied; the relative differences in electoral behavior between group members and non-group members and among the groups are compared; and some hypotheses are developed about the political salience of primary and secondary groups in politics.[34]

In analyzing the inter-relationship of social class and political behavior, in addition, the authors develop the concept of *status polarization.*[35] They use it as a gauge to determine the "intensity and extent of class identifications" in a society at any point in time.[36] The two Eisenhower elections exemplify periods of low status polarization; and the elections of Franklin Roosevelt in the 1930's represent periods of high status polarization.

Over-all, *The American Voter* is an impressive substantive and methodological advance toward a science of electoral behavior, particularly as it extends the lines of inquiry anticipated in *The Voter Decides*, but unfortunately its publication has introduced a period of unwarranted complacency into the study of voting behavior. In one sense, it has over-awed scholars with more limited resources. Yet there is a need for a theoretical extension of the results and basic assumptions in voter decision-making, as well as for the exploitation of a number of potentially valuable research avenues. The next two sections deal with these topics.

## IV. TOWARD A THEORY OF ELECTORAL BEHAVIOR: THE PATTERN MODEL AND THE DEDUCTIVE MODEL

Voting research patently is "going"; but it has a long way to go, and its progress will depend on what has gone before. Consider the distinction that Abraham Kaplan draws between *pattern models* and *deductive models.*[37] The two aid in appraising voting studies. One model characterizes the present stage of voting research; and the other provides methodological direction for the future.

The *pattern model* is more appropriate for early stages of social inquiry. Less formal than the deductive model, its emphasis is on developing a cognitive map of the relations among variables. An analytic unit is not known by its intrinsic properties, but rather through its position in a web of relationships. As Kaplan points out:

> According to the pattern model . . . something is explained when it is so related to a set of other elements that together they constitute a unified system. We understand something by identifying it as a specific part in an organized whole. There is a figure consisting of a long vertical straight line with a short one branching upwards from it near the top, and a sharp curved line joining it on the same side near the bottom. . . . We understand the figure by being brought to see the whole picture, of which what is to be explained is only a part. It is in this way that familiarity may come into play: the unknown is identified with something known, though not by way of its local properties but in terms of its place in a network of relations.[38]

Consequently, pattern models characterize the natural-history stage of scientific development, serving as a springboard for the development of theoretical propositions of the middle range and beyond.

The pattern model implies the dynamics of its own replacement. Research success in filling in the blanks in any pattern model expands that model. But the process cannot continue indefinitely. At some point, a more generalized theoretical structure must be developed. The pattern model is a valuable exploratory device, but it has limited predictive ability.

A deductive model is more rigid, in contrast, but it is also more powerful. The model characterizes advanced scientific stages. That is, it permits a more formal and logical ordering of data, and it facilitates prediction. The deduction model accounts for relations between variables in ways that are parsimonious and logically inevitable. Kaplan explains that:

> The various types of explanation . . . are differentiated by the nature of the general statements that serve, together with the particular antecedent conditions, as premises for the explanatory deductions. It is not the premises alone that explain, however, but the fact that what is to be explained follows from them. Only this following makes clear why something *must* be the case. A fact that *is* unexplained is merely contingent, and a law merely "empirical." The factor law just happens to be thus and not otherwise; there is no reason for it—or better, if there is a reason we do not know what it is. That we do not know is what is meant by saying that something is unexplained. The explanation shows that, on the basis of what we already know, the something could not be otherwise. Whatever provides this element of necessity serves as an explanation. The great power of the deductive model consists in the clear and simple way in which the necessity is accounted for.[39]

*The American Voter* develops the most explicit and most systematic statement of its theoretical ambitions, and it clearly casts its lot with the pattern model.[40] The evidence is unambiguous. First, its authors are more concerned that their concepts promote understanding rather than possess predictive capacities. Second, their design does not emphasize causal factors. The authors are content with illustrating the interrelations among variables. That is, the design does not determine whether Variable A is a cause or effect of Variable B, or whether both are the products of a third variable. Third, the authors employ a conceptual framework they label the "funnel of causality." Summarily, they caution their readers that: "We wish to account for a single behavior [voting] at a fixed point in time [election day]. But [that behavior] stems from a multitude of prior factors. We can visualize the chain of events with which we wish to deal as contained within a *funnel of causality*."[41]

The funnel of causality constitutes a pattern model. It relates a diverse set of factors that help explain the behavior of ultimate interest, the vote. The funnel can be visualized as a horizontal cone that extends through time, as in Figure XII.1. The variables that affect the ultimate decision are temporally ordered. For example, the political attitudes of the family and their contribution to conditioning the individual's political sensitivity occur initially, as it were, far back in the cone. Other variables affect other regions. Party identification, to illustrate, is more proximate to the behavioral outcome than are childhood experiences. And the specific issues, candidates, and the campaign operate even closer to the ultimate vote.[42]

Figure XII.1 admits a theoretical richness. The flow of movement in the funnel of causality is from $t_1$ to $t_4$, the latter representing the point at which the act being explained occurs. Over time, a continual processing of the factors relevant to the ultimate decision occurs. For example, $t_2$ and $t_3$ represent cross-sections of the funnel at specified points in time. The conditions of relevance at $t_2$ have been selectively focused at $t_3$, and so on. Point $t_4$ is an observable and definite act; $t_1$ is more diffuse. In actuality, $t_2$ includes all influences of relevance in influencing the decision. The authors of *The American Voter* also make a number of other distinctions in their pattern model useful for organizing their data. These distinctions are described by Keys 2–4 in Figure XII.1.

The application of the funnel of causality in *The American Voter* has major limitations, over and above those limitations always associated with pattern models. In effect, for example, the authors of *The American Voter* have abstracted for examination a cross-section of the funnel between $t_3$ and $t_4$, and much closer to $t_4$ or to the behavior they intend to explain. Relying on field theory, they assume that events preceding this point will be somehow reflected in their analysis. Obviously, this is a convenient but limiting assumption. In addition, the design neglects the decision's aftermath. To illustrate, the design neglects feedback into the funnel from the frustration of a vote for a losing candidate.

These and other problems with the application of the funnel of causality in *The American Voter* have formidable consequences and costs. The application tends to be static rather than dynamic; it is narrowly conceived; it stops at one point in time; and it does not account for effects of the voting decision on the voter at some subsequent time $t_5$. The costs are proportionately great. The specific influences that condition developing political perceptions and attitudes are only hinted at in gross tabula-

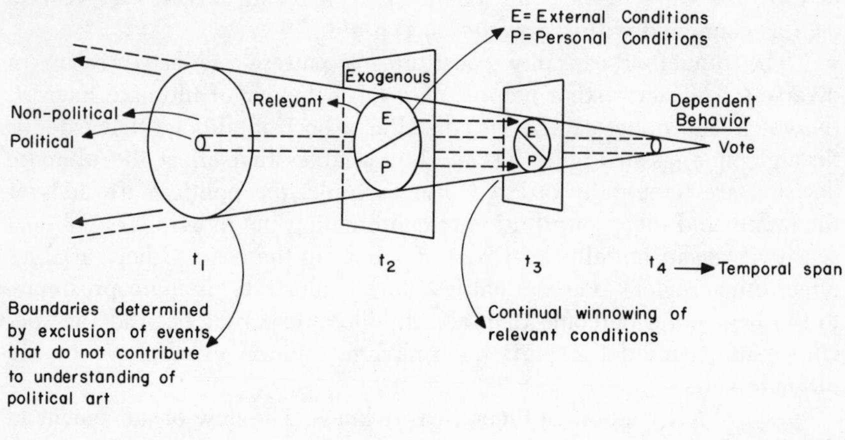


*Key: Ordering Dimensions in the Funnel*

1. Time—the temporal span is one way of relating events leading to the first decision. For example:

   $t_1$—can project backwards as far as necessary in time to include relevant political data, e. g., Civil War, Great Depression, condition behavior of some voters in any given presidential election.

   $t_4$—fixed date, election day.

   $t_2$, $t_3$—convergence of forces leading to vote decision at points in time prior to election, abstracted from funnel.

2. Distinction between *exogenous* factors and *relevant* conditions:
   a. exogenous factors—by definition not of theoretical interest, e.g., non-voting caused by flat tire on way to the polls.
   b. relevant conditions—of theoretical assistance in exploring dependent behavior, e.g., non-voting related to apathy, lack of attraction to either of candidates, strains on traditional party loyalty, etc., rather than environmental conditions over which actor has no control.

3. Distinction between *personal* and *external* conditions:
   a. personal conditions—events and conditions within the funnel of which the actor is aware.
   b. external conditions—events beyond the awareness of the actor, but of significance in understanding the actor's later political behavior.

4. Distinction between *political* and *non-political* conditions:
   a. political conditions—core of funnel represents political factors, determined by investigator's interest in them and their direct contribution to explaining dependent behavior.
   b. non-political conditions—utilizing same criteria, these factors not considered political, but still relevant, form shell around central core.

FIGURE XII.1 The Funnel of Causality in Voting Research.

tions, but these hints reek of significance. For instance, individuals from families with intense partisan identifications are sensitized to politics earlier and also form stronger and more lasting bonds to particular parties.[43] The specific developmental patterns await exploration.

A balanced condition emerges from such considerations. Research on electoral behavior has not reached the stage of scientific maturation that can develop a deductive model, but data generated by the pattern model will facilitate reaching this stage. To quote Angus Campbell: "It is often said that good theory leads to the discovery of new data, but it is probably no less valid to say that good data lead to the development of new theory."[44]

## V. SOME PATHWAYS OF FUTURE RESEARCH

The research on electoral behavior has focused on identifying the interaction patterns immediately preceding the vote decision, and it must be extended both backward and forward in the funnel of causality. Figure XII.2 indicates some of the forces of analytic importance that precede, and some of the consequences of, the vote decision. The major studies, however, have been narrowly conceived to explain only the individual's perception of immediate campaign stimuli and the extent to which these contribute to the decision. Even here the gaps are significant. The campaign itself has not been adequately investigated. Moreover, political institutions—the party organization and its operations, interest groups, the electoral setting in which the individual operates—have received little attention. In addition, the bulk of studies consider voter decision-making at the presidential level only. From this core future comparative research at many levels can build more general theories of political attitude formation.

The techniques and concepts of the studies on presidential voting research have not been extended to state and local analyses of voting behavior, a neglect which illustrates the research areas that need attention and the type of problems that can be investigated. With the exception of a few competent aggregative studies such as those by Key,[45] the atypical research is scattered and primitive. This neglect is puzzling for the most part. The proximity of the data and the institutional and socio-economic differences between localities and states provide the researcher with natural laboratories for exploring topics not extensively developed in the more inclusive studies, as well as for experimenting with new research techniques.[46] Research at the state and local level thus might reveal a greater sense of discrimination in party perception and an ordering and balancing of influences unlike those operative in national elections. Granted, the immediate analytic problems faced by any investigator may prove difficult. But regional and personal factors that are neutralized in a nationwide analysis might assume greater importance in state elections. Party identification also might prove less salient.

Moreover, the opportunities in comparative analysis for employing useful techniques also are numerous. For example, the local community permits experimentation with techniques, e.g., Agger and his associates' index of cynicism,[47] to tackle problems whose investigation would be awkward at other governmental levels. Similarly, an expansion of the "opinion leader" concept first advanced in *The People's Choice* and more fully developed in *Personal Influence*[48] is a manageable problem that would not unduly tax the empirical skills of the researcher.

Oppositely, however, the research on local electoral systems has been technique-poor and narrowly conceived to deal with specialized local problems. Methodologically and conceptually, the studies suffer. A few studies of local party organizations and their effects on municipal electorates[49] exist; and some research investigates the influence on community politics of particular types of electoral systems, especially in relation to non-partisan elections.[50] Over-all, however, electoral research on the local level has remained remarkably impervious to the advances pioneered by the Survey Research Center in their nationwide studies. The concern with psychological variables and the use of sophisticated research designs, particularly, have made no great headway in political research on community politics.[51]

Guides for filling the need for comparative studies at various levels of government do exist, fortunately. For example, Matthews and Prothro provide some guidance for such analysis in the development of their notion of "party image."[52] They observed divergent perceptions of the same parties by southern whites and negroes. Similar differences in perceptions of parties may also exist at national and local levels.[53] Such perceptual differences may be approached, for example, via the concept of "cross-pressures."[54] The concept was formulated within a sociological frame of reference. It postulates delay in decision-making and then either one of two alternatives, non-voting or voting. Actually, a number of other alternatives are offered by our electoral systems to the reluctant voter. He can abstain from voting at one level, and vote a straight party ticket for every other state and local office on the ballot. Or he can split his votes among the candidates of the two parties. States and localities provide laboratories for relating such alternatives to the notion of cross-pressure, opportunities that do not exist in such richness at the presidential level or the federal level alone.

Murray Levin's study of the 1960 gubernatorial race in Massachusetts suggests yet another approach to encompassing diverse campaign phenomena in comparative analysis. Levin's research design has significant limitations.[55] Essentially, however, he focused on the contenders in the party primaries and in the general election. Interviews of principals emphasized assessment of the strengths and weaknesses of their campaign strategy. The realism of the candidate strategies also was estimated. The criteria for judgment included the use of a random sample of the electorate to ascertain their evaluation of the various contenders, the issues they perceived to be important, and the factors motivating individuals to vote for or against any particular candidate. In sum, Levin's work combines the survey techniques of the national studies and a "political" framework, thus lessening the sting of the charge that the voting studies are essentially non-political in nature.[56] Such a research focus also compensates for the common emphasis on socio-economic variables.[57] To date, political institutions have not been adequately accounted for in electoral analysis.[58]

The computer simulation of campaigns to predict specific voter reactions represents another approach of value for developing a deductive theory of electoral behavior and for practical application. Simulation is a new field of exploration. How new may be dated exactly for all practical purposes. During the 1960 campaign, social scientists at the Massachusetts Institute of Technology engaged in simulating voter response to potential issues proposed by a candidate for office. The results of this Simulmatics Project were of value to the 1960 Democratic candidate for the presidency.

The dating of Simulmatics is not accidental. That is, electoral simulation depends on three conditions: a candidate must have a number of policy alternatives; relevant theory must be available; and data relevant to the model must be accessible.[59] These three conditions were first met in 1960. The candidates, of course, did have potential alternative strategies that they could pursue. *The American Voter* provided a theory of voter decision-making. And a series of 66 polls—covering the period 1952–1960 and including 130,000 different interviews on issues of civil rights, social welfare policies, and foreign affairs—provided the data base.[60]

The Simulmatics Project blended research and practice. The Project turned out a modest series of reports on the images of party candidates, the religious issue, the race question, and foreign policy. Whatever the focus, however, the purpose was to anticipate voter reaction and to influence strategic decision-making. Many of the calculations were projected from a data base employing information on only the years 1952–

1953, but the Project had many more aspects. The reports did have an impact on Democratic decision-making during the campaign and, in general, the experiment was successful. Prediction and application are dual values of the simulation of electoral behavior that help to break through the time-boundedness of the major voting studies. A re-analysis of the systematic accumulation of data on every presidential campaign since 1952 by the Survey Research Center also may help broaden perspectives on the factors influencing electoral decision-making.

Despite the opportunities, in sum, little has been done to exploit them in comparative electoral analysis. Generally, the data do not provide the consensus necessary even for a pattern model of local voting behavior. One example will illustrate the point. Boskoff and Zeigler interpret Dahl's analysis in *Who Governs?*[61] to mean that status polarization is not as important in local elections as it is in national elections. This is contrary to the burden of previous research. Boskoff and Zeigler themselves believe "... that the voter in local elections reflects more 'class awareness' than the national voter."[62] They indicate that the various indices of economic position—income, residential area, socio-economic status, and possibly occupation—correlate with voting phenomena in ways that suggest the relevance of "class."[63] This hypothesis had been generally accepted in urban electoral research. Given the design inadequacies of most existing research, however, the point must remain moot.

The lack of relevant data is quite general. For example, the phenomena associated with political participation in suburban politics are not well understood. More specifically, the relative salience of the locality vs. the core city in affecting political behavior has not been systematically examined. Similarly, participation in suburban political decision-making has not been extensively investigated. And the changes the newcomer undergoes in moving his residence from the central city to the suburbs also might be analyzed profitably. *The American Voter* has given this problem suggestive examination that could provide guidelines for appropriate research.[64]

A similar point holds if we enlarge our focus. That is, the discussion above has been primarily concerned with Stages C, D, and possibly B in Figure XII.2. Current research on political socialization promises to yield the data necessary for elaborating Stage A of the diagram and in setting the background for Stage B. This includes "direct" attempts of a government or a family[65] to indoctrinate its youngsters with a particular point of view. It also includes "indirect" political socialization, which occurs as the child assimilates attitudes and values from his observations of others and as he learns "types" of information of political relevance. In Stage A, the individual is sensitized to categories of knowledge that

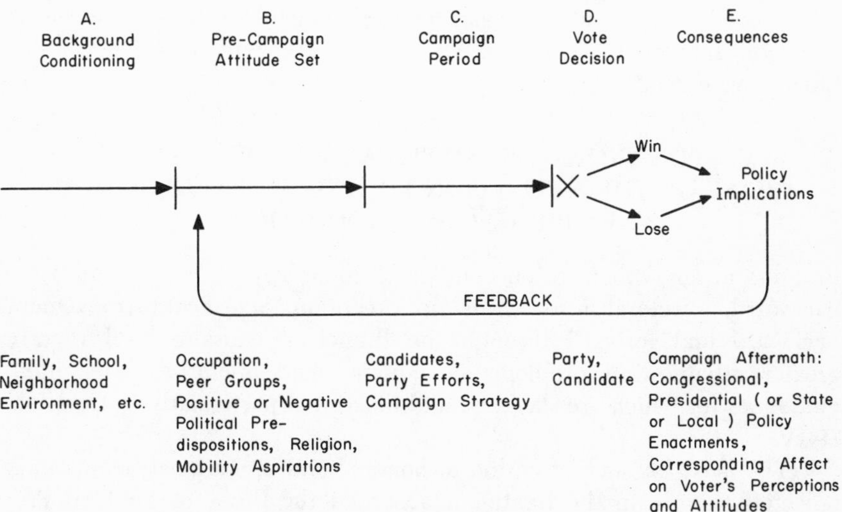


FIGURE XII.2 The Formation of Political Attitudes.

include cultural values, affective orientations toward politics and the political system, orientations toward instruments of tension management in the society, motivation to participate in varying capacities in politics, and information concerning the manner in which political institutions operate. Various agencies perform the socializing function with varying degrees of success. The most important socializing institutions are generally conceded to be the family, the school, and the peer group. The rich potential of the area is just beginning to be exploited, as by Easton, Hess, and Dennis[66] and Greenstein.[67] Adult socialization has received much less attention.[68]

Research progress also must be made in exploiting the E-Region in Figure XII.2. The Survey Research Center has expanded its initial concern with presidential elections to include the analyses of congressional politics. The research concerns problems in Stages C, D, and E in Figure XII.2, including the feedback process from E to B. Warren Miller and Donald Stokes[69] of the SRC have been concerned with the implications of policy positions both in conditioning the environment of the campaign and in providing through the election a communications channel between voter and representative. They also analyze the factors influential in the congressman's decision for or against specific measures in specified areas of policy concern—civil rights, foreign affairs, and social welfare legislation.[70] The conception of these studies is broader than the focus on voter decision-making in presidential campaigns and exemplifies the research needed to provide the basis for a more inclusive theory of electoral behavior. Inter-nation comparative research also will be a part of this broader research.[71]

## VI. THE INDEX OF POLITICAL PREDISPOSITION: A CASE OF THE ATTENTION TO, AND THE NEGLECT OF, EMPIRICAL METHODOLOGY

Progress in any sphere often consists of some steps forward, and some backward. Electoral research is no exception. Specifically, movement backward and forward through the funnel of causality will require greater attention to problems of nominal and operational definition, guidelines for which are sketched and illustrated particularly in Chapters II–IV.

The need for such attention to nominal and operational definition is reflected sharply in the treatment accorded the Index of Political Predisposition. That treatment flirts with the methodological guidelines for empirical science, takes those tentative first two or three steps forward, gains experience, and then retreats blushing but unconsummated.

Let us support this airy metaphor with specific detail. The Index of Political Predisposition was introduced in *The People's Choice*. That research assigned perhaps 25 per cent of the variance in voting decisions to the sociological variables focused upon.[72] The "greatest part" of this statistical relation, we are told, could be attributed to three factors: socioeconomic status (SES), religion, and urban-rural residence.[73] Eschewing various possible statistical tools, index numbers 1–7 were assigned to individual voters following the schedule in Table XII.3. In terms of their analysis, index numbers 1 and 2 should identify the "most Republican" voters; 6 and 7 the "most Democratic"; and individuals scoring 3–5

**TABLE XII.3a Schedule for Assigning IPP Index Numbers to Voters**

| *Socio Economic Status* | *Protestant* | | *Catholic* | |
|---|---|---|---|---|
| | *Rural* | *Urban* | *Rural* | *Urban* |
| A,B (High) | 1 | 2 | 3 | 4 |
| C+ | 2 | 3 | 4 | 5 |
| C− | 3 | 4 | 5 | 6 |
| D (Low) | 4 | 5 | 6 | 7 |

Source: From Paul F. Lazarsfeld, Bernard Berelson, and Hazel Gaudet, *The People's Choice* (2nd ed.; New York: Columbia University Press, 1948), p. 17.

should experience "cross-pressures," thereby meriting more mixed identifications as voters.

Conceptually and operationally, the Index (IPP) has questionable foundations. Conceptually, indeed, IPP was not thought by the authors to be a dimension of reality. Rather, IPP was a convenient device to test the generality of the pattern of results isolated. Hence the nominal definition of IPP is both relatively unspecific and questionable. Its lack of specificity may be illustrated easily. As the authors broadly explain: "The people with the best homes, furniture, clothes, etc., i.e., the ones with the most money, would be classed as A's."[74] Questions about the concept's validity also can be raised, although they cannot be settled here. Consider the difference between SES as "objective" and as "subjective." Despite their "objective" nominal definition, to suggest the point, the authors of *The People's Choice* recognize that "the identifications which people make in their own minds are more important in determining their vote than is their objective occupation."[75]

Questions about the conceptual specificity and validity make problematic the degree to which objective SES corresponds to a meaningful *something* useful for describing and predicting reality. When the face-validity of SES ratings was tested, measures of objective status, such as "occupation," helped little in accounting for more of the variance in voting decisions. On the other hand, subjective or attitudinal criteria differentiated in significant senses between individuals having the same SES scores. For example, identification with "business" or "labor" was one important attitudinal variable intervening between SES level and voting decision. Consider only the subjects rated C+ on SES. Only 38 per cent of those who identified with "business" voted Democratic. In contrast, fully 53 per cent of C+ subjects who identified with "labor" voted Democratic.[76] In short, specifying this one attitudinal variable would have sharply increased the power of IPP to predict outcomes. Curiously, the authors of *The People's Choice* made little further use of this type of subjective variable. Such use would have complemented the focus in *The People's Choice* on objective categoric groupings; and such use would have done much to expand the scope of their research. Just such subjective variables —identification with party, for example—led to the more recent and surer analytic ventures found in Category III studies.

Operationally, moreover, IPP rested on a problematic base. The operational grounds for determining a voter's SES were quite general, at least in the public record. We can only sample the operational difficulties. Thus we are told that: "Interviewers are trained to assess the homes, possessions, appearance, and manner of speech of the respondents and to classify them into their proper stratum in the community according to a set quota."[77] The operational difficulties are patent, especially in connection with inter-observer reliability. Whatever "set quota" means, in any case, the interviewers apparently had difficulty doing the job. The bulk of those rated (63 per cent) fell into SES category C. An operational refinement—introducing the factor of possession or lack of a telephone—in turn dichotomized this unsatisfactory clustering of cases into SES categories C+ and C−. Moreover, interviewers were instructed to rank highest those individuals with "money *and* family status"; next came those who qualify "on only one of these points"; and last came those "who had neither money nor a time-honored name."[78] Thus—although the ground rules were far from clear in the written record—family name and prestige were to be part of the operational definition of SES. And SES scores, in turn, were important components of IPP.

Derivative operational difficulties are great, both in principle and practice. In principle, the operational ground rules are unclear. Moreover, the operational definition makes some provision for subjective SES in family name and prestige. Nominal definition of SES, in contrast, fixated on objective SES. This is inelegant.

In practice, the difficulties of uneven operational definition were not avoided. Measures of the performance of raters making assignments to SES classes suggest the point. We are told that a substantial proportion of the panel sample in Erie County could not be assigned an SES level.[79] Moreover, the reliability of the observer assignments actually made was relatively low. Intra-observer assignments of the same cases correlated only +.8, which accounts for some 65 per cent of the variance in the assignments. When different observers rated the same cases, the correlation dropped to ".6 or .7."[80] These relatively low coefficients imply much room for conceptual-operational refinement.

Conceptual and operational difficulties aside, IPP seemed to touch some part of something vital in reality. Table XII.3 reflects the point. In

**TABLE XII.3b IPP as a Predictor of Voting Outcomes**

| *Index of Political Predisposition* | *Percentage of Vote* | |
|---|---|---|
| | *Republican* | *Democratic* |
| 1 | 74 | 26 |
| 2 | 73 | 27 |
| 3 | 61 | 39 |
| 4 | 44 | 56 |
| 5 | 30 | 70 |
| 6,7 | 17 | 83 |

SOURCE: Data from Paul F. Lazarsfeld, Bernard Berelson, and Hazel Gaudet, *The People's Choice* (2nd ed.; New York: Columbia University Press, 1948), p. 26.

brief, variations in IPP coincided with variations in voter allegiance. Although IPP obviously does not account for all cases, the record of 74–83 cases out of 100 is a formidable one indeed for social and political phenomena.

Although the authors of *The People's Choice* therefore conclude broadly that "social characteristics determine political preference,"[81] the social characteristics comprising IPP did no more than touch some part of something vital in reality. The limits of these three characteristics—SES level, religion, and urban-rural residence—may be suggested. The authors use IPP throughout the analysis, and success and failure exist cheek by jowl. For example, individuals who score as Republicans on the IPP and who changed their vote intention, return to the Republican party in a ratio of 6:1.[82] This is very positive support. However, Democratic changers scoring high on IPP break the pattern. Sixteen per cent of them go from Democratic intention to Republican vote; and 10 per cent go from Republican to Democrat. This indicates that IPP neglects variables of importance—intensity of attachment to the parties, perception of political involvement, motivation, and social reinforcement. The nature of the neglected variables is not obscure. When the May "undecideds" are classified by IPP score on a six-part continuum ranging from "strongly Republican" to "strongly Democratic" in regard to their October intentions, for example, results suggest the importance of the reliable party identification measures developed later by the researchers at the Survey Research Center. That is, those voters who incline toward one party usually end up declaring their support for that party's nominee. Although the *N*'s are small, the most pronounced rate of "crystallization" (a 3:1 ratio) is found at each end of the continuum, among those classified as most strongly supportive of one party or the other.[83]

In replications of the original IPP findings,[84] some methodological guidelines for empirical work have been violated and others respected. The research of Janowitz and Miller, who used survey research techniques on a national sample, illustrates both the progress and the limitations of the subsequent research. Janowitz and Miller rested their replication on the soundest of foundations. Replication was necessary to guard against the results of any study reflecting only the uniqueness of the population studied or the uniqueness of the conditions under which the study was conducted. The rationale for their study was uncomplicated, therefore. "Such comparisons of similar studies," Janowitz and Miller explained, "are essential to the progress of social research in that they guard against unwitting selection or exclusion of crucial variables in the studies."[85]

The two scholars imply the need to test the generality of any pattern model in empirical science. The IPP—being an index composed of separate personal characteristics of respondents, each of which had some individual relation to voting decisions—was such a model. As such, replication of that pattern was a necessary prelude to the task of developing a deductive model. The possible outcomes of replications are two: they might discard the pattern model; or they might develop a unique theoretical explanation of the pattern in a deductive model. The rationale of Janowitz and Miller differs basically in vocabulary only. "Each of the personal characteristics or attitudes included [in such analysis] has some explanatory value," they note. "Combination of the relevant correlates is undertaken, consequently, in order to increase the number of respondents whose behavior can be explained in terms of the selected characteristics." The approach has real limits, however, and it was these limits which Janowitz and Miller sought to test. "Theoretical considerations are not usually paramount in such a method of analysis, although the correlates selected for combination are usually both statistically related and logically plausible in broad theoretical terms."[86] Hence Janowitz and Miller relied on a national sample, rather than a community sample. And they used survey research techniques. This facilitated exploring the characteristics of individual voters who are aggregatively reflected in IPP analysis in the main.

The results of Janowitz and Miller's replication are mixed, if mixed has a variable and undefinable meaning. Verbally, Janowitz and Miller report moderately that "the IPP, although it has explanatory value, requires considerable refinement . . ."[87] The data reported give much less the better of it to *The People's Choice.*

Our interpretation of the replicatory findings as contributing to the scientific dialectic also must be mixed. Without arguing for the resurrection of IPP, we briefly note several significant methodological difficulties with the replication. Apparently minor issues will be neglected. For example, the samples for the replication are somewhat different, as judged along several dimensions,[88] but the differences do not seem significant.

First and most elemental, the reporting of results requires tentativeness. Consider the matter of voting versus non-voting. In accordance with IPP analysis, non-voters should be clustered in the middle ranges of IPP scores. Remember, the intermediate scorers are "cross-pressured," and one way of escaping a voting decision is to decide to stay away from the polls. Similarly, there should be significantly more voters than non-voters having IPP scores 1 or 2 and 6 or 7.

Relying on the data in Columns 1 and 2 in Table XII.4, Janowitz and Miller came to two conclusions about the generality of IPP in differentiating voters and non-voters. First, "differences between voters and

**TABLE XII.4 Two Ways of Viewing Janowitz and Miller's Data from Replication of IPP Pattern Model**

| | Janowitz and Miller Data (columns as percentage bases) | | | Our Recalculations (rows as percentage bases) | | | |
|---|---|---|---|---|---|---|---|
| | (1) | (2) | (3) | (4) | (5) | (6) | (7) |
| IPP Scores | Voters (per cent) | Non-Voters (per cent) | Total (per cent) | Voters (per cent) | Non-Voters (per cent) | Totals (per cent) | No. of Cases |
| 1 & 2 | 18 | 14 | 17 | 64.4 | 35.6 | 100 | 87 |
| 3 | 28 | 27 | 28 | 59.9 | 40.1 | 100 | 146 |
| 4 | 18 | 31 | 22 | 45.1 | 54.9 | 100 | 124 |
| 5 | 24 | 18 | 22 | 65.5 | 34.5 | 100 | 113 |
| 6 & 7 | 12 | 10 | 11 | 62.7 | 37.3 | 100 | 59 |
| Total | | | | | | | |
| (per cent) | 100 | 100 | 100 | | | | |
| No. of Cases | (310) | (218) | (528) | | | | |

Columns (1), (2), and (3) are from Morris Janowitz and Warren E. Miller, "The Index of Political Participation in the 1948 Election," *Journal of Politics*, 14 (November, 1952), Table 3, p. 716.

non-voters at the extremes of the IPP were slight," whereas the original results implied a large difference. Second, they saw "some support" for IPP in that "a markedly higher concentration of non-voters was found" in category 4.[89]

These dual conclusions can be questioned, however. Specifically, the authors' rationale for using total column entries as the bases for percentages is not available, but it seems to hide relations in nature. Consider only Columns 1 and 2. Patently, there seems little difference in IPP categories 1 and 2 between voters and non-voters (18 and 14 per cent, respectively). Similarly, moderate differences also seem to exist between voters and non-voters in Categories 6 and 7 (12 and 10 per cent, respectively). But those small differences in Columns 1 and 2, in part, are dependent on the fact that the paired percentages have different base-numbers (310 and 218, respectively) in Janowitz and Miller's data. Where such independence does not exist, as in Columns 4 and 5, the original IPP results receive dual support. That is, "substantial" differences between voters and non-voters do exist in the extreme categories. Moreover, the greatest concentration of non-voters still appears in IPP Category 4. The recalculations also have a pleasing symmetry. We have not determined whether the recalculated results are statistically significant. In any case, the recalculations require adding some force to the faint support of IPP provided by Janowitz and Miller.

Second, conceptual differences and problems inhibit interpretation of the replication by Janowitz and Miller. In regard to differences, for example, the conceptual focus of the SES component of their version of IPP shifted from that based on interviewer ratings of respondents in *The*

*People's Choice.* Three variables—education, occupation, and dollar income—comprise the bases for rating SES level in the replication.[90] How this shift affected results is not known, but interpretive caution seems appropriate. As an example of conceptual problems, at even a surface level, the focus of the replication is still on objective SES levels. The use of survey techniques permitted some attempt to tap subjective or attitudinal SES levels, but the opportunity was apparently not taken. An analysis of the co-variation of objective and subjective concepts, appropriately defined operationally, would have provided useful information on the validity of the original IPP results and of the replication as well. As it is, we can only raise the potential problems associated with conceptual definition of IPP.

Third, Janowitz and Miller's replication also reflects differences and problems with operational definition. On balance, except in the case of the specific comparison intended, the operational changes seemed to imply progress. Any operational changes between any two studies, however, raise the knotty issues of operational coincidence and thus of the comparability of results. Operational differences are acknowledged by Janowitz and Miller, but this does not avoid these two significant issues. In addition, the usual operational problems are raised by the use of survey techniques. Thus respondent veracity becomes an issue. But that problem is always with us. Moreover, the operations employed by Janowitz and Miller provided many substantial countervailing advantages, as in increasing the percentage of subjects classifiable in IPP categories.[91]

The purpose here is not to flog a dead historical moment, but to extract methodological insight from it. That is, the task of isolating the dimensions of reality appropriate to a voting theory of the middle range remains unfinished. Janowitz and Miller pointed to this task in noting that their purpose was neither "to develop new composite group indices of electoral behavior or to elaborate new theoretical explanations." As they explained:

> Such new theoretical explanations will of necessity encompass not only indices of the group characteristics of the population, but in addition, consideration of such items as the nature of the political campaign, the existence of partisan affiliation, ideological commitments of voters, the character of candidates, and the organizational effectiveness of the political parties involved.[92]

Researchers on voting behavior seem to be girding their loins for just such a comprehensive assault on isolating dimensions of reality. When that assault comes, as it surely will, the methodological questions raised in the development and replication of IPP will be resurrected in their complexity, and this section is dedicated to the proposition that one can learn from history.

## VII. CONCLUSION

Research on electoral behavior has progressed far in a relatively short period of time. The development has been marked by a methodological sophistication and a systematic extension of understanding that is rare in Political Science. The scientific nature of the research has drawn comment, not all of it favorable. Some critics have been concerned by the non-normative nature of the investigations. Other observers are more concerned that the research be broadly conceived and that the data base be extended so that reliable prediction becomes possible. Eventually, a deductive theory relevant to the formation and expression of political attitudes will realize the methodological promise of a science of electoral behavior. Only then will a true reconciliation of the normative and empirical emphases—in goal-based empirical theories—occur.

## NOTES

1. Walter Berns, "Voting Studies," in Herbert J. Storing (ed.), *Essays on the Scientific Study of Politics* (New York: Holt, Rinehart & Winston, 1962), pp. 1–62.

2. *Ibid.*, p. 55.

3. *Ibid.*

4. *Ibid.*, p. 50. Emphasis added.

5. *Ibid.*, p. 52.

6. *Ibid.*, p. 45.

7. *Ibid.*, pp. 22, 33–34. The pitfalls of relying on "common sense"—which Berns contends reveals much of what the voting studies have to offer—and the value of rigorous methodological experimentation are expounded in Karl W. Deutsch, "The Limits of Common Sense," *Psychiatry*, 22 (May, 1959), 105–12; and Paul F. Lazarsfeld and Morris Rosenberg (eds.), *The Language of Social Research* (Glencoe, Ill.: The Free Press, 1955), pp. 9–12.

8. Walter Berns, "The Behavioral Sciences and the Study of Political Things," *American Political Science Review*, 55 (September, 1961), 550–59.

9. Berns' treatment of three of the major studies—*The People's Choice, Voting,* and *The Voter Decides*—is harsh. He is somewhat more receptive to *The American Voter*, although its late publication necessitated its receiving only brief mention in an appendix to Berns' original observations. The more recent Survey Research Center research pieces collected in Angus Campbell, Philip E. Converse, Warren E. Miller, and Donald E. Stokes, *Elections and the Political Order* (New York: Wiley, 1966) also, of course, did not receive attention.

10. At least, Berns is unwilling to consider the voting studies as making a contribution to normative philosophic concerns. For example, he dismisses efforts of the authors of *Voting* to interrelate the normative and empirical.

11. Leslie A. Fiedler, "Voting and Voting Studies," in Eugene Burdick and Arthur J. Brodbeck (eds.), *American Voting Behavior* (Glencoe, Ill.: The Free Press, 1959), p. 186.

12. Little is gained from an extensive recounting of the specific evolution of each of the major voting publications. This has been done quite adequately elsewhere. See, in particular: Peter H. Rossi, "Four Landmarks in Voting Research," in Eugene Burdick and Arthur J. Brodbeck (eds.), *American Voting Behavior* (Glencoe, Ill.: The Free Press, 1959), pp. 5–54; Rossi, "Trends in Voting Behavior Research: 1933–1963," in Edward C. Dreyer and Walter A. Rosenbaum (eds.), *Political Opinion and Electoral Behavior: Essays and Studies* (Belmont, Calif.: Wadsworth, 1966), pp. 67–77; and S. M. Lipset, Paul F. Lazarsfeld, Allen H. Barton, and Juan Linz, "The Psychology of Voting: An Analysis of Political Behavior," in Gardner Lindzey (ed.), *Handbook of Social Psychology* (Cambridge, Mass.: Addison-Wesley, 1954), II, 1124–75.

13. Morris Janowitz and Warren E. Miller, "The Index of Political Predisposition in the 1948 Election," *Journal of Politics*, 14 (November, 1952), 710–11.

14. By a "truncated" panel design, Rossi is referring to one approach of the Survey Research Center of the University of Michigan. The SRC sponsored *The Voter Decides, The American Voter,* and the research reported in *Elections and the Political Order*. One SRC design involved interviewing the same nationwide sample of respondents twice, once preceding the election and once immediately after. The Bureau of Applied Social Research at Columbia University utilized seven interview waves to obtain data from the same panel of respondents. Rossi, *op. cit.*, p. 38.

15. Austin Ranney, "The Utility and Limitation of Aggregate Data in the Study of Electoral Behavior" in Austin Ranney (ed.), *Essays on the Behavioral Study of Politics* (Urbana: University of Illinois Press, 1962), p. 92. This selection is particularly good for constructively analyzing some of the contributions that aggregate data analysis can make.

16. Stuart A. Rice, *Quantitative Methods in Politics* (New York: Knopf, 1928).

17. V. O. Key, Jr., *Southern Politics* (New York: Knopf, 1949). See also

Key's *American State Politics: An Introduction* (New York: Knopf, 1956) and his *Politics, Parties, and Pressure Groups* (5th ed.; New York: Crowell, 1964). In the former, for example, he ingeniously relates aggregate data to the structural characteristics of the party.

18. Key, *Politics, Parties, and Pressure Groups,* pp. 228–53; Herbert Agar, *The Price of the Union* (Boston: Houghton Mifflin, 1950); and Arthur Holcombe, *The New Party Politics* (New York: Norton, 1933).

19. One example from the many possible is M. Kent Jennings and L. Harmon Zeigler, "A Moderate's Victory in a Southern Congressional District," *Public Opinion Quarterly,* 28 (Winter, 1964), 595–603.

20. For examples of these potentialities, consult E. E. Schattschneider, *The Semi-Sovereign People* (New York: Holt, Rinehart & Winston, 1960); and Charles Sellers, "The Equilibrium Cycle in Two-Party Politics," *Public Opinion Quarterly,* 29 (Spring, 1965), 16–38. Trend analysis along these lines should be facilitated by the project in progress by the Inter-University Consortium for Political Research to collect and store voting data at the county level for many past elections. The intentions of the Consortium are discussed in Philip E. Converse, "A Network of Data Archives for the Behavioral Sciences," *Public Opinion Quarterly,* 28 (Summer, 1964), 273–86.

21. William S. Robinson, "Ecological Correlations and the Behavior of Individuals," *American Sociological Review,* 15 (June, 1950), 351–57.

22. S. M. Lipset, *Political Man* (Garden City, N.Y.: Doubleday Anchor Books, 1963); and Ralph H. Retzlaff, "The Use of Aggregate Data in Comparative Political Analysis," *Journal of Politics,* 27 (November, 1965), 797–817.

23. Discussions of the panel design can be found in Lipset et al., *op. cit.;* Eleanor E. Maccoby and Ray Hyman, "Measurement Problems in Panel Studies," in Eugene Burdick and Arthur J. Brodbeck (eds.), *American Voting Behavior* (Glencoe, Ill.: The Free Press, 1959), pp. 68–79; and James A. Davis, "Panel Analysis: Techniques and Concepts in the Interpretation of Repeated Measures" (Chicago: National Opinion Research Center, November, 1963), (mimeographed).

24. See the development of this idea in the later work by Elihu Katz and Paul F. Lazarsfeld, *Personal Influence* (Glencoe, Ill.: The Free Press, 1955), and the ingenious, if restricted, experimental field research on the concept presented in Verling C. Troldahl, "A Field Test of a Modified 'Two Step Flow of Communication' Model," *Public Opinion Quarterly,* 30 (Winter, 1966), 609–723.

25. Angus Campbell, Philip E. Converse, Warren E. Miller, and Donald E. Stokes in *The American Voter* (New York: Wiley, 1960) estimated that at the beginning of the campaign or by convention time, about two-thirds (in 1952) to three-quarters (1956) of the electorate had made their decision. Some supporting data may be found in Table 4:4, p. 78.

26. "Cross-pressure" theory becomes attitudinal conflict in *The American Voter,* and its implications are more refined. See also Angus Campbell and Warren E. Miller, "The Motivational Basis of Straight and Split Ticket Voting," *American Political Science Review,* 51 (June, 1957), 293–312. The feasibility of the Index of Political Predisposition is discussed in Janowitz and Miller, *op. cit.*

27. Bernard R. Berelson, Paul F. Lazarsfeld, and William N. McPhee, *Voting* (Chicago: University of Chicago Press, 1954), pp. 153–81.

28. Alternative designations—"position-issues" and "valence-issues"—are advanced and their meaning is clarified by Donald E. Stokes in "Spatial Models of Party Competition," Chap. 9, in Campbell, et al., *Elections and the Political Order, op. cit.*

29. Paul F. Lazarsfeld, Bernard Berelson, and Hazel Gaudet, *The People's Choice* (New York: Columbia University Press, 1948), p. 27.

30. These explanatory variables are expanded in *The American Voter* to include "interest in the campaign" and "concern with election outcome" in analyzing voter turnout. *Op. cit.,* pp. 101–7. The political aspects of the analysis are extended further in the reports in *Elections and the Political Order.*

31. *Ibid.*, pp. 500–503.

32. Kurt Lewin, *Field Theory and Social Science,* edited by Dorwin Cartwright (New York: Harper, 1951).

33. Philip E. Converse, Angus Campbell, Warren E. Miller, and Donald E. Stokes, "Stability and Change in 1960: A Reinstating Election," *American Political Science Review,* 55 (June, 1961), 269–30; and Philip E. Converse, Aage R. Clausen, and Warren E. Miller, "Electoral Myth and Reality: The 1964 Election," *American Political Science Review,* 59 (June, 1965), 321–36.

34. Campbell, et al., *The American Voter,* pp. 295–332.

35. *Ibid.*, pp. 338–40.

36. *Ibid.*, p. 339. Emphasis in the original omitted.

37. Abraham Kaplan, *The Conduct of Inquiry* (San Francisco: Chandler, 1964), pp. 327–46.

38. *Ibid.*, p. 333.

39. *Ibid.*, p. 339.

40. Campbell, et al., *The American Voter,* pp. 18–37.

41. *Ibid.*, pp. 23–24. Causal model analysis does prove useful in predicting from consituency policy views either as perceived by a congressman or in conjunction with his own policy beliefs to congressional roll call behavior. A. Campbell, et al., *Elections and the Political Order, op. cit.*, pp. 351–72, and Charles F. Cnudde and Donald J. McCrone, "The Linkage Between Constituency Attitudes and Congressional Voting: A Causal Model," *American Political Science Review,* 60 (March, 1966), 66–72.

42. Bernard Hennessy evaluates the contribution of the funnel of causality to the understanding of the broader subject of public opinion in *Public Opinion* (Belmont, Calif.: Wadsworth, 1965), pp. 156–70.

43. For a different treatment of similar problems, consult Ulf Himmelstrand, *Social Pressures, Attitudes, and Democratic Processes* (Stockholm: Almqvist and Wiksell, 1960); and Himmelstrand, "Verbal Attitudes and Behavior: A Paridigm for the Study of Message Transmission and Transformation," *Public Opinion Quarterly,* 24 (Summer, 1960), 224–50.

44. Angus Campbell, "Recent Developments in Survey Studies of Political Behavior," in Austin Ranney (ed.), *Essays on the Behavioral Study of Politics* p. 45.

45. V. O. Key, Jr. and Frank Munger, "Social Determinism and Electoral Decision: The Case of Indiana," in Burdick and Brodbeck, *op. cit.*, pp. 281–99; and Key's *American State Politics: An Introduction, op. cit.*, and *Southern Politics, op. cit.*, are representative examples of his work.

46. Robert E. Agger, Daniel Goldrich, and Bert E. Swanson, *The Rulers and the Ruled* (New York: Wiley, 1964); and Bradbury Seasholes and Frederick N. Cleaveland, "Negro Political Participation in Two Piedmont Crescent Cities." in F. Stuart Chapin, Jr. and Shirley F. Weiss (eds.), *Urban Growth Dynamics in a Regional Cluster of Cities* (New York: Wiley, 1962), pp. 260–308.

47. Robert E. Agger, Marshall M. Goldstein, and Stanley A. Pearl, "Political Cynicism: Measurement and Meaning," *Journal of Politics,* 23 (August, 1961), 477–506. The same index is applied in a different setting by Edgar Litt, "Political Cynicism and Political Futility," *Journal of Politics,* 25 (May, 1963), 312–23.

48. Katz and Eldersveld, *op. cit.* This is a particularly promising focus for revealing the political communications network in which the individual is imbedded. The Decatur Study reported in *Personal Influence* is crude and the data insufficient for following up the suggestive leads uncovered in the analysis. The field work on the study was executed in 1945, although the findings did not appear in print for a decade. Nonetheless, the report does show far fewer opinion leaders in public affairs than a breakdown of the more "typical" leadership patterns discovered in marketing, fashions, and movies (one sign of the work's age). The study does discuss the role of men in political opinion-making (unlike the other subjects examined), the low salience of politics for women sampled, the greater demands, implicitly at least, placed on leaders in this area, and, even more implicitly, the role of family interaction in structuring political opinions. The latter, by itself, is a promising and

unexploited area for serious research. See, for example, James G. March, "Husband-Wife Interaction Over Political Issues," *Public Opinion Quarterly,* 17 (Winter, 1953–1954), 461–470; William A. Glaser, "The Family and Voting Turnout," *Public Opinion Quarterly,* 23 (Winter, 1951), 563–70; and Herbert McClosky and Harold E. Dahlgren, "Primary Group Influence on Party Loyalty," *American Political Science Review,* 53 (September, 1959), 757–76.

49. Daniel Katz and Samuel J. Eldersveld, "The Impact of Local Party Activity upon the Electorate," *Public Opinion Quarterly,* 25 (Spring, 1961), 1–24; and the work of Peter H. Rossi and Phillips Cutright as exemplified by "The Impact of Party Organization in an Industrial Setting," in Morris Janowitz (ed.), *Community Political Systems* (Glencoe, Ill.: The Free Press, 1961), pp. 81–116. See also Samuel J. Eldersveld, *The Political Party: A Behavioral Analysis* (Chicago: Rand McNally, 1964).

50. Charles R. Adrian, "Some General Characteristics of Nonpartisan Elections," *American Political Science Review,* 46 (September, 1952), 766–76; and J. Leiper Freeman, "Local Party Sytems: Theoretical Considerations and a Case Analysis," *American Journal of Sociology,* 64 (November, 1958), 282–89.

51. Alvin Boskoff and Harmon Zeigler, *Voting Patterns in a Local Election* (Philadelphia: Lippincott, 1964), pp. 1–29. This book provides a good review of the literature and places it within the broader perspective of the nationwide studies, as well as contributing an empirical analysis of its own. A paper by John C. Croft and Stephen N. Stivers, *Voting Behavior in School Elections* (Eugene, Ore.: Center for the Advanced Study of Educational Administration, mimeographed, n. d.) details the dearth of reliable research.

52. Donald R. Matthews and James W. Prothro, "Southern Images of Political Parties: An Analysis of White and Negro Attitudes," in Avery Leiserson (ed.), *The American South in the 1960's* (New York: Praeger, 1964), pp. 82–111, and Matthews and Prothro, *Negroes and the New Southern Politics* (New York: Harcourt, Brace & World, 1966), pp. 369–404.

53. Campbell and Miller, *op. cit.*

54. Matthews and Prothro, *op. cit.*

55. Murray Levin, *The Compleat Politician* (Indianapolis: Bobbs-Merrill, 1962). Unfortunately, Levin tests the reality of the political decision-makers' perceptions of their electorates against polls taken in several communities supposedly typical of voting patterns for different categories of the electorate. This can be misleading.

56. Key and Munger, *op. cit.,* p. 281; and V. O. Key, Jr., "The Politically Relevant in Surveys," *Public Opinion Quarterly,* 24 (Spring, 1960), 54–61. A. Campbell, et al. in *Elections and the Political Order* tried to deal with some of these shortcomings. Berns' "Voting Studies," *op. cit.,* also makes the same charge.

57. Campbell, *op. cit.,* pp. 41–42.

58. *Ibid.,* pp. 32–36. Encouragingly, the trend is in this direction.

59. Ithiel de Sola Pool, Robert P. Abelson, and Samuel L. Popkin, *Candidates, Issues, and Strategies* (Cambridge, Mass.: M.I.T. Press, 1964), p. 6. See also the discussion of simulation by William N. McPhee in "Note on Campaign as Simulator," *Public Opinion Quarterly,* 25 (Summer, 1961), 184–93. Also consult Chapters I and IX above for an extended discussion of simulation problems and in particular for their treatment of the difficulties involved in isolating dimensions of reality.

60. Pool, et. al., *op. cit.,* p. 15.

61. Robert A. Dahl, *Who Governs?* (New Haven, Conn.: Yale University Press, 1961).

62. Boskoff and Zeigler, *op. cit.,* p. 28.

63. *Ibid.,* pp. 25–28.

64. Campbell, et al., *The American Voter,* pp. 453–72. On various aspects of suburban politics, consult: Robert C. Wood, *Suburbia* (Boston: Houghton Mifflin, 1959); Fred I. Greenstein and Raymond E. Wolfinger, "The Suburbs and Shifting Party Loyalty," *Public Opinion Quarterly,* 22 (Winter, 1958), 473–82; James G. Manis and Leo C. Stine, "Suburban Residents and Political Behavior," *Public Opinion Quarterly,* 22

(Winter, 1958), 483–89; and Frederick M. Wirt, "The Political Sociology of American Suburbia: A Reinterpretation," *Journal of Politics,* 27 (August, 1965), 647–66.

65. Apparently this occurs in Canada when partisan loyalties and strong ideological attachments are held by the parents. Allan Kornberg and Norman Thomas, "The Political Socialization of National Legislative Elites in the United States and Canada," *Journal of Politics,* 27 (November, 1965), 761–75.

66. Two examples of their work are: David Easton and Robert D. Hess, "Youth and the Political System," in S. M. Lipset and Leo Lowenthal (eds.), *Culture and Social Character* (New York: The Free Press of Glencoe, 1961), pp. 226–51; and David Easton and Jack Dennis, "The Child's Image of Government," in Roberta Sigel (ed.), *Political Socialization: Its Role in the Political Process,* in *Annals* (Philadelphia: American Academy of Political and Social Science, September, 1965), 40–57.

67. Fred I. Greenstein, *Children and Politics* (New Haven, Conn.: Yale University Press, 1965).

68. Somewhat dated introductions to the study of socialization are: Irwin L. Child, "Socialization," in Gardner Lindzey (ed.), *Handbook of Social Psychology* (Reading, Mass.: Addison-Wesley, 1954), I, 655–92; and Herbert H. Hyman, *Political Socialization* (Glencoe, Ill.: The Free Press, 1959).

69. Donald E. Stokes and Warren E. Miller, "Party Government and the Saliency of Congress," in Campbell, et al., *Elections and the Political Order, op. cit.,* pp. 194–211, and Warren E. Miller and Donald E. Stokes, "Constituency Influence in Congress," *American Political Science Review, op. cit.*

70. Miller and Stokes, "Constituency Influence in Congress."

71. Representative examples are: Philip E. Converse and Georges Dupeux, "Politicization of the Electorate in France and the United States," *Public Opinion Quarterly,* 26 (Spring, 1962), 1–23; Stein Rokkan and Angus Campbell, "Norway and the United States of America," *International Social Science Journal,* 12 (1960), 69–99; and Angus Campbell and Henry Valen, "Party Identification in Norway and the United States," *Public Opinion Quarterly,* 25 (Winter, 1961), 505–25. A major study of British electoral behavior under the general supervision of Donald Stokes of the Survey Research Center is in the analysis stage. Also consult the discussion of the methodological problems involved in cross-cultural analysis and the introduction to the repositories of data presented by "Data in Comparative Research," *International Social Science Journal,* 16 (1964). A more primitive data base has received a secondary analysis for electorates in four countries—Great Britain, Australia, Canada, and the United States —in Robert R. Alford, *Party and Society: The Anglo-American Democracies* (Chicago: Rand McNally, 1963). Political participation, including voting, and political values are subject to extended treatment in the five nation comparative study reported in Gabriel A. Almond and Sidney Verba, *The Civic Culture* (Princeton, N.J.: Princeton University Press, 1963).

72. Lazarsfeld, Berelson, and Gaudet, *op. cit.,* p. 26.

73. *Ibid.,* pp. 25–26.

74. *Ibid.,* p. 17.

75. *Ibid.,* p. 20

76. *Ibid.,* pp. 20–21. For another example of the neglect of the same discovery, consult footnote 2, Chapter XII, p. 167. There the authors show that the expectation of victory has an independent effect on the vote, IPP scores being controlled.

77. *Ibid.,* p. 17.

78. *Ibid.,* p. 18.

79. Janowitz and Miller, *op. cit.,* p. 727.

80. Lazarsfeld, Berelson, and Gaudet, *op. cit.,* p. 17.

81. *Ibid.,* p. 27.

82. *Ibid.,* p. 139.

83. *Ibid.,* p. 164.

84. *Ibid.,* p. xvi.

85. Janowitz and Miller, *op. cit.,* p. 710.

86. *Ibid.,* p. 712.

87. *Ibid.,* p. 714.

88. *Ibid.,* p. 715.

89. *Ibid.,* pp. 716–17.

90. *Ibid.,* pp. 726–27.

91. *Ibid.,* p. 727.

92. *Ibid.,* p. 713.

# PART FOUR

## Two Methodological Perspectives Toward an Integrative Political Science

# xiii

# Models in the Social Sciences: A *General* View

Fundamentally, all explanation proceeds in terms of models.[1] The construction of a general theory of behavior requires effective procedures for determining the application of such a theory at a variety of levels, for example, in which task models are useful. Further, the historical importance of models also is clear in a broader context. For example, we have repeatedly developed metaphysical systems to give order to our existence. This industry implies an apparent necessity to conceptualize reality in terms of abstracted systems, or models.[2]

Because models are so central, persons interested in promoting scientific research accord model-building a pre-eminence. Hence the focus throughout this volume on reasonably explicit models in political research.

If nothing else, however, this volume sounds at least one discordant note in connection with disciplinary model-building. Research Everyman in Political Science labors to build some kind of model of politics for some purpose, but few pause over what a model *is*. Each proceeds merrily, utilizing (explicitly or implicitly) some sort of analytic structure. Perhaps that structure amounts to nothing more than a set of unarticulated assumptions, or a set of loosely connected definitions of nonsystematically selected concepts. But a structure there is, even if only a small number of philosophers of science give it any real attention. No one interested in explanation, prediction, or verification can avoid using models. Models—or at least, analytic structures which are often called models—are present in every piece of research, certainly in any research which goes beyond the mere accumulation of data. Hence this chapter.

This chapter hopes to contribute both to defining the concept *model* and to evaluating specific models. Certainly, sharper definition is necessary in the social sciences. Significantly different concepts of model exist. And no wonder, for no agreement exists about the characteristics relevant for defining model. Further, the social sciences have developed little agreement about criteria for evaluating models. All pieces of research aimed toward a science of human behavior should be evaluated in identical, or at least complementary, terms. But even the briefest glance at the literature reviewed in this volume suggests three critical problems: (1) some research, while clearly making use of rigorous, systematic methods, is not undertaken with a view to its science-building contribution; (2) there is substantial disagreement as to whether building a science of behavior is an acceptable purpose of scholarly inquiry; and (3) most important, there is some inconsistency in the demands of empirical theory-building, as between the twin requisites of operationality and generality.

Little has been done about definitely rejecting the legacy of the past, clearly. There have been few efforts to devise standardized criteria for problem selection; and there has been little concern in Political Science for specifying a set of general criteria by which all models might be evaluated. The expected result has been a confused (and confusing) babble of inconsistent and uncertain voices. Implicitly, we have almost come to the point of treating the concept *model* as an undefinable "primitive term" in our professional vocabulary, a distinction for which it appears not to qualify.[3]

This chapter proposes to catalog the reigning confusion while, it is hoped, introducing a degree of order. Specifically, first, we have three definitional aims. We will sample opinions as to what classificatory designations are useful for explicating the concept of *model;* a synthesized definition of model will be proposed; and the uses to which models are put in the social sciences will be examined. Second, these pages also will advance a set of criteria for the evaluation of models. These criteria will be methodologically, although not terminologically, quite close to the three criteria which have been used for evaluative purposes throughout the book. These three base-line minima are: methodological compatibility with work in other fields, external confirmation or disconfirmation, and usefulness in isolating the dimensions of reality.

## I. DIFFICULTIES WITH ORDERING THE UNIVERSE OF MODELS

The tasks we have set for ourselves are neither easy nor well defined. Consider only two difficulties with attempting to impose order on the universe of models. First, any such order is arbitrary. Unfortunately, an attempt at ordering is often necessary, although orderliness takes no general preference over vigor and thoughtful dissent. Moreover, the appropriateness of a given conceptual (or operational) definition may not be separable from the specific research context in which it is used. Yet we believe that the consistent usage of critical terminology is a prerequisite for meaningful communication within and among scholarly disciplines. Indeed, standardized terminology seems necessary for engineering the collapse of traditional disciplinary boundaries.

Second, our attempt at order does not escape the prevailing tendency to draw little verbal distinction between the definition of model and the evaluation of models. That is, the characteristics commonly referred to in *defining* a model almost always turn up again as bases for *evaluating* models. For example, a question commonly asked in attempting to define model is: To what degree need an analytic structure correspond to "reality" before we consider it a model? At the same time, the congruence between the "reality" from which a model is abstracted, and the structure (or content) of the model may be one of the bases upon which the usefulness of the model is judged.

We do not consider definitional/evaluational overlap as particularly troublesome. As a matter of fact, the practice of using the same dimensions for definition and evaluation is common, both in everyday language and in scientific discourse. Before a vehicle may be a "*good* automobile" it must qualify as an "automobile." One of the definitional characteristics of an automobile might be that it rolls on wheels, for example. Yet we also evaluate the performance of that auto partly in terms of how well the wheels operate. Definitions are minimal (necessary and sufficient) specifications of characteristics; evaluations pick up where definitions end. Evaluations *may be* assessments of the degrees to which whatever we are focusing on possesses certain attributes. That is, the difference between definition and evaluation is not merely one of kind. Differences in degree may be distinguished along each of the dimensions used for definition. In addition, differences of kind should exist between dimensions.

Ordering the universe of models also requires subsequent refinement of the general terms used above, particularly the term *theory.* Let us clarify what the notion of theory embraces. Loose, everyday usage may dignify any hunch as theory. Similarly, theory may be thought of as the speculative and idealized counterpart of practice, an approach which parades theory as a kind of systematic and persistent pursuit of the irrelevant. More generally, following McClelland

> it is recognized commonly that theory may mean the history of ideas, the analysis of systems of political or social thought, the product of creative efforts to state or restate moral philosophies, or the formulation of strict schemes of explanation to account for observed events and states of affairs.[4]

From the mélange of notions of what theory is supposed to be, we can abstract two core-notions. A Theory is a set of ideas *about ideas;* and theory is a set of ideas *about concrete data* observed in the real world. The dispute over what role normative theory (i.e., philosophy) should play in contemporary academic enterprises exemplifies a theoretical question of the first type, for example. Systematic, empirical explanations fall into the second category.

McClelland sharpens these core-notions. He differentiates subject Theory from subject-matter theory, a classification which roughly corresponds with the distinction made above between idea-centered thought and data-centered thought. A Theory will be thought of as the content of thinking about intellectual policy in academic fields. In several senses, then, this volume is about Theory, for our methodological interests reflect ideas about the appropriateness of given approaches to reality. Initially, the products of our Theory will be middle-range empirical theories, or schemes for relating observational phenomena.[5] Ultimately, also, our methodological Theory will generate a higher-level deductive Theory whose major concepts are not rooted in immediately apprehended data but are logically deduced from a model of relations.

This rudimentary distinction focuses the thrust of this chapter. Generally, we hope to contribute to Theory (read: methodological development) in Political Science by attempting to clarify the discipline's thinking about models. In outlining the criteria by which models should be evaluated, at the same time, we also raise the question of how models are related to theories. To summarize in advance, we see models as intermediate steps along the road to theory. How far along the pathway a given model has come depends upon its performance as judged against our six criteria. Some criteria (especially generality) are more relevant than others to a model's theoretical promise. Each criterion, however, purports to be an index of progress toward theory. Subject-matter theories thus may be viewed as highly sophisticated models. In this chapter then we are embarking on an essay on Theory, which has reference to the means by which theories are built.

## II. THE DEFINITION/EVALUATION MIX

Let us boldly approach the definition/evaluation of *model.* The criteria being proposed in this chapter for the evaluation of models are validity, flexibility, generality, measurement sophistication, significance, and internal logic. The argument shall be that, other things being equal, a model having more of one of these attributes is to be preferred by the social scientist to one having less. All these criteria constitute the more general criterion which is most important: predictive capacity. In the last analysis, we are searching for models which will aid us in making verifiable predictions.

Note again, further, that the dimensions in terms of which models are defined and evaluated are similar. In fact, combining evaluative criteria and their corresponding definitional elements would seem to be the most efficient way to organize the next segment of this chapter. *How we evaluate models* (or anything else, for that matter) *must depend in part on what it is we are evaluating*. Thus, within the discussion of each criterion of evaluation we will talk about relevant questions concerning the definition of the concept. Later in the chapter, questions of definition will be pulled together, pursuant to our interest in arriving at a synthesized definition of the concept *model*.

Our approach, it is important to note, shies away from two well-worn paths. That is, there are two common broad approaches to the evaluation of model-building in the contemporary social science literature, the *simplicity criterion* approach and the *interdependence postulate* approach.

The simplicity approach emphasizes criteria of convenience. Its typical judgmental questions ask: Is the model so complex that the operational design of research is rendered laborious, expensive, and time-consuming? Are the hypotheses deduced from, or inferred from, the model reasonably simple and direct, or are there numerous intervening variables, the control of which would prove difficult? Such judgmental questions have a common home in this question: Is the model relatively easy to apply, and does it offer a reasonable chance of a pay-off in a short time?

The interdependence postulate approach lusts rather after "plausibility," commonly defined in terms of the congruence of the model with the data to which it refers. Thus models of complex real-world processes are expected to be equally complex. Almost all simplification tends to be viewed as over-simplification. Short-run utility is rejected in favor of comprehensiveness, closure, and predictability based on near-isomorphism with reality. The supporters of the "plausibility" posture would rather be cumbersomely explicit than parsimoniously suggestive, in short.

Opinion has not polarized around these two approaches, but there is little consolation in noting that many social scientists have adopted in varying degrees a kind of combined "simplicity-plausibility" approach. DeFleur and Larsen, for example, contend that a model should be evaluated on the basis of "how well it accounts for the observations, the number of parameters necessary to predict the data, and the adequacy of its rationale."[6] Unfortunately, DeFleur and Larsen share the difficulty that plagues most middle-of-the-road postures on questions of Theory. These scholars neither adequately specify what they mean by their criteria (i.e., how to apply them), nor do they deal with the apparent partial inconsistencies within their evaluative criteria.

We shall not avoid our own challenge. How adequately specified are our own criteria for evaluation?

### A. Validity

Certainly we pick no easy place to start. Indeed, when we speak of the *validity* of a model, we refer to three elements. These include: the correspondence of the elements of a model with the reality it purports to represent; the model's susceptibility to operationalization; and the possible existence of errors of structural commission. Each of these more specific sub-criteria, of course, concerns the linkage between the model and the real-world phenomena from which it has been abstracted.

#### *1. Correspondence to Reality*

The literature has been fascinated by (and nearly fixated on) the question of correspondence to reality, both in evaluation and definition. Consider two leading questions:

I. Is a model only structure or must it have variables with direct empirical referents?

II. To be considered a model, to what degree must an analytic structure (with or without direct empirical import) correspond with reality?

A brief cataloging of views on these two questions should move us toward an acceptable definition of model. The cataloging also should aid us in appreciating the problems attendant on judging the validity of models.

Among social scientists generally, the majority opinion on the first question is that models consist only of "structure." That is, it is widely supposed that models are not tied to any specific set of data, but rather are intended to apply to several discrete observations. In a sense, then, all models would be mathematical, insofar as they represent abstract formalizations of empirically determined relationships, or of some set of postulates. F. H. George, for example, sees models as "relational structures . . . sets of marks open to interpretation as languages which may be used for any purpose whatsoever that is consistent with the interpretation placed on the marks."[7] He has strong support. Paul Meadows contends that a model is a "pattern of symbols, rules, and processes regarded as matching, in part or in totality, *an existing perceptual complex*."[8] To J. M. Beshers, a model is "a set of assumptions . . . not being directly tested."[9] Such models identify and state the relationships among a set of factors in an abstracted form. Karl Deutsch concurs, defining models as "symbols which are put in relations or sequences according to operating rules."[10] These examples will suffice, but we might note that this general position is also supported by Anatol Rapoport,[11] Kenneth Arrow,[12] Karl Pearson,[13] and Ivan London.[14]

The minority position is well represented by the views of Herbert Simon and Allan Newell.[15] They accept what they call "contemporary usage," which makes model simply a synonym for theory. Thus, models have both form (a set of sentences, expressing certain relationships) and content ("the totality of empirical assertions that the theory makes explicitly or implicitly, about the real world phenomena to which it refers"). They further divide content into logical properties (the facts that can be extracted from the model by applying the laws of logic) and psychological content (the empirical propositions that scientists are in fact able to derive from it).

There is a growing group of scholars with a proverbial foot in each camp. They see dangers in excluding content from the definition of model. But they also agree with the position that models are structures *from which* empirical propositions are derived. Hence typologies have been developed in which some models consist only of structure, while others embrace content as well. Marion Levy has identified both mathematical models (ways of ordering abstractions about empirical phenomena) and empirical models (ways of ordering directly observable concepts about empirical phenomena).[16] Similarly, Rosenblueth and Wiener have differentiated formal models (structure only) and material models (having concepts with empirical referents).[17] And while Herman Meyer's mechanistic and arithmetical models appear to be devoid of empirical content, his notion of the axiomatic model is described in terms of a set of physical propositions, in which "observables" have been substituted for the variables in the "empty formulae" derived from the axioms on which the model rests.[18] A similar middle-of-the-road position has also been taken by M. L. DeFleur and O. N. Larsen.[19]

We avoid these definitional wars without denying their justice. Pragmatically, we are content with the general agreement on the processes by which models are constructed, and by which they are applied to empirical phenomena. Moreover, most social scientists recognize the importance of abstract formalization and manipulation of variables, as well as of concrete characterization of concepts with empirical referents. The disagreement is whether both constitute a model. Perhaps it is not too great a simplification to say that the differences are semantic. It would be unfortunate, however, to assume that personal preference should be the controlling criterion for selection of a definition of model. Indeed, this chapter presumes to suggest alternative criteria.

Similarly, nothing approaching consensus emerges from the literature concerning the second query about the degree to which an analytic structure must correspond with "reality" to be considered a model. As Meadows says, "each model stipulates . . . some correspondence with reality."[20] Beshers asserts that models "should be structurally congruent with the data they are supposed to represent."[21] Deutsch and Arrow take a similarly vague position.[22] However, congruence with reality is a matter of degree. To state that there must be "some correspondence" is not helpful in formulating a definition of model. Nor is it helpful in evaluating existing models, although the statement may permit useful comparison of models. There is a need for more specificity.

Tentative efforts to provide greater specificity reflect significant difficulties, however. Thus London distinguishes models whose every point is in one-to-one correspondence with a presumed reality and those models "having only punctuate correspondences" between themselves and the reality they attempt to comprehend into theory.[23] The first type of model is derived from classical physics, the latter from quantum mechanics. By deriving these definitions of model from their origins, London provides some aid in evaluating models. But his aid extends only to judging models against what they were originally intended to be, not what they "ought" to be. Further, the term "punctuate correspondences" in the second type of model is hardly more specific than "some congruence."

Simon and Levy go further in asserting that models need have very little correspondence with reality. Simon contends that all types of models (for him, verbal, mathematical, and analogic) "have a great deal of content that has no correspondence with the phenomena to which they are applied." Simon's position is based in large part upon his contention that "at a sufficiently microscopic level a theory will more closely mirror the neurological and psychological properties of its information-processing system (e.g., the human brain) than it will anything to be found in the outside world."[24] Levy similarly says that "models do not reflect empirical phenomena with very detailed accuracy. . . . The most rarefied and abstract models may prove to be extremely useful. When results deviate from predictions, attention is focused on those factors causing the deviations. More than this is not to be expected from models."[25] Moreover, the congruence of the model's assumptions with reality may have no direct relation to the predictive capacity of the model, as DeFleur and Larsen have indicated. Many models with "unrealistic" assumptions, and containing structural relationships not analogous to relationships among the empirical phenomena in question, have yielded accurate predictions about real-world outcomes.[26]

Many refuse to join Simon in solving by definition the reality-status of models. Indeed, some observers go to the opposite extreme. Thus

Meyer appears to propose a definition involving a strictly isomorphic relationship between the model and the reality it describes. For him, "models may be called interpretations of mathematical theories . . . but it would be equally correct to say that physical theories are mathematical formulae expressing relations between ideal elements of the model. These relations and the models are *strictly isomorphic*."[27] Now, it follows that physical theories (having concepts with empirical referents) express relationships which must be totally isomorphic with the models. Since these relationships constitute the structure of the theory, and since the theory embodies the empirical phenomena, total congruence between model and reality is being called for here. May Brodbeck is rather more direct. She calls for a "one-to-one correspondence between the elements of the model and the elements of the thing of which it is a model."[28]

With this extensive sampling of opinion in mind, we will parsimoniously suggest how the criterion of validity may be applied in evaluating models. We propose that models need not be totally congruent with a perceived reality; we ask for no more than limited correspondence. As the existing correspondence declines, however, so increases the danger of falling into utopian theory.

### 2. *Operationality of the Model*

More central than any requirement for correspondence with reality is the operationality of the model. That is, the model must continually be referred back to empirical phenomena, via the testing of derived propositions. If the model is of what shall subsequently be called the empirical type, the model itself should contain propositions dealing with observables. Alternately, such propositions should be deducible from the model. This orientation toward testing is a prime safeguard against utopian theorizing, whatever the required correspondence of a model with reality.

Our emphasis on operationality avoids one pseudo difficulty. "Reality" is not the solid, determinate point of reference which some assume it to be. When we speak of the correspondence of a model to "reality" we are actually relating the model to individual *perceptions* of the real world. No two perceptions of reality are identical, as Simon dramatically noted in stressing the dominant intervening position of any information processing system (especially including the human brain) between the real world and perceptions of it. This is not the place to entertain the philosophical implications of this problem. If reality is not self-evident, however, its dimensions are differentially perceived and cataloged.

### 3. *Errors of Structural Commission*

Operationality guards against errors of structural commission, as well as errors of omission. The former severely restrict the validity of a model, positing as they do a relation between two variables which does not in fact exist. Validity is not necessarily greatly compromised, on the other hand, when a model contains variables having no counterparts in reality. If the variables do not centrally interact with other variables in the model, this would be an error of elemental commission. Such a non-harmful error of commission can occur only in certain types of models (see the typology offered below), and only when those models are used for description alone.

**B. Flexibility and Generality**

The second and third criteria offered here for the evaluation of models are *flexibility* and *generality.* Flexibility refers to the susceptibility of the model to changes in the number, nature, or interrelation of variables during the model's use as a guide to research. Generality refers to the breadth of relevance of the model. That is, it refers to the number of sets (or systems) of empirical phenomena to which any model may usefully be applied.

Again, the questions concerning evaluation of a model are closely related to questions of definition. Perspective may be gained by making two inquiries of the literature on models:

I. How extensive must the structure of an analytic scheme be before it may be called a model?

II. Must an analytic scheme be so constructed as to permit application to some set of phenomena other than that from which it was abstracted before it may be considered a model?

The first question is closely related to, but still distinct from, the issue of correspondence with reality. Any model whose variables and inter-variable relationships were nearly or totally isomorphic with reality would eventually have a rather extensive structure. Since a model is developmental, however, at any point in time it: (1) may simply *identify* a set of variables; (2) may identify a set of phenomena, and state that they *interact;* (3) may identify a set of phenomena and indicate the *pattern* of their interaction; or (4) it may identify a set of phenomena, identify the pattern of their interaction, and attempt explicitly to account for all possible *variance* in their relationships. Each successive stage implies more extensive structure in the model.

Flexibility and generality are principally concerned with the degree to which the relationships among a model's variables need to be made explicit. Although Meyer[29] calls for a strict isomorphism of relations as well as elements, the literature tends toward two more moderate positions. First, some argue that to qualify as a model, an analytic structure must merely specify which variables interact with which others. The frequencies, magnitudes, and direction of influence of the relationships need not be specified, according to this view. Second, other social scientists have argued that, without some indication of the *kinds* of relationships which hold among variables, a conceptual scheme is of little utility and thus cannot qualify as a model.

The two common positions may be illustrated briefly. First, some observers stress the need for extensiveness, if their insistence varies. To Meadows, for example, a model must have *elements* which are "logically interdependent." Further, every model must contain the description of *processes*.[30] Beshers similarly, but less restrictively, indicates that a model must show in a general way the *kinds* of relationships which hold among variables.[31] London's position is similar, although he is also concerned with the comprehensiveness of the model's structure.[32]

Second, by contrast, Rapoport contends that the structure of a model need not be extensive at all. Recognizing that, for the social scientist, a "theory is often (in effect) a system of reference, that is, merely a multitude of definitions," he contends that "most models are too simple to fit into the exceedingly involved interplay of variables associated with human behavior." It is sufficient, he says, if an analytic scheme "contains the essentials, no matter how crudely simplified, of some social process."[33] If it does this, it is a model. Levy's position is similar. DeFleur and Larsen similarly assert that the function of a model is "to point out where to look, and under what conditions to make the observations or discriminatory responses."[34] For them, also, a scheme need have little extensiveness of structure to be considered a model.

By referring to generality in terms of the breadth of application of a model, we do not wish to slight what is probably a more common usage of *generality*. This usage emphasizes the level of abstraction at which a model operates. As a matter of fact, breadth of application and level of abstraction are often very closely related. Among philosophers of science, both characteristics often are subsumed under the rubric of generality. To a considerable degree, the generality of a model is an inverse function of the extensiveness of its structure and of the degree to which the model corresponds with reality.

We may press toward a dual conclusion. Social scientists basically agree that, in order to be considered a model, an analytic structure need not be applicable to sets of phenomena other than that from which it was abstracted. But there is equally strong agreement that the greater the generality and flexibility of the model, the more fruitful it is for science.

Let us develop some sense of the best of both worlds on the issue of generality. George has called for a "flexible framework which would serve as a scientific tool for research to encompass the experimental work in progress, and be precise enough to avoid the pitfalls of ordinary language; and yet again be capable of being used as approximate models for theories to answer questions of varying generality at any time."[35] Moreover, in London's terms, "two radically different models may have the same punctuate correspondences" with a given set of observations.[36] Thus greater generality would facilitate the choice between such competing models. Trade-offs do exist, of course. Particularistic models often provide advantages of exactitude, as well as validity. But again, "to stay within the confines of the [particularistic] model yields exactitude at the price of fullness, validity at the cost of generality."[37] Perhaps the evaluation of the generality of a model must depend in part on the scientific function being served by the model at any given point in time. As we suggest in a subsequent section of this chapter, the uses to which models are put are logically interdependent, but these uses are sometimes operationally discrete.

What, then, can be said in summary about the criteria of flexibility and generality? With regard to the former, a useful model will permit the introduction of new data and even new concepts, without negating any of the originally stated inter-variable relationships. Models which we shall subsequently characterize as *empirical* must provide the basis for answering particularistic questions to explain the processes or relationships in reality to which the model refers. Of course, no model can initially represent a comprehensive picture of reality. Rather, the model must be so constructed that, as new research suggests additional meaningful questions, the model may be expanded without being reconstructed.

With respect to the criterion of generality, our argument is straightforward. The greater the generality of the model, the greater its promise for scientific inquiry. However, generality is often gained at the expense of validity; therefore, caution must be exercised in designing any given model for diverse ranges of phenomena.

Our treatment of generality also has an implied thrust. Models may be thought of as formalized analogies, and thus as appropriate targets for the substantial criticisms made of analogic thinking.[38] To be sure, the usefulness of models often is judged in terms of the care with which the model's architect has extracted generalizations from reality, or in terms of the skill with which he has isolated analogous circumstances in different systems of behavior. This is particularly true at higher levels of generality. Thus, generality is often considered a product of analogic logic; hence the vogue of utopian work.

Testing the generality of models, however, involves their application to sets of phenomena other than those from which they were abstracted. That is, the generality of a model is as much an empirical question as it is a logical one. In fact, rather than the skill of the model-builder, the configuration of real-world events (and our ability to observe them in a consistent way) determines the generality of models. If there are indeed identifiable regularities among different types (or systems) of phenomena, then we should be able to devise models with substantial generality. But a model cannot genuinely do what reality does not.

### C. Measurement Sophistication

Social scientists blithely use related terms such as *measurement, quantification,* and *mathematization* as if they were interchangeable. We will distinguish briefly among the terms, their importance for our purposes over-balancing the danger of forgetting that definitions cannot win the day.

Broadly speaking, the act of *measurement* involves assigning numbers to observations. Contrary to popular assumption, however, all measurement is not quantitative. According to Coombs, "The theory of measurement consists of a system of distinct theories, each corresponding to what may be called a level of measurement. . . . a given set of data may satisfy (permit the valid use of) some of these levels of measurement but not others."[39]

*Quantitative* measurement involves the use of measurement theory, which includes the theories of interval and ratio scales. *Qualitative* measurement involves the application of *scaling theory,* which includes the theories of the ordered metric and less powerful scales (i.e., nominal, partially ordered, and ordinal scales). Thus, quantification is a more sophisticated form of measurement.

Quantification, we might stress, is by definition an act of simplification. It is undertaken because of the perceived need to compare two or more phenomena which *superficially* may appear not to be comparable. The "quantity" involved is thus not inherent in the thing quantified, but in the operations associated with quantification.[40] Indeed, operationism is the principle that the meaning to be given to a concept resides in the operations which give rise to the measure of the concept.[41]

Mathematics, on the other hand, may have nothing to do with numbers. *Mathematization* involves the formalization of relationships which have been abstracted from their substantive (empirical) referents, focusing on the logical explication and elaboration of these relationships.[42] Thus mathematics is "a study of the form of arguments and . . . is entirely devoid of subject matter." Mathematics is advanced logic. In Kemeny's words, "all scientific theories—numerical or other—are mathematical. . . .

When a scientist *states a theory precisely* and is interested in knowing just exactly what his theory involves, he is practicing mathematics."[43]

With this terminology at least broadly under control, we can turn back to our criterion of measurement sophistication. Social scientists express consensus that models need not make use of measurement theory to be useful. At the same time, most agree that the greater the degree of measurement sophistication, the greater the scientific value of the model.

Granting that many useful models do not make use of quantitative measurement, it is still necessary to confront the question: Must *some kind* of measurement be a part of any model? Little explicit comment on this question exists in the literature, but that little does reflect the assumption that at least ordinal measurement (more precisely, ordinal *scaling*) is necessary in model construction.[44] Thus a presupposition exists that scientific knowledge should be interpersonally valid and transmittable, and hence couched in an objective, consistent language. Moreover, Arrow contends that "any intuitive knowledge can always be reduced to mathematical terms."[45] If this is so, and given the goals of science, it seems safe to say that at least ordinal scaling must be used in models. Naturally, it is hoped that more sophisticated levels of measurement will be achieved.

At the same time, considerable caution must be applied in evaluating the measurement sophistication of models. As Arrow has pointed out, "it is unfortunately true that it is very easy to formulate theoretical models in which the determination of the optimum statistical (quantitative) methods leads to mathematical problems which have not been solved."[46] Quantification must not become an end in itself. We wish to quantify only as it helps us predict, or verify. Numerical designation has little value in itself. Its real worth lies in facilitating the construction of science.

### D. Significance

A fifth criterion, and one which is both uncontested and troublesome, is *significance*. By acclamation, a model should be applicable to sets of phenomena which represent important problems to be investigated by social scientists. However, few systematic attempts to devise criteria for problem selection have been undertaken. A glance at the articles appearing in any major journal suggests strong disagreement among their authors on this question. We can only highlight the absence of agreement and stress the need for specifying such criteria prior to attempts at model-building. Once criteria for problem selection have been laid out, the significance of models with respect to these criteria should be carefully evaluated.

We do not propose to glide lightly past the issue of significance without acknowledging that some social scientists are convinced of the impossibility of devising standardized criteria for problem selection.[47] Earlier chapters in this volume have noted that, philosophically, problem selection must be a personal evaluative act and cannot be objective. But we should not despair of at least broad professional agreement on criteria for problem selection, especially if those criteria are primarily methodological rather than substantive. Similarly, criteria do not have to be "value-free" (as indeed they cannot be) to be standardized. This is an important problem of intellectual policy. In McClelland's terms, it is a problem of Theory to which more attention surely should be given.

**E. Internal Logic**

Finally, a model should possess internal logic. This reference includes such obvious needs as that for transitive relationships. And it also extends to the premium placed on a model which is so constructed that empirical propositions can be logically deduced from its structure. It is one thing for a model to suggest observations; it is quite another for specific propositions to be deducible from it.

Others extend the notion of "internal logic" beyond our tastes. Consider the question of whether a model can explain *why* as well as *how*. Indeed, models are sometimes classified in terms of whether or not they reveal the "first principles," or initial causes, of a set of events—the "why of things." General support exists, however, for London's contention that models cannot demonstrate *why*. His argument has two major thrusts. First, the determination of *why* is almost always dependent upon the capacity to establish the truth of the assumptions upon which the model is based. But such a determination often is not possible. For many models contain assumptions that cannot be "proved," in the sense of determining their congruence with a set of empirical observations. Moreover, many models incorporate assumptions which are pre-acknowledged to be deviant from reality.

Second, London argues that *why* formulations "can in every case be shown to be not only equivalent to, but actually deducible from, basic formulations expressed strictly in terms of 'how.'" London contends that "as a first principle, the 'why' is illusory." Indeed, that *why* must escape the user of models. For the *how* formulations in the model "reflect the inner mechanism, not of reality, but of the arbitrary model. The 'how' reflects reality less than it does (the scientist's) method of grappling with it."[48]

London convinces us that the "why-how" argument does not even merit the emotional and intellectual energies already expended on it.

For our purposes, the issue relates particularly to the *uses* of models, and we try to suggest later in this chapter that the various uses of models can be established without troubling over the "why-how" debate.

We do not wish to leave the issue of classification hanging, however, on our bare agreement with London that the "why-how" classification is not useful for characterizing models. Consequently, we submit four criteria to guide the classification of models:

(1) All classifications should be first-order differentiations; that is, no classification should represent a characteristic which is completely a function of some other characteristic.

(2) No classification should be totally a function of the nature of the empirical phenomena which the variables in the model purport to represent (in which case the classification would be applicable to the phenomena, but not to the model).

(3) All classifications should be applicable to all types of models; that is, the classifications should be "universal."

(4) All classifications must afford a basis for differentiating models.

## III. A PROPOSED DEFINITION OF *MODEL*

The widely differing opinions as to what constitutes a model have been woven by their supporters into an equally confusing set of typologies. In a sampling of 22 articles in which typologies of models were advanced, 10 distinct typologies were noted, and they included no less than 20 different types. The literature refers to logical nets, mathematical structures, physical systems, verbal models, analogies, empirical models, rational models, empirical-mathematical models. It also recognizes pictorial, descriptive, correlational, mechanistic, organismic, arithmetical, axiomatic, operating, causal, and statistical models. And even typologies and constructs are sometimes called "models."

We can give form to the strategy which follows. No one can eliminate the complexity inducing this designational chaos. Nor can we settle for some simple and sovereign definition of model. For the great diversity of subject matters in the social sciences has led to the use of models which are sufficiently different to frustrate any broad definition. The complex typology is necessarily with us in our efforts to define model. Our only resort is to make our typology as comprehensive, and as clear and direct, as possible. We will adopt a general definition of model, within which may be found four distinct sub-types: empirical, elementally isomorphic, structurally isomorphic, and quantitative. An entity meeting all the points of the general definition, and also representing all four sub-types, will be referred to as a theoretical model.

In turn, we define model and distinguish sub-types. A *model* is a structure embodying a set of variables having a specified set of interrelations, but which variables and relationships need have only limited correspondence with the empirical phenomena and relations among empirical phenomena to which they refer. A model is characterized by the use of measurement, at least at the ordinal level, in abstracting variables from empirical phenomena.

Within the scope of this definition, we isolate four sub-types.

An *empirical* model contains "observables," i.e., variables having direct empirical import.

An *elementally isomorphic* model is one whose every variable is in a one-to-one correspondence with a presumed reality.

A *structurally isomorphic* model is one in which all specified relationships among variables are isomorphic with relationships among corresponding empirical phenomena in a presumed reality.

A *quantitative* model is one in which the abstraction of variables from empirical phenomena is accomplished through the application of measurement theory (as opposed to scaling theory), that is, through interval or ratio measurement.

We also isolate one combinatorial sub-type.

A *theoretical* model is one which is empirical, elementally isomorphic, structurally isomorphic, and quantitative. A theoretical model may be considered a low-level theory; by definition, however, it operates at a low level of generality. An empirical, quantitative model operates at a high level of generality.

These four sub-types of models generate several combinatory types. To begin, one may conceive of a model generic to the broad definition, but not representative of any sub-type. This case may be characterized as a general or generic model. The four major sub-types above thus generate 13 possible types of models: (1) (general) model, (2) empirical, (3) empirical-elementally isomorphic, (4) empirical-structurally isomorphic, (5) empirical-quantitative, (6) elementally and structurally isomorphic, (7) elementally isomorphic-quantitative, (8) structurally isomorphic-quantitative, (9) empirical-elementally and structurally isomorphic, (10) quantitative-elementally and structurally isomorphic, (11) empirical-elementally isomorphic-quantitative, (12) empirical-structurally isomorphic-quantitative, and (13) theoretical.

Referents for some of the specified sub-types may be suggested. Most models in use in the social sciences today are empirical models. For example, the policy-making models of Lasswell,[49] Snyder,[50] and Dahl and

Lindblom,[51] fall into this category. Downs' *An Economic Theory of Democracy*[52] represents an empirical-quantitative model which may, in fact, be a theory. In *Models of Man*,[53] Simon presents several empirical-quantitative models, and a few strictly quantitative ones.

## IV. THE USES OF MODELS IN THE SOCIAL SCIENCES

Models may be used to *describe, explain, predict,* and *verify.* Some observers also stress the operating use of models. We shall attempt to illustrate each use in turn. To be sure, the uses of models are interdependent. But the uses do differ meaningfully from one another, and the differences are distinct enough in an analytical sense. Although pure description may help us in preparing our explanations, for example, a model may describe accurately up to a point without providing much explanatory guidance.

*Description.* Most models are descriptive. Those models which are only descriptive have little scientific value, although they may be extremely helpful in conceptualizing particular problems. The epitome of a purely descriptive model would be one which is elementally isomorphic with reality, but which has a very low degree of structural isomorphism.

A descriptive model indicates that there are certain variables, then, characterizes them in some way, and states that they interact in some way. This type of model is an aid in *identifying* a set of phenomena, or relations among phenomena, which are indeterminately (so far as the model is concerned) inter-related.

*Explanation.* A model which is explanatory indicates specific relations among specific variables. It stresses *how*, detailing which certain events have constant relations to certain others. Thus, such a model is an aid in *understanding* a *process* of *determinate* relations.

Explanatory models often have more extensive structure than descriptive models, although not necessarily so. Their structure also tends to be considerably more extensive than predictive models, especially those with high generality.

*Prediction.* Predictive models are usually more general in application, and less extensive in structure, as has been suggested. Still, their generality conceals considerable danger for the scientist who does not recognize that generality requires selective application. As London says, "the fact that our models have . . . permitted us frequent rich penetration into the unknown should not blind us to the hazardous aspects of complete trust . . . in the cleverness of our conceptual constructions and the sureness of our extrapolatory ventures."[54]

Some kind of predictive power generally is considered to be the highest attribute of a model. A predictive model is an aid in *projecting* our understanding of a process of determinate relationships. Predictive models may be utilized in two ways. First, they may attempt to predict reality. Or second, they may provide only an indeterminate approximation thereto. The latter use involves a *rational* model—a statement of relationships among variables, assuming certain untested (or untestable) postulates. Such a model may have little resemblance to reality. We use it in order to measure deviations from reality, to determine when and how reality and the model's predictions diverge. One major pay-off is concentrating investigations in those areas most congenial to the eventual formulation of a model conforming closely to reality. As noted in Chapter II, however, such rational ventures often degenerate into self-fulfilling utopian theories.

The rational model has at its core some simplifying assumptions, such as that of utility-maximizing "economic man." A number of objections have been raised to the use of such models for predictive purposes. First, if the complicated nature of the range of choices possible in an actual social situation is even approximately taken into account in the theoretical model, the mathematical problems to be solved in the maximization of utility become exceedingly complex. Results which have direct meaning are consequently difficult to derive. Second, no reason exists for supposing that individual behavior does conform to the principle of rationality. Third, the concept of rationality in a social situation implies a fundamental ambiguity.[55]

Supporters of the use of these rational models do have a case, however. They rightly point out that accurate predictions do not necessarily rest on "realistic" assumptions. Yet it may be true that under such conditions, accurate predictions can be made only by chance. In addition, supporters note that the three criticisms above do not destroy the usefulness of this model as an indicator of fruitful foci for future inquiry. However, these criticisms reduce the force of their argument.

*Verification.* As R. B. Braithwaite has indicated, we often use models in applying hypotheses to testable particulars, after generating data into "untested theories."[56] With a model, one can "verify" either (1) the empirical propositions of a theory, or (2) the generality of a theory. That is, one can determine whether the content of the theory has truth-value; and one can also establish the range of phenomena to which the structure of a theory is applicable.

*Verifactory* models are used to lend *scientific certainty* to our projections of understanding of a process of determinate relationships. As with prediction, we can verify by attempting to determine reality with our model, or by determining what reality is *not,* through "rational" use of the model.

*Operating Use.* Some students also distinguish the *operating* use of models. For example, Brody considers operating models a separate type. These he defines as "physical and/or biological representations of systems which attempt to replicate socio-political processes."[57] Three sub-types of operating models are identified: (1) machine or computer simulations, (2) mixed or man-machine simulations, and (3) games.

This is not the place to argue the (perhaps trivial) point of whether the term *operating* may rightfully be attached to a distinct type, or a distinct use, of models. From the viewpoint being advanced here, operating models are "physical and/or biological representations" of *other models* (explicit or implicit), and thus might be sub-types within the general categories. Mention of them is made here primarily to take note of the increasing use of simulation as a technique of theory-building in social science.

## V. CONCLUSION

The critical importance of model construction—that is, the organization of variables into systems—in scientific endeavor is clear. These comments have attempted to impose arbitrary order where intellectual disorder has prevailed in the literature dealing with models. As we have said, orderliness is not necessarily preferable to vigorous and thoughtful disagreement. It is naturally the minimum hope of the "synthesizers" that their efforts will provoke more such dissent.

## NOTES

1. Ivan D. London, "The Role of the Model in Explanation," *Journal of Genetic Psychology,* 74 (June, 1949), 165.

2. Paul Meadows, "Models, Systems, and Science," *American Sociological Review,* 22 (February, 1957), 3.

3. See Carl G. Hempel, *Fundamentals of Concept Formation in Empirical Science* (Chicago: University of Chicago Press, 1952), especially pp. 14–20.

4. Charles A. McClelland, "The Function of Theory in International Relations," *Conflict Resolution,* 4 (1960), 304.

5. *Ibid.,* p. 305.

6. M. L. DeFleur and O. N. Larsen, *The Flow of Information* (New York: Harper, 1958), p. 92.

7. F. H. George, "Models and Theories in Social Psychology," in Llewellyn Gross, (ed.), *Symposium on Sociological Theory* (Evanston, Ill.: Row, Peterson, 1959), p. 335.

8. Meadows, *op. cit.,* p. 4.

9. J. M. Beshers, "Models and Theory Construction," *American Sociological Review,* 22 (February, 1957), 34.

10. Karl W. Deutsch, "Mechanism, Organism, and Society: Some Models in Natural and Social Science," *Philosophy of Science,* 28 (July, 1951), 230.

11. Anatol Rapoport, "Uses and Limitations of Mathematical Models in Social Science," in Llewellyn Gross, (ed.), *Symposium on Sociological Theory* (Evanston, Ill.: Row, Peterson, 1959), pp. 348–72.

12. Kenneth J. Arrow, "Mathematical Models in the Social Sciences," in Daniel Lerner and Harold D. Lasswell, (eds.), *The Policy Sciences* (Stanford, Calif.: Stanford University Press, 1951), pp. 129–54.

13. Karl Pearson, *The Grammar of Science* (London: A. and C. Black, 1900), p. 357.

14. London, *op. cit.,* pp. 165–76.

15. Herbert A. Simon and Allan Newell, "Models: Their Uses and Limitations," in Leonard D. White, (ed.), *The State of the Social Sciences* (Chicago: University of Chicago Press, 1955), pp. 66–83.

16. Marion J. Levy, Jr., *The Structure of Society* (Princeton, N.J.: Princeton University Press, 1952), pp. 29–33.

17. A. Rosenbleuth and Norbert Wiener, "The Role of Models in Science," *Philosophy of Science,* 12 (1945), 317–18.

18. Herman Meyer, "On the Heuristic Value of Scientific Models," *Philosophy of Science,* 28 (April, 1951), 111–23.

19. DeFleur and Larsen, *op. cit.,* pp. 79–97.

20. Meadows, *op. cit.,* p. 4.

21. Beshers, *op. cit.,* p. 34.

22. Deutsch, *op. cit.,* p. 230; Arrow, *op. cit.,* p. 132.

23. London, *op. cit.,* p. 165.

24. Simon and Newell, *op. cit.,* p. 74.

25. Levy, *op. cit.,* pp. 30–31.

26. DeFleur and Larsen, *op. cit.,* p. 91.

27. Meyer, *op. cit.,* p. 118.

28. May Brodbeck, "Models, Meanings, and Theories," in D. Willner, (ed.), *Decisions, Values, and Groups* (London: Pergamon Press, 1960), pp. 9–10.

29. *Cf.* Meyer, *op. cit.,* p. 121.

30. Meadows, *op. cit.,* pp. 3, 4.

31. Beshers, *op. cit.,* p. 33.

32. London, *op. cit.,* pp. 165–67.

33. Rapoport, *op. cit.,* pp. 351, 363, 371.

34. DeFleur and Larsen, *op. cit.,* p. 86.

35. George, *op. cit.,* p. 334.

36. London, *op. cit.,* p. 167.

37. Meadows, *op. cit.,* p. 7.

38. See W. H. Watson, "On Methods of Representation," in A. Danto and S. Morgenbesser, *Philosophy of Science* (New York: Meridian Books, 1960), pp. 226–44.

39. See C. H. Coombs, "Theory and Methods of Social Measurement," in Leon Festinger and Daniel Katz (eds.), *Research Methods in the Behavioral Sciences* (New York: The Dryden Press, 1953), pp. 471–535; also see S. S. Stevens, "On the Theory of Scales of Measurement," in A. Danto and S. Morgenbesser, *Philosophy of Science* (New York:

Meridian Books, 1960), pp. 141–49.

40. See Anatol Rapoport, "Quantification," in his *Operational Philosophy: Integrating Knowledge and Action* (New York: Harper, 1953).

41. Coombs, *op. cit.*

42. See J. G. Kemeny, *A Philosopher Looks at Science* (New York: Van Nostrand, 1959), especially pp. 14–35, 141.

43. *Ibid.*, p. 33.

44. Technically, the use of ordinal scales is part of scaling theory, not measurement theory. The "measurement" done with them is qualitative, not genuinely quantitative. *Cf.* C. H. Coombs, *op. cit.*, pp. 471-535.

45. Arrow, *op. cit.*, p. 130.

46. *Ibid.*, p. 132.

47. A notable exception is James A. Robinson, "The Major Problems of Political Science," in Lynton K. Caldwell (ed.), *Politics and Public Affairs* (Bloomington: Indiana University Press, 1962), pp. 161–88.

48. London, *op. cit.*, pp. 169–72.

49. See Harold D. Lasswell, *The Decision Process: Seven Categories of Functional Analysis* (College Park: Bureau of Governmental Research, University of Maryland, 1956); Harold D. Lasswell and Abraham Kaplan, *Power and Society: A Framework for Political Inquiry* (New Haven, Conn.: Yale University Press, 1950); Harold D. Lasswell and M. McDougal, "Legal Education and Public Policy: Professional Training in the Public Interest," in McDougal and associates, *Studies in World Public Order* (New Haven, Conn.: Yale University Press, 1960), pp. 42–154.

50. See Richard C. Snyder, "A Decision-Making Approach to the Study of Political Phenomena," in Roland Young, (ed.), *Approaches to the Study of Politics* (Evanston, Ill.: Northwestern University Press, 1958), pp. 3–38 and *The Korean Decision (1950) and the Analysis of Crisis Decision-Making*, Paper presented at Stanford University Conference on Decision-Making in Crises, January 12–13, 1962; and Richard C. Snyder and Glenn D. Paige, "The United States Decision to Resist Aggression in Korea: The Application of an Analytical Scheme," *Administrative Science Quarterly*, 3, No. 3 (December, 1958), 341–78.

51. See Robert A. Dahl and Charles E. Lindblom, *Politics, Economics, and Welfare* (New York: Harper, 1953).

52. Anthony Downs, *An Economic Theory of Democracy* (New York: Harper, 1957).

53. Harold A. Simon, *Models of Man: Social and Rational* (New York: John Wiley and Sons, 1957).

54. London, *op. cit.*, p. 169.

55. Arrow, *op. cit.*, p. 136.

56. R. B. Braithwaite, *Scientific Explanation* (Cambridge: Cambridge University Press, 1953).

57. R. A. Brody, *Political Games for Model Construction in International Relations*, Unpublished Paper, Northwestern University, Department of Political Science, June, 1961, pp. 1–6.

## xiv

# Political Science as Blending Empirical and Normative Elements: Organization as a Moral Problem

However elegant and precise the formulations, Political Science cannot rest content with the development of empirical propositions or of typologies of models. Empirical preoccupation never has sufficed to encompass the full spectrum of interests relevant in the discipline, and it never will. Hence this chapter, which merely exemplifies what is necessary *and* mutually possible in developing empirical and normative elements in the discipline. The happy congruence of the necessary and the possible powerfully motivates this chapter, and the cursory treatment here only reflects the fact that a full-blown development of a widely ranging empirical argument appears in Golembiewski's *Men, Management, and Morality*. The normative issues involved have nowhere been accorded detailed attention, however.

## I. SOME POSITIVE MOTIVATORS

In addition to the fortunate congruence of necessity and possibility in the matter of developing empirical and normative elements within the scope of Political Science, four other factors motivate this chapter. First, a contemporary stand-off (if nothing worse) exists within the discipline between the empirically oriented and those for whom normative issues are primary. The issue is most sharply joined between some adherents of the philosophic persuasion and the behavioralists, but the contraposition is fairly general in the discipline.[1] Moreover, the jockeying is particularly intense among those who are (or wish to be) disciplinary arbiters of research tastes. Perhaps it is always thus, but this does not alleviate the problem a whit.

---

The basic argument of this chapter appeared as "Organization as a Moral Problem," *Public Administration Review,* 22 (Spring, 1962), 51–58. The original article was modified for present purposes.

Second—perhaps we merely rephrase the first point—little sign exists of a general effort to encourage complementary use of the empirical and the normative. Some peacemakers have spoken out in the discipline,[2] to be sure, and this may bode well for the future. Our contrasting belief is that more positive action is required lest the proposed "reduction of tensions" abort in a kind of more or less peaceful co-existence. Rather, we seek a real integration of the normative and the empirical in the process of developing goal-based, empirical theories.

Growing evidence establishes that we are far from alone in our desire to get on with developing the empirical and the normative. Indeed, James Q. Wilson felt it necessary to complain broadly about the unrelieved empirical stress he saw in his area of special interest. Wilson noted:[3]

> I think this has gone on long enough. The methodological issue—how we study urban politics—is not a trivial issue; but it is not the fundamental one, either. It was a secondary issue when it was first raised, and it is a secondary issue now. The basic issue is not how we answer questions but what questions we want to answer; ultimately, we should be more concerned with where we are going than with how we get there.

Like Wilson, we stress the normative. But we do not consider it as primary or secondary. Rather, we stress the integration of the empirical and the normative in goal-based, empirical theories.

Third, the area within Political Science chosen here to illustrate the articulation of empirical and normative elements is an important one. Generally, organization analysis has a high priority in the study of Public Administration. Moreover, it has relevance to a substantial cross-section of matters of concern to the political scientist. In addition, although the point is often made stridently, one cannot fault the moderate assertion that no small part of the issue of human freedom will be decided by the ways in which our various bureaucracies behave qua organizations. All the goodwill in the world may not prevail in the absence of the development of knowledge about life in organizations and the disciplining of this knowledge to generally accepted values. The development of appropriate goal-based, empirical theories relevant to organizations thus takes on a compelling quality.

Fourth, normative preachment within the organization area can be complemented by a relatively solid empirical literature. Moreover, that literature is not merely descriptive. It permits prescriptions of appropriate ways of achieving such desirable goals as high productivity while respecting super-ordinate values. This happy congruence does not characterize many areas of relevance to the political scientist in which empirical and normative elements must be mutually developed.

We do not wish to appear pollyannish, but the convenient existence of a great and growing empirical literature helps in moderating some aspects of the troublesome controversy between the adherents of the philosophic persuasion and those of the behavioral persuasion. Consider the realistic concern that behavioral research can be used to more effectively enslave or to manipulate wide segments of the population. "Those who wield power," Kariel observed about existing behavioral research, "may now choose more effectively among concensus-creating techniques . . ."[3a] This is a realistic danger, but unfortunately the alternative of neglecting behavioral research is not really open to us. Patently, we have already bitten deeply into that particular piece of fruit in the garden of knowledge, and (for good or for evil) we can no longer yearn to be children of innocence. Indeed, moreover, there is in any case no human alternative to empirical research on behavior. For man's humanity is reflected in his growing ability to predict consequences and to prescribe ways of achieving specific ends. If man does not value what his science describes and predicts, then man must use his science to attempt to change the state of what exists. Man cannot change for the better, in short, unless he can both describe and explain the empirical patterns in reality.

So empirical research there will and must be, and we can only be more or less effective in using the resulting knowledge for our own moral ends. Rest assured that if we do not put that knowledge to our service, someone will use that knowledge to put us to their service.

One of the more difficult problems with exercising such oversight, however, inheres in the fact that the existing empirical literature has in general not progressed beyond the descriptive, or natural-history, stage of its development. This datum has been a particular source of contention between adherents of the two persuasions, philosophic and behavioral.

With only a little carelessness on both sides, this simple datum can cause great mischief. If the empirical results are trumpeted a little too loudly, their descriptive status might be lost sight of. And if the behavioral descriptions of what exists are not particularly attractive to man, or if the description takes on a be-all and end-all patina, it is easy to understand why scholars challenge such results and accuse their formulators of denying man's rationality and humanity. In point of fact, behavioralism is not at fault. Rather, failure lies in missing the point that description differs sharply from the ability to predict and prescribe inherent in later stages of empirical scientific development.[4]

The happy complementaries of value and fact in the organization area, needless to say, particularly motivate this chapter. These complementaries, it is hoped, also will inspire the required methodological applications in other areas of relevance to Political Science. Opportunities certainly exist. Enough is known about voting behavior, for example, to begin developing appropriate goal-based, empirical theories in that area.[5]

## II. ORGANIZATION AS TECHNICAL SIMPLEX

The act of organizing often has been considered a technical problem, and a low-level technical problem at that. Hence the uncomplicated, Tinker Toy-like terms in which the study of organization commonly is formulated. To Lepawsky, for example, organization is to administration as skeletology is to medicine. "An organization," he noted, "can be sketched and charted just as the human body can be physically depicted." The graphics are not of overpowering difficulty. Indeed, organization is "mainly a matter of structure" and, Lepawsky concluded, organization is the "most elementary aspect of administration."[6]

Such analysis has tended to paralyze thought about organization, and it has contaminated organizationally relevant work with a scope that includes much of the discipline of Political Science. Virtually all of the literature on the American presidency, for example, has roots in this uncomplicated tradition. The study of legislatures, state and local governments, and international relations also has been similarly affected, as have other specialties within Political Science.[7] Only the occasional exception exists.[8] Indeed, that exceptions can exist is seldom recognized, so pervasive is the organizational orthodoxy.[9]

Basically, the difficulty with organization conceived as a technical problem is the analogy of the healthy body, or the well-oiled machine, which lies just below the surface of the concept. The mirage of *a* "healthy" organization, of *an* optimum and invariant arrangement of parts, has guided many students and practitioners. The early work in "scientific management" illustrates the point. This early work assumed that "the system emerges from and is immanent in the 'facts' of existence and emerges from them when they are recorded and manipulated"[10] in much the same way that observation reveals the proper relation of the bones of a body or the parts of a machine. Time has not eliminated this bias. Recent observers still stress the search for *the* organization theory.[11]

This view of organization may be challenged from many points of approach. One of these approaches will be taken here—that the emphasis upon one single organization theory forecloses a moral evaluation of organization.

## III. THE COMPLEX PROBLEM OF ORGANIZATION

The neglect of organization as a moral problem cannot be condoned. For the man-to-man relations implied in organization structures and procedures have more than a technical aspect. Organization, in this sense, is more akin to psychiatry than to skeletology. The concept of *healthy* in skeletology can be determined (for general purposes) by observing many specimens. Observing individuals or organizations, in contrast, merely describes. Observation does not determine moral health.

The implied methodological inelegance is patent. Organization theorists have tended to neglect an important distinction between types of theories. The complex problem of organization derives from the two types of questions which must be treated: What is related to what in organizations? and, What relations are desirable and how are they to be achieved in organizations? The first question implies an empirical theory. Considerable progress has been made of late toward such a theory. The second question requires a moral, or value, orientation. Values may guide the prescription of how various desired states may be achieved, given a knowledge of the important relations which exist under the full range of conditions encountered in organizations. These prescriptions, or guides for action, have been called goal-based, empirical models in Chapter II. Their development has been conspicuously lacking, specifically in organization theory as well as generally in Political Science.

The development of goal-based, empirical theories complicates the study of organization substantially. This is the case in a number of senses. Of course, there can be many goal-based, empirical theories of organization. Gone, therefore, is the solace of *an* organization theory. The point may be put tersely. There will *eventually* be *one* general empirical theory of organization. Of course, this theory will change substantially over time as it is extended to more and more phenomena, and this general theory will develop from the trial-by-testing of numerous and often conflicting theoretical systems. Empirical theory in the physical sciences, for example, has followed this course while working toward a single network of propositions which uniquely and convincingly describe reality. There will *always* be a *large number* of possible goal-based, empirical theories, in contrast, whatever the developmental state of this general empirical theory.

Other complications implicit in distinguishing the two types of theories also must be recognized. For example, not every goal-based, empirical theory is "right" in a moral sense. For example, such a theory could be developed around the goal of increasing friendly social contact on the job. Similarly, a goal-based, empirical theory could be developed—relying heavily on the experience with SS officers during World War II—to guide selection and training consistent with the goal of a smoothly run extermination program. These theories are generically similar. But, they do raise different moral issues.

These considerations suggest the following approach. First, one set of values which might guide the act of organizing will be hazarded. These values—J-C Ethic, for convenience—derive from the Judaeo-Christian tradition. Second, some behavioral findings relevant to organization will be reviewed to determine whether they support the values implied in traditional organization theory or the J-C values. Those findings support one important point. Those findings proclaim the realism and usefulness of approaching the Judaeo-Christian values in organizing.

## IV. MAN IN ORGANIZATION

To develop a contrast, let us remove the human from organizations. If organizations were a complex of gears and drive shafts, the development of theories or organization would not be onerous. It would be necessary to deal mostly with empirical properties in achieving desired states. That is, if a design were decided upon (a value choice), only factors like gear speed and the nature of materials would require attention. Such part-to-part relations are relatively uncomplicated.

But man is a prime component of organizations.[12] Man-to-man relations add important dimensions to the difficulty of developing goal-based, empirical theories of organization. For instance, it is necessary to know that such-and-such a leadership style will have such-and-such consequences upon the behavior of employees performing some specific task. In addition, however, the moral desirability of those behavioral consequences must be determined.

There is an even more confusing aspect of the problem, finally. The choice of a leadership style, for example, might be based upon a value-preference for authoritarian supervision. The use of this style, in turn, might have the self-fulfilling effect of causing employees to act as if such a style were certainly necessary to restrain them. The employees, then, might be expressing their dissatisfaction with the style of leadership by various forms of behavior considered undesirable by management (which the research literature tells us often happens). Such behavior easily could be interpreted as proof that an authoriarian style is not only desirable, but necessary as well. This visible reinforcement of a value by an apparent necessity often makes it difficult to raise the question of values, for it can be argued that, realistically, no choice exists.[13] We must challenge this self-fulfilling prophecy.

More difficulties of providing for the human in organizing might be detailed, but the challenge is clear. We are not ready to cope successfully with the difficulties of mutually developing facts and values; but neither are we willing to postpone testing our degree of readiness. That is, no one has developed a full set of values to guide man-to-man relations in organization. Also, we are less than perfect in consistently respecting the partial set of guidelines which have been developed. But the Judaeo-Christian tradition implies a partial set of values applicable to man-to-man relations in organizations. Consider this possible set of values, the J-C Ethic. It is offered without pretense of completeness,[14] but with intense conviction that the dialectic must begin somewhere. Specifically, the J-C Ethic provides that:

1. work must be psychologically acceptable to the individual; that is, its performance cannot generally threaten the individual;
2. work must allow man to develop his faculties;
3. the work task must allow the individual considerable room for self-determination;
4. the worker must have the possibility of controlling, in a meaningful way, the environment within which the task is to be performed; and
5. the organization should not be the sole and final arbiter of behavior; both the organization and the individual must be subject to an external moral order.

For those who balk at asserting a preference for any moral values, the J-C Ethic can be considered as illustrative rather than prescriptive. For the purposes of this book, it does not matter. The purpose here is to demonstrate how scientific research can be used to complement goal-oriented thought.

These five value guidelines are goals toward which the act of organizing should point. Any organization-in-being, then, will fall somewhere along a continuum (for example, from 0 to 100 per cent compliance) for each of the five values. The question is: Where?

This may seem a formidable *Where?* Traditional organization theory, however, provides a convenient benchmark for this analysis. The theory has been an important guide in planning many organizations. Therefore, traditional organization theory is not an analytical straw man. But it does outline a more extreme set of conditions than often exists in practice. Evaluating traditional organization theory in terms of the J-C values is meaningful, then, even if some modifications are necessary to fit particular organizing efforts.

## V. MAN IN TRADITIONAL ORGANIZATION THEORY

Traditional organization theory—despite its limitations for present purposes—has an immense advantage as a frame of reference for this analysis. One need not search for it. Indeed, one cannot avoid it. Almost any textbook on organization or administration is a source. Nor is there great disagreement about the properties of this theory. For present purposes, four properties of this traditional organization theory—or perhaps more appropriately, traditional philosophy—may be emphasized. The theory provides that:

1. authority should be "one-way"; it should flow in a single stream from organization superiors to subordinates;
2. supervision should be detailed and the span of control should be narrow;
3. the organization of work should respect only the physiological properties of the individual, who is considered as a social isolate; and
4. work should be routinized.

Traditional organization theory has little sensitivity for the J-C Ethic outlined above. Indeed, the two lists negate one another. The traditional theory of organization calls for a routinized job, whose performance is monitored closely by a supervisor with a narrow span of control, in an organization in which authority is a one-way relation. The contrast could not be more pointed. Less superficial behavioral analysis reinforces this conclusion.[15]

The disregard of man-as-an-end in traditional organization theory has many reflections in practice. The "boon of stupidity," for example, has been cited by a testing expert as the most desirable quality of workers on some routinized operations. More to the point, the dehumanization of work has gone so far that morons[16] and (believe it or not) pigeons have replaced "normal" human beings on some operations with marked success. These, of course, are extreme cases. Much work—both in industrial operations and in the so-called "administration of paper"—also leans in the same direction, if not so markedly. Moreover, although the point cannot be developed fully here, the traditional theory has similar consequences at high levels of organization as well as at low levels.[17]

## VI. MAN-CENTERED ORGANIZATION: SOME HARDHEADED SUPPORT

Let us begin with a conclusion. There seem to be substantial limits on the degree to which work, especially in our developed economy, can violate the values derived from the Judaeo-Christian tradition without paying a heavy price.

Our position contradicts commonly held views. For example, the Marxian analysis assumes an inevitable conflict between the "forces of production" (roughly, the technology) and the "relations of production" (roughly, the values which give meaning to man's life). Traditional organization theory seems to support this analysis. That is, the closer the approach to the traditional theory, the greater the tension between the technology and the J-C values which have given meaning to western man's "relations of production."

The conflict predicated by Marx does not seem to be inevitable. Indeed, the "forces of production" and the "relations of production" can (and perhaps must) complement one another under certain conditions. Consider only two such conditions. First, the mass-production model is at the heart of the traditional theory of organization and the Marxian analysis as well. But that model grows increasingly inapplicable. Technicians characterize the new economy, not unskilled operatives; and services increasingly displace manufacturing as employers of men. Such changes improve the chances of approaching the J-C Ethic.

Second, the development of a particular "force of production," the technology of behavioral science, also makes it possible (and reasonable) to approach more closely the J-C values. Some main elements of this behavioral research will be summarized later. Basically, the new behavioral science technology forces this point: the more closely work approximates the set of J-C values outlined above, under imprecisely known but general conditions, the more effective performance will be.

The general analysis is summarized in Table XIV.1. The table presents two types of information: (1) the values which should underlie man-to-man relations; and (2) the conditions isolated by behavioral research which approach this set of values and which are associated with high output and high satisfaction. Table XIV.1, of course, summarizes large aggregates of data from behavioral research. The findings thus will not always apply to individual cases.[18] Hence the behavioral findings reviewed here are presented in the sense of central tendencies, of more or less dominant relations which have been isolated in the study of man in organization.

Evidence for each of the conditions in the right-hand column of Table VIV.1 could be cited. Only the asterisked conditions—one for each

**TABLE XIV.1 Behavioral Conditions Associated with High Output Consistent with Judaeo-Christian Values Which Should Guide Man-to-Man Relations in Organizations**

| *Values Guiding Man-to-Man Relations* | *Conditions Associated with High Output* |
|---|---|
| 1. work must be psychologically acceptable, generally non-threatening | 1. congruence of personality and job requirements |
| | 1a. compatibility of personalities of work-unit members* |
| 2. work must allow man to develop his faculties | 2. job enlargement |
| | 2a. job rotations* |
| | 2b. training, on and off the job |
| | 2c. decentralization |
| 3. the task must allow the individual room for self-determination | 3. job enlargement |
| | 3a. general supervisions* |
| | 3b. wide span of control |
| 4. the worker must influence the environment within which he works | 4. group decision-making* |
| | 4a. peer representation in promotion |
| | 4b. self-choice of work-unit members |
| | 4c. decentralization |
| 5. the formal organization must not be the sole and final arbiter of behavior | 5. decentralization* |
| | 5a. group decision-making |

N.B. An * designates a condition that will be specifically discussed below.

of the five values—will be supported here, however, and those only briefly.

## A. Psychological Acceptability of Work

Consider, to begin, the psychological acceptability of work. Personality and aptitude testing often are used to determine the "fit" between the specific traits or characteristics of people and specific jobs. Much money and energy are expended for the purpose each year. And substantial progress in the area cannot be denied. But, if we can look forward to the future pay-offs of testing, our knowledge of the dimensions of personality leaves much to be desired.[19] Consider the testing of intelligence, which is quite advanced.[20] Intelligence scores have substantial limits in the prediction of performance in organizations. Many dullards perform well; and many of the gifted do not. Other personality characteristics must be known to increase the accuracy of predictions. Measures of ability commonly account for perhaps a quarter of the variance in performance scores.[21]

Recent work has attempted with some success to isolate and measure "basic" personality characteristics, what may be called "general predispositions to action." This work has great promise. William Schutz, for example, experimented with three major behavioral predispositions of individuals.[22] They were:

1. a *power orientation,* referring to the predisposition of an individual to become a power figure or to be subject to a power figure;
2. a *personalness—counter-personalness orientation,* referring to an individual's predisposition to seek close personal relations; and
3. an *assertiveness orientation,* referring to an individual's predisposition to make his views known in a group.

On the basis of these predispositions, Schutz constructed experimental groups which were "compatible" and "incompatible." An "incompatible" group, for example, includes individuals with extremely different scores on the personalness—counter-personalness orientation.

Schutz's manipulations proved their point. "Compatible" groups were more effective on a number of tasks. Output, satisfaction, and group cohesiveness were among the measures employed. Cruder but similar managerial techniques—such as self-choice[23]—have had similar consequences.

While most available measuring instruments have been crudely defined, testing for basic personality characteristics has enormous potential for assuring that work is psychologically acceptable to employees.[24] This is the case despite the cries of critics, such as William H. Whyte, Jr., for whom testing means only a violation of the privacy of individuals. There are risks in the use of testing, to be sure, and quackeries aplenty in its practice. But the pay-offs—for individuals and for the organization —seem well worth the risks and the humbug.

**B. Development of Individual Faculties**

Next, the literature seems quite definite on the point that techniques which allow the individual to develop his faculties generally are associated with high output. Job enlargement, therefore, has gained quite a reputation.[25] Humbler techniques—such as the simple rotation between routine jobs—often have a similar impact.[26] Effective assembly lines, for example, have been found to practice (quite secretly) job rotation. The experience at the Endicott, New York, plant of IBM seems typical. There, while the boss was away, employees began to rotate jobs informally to break the monotony. Rotation was a tonic:[27]

> By the time the switch was discovered, the men were all doing so much better that the boss decided to rotate jobs in his department ... as a matter of policy. That was a year ago. Since then manufacturing costs in the department have dropped about 19 per cent.

The value of allowing the individual to develop his faculties, in short, is an attractive proposition in terms of cost as well as from a moral standpoint. This relation seems to hold for all organization levels, which makes it particularly noteworthy. Moreover, job enlargement often will have the effects of reducing supervisory costs and of freeing supervisors to perform functions of management other than surveillance.

### C. Room for Self-Determination

Tasks which allow the individual room for self-determination, the third value of the J-C Ethic, also have a double-barrelled effect which is attractive from a cost standpoint. They approach one of the values which should guide man-to-man relations in organization, and they are associated with high output.

For example, "general supervision" allows the individual room for self-determination on the task. A wide span of control has a similar effect.[28] Output tends to respond favorably. This was the case, for example, for about three-quarters of the supervisors in one sample.[29] First-line supervisors who utilized general supervision—setting objectives and allowing the worker considerable leeway in reaching them—tended overwhelmingly to have work units with high productivity. In contrast, "close supervision" was associated very strongly with low output. Close supervision may be defined in terms of constant overseeing, minute specification of instructions, and constant check-ups.

The rationale can be extended. Consistently, second-line supervisors who employed general supervision almost always had subordinate foremen who used the same style. Those employing close supervision also had subordinates who used the same style. The point, then, seems to hold for all organization levels.[30]

### D. Controlling the Environment

The fourth value which should guide man-to-man relations—the possibility of employee control over the work environment—covers a far broader field than allowing the individual room for self-determination on the task. It extends to the general environment within which the task is performed. Again, techniques which approach this value tend to be associated with high output.

Group decision-making concerning changes in jobs or output levels—certainly among the more important aspects of the environment within which a task is performed—illustrates the point. The basic technique is a simple, if revolutionary, one.[31] A typical application involves the setting by management of general goals, for example, to meet increasingly sharp competition. Work units in the concern, cognizant of these general goals, determine and enforce a specific level of output. Traditional organization theory, of course, countenances no such falderal. In its terms, an order would suffice.

Group decision-making generally leads to increased output, although what precisely makes for success (or failure) is not known. This may seem surprising, but the explanation is plausible. Group decision-making implies a low degree of threat, as opposed to exhortation by management. Consequently, less resistance results (for example, to high levels of output). Moreover, the group is free to develop and enforce a norm. This norm, in turn, often serves as a very potent guide for the behavior of members, even when the supervisor is away. The group makes strong medicine then.[32] More significantly, the medicine is often far stronger than management can brew under present economic and cultural conditions.

Despite the fuzziness surrounding the concept, group decision-making seems to encourage participation and, therefore, increases the probability of involvement in decisions by those who must carry them out.[33] One experiment strikingly makes the point. Three degrees of participation in a minor change in a job were studied: *total participation,* or group decision-making by a formal work unit; *representative participation,* in which members of a work unit chose representatives to participate in the decision-making; and *no participation,* in which the workers were simply told that a change was necessary and that it would be made.

The degree of participation made a substantial difference. Originally, the work units had comparable output levels which clustered around 60 units per hour. *Total participation* led to the highest output after the change, substantially above the levels reached before the change. *No participation* resulted in the lowest output. Indeed, the *no-participation* unit fell far below its previous output and did not recover during a 32-day period of observation. The data in Table XIV.2 summarize these results.

Curiously, the principle of group decision-making has had few full-

**TABLE XIV.2 Varying Degrees of Participation in Decisions on Introducing Minor Changes and Their Effects on Output**

| *Condition* | *Production (in units per hour) at Five-Day Intervals After the Change in the Job* | | | | | |
|---|---|---|---|---|---|---|
| | 5 | 10 | 15 | 20 | 25 | 30 |
| Total Participation | 64 | 63 | 75 | 71 | 71 | 72 |
| Representative Participation | 50 | 53 | 60 | 68 | 64 | 66 |
| No Participation | 45 | 53 | 55 | 51 | 49 | 55 |

Approximated from a graph in Lester Coch and John R. P. French, Jr., "Overcoming Resistance to Change," in Dorwin Cartwright and Alvin Zander (eds.), *Group Dynamics: Research and Theory* (Evanston, Ill.: Row, Peterson, 1953).

fledged applications. Various bastardized "participation plans" do exist, of course. Often they attempt to get without giving and must take their place in the storehouse of gimmicks that might (or might not) work in the short run and are likely to fail in the longer run. The Scanlon Plan, in contrast, attempts to exploit the possibilities of participation *and* distributes the benefits among all. It does not pussyfoot. The heart of the Plan is a Production Committee, composed of equal numbers of management personnel and hourly employees who are elected periodically. The Committee considers the spectrum of management problems and plays an important role in communicating decisions.

The available evidence, none of it very complete, suggests that such full-scale participative efforts as the Scanlon Plan have much to offer employees and management.[34] Co-determination (as practiced in Yugoslavia, for example) can have similar effects.

Of whatever scope, the possibility of the worker influencing the productive environment tends to pay off in increased output and heightened satisfaction. Again, efforts to establish conditions approximating this fourth value governing man-to-man relations have behind them practical support as well as moral force.

Indeed, management has only a limited choice in such areas as group decision-making. For denying the worker such "legitimate" means of influencing the environment often means only that the environment will be controlled informally in ways unfavorable to management. For example, informal groups will develop which control the behavior of employees in the matter of output. This is a substantial way of influencing the work environment, and the informal group has a relatively clear field. It controls the rewards of status, affect, and emotional support which can be provided best (perhaps, only) by a small informal group. In contrast, management often cannot provide such satisfactions directly and continuously for most employees.

At best, then, management has no real choice. It can attempt to mesh the norms of the informal group with the goals of the formal organization. Or it can thrust its head into the proverbial sand by ignoring the need for employee participation.

### E. Subjection to an External Moral Order

The fifth value which should govern man-to-man relations, finally, is in many senses the linchpin of the J-C Ethic. For if the organization is the ultimate measure of man, the first four values could hardly be attained in great measure. The subordinacy of "the organization" to an external moral order was stressed in the war trials following World War II, for example. Similarly, the military organizations of many Western countries often have emphasized that an immoral order need not be obeyed.[35] And many public and business organizations have policies and procedures to provide "alternative channels" for appeals against the hierarchy. Unions have demanded such alternative channels; and management, often unilaterally, has granted them.[36]

With relative certainty, we can paint a likeness of an organization qua monolith. For example, creativity seems more common in organizations in which the "true believer" is rare. This might seem to apply with most force to upper levels of the organization. But fortunate is the organization which can tap the enormous pool of creativity among its lower-level operatives. In addition, the person who accepts the organization as the sole and final arbiter is a caricature of a man who might find it difficult to supply the most miniscule adaptations required by his work until they were programmed. Moreover, communication in an organization of true believers would have an Alice-in-Wonderland quality. The German experience in World War II is instructive on this score. Intelligence percolating up to Hitler told him what he wanted to hear rather than what he should hear. For the head of the German government had made it very clear—sometimes by executions—that he had already predicted what would happen and that intelligence ought not contradict the predictions. Consequently, some of the most incredible decisions imaginable were made; for example, one such ruling emasculated a jet aircraft program which was far ahead of similar Allied programs. Too much obedience to the organization, clearly, prejudiced its chances for survival. Admittedly Hitler's techniques were extreme, but the lesson of the example has many applications.

In these terms, White's conclusion that the successful executive typically has a somewhat jaundiced view of "the organization" rings true.[37] The successful executive seems to support the organization only so long as it generally supports his needs and values. Is it reasonable to expect any employee to sacrifice his personality without exacting a high pay-off for so doing? And can you really trust someone who would do anything to keep his job, even if it means sacrificing his needs and values?

Greater tentativeness is in order concerning specific approaches to attaining the fifth value of the J-C Ethic than was the case with previous examples. The multiplicity of variables complicates all comparisons. However, a convincing case can be developed for the position that consciousness of this fifth value has useful consequences for administration. For example, decentralization seems the major structural technique which approaches the value that the formal organization is not the sole and final arbiter of behavior. Indeed, a decentralized system requires precisely the kind of manager who has the strength of character and ability to make his decisions and to let others make theirs. The very act of decentralization—of setting an individual loose within general boundaries—is optimistic.[38] Decentralization also implies that there is much to be gained in terms of increasing the chances for adaptation, training, and involvement at lower levels. This is accomplished by cultivating the attitude that the formal organization above an officer's level is not the sole and final arbiter of behavior.

With some reservations, then, the fifth value which should guide man-to-man relations seems to contribute to organization effectiveness.[39] This is the case despite the patent difficulty of saying "when" to attempts at decentralization, of training personnel, and of developing suitable controls.[40]

Indeed, the position here may be over-cautious. The experience of firms like Sears, Roebuck & Co. supports the usefulness of decentralization. Its middle-sized stores with internal decentralized structures had higher sales and developed more promotable executives than stores with centralized patterns.[41] The returns of a 1935-39 decentralization at Westinghouse, similarly, appear to have been very substantial.[42] And the comparison of a sample of centralized and decentralized firms favored the latter on such significant measures as turnover of the work force, absenteeism, and accident severity and frequency.[43]

Data concerning decentralization in government agencies are in far shorter supply. But agencies like the Internal Revenue Service, the Post Office, and the Civil Service Commission—often out of dire necessity[44]—have begun programs of decentralization, and the results seem generally positive.[45]

## VII. CONCLUSION

The data above support a dual conclusion. First, there is considerable evidence that in organizing, it is advisable to establish conditions that permit attainment of those values relevant to man-to-man relations which have been accepted in general at an intellectual level in Western cultures. Second, however, the difficulty of facilitating approaches to these values should not be underestimated. One must have acute ideological foresight indeed to envision the time when these values will be achieved in substantial measure. Even inch-by-inch advances will often come dearly. Major changes in attitudes and techniques will be required. Also, fundamental changes in traditional organization theory must be made.[46] Job enlargement, for example, is not consistent with that theory empirically or in a value sense.

Whether these changes are made or not, however, one point cannot be neglected: *organization is a moral problem.* Findings such as those cited above help us recognize the point. But a moral problem is a moral problem, whatever the research technology tells us. Conveniently, the research technology gives a generally clear go-ahead to efforts to face this moral problem in practice.

At another level, the present argument illustrates the kind of goal-based, empirical inquiry which probably will and certainly should become an increasing preoccupation in Political Science. Of course, notable achievements of this kind are already on the record, as in our constitutional innovation of a government strong enough to preserve its integrity but not so strong as to be able to do so at the expense of its people's liberties. But present achievement pales before that which needs doing. It is only clear that the effort will have important consequences. The processes of developing goal-based, empirical models imply many possibilities for mutual development of value and empirical approaches. Thus the philosophical analysis of a specific normative issue—the preservation of political dissent—may point up the existing inadequacy of knowledge and trigger empirical work on the processes of deviation from group norms and the characteristics of deviators. Similarly, empirical work may point up the lack of specificity of normative imperatives, as by isolating existential states that are beyond the capacity of some normative system for which a goal-based, empirical model was developed. Value clarification may result from such empirical findings or discoveries.[47]

## NOTES

1. Albert Somit and Joseph Tannenhaus, *American Political Science: A Profile of a Discipline* (New York: Atherton Press, 1964).

2. Robert A. Dahl, "The Behavioral Approach," *American Political Science Review,* 55 (December, 1961), 763–72.

3. James Q. Wilson, "Problems in the Study of Urban Politics," in Edward H. Buehrig (ed.), *Essays in Political Science* (Bloomington: Indiana University Press, 1966), p. 131.

3a. Henry S. Kariel, "The Political Relevance of Behavioral and Existential Psychology," *American Political Science Review,* 61 (June, 1967), p. 335.

4. Much of value can be made of the differences between description and explanation, as in Ernest Nagel, *The Structure of Science* (New York: Harcourt, Brace and World, 1961); and in Robert Brown, *Explanation in Social Science* (Chicago: Aldine, 1963).

5. Such an effort, indeed, has been begun by Robert A. Dahl, *Modern Political Analysis* (Englewood Cliffs, N.J.: Prentice-Hall, 1964), pp. 55–71.

6. Albert Lepawsky (ed.), *Administration: The Art and Science of Organization and Management* (New York: Knopf, 1952), p. 219.

7. The point is amply established by Dwight Waldo, *The Administrative State* (New York: Ronald Press, 1948).

8. Bowdoin Commission Report, *Georgia Game and Fish Department: Management and Operations* (February 4, 1964).

9. James Burnham, *Congress: The American Tradition* (Chicago: Regnery, 1959), especially pp. 121–22, neatly develops the point in relation to Congress.

10. Waldo, *op. cit.,* p. 178.

11. William G. Scott, "Organization Theory: An Over-View and Appraisal," *Journal of the Academy of Management,* 4 (April, 1961), especially 22–26.

12. And he is likely to remain so for a long time, cybernation and automation notwithstanding. Indeed, evidence suggests that the management of human resources becomes more (rather than less) critical under advanced technological conditions. See Charles R. Walker, *Toward the Automated Factory* (New Haven, Conn.: Yale University Press, 1957).

13. This core-insight preoccupies Douglas McGregor in *The Human Side of Enterprise* (New York: McGraw-Hill, 1960) as he contrasts Theory X and Theory Y.

14. The religious-humanitarian roots of these values are suggested in Robert T. Golembiewski, *Men, Management, and Morality,* (New York: McGraw-Hill, 1965), especially pp. 63–65.

15. Robert T. Golembiewski, *Behavior and Organization: O & M and the Small Group* (Chicago: Rand McNally, 1962).

16. Niall Brennan, *The Making of a Moron* (New York: Sheed and Ward, 1953), p. 16.

17. Golembiewski, *Men, Management, and Morality,* especially pp. 203–90.

18. For some of the qualifications necessary for more precise prediction, see Robert T. Golembiewski, "The Small Group and Public Administration," *Public Administration Review,* 19 (Summer, 1959), 154–56.

19. Saul W. Gellerman, "A Hard Look at Testing," *Personnel,* 38 (May-June, 1961), 8–15. See *American Psychologist,* 20 (November, 1965), for analysis of recent attacks against government use of such tests.

20. Jacob W. Getzels and Philip W. Jackson, *Creativity and Intelligence* (New York: Wiley, 1962) have spotlighted some of the limitations of imputing too much to measures of intelligence.

21. One large batch of Graduate Record Examination scores, for example, accounted for less than 10 per cent of the variance in subsequent scholastic records.

22. William C. Schutz, "What Makes Groups Productive?" *Human Relations,* 8 (November, 1955), 429–66.

23. In this connection, see Raymond H. Van Zelst, "Validation of Sociometric Regrouping Procedure," *Journal of Abnormal and Social Psychology,* 47 (April, 1952), 299–301.

24. The power of such work is suggested by much research. Consider the

comparison of effective and relatively ineffective experimental groups. Members of the effective groups tended to have personality characteristics such as: less need for aggression; stronger feelings of adequacy; greater acceptance of social affiliation; and fewer negative self-concepts. Paul H. Mussen and Lyman W. Porter, "Personal Motivations and Self-Conceptions Associated with Effectiveness and Ineffectiveness in Emergent Groups," *Journal of Abnormal and Social Psychology*, 59 (July, 1959), 23–27.

25. Chris Argyris, *Personality and Organization* (New York: Harper, 1957), pp. 177–87; and Argyris *Integrating the Individual and the Organization* (New York: Wiley, 1964), pp. 78–82.

26. By way of qualification, there is job rotation and job rotation. Administrative difficulties inhere in some varieties because, for example, of the difficulties of assigning responsibility for performance. On this point, see Louis E. Davis, "Job Design and Productivity: A New Approach," *Personnel*, 33 (March, 1957), 425–26.

27. Argyris, *Personality and Organization*, p. 276.

28. The relation is a complicated one, to be sure. For support of the crude generalization above, however, see Golembiewski, *Men, Management, and Morality*, pp. 169–79.

29. Robert L. Kahn and Daniel Katz, "Leadership Practices in Relation to Productivity and Morale," in Dorwin Cartwright and Alvin Zander (eds.), *Group Dynamics: Research and Theory* (Evanston, Ill.: Row, Peterson, 1953), p. 615. Individuals scoring high on "authoritarianism," however, would probably respond less favorably. More precise predictions would specify such personality differences, although respondents in existing studies tend to include only a smallish percentage of high authoritarian scorers.

30. *Ibid.*

31. For the range of related techniques, see Golembiewski, *Men, Management, and Morality*, pp. 212–27.

32. Robert T. Golembiewski, *The Small Group: An Analysis of Research Concepts and Operations* (Chicago: University of Chicago Press, 1962), pp. 9–26.

33. For experimental work with other relevant conditions under which group decision-making works, see Edith B. Bennett, "Discussion, Decision, Commitment, and Consensus in 'Group Decision,'" *Human Relations*, 8 (1955), 251–74.

34. Argyris, *Integrating the Individual and the Organization*, pp. 205–8.

35. The interesting history of the "legitimate order" in the military of many Western societies is detailed in Guenter Lewy, "Superior Orders, Nuclear Warfare, and the Dictates of Conscience: The Dilemma of Military Obedience in the Atomic Age," *American Political Science Review*, 55 (March, 1961), 3–23.

36. William G. Scott, *The Management of Conflict: Appeals Systems in Organizations* (Homewood, Ill.: Irwin-Dorsey, 1965).

37. Similarly, Elliot Jaques noted that the successful executive practiced "adaptive segregation" to insulate some part of himself from job pressures. See *The Changing Culture of a Factory* (New York: Dryden Press, 1952), pp. 302–3.

38. Each general manager of the 100 operating departments of General Electric is allowed to expend up to $500,000 for capital projects without specific authorization by headquarters, for example.

39. For a statement of some additional qualifications, see Mayer Zald, "Decentralization—Myth and Reality," Paper delivered at Twelfth Annual Management Conference, University of Chicago School of Business, March, 1964.

40. Some of these problems with decentralization are detailed by Andrew Whinston, "Price Guides in Decentralized Organizations," in William W. Cooper, Harold J. Leavitt, and Maynard W. Shelly, II (eds.), *New Perspectives in Organization Research* (New York: Wiley, 1964), pp. 405–48.

41. James C. Worthy, as cited in William F. Whyte, *Man and Organization* (Homewood, Ill.: Irwin, 1959), pp. 11–16. See also Paul R. Lawrence, *The Changing of Organizational Behavior Patterns* (Cambridge, Mass.: Harvard University Graduate School of Business Administration, 1958).

42. Ernest Dale, "Some New Per-

spectives on Decentralization," *Advanced Management,* 24 (January, 1959), 16–20.

43. From a study reported in Ernest Dale, "Centralization Versus Decentralization," *Advanced Management,* 21 (June, 1956), 15.

44. See Bernard H. Baum, *Decentralization of Authority in a Bureaucracy* (Englewood Cliffs, N.J.: Prentice-Hall, 1961), p. 79.

45. Frank J. McKenna, "Decentralization of Federal Disbursing Functions," *Public Administration Review,* 16 (Winter, 1956), 37–39; Clara Penniman, "Reorganization and the Internal Revenue Service," *Public Administration Review,* 21 (Summer, 1964), 121–30; and, for a general review, Golembiewski, *Men, Management, and Morality,* Chapter 8.

46. Considerable experience with the problems of achieving related attitudinal and structural change has been accumulated. See Edgar H. Schein and Warren G. Bennis (eds.), *Personal and Organizational Change Through Group Methods* (New York: Wiley, 1965).

47. Just such a sequence describes the change in widespread values concerning mental illness and addiction. Empirical findings and discoveries challenged (or permitted challenging) common values about mental illness. In turn, this challenge encouraged new norms about (for example) the treatment of the "insane," about their hiring, and so on. Various new drugs were the prime empirical goads to normative clarification. As Nature gives, however, so she also commonly takes away. Thus some uses of these new drugs, as for example LSD, have raised fresh ethical questions which increasingly demand attention.

# AUTHOR INDEX

# SUBJECT INDEX

PRINTED IN U.S.A.